Solutions Manual for

Introduction to Modern Economic Growth

STUDENT EDITION

Michael Peters
Alp Simsek

Princeton University Press

Princeton and Oxford

Published by Princeton University Press, 41 William Street, Princeton, New Jersey 08540

In the United Kingdom: Princeton University Press, 6 Oxford Street, Woodstock, Oxfordshire OX20 1TW

ISBN (pbk.) 978-0-691-14163-3

The publisher would like to acknowledge the author of this volume for providing the camera-ready copy from which this book was produced.

press.princeton.edu

Printed in the United States of America

For you, Edna. -M.P.

To my parents and my brothers, -A.S.

Contents

Introduction

This manual contains solutions to selected exercises from *Introduction to Modern Economic Growth* by Daron Acemoglu. Our exercise selection has been guided by a number of principles. First, we have tried to include the exercises that facilitate the understanding of the material covered in the book, for example, the ones that contain proofs to propositions or important extensions of the baseline models. Second, we have included exercises which we have found relatively more useful for improving economic problem-solving skills or building economic intuition. Third, we made an effort to include exercises which seemed particularly challenging. Fourth, we also tried to strike a balance across the chapters. Even with these criteria, making the final selection has not been easy and we had to leave out many exercises which are no doubt important and interesting. We hope the readers will find our selection useful and we apologize up front for not providing the solution of an exercise which may be of interest.

A word on the organization and the equation numbering of the solutions manual may be helpful. The exercises are presented in the same chapters they belong to in the book. Our solutions regularly refer to equations in the book and also to equations defined within the manual. To avoid confusion between the two types of references, we use the prefix "S" for the labels of the equations defined in the solutions manual. For example Eq. (5.1) would refer to the first labeled equation in Chapter 5 of the book, whereas Eq. (S5.1) would refer to the first labeled equation in Chapter 5 of this manual.

Although this version of the manual went through various stages of proofreading, there are no doubt remaining errors. To partly make up for the errors, we will post an errata document on our personal websites which we will commit to updating regularly. In particular we would appreciate it if readers could e-mail us concerning errors, corrections or alternative solutions, which we will include in the next update of the errata document. Our present e-mail and website addresses are as follows:

Michael Peters, mipeters@mit.edu, http://econ-www.mit.edu/grad/mipeters

Alp Simsek, alpstein@mit.edu, http://econ-www.mit.edu/grad/alpstein

An errata document and additional information will also be posted on the companion site for *Introduction to Modern Economic Growth* at: http://press.princeton.edu/titles/8764.html

Acknowledgments.

We would like to thank Daron Acemoglu for his help with the exercise selection and for useful suggestions on multiple solutions. We would also like to thank Camilo Garcia Jimeno and Suman Basu for various contributions and suggestions, and to thank Samuel Pienknagura for providing his own solutions to some of the exercises in Chapter 22. A number of exercises have also been assigned as homework problems for various economics classes at MIT and we have benefited from the solutions of numerous graduate students in these classes.

Chapter 2: The Solow Growth Model

Exercise 2.11

Exercise 2.11, Part (a). Recall that the capital accumulation in the Solow (1956) model is characterized by the differential equation

$$\dot{K}(t) = sY(t) - \delta K(t). \tag{S2.1}$$

Let $k(t) = K(t)/L(t)$ denote the . Using the production function $Y(t) = L(t)^{\beta} K(t)^{\alpha} Z^{1-\alpha-\beta}$ and the assumption that the population is constant, the evolution of the is given by

$$\frac{\dot{k}(t)}{k(t)} = \frac{\dot{K}(t)}{K(t)} = sL^{\beta}K(t)^{\alpha-1}Z^{1-\alpha-\beta} - \delta$$

$$= sk(t)^{\alpha-1}z^{1-\alpha-\beta} - \delta,$$

where the first line uses Eq. (S2.1) and the second line defines $z \equiv Z/L$ as the land to labor ratio. Setting $\dot{k}(t) = 0$ in this equation, the unique positive steady state can be solved as

$$k^* = \left(\frac{sz^{1-\alpha-\beta}}{\delta}\right)^{1/(1-\alpha)}. \tag{S2.2}$$

The steady state output per capita is in turn given by

$$y^* = s\left(k^*\right)^{\alpha}(z^*)^{1-\alpha-\beta} \tag{S2.3}$$

$$= \left(\frac{s}{\delta}\right)^{\alpha/(1-\alpha)} z^{(1-\alpha-\beta)/(1-\alpha)}$$

To prove that the steady state is globally stable, let us define $g(k) \equiv sz^{1-\alpha-\beta}k^{\alpha-1} - \delta$. Since $g(k)$ is a decreasing function of k and since $g(k^*) = 0$, we have

$$g(k(t)) > 0 \text{ for } k(t) \in (0, k^*) \text{ and}$$
$$g(k(t)) < 0 \text{ for } k(t) \in (k^*, \infty).$$

Since $\dot{k}(t) = k(t)g(k(t))$, the previous displayed equation implies that $k(t)$ increases whenever $0 < k(t) < k^*$ and decreases whenever $k(t) > k^*$. It follows that starting from any $k(0) > 0$, the converges to the unique positive steady state level k^* given in Eq. (S2.2). Intuitively, the land to labor ratio remains constant since there is no population growth. This in turn implies that there is a unique steady state with a positive despite the fact that the production function exhibits diminishing returns to jointly increasing capital and labor.

Exercise 2.11, Part (b). As Eq. (S2.3) continues to apply, the evolves according to

$$\dot{k}(t) = sz(t)^{1-\alpha-\beta}k(t)^{\alpha} - (\delta + n)k(t). \tag{S2.4}$$

1

In this case the land to labor ratio $z(t) = Z/L(t)$ is decreasing due to population growth, that is

$$\frac{\dot{z}(t)}{z(t)} = -n. \tag{S2.5}$$

The equilibrium is characterized by the system of differential equations (S2.5) and (S2.4) along with the initial conditions $k(0) = K(0)/L(0)$ and $z(0) = Z/L(0)$.

First, we claim that the only steady state of this system is given by $k^* = z^* = 0$. By Eq. (S2.5), $\lim_{t\to\infty} z(t) = 0$ hence $z^* = 0$ is the only steady state. Plugging $z^* = 0$ in Eq. (S2.4) and solving for $\dot{k}(t) = 0$, the only steady state is $k^* = 0$, proving our claim. Next, we claim that starting from any initial condition, the system will converge to this steady state. Note that Eq. (S2.5) has the solution $z(t) = z(0)\exp(-nt)$. Plugging this expression in Eq. (S2.4), we have the first-order nonlinear differential equation

$$\dot{k}(t) = sz(0)^{1-\alpha-\beta}\exp(-n(1-\alpha-\beta)t)k(t)^{\alpha} - (\delta+n)k(t).$$

To convert this to a linear differential equation, define $x(t) = k(t)^{1-\alpha}$ and note that the evolution of $x(t)$ is given by $\frac{\dot{x}(t)}{x(t)} = (1-\alpha)\frac{\dot{k}(t)}{k(t)}$, or equivalently

$$\dot{x}(t) = s(1-\alpha)z(0)^{1-\alpha-\beta}\exp(-n(1-\alpha-\beta)t) - (1-\alpha)(\delta+n)x(t).$$

The solution to this linear first-order differential equation is given by (see Section B.4)

$$
\begin{aligned}
x(t) &= \exp(-(1-\alpha)(\delta+n)t)\left[x(0) + \int_0^t s(1-\alpha)z(0)^{1-\alpha-\beta}\exp((n\beta+(1-\alpha)\delta)t')\,dt'\right] \\
&= \left[x(0) - \frac{s(1-\alpha)z(0)^{1-\alpha-\beta}}{n\beta+(1-\alpha)\delta}\right]\exp(-(1-\alpha)(\delta+n)t) \\
&\quad + s(1-\alpha)z(0)^{1-\alpha-\beta}\frac{\exp(-n(1-\alpha-\beta)t)}{n\beta+(1-\alpha)\delta}
\end{aligned}
$$

Using $x(t) = k(t)^{(1-\alpha)}$, the previous equation implies

$$
k(t) = \left(
\begin{array}{c}
\left[k(0)^{1-\alpha} - \frac{s(1-\alpha)z(0)^{1-\alpha-\beta}}{n\beta+(1-\alpha)\delta}\right]\exp(-(1-\alpha)(\delta+n)t) \\
+ \frac{s(1-\alpha)z(0)^{1-\alpha-\beta}}{n\beta+(1-\alpha)\delta}\exp(-n(1-\alpha-\beta)t)
\end{array}
\right)^{1/(1-\alpha)}, \tag{S2.6}
$$

which provides an explicit form solution for $k(t)$. Since $\alpha + \beta < 1$, this expression also implies that $\lim_{t\to\infty} k(t) = 0$, proving that the economy will converge to the steady state capital-labor ratio $k^* = 0$ starting from any initial condition.

Eq. (S2.6) demonstrates a number of points worth emphasizing. First, since $1 - \alpha > 0$ the first component always limits to zero, hence the initial condition has no impact on the limiting value of capital-labor ratio in the Solow model. Second, the second component limits to zero if $\alpha + \beta < 1$, but limits to a positive value if $\alpha + \beta = 1$ or if $n = 0$ (which corresponds to the case studied in Part (a) of this problem). Hence, the assumptions that drive the results of this exercise are the joint facts that the production function has diminishing returns in capital and labor and that the population is increasing. Intuitively, as the population grows, each unit of labor commands less land for production and the output of each worker declines (and limits to zero) since land is an essential factor of production.

We next claim that the aggregate capital and output limit to infinity. To see this, note that $\lim_{t \to \infty} k(t) L(t) =$

$$\lim_{t \to \infty} \left(\frac{\left[k(0)^{1-\alpha} - \frac{s(1-\alpha)z(0)^{1-\alpha-\beta}}{n\beta + (1-\alpha)\delta} \right] \exp\left(-(1-\alpha)(\delta+n)t \right) +}{\frac{s(1-\alpha)z(0)^{1-\alpha-\beta}}{n\beta + (1-\alpha)\delta} \exp\left(-n(1-\alpha-\beta)t \right)} \right)^{1/(1-\alpha)} L(0) \exp(nt)$$

$$= \lim_{t \to \infty} \left(\frac{\left[k(0)^{1-\alpha} - \frac{s(1-\alpha)z(0)^{1-\alpha-\beta}}{n\beta + (1-\alpha)\delta} \right] \exp\left(-(1-\alpha)\delta t \right) +}{\frac{s(1-\alpha)z(0)^{1-\alpha-\beta}}{[n\beta + (1-\alpha)\delta]} \exp(n\beta t)} \right)^{1/(1-\alpha)} L(0) = \infty.$$

Consequently, $Y(t) = F(K(t), L(t), Z)$ also limits to infinity, since both $K(t)$ and $L(t)$ limit to infinity. The previous displayed equation also shows that the aggregate capital grows at rate $n\beta/(1-\alpha) < n$, that is, the aggregate variables still grow at an exponential rate but just not fast enough to compensate for the population growth and sustain a positive level of capital-labor ratio and output per capita.

We claim that the returns to land also limit to infinity. Land is priced in the competitive market, hence returns to land are given by

$$p^z(t) \equiv (1 - \alpha - \beta) L(t)^\beta K(t)^\alpha Z^{-\alpha-\beta},$$

which limits to infinity since $K(t)$ and $L(t)$ are increasing. Alternatively, one can also see this by noting that the share of land in aggregate output is constant due to the Cobb-Douglas form of the production function, that is, $p^z(t)Z = (1 - \alpha - \beta)Y(t)$. Since output grows, returns to land also grow and limit to infinity. Intuitively, land is the scarce factor in this economy and as other factors of production (and output) grow, the marginal product of land increases. We finally claim that the wage rate limits to zero. The wage rate is given by

$$\begin{aligned} w &= \beta L^{\beta-1} K^\alpha Z^{1-\alpha-\beta} \\ &= \beta k^\alpha z^{1-\alpha-\beta}, \end{aligned}$$

which limits to zero since both k and z limit to zero. Labor complements land and capital in production, therefore, as capital-labor ratio and land-labor ratio shrink to zero, wages also shrink to zero. Intuitively, every worker has less machines and less land to work with, hence has lower productivity and receives lower wages in the competitive equilibrium.

An alternative (simpler and more elegant) analysis. Define the normalized variable

$$\tilde{L}(t) = \left(L(t)^\beta Z^{1-\alpha-\beta} \right)^{1/(1-\alpha)},$$

which grows at the constant rate $\beta n/(1-\alpha) < n$. The production function can be rewritten in terms of this normalized variable as

$$F\left(K(t), \tilde{L}(t) \right) = K(t)^\alpha \tilde{L}(t)^{1-\alpha}.$$

Then, if we interpret $\tilde{L}(t)$ as the labor force in a hypothetical economy, the textbook analysis of the Solow model shows that this hypothetical economy has a unique steady state capital-labor ratio $\tilde{k}^* = \left(K(t)/\tilde{L}(t) \right)^*$, and starting at any $K(t) > 0$ and $\tilde{L}(t) > 0$, the economy converges to this level of capital-labor ratio. By construction, the aggregate capital in the original economy is equal to the aggregate capital in the hypothetical economy. Thus, capital in the original economy satisfies

$$\lim_{t \to \infty} \frac{K(t)}{\tilde{L}(t)} = \tilde{k}^*,$$

which shows that the aggregate capital $K(t)$ asymptotically grows at rate $\beta n/(1-\alpha)$ (which is the growth rate of $\tilde{L}(t)$). Since $\beta n/(1-\alpha) < n$, population grows faster than aggregate capital, hence the capital-labor ratio limits to zero. The remaining results are obtained as in the above analysis.

Exercise 2.11, Part (c). We would expect both s and n to change. When we endogenize savings as in Chapter 8, we see that s in general depends on a number of factors including preferences for intertemporal substitution and factor prices. Nevertheless, the analysis in the preceding parts applies even when $s = 1$ (i.e. individuals save all their income), thus the capital-labor ratio and the output per capita would limit to zero also in the economy with endogenously determined saving rate. Intuitively, savings cannot provide enough of a force to overcome diminishing returns and immiseration in this economy.

The stronger stabilizing force comes from endogenizing the demographics in the model, that is, endogenizing n. A simple way of doing this is to use the idea proposed by Malthus (1798), which we can incorporate in our model as:

$$\frac{\dot{L}(t)}{L(t)} = n(y(t)), \tag{S2.7}$$

where $n'(y) > 0$, $\lim_{y\to\infty} n(y) = \bar{n} > 0$ and $\lim_{y\to\infty} n(y) = \underline{n} < 0$. The intuition behind Eq. (S2.7) is that when output per capita is higher, people live longer, healthier and they have more children (abstracting from a lot of considerations such as birth control measures) which increases the population growth. Note that when the output per capita is very low population may shrink, and note also that there is a unique value of output per labor, y^*, that satisfies $n(y^*) = 0$, i.e. population remains constant when output per labor is at y^*.

The system that describes the equilibrium in this economy constitutes of Eqs. (S2.7), (S2.5), and (S2.4). This system has a unique steady state, (y^*, z^*, L^*), where y^* is the unique solution to $n(y^*) = 0$, z^* is the unique solution to

$$y^* = \left(\frac{s}{\delta}\right)^{\alpha/(1-\alpha)} (z^*)^{(1-\alpha-\beta)/(1-\alpha)},$$

and $L^* = z^*Z$. Starting from any value of $L(0)$, *the level of population* will adjust, that is $\lim_{t\to\infty} L(t) = L^* = z^*Z$ so that land per labor is z^*, the output per labor is y^*, and population growth is $n(y^*) = 0$. Intuitively, as output per capita limits to 0, population growth slows down, which increases the amount of land that each person commands, and consequently increases output per capita.[1] Hence endogenizing demographics creates a stabilizing force that sustains positive levels of output per capita. The result of Part (b), in particular the result that output per capita and the capital-labor ratio limit to zero, are largely artifacts

---

[1] On the other hand, with Assumption (S2.7), sustained increases in output per capita are not possible either, even with modest amounts of technological progress. An increase in output per capita increases population which in turn decreases and stabilizes output per capita. This is the so-called Malthusian trap: In a Malthusian world, modest amounts of technological progress result in higher population but not necessarily higher output per capita. The Malthusian model roughly matches the evolution of output per capita before the Industrial Revolution. For example, despite technological progress, the real wages in England in the 17th century were similar to those in the 13th century (Clark (2004)). Again consistent with this model, measures of urbanization and population density are good proxies for technological progress of ancient societies (see Acemoglu, Johnson, Robinson (2002)). However, a sufficiently fast technological change might overturn this result, in particular, once we add labor-augmenting technological change in the model, the Malthusian trap is less likely the larger the labor-augmenting technological progress and the smaller $\bar{n}$ (the maximum rate of population growth). Hence, one can argue that the Industrial Revolution (which increased technological progress) and the demographic transition (which one may interpret as reducing $\bar{n}$) were crucial for the human societies to get out of the Malthusian trap.

of taking n and s constant, which suggests that we should be careful in using the Solow model since the model relies on reduced form assumptions on population dynamics and consumer behavior.

Exercise 2.14*

Exercise 2.14, Part (a). We will construct an example in which $K(t), Y(t)$ and $C(t)$ asymptotically grow at constant but different rates. Consider paths for $Y(t), C(t)$ given by

$$Y(t) = Y(0) \exp(gt), \quad C(t) = C(0) \exp\left(\frac{g}{2}t\right)$$

where $g > 0$ and $C(0) < Y(0)$, and define $K(t)$ as the solution to $\dot{K}(t) = Y(t) - C(t) - \delta K(t)$. Note that $\dot{Y}(t)/Y(t) = g$ and $\dot{C}(t)/C(t) = g/2$ for all t. Define $\chi(t) = K(t)/Y(t)$ and note that

$$\frac{\dot{\chi}(t)}{\chi(t)} = \frac{\dot{K}(t)}{K(t)} - g = \frac{1}{\chi(t)} - \frac{C(t)}{Y(t)} \frac{1}{\chi(t)} - \delta - g \qquad (S2.8)$$

hence

$$\dot{\chi}(t) = 1 - \frac{C(0)}{Y(0)} \exp\left(-\frac{g}{2}t\right) - (\delta + g)\chi(t).$$

As $t \to \infty$, the middle term on the right hand side goes to zero and $\chi(t) = K(t)/Y(t)$ converges to the constant $1/(\delta + g)$, so we have $\lim_{t\to\infty} \dot{K}(t)/K(t) = g$. Hence, in this example $Y(t)$ and $K(t)$ asymptotically grow at rate g while $C(t)$ asymptotically grows at rate $g/2$, proving that Part 1 of Theorem 2.6 is not correct without further conditions.

Note that this example features $C(t)$ growing at a constant rate slower than both $K(t)$ and $Y(t)$ so in the limit all output is invested and both capital and output grow at the same constant rates. To rule out such examples, let us assume that

$$\lim_{t\to\infty} C(t)/Y(t) = \eta^* \in (0,1) \qquad (S2.9)$$

so that $g_C = g_Y$. Taking the limit of Eq. (S2.8), we have as $t \to \infty$

$$\dot{\chi}(t) \approx 1 - \eta^* - (\delta + g)\chi(t).$$

This equation shows that $\lim_{t\to\infty} \chi(t) = (1 - \eta^*)/(\delta + g) \in (0,\infty)$, which in turn shows that $K(t)$ and $Y(t)$ asymptotically grow at the same constant rates, that is $g_K = g_Y$. Hence Condition (S2.9) is sufficient to ensure that the limiting growth rates of $Y(t), K(t)$ and $C(t)$ are equal to each other.

Exercise 2.14, Part (b). We assume that Condition (S2.9) is satisfied so $g_C = g_Y = g_K \equiv g$. We also assume that both $g_Y(t)$ and $g_K(t)$ converge to g at a rate faster than $1/t$, that is, there exists a sequence $\{\varepsilon_T\}_{T=1}^{\infty}$ with $\lim_{T\to\infty} \varepsilon_T T = 0$ such that, $|g_Y(t) - g_Y| < \varepsilon_T/2$ and $|g_K(t) - g_Y| < \varepsilon_T/2$ for all T and $t \geq T$.

Repeating the steps as in the proof of Theorem 2.6 as suggested in the exercise gives

$$Y(t) = \tilde{F}\left[\exp\left(\int_T^t (g_Y(s) - g_K(s))\,ds\right)K(t), \exp\left(\int_T^t (g_Y(s) - n)\,ds\right)L(t), \tilde{A}(T)\right]. \tag{S2.10}$$

For each T, we let $A(t) = \exp((g_Y - n)t)$ and we define the production function

$$F_T(K(t), A(t)L(t)) \equiv \tilde{F}\left[K(t), \frac{A(t)L(t)}{A(T)}, \tilde{A}(T)\right],$$

and the production function $F\left(K\left(t\right),A\left(t\right)L\left(t\right)\right)$ as the limit

$$F\left(K\left(t\right),A\left(t\right)L\left(t\right)\right)=\lim_{T\to\infty}F_T\left(K\left(t\right),A\left(t\right)L\left(t\right)\right).$$

We claim that F provides an asymptotic representation for $\tilde{F}$, that is $\lim_{t\to\infty}\frac{\tilde{F}\left(K(t),L(t),\tilde{A}(t)\right)}{F(K(t),A(t)L(t))}=1$. To see this, we first claim that

$$\exp\left(-\varepsilon_T\left(t-T\right)\right)\leq\frac{\tilde{F}\left(K\left(t\right),L\left(t\right),\tilde{A}\left(t\right)\right)}{F_T\left(K\left(t\right),A\left(t\right)L\left(t\right)\right)}\leq\exp\left(\varepsilon_T\left(t-T\right)\right).\qquad\text{(S2.11)}$$

To prove the right hand side, note that

$$\begin{aligned}\frac{\tilde{F}}{F_T}&=\frac{\tilde{F}\left[\exp\left(\int_T^t\left(g_Y\left(s\right)-g_K\left(s\right)\right)ds\right)K\left(t\right),\exp\left(\int_T^t\left(g_Y\left(s\right)-n\right)ds\right)L\left(t\right),\tilde{A}\left(T\right)\right]}{\tilde{F}\left[K\left(t\right),\exp\left(\int_T^t\left(g_Y-n\right)ds\right)L\left(t\right),\tilde{A}\left(T\right)\right]}\\[2mm]&\leq\frac{\tilde{F}\left[K\left(t\right)\exp\left(\varepsilon_T\left(t-T\right)\right),\exp\left(\int_T^t\left(g_Y-n\right)ds\right)L\left(t\right)\exp\left(\varepsilon_T\left(t-T\right)\right),\tilde{A}\left(T\right)\right]}{\tilde{F}\left[K\left(t\right),\exp\left(\int_T^t\left(g_Y-n\right)ds\right)L\left(t\right),\tilde{A}\left(T\right)\right]}\\[2mm]&=\exp\left(\varepsilon_T\left(t-T\right)\right),\end{aligned}$$

where the first line uses Eq. (S2.10), the inequality follows since $\left|g_Y\left(s\right)-g_Y\right|<\varepsilon_T/2$ and $\left|g_K\left(s\right)-g_Y\right|<\varepsilon_T/2$ for $s\geq T$, and the last line follows since $\tilde{F}$ is constant returns to scale. The left hand side of Eq. (S2.11) is proved similarly. Letting $t=\xi T$ for some $\xi>1$ and taking the limit of Eq. (S2.11) over T, we have

$$\lim_{T\to\infty}\exp\left(-\left(\xi-1\right)\varepsilon_T T\right)\leq\lim_{T\to\infty}\frac{\tilde{F}\left[K\left(\xi T\right),L\left(\xi T\right),\tilde{A}\left(\xi T\right)\right]}{F_T\left[K\left(\xi T\right),A\left(\xi T\right)L\left(\xi T\right)\right]}\leq\lim_{T\to\infty}\exp\left(\left(\xi-1\right)\varepsilon_T T\right).$$

Since $\lim_{T\to\infty}\varepsilon_T T=0$, the limits on the left and the right hand side of the inequality are equal to 1, which implies that the middle limit is also equal to 1. Using $t=\xi T$, the middle limit can be rewritten as

$$\lim_{t\to\infty}\frac{\tilde{F}\left[K\left(t\right),L\left(t\right),\tilde{A}\left(t\right)\right]}{F_{T=\xi t}\left[K\left(t\right),A\left(t\right)L\left(t\right)\right]}=1,$$

which holds for all $\xi>1$. Taking the limit of the above expression over ξ we have

$$\begin{aligned}1&=\lim_{\xi\to\infty}\lim_{t\to\infty}\frac{\tilde{F}\left[K\left(t\right),L\left(t\right),\tilde{A}\left(t\right)\right]}{F_{T=\xi t}\left[K\left(t\right),A\left(t\right)L\left(t\right)\right]}\\[2mm]&=\lim_{t\to\infty}\frac{\tilde{F}\left[K\left(t\right),L\left(t\right),\tilde{A}\left(t\right)\right]}{\lim_{\xi\to\infty}F_{T=\xi t}\left[K\left(t\right),A\left(t\right)L\left(t\right)\right]}\\[2mm]&=\lim_{t\to\infty}\frac{\tilde{F}\left[K\left(t\right),L\left(t\right),\tilde{A}\left(t\right)\right]}{F\left[K\left(t\right),A\left(t\right)L\left(t\right)\right]},\end{aligned}$$

where the last line follows from definition of F. This proves $\lim_{t\to\infty}\tilde{F}/F=1$, that is, F provides an asymptotic representation for $\tilde{F}$ as desired.

Note that our proof relies on the inequality in (S2.11), which does not necessarily hold when either $g_K\left(t\right)$ or $g_Y\left(t\right)$ converges to g at a rate slower than $1/t$. In this case, $\tilde{F}$ does not necessarily have an asymptotic representation with labor-augmenting technological progress.

Exercise 2.17

Exercise 2.17, Part (a). Let F take the Cobb-Douglas form, that is, assume

$$F[A_K K, A_L L] = C(A_K K)^\alpha (A_L L)^{1-\alpha},$$

for some constants C and α. Then, F can be rewritten as

$$F[A_K K, A_L L] = CK^\alpha \left(\left[A_L A_K^{\alpha/(1-\alpha)} \right] L \right)^{1-\alpha}.$$

Note that, when written in this form, the technological change is essentially labor-augmenting. Then the textbook analysis for the Solow model with technological progress applies in this case as well. In particular, define $A(t) \equiv A_L(t) A_K(t)^{\alpha/(1-\alpha)}$ as the labor-augmenting technological progress and $k(t) = K(t)/(A(t) L(t))$ as the effective capital-labor ratio, and note that

$$
\begin{aligned}
\frac{\dot{k}(t)}{k(t)} &= \frac{sF[A_K(t)K(t), A_L(t)L(t)] - \delta K(t)}{K(t)} - \frac{\dot{A}(t)}{A(t)} - \frac{\dot{L}(t)}{L(t)} \\
&= sCk(t)^{\alpha-1} - \delta - g_L - \frac{\alpha}{1-\alpha} g_K.
\end{aligned}
$$

Solving for $\dot{k}(t) = 0$, there exists a globally stable steady state with effective capital-labor ratio

$$k^* = \left(\frac{sC}{\delta + g_L + \frac{\alpha}{1-\alpha} g_K} \right)^{\frac{-1}{1-\alpha}}.$$

It follows that the economy admits a balanced growth path in which the effective capital-labor ratio is constant and the capital-labor ratio and output per capita grow at the constant rate

$$g \equiv g_L + \frac{\alpha}{1-\alpha} g_K.$$

Starting from any level of effective capital-labor ratio, the economy converges to this effective capital-labor ratio, that is, if $k(0) < k^*$, then the economy initially grows faster than g and $k(t) \uparrow k^*$, and similarly, if $k(0) > k^*$, then the economy initially grows slower than g and $k(t) \downarrow k^*$.

Exercise 2.17, Part (b). We first prove a general result that will be useful to solve this exercise. We claim that the effective capital-labor ratio in this economy limits to infinity, that is

$$\lim_{t \to \infty} k(t) \equiv A_K(t) K(t) / (A_L(t) L) = \infty. \tag{S2.12}$$

The intuition for this result is as follows: the capital stock would asymptotically grow at rate g_L if $A_K(t)$ were constant. Hence, with the added technological progress in $A_K(t)$, the economy does not do worse and capital stock continues to grow at least at rate g_L. It follows that the effective capital stock, $A_K(t) K(t)$ grows strictly faster than g_L, leading to Eq. (S2.12). The following lemma and the proof formalizes this idea.

LEMMA S2.1. *Suppose that the production function takes the form $Y(t) = F(A_K(t) K(t), A_L(t) L(t))$ and suppose $A_L(t)$ grows at the constant rate g_L and $A_K(t) \geq A_K(0)$ for all t. Let $\hat{k}(t) = K(t)/(A_L(t) L(t))$ denote the capital to effective labor ratio in this economy and $\tilde{k}(t)$ denote the capital to effective labor ratio in the hypothetical economy which has the same initial conditions but in which the production function is* *given by $\tilde{Y}(t) = F(A_K(0) K(t), A_L(t) L(t))$, that is, the hypothetical economy has labor-augmenting technological change at the same rate g_L but it has no capital-augmenting technological change. Then, $\hat{k}(t) \geq \tilde{k}(t)$ for all t. In particular, $\lim_{t \to \infty} \hat{k}(t) \geq \tilde{k}^*$, and moreover, $\lim_{t \to \infty} k(t) = \lim_{t \to \infty} A_K(t) \hat{k}(t) = \infty$ whenever $\lim_{t \to \infty} A_K(t) = \infty$.*

PROOF. Let $f\left(\hat{k}\right) = F\left(\hat{k}, 1\right)$ and note that $\hat{k}$ accumulates according to

$$
\begin{aligned}
d\hat{k}/dt &= sf\left(A_K \hat{k}\right) - (\delta + n)\hat{k} \\
&\geq sf\left(A_K(0)\hat{k}\right) - (\delta + n)\hat{k},
\end{aligned}
\tag{S2.13}
$$

where the inequality follows since $A_K(t) \geq A_K(0)$. Similarly, capital to effective labor ratio in the hypothetical economy, $\tilde{k}$, satisfies

$$
d\tilde{k}/dt = sf\left(A_K(0)\tilde{k}\right) - (\delta + n)\tilde{k},
\tag{S2.14}
$$

with the same initial condition, that is, $\tilde{k}(0) = \hat{k}(0)$. Suppose, to get a contradiction, that $\hat{k}(t) \leq \tilde{k}(t)$ for some $t > 0$. Since both $\hat{k}$ and $\tilde{k}$ are continuously differentiable in t, and since $\hat{k}(0) = \tilde{k}(0)$, there exists some $t' \in [0, t]$ where $\tilde{k}$ just gets ahead of $\hat{k}$, that is $\hat{k}(t') = \tilde{k}(t')$ and $d\hat{k}(t')/dt < d\tilde{k}(t')/dt$. Since $\hat{k}(t') = \tilde{k}(t')$, this yields a contradiction to Eqs. (S2.13) and (S2.14), showing that $\hat{k}(t) \geq \tilde{k}(t)$ for all t. Note that the textbook analysis of the Solow model with labor-augmenting technological progress shows that $\lim_{t \to \infty} \tilde{k}(t) = \tilde{k}^* > 0$, which in turn implies $\lim_{t \to \infty} \hat{k}(t) \geq \tilde{k}^* > 0$. Finally, this also implies that Eq. (S2.12) holds when $\lim_{t \to \infty} A_K(t) = \infty$, as desired. □

We next turn to the present problem. We prove the result by contradiction, that is, we suppose there is a steady state equilibrium and we show that the production function must have a Cobb-Douglas representation. Consider a BGP equilibrium in which both K and Y grow at constant rates g^K and g^Y. We use superscripts for these growth rates so that the growth rates of capital and output are not confused with the productivity growth rates.

We first show that K and Y must grow at the same rate, that is $g^K = g^Y$. To see this, consider the capital accumulation equation

$$
\dot{K} = sY - \delta K.
$$

Since K and Y grow at constant rates, we have $K(t) = K(0)\exp\left(g^K t\right)$ and $Y(t) = Y(0)\exp\left(g^Y t\right)$. Plugging these expressions in the previous displayed equation, we have

$$
g^K K(0)\exp\left(g^K t\right) = sY(0)\exp\left(g^Y t\right) - \delta K(0)\exp\left(g^Y t\right),
$$

which further implies

$$
\frac{g^K K(0) + \delta K(0)}{sY(0)} = \exp\left(\left(g^Y - g^K\right)t\right).
$$

The left hand side is constant, hence this equation can only be satisfied if $g^Y = g^K$. We refer to the common growth rate of Y and K as g.

Second, we define $f(k) = F(k, 1)$ and we claim that $f(k) = Ck^\alpha$ for some constants C and $\alpha \in (0, 1)$. To see this, consider

$$
\begin{aligned}
\frac{Y(t)}{L} &= A_L(t) F\left[\frac{A_K(t)}{A_L(t)} \frac{K(t)}{L(t)}, 1\right] \\
&= A_L(t) f\left(\frac{A_K(t)}{A_L(t)} \frac{K(t)}{L(t)}\right),
\end{aligned}
$$

Plugging $K(t) = K(0)\exp(gt)$ and $Y(t) = Y(0)\exp(gt)$, $A_L(t) = A_L(0)\exp(g_L t)$ and $A_K(t) = A_K(0)\exp(g_K t)$ in this expression, we have

$$\frac{Y(0)}{A_L(0)L}\exp((g - g_L)t) = f(k(0)\exp((g_K - g_L + g)t)). \qquad (S2.15)$$

By Lemma S2.1, $k(t) = k(0)\exp((g_K - g_L + g)t)$ is growing. Then, considering the following change of variables between t and k

$$k(0)\exp((g_K - g_L + g)t) = k$$

in Eq. (S2.15), $f(k)$ can be calculated for all $k \geq k(0)$. In particular, we have

$$
\begin{aligned}
f(k) &= \frac{Y(0)}{A_L(0)L}\exp\left(\frac{g - g_L}{g_K - g_L + g}\ln\frac{k}{k(0)}\right) \\
&= \frac{Y(0)}{A_L(0)L}\left(\frac{1}{k(0)}\right)^{\frac{g-g_L}{g_K-g_L+g}} k^{\frac{g-g_L}{g_K-g_L+g}} \\
&= Ck^\alpha
\end{aligned}
$$

for some constant C, where the last line defines $\alpha \equiv \frac{g-g_L}{g_K-g_L+g}$.

Finally, note that $f(k) = Ck^\alpha$ implies

$$
\begin{aligned}
F(A_K K, A_L L) &= A_L L f(k) \qquad\qquad\qquad\qquad\qquad\qquad (S2.16)\\
&= C(A_K K)^{(g-g_L)/(g_K-g_L+g)}(A_L L)^{g_L/(g_K-g_L+g)},
\end{aligned}
$$

proving that the production function takes the Cobb-Douglas form.

An alternative proof based on the fact that factor shares are constant. Suppose, as before, that we are on a BGP on which Y and K grow at constant rates g^Y and g^K. The same argument as above shows that we must have $g^Y = g^K = g$. We first claim that the factor shares should also be constant on any such BGP. Let

$$\alpha_K = \frac{RK}{Y} = \frac{F_1 A_K K}{F} \quad \text{and} \quad \alpha_L = \frac{wL}{F} = \frac{F_2 A_L L}{F},$$

denote the shares of capital and labor in output. Here, F_1 and F_2 denote the first and second derivatives of the function $F(A_K K, A_L L)$.

We first claim that $\alpha_K(t)$ is a constant independent of time. Differentiating $Y(t) = F(A_K(t)K(t), A_L(t)L(t))$ with respect to t and dividing by F, we have

$$
\begin{aligned}
\frac{\dot{Y}}{Y} &= \frac{F_1 A_K K}{F}\left(\frac{\dot{K}}{K} + g_K\right) + \frac{F_2 A_L L}{F}\left(\frac{\dot{L}}{L} + g_L\right) \\
&= \alpha_K(t)\left(\frac{\dot{K}}{K} + g_K\right) + \alpha_L(t)\left(\frac{\dot{L}}{L} + g_L\right) \\
&= \alpha_K(t)\left(\frac{\dot{K}}{K} + g_K\right) + (1 - \alpha_K(t))\left(\frac{\dot{L}}{L} + g_L\right), \qquad (S2.17)
\end{aligned}
$$

where the last line uses $\alpha_K(t) + \alpha_L(t) = 1$. By assumption, we have $\dot{Y}/Y = g$, $\dot{K}/K = g$, and $\dot{L}/L = 0$. Moreover, Lemma S2.1 shows that $g \geq g_L$, which also implies $g_K + g > g_L$. Consequently, by Eq. (S2.17), $\alpha_K(t)$ can be solved in terms of the growth rates and is given by

$$\alpha_K(t) = \alpha_K \equiv \frac{g - g_L}{g + g_K - g_L}. \qquad (S2.18)$$

This expression is independent of t, which proves our claim that $\alpha_K(t)$ is constant.

Second, we use Eq. (S2.18) to show that F takes the Cobb-Douglas form. Note that we have

$$\alpha_K(t) = \frac{F_1 A_K K}{F} = \frac{f'(k)}{f(k)} \frac{A_K K}{A_L L} = \frac{f'(k)\, k}{f(k)},$$

where recall that we have defined $k = (A_K K)/(A_L L)$. Using the fact that $\alpha_K(t)$ is constant, we have

$$\frac{d \log f(k)}{dk} = \frac{f'(k)}{f(k)} = \frac{\alpha_K}{k}.$$

Note that by Lemma S2.1, we have that $k(t)$ is growing. Then, the previous equation is satisfied for all $k \geq k(0)$, thus we can integrate it to get

$$\log f(k) = \alpha_K \log k + \log C,$$

where $\log C$ is a constant of integration. From the previous expression, we have $f(k) = Ck^{\alpha_K}$, which again leads to the Cobb-Douglas production function $F(A_K K, A_L L) = C(A_K K)^{\alpha_K}(A_L L)^{1-\alpha_K}$. In view of the expression for α_K in Eq. (S2.18), the representation obtained in the alternative proof is exactly equal to the representation obtained earlier in Eq. (S2.16).

The second proof brings out the economic intuition better. From the growth accounting equation (S2.17), when effective factors grow at different constant rates (in particular, when effective capital grows faster than effective labor, as implied by Lemma S2.1), output can grow at a constant rate only if factor shares remain constant. But when effective factors grow at different rates, the only production function that keeps factor shares constant is the Cobb-Douglas production function.

Exercise 2.18*

We first note that, by Lemma S2.1, the effective capital-labor ratio in this economy limits to infinity, that is

$$\lim_{t\to\infty} A_K(t) K(t) / (A_L(t) L) = \infty. \qquad (S2.19)$$

Next, we claim that capital, output, and consumption asymptotically grow at rate g_L. To see this, let $\hat{k}(t) = K(t) / (A_L(t) L)$ denote the capital to effective labor ratio and note that

$$d\hat{k}(t)/dt = s\left[\gamma_K \left(A_K(t)\hat{k}(t)\right)^{(\sigma-1)/\sigma} + \gamma_L\right]^{\sigma/(\sigma-1)} - (\delta + n)\hat{k}(t).$$

Using the limit expression in (S2.19) and the fact that $\sigma < 1$, this differential equation approximates

$$d\hat{k}(t)/dt \approx s\gamma_L^{\sigma/(\sigma-1)} - (\delta + n)\hat{k}(t).$$

Hence, we have

$$\lim_{t\to\infty} d\hat{k}(t)/dt = 0 \quad \text{and} \quad \lim_{t\to\infty} \hat{k}(t) = s\gamma_L^{\sigma/(\sigma-1)}/(\delta + n).$$

Since $\hat{k}(t)$ asymptotes to a constant, we have that $K(t) = A_L(t) L\hat{k}(t)$ asymptotically grows at rate g_L. Moreover, we have

$$
\begin{aligned}
Y(t) &= A_L(t) Lf\left(A_K(t)\hat{k}(t)\right) \\
&= A_L(t) L\left[\gamma_K\left(A_K(t)\hat{k}(t)\right)^{(\sigma-1)/\sigma} + \gamma_L\right]^{\sigma/(\sigma-1)} \\
&\to \gamma_L^{\sigma/(\sigma-1)} A_L(t) L \text{ as } t \to \infty, \quad\quad\quad\quad\quad\quad (S2.20)
\end{aligned}
$$

hence asymptotically $Y(t)$ also grows at the constant rate g_L. Finally, consumption in the Solow model is a constant share of output and hence also grows at rate g_L, proving our claim.

Finally, we claim that the share of labor in national income tends to 1. Note that the wages can be solved from

$$
\begin{aligned}
w(t) &= \frac{d}{dL}\left(\left[\gamma_K\left(A_K(t)K(t)\right)^{(\sigma-1)/\sigma} + \gamma_L\left(A_L(t)L\right)\right]^{(\sigma-1)/\sigma}\right)^{\sigma/(\sigma-1)} \\
&= \gamma_L A_L(t)^{(\sigma-1)/\sigma} L^{-1/\sigma} Y(t)^{1/\sigma}.
\end{aligned}
$$

The share of labor in national income is then given by

$$
\begin{aligned}
\frac{w(t) L}{Y(t)} &= \frac{\gamma_L A_L(t)^{(\sigma-1)/\sigma} L^{(\sigma-1)/\sigma} Y(t)^{1/\sigma}}{Y(t)} \\
&= \frac{\left[\gamma_L^{\sigma/(\sigma-1)} A_L(t) L\right]^{(\sigma-1)/\sigma}}{Y(t)^{(\sigma-1)/\sigma}},
\end{aligned}
$$

which limits to 1 from Eq. (S2.20), proving our claim.

Intuitively, when $\sigma < 1$, capital and labor are not sufficiently substitutable and labor becomes the bottleneck in production. Hence, despite deepening of effective capital to effective labor, capital and output can only grow at the same rate as effective labor. A complementary intuition comes from considering the approximation in Eq. (S2.20): with $\sigma < 1$, capital deepening causes an abundance of effective capital so that the limit production is essentially determined by how much effective labor the economy has. This exercise provides a robust counter-example to the general claim sometimes made in the literature that capital-augmenting technological progress is incompatible with balanced growth. Note, however, that the share of labor in this economy goes to one which suggests that the claims in the literature can be remedied by adding the requirement that the shares of both capital and labor stay bounded away from 0.

Exercise 2.19*

Exercise 2.19, Part (a). Similar to the construction in the proof of Theorem 2.6, note that, in this case we have

$$
\begin{aligned}
\tilde{F}\left(K(t), L(t), \tilde{A}(t)\right) &= K(t)^{\tilde{A}(t)} L(t)^{1-\tilde{A}(t)} \\
&= K(t)^{\tilde{A}(T)} L(t)^{1-\tilde{A}(T)}.
\end{aligned}
$$

where the second line uses the fact that $K(t) = L(t) = \exp(nt) K(0)$. Defining $A(t) = 1$ for all t, and

$$
F_T\left(K(t), A(t) L(t)\right) = K(t)^{\tilde{A}(T)}\left(A(t) L(t)\right)^{1-\tilde{A}(T)}, \quad\quad\quad\quad (S2.21)
$$

we have $\tilde{F}\left(K\left(t\right),L\left(t\right),\tilde{A}\left(t\right)\right)=F_T\left(K\left(t\right),A\left(t\right)L\left(t\right)\right)$, hence the expression in (S2.21) provides a class of functions (one for each T) as desired.

Exercise 2.19, Part (b). The derivatives do not agree since

$$\frac{dF_T\left(K\left(t\right),A\left(t\right)L\left(t\right)\right)}{dK\left(t\right)}=\tilde{A}\left(T\right)\left(\frac{K\left(t\right)}{A\left(t\right)L\left(t\right)}\right)^{\tilde{A}(T)-1}=\tilde{A}\left(T\right),$$

where we have used $A\left(t\right)=1$ and $K\left(t\right)=L\left(t\right)$, while

$$\frac{d\tilde{F}\left(K\left(t\right),L\left(t\right),\tilde{A}\left(t\right)\right)}{dK\left(t\right)}=\tilde{A}\left(t\right)\left(\frac{K\left(t\right)}{L\left(t\right)}\right)^{\tilde{A}(t)-1}=\tilde{A}\left(t\right).$$

Hence, for any fixed T, the derivatives of $\tilde{F}\left(K\left(t\right),L\left(t\right),\tilde{A}\left(t\right)\right)$ and $F_T\left(K\left(t\right),A\left(t\right)L\left(t\right)\right)$ will be different as long as $\tilde{A}\left(t\right)\neq\tilde{A}\left(T\right)$.

Exercise 2.19, Part (c). Note that, in this economy, capital, labor, output, and consumption all grow at rate n. However, the share of capital is given by

$$\frac{\tilde{F}_K\left(K\left(t\right),L\left(t\right),\tilde{A}\left(t\right)\right)K\left(t\right)}{\tilde{F}\left(K\left(t\right),L\left(t\right),\tilde{A}\left(t\right)\right)}=\frac{\tilde{A}\left(t\right)K\left(t\right)}{K\left(t\right)^{\tilde{A}(t)}L\left(t\right)^{1-\tilde{A}(t)}}=\tilde{A}\left(t\right),$$

where we have used $K\left(t\right)=L\left(t\right)$. Hence even though all variables grow at a constant rate, the share of capital will behave in an arbitrary fashion. When, for example, $\tilde{A}\left(t\right)=\left(2+\sin\left(t\right)\right)/4$, the share of capital will oscillate.

Exercise 2.20

Exercise 2.20, Part (a). Let $k\left(t\right)=K\left(t\right)/L$ denote the capital-labor ratio in this economy. Note that $w\left(k\right)\equiv f\left(k\right)-kf'\left(k\right)$ is increasing in k. There are two cases to consider. First, suppose

$$\lim_{k\to\infty}w\left(k\right)<\overline{w},$$

that is, the minimum wage level is so high that, even with abundant levels of capital-labor ratio, labor's productivity would be short of $\overline{w}$ (this is the case, for example, with the CES production function with $\sigma<1$ when $\overline{w}$ is sufficiently large). In this case, no firm can afford to pay wages $\overline{w}$ regardless of the capital used by each unit of labor, hence the equilibrium employment is always zero, that is $L^d\left(t\right)=0$ and equilibrium unemployment is L. The more interesting case is when $\lim_{k\to\infty}f\left(k\right)-kf'\left(k\right)>\overline{w}$, so there exists a unique $\overline{k}$ such that

$$w\left(\overline{k}\right)=f\left(\overline{k}\right)-\overline{k}f'\left(\overline{k}\right)=\overline{w}.$$

In this case, suppose first that $k\left(t\right)<\overline{k}$. As each employed worker commands capital $\overline{k}$, that is $K\left(t\right)/L^d\left(t\right)=\overline{k}$, the employment rate $l^d\left(t\right)$ is given by

$$l^d\left(t\right)\equiv\frac{L^d\left(t\right)}{L}=\frac{K\left(t\right)}{L\overline{k}}=\frac{k\left(t\right)}{\overline{k}}.$$

Then, output per capita is given by

$$
\begin{aligned}
y(t) &= l^d(t) f\left(\overline{k}\right) \\
&= k(t) \frac{f\left(\overline{k}\right)}{\overline{k}} \\
&< k(t) \frac{f(k(t))}{k(t)} = f(k(t)),
\end{aligned}
$$

where the inequality follows since $f(k)/k$ is a decreasing function. The second line shows that the production function is essentially linear when $k(t) < \overline{k}$. The inequality shows that output per capita is depressed by the minimum wage requirement since some laborers in the economy remain unemployed. Next, suppose that $k(t) > \overline{k}$. Then each employed worker commands capital $k(t)$, all labor is employed, that is $l^d(t) = 1$, and output per capita is given by $y(t) = f(k(t))$.

Combining these two cases, capital-labor ratio in this economy evolves according to

$$
\dot{k} = \left[s \min\left(\frac{f\left(\overline{k}\right)}{\overline{k}}, \frac{f(k)}{k} \right) - \delta \right] k, \tag{S2.22}
$$

given the initial condition $k(0) \equiv K(0)/L$. Recall that $k^* < \overline{k}$, so

$$
\min\left(\frac{f\left(\overline{k}\right)}{\overline{k}}, \frac{f(k)}{k} \right) \le \frac{f\left(\overline{k}\right)}{\overline{k}} < \frac{f(k^*)}{k^*} = \frac{\delta}{s}.
$$

By Eq. (S2.22), this implies that $\dot{k}(t) < 0$ for any $k(t)$, that is $k(t)$ is always decreasing, and in particular,

$$
\lim_{t \to \infty} k(t) = 0.
$$

Hence the capital-labor ratio and output per capita in this economy converges to 0 starting from any initial condition. Note that the unemployment rate, given by $1 - l^d(t) = 1 - \min\left(k(t)/\overline{k}, 1\right)$, is weakly increasing and tends to 1 in the limit.

Intuitively, output per capita and capital accumulation is depressed due to the minimum wage requirement since not all labor can be competitively employed at the required minimum wages. Somewhat more surprisingly the dynamic effects of the minimum wage requirement are so drastic that the capital-labor ratio and output per capita in the economy tend to 0 and unemployment rate tends to 1. The minimum wage requirement is equivalent to requiring each employed worker to command a minimum amount of machines, $\overline{k}$, regardless of the capital-labor ratio in this economy. Consequently, as aggregate capital falls, fewer people are employed which reduces aggregate savings and further reduces aggregate capital, leading to immiseration in the long run.[2]

Exercise 2.20, Part (b). In this case, the dynamic equilibrium path for capital-labor ratio is identical to the textbook Solow model. More specifically, since all agents in this economy save a constant share s of their income, the distribution of income between employees and employers does not change the capital accumulation equation, which is still given by

$$
\dot{k}(t) = sf(k(t)) - \delta k(t).
$$

---

[2]In contrast with the standard Solow model, marginal productivity of capital does not increase as the capital-labor ratio falls. By requiring that each labor commands a capital level $\overline{k}$, the minimum wage law effectively shuts down the diminishing returns to capital channel, which would typically ensure an equilibrium with positive capital-labor ratio.

Hence, starting with any $k(0)$, capital-labor ratio in this economy converges to $k^* > 0$ that is the unique solution to $f(k^*)/k^* = \delta/s$. However, the distribution of income between capital owners and workers will be different since the wages along the equilibrium path are now given by $\lambda f(k(t))$ instead of $f(k(t)) - k(t)f'(k(t))$. Depending on λ and the form of the production function, the workers could be better or worse off relative to the case with competitive labor markets.

Exercise 2.23

Exercise 2.23, Part (a). We consider the Solow model in continuous time and note that output per capita is given by the CES production function (first introduced by Arrow, Chenery, Minhas, Solow (1961))

$$f(k) = A_H \left[\gamma (A_K k)^{\frac{\sigma-1}{\sigma}} + (1-\gamma)(A_L)^{\frac{\sigma-1}{\sigma}} \right]^{\frac{\sigma}{\sigma-1}}. \tag{S2.23}$$

The capital-labor ratio accumulates according to

$$
\begin{aligned}
\dot{k}(t) &= sf(k(t)) - (\delta + n)k(t) \tag{S2.24}\\
&= sA_H \left[\gamma (A_K k(t))^{\frac{\sigma-1}{\sigma}} + (1-\gamma)(A_L)^{\frac{\sigma-1}{\sigma}} \right]^{\frac{\sigma}{\sigma-1}} - (\delta + n)k(t).
\end{aligned}
$$

Since $\sigma > 1$, we have that $f(k)/k = A_H \left[\gamma (A_K)^{\frac{\sigma-1}{\sigma}} + (1-\gamma)(A_L)^{\frac{\sigma-1}{\sigma}} k^{\frac{1-\sigma}{\sigma}} \right]^{\frac{\sigma}{\sigma-1}}$ is decreasing in k with limits

$$\lim_{k \to 0} f(k)/k = \infty \text{ and } \lim_{k \to \infty} f(k)/k = A_H A_K \gamma^{\frac{\sigma}{\sigma-1}}.$$

Then there are two cases to consider.

First, if the following condition holds,

$$A_H A_K \gamma^{\frac{\sigma}{\sigma-1}} < \frac{\delta + n}{s}, \tag{S2.25}$$

then there is a unique $k^* > 0$ that solves $f(k^*)/k^* = (\delta + n)/s$, which is the unique steady state capital-labor ratio in the economy. Moreover, From Eq. (S2.24), when $k(t) > k^*$, we have $\dot{k}(t) < 0$ and when $k(t) < k^*$, we have $\dot{k}(t) > 0$, which implies that the steady state is globally stable. Hence, this case is very similar to the baseline analysis and the economy converges to the unique steady state starting from any initial capital-labor ratio.

Second, if Condition (S2.25) fails, that is, if $A_H A_K \gamma^{\frac{\sigma}{\sigma-1}} \geq (\delta + n)/s$, then Eq. (S2.24) implies that $\dot{k}(t) > 0$ for any $k(t) > 0$, hence $\lim_{t \to \infty} k(t) = \infty$ starting from any initial condition. Moreover, we have

$$\lim_{k \to \infty} \frac{f(k)}{A_H A_K \gamma^{\sigma/(\sigma-1)}k} = 1. \tag{S2.26}$$

Then, as $t \to \infty$, the system in Eq. (S2.24) approximates $\dot{k}(t) = \left(sA_H A_K \gamma^{\sigma/(\sigma-1)} - \delta - n \right) k(t)$, and the asymptotic growth rate of $k(t)$ is $g_k \equiv sA_H \gamma^{\sigma/(\sigma-1)} - \delta - n$. By Eq. (S2.26), the asymptotic growth rate of output and consumption is also g_k.

Hence, if the productivity and the saving rate are sufficiently high, the production function in the limit resembles the AK production function in Exercise 2.22, the economy behaves similarly and features sustained growth. Intuitively, when $\sigma > 1$, part of Assumption 2 fails and the marginal product of capital remains positive if there is an abundance of capital.

Consequently, when the productivity is sufficiently high, sustained growth is possible just like in the AK economy.

Exercise 2.23, Part (b). Before we start the present exercise, for completeness we also characterize the equilibrium with the CES production function when $\sigma \leq 1$. When $\sigma = 1$, the production function is Cobb-Douglas and satisfies Assumptions 1 and 2 in the text, hence the analysis in the text applies without change, proving that there is a unique steady state equilibrium with positive capital-labor ratio.

Next consider the same CES production function (S2.23) in Part (a) with $\sigma < 1$. We have $f(k)/k$ is decreasing in k with limits

$$\lim_{k \to 0} f(k)/k = A_H A_K \gamma^{\frac{\sigma}{\sigma-1}}, \text{ and } \lim_{k \to \infty} f(k)/k = 0.$$

There are two cases to consider.

First, if the opposite of Condition (S2.25) holds, that is, if $A_H A_K \gamma^{\frac{\sigma}{\sigma-1}} > (\delta + n)/s$, then there is a unique $k^* > 0$ that solves $f(k^*)/k^* = (\delta + n)/s$, which is the unique steady state capital-labor ratio in the economy. Moreover, from Eq. (S2.24), when $k(t) > k^*$, we have $\dot{k}(t) < 0$ and when $k(t) < k^*$, we have $\dot{k}(t) > 0$, which implies that the steady state is globally stable. This case is very similar to the baseline analysis and the economy converges to the unique steady state starting from any initial capital-labor ratio.

Second, if Condition (S2.25) holds as a weak inequality, that is, if $A_H A_K \gamma^{\frac{\sigma}{\sigma-1}} \leq (\delta + n)/s$, then Eq. (S2.24) implies that $\dot{k}(t) < 0$ for all $k(t) > 0$ and there is a unique, globally stable steady state at $k^* = 0$. In this case, the productivity in the economy and the saving rate is sufficiently low that, even for very low levels of capital-labor ratio, new investment is not sufficient to cover the effective depreciation of the capital and the capital-labor ratio limits to 0 in the long run.

We next turn to the present exercise with the Leontief production function, $f(k) = \min\{A_K k; A_L\}$, which is the limit of the CES production function (S2.23) as $\sigma \to 0$.[3] In this case, the capital-labor ratio accumulates according to

$$\dot{k}(t) = sA_H \min\{A_K k(t); A_L\} - (\delta + n)k(t). \tag{S2.27}$$

There are three cases to consider.

First, since this case is the limit of the case analyzed in Part (b), we conjecture that when the analogue of the opposite of Condition (S2.25) as $\sigma \to 0$ holds, i.e. when

$$A_H A_K > (\delta + n)/s, \tag{S2.28}$$

there is a steady state with positive capital-labor ratio. In this case, we have

$$A_K k^* \geq A_L \tag{S2.29}$$

(verified below) hence from Eq. (S2.27), the steady state capital-labor ratio can be solved as

$$k^* = \frac{sA_H A_L}{\delta + n}.$$

Plugging in the expression for k^*, we verify that Eq. (S2.29) holds since Eq. (S2.28) holds, proving that there is a steady state with positive capital-labor ratio. From Eq. (S2.27), it can also be seen that, starting from any $k(0)$, the economy converges to the capital-labor ratio k^*. Note that, at this steady state, Eq. (S2.29) holds with strict inequality. Hence

---

[3]There is a typo in Chapter 2 and the exercise statement. As $\sigma \to 0$, the correct limit of the CES production function in Eq. (S2.23) is this expression.

there is idle capital and the price of capital at the steady state is zero, that is $R^* = 0$. The price of labor at steady state is given by $w^* = A_H A_L$.

Second, we claim that when the opposite of Condition (S2.28) hold, that is, if $A_H A_K < (\delta + n)/s$, then the economy converges to a unique steady state in which the capital-labor ratio is 0. In this case, we claim that $\dot{k}(t) < 0$ for all $k(t) > 0$. For $k(t) > A_L/A_K$, the capital accumulation equation in Eq. (S2.27) implies

$$\dot{k}(t) = s A_H A_L - (\delta + n) k(t) < s A_H A_L - (\delta + n) \frac{A_L}{A_K} \leq 0,$$

where the first inequality follows since $k(t) > A_L/A_K$ and the second inequality follows since Condition (S2.28) does not hold. For $k(t) \leq A_L/A_K$, the capital accumulation equation now implies $\dot{k}(t) = (s A_H A_K - \delta - n) k(t) < 0$ since Condition (S2.28) does not hold. This proves that $k(t)$ is decreasing whenever it is positive. Moreover, $k^* = 0$ is indeed a steady state of the system in (S2.27), hence starting with any capital-labor ratio, the economy converges to the globally stable steady state $k^* = 0$. Note that, at this steady state, there is idle labor hence the steady state wages are equal to zero, that is, $w^* = 0$. The steady state price of capital is given by $R^* = A_H A_K$.

Finally, in the degenerate case in which $A_H A_K = (\delta + n)/s$, we have, $\dot{k}(t) < 0$ for $k(t) > A_L/A_K$, and we also have that any value of $k^* \in [0, A_L/A_K]$ is a steady state of the system in Eq. (S2.27). Hence, starting with too high a capital-labor ratio, more specifically when $k(0) > A_L/A_K$, the capital-labor ratio declines and settles at $k^* = A_L/A_K$, and at this steady state there is no idle capital or labor. At this steady state, wages and the price of capital are indeterminate, i.e. the only condition imposed by equilibrium is $w^* + R^* k^* = f(k^*)$. Starting with a lower level of capital-labor ratio, more specifically when $k(0) \in [0, A_L/A_K]$, the economy stays at $k^* = k(0)$. At these steady states, there is idle labor and the factor prices are $w^* = 0, R^* = A_H A_K$. This completes the characterization of the Leontief economy.

Note that, except for the degenerate case of $A_H A_K = (\delta + n)/s$ and sufficiently high capital-labor ratio, the Leontief economy has either idle capital or idle labor at the steady state. Such equilibria are arguably pathological and we would not expect to observe them in practice (there is much unemployment observed in practice, but there are many more plausible explanations for this phenomenon).

The first reason why these equilibria are unrealistic is because, in reality, factors are not supplied inelastically (as in the case of labor in the Solow model) or mechanically (as in the case of capital in the Solow model) but adjust to factor returns. Consider, for example a steady state equilibrium with idle labor, i.e. consider the second case above. The labor is earning zero wages, hence we would expect individuals not to work and leave the labor force until there is no idle labor and wages become positive again. Similarly, if capital was idle, the net return to capital would be lower than 1 and individuals would not invest their savings in the productive technology (but rather save resources under their pillows!). Hence, the idle capital and labor equilibria of this model are artifacts of our simplifying assumptions for factor supplies and do not represent interesting economic phenomena.

The second reason why these equilibria are unrealistic is because, in reality, technology is not fixed but endogenously supplied and technological progress may be guided by factor returns. Consider, for example, the steady state equilibrium with idle labor. In this case, research and development activities would be directed towards capital-augmenting technologies (i.e. towards increasing A_K) and the effective capital-labor ratio would increase until labor is no longer idle. Hence, endogenizing technology and considering the possibility that further technological progress might be directed towards utilizing the idle factor (i.e. by increasing the effective amount of the complementary factor), we have further reason to doubt the relevance of the idle factor equilibria of the Solow model with Leontief production function.

Exercise 2.27

Exercise 2.27, Part (a). Let the population grow at rate n. Let $k(t) = K(t)/L(t)$ and define the function $f(k) = F(k, 1)$. The capital-labor ratio accumulates according to

$$\dot{k}(t) = sq(t) f(k(t)) - (\delta + n) k(t).$$

Suppose there is a BGP in which capital-labor ratio grows at rate $g_k \geq 0$. Then, we can solve for $k(t)$ and $q(t)$ as $k(t) = k(0) \exp(g_k t)$ and $q(t) = q(0) \exp(\gamma_K t)$. Plugging in the previous equation, we have

$$g_k k(0) \exp(g_k t) = sq(0) \exp(\gamma_K t) f(k(0) \exp(g_k t)) - (\delta + n) k(0) \exp(g_k t),$$

which can be further simplified to

$$\frac{k(0)}{sq(0)} (g_k + \delta + n) \exp[(g_k - \gamma_K) t] = f(k(0) \exp(g_k t)).$$

First, consider the possibility that $g_k = 0$. This clearly yields a contradiction, for in this case, the left hand side goes to zero while the right hand side is constant. Hence, we must have $g_k > 0$. But then, capital per labor and hence the argument of $f(.)$ on the right hand side is growing to infinity. Thus we can solve for $f(k)$ for any $k \in [k(0), \infty)$. Using a change of variables between t and k, in particular $k = k(0) \exp(g_k t)$ (or equivalently $t = \ln\left(\frac{k}{k(0)}\right)/g_k$), we have

$$f(k) = \frac{k(0)}{sq(0)} (g_k + \delta + n) \frac{1}{(k(0))^{(g_k - \gamma_K)/g_k}} k^{(g_k - \gamma_K)/g_k} \text{ for all } k \in [k(0), \infty),$$

which can be rewritten, for some constant $C > 0$, as

$$f(k) = Ck^{(g_k - \gamma_K)/g_k}, \text{ for all } k \in [k(0), \infty).$$

For the production function F, we have

$$F(K, L) = Lf(k) = CK^{(g_k - \gamma_K)/g_k} L^{\gamma_K/g_k}.$$

In other words, a balanced growth path is only possible if F takes the Cobb-Douglas form. This proves, in particular, that for general production functions this model will not feature a balanced growth path. Any production function that is not Cobb-Douglas can be provided as an example in which this model does not feature balanced growth.

To see the intuition, consider a hypothetical economy with production function

$$\tilde{F}(K, L) = qF(K, L).$$

In this hypothetical economy, the accumulation of capital is identical to the original economy. Note that $q(t)$ acts as a Hicks neutral technological change in the hypothetical economy. From Uzawa's Theorem (cf. Theorem 2.6), balanced growth is only compatible with labor-augmenting (or Harrod neutral) technological change. The only exception to this is the Cobb-Douglas production function, which, since the elasticity of substitution between factors is equal to 1, makes all kinds of technological progress equivalent. It follows that the only production function that is consistent with balanced growth in the hypothetical economy (and thus the original economy) is the Cobb-Douglas production function.

Exercise 2.27, Part (b). We suppose that the production function is Cobb-Douglas, that is, $f(k) = k^\alpha$ and we continue to assume that $\dot{q}(t)/q(t) = \gamma_K$. The capital accumulation is given by

$$\frac{\dot{k}(t)}{k(t)} = sqk(t)^{\alpha-1} - (\delta + n). \tag{S2.30}$$

On a BGP, the left hand side is constant, hence the right hand side is also constant. In particular, $q(t)k(t)^{\alpha-1}$ is not growing, that is, $\frac{d\left(q(t)k(t)^{\alpha-1}\right)/dt}{q(t)k(t)^{\alpha-1}} = 0$, which implies

$$\frac{\dot{q}(t)}{q(t)} + (\alpha - 1)\frac{\dot{k}(t)}{k(t)} = 0.$$

Hence $g_k \equiv \dot{k}(t)/k(t) = \gamma_K/(1-\alpha)$ is the only possible growth rate of capital-labor ratio that is consistent with balanced growth.

Next, we claim that there exists a BGP over which $k(t)$ grows at rate g_k. To see this, define the normalized capital-labor ratio as

$$\hat{k}(t) \equiv \frac{k(t)}{q(t)^{1/(1-\alpha)}} = \frac{k(t)}{q(0)\exp\left(\gamma_K/(1-\alpha)t\right)}. \tag{S2.31}$$

Then, using Eq. (S2.30), we have

$$
\begin{aligned}
\frac{d\hat{k}/dt}{\hat{k}(t)} &= \frac{\dot{k}(t)}{k(t)} - \frac{\gamma_K}{1-\alpha} \\
&= sq(t)k(t)^{\alpha-1} - \delta - n - \frac{\gamma_K}{1-\alpha} \\
&= sq(t)\left[\hat{k}(t)q(t)^{1/(1-\alpha)}\right]^{\alpha-1} - (\delta + n) - \frac{\gamma_K}{1-\alpha} \\
&= s\hat{k}(t)^{\alpha-1} - \delta - n - \frac{\gamma_K}{1-\alpha} \equiv g\left(\hat{k}(t)\right)
\end{aligned}
$$

where the third line follows by using Eq. (S2.31) and the last line defines the function $g\left(\hat{k}\right)$. Then, we have that the normalized capital-labor ratio

$$\hat{k}^* = \left(\frac{s}{\delta + n + \frac{\gamma_K}{1-\alpha}}\right)^{1/(1-\alpha)},$$

represents a steady state equilibrium on which $k(t)$ grows at the constant rate g_k, proving our claim.

Next, note that since $g\left(\hat{k}\right)$ is a decreasing function and since $g\left(\hat{k}^*\right) = 0$, we have

$$g\left(\hat{k}(t)\right) > 0 \text{ if } \hat{k}(t) < \hat{k}^*, \text{ and } g\left(\hat{k}(t)\right) < 0 \text{ if } \hat{k}(t) > \hat{k}^*,$$

so that the steady state normalized capital-labor ratio $\hat{k}^*$ is globally stable. Starting with any $\hat{k}(0)$, the normalized capital-labor ratio in this economy converges to $\hat{k}^*$ and the capital-labor ratio asymptotically grows at the rate g_k.

Finally, we consider the path of output per capita, which is given by $y(t) = k(t)^\alpha$ and hence grows at rate

$$g_y(t) \equiv \frac{\dot{y}(t)}{y(t)} = \alpha\frac{\dot{k}(t)}{k(t)}.$$

It follows that the asymptotic growth rate of output (or its growth rate on a BGP equilibrium) is given by $g_y \equiv \alpha g_k = \frac{\alpha}{(1-\alpha)}\gamma_K$, proving that output per capita also grows at a constant rate on BGP.

Exercise 2.27, Part (c). We have that $k(t)$ grows at rate $g_k = \gamma_K / (1 - \alpha)$ but output per capita grows at rate $g_y = \gamma_K \alpha / (1 - \alpha) < g_k$. Hence, physical capital grows faster than output. In particular, on the BGP, we have

$$\frac{K(t)}{Y(t)} \to \infty,$$

which is, strictly speaking, not consistent with the Kaldor facts. Capital in this model grows faster since the price of capital in terms of the consumption good is constantly decreasing which enables the economy to accumulate capital at higher rates.

Note that we can interpret $q(t)$ as the inverse of the price of capital in terms of consumption goods. Then, instead of considering capital output ratio, we might instead consider the relative value of aggregate capital to output, that is, the ratio of $K(t)/q(t)$ to $Y(t)$. For the growth rate of this ratio, note that

$$\frac{d(K(t)/q(t))/dt}{K(t)/q(t)} = \frac{\dot{K}(t)}{K(t)} - \frac{\dot{q}(t)}{q(t)} = g_k + n - \gamma_K$$

$$= \frac{1}{1-\alpha}\gamma_K - \gamma_K + n$$

$$= \frac{\alpha}{1-\alpha}\gamma_K + n = g_y + n = \frac{\dot{Y}(t)}{Y(t)}.$$

Hence, $K(t)/q(t)$ and $Y(t)$ grow at the same rate, and in particular, their ratio is constant on the BGP. Hence, even though physical capital increases faster than output, the value of aggregate capital in terms of output remains constant. In practice, we do not measure the number of machines, but we measure the value of aggregate machines as the level of capital—in fact, the standard way to calculate aggregate capital is to add up investment (which includes prices of machines as well as quantities) going back to far enough in the past. Hence, if this model were correct, we would still observe constant capital value to output in practice, thus the model is not necessarily contradicting the Kaldor facts broadly interpreted.

Chapter 3: The Solow Model and the Data

Exercise 3.1

Let $k\left(\tilde{t}\right) = K\left(\tilde{t}\right)/L\left(\tilde{t}\right)$ and $y\left(\tilde{t}\right) = Y\left(\tilde{t}\right)/L\left(\tilde{t}\right)$ respectively denote capital-labor ratio and output per capita at dates $\tilde{t} \in \{t, t+T\}$, and define

$$g_y\left(t, t+T\right) \equiv g_Y\left(t, t+T\right) - g_L\left(t, t+T\right) = \ln\left(\frac{y\left(t+T\right)}{y\left(t\right)}\right) \qquad \text{(S3.1)}$$

$$\text{and } g_k\left(t, t+T\right) \equiv g_K\left(t, t+T\right) - g_L\left(t, t+T\right) = \ln\left(\frac{k\left(t+T\right)}{k\left(t\right)}\right)$$

as their growth between t and $t+T$. Using $\alpha_L\left(\tilde{t}\right) = 1 - \alpha_K\left(\tilde{t}\right)$, the TFP estimates using beginning and end factor shares can be expressed as

$$\hat{x}^b\left(t, t+T\right) = g_y\left(t, t+T\right) - \alpha_K\left(t\right) g_k\left(t, t+T\right), \qquad \text{(S3.2)}$$

$$\hat{x}^e\left(t, t+T\right) = g_y\left(t, t+T\right) - \alpha_K\left(t+T\right) g_k\left(t, t+T\right).$$

Suppose we observe $Y\left(\tilde{t}\right), K\left(\tilde{t}\right), L\left(\tilde{t}\right)$ (hence $k\left(\tilde{t}\right)$ and $y\left(\tilde{t}\right)$) along with competitive prices $w\left(\tilde{t}\right) = F_L\left(K\left(\tilde{t}\right), L\left(\tilde{t}\right)\right)$ at the two dates $\tilde{t} \in \{t, t+T\}$. From this information, we can calculate

$$\alpha_L\left(\tilde{t}\right) = \frac{w\left(\tilde{t}\right)L\left(\tilde{t}\right)}{Y\left(\tilde{t}\right)} \text{ and } \alpha_K\left(\tilde{t}\right) = 1 - \alpha_L\left(\tilde{t}\right)$$

at the the two dates. We can also calculate $g_y\left(t, t+T\right)$ and $g_k\left(t, t+T\right)$ from Eq. (S3.1), obtaining the estimates in (S3.2) for the TFP growth (as first suggested by Solow (1957)).

We claim, however, that both estimates $\hat{x}^b\left(t, t+T\right)$ and $\hat{x}^e\left(t, t+T\right)$ that we calculate in this manner could be arbitrarily different from the true TFP growth $x\left(t, t+T\right)$. Suppose that the production function is given by $AF\left(K, L\right)$, where the technology takes the Hicks-neutral form, and let $\dot{A}/A = g$ so that the true TFP growth is

$$x\left(t, t+T\right) = \ln\left(\frac{A\left(t+T\right)}{A\left(t\right)}\right) = gT.$$

Suppose also that L is constant and K grows at some rate g^K. Note that per labor output function is given by $Af\left(k\right)$ where $f\left(k\right) = F\left(k, 1\right)$, the rental rate of capital is $Af'\left(k\right)$ and the share of capital is given as a function of capital-labor ratio as

$$\alpha_K\left(k\right) = Af'\left(k\right)k/\left(Af\left(k\right)\right) = f'\left(k\right)k/f\left(k\right).$$

In this case, the estimate $\hat{x}^b(t, t+T)$ in Eq. (S3.2) can be rewritten as

$$
\begin{aligned}
\frac{\hat{x}^b(t, t+T)}{T} &= \frac{1}{T}\ln\left(\frac{y(t+T)}{y(t)}\right) - \frac{k(t)f'(k(t))}{f(k(t))}g^K \\
&= \frac{1}{T}\ln\left(\frac{A(t+T)f(k(t+T))}{A(t)f(k(t))}\right) - \frac{k(t)f'(k(t))}{f(k(t))}g^K \\
&= g + \left[\frac{1}{T}\ln\left(\frac{f(k(t)\exp(g^K T))}{f(k(t))}\right) - \frac{k(t)f'(k(t))}{f(k(t))}g^K\right].
\end{aligned}
\tag{S3.3}
$$

The estimate $\hat{x}^b(t, t+T)/T$ for the average growth rate will be wrong whenever the term in brackets in the last displayed equation is non-zero. This term is typically non-zero for any function but the Cobb-Douglas production function. To see this, consider, for example a CES production function $f(k) = \left(k^{(\varepsilon-1)/\varepsilon} + 1\right)^{\varepsilon/(\varepsilon-1)}$. Plugging this in (S3.3), we have

$$
\frac{\hat{x}^b(t, t+T)}{T} = g + \frac{1}{T}\frac{\varepsilon}{\varepsilon-1}\ln\left(\frac{\left[k(t)\exp(g^K T)\right]^{(\varepsilon-1)/\varepsilon} + 1}{k(t)^{(\varepsilon-1)/\varepsilon} + 1}\right) - \frac{k(t)^{(\varepsilon-1)/\varepsilon}}{k(t)^{(\varepsilon-1)/\varepsilon} + 1}g^K.
\tag{S3.4}
$$

Let $\varepsilon < 1$ and note that

$$
\lim_{g^K \to \infty}\frac{\hat{x}^b(t, t+T)}{T} = g + \frac{1}{T}\frac{\varepsilon}{\varepsilon-1}\ln\left(\frac{1}{k(t)^{(\varepsilon-1)/\varepsilon} + 1}\right) - \infty = -\infty.
$$

In particular, with $\varepsilon < 1$ and sufficiently large g^K, the estimate $\hat{x}^b(t, t+T)/T$ will underestimate the average TFP growth rate, and this underestimation can be arbitrarily large. With $\varepsilon < 1$ and sufficiently fast capital deepening the share of capital will decrease rapidly. Consequently, using the initial share of capital overestimates the contribution of capital accumulation to growth and underestimate the TFP growth.

Consider also the case with $\varepsilon > 1$ and note that, taking the limit of Eq. (S3.4) in this case, we have

$$
\begin{aligned}
\lim_{g^K \to \infty}\frac{\hat{x}^b(t, t+T)}{T} &= g + \lim_{g^K \to \infty}\left\{g^K + \frac{1}{T}\frac{\varepsilon}{\varepsilon-1}\ln\frac{k(t)^{(\varepsilon-1)/\varepsilon}}{k(t)^{(\varepsilon-1)/\varepsilon} + 1} - \frac{k(t)^{(\varepsilon-1)/\varepsilon}}{k(t)^{(\varepsilon-1)/\varepsilon} + 1}g^K\right\} \\
&= g + \lim_{g^K \to \infty}\left\{\frac{1}{T}\frac{\varepsilon}{\varepsilon-1}\ln\left(\frac{k(t)^{(\varepsilon-1)/\varepsilon}}{k(t)^{(\varepsilon-1)/\varepsilon} + 1}\right) + \frac{1}{k(t)^{(\varepsilon-1)/\varepsilon} + 1}g^K\right\} \\
&= +\infty,
\end{aligned}
$$

where the first uses the fact that the 1 in the numerator can be ignored when evaluating the limit of $\frac{1}{T}\frac{\varepsilon}{\varepsilon-1}\ln\left(\frac{[k(t)\exp(g^K T)]^{(\varepsilon-1)/\varepsilon}+1}{k(t)^{(\varepsilon-1)/\varepsilon}+1}\right)$ which simplifies the expression, and the second line collects the g^K terms together. That is, with $\varepsilon > 1$ and sufficiently large g^K, the estimate $\hat{x}^b(t, t+T)/T$ will overestimate the average TFP growth rate, and this overestimation can be arbitrarily large. In this case, the share of capital is increasing and using the initial value of the share of capital underestimates the contribution of capital accumulation to output growth and hence overestimates the TFP growth.

A similar analysis also establishes that, in the same example with the CES production function, the estimate, $\hat{x}^e(t, t+T)/T$, that uses the last period share of capital can be arbitrarily different than $x(t, t+T)/T = g$ when the rate of capital accumulation, g^K, is high. When $\varepsilon < 1$, using the last period underestimates the contribution of capital accumulation and overestimates the TFP growth, while when $\varepsilon > 1$, using the last period overestimates the contribution of capital accumulation and underestimates the TFP growth.

The intuition we have provided also explains the role of the differences in factor proportions in these results. If effective factor ratios $\frac{A_K K}{A_L L}$ were the same over time, a neoclassical production function $F(A_K K, A_L L)$ would have constant factor shares and the approximation using either beginning or end value for factor shares would yield the correct TFP. When the effective factor proportions change, factor shares also change for any production function other than Cobb-Douglas, hence the estimations using the initial or end values for factor shares might be biased.

Exercise 3.9

Exercise 3.9, Part (a). Capital accumulates according to

$$\dot{K}(t) = sF(K(t), H(t)) - \delta K(t).$$

Since $F(K, H)/K$ is decreasing in K, there is a unique steady state K^*, found by solving

$$\frac{F(K^*, H)}{K^*} = \frac{\delta}{s}. \tag{S3.5}$$

Exercise 3.9, Part (b). The steady state return to a unit of human capital is given by $F_H(K^*, H)$, hence an individual with human capital h_i earns income $F_H(K^*, H) h_i$. If she increases her human capital by 10%, that is to $1.1 \times h_i$, then her income will increase to $1.1 \times F_H(K^*, H) h_i$, which is 10% higher than $F_H(K^*, H) h_i$. Hence, a 10% increase in individual human capital leads to a $a \equiv 10\%$ increase in income.

At the aggregate level, the aggregate human capital increases from H to $1.1 \times H$. Hence, the new steady state capital stock is found by solving

$$\frac{F(K^{new}, 1.1 \times H)}{K^{new}} = \frac{\delta}{s}.$$

Comparing this equation with Eq. (S3.5) and using the fact that F is constant returns to scale in K and H, we have $K^{new} = 1.1 \times K^*$, that is, the steady state capital level also increases by 10%. The new steady state output is given by

$$F(K^{new}, 1.1 \times H) = F(1.1 \times K^*, 1.1 \times H) = 1.1 \times F(K^*, H),$$

that is, the steady state output also increases by 10%, as desired. Intuitively, since the Solow model features constant returns to scale, as aggregate human capital increases, the aggregate capital stock adjusts by the same rate, and consequently output increases by the same rate.

Next we consider the change in output before the capital stock adjusts. The change in output before the adjustment of the capital stock satisfies the inequality

$$1 < \frac{F(K^*, 1.1 \times H)}{F(K^*, H)} < \frac{F(1.1 \times K^*, 1.1 \times H)}{F(K^*, H)} = 1.1.$$

Hence, initially output increases but by less than 10%. Intuitively, this is because there are diminishing returns to human capital at the aggregate level even though there are constant returns to scale at the individual level (which is what we measure). At the time of the change, there is less physical capital per human capital, hence each unit of human capital produces less than the previous steady state. This in turn implies that the aggregate output increases by a rate less than the rate of increase in aggregate human capital. Once capital adjusts, the physical capital to human capital ratio increases to its previous level and the increase in output matches the increase in aggregate human capital.

Chapter 4: Fundamental Determinants of Differences in Economic Performance

Exercise 4.3

Exercise 4.3, Part (a). This trivially follows from the mechanical assumption that $L(t) = \phi Y(t)$. By assumption, any increase in output translates to a population increase so output per capita is constant at $1/\phi$ throughout.

Exercise 4.3, Part (b). The modified equation,

$$L(t) = \phi Y(t)^\beta \tag{S4.1}$$

with $\beta \in (0,1)$, suggests that the Malthusian channels are present but are weaker. In particular, an output growth rate of g translates into a population growth rate of βg, which in turn allows output per capita to grow at rate $(1-\beta)g$. This equation may be justified as follows. The Malthusian channel is typically associated with richer individuals living longer and having more children, and the children facing a lower probability of death, again thanks to the riches of their parents. This reasoning does not necessarily imply a linear functional form between output and population. In fact, since there are natural limits to how long an individual could live and how many children a couple may have, it is more sensible to assume that the Malthusian channel implies that population increases in response to increases in output, but at a diminishing rate. The modified functional form in (S4.1) captures just that.

We next derive the law of motion of technology and income in the first scenario, in which technology evolves according to Eq. (4.1). Using the production function in Eq. (S4.1), we have the following relationship between population and technology

$$L(t) = \phi^{1/(1-\alpha\beta)} A(t)^{\beta/(1-\alpha\beta)}. \tag{S4.2}$$

Plugging this in Eq. (4.1), we obtain the technology evolution equation

$$\dot{A}(t) = \lambda \phi^{1/(1-\alpha\beta)} A(t)^{\frac{(1-\alpha)\beta}{1-\alpha\beta}}. \tag{S4.3}$$

Note that this expression can be rearranged into a separable differential equation as

$$A^{-\frac{(1-\alpha)\beta}{1-\alpha\beta}} dA = \lambda \phi^{1/(1-\alpha\beta)} dt.$$

Integrating this expression, we have

$$\frac{A(t)^{1-\frac{(1-\alpha)\beta}{1-\alpha\beta}}}{1-\frac{(1-\alpha)\beta}{1-\alpha\beta}} = \lambda \phi^{1/(1-\alpha\beta)} t + C,$$

where C is a constant of integration. Solving for C using the initial condition $A(0)$, the previous expression yields

$$A(t) = \left[\lambda \phi^{1/(1-\alpha\beta)} \frac{1-\beta}{1-\alpha\beta} t + A(0)^{(1-\beta)/(1-\alpha\beta)} \right]^{(1-\alpha\beta)/(1-\beta)}.$$

Hence, as in the baseline case, $A(t)$ limits to infinity so technology increases as a result of the accumulation of population and ideas. Note also that, by Eq. (S4.3), we have

$$\frac{\dot{A}(t)}{A(t)} = \lambda \phi^{1/(1-\alpha\beta)} A(t)^{\frac{-(1-\beta)}{1-\alpha\beta}}.$$

Since $-(1-\beta)/(1-\alpha\beta) < 0$ and $A(t)$ is increasing, different than the baseline case, in this case technology grows at a decreasing rate. The reason for this result is the assumption that Malthusian forces are weaker as the economy develops, so population, and hence ideas, grow at an ever slower rate. Using Eqs. (S4.1) and (S4.2), we can also calculate the income per capita as

$$\frac{Y(t)}{L(t)} = \phi^{-\frac{1-\alpha}{1-\alpha\beta}} A(t)^{\frac{1-\beta}{1-\alpha\beta}}, \tag{S4.4}$$

which grows at rate

$$g_{Y/L}(t) = \frac{1-\beta}{1-\alpha\beta} \frac{\dot{A}(t)}{A(t)} = \lambda \phi^{1/(1-\alpha\beta)} \frac{1-\beta}{1-\alpha\beta} A(t)^{-\frac{(1-\beta)}{1-\alpha\beta}},$$

which is decreasing and limits to 0. Hence, different than the baseline model, income per capita is increasing in this model, but at ever decreasing rates. This is a slight improvement over the baseline model, but is still unrealistic in view of the recent emergence of modern growth and acceleration of income per capita growth.

To make the predictions of the model more realistic, consider the second scenario in which technology evolves according to

$$\frac{\dot{A}(t)}{A(t)} = \lambda L(t).$$

Using Eq. (S4.2), the technology evolution equation can be rewritten as

$$\dot{A}(t) = \lambda A(t)^{\frac{(1-\alpha)\beta}{1-\alpha\beta}+1} \phi^{1/(1-\alpha\beta)}.$$

Similar to above, this expression can be rearranged into a separable differential equation and integrated to give

$$A(t) = \left(\frac{1}{\frac{-\lambda \phi^{1/(1-\alpha\beta)}}{\frac{(1-\alpha)\beta}{1-\alpha\beta}+1} t + A(0)^{-\frac{(1-\alpha)\beta}{1-\alpha\beta}}} \right)^{\frac{1-\alpha\beta}{(1-\alpha)\beta}}.$$

Hence we recover the accelerating pattern as in the baseline analysis: $A(t)$ grows and the growth rate of $A(t)$ is given by

$$\frac{\dot{A}(t)}{A(t)} = \lambda A(t)^{\frac{(1-\alpha)\beta}{1-\alpha\beta}} \phi^{1/(1-\alpha\beta)},$$

which is increasing since $\frac{(1-\alpha)\beta}{1-\alpha\beta}$ is positive. Moreover, income per capita is still given by Eq. (S4.4) and its growth rate in this case is given by

$$g_{Y/L}(t) = \frac{1-\beta}{1-\alpha\beta} \frac{\dot{A}(t)}{A(t)} = \lambda \phi^{1/(1-\alpha\beta)} \frac{1-\beta}{1-\alpha\beta} A(t)^{\frac{(1-\alpha)\beta}{1-\alpha\beta}},$$

which is increasing and limits to infinity. Hence income per capita grows at an accelerating rate. This modification may be viewed as an improvement over the baseline model since it gets the model's predictions for income per capita closer to reality.

Chapter 5: Foundations of Neoclassical Growth

Exercise 5.9

First, we formally state the optimization problem that an individual solves to choose time 0 bond trades and time t commodity trades, $(\mathbf{x}^{**}, \mathbf{b}^{**})$, given prices $(\mathbf{q}^{**}, \mathbf{p}^{**})$. We invoke the result we have obtained in Exercise 5.1, that is, since the individual's preferences are time-consistent, at time t she follows exactly the plan that she had made at time 0. At time 0 (before time 0 endowments are allocated) she solves

$$\max_{\{b_t^h\}_t, \{x_{j,t}^h\}_{j,t}} \sum_{t=0}^{T} \left(\beta^h\right)^t u^h \left(x_{1,t}^h, ..., x_{N,t}^h\right), \tag{S5.1}$$

$$\text{s.t.} \quad \sum_{j=1}^{N} p_{j,t}^{**} x_{j,t}^h \leq \sum_{j=1}^{N} p_{j,t}^{**} \omega_{j,t}^h + b_t^h \text{ for } t \in \{0, 1, ..., T\}, \tag{S5.2}$$

$$\sum_{t=0}^{T} q_t^{**} b_t^h \leq 0. \tag{S5.3}$$

Here, to simplify notation and without loss of generality, we treat time 0 symmetrically as any time $t \geq 1$ and allow the individual to hold bonds also for time 0. The individual engages in all bond trades before time 0 endowments are allocated leading to constraint (S5.3) which states that the individual's intertemporal bond trades should break even.

The crux of the argument is to observe that the constraints (S5.2) and (S5.3) are essentially equivalent to a lifetime budget constraint. In particular, substituting the constraints (S5.2) in the constraint (S5.3) to eliminate the b_t^h terms, we get the lifetime budget constraint

$$\sum_{t=0}^{T} \sum_{j=1}^{N} q_t^{**} p_{j,t}^{**} x_{j,t}^h \leq \sum_{t=0}^{T} \sum_{j=1}^{N} q_t^{**} p_{j,t}^{**} \omega_{j,t}^h. \tag{S5.4}$$

Conversely, for any $\mathbf{x}^h$ that satisfies Eq. (S5.4), one can construct

$$b_t^h = \sum_{j=1}^{N} p_{j,t}^{**} \left((x^{**})_{j,t}^h - w_{j,t}^h\right) \tag{S5.5}$$

so that the resulting pair $\left(\mathbf{x}^h, \mathbf{b}^h\right)$ satisfies both of the constraints (S5.2) and (S5.3). Consequently, we have that the individual's problem is essentially identical in the Arrow-Debreu and the sequential equilibria, which in turn will show that there is a one-to-one mapping between the two equilibria. Next, we prove Theorem 5.8 by formalizing this argument.

To prove the first part of the theorem, let $(\mathbf{p}^*, \mathbf{x}^*)$ be an Arrow-Debreu equilibrium. As in the theorem statement, construct the bundle $(\mathbf{p}^{**}, \mathbf{q}^{**}, \mathbf{x}^{**})$ such that $\mathbf{x}^{**} = \mathbf{x}^*$, $p_{j,t}^{**} = p_{j,t}^*/p_{1,t}^*$ for all j and t and $q_t^{**} = p_{1,t}^*$ for all $t > 0$. Also construct $\mathbf{b}^{**}$ as in Eq. (S5.5), so that the bond payoffs at time t are just enough for the individual to purchase $\left\{ (x^*)_{j,t}^h \right\}_{j=1}^N$ at time t. We claim that $(\mathbf{p}^{**}, \mathbf{q}^{**}, \mathbf{x}^{**}, \mathbf{b}^{**})$ corresponds to a sequential trading equilibrium. The commodity markets clear since $\mathbf{x}^{**} = \mathbf{x}^*$ and $\mathbf{x}^*$ is part of an Arrow-Debreu equilibrium. The bond markets clear since

$$\sum_{h \in \mathcal{H}} (\mathbf{b}^{**})_t^h = \sum_{h \in \mathcal{H}} \sum_{j=1}^N p_{j,t}^{**} \left((x^*)_{j,t}^h - w_{j,t}^h \right)$$

$$= \sum_{j=1}^N \frac{p_{j,t}^*}{p_{j,1}^*} \sum_{h \in \mathcal{H}} \left((x^*)_{j,t}^h - w_{j,t}^h \right) \leq 0,$$

where the inequality follows since $\sum_{h \in \mathcal{H}} \left((x^*)_{j,t}^h - w_{j,t}^h \right) \leq 0$ for each j, t due to the market clearing constraints in the Arrow-Debreu economy. Hence, the only thing left to check is that each individual's bond and commodity trades, $\left((\mathbf{x}^{**})^h, (\mathbf{b}^{**})^h \right)$ solve Problem (S5.1). To see this, consider any $\left((\tilde{\mathbf{x}}^{**})^h, \left(\tilde{\mathbf{b}}^{**} \right)^h \right)$ which satisfies Constraints (S5.2) and (S5.3), which implies by our earlier analysis that it satisfies the budget constraint (S5.4). Using $q_t^{**} p_{j,t}^{**} = p_{j,t}^*$, $\left((\tilde{\mathbf{x}}^{**})^h, \left(\tilde{\mathbf{b}}^{**} \right)^h \right)$ also satisfies the lifetime budget constraint

$$\sum_{t=0}^T \sum_{j=1}^N p_{j,t}^* \tilde{x}_{j,t}^h \leq \sum_{t=0}^T \sum_{j=1}^N p_{j,t}^* \omega_{j,t}^h, \tag{S5.6}$$

that is $(\tilde{\mathbf{x}}^{**})^h$ is in the budget set for household h in the Arrow-Debreu economy. Since $(\mathbf{x}^{**})^h$ is an Arrow-Debreu equilibrium allocation, it attains a higher utility than $(\tilde{\mathbf{x}}^{**})^h$. Since $\left((\tilde{\mathbf{x}}^{**})^h, \left(\tilde{\mathbf{b}}^{**} \right)^h \right)$ is an arbitrary allocation that satisfies the constraints of Problem (S5.1), it follows that $\left((\mathbf{x}^{**})^h, (\mathbf{b}^{**})^h \right)$ solve this problem, proving that $(\mathbf{p}^{**}, \mathbf{q}^{**}, \mathbf{x}^{**}, \mathbf{b}^{**})$ is a sequential trading equilibrium.

To prove the second part of the theorem, we let $(\mathbf{p}^{**}, \mathbf{q}^{**}, \mathbf{x}^{**}, \mathbf{b}^{**})$ be a sequential trading equilibrium and we claim that

$$\left(\mathbf{p}^* \equiv \left\{ p_{j,t}^* = \frac{p_{j,t}^{**}}{p_{1,t}^{**}} q_t^{**} \right\}_{j,t}, \mathbf{x}^* \equiv \mathbf{x}^{**} \right)$$

is an Arrow-Debreu equilibrium. Since commodity markets clear in the sequential equilibrium and since $\mathbf{x}^* \equiv \mathbf{x}^{**}$, commodity markets also clear in the Arrow-Debreu equilibrium. The only thing left to check is that each individual's commodity choices $(\mathbf{x}^*)^h$ maximize her utility subject to the lifetime budget constraint (S5.6). Suppose, to reach a contradiction, that there exists an individual $h \in \mathcal{H}$ and a vector $(\tilde{\mathbf{x}}^*)^h$ which satisfies Eq. (S5.6) and attains higher utility for individual h than $(\mathbf{x}^*)^h$. First, observe that since $p_{j,t}^* = \frac{p_{j,t}^{**}}{p_{1,t}^{**}} q_t^{**}$ for each j, the lifetime budget constraints (S5.6) and (S5.4) are equivalent and $(\tilde{\mathbf{x}}^*)^h$ also satisfies the latter. Next, construct $\left(\tilde{\mathbf{b}}^{**} \right)^h$ as in Eq. (S5.5) given $(\tilde{\mathbf{x}}^*)^h$, and let $(\tilde{\mathbf{x}}^{**})^h \equiv (\tilde{\mathbf{x}}^*)^h$. By the observation we have made earlier, since $(\tilde{\mathbf{x}}^*)^h$ satisfies (S5.4), the pair $\left((\tilde{\mathbf{x}}^{**})^h, \left(\tilde{\mathbf{b}}^{**} \right)^h \right)$

satisfies Constraints (S5.2) and (S5.3). Since $\left((\tilde{\mathbf{x}}^{**})^h = (\tilde{\mathbf{x}}^*)^h, \left(\tilde{\mathbf{b}}^{**}\right)^h \right)$ attains a higher utility for individual h than the pair $\left((\mathbf{x}^{**})^h = (\mathbf{x}^*)^h, (\mathbf{b}^{**})^h \right)$, we have a contradiction to the fact that $\left((\mathbf{x}^{**})^h, (\mathbf{b}^{**})^h \right)$ solves Problem (S5.1). This completes the proof of the theorem.

Exercise 5.11

Assume that u is strictly concave and strictly increasing with $u'(0) = \infty$. We claim that for any such u, this economy does not feature a representative consumer. First, note that the consumption of household h in group $j \in \{A, B\}$ solves

$$\max_{\left(c_1^h, c_2^h\right) \geq 0} \quad u\left(c_1^h\right) + \beta_j u\left(c_2^h\right)$$

$$\text{s.t.} \quad c_1^h + c_2^h/R \leq y_j.$$

With our assumptions on u, for any $y_j > 0$ this problem has a unique interior solution characterized by the Euler equation

$$u'\left(c_1^j\right) = \beta_j R u'\left(R\left(y_j - c_1^j\right)\right) \tag{S5.7}$$

We denote the unique solution by the function $c_1^j(y_j, R)$ and we also define $c_2^j(y_j, R) \equiv R\left(y_j - c_1^j(y_j, R)\right)$.

We next claim that

$$c_1^A(y, R) < c_1^B(y, R) \tag{S5.8}$$

for any $y > 0$ and R, that is, given the same income and prices the more patient group consumes strictly less today than the less patient group. To see this, define the function

$$f(c) = u'(c) - \beta_B R u'\left(R(y - c)\right), \text{ for } c < y,$$

and note that this function is strictly decreasing in c. We then have

$$
\begin{aligned}
f\left(c_1^A(y, R)\right) &= u'\left(c_1^A(y, R)\right) - \beta_B R u'\left(R\left(y - c_1^A(y, R)\right)\right) \\
&> u'\left(c_1^A(y, R)\right) - \beta_A R u'\left(R\left(y - c_1^A(y, R)\right)\right) \\
&= 0,
\end{aligned}
$$

where the second line follows since $\beta_B < \beta_A$, and the last line follows by the Euler equation (S5.7) for $c_1^A(y, R)$. The Euler equation for $c_1^B(y, R)$ is equivalent to $f\left(c_1^B(y, R)\right) = 0$. Since $f\left(c_1^A(y, R)\right) > 0 = f\left(c_1^B(y, R)\right)$ and since f is strictly decreasing in c, the claim in (S5.8) follows.

Finally, we claim that there exists no representative consumer. Let $C_1(y_A, y_B, R)$ denote the aggregate demand function for consumption today given a wealth distribution (y_A, y_B) and price R, that is, let

$$c_1(y_A, y_B, R) = N_A c_1^A(y_A, R) + N_B c_1^B(y_B, R),$$

and let $C_2(y_A, y_B, R)$ be defined likewise. A representative consumer exists only if the aggregate consumption demand is independent from the way wealth is distributed in the economy, that is, only if the aggregate demand remains constant as we redistribute the aggregate wealth $Y \equiv N_A y_A + N_B y_B$ in the economy. To simplify the algebra, we assume that we can actually target individuals within groups when we redistribute wealth.[1] Let h_A, h_B denote two individuals, one from each group. We consider two income distributions that leave everybody else's income the same except for these two individuals. Distribution A, represented by function $y^A(h)$, favors household h^A, that is, $y^A(h^A) = y_A + y_B$, $y^A(h^B) = 0$, while the distribution B, represented by $y^B(h)$, favors household h^B, that is $y^B(h^A) = 0$, $y^A(h^B) = y_A + y_B$. The difference in aggregate demand for distributions A and B is given by

$$C_1\left(\{y^A(h)\}_h, R\right) - C_1\left(\{y^B(h)\}_h, R\right)$$
$$= c_1^A(y_A + y_B, R) + c_1^B(0, R) - c_1^A(0, R) - c_1^B(y_A + y_B, R)$$
$$= c_1^A(y_A + y_B, R) - c_1^B(y_A + y_B, R) < 0$$

where the second equality follows since consumption is 0 with 0 wealth and the inequality follows by Claim (S5.8). Hence the aggregate demand does not remain constant for arbitrary distributions of income, proving that there exists no representative consumer. More specifically, we have shown that, the more of the income is held by the more patient consumers, the less today's consumption will be.

An alternative solution using example utility functions. We consider the log utility, $u(c) = \log c$, as a simple example to demonstrate the effects of the distribution of income. With log utility, the Euler equation (S5.7) has the solution

$$c_1^j(y_j, R) = \frac{1}{1 + \beta_j} y_j.$$

Aggregate demand is given by

$$C_1(y_A, y_B, R) = \frac{N_A y_A}{1 + \beta_A} + \frac{N_B y_B}{1 + \beta_B}.$$

Clearly, this expression is not independent of how we distribute aggregate wealth $Y \equiv N_A y_A + N_B y_B$. In particular, the larger y_A relative to y_B keeping Y constant (that is, the more of the wealth is held by the patient group), the less current consumption $C_1(y_A, y_B, R)$ will be. Consequently, there exists no representative consumer.

Exercise 5.12

Exercise 5.12, Part (a). An Arrow-Debreu commodity in this economy is the final good at different times $t \in \{0, 1, .., \infty\}$. We denote the price of the Arrow-Debreu commodity for time t as p_t. Note that there are countably infinite Arrow-Debreu commodities. Note also that, even though there is no production technology in this economy, we can essentially view saving as a production technology (in the Arrow-Debreu sense) hence the production sets in the Arrow-Debreu economy can be represented by

$$Y^t = \{(y_0 = -y, y_t = y) \mid y \in \mathbb{R}_+\}, \text{ for each } t \in \{1, 2..\} \tag{S5.9}$$

that is, we can suppose that there are competitive time t firms that convert time 0 goods to time t goods. Other representations for the production set are also possible, for example, instead, we could have introduced production technologies that convert time t goods to time $t + 1$ goods. These other representations would capture the same economic environment and yield the same equilibria and Pareto optimal allocations, hence for simplicity we consider the representation in (S5.9).

---

[1]The result holds also in the case we cannot target an individual from each group and we must provide all group members with the same wealth.

Exercise 5.12, Part (b). A Pareto optimal allocation in this economy is a set of consumption paths $\left\{c^h\left(t\right)\right\}_{t=1,h\in\{1,..,N\}}^{\infty}$ that satisfies the resource constraints,

$$\sum_{t=0}^{\infty}\sum_{h=1}^{N}c^h\left(t\right)\le y, \text{ and } c^h\left(t\right)\ge 0 \text{ for each } h \text{ and } t, \tag{S5.10}$$

such that there is no other set of consumption paths, $\left\{\tilde{c}^h\left(t\right)\right\}_{t=1,h\in\{1,..,N\}}^{\infty}$, that satisfies the resource constraints, makes one household strictly better off and makes everyone else at least as well off. Under standard assumptions (when u is strictly increasing and strictly concave), the set of Pareto optimal allocations can be found by solving the following Pareto problem:

$$P\left(\left\{\lambda^h\right\}_{h=1}^{N}, \lambda\ge 0, \lambda\ne 0\right) \quad : \quad \max_{\left\{c^h(t)\right\}_{h,t}\ge 0}\sum_{h=1}^{N}\lambda^h\sum_{t=0}^{\infty}\beta^t u\left(c^h\left(t\right)\right) \tag{S5.11}$$

$$\text{s.t.} \quad \sum_{h=1}^{N}\sum_{t=0}^{\infty}c^h\left(t\right)\le y.$$

That is, every Pareto optimal allocation maximizes a weighted-sum of household utilities subject to economy-wide resource constraints, where the weight of an household λ^h, loosely speaking, denotes the importance of the household h in this Pareto allocation.[2]

We next characterize the Pareto set by solving Problem (S5.11) for arbitrary set of Pareto weights $\left\{\lambda^h\right\}_{h=1}^{N}, \lambda\ge 0, \lambda\ne 0$. First note that, households with zero Pareto weights will always be given 0 consumption, that is

$$c^h\left(t\right)=0 \text{ for all } h \text{ s.t. } \lambda^h=0.$$

Next, let the Lagrange multiplier on the resource constraint be γ, then the first-order conditions for $c^h\left(t\right)$ where $\lambda^h>0$ are

$$\lambda^h\beta^t u'\left(c^h\left(t\right)\right)\le\gamma \text{ with equality if } c^h\left(t\right)>0. \tag{S5.12}$$

Then given γ, the consumption of household h at time t is given by

$$c^h\left(t\right)=\max\left(0,u'^{-1}\left(\frac{\gamma}{\lambda^h\beta^t}\right)\right) \text{ for all } h \text{ where } \lambda^h>0, \tag{S5.13}$$

which is weakly increasing in γ. The Lagrange multiplier γ can then be uniquely solved from the aggregate budget constraint

$$\sum_{h=1}^{N}\sum_{t=0}^{\infty}c^h\left(t\right)=\sum_{h\in\{1,..,N\}\ |\ \lambda^h>0}\ \sum_{t=0}^{\infty}\max\left(0,u'^{-1}\left(\frac{\gamma}{\lambda^h\beta^t}\right)\right)=y. \tag{S5.14}$$

Hence, for any given set of Pareto weights, $\left(\left\{\lambda^h\right\}_{h=1}^{N}, \lambda\ge 0, \lambda\ne 0\right)$, there is a unique solution characterized by Eqs. (S5.13) and (S5.14), characterizing the set of Pareto optima.

We next note a number of interesting properties of the Pareto optima. First, considering the first-order condition (S5.12) for $c^h\left(t\right)$ and $c^h\left(t+1\right)$ shows that the following Euler equation holds for any Pareto optimal allocation

$$u'\left(c^h\left(t\right)\right)\ge\beta u'\left(c^h\left(t+1\right)\right) \text{ with equality if } c^h\left(t+1\right)>0. \tag{S5.15}$$

---

[2]MasColell, Whinston and Green (1995), Section 16.E provides the exact conditions under which solving this problem (with different weights) gives all Pareto optimal allocations.

This is the relevant Euler equation since interest rate in any equilibrium is equal to 1 as we explain below. Intuitively, there are no externalities in the economy and distorting the intertemporal substitution of a household only hurts that household without any benefits for the remaining households. Hence the social planner does not want to distort the intertemporal substitution of any household, as shown in Eq. (S5.15). This equation also shows that each household in each Pareto optimum has a decreasing consumption profile due to discounting. Second, for two households with $\lambda^h > \lambda^{h'} > 0$, we have

$$c^h(t) = \max\left(0, u'^{-1}\left(\frac{\gamma}{\lambda^h \beta^t}\right)\right) \geq c^{h'}(t) = \max\left(0, u'^{-1}\left(\frac{\gamma}{\lambda^{h'} \beta^t}\right)\right)$$

since u'^{-1} is a decreasing function, showing that a household with the higher Pareto weight will consume more at all times than a household with lower Pareto weight.

Exercise 5.12, Part (c). The Second Welfare Theorem applies if we make the standard assumptions on preferences that u is strictly increasing, concave, and continuous. Under these assumptions for u, we claim that the assumptions of Theorem 5.7 are satisfied. The most important assumptions to check are the convexity assumptions for the consumption and production sets and concavity of the utility functions, since this allows for a separation argument (separation of the better than set and the production set with a hyperplane) that is at the heart of the Second Welfare Theorem. There are also a number of technical assumptions, most importantly, the tail assumption, which we need to check to ensure that the linear functional that we get from the separating hyperplane corresponds to a valid price function and not to some ill behaved linear functional that puts all weight at infinity. We check these assumptions in turn.

First, we claim that the consumption and production sets are convex and the production set is a cone. Production sets defined in (S5.9) are both convex and cones. The consumption set of a household is $\mathbb{R}_+^\infty$, which is convex, proving our claim. Second, we claim that the utility function $U(\{c(t)\}_{t=0}^\infty) = \sum_{t=0}^\infty \beta^t u(c(t))$ is continuous, concave, and satisfies local non-satiation. Continuity in $\mathbb{R}_+^\infty$ (in the sup norm) follows from continuity of u. The fact that U is concave follows since u is concave. Finally, local non-satiation of U follows since u is strictly increasing, proving our claim. Third, we note that $\sum_{h \in \mathcal{H}} c_{j,t}^h \leq y$ from the resource constraints hence the boundedness requirement of Theorem 5.7 is satisfied with $\chi = y$.

Fourth, we claim that the tail assumptions of Theorem 5.7 hold. In particular, for any pair of $c = \{c(t)\}_{t=0}^\infty, c' = \{c'(t)\}_{t=0}^\infty \in \mathbb{R}_+^\infty$ such that $U(c) > U(c')$, we claim that there exists $\bar{T}$ such that for all $T > \bar{T}$, $U(c[T]) > U(c')$, where recall that $c[T] = (c(0), c(1), .., c(T), 0, 0, ..)$. This assumption essentially holds due to discounting and the fact that utility is bounded over the interval $[0, y]$. To prove formally, let $\bar{T}$ be sufficiently large that

$$\frac{\beta^{\bar{T}}}{1-\beta} u(y) < U(c) - U(c'). \tag{S5.16}$$

Then, for any $T > \overline{T}$

$$
\begin{aligned}
U\left(c\left[T\right]\right) &= U\left(c\right) + \sum_{t=T+1}^{\infty} \beta^t \left(u\left(0\right) - u\left(c\left(t\right)\right)\right) \\
&\geq U\left(c\right) - \sum_{t=T+1}^{\infty} \beta^t u\left(y\right) \\
&= U\left(c\right) - \frac{\beta^T}{1-\beta} u\left(y\right) > U\left(c'\right),
\end{aligned}
$$

where the first inequality follows since $u\left(0\right) = 0$ and $u\left(c\left(t\right)\right) \leq u\left(y\right)$, and the last inequality follows from the choice of $\overline{T}$ in (S5.16). Hence, the tail assumption for consumption sequences holds. The corresponding assumption for production sequences trivially hold, since any production vector in (S5.9) has only two non-zero elements.

It then follows that the assumptions of Theorem 5.7 are satisfied and the Second Welfare Theorem applies to this economy.

Exercise 5.12, Part (d). An equilibrium is a set of allocations $\left\{c^h\left(t\right)\right\}_{t=0, h\in\{1,..,N\}}^{\infty}$, prices $\{p_0, p_1.., \}$, and production vectors[3] such that:

- Firms maximize given prices $\{p_0, p_1.., \}$ over the sets in (S5.9). This implies that, prices must satisfy

$$
p_0 \geq p_t, \text{ with equality if } y_t = \sum_{h=1}^{N} c^h\left(t\right) > 0.
$$

That is, if there is positive consumption at a period, then the price of the good in that period is equal to p_0. The prices could, in principle, be declining, but this is only possible if there is consumption at period t. The intuition for this is as follows. If $p_t > p_0$, then the period t firm would produce infinite amount of the period t good and the market clearing condition (condition 3 below) would be violated. If $p_0 > p_t$, then, firm t must shut down, otherwise it would lose money. But this means that firm t is not producing hence there is no period t good in equilibrium, which is only possible if consumption demand at t is 0.

In the case in which demand for the period t good is 0, it is in principle possible to have $p_t < p_0$. But if this is the case, then $p'_t = p_0$ is also always an equilibrium. If a consumer demands 0 consumption at time t, then she will continue to demand 0 if the price at time t is raised from $p_t < p_0$ to $p'_t = p_0$. Consequently, we can take $p_t = p_0$ (or equivalently, $R_{t+1} = 1$ for the interest rate) for all t without loss of generality.[4] We normalize $p_0 = 1$ and have $p_t = 1$ for all t for the rest of the analysis.

---

[3] We subsume the notation for production vectors for simplicity: these vectors convert time 0 goods to time t goods, hence once we are given the aggregate consumption vector in the economy, we can easily solve for the production vectors implied by that consumption vector.

[4] We provide a complementary intuition for why we can take the interest rates between periods equal to 1 (which correspond to all Arrow-Debreu prices being equal), by considering a household that chooses consumption, trades bonds, and has access to a saving technology can convert one unit at period t to one unit at period $t+1$. Suppose $R_{t+1} < 1$ for some t, that is, there are bonds traded at period t that return $R_{t+1} < 1$ next period. Then, the household would sell bonds, buy time t goods in the market, save these goods until period $t+1$, pay his debtors and end up with net profits. This is an arbitrage opportunity and any rational household would do this at infinite amounts, which would violate market clearing. Consider now the case in which $R_{t+1} > 1$. Suppose that some household is consuming a positive amount at $t+1$. Then at least one household must be saving resources until period $t+1$. Then that household has the following arbitrage

- The second equilibrium condition is that each household h solves

$$\max_{\{c^h(t)\}_{t=0}^{\infty}} \sum_{t=0}^{\infty} \beta^t u\left(c\left(t\right)\right) \tag{S5.17}$$

$$\text{s.t.} \quad \sum_{t=0}^{\infty} p_t c^h\left(t\right) \leq p_0 y^h.$$

- The last equilibrium condition is market clearing, which after netting out production vectors for the firms in (S5.9), is given by

$$\sum_{h=1}^{N} \sum_{t=0}^{\infty} c^h\left(t\right) = \sum_{h=1}^{N} y^h = y.$$

We next characterize the equilibrium allocations. From the first-order conditions for Problem (S5.17), each individual's consumption path $\{c^h(t)\}_{t=0}^{\infty}$ satisfies the same Euler equation as the Pareto optimal allocations (S5.15). Using the Euler equation and the budget constraint $\sum_{t=0}^{\infty} c^h(t) = y^h$, the consumption path $\{c^h(t)\}_{t=0}^{\infty}$ of each household is uniquely solved as a function of y^h. Hence, the equilibrium is characterized by these allocations along with the essentially unique prices, $p_t = 1$ for all t.

Exercise 5.12, Part (e). The competitive equilibria are Pareto optimal since the standard proof of Pareto optimality apply to this problem in view of the fact that the relevant sums are finite. To see this, consider a competitive equilibrium allocation $\{c^h(t)\}_{t=0, h \in \{1,..,N\}}^{\infty}$ (with corresponding prices $\{p_t = 1\}_{t=0}^{\infty}$). Suppose, to reach a contradiction, that there exists another allocation $\{\tilde{c}^h(t)\}_{t=0, h \in \{1,..,N\}}^{\infty}$ for which resource constraints (S5.10) hold, one household is strictly better off, that is

$$\sum_{t=0}^{\infty} \beta^t u\left(\tilde{c}^{\tilde{h}}\left(t\right)\right) > \sum_{t=0}^{\infty} \beta^t u\left(c^{\tilde{h}}\left(t\right)\right) \tag{S5.18}$$

for some $\tilde{h}$, and all other households are at least as well off, that is

$$\sum_{t=0}^{\infty} \beta^t u\left(\tilde{c}^h\left(t\right)\right) \geq \sum_{t=0}^{\infty} \beta^t u\left(c^h\left(t\right)\right) \quad \text{for all } h. \tag{S5.19}$$

By Eq. (S5.18), we have

$$\sum_{t=0}^{\infty} \tilde{c}^{\tilde{h}}\left(t\right) > \sum_{t=0}^{\infty} c^{\tilde{h}}\left(t\right)$$

---

opportunity: she should save less to period $t+1$ and use those resources instead to buy bonds at period t. The bonds yield her more at period $t+1$ than what she would have had by saving, hence the household ends up with net profits at period $t+1$. This is an arbitrage opportunity that would continue until the consumption at period $t+1$ falls to zero.

The case in which $R_{t+1} > 1$ and all households consuming nothing at period $t+1$ is in principle possible (corresponds to the $p_t < p_0$ and no consumption case that we have noted above). But if this is the case, then allocations do not change if we instead set $R'_{t+1} = 1$. Since households were not buying any bonds at the higher rate $R_{t+1} > 1$, they will continue not buying bonds at the lower rate $R_{t+1} = 1$. It follows that we can take $R'_{t+1} = 1$ without loss of generality.

since, otherwise, $\left\{\tilde{c}^{\tilde{h}}(t)\right\}_{t=0}^{\infty}$ would be in household $\tilde{h}$'s budget set and she would rather consume this allocation in equilibrium. Similarly, we claim that Eq. (S5.19) implies

$$\sum_{t=0}^{\infty}\tilde{c}^h(t) \geq \sum_{t=0}^{\infty} c^h(t), \text{ for all } h.$$

Suppose this does not hold. Then by consuming $\left\{\tilde{c}^h(t)\right\}_{t=0}^{\infty}$ instead of $\left\{c^h(t)\right\}_{t=0}^{\infty}$ household h would attain at least the same utility and save some money. By non-satiation (which in turn follows since we assume u is strictly increasing), she can use these extra funds to further increase utility, hence she would not choose $\left\{c^h(t)\right\}_{t=0}^{\infty}$ in equilibrium. This yields a contradiction and proves the previous displayed equation. Summing over the last two displayed equations, and using the fact that $\left\{\tilde{c}^h\right\}_{t,h}$ satisfies the resource constraints (S5.10), we have

$$y \geq \sum_{h=1}^{N}\sum_{t=0}^{\infty}\tilde{c}^h(t) > \sum_{h=1}^{N}\sum_{t=0}^{\infty} c^h(t) = y,$$

which yields a contradiction since y is finite. This proves our claim that the First Welfare Theorem applies to this economy and every competitive equilibrium is Pareto optimal. The last step, in particular, the fact that y is finite, is critical to apply the First Welfare Theorem. The sum over all household of all commodities (which is consumption at different dates in this model) should be finite, otherwise that step does not necessarily go through and the First Welfare Theorem does not necessarily apply.

Exercise 5.12, Part (f). We have already seen in Part (b) that the social planner does not want to distort the intertemporal decision of the consumers, since the Pareto optimal allocations and the equilibrium allocation satisfy the same Euler equation (S5.15). Hence, given a Pareto optimal allocation $\left\{c_p^h(t)\right\}_{t=0,h\in\{1,..,N\}}^{\infty}$, we can decentralize it by giving each household the endowment

$$y^h \equiv \sum_{t=0}^{\infty} c_p^h(t). \tag{S5.20}$$

That is, the social planner gives each household an endowment just enough to consume what he wants her to consume, and the household ends up consuming the same allocation since the incentives of the planner and the household are lined up for intertemporal substitution.

We claim, more formally, that for the endowments defined as in (S5.20), we have $c_{eq}^h(t) = c_p^h(t)$ for all t and h'. Suppose, to reach a contradiction, that $\left\{c_{eq}^{h'}(t)\right\}_{t=0}^{\infty} \neq \left\{c_p^{h'}(t)\right\}$ for one household h'. Then, since the household h's Problem (S5.17) is a strictly concave problem and since $\left\{c_p^{h'}(t)\right\}$ is also in the feasible set for the household (by choice of y^h in (S5.20)), it must be the case that

$$\sum_{t=0}^{\infty}\beta^t u\left(c_{eq}^{h'}(t)\right) > \sum_{t=0}^{\infty}\beta^t u\left(c_p^{h'}(t)\right).$$

But then $\left\{c_p^h(t)\right\}_{t=0,h\in\{1,..,N\}}^{\infty}$ cannot be a Pareto optimal allocation, since the social planner could change household h's allocation to $\left\{c_{eq}^h(t)\right\}_{t=0}^{\infty}$ while leaving all other allocations unchanged. This change would satisfy the resource constraints, it would strictly improve household h's utility and leave all other households as well off, yielding a contradiction. This proves our claim that the equilibrium coincides with the Pareto optimal allocation given the endowments in (S5.20).

Exercise 5.14*

Exercise 5.14, Part (a). Note that we have $\lim_{c \to 0} u(c) = -\infty$ for $\theta \geq 1$. Then, no matter how large T is, $x^h[T] = \left(x^h(0), x^h(1), ..., x^h(T), 0, 0, ..\right)$ gives the individual a utility $-\infty$, which is potentially very different than $U^h(x^h)$. More specifically, let $X^h = X$ be a compact set, $\beta < 1$, and consider some $x^h, \bar{x}^h \in X$ such that $x^h(t), \bar{x}^h(t) \geq \varepsilon > 0$ for all t and $U^h(x^h) > U^h(\bar{x}^h)$. Then, for any $\bar{T} < \infty$, we have

$$
\begin{aligned}
U^h\left(x^h[\bar{T}]\right) &= \sum_{t=0}^{\bar{T}} \beta^t u\left(x^h(t)\right) + \sum_{t=\bar{T}+1}^{\infty} \beta^t u(0) \\
&= \sum_{t=0}^{\bar{T}} \beta^t u(c) - \infty \\
&< U^h\left(\bar{x}^h\right),
\end{aligned}
$$

where the last inequality follows since $\sum_{t=0}^{\bar{T}} \beta^t u\left(x^h(t)\right)$ and $U^h(x^h)$ are finite due to the assumptions that X is compact, $\beta < 1$, and $x^h, \bar{x}^h \geq \varepsilon > 0$. Regardless of how large $\bar{T}$ is chosen, an individual that prefers x_t^h to $\bar{x}_t^h$ will prefer $\bar{x}_t^h$ to $x_t^h[T]$ and the individual's choices will be overturned by truncating her consumption. Consequently, the truncation (tail) assumption of Theorem 5.7 is not satisfied and the theorem does not apply. Intuitively, truncations even very far in the future affects the agent's choices since the agent extremely dislikes zero consumption.

Exercise 5.14, Part (b). We will provide a more general theorem which does not require X^h to be restricted but instead slightly weakens the requirement for the preferences U^h (see assumption (iii) below) so that we can accommodate economies as in Part (a). For a given vector $x^h \in X^h$ and for $\varepsilon \geq 0$, let $x_\varepsilon^h[T] = \left(x^h(0), .., x^h(T), \varepsilon, \varepsilon, ..\right)$ denote the vector in which the entries after T are truncated to ε and let $\underline{\varepsilon} = (\varepsilon, \varepsilon, ..)$ denote the vector with all elements equal to ε.

THEOREM S5.1. *(Second Welfare Theorem II) Consider a Pareto optimal allocation* $(\mathbf{x}^*, \mathbf{y}^*)$ *in an economy with endowment vector* ω, *production sets* $\left\{Y^f\right\}_{f \in \mathcal{F}}$, *consumption sets* $\left\{X^h\right\}_{h \in \mathcal{H}}$, *and utility functions* $\left\{U^h(\cdot)\right\}_{h \in \mathcal{H}}$. *Suppose that all production and consumption sets are convex, all production sets are cones, and all utility functions* $\left\{U^h(\cdot)\right\}_{h \in \mathcal{H}}$ *are continuous and quasi-concave and satisfy local non-satiation. Moreover, suppose also that (i) there exists* $\chi < \infty$ *such that* $\sum_{h \in \mathcal{H}} x_{j,t}^h < \chi$ *for all* j *and* t; *(ii)* $\underline{0} \in X^h$ *for each* h; *(iii) For any* h *and* $x^h, \bar{x}^h \in X^h$ *such that* $U^h(x^h) > U^h(\bar{x}^h)$ *and for any* $\varepsilon > 0$, *there exists* $\bar{T}$ *(possibly as a function of* $h, x^h, \bar{x}^h$ *and* ε) *such that* $U^h\left(x_\varepsilon^h[T]\right) > U^h(\bar{x}^h)$ *for all* $T \geq \bar{T}$; *and (iv) for any* f *and* $y^f \in Y^f$, *there exists* $\tilde{T}$ *such that* $y^f[T] \in Y^f$ *for all* $T \geq \tilde{T}$. *Then, there exist a price vector* p^* *and endowment and share allocations* $(\boldsymbol{\omega}^*, \boldsymbol{\theta}^*)$ *such that in the economy* $\mathcal{E} \equiv (\mathcal{H}, \mathcal{F}, \mathbf{U}, \boldsymbol{\omega}^*, \mathbf{Y}, \mathbf{X}, \boldsymbol{\theta}^*)$,

(a) *the endowment allocation* $\boldsymbol{\omega}^*$ *satisfies* $\omega = \sum_{h \in \mathcal{H}} \omega^{h*}$;

(b) *for all* $f \in \mathcal{F}$,

$$p^* \cdot y^{f*} \geq p^* \cdot y^f \text{ for any } y^f \in Y^f;$$

(c) *for all* $h \in \mathcal{H}$,

$$\text{if } U^h\left(x^h\right) > U^h\left(x^{h*}\right) \text{ for some } x^h \in X^h, \text{ then } p^* \cdot x^h \geq p^* \cdot w^{h*},$$

where $w^{h*} \equiv \omega^{h*} + \sum_{f \in \mathcal{F}} \theta_f^{h*} y^{f*}$.

Moreover, if $p^* \cdot w^{h*} > 0$ for each $h \in \mathcal{H}$, then the economy $\mathcal{E}$ has a competitive equilibrium $(\mathbf{x}^*, \mathbf{y}^*, p^*)$.

PROOF. Part 1 of the proof of Theorem 5.7 applies to this case without any changes and shows that there exists a non-zero continuous linear functional ϕ that separates the sets Y' and P, that is

$$\phi(y) \le \phi(x^*) \le \phi(x) \text{ for all } y \in Y' \text{ and } x \in P, \tag{S5.21}$$

where recall that Y' is the sum of the "more preferred" sets for households and P is the sum of the production sets shifted by the endowment vector. To prove the analogue of Part 2 in this case, define $\bar{\phi}(x)$ the same way as in the text with $\bar{\phi}(x) = \lim_{T \to \infty} \phi(x_0[T])$. The same steps as in the main text show that $\bar{\phi}$ is a continuous linear functional and that there exists a price vector p^{**} such that $\bar{\phi}(x) = \lim_{t \to \infty} p^{**} \cdot x$. We claim that $\bar{\phi}$ can be used instead of ϕ as the separating function also in this case. This result will follow from establishing steps (a)-(d) as in the proof of Theorem 5.7. Moreover, steps (b), (c) and (d) go through without change. So all we need to check is step (a), that is,

$$\phi(x^*) \le \bar{\phi}(x) \text{ for all } x \in P.$$

Suppose, to reach a contradiction, that there exists $x \in P$ such that $\bar{\phi}(x) < \phi(x^*)$. By linearity of $\bar{\phi}$ and ϕ, there exists h such that $\bar{\phi}(x^h) < \phi(x^{h*})$. Since ϕ and $\bar{\phi}$ are both continuous functionals at 0 with $\phi(\underline{0}) = \bar{\phi}(\underline{0}) = 0$, there exists sufficiently small $\varepsilon > 0$ such that

$$\left| \phi(\underline{\varepsilon}) - \bar{\phi}(\underline{\varepsilon}) \right| < \phi\left(x^{h*}\right) - \bar{\phi}\left(x^h\right). \tag{S5.22}$$

Since $x^h \in P^h$, we have $U^h(x^h) > U^h(x^{h*})$. Applying assumption (iii) for this choice of ε, there exists $\bar{T}$ sufficiently large so that $U^h(x_\varepsilon^h[T]) > U^h(x^{h*})$ for all $T > \bar{T}$. This implies $x_\varepsilon^h[T] \in P^h$, which, by Eq. (S5.21), implies

$$\phi\left(x_\varepsilon^h[T]\right) \ge \phi\left(x^{h*}\right) \text{ for all } T > \bar{T}. \tag{S5.23}$$

Note also that

$$
\begin{aligned}
\phi\left(x_\varepsilon^h[T]\right) &= \phi(\underline{\varepsilon}) + \phi\left(x_\varepsilon^h[T] - \underline{\varepsilon}\right) \\
&= \phi(\underline{\varepsilon}) + \bar{\phi}\left(x_\varepsilon^h[T] - \underline{\varepsilon}\right) \\
&= \phi(\underline{\varepsilon}) - \bar{\phi}(\underline{\varepsilon}) + \bar{\phi}\left(x_\varepsilon^h[T]\right),
\end{aligned}
\tag{S5.24}
$$

where the second line follows since $x_\varepsilon^h[T] - \underline{\varepsilon}$ is a vector with 0's after the T'th element and the functionals ϕ and $\bar{\phi}$ agree for such vectors, and the last line follows since $\bar{\phi}$ is linear. Combining Eqs. (S5.23), (S5.24) and taking the limit over T, we have

$$
\begin{aligned}
\phi\left(x^{h*}\right) &\le \phi(\underline{\varepsilon}) - \bar{\phi}(\underline{\varepsilon}) + \lim_{T \to \infty} \bar{\phi}\left(x_\varepsilon^h[T]\right) \\
&= \phi(\underline{\varepsilon}) - \bar{\phi}(\underline{\varepsilon}) + \bar{\phi}\left(x^h\right),
\end{aligned}
\tag{S5.25}
$$

where the second line follows from the definition of $\bar{\phi}$. The inequalities in (S5.22) and (S5.25) provide a contradiction, proving step (a) and completing the proof of the theorem. $\square$

Exercise 5.14, Part (c). Consider the neoclassical optimal growth economy with no population growth and no technological progress. An equilibrium in this economy can be represented as a path of per capita allocations and prices $[c(t), k(t), R(t), w(t)]_t$ such that the representative household maximizes her utility given initial asset holdings $K(0) > 0$, firms maximize profits taking the time path of factor prices $[w(t), R(t)]_{t=0}^{\infty}$ as given, and factor prices $[w(t), R(t)]_{t=0}^{\infty}$ are such that all markets clear (cf. Definitions 8.1 and 8.2). The social planner's problem can be described as the optimal growth problem of maximizing the utility of the representative household subject to the resource constraints (cr. Section 8.3).

Denote the optimal growth solution by $[c(t), k(t)]_{t=0}^{\infty}$. Our goal is to use the Second Welfare Theorem II of Part (b) to show that $[c(t), k(t)]_{t=0}^{\infty}$ corresponds to an equilibrium allocation. Note that all continuity and convexity assumptions are satisfied, and that the preferences in (8.3) are non-satiated. Moreover, let $y^{\max} = \max_k F(k, 1) - \delta k$ and note that output in any period in this economy cannot be larger than $y^{\max}$, therefore we can take $\chi = y^{\max}$ so that $\sum_{h \in \mathcal{H}} c_t^h < \chi$ for all t. We need to check our new assumption (iii). Let $[c(t)]_{t=0}^{\infty}$ and $[\bar{c}(t)]_{t=0}^{\infty}$ be such that $U^h([c(t)]_{t=0}^{\infty}) > U^h([\bar{c}(t)]_{t=0}^{\infty})$ and consider some $\varepsilon > 0$. Note that, different than $u(0)$ used in Part (a), $u(\varepsilon)$ is a finite number, even though it can be very small. Moreover, $u(c(t))$ is also bounded above by $u(y^{\max}) < \infty$. Therefore, there exists $\bar{T}$ sufficiently large that

$$\frac{\beta^{\bar{T}+1}}{1-\beta}\left(u(y^{\max}) - u(\varepsilon)\right) < U^h([c(t)]_{t=0}^{\infty}) - U^h([\bar{c}(t)]_{t=0}^{\infty}). \tag{S5.26}$$

Note that, for any $T > \bar{T}$, we have

$$
\begin{aligned}
U^h(c_\varepsilon[T]) &= \sum_{t=0}^{\infty} \beta^t u(c(t)) + \sum_{t=T+1}^{\infty} \beta^t \left(u(\varepsilon) - u(c(t))\right) \\
&\geq U^h([c(t)]_{t=0}^{\infty}) - \frac{\beta^{T+1}}{1-\beta}\left(u(y^{\max}) - u(\varepsilon)\right) \\
&> U^h([\bar{c}(t)]_{t=0}^{\infty}),
\end{aligned}
$$

where the first inequality follows since $c(t) \leq y^{\max}$ for all t, and the last line inequality follows from Eq. (S5.26) since $T > \bar{T}$. This proves that $U^h(c_\varepsilon[T]) > U^h([\bar{c}(t)]_{t=0}^{\infty})$ for all $T > \bar{T}$ and assumption (iii) is also satisfied. Assumption (iv) is satisfied as shown in Part (b) of Exercise 5.13. Consequently, the Second Welfare Theorem II from Part (b) applies and shows that there exists prices $p^* \equiv [R(t), w(t)]_{t=0}^{\infty}$ such that statements (a)-(c) hold for this economy. In particular, there exist prices $[R(t), w(t)]_{t=0}^{\infty}$ such that

$$
\begin{aligned}
&F(k(t)L(t), L(t)) - R(t)k(t)L(t) - w(t)L(t) \\
&\geq F\left(\tilde{K}(t), \tilde{L}(t)\right) - R(t)\tilde{K}(t) - w(t)\tilde{L}(t) \text{ for all } \tilde{K}(t) \geq 0, \tilde{L}(t) \geq 0 \text{ and all } t.
\end{aligned}
$$

Since F satisfies Assumptions 1 and 2 in Section 2, the previous equation implies $R(t), w(t) \in (0, \infty)$ for each t. Since the prices are positive and there is a single representative household that holds the entire endowment in the economy, we have $p^* \cdot \omega^{h*} > 0$ for $h \in \mathcal{H}$. Consequently, the last part of the Second Welfare Theorem II also applies and shows that $[c(t), k(t), R(t), w(t)]_{t=0}^{\infty}$ corresponds to an equilibrium of the neoclassical economy, as desired.

Chapter 6: Infinite-Horizon Optimization and Dynamic Programming

Exercise 6.2*

To prove this claim, let us define the operator $W = T^n$. By construction W is a contraction, so that all the results derived in Section 6.4 apply. In particular we know that W has a unique fixed point, i.e. there exists a unique $\hat{z} \in S$ such that

$$W\hat{z} = \hat{z}.$$

Using this, we can now prove that T has a unique fixed point by contradiction. We first show that $\hat{z}$ is a fixed point of the operator T. Then we show that it is the unique one. So suppose that $\hat{z}$ was not a fixed point of T, i.e.

$$T\hat{z} = \tilde{z} \neq \hat{z}. \tag{S6.1}$$

As $\hat{z}$ is the unique fixed point of the operator $W = T^n$, we get

$$\hat{z} = W\hat{z} = T^n\hat{z} = T^{n-1}T\hat{z} = T^{n-1}\tilde{z}.$$

But this implies that

$$T\hat{z} = TT^{n-1}\tilde{z} = T^n\tilde{z}. \tag{S6.2}$$

Together with $T\hat{z} = \tilde{z}$ (from (S6.1)), (S6.2) reads

$$\tilde{z} = T^n\tilde{z} = W\tilde{z},$$

i.e. $\tilde{z}$ is a fixed point of W. But this is a contradiction, as $\hat{z}$ is the unique fixed point of the operator W and $\tilde{z} \neq \hat{z}$. This shows that $\hat{z}$ is also a fixed point of the operator T.

To prove uniqueness, suppose that T would have another fixed point $z' \neq \hat{z}$. This would imply that

$$Wz' = T^nz' = T^{n-1}Tz' = T^{n-1}z' = T^{n-2}Tz' = \dots = Tz' = z',$$

i.e. z' would also be a fixed point of W. Again this contradicts the fact that W has a unique fixed point. Hence, T has a unique fixed point, which is $\hat{z}$. This concludes the proof.

Exercise 6.8

Exercise 6.8, Part (a). To set up the dynamic programming version of the maximization problem, it is again helpful to first eliminate the control variable $c(t)$. Specifically we can use the constraint to express consumption as

$$c(t) = Ak(t) - k(t+1).$$

Using this in the utility function, the recursive formulation of the problem results in

$$V(k) = \max_{k' \in [0, Ak]} \left\{ Ak - k' - \frac{a}{2}(Ak - k')^2 + \beta V(k') \right\}$$

where the constraint $k' \leq Ak$ stems from the fact that consumption must not be negative.

Exercise 6.8, Part (b). To make some progress in determining if a solution (both in terms of the value function and the policy function) exists, let us go back to the results which were derived in Chapter 6. Specifically recall Theorem 6.3, which showed that a *unique* value function and *some* policy function exist, if Assumptions 6.1 and 6.2 hold true. Hence, let us verify those assumptions for our problem.

Let us start with Assumption 6.1. We have to check that the value function of the sequence problem is well-defined in the sense that $\lim_{n \to \infty} \sum_{t=0}^{n} \beta^t U(x(t), x(t+1))$ exists and is finite. To check this condition, let us rewrite the sequence version of the maximization problem as

$$V^*(k(0)) = \sup_{\{k(t+1)\}_0^\infty} \sum_{t=0}^{\infty} \beta^t [Ak(t) - k(t+1) - \frac{a}{2}(Ak(t) - k(t+1))^2]$$

$$\text{s.t. } k(t) \in [0, \bar{k}].$$

Now note that we can bound the value of $V^*(k(0))$ by recognizing that each of the terms

$$Ak(t) - k(t+1) - \frac{a}{2}(Ak(t) - k(t+1))^2$$

is bounded by

$$Ak(t) - k(t+1) - \frac{a}{2}(Ak(t) - k(t+1))^2 < Ak(t) < A\bar{k},$$

as $k(t) \in [0, \bar{k}]$. Hence it is clear that

$$V^*(k(0)) \leq V^*(\bar{k}) < \sum_{t=o}^{\infty} \beta^t A\bar{k} = A\bar{k} \frac{1}{1-\beta} < \infty.$$

The fact that $V^*(k(0)) \leq V^*(\bar{k})$ is immediate, as starting with a capital stock $\bar{k} \geq k(0)$, the optimal consumption plan when starting with $k(0)$ can be replicated and consumption can be increased in the first period. Recall that we assumed $\bar{k}$ to be such that utility is increasing in consumption. Hence, starting with a higher level of capital will increase the value of the program. This proves that the limit exists and is finite. We also have to show that the constraint correspondence is non-empty. But the constraint correspondence in this problem is just given by $G(k) = [0, Ak]$, which is non-empty. This verifies the conditions of Assumption 6.1.

Now consider Assumption 6.2. That the instantaneous utility function U is continuous is obvious. By assumption we have that $k(t) \in [0, \bar{k}]$, which is clearly a compact subset. To finally show that the constraint correspondence is continuous and compact-valued, recall that $G(k) = [0, Ak]$ which satisfies these requirements. Hence, the requirements for Assumption 2 are also satisfied, so that Theorem 6.3 is applicable. This proves the existence of both a unique value function and some optimal plan. However, we can apply Theorem 6.4 to strengthen those results as G is convex and the utility function is strictly concave. Hence, there is a unique optimal plan and the policy function is in fact a function, i.e. single-valued. Using those results let us now characterize this solution.

Exercise 6.8, Part (c). Following the analysis in Chapter 6, the policy function can be characterized by the first-order condition and the Envelope Condition The optimality condition for tomorrow's capital stock $k' = \pi(k)$ is given by

$$-1 + a(Ak - \pi(k)) + \beta V'(\pi(k)) = 0, \tag{S6.3}$$

where π denotes the policy function. The Envelope Condition is given by

$$V'(k) = A - a(Ak - \pi(k))A = A(1 - aAk + a\pi(k)). \tag{S6.4}$$

Substituting (S6.4) into (S6.3) yields

$$\begin{aligned}
1 &= a(Ak - \pi(k)) + \beta A(1 - aA\pi(k) + a\pi(\pi(k))) \\
&= \beta A + aAk - a(1 + A^2\beta)\pi(k) + \beta Aa\pi(\pi(k)). \tag{S6.5}
\end{aligned}$$

By looking at (S6.5) we can already get a feeling for the form of the solution. Note first that (S6.5) has to hold for all levels of the state variable k. As there is already a constant $(\beta A - 1)$ and a linear term (aAk) it is natural to conjecture that the policy function is linear and has an intercept. Hence let us conjecture that

$$\pi(k) = \varphi k + \gamma,$$

where φ and γ are coefficients to be determined. As this implies that

$$\pi(\pi(k)) = \varphi(\varphi k + \gamma) + \gamma = \varphi^2 k + \gamma(1 + \varphi),$$

(S6.5) requires that

$$1 = \beta A - a(1 + A^2\beta)\gamma + \beta Aa\gamma(1 + \varphi) + (aA - a(1 + A^2\beta)\varphi + \beta Aa\varphi^2)k. \tag{S6.6}$$

As (S6.6) has to hold for all k, the RHS cannot depend on k, i.e.

$$(aA - a(1 + A^2\beta)\varphi + \beta Aa\varphi^2) = 0.$$

Conveniently, this expression does not involve γ so that we can simply solve for φ. Factoring out the a we get that

$$0 = A - (1 + A^2\beta)\varphi + \beta A\varphi^2 = A - \varphi - A^2\beta\varphi + \beta A\varphi^2 = (A - \varphi)(1 - A\beta\varphi). \tag{S6.7}$$

From (S6.7) it is clear that there are two potential solutions for φ. But did we not argue that the policy function was unique (by the strict concavity of the utility function)? This is indeed the case, i.e. only one of the solutions to Eq. (S6.7) corresponds to the optimal policy. In particular, $\varphi = A$ solves Eq. (S6.7) but does not correspond to the optimal policy. To see this, recall that (by Theorem 6.5) the value function is strictly increasing in the state variable k.[1] So suppose $\varphi = A$ would be solution. Using (S6.6), the corresponding solution for γ has to solve the equation

$$1 = \beta A - a\gamma[1 + A^2\beta \doteq \beta A - \beta A\varphi],$$

i.e. $\gamma = -\frac{1}{a}$. But going back to the Envelope Condition in (S6.4), this would imply that

$$V'(k) = A(1 - aAk + a\pi(k)) = A(1 - aAk + a(Ak - \frac{1}{a})) = 0,$$

which would violate the strict monotonicity of the value function. Hence, let us focus on the other solution $\varphi = \frac{1}{A\beta}$. Some algebra shows that (S6.6) implies $\gamma = -\frac{1 - \beta A}{aA\beta(A-1)}$ so that the policy function is given by

$$\pi(k) = \frac{1}{A\beta}k - \frac{1 - \beta A}{aA\beta(A - 1)}. \tag{S6.8}$$

Consequently, the consumption level is given by

$$c(t) = Ak(t) - \pi(k(t)) = \frac{A^2\beta - 1}{A\beta}k + \frac{1 - \beta A}{aA\beta(A - 1)}. \tag{S6.9}$$

---

[1] Recall that we assumed that $a < \bar{k}^{-1}$ so that the objective function (here the utility function) is increasing in consumption in the relevant range.

Using again the Envelope Condition (S6.4), we see that now

$$
\begin{aligned}
V'(k) = A(1 - aAk + a\pi(k)) &= A(1 - aAk + \frac{a}{A\beta}k - \frac{1 - \beta A}{A\beta(A - 1)}) \\
&= \frac{A^2\beta - 1}{\beta(A - 1)} + a\frac{1 - A^2\beta}{\beta}k \\
&= \frac{A^2\beta - 1}{\beta}(\frac{1}{A - 1} - ak).
\end{aligned} \tag{S6.10}
$$

Hence, the value function is quadratic (as the derivative is linear in k), i.e. takes the form

$$
V(k) = \psi_2 k^2 + \psi_1 k + \psi_0.
$$

In order to solve for V we only have to find the coefficients $\psi_0, \psi_1,$ and ψ_2. The two coefficients ψ_1 and ψ_2 are already determined by (S6.10) and given by

$$
\psi_2 = -\frac{1}{2}\frac{A^2\beta - 1}{\beta}a \tag{S6.11}
$$

$$
\psi_1 = \frac{A^2\beta - 1}{\beta}\frac{1}{A - 1}. \tag{S6.12}
$$

To determine ψ_0, recall that the value function V is recursively defined as

$$
\begin{aligned}
V(k) &= U(k, \pi(k)) + \beta V(\pi(k)) \\
&= c(t) - \frac{a}{2}c(t)^2 + \beta(\psi_2\pi(k)^2 + \psi_1\pi(k) + \psi_0),
\end{aligned} \tag{S6.13}
$$

where the second line already imposed that V is a quadratic. The policy function was given in (S6.8) as

$$
\pi(k) = \frac{1}{A\beta}k - \frac{1 - \beta A}{aA\beta(A - 1)} \equiv \frac{1}{A\beta}k - \chi,
$$

where we defined $\chi = \frac{1 - \beta A}{aA\beta(A - 1)}$ to save on notation. Substituting this into the expression for consumption (S6.9), we get that

$$
c(t) = \frac{A - 1}{A}\psi_1 k + \frac{1 - \beta A}{aA\beta(A - 1)} = \frac{A - 1}{A}\psi_1 k + \chi.
$$

Hence we can express (S6.13) as

$$
\begin{aligned}
V(k) &= \frac{A - 1}{A}\psi_1 k + \chi - \frac{a}{2}((\frac{A - 1}{A}\psi_1 k)^2 + \chi^2 + 2\frac{A - 1}{A}\psi_1 k\chi) \\
&\quad + \beta(\psi_2((\frac{1}{A\beta})^2 k^2 - 2(\frac{1}{A\beta}k\chi) + \chi^2) + \psi_1(\frac{1}{A\beta}k - \chi) + \psi_0).
\end{aligned} \tag{S6.14}
$$

Now recall that we needed the recursive formulation only to determine the constant term ψ_0 in the value function. Hence we do not have to consider the terms that depend on k. Using (S6.14) we therefore find that

$$
\psi_0 = \chi - \frac{a}{2}\chi^2 + \beta\psi_2\chi^2 - \beta\psi_1\chi + \beta\psi_0.
$$

so that ψ_0 is given by

$$
(1 - \beta)\psi_0 = (1 - \frac{a}{2}\chi + \beta\psi_2\chi - \beta\psi_1)\chi. \tag{S6.15}
$$

Upon substituting ψ_1 and ψ_2 from (S6.11) and (S6.12) and after some algebra, (S6.15) reduces to

$$(1-\beta)\psi_0 = \frac{1}{2}\frac{A(1-A\beta)}{(A-1)}\chi,$$

so that

$$\psi_0 = \frac{1}{2}\frac{1}{(1-\beta)}\chi\frac{A(1-A\beta)}{(A-1)} = \frac{1}{2}\frac{1}{a\beta(1-\beta)}\left(\frac{1-A\beta}{A-1}\right)^2. \qquad (S6.16)$$

Hence the final value function is given by

$$V(k) = \psi_0 + \psi_1 k + \psi_2 k^2,$$

with the coefficients given in (S6.11), (S6.12) and (S6.16).

Exercise 6.9

Using Theorem 6.4 and Theorem 6.6 we can immediately conclude that the unique value function is strictly concave and differentiable with its derivative (as x is a scalar in our example) given by

$$V'(x) = \frac{\partial}{\partial x}U(x,\pi(x)).$$

Assuming that V is twice differentiable (we will come back to this assumption below) the desired result follows directly from the Euler equations (6.25)

$$\frac{\partial}{\partial y}U(x,\pi(x)) + \beta V'(\pi(x)) = 0. \qquad (S6.17)$$

To see this, recall that (S6.17) has to hold for all x. Differentiating this condition with respect to the state variable x and rearranging terms yields

$$\pi'(x) = -\frac{\frac{\partial^2}{\partial y\partial x}U(x,\pi(x))}{\frac{\partial^2}{\partial x\partial x}U(x,\pi(x)) + \beta V''(\pi(x))} \geq 0,$$

as the denominator is strictly negative due to the strict concavity of the value and the utility function. Note however that V is an endogenous object and we did not establish that V'' would even exist. Hence let us also show this result without this assumption. Consider $x_2 > x_1$ and suppose by contradiction that $\pi(x_2) < \pi(x_1)$. As (S6.17) has to hold for all x, i.e. particularly for x_2 and x_1, we can combine the two equations to get

$$\frac{\partial}{\partial y}U(x_2,\pi(x_2)) - \frac{\partial}{\partial y}U(x_1,\pi(x_1)) + \beta(V'(\pi(x_2)) - V'(\pi(x_1))) = 0. \qquad (S6.18)$$

As the value function is strictly concave by Theorem 6.4, it is clear that $V'(\pi(x_2)) > V'(\pi(x_1))$ (under the hypothesis that $\pi(x_2) < \pi(x_1)$). Expanding (S6.18) by $\frac{\partial}{\partial y}U(x_1,\pi(x_2))$ we get that

$$\frac{\partial}{\partial y}U(x_2,\pi(x_2)) - \frac{\partial}{\partial y}U(x_1,\pi(x_2)) + \frac{\partial}{\partial y}U(x_1,\pi(x_2)) - \frac{\partial}{\partial y}U(x_1,\pi(x_1)) < 0.$$

Again we have from concavity of U that $\frac{\partial}{\partial y}U(x_1,\pi(x_2)) > \frac{\partial}{\partial y}U(x_1,\pi(x_1))$ so that the above implies that

$$\frac{\frac{\partial}{\partial y}U(x_2,\pi(x_2)) - \frac{\partial}{\partial y}U(x_1,\pi(x_2))}{x_2-x_1} < 0.$$

Taking the limit $x_2 \to x_1$ yields

$$\lim_{x_2 \to x_1} \frac{\frac{\partial}{\partial y}U(x_2, \pi(x_2)) - \frac{\partial}{\partial y}U(x_1, \pi(x_2))}{x_2 - x_1} = \left.\frac{\partial^2 U(x,y)}{\partial x \partial y}\right|_{y=\pi(x)} < 0.$$

This however contradicts our assumption that $\partial^2 U(x,y)/\partial x \partial y \geq 0$. Hence, $\pi(x_2) \geq \pi(x_1)$ whenever $x_2 > x_1$. This shows that the policy function is nondecreasing.

Chapter 7: An Introduction to the Theory of Optimal Control

Exercise 7.1

Similar to the analysis in Section 7.1, we define the variation of the function $\hat{y}(t)$ with

$$y(t, \varepsilon) = \hat{y}(t) + \varepsilon \eta(t) \tag{S7.1}$$

for all $t \in [0, t_1]$ and we define $x(t, \varepsilon)$ as the solution to

$$\dot{x}(t, \varepsilon) = g(t, x(t, \varepsilon), y(t, \varepsilon)) \text{ for all } t \in [0, t_1] \text{ with } x(0, \varepsilon) = x_0. \tag{S7.2}$$

The same steps as in Section 7.1 give us

$$0 \equiv W'(0) = \int_0^{t_1} \left[f_x(t, \hat{x}(t), \hat{y}(t)) + \lambda(t) g_x(t, \hat{x}(t), \hat{y}(t)) + \dot{\lambda}(t) \right] x_\varepsilon(t, 0) \, dt \tag{S7.3}$$

$$+ \int_0^{t_1} [f_y(t, \hat{x}(t), \hat{y}(t)) + \lambda(t) g_y(t, \hat{x}(t), \hat{y}(t))] \eta(t) \, dt$$

$$- \lambda(t_1) x_\varepsilon(t_1, 0),$$

which has to hold for all choices of continuous $\eta(t)$ and continuously differentiable $\lambda(t)$. Unlike in Section 7.1, we choose $\lambda(t)$ so that the second integral in Eq. (S7.3) is zero, that is we define

$$\lambda(t) \equiv -f_y(t, \hat{x}(t), \hat{y}(t)) / g_y(t, \hat{x}(t), \hat{y}(t)).$$

We claim that if the condition

$$\dot{\lambda}(t) = -[f_x(t, \hat{x}(t), \hat{y}(t)) + \lambda(t) g_x(t, \hat{x}(t), \hat{y}(t))] \text{ for all } t \in (t', t'') \tag{S7.4}$$

is violated over an interval (t', t''), then we can indirectly control $x_\varepsilon(t, 0)$ (through controlling $\eta(t)$) in a way to violate Eq. (S7.3). To see this, we first claim that we can induce any continuously differentiable $x_\varepsilon(t, 0)$ through Eq. (S7.2) by controlling $\eta(t)$.

CLAIM 1. *For any given continuously differentiable function $\psi(t) : [0, t_1]$ such that $\psi(0) = 0$, there exists a unique continuous $\eta(t)$ such that*

$$x_\varepsilon(t, 0) = \psi(t) \text{ for all } t \in [0, t_1].$$

PROOF. First note that, by integrating Eq. (S7.2), $x(t, \varepsilon)$ satisfies

$$x(t, \varepsilon) = x_0 + \int_0^t g(t', x(t', \varepsilon), \hat{y}(t') + \varepsilon \eta(t')) \, dt'.$$

Hence, the derivative x_ε evaluated at $\varepsilon = 0$ satisfies the following (implicit) equation for all $t \in [0, t_1]$

$$x_\varepsilon(t, 0) = \int_0^t [g_x(t', \hat{x}(t'), \hat{y}(t')) x_\varepsilon(t', 0) + g_y(t', \hat{x}(t'), \hat{y}(t')) \eta(t')] \, dt',$$

which also implies $x_\varepsilon (0,0) = 0$. By Leibniz' rule, $x_\varepsilon (t,0)$, when viewed as a function of t, satisfies the differential equation

$$\dot{x}_\varepsilon (t,0) = g_x (t, \hat{x} (t), \hat{y} (t)) x_\varepsilon (t,0) + g_y (t, \hat{x} (t), \hat{y} (t)) \eta (t) \text{, with } x_\varepsilon (0,0) = 0. \qquad \text{(S7.5)}$$

Next, consider any continuously differentiable function $\psi (t)$ with $\psi (0) = 0$. Define $\eta (t)$ as

$$\eta (t) = \frac{\dot{\psi} (t) - g_x (t, \hat{x} (t), \hat{y} (t)) \psi (t)}{g_y (t, \hat{x} (t), \hat{y} (t))}, \text{ for all } t \in [0, t_1],$$

which is well defined since we are given $g_y \neq 0$. Under regularity conditions (i.e. when g_x and g_y are Lipschitz continuous), the differential equation in Eq. (S7.5) has a unique solution for the given initial value $x_\varepsilon (0,0) = 0$. Since, by definition, $\psi (t)$ solves the differential equation, it must be the unique solution, that is $x_\varepsilon (t,0) = \psi (t)$, as desired. $\qquad \square$

The rest of the argument is now straightforward. Recall that, we have made the second integral in Problem (S7.3) zero by our choice of $\lambda (t)$. Now, suppose Eq. (S7.4) is violated over (t', t'') and define the continuous function

$$h (t) \equiv \dot{\lambda} (t) + f_x (t, \hat{x} (t), \hat{y} (t)) + \lambda (t) g_x (t, \hat{x} (t), \hat{y} (t)).$$

By construction $h (t)$ never hits 0 over $t \in (t', t'')$, i.e. it is either positive or negative over all of this interval. Without loss of generality suppose it is positive everywhere. Let $\psi (t)$ be a continuously differentiable function that is positive over (t', t'') and is zero at $t = t_1$. By Claim (1), there exists some $\eta (t)$ such that with the choice of $\eta (t)$, we have $x_\varepsilon (t,0) = \psi (t)$. Then, with this choice of $\eta (t)$, we have that the first integral in (S7.3) is positive, the second integral is zero by our choice of $\lambda (t)$, and the last term is zero as $x_\varepsilon (t_1,0) = \psi (t_1) = 0$. Hence Eq. (S7.3) is violated, providing the desired contradiction. Similarly, $\lambda (t_1) = 0$ is a necessary condition since otherwise we can choose $\eta (t)$ that leads to $x_\varepsilon (t_1,0) = -\lambda (t_1)$, violating Eq. (S7.3).

A simpler and correct solution that looks like cheating. As in Section 7.1, let us define $\tilde{\lambda} (t)$ so that the first and the third terms in (S7.3) are zero, that is let $\tilde{\lambda} : [0, t_1] \to \mathbb{R}$ be the solution to

$$\frac{d\tilde{\lambda} (t)}{dt} = -f_x (t, \hat{x} (t), \hat{y} (t)) - \tilde{\lambda} (t) g_x (t, \hat{x} (t), \hat{y} (t)) \text{ and } \tilde{\lambda} (t_1) = 0. \qquad \text{(S7.6)}$$

Eq. (S7.3) then implies

$$f_y (t, \hat{x} (t), \hat{y} (t)) + \tilde{\lambda} (t) g_y (t, \hat{x} (t), \hat{y} (t)) = 0,$$

since otherwise we would get a contradiction to Eq. (S7.3) in view of the fact that $\eta (t)$ can be chosen freely. But, since $g_y > 0$, the last displayed equation implies

$$\tilde{\lambda} (t) = \frac{-f_y (t, \hat{x} (t), \hat{y} (t))}{g_y (t, \hat{x} (t), \hat{y} (t))} = \lambda (t),$$

that is, the $\tilde{\lambda} (t)$ we have constructed must almost everywhere agree with $\lambda (t)$ defined by Eq. (7.12) in the problem statement. Since $\tilde{\lambda} (t)$ satisfies Eq. (S7.6) but $\lambda (t)$ violates that same differential equation over (t', t'') [cf. Eq. (S7.4)], this yields a contradiction hence $(\hat{x} (t), \hat{y} (t))$ cannot be an interior continuous solution attaining the optimum.

The reason this argument looks like cheating is because it defies the whole point of the problem. The purpose of the problem was to get us to think about an alternative way of proving the necessary conditions, that is, by getting a contradiction through controlling $x_\varepsilon (t, \varepsilon)$ indirectly, rather than $\eta (t)$ directly. But this proof gets around that alternative approach by providing the same exact argument as in Section 7.1 and noting that the λ defined by the two approaches must be equivalent.

Exercise 7.10

The proof is similar to the proof of Theorem 7.1 in Section 7.1. We construct the variation policy $y(t, \varepsilon)$ and the corresponding $x(t, \varepsilon)$ as in Eqs. (S7.1) and (S7.2), but with the added requirement that $\eta(t) \geq 0$ holds for all $t \in [0, t_1]$. The same steps as in the proof of Theorem 7.1 lead to Eq. (S7.3). We construct $\lambda(t)$ as the solution to the differential equation (7.11) with the boundary condition $\lambda(t_1) = 0$. With this choice of $\lambda(t)$, the first and the third terms in Eq. (S7.3) vanish and the equation reduces to

$$\int_0^{t_1} [f_y(t, \hat{x}(t), \hat{y}(t)) + \lambda(t) g_y(t, \hat{x}(t), \hat{y}(t))] \eta(t) \, dt = 0, \tag{S7.7}$$

which must hold for all continuous deviation functions $\eta(t)$ such that $\eta(t) \geq 0$. We claim that $H_y(t, \hat{x}(t), \hat{y}(t), \lambda(t)) \leq 0$ for all $t \in [0, t_1]$. Suppose the contrary. Since H_y is continuous, this implies that there is some $\delta > 0$ and an interval $[t', t'']$ such that $H_y(t, \hat{x}(t), \hat{y}(t), \lambda(t)) \geq \delta$ for all $t \in [t', t'']$. Consider a continuous function $\eta(t)$ such that $\eta(t) = 0$ for all $t \notin [t', t'']$, $\eta(t) \geq 0$ for $t \in [t', t'']$, and $\eta(t) \geq 1$ for $t \in [t' + \varepsilon, t'' - \varepsilon]$ for $\varepsilon = (t'' - t')/4$. Then, $\eta(t)$ is a feasible variation and the integral in Eq. (S7.7) is at least as large as $(t'' - t') \delta/2 > 0$, which yields a contradiction, proving our claim. Eq. (7.11) holds by construction of $\lambda(t)$, and the fact that $\dot{x}(t) = H_\lambda(t, \hat{x}(t), \hat{y}(t), \lambda(t))$ for all $t \in [0, t_1]$ holds since $(\hat{x}(t), \hat{y}(t))$ is a feasible path, competing the proof.

Our proof shows that the necessary condition $H_y(t, \hat{x}(t), \hat{y}(t), \lambda(t)) \leq 0$ can actually be strengthened to a complementary slackness condition, $H_y(t, \hat{x}(t), \hat{y}(t), \lambda(t)) \hat{y}(t) = 0$ with $H_y(t, \hat{x}(t), \hat{y}(t), \lambda(t)) \leq 0$ and $\hat{y}(t) \geq 0$. To prove this stronger condition, we only need to show that $H_y(t, \hat{x}(t), \hat{y}(t), \lambda(t)) = 0$ for all t such that $\hat{y}(t) > 0$. Consider such $t \in [0, t_1]$. Then, in a neighborhood of t, the variation $\eta(t)$ is essentially unconstrained since, for a sufficiently small neighborhood $(t - \delta, t + \delta)$ and sufficiently small ε, $y(\tilde{t}) + \varepsilon \eta(\tilde{t}) > 0$ for all $\tilde{t} \in (t - \delta, t + \delta)$ due to continuity of $\hat{y}(t)$ and $\eta(t)$.[1] Then, the same argument above implies $H_y(t, \hat{x}(t), \hat{y}(t), \lambda(t)) = 0$, proving the stronger complementarity condition.

Exercise 7.17*

We claim that the generalized version of the transversality condition

$$\lim_{t \to \infty} \lambda(t) \hat{x}(t) = 0 \tag{S7.8}$$

holds for non-discounted problems that satisfy the stronger version of Assumption 7.1 in the exercise statement. Theorem 7.12 also applies to non-discounted problems and shows that the following weaker form of the transversality condition holds

$$\lim_{t \to \infty} f(t, \hat{x}(t), \hat{y}(t)) + \lambda(t) g(t, \hat{x}(t), \hat{y}(t)) = 0.$$

Since $\lim_{t \to \infty} V(t, \hat{x}(t)) = \lim_{t \to \infty} \int_t^\infty f(t, \hat{x}(t), \hat{y}(t))$ exists and is finite, we have that $\lim_{t \to \infty} f(t, \hat{x}(t), \hat{y}(t)) = 0$, hence the weaker form of the transversality condition implies

$$\lim_{t \to \infty} \lambda(t) g(t, \hat{x}(t), \hat{y}(t)) = \lim_{t \to \infty} \lambda(t) \dot{x}(t) = 0.$$

---

[1] In general, $\hat{y}(t)$ may be discontinuous, but the conditions are necessary only at points of continuity, so there is no loss of generality in assuming that $\hat{y}(t)$ is continuous.

Let us define $\mu(t) \equiv \lambda(t) \exp(\kappa t)$ for each t, then the previous equation can be written as

$$\lim \mu(t) \exp(-\kappa t) \dot{x}(t) = 0. \tag{S7.9}$$

Moreover, the generalized transversality condition (S7.8) can be written in terms of $\mu(t)$ as

$$\lim_{t\to\infty} \exp(-\kappa t) \mu(t) \hat{x}(t) = 0. \tag{S7.10}$$

We claim that $\mu(t)$ is bounded, that is, there exists $B > 0$ such that $|\mu(t)| < B$ for all t. Suppose, to reach a contradiction, that there exists a subnet $\{\mu(t)\}_{t\in T}$ which limits to $+\infty$ or $-\infty$. By the Maximum Principle (cf. Theorem 7.12), we have

$$f_y(t, \hat{x}(t), \hat{y}(t)) + \lambda(t) g_y(t, \hat{x}(t), \hat{y}(t)) = 0, \text{ or equivalently}$$
$$\exp(\kappa t) f_y(t, \hat{x}(t), \hat{y}(t)) + \mu(t) g_y(t, \hat{x}(t), \hat{y}(t)) = 0.$$

Since $\mu(t)$ limits to $\pm\infty$, and since $|g_y(t, \hat{x}(t), \hat{y}(t))| > m > 0$ by part (ii) of Assumption 7.1, the previous displayed equation implies that $\lim_{t\to\infty} \exp(\kappa t) |f_y(t, \hat{x}(t), \hat{y}(t))| = \infty$, which contradicts part (iii) of Assumption 7.1, proving our claim.

As in the proof of Theorem 7.13, we analyze two cases in turn. First, suppose $\lim_{t\to\infty} \hat{x}(t) = \hat{x}^* \in \mathbb{R}$. Note that we have $\lim_{t\to\infty} \exp(-\kappa t) \mu(t) = 0$ since $|\mu(t)| < B$. Then,

$$\lim_{t\to\infty} \exp(-\kappa t) \mu(t) \hat{x}(t) = \lim_{t\to\infty} \exp(-\kappa t) \mu(t) \lim_{t\to\infty} \hat{x}(t) = 0,$$

proving Eq. (S7.10) for this case.

Second, suppose that $\lim_{t\to\infty} \dot{x}(t)/\hat{x}(t) = \chi > 0$. Then, for each $\varepsilon \in (0, \chi)$, there exists $T < \infty$ such that $|\dot{x}(t)| \geq |\chi - \varepsilon| |\hat{x}(t)|$ for all $t > T$. Multiplying both sides of this inequality with $|\exp(-\kappa t) \mu(t)|$ and taking limits, we have

$$\lim_{t\to\infty} |\exp(-\kappa t) \mu(t)| |\dot{x}(t)| \geq |\chi - \varepsilon| \lim_{t\to\infty} |\exp(-\kappa t) \mu(t)| |\hat{x}(t)| \geq 0.$$

The left hand side is 0 from Eq. (S7.9), which shows that the middle term is also 0, proving Eq. (S7.10) for this case and completing the proof.

Exercise 7.18

Exercise 7.18, Part (a). Part (iii) of Assumption 7.1 is not satisfied since $|f_y(x, 0)| = \infty > M$ and $y = 0$ is a feasible choice variable.

Exercise 7.18, Part (b). The current value Hamiltonian is

$$\hat{H}(x(t), y(t), \mu(t)) = \log y(t) - \mu(t) y(t),$$

and the Maximum Principle implies that the following first-order conditions are necessary:

$$\hat{H}_y(x(t), y(t), \mu(t)) = 0 \implies \frac{1}{y(t)} = \mu(t)$$

$$\hat{H}_x(x(t), y(t), \mu(t)) = \rho\mu(t) - \dot{\mu}(t) \implies \frac{\dot{\mu}(t)}{\mu(t)} = \rho.$$

Solving the second equation, we have $\mu(t) = \mu(0) \exp(\rho t)$. Plugging this in the first equation, we have

$$y(t) = \frac{1}{\mu(0)} \exp(-\rho t), \tag{S7.11}$$

as desired.

At this point of the analysis, we typically use the strong version of the transversality condition to solve for $\mu(0)$. However, as we will see in Part (d), the typical transversality condition does not apply in this problem. Another line of attack is to solve for the plan

$(x(t), y(t))$ for each $\mu(0)$ and pick the plan (i) that satisfies the constraints, in particular, the constraint that $\lim_{t\to\infty} x(t) \geq x_1$, (ii) that results in the highest value for the objective function. The solution that satisfies (i) and (ii) must be the optimal solution, since it is feasible, satisfies the necessary conditions and yields the agent the highest utility among all feasible solutions that satisfy the necessary conditions. To operationalize this approach, we plug Eq. (S7.11) in the differential equation $\dot{x}(t) = -y(t)$ and solve for $x(t)$ as

$$x(t) = x_0 - \frac{1}{\mu(0)\rho}(1 - \exp(-\rho t)).$$

The objective function can also be written in terms of $\mu(0)$ as

$$\int_0^\infty \exp(-\rho t) \log\left(\frac{1}{\mu(0)}\exp(-\rho t)\right) dt.$$

From the last two displayed equations, we would like to choose $\mu(0)$ as small as possible to maximize the objective function, but not too small so as to violate the constraint $\lim_{t\to\infty} x(t) \geq x_1$. This reasoning implies that $\mu(0)$ should be chosen so that $\lim_{t\to\infty} x(t) \geq x_1$ is satisfied with equality, that is

$$\lim_{t\to\infty} x_0 - \frac{1}{\mu(0)\rho}(1 - \exp(-\rho t)) = x_0 - \frac{1}{\mu(0)\rho} = x_1,$$

which gives

$$\mu(0) = \frac{1}{\rho(x_0 - x_1)}.$$

The optimal solution is then given by

$$\begin{aligned} y(t) &= (x_0 - x_1)\rho\exp(-\rho t) \text{ and} \\ x(t) &= x_0 - (x_0 - x_1)(1 - \exp(-\rho t)) = x_1 + (x_0 - x_1)\exp(-\rho t). \end{aligned}$$

Intuitively, the optimal solution is to deplete the remaining stock $x(t) - x_1$ at a constant rate (that matches the discount rate ρ) so that the limit stock is exactly x_1, the constraint value.

Exercise 7.18, Part (c). Note that the solution we have found in the previous part satisfies

$$\begin{aligned} \lim_{t\to\infty} \exp(-\rho t)\hat{H}(x(t), y(t), \mu(t)) &= \lim_{t\to\infty} \exp(-\rho t)\log(y(t)) - \exp(-\rho t)\mu(t)y(t) \\ &= \lim_{t\to\infty} \exp(-\rho t)\log\left(\frac{1}{\mu(0)}\exp(-\rho t)\right) - \exp(-\rho t) \\ &= \lim_{t\to\infty} \exp(-\rho t)[-\log\mu(0) - \rho t - 1] = 0, \end{aligned}$$

where the second equality uses the first-order condition $\mu(t)y(t) = 1$ and Eq. (S7.11), and the last equality uses the fact that $\mu(0) = 1/\rho(x_0 - x_1) > 0$ (so $\log\mu(0)$ is finite) and the fact that $\lim_{t\to\infty} \exp(-\rho t)t = 0$. Hence, consistent with Theorem 7.12, the solution satisfies the weak form of the transversality condition.

Exercise 7.18, Part (d). The solution we have found in Part (b) satisfies

$$\begin{aligned} \lim_{t\to\infty}[\exp(-\rho t)\mu(t)x(t)] &= \lim_{t\to\infty}\left[\exp(-\rho t)\frac{1}{\rho(x_0-x_1)}\exp(\rho t)[x_1 + (x_0 - x_1)\exp(-\rho t)]\right] \\ &= \frac{x_1}{\rho(x_0-x_1)} \neq 0, \end{aligned}$$

in particular, the strong form of the transversality condition is not satisfied. This does not contradict Theorem 7.13 since this problem does not satisfy Assumption 7.1 as we have shown in Part (a).

Exercise 7.18, Part (e). The fact that transversality condition is not satisfied in this problem can be explained both from a mathematics and an economics perspective. From the mathematics point of view, the failure of the transversality condition is possible since the optimization problem does not satisfy Assumption 7.1 due to the logarithmic objective function. From an economics point of view, the typical economic argument for the strong transversality condition does not apply to this problem. The typical argument goes like this: since $\lambda(t) = \exp(-\rho t)\mu(t)$ measures the marginal time 0 value of an additional stock variable, $\lim_{t\to\infty} \exp(-\rho t)\mu(t)x(t)$ should be zero since it should be optimal to deplete all the stock available, that is, it cannot be optimal to plan to leave some stock unused. But the typical reasoning does not apply to this problem since there is an exogenous constraint, $\lim_{t\to\infty} x(t) \geq x_1$, which prevents the full depletion of the stock. Applying the same economic rationale to this problem, we would expect instead the following transversality condition to hold

$$\lim_{t\to\infty} [\exp(-\rho t)\mu(t)(x(t)-x_1)] = 0,$$

which in fact holds since the limit is equal to $[\rho(x_0-x_1)]^{-1}(x_1-x_1) = 0$.

This exercise then suggests a cautionary note for using the transversality condition. The transversality condition typically holds and is often useful in characterizing the optimal solution. However, it is important to bear in mind the economic rationale behind the transversality condition, which might imply different versions of the condition for different problems (see Michel (1982, 1990) for generalizations and further clarifications of the transversality condition).

Exercise 7.21

Exercise 7.21, Part (a). The Hamiltonian is

$$H(t,k(t),c(t),\lambda(t)) = u(c(t)) - u(c^*) + \lambda(t)[f(k(t)) - c(t) - \delta k(t)].$$

Exercise 7.21, Part (b). The first-order optimality conditions are

$$H_c = 0 \implies u'(c(t)) = \lambda(t),$$
$$H_k = -\dot\lambda(t) \implies \dot\lambda(t) + \lambda(t)(f'(k(t)) - \delta) = 0.$$

Combining these conditions, we obtain the Euler equation without discounting

$$\frac{\dot c(t)}{c(t)} = \frac{-c(t)u'(c(t))}{u''(c(t))}(f'(k(t)) - \delta). \tag{S7.12}$$

The solution also satisfies the capital accumulation equation

$$\dot k(t) = f(k(t)) - c(t) - \delta k(t), \tag{S7.13}$$

with the initial condition $k(0)$.

Note that Eqs. (S7.12) and (S7.13) constitute two differential equations in two variables and only one initial condition. Therefore we are one condition short of calculating the optimal path. We will pin down the optimal path by considering all possible paths of $k(t)$ and $c(t)$ that satisfy these conditions and eliminating sub-optimal ones. Note that for each choice of the initial consumption, $c(0)$, the whole path $[k(t),c(t)]_{t=0}^{\infty}$ is uniquely determined, hence we go through possible choices for $c(0)$ and eliminate the sub-optimal ones.

(1) If $c(0)$ is above the stable arm, then using the standard phase diagram for the differential equations (S7.12) and (S7.13), we have that $k(t)$ becomes 0 at some finite time $\bar{t}$ and $c(t)$ is 0 after this time. Since $\lim_{T\to\infty} \int_{\bar{t}}^{T} [u(0) - u(c^*)]\, dt = -\infty$, this path yields an objective value of $-\infty$ and is not optimal.

(2) If $c(0)$ is below the stable arm, then it can be seen from the phase diagram that $c(t)$ limits to 0, which implies that there exists some $\varepsilon > 0$ and $\bar{t} > 0$ such that $c(t) < c^* - \varepsilon$ for all $t > \bar{t}$. This further implies

$$\lim_{T\to\infty} \int_{\bar{t}}^{T} [u(c(t)) - u(c^*)]\, dt \leq \lim_{T\to\infty} \int_{\bar{t}}^{T} [u(c^* - \varepsilon) - u(c^*)]\, dt = -\infty,$$

that is, this path also yields a value of $-\infty$ and is not optimal.

(3) If $c(0)$ is on the stable arm, then, $c(t) \to c^*$ and $k(t) \to k^*$ along the saddle path, where $c^* = f(k^*) - \delta k^*$ and k^* is the solution to $f'(k^*) = \delta$. This path yields a finite value and thus is the optimal path, characterizing the solution to the optimal growth problem.

Exercise 7.21, Part (c). Note that $\lambda(t) = u'(c(t)) \to u'(c^*) \neq 0$ hence

$$\lim_{t\to\infty} \lambda(t) k(t) = k^* u'(c^*) \neq 0.$$

The optimal path does not satisfy the strong form of the transversality condition, that is, the value of the capital stock does not limit to 0. The reason for this is the absence of discounting. Depleting the capital stock at periods far in the future is not profitable since this would cause a utility loss for all of the remaining periods, and without discounting these periods are still significant from the time 0 point of view. Hence, the capital stock always yields future benefits and the value of holding additional capital stock is always positive. Note that the weaker form of the transversality condition (of Michel (1982)) is satisfied, that is

$$\lim_{t\to\infty} H(t, k(t), c(t), \lambda(t)) = \lim_{t\to\infty} u(c^*) - u(c^*) + u'(c^*)[f(k^*) - c^* - \delta k^*]$$
$$= 0,$$

where the last line follows from the fact that $\dot{k}(t) = 0$ at steady state.

This exercise further provides a cautionary note for using the strong version of the transversality condition. We always need to keep in mind the economic rationale behind this condition and use the condition only when the rationale applies to the problem. This exercise suggests that the economic rationale of this condition may not apply to problems in which the objective value has no discounting (see also Part (e) of Exercise 7.18).

Exercise 7.24*

First, we consider the unconstrained problem[2]

$$\max_{[k(t)\geq 0, c(t)]_t} \int_0^\infty \exp(-\rho t)\, c(t)\, dt \tag{S7.14}$$

$$\text{s.t. } \dot{k}(t) = f(k(t)) - \delta k(t) - c(t),\ k(0) = k^*.$$

---

[2]Note that there is a typo in the problem statement. The intertemporal substitution should be perfectly elastic, that is, the utility function should be given by $\int_0^\infty \exp(-\rho t)\, c(t)\, dt$ instead of the more general form $\int_0^\infty \exp(-\rho t)\, u(c(t))\, dt$. For strictly concave utility functions, the alternating policy suggested in the hint would result in first order utility losses and would not approximate the unconstrained optimum policy.

It follows by Theorem 7.14 that $k(t) = k^*$ and $c(t) = c^* \equiv f(k^*) - \delta k^*$ is the unique solution to this problem.

Second we note that the path $[k(t) = k^*]_t$ is not a solution in the constrained problem of this exercise since it is not feasible. Suppose, to reach a contradiction, that it is feasible. Then there must be investment just enough to replenish the depreciated capital otherwise capital would either increase or depreciate, that is

$$f(k(t)) - c(t) = \delta k(t) = \delta k^*.$$

But since $\delta k^* < \underline{k}$, this level of investment violates the minimum size requirement hence we must have $\dot{k} = -\delta k$, which is a contradiction to the fact that $k(t)$ remains constant.

Third, we get a minor issue out of the way. We note that a path $[k(t), c(t)]_{t=0}^{\infty}$ that is feasible for the constrained problem is not necessarily feasible for the unconstrained problem, but it can always be improved by a path $\left[\tilde{k}(t), \tilde{c}(t)\right]_{t=0}^{\infty}$ that is feasible for both problems. The issue is that there are paths $[k(t), c(t)]_{t=0}^{\infty}$ feasible for the constrained problem that sometimes satisfy $f(k(t)) - c(t) \in (0, \underline{k})$, that is, at some periods there is positive investment even though this investment does not meet the minimum investment requirement (so the positive investment does not contribute to output and goes to waste). Such paths do not satisfy the law of motion of the unconstrained problem (S7.14). But these paths are clearly sub-optimal since the household is better off by consuming the investment that goes to waste without affecting the accumulation of capital. It follows that we can ignore these paths without loss of generality, and any remaining paths feasible for the constrained problem are also feasible for the unconstrained problem. This also implies that the optimal value of the constrained problem is weakly lower than the optimal value of the unconstrained problem.

Fourth, as the crux of the argument, we claim that there are feasible paths $[k(t), c(t)]_{t=0}^{\infty}$ for the constrained problem that yield value arbitrarily close to the value $\int_0^{\infty} \exp(-\rho t) c^* dt = c^*/\rho$ of the unconstrained problem. The idea is to construct a path that alternates very frequently between not investing and investing at the minimum size requirement so as to keep average capital close to k^* at all points in time. Since the firm operates close to optimal scale at all points in time, average consumption will also be close to c^* (but it will not be smooth, in fact it will be very jumpy). Since we assume that the period utility is linear, the intertemporal substitution is perfectly elastic and an alternating policy of this kind will yield a utility arbitrarily close to c^*/ρ.

To formalize this argument, we define the investment $i(t) \equiv f(k(t)) - c(t)$ and for convenience we construct the path using the investment variable rather than consumption. We fix some $\Delta_1 > 0$ and we consider a path along which there is no investment for a period of length Δ_1 and the investment is at the minimum required level $\underline{k}$ for a period of length $\Delta_2 - \Delta_1$ for an appropriately chosen $\Delta_2 > \Delta_1$. More specifically, we consider the path $[i(t)]_{t=0}^{\Delta_1+\Delta_2}$ given by

$$i(t) = \begin{cases} 0, & \text{for } t \in [0, \Delta_1] \\ \underline{k}, & \text{for } t \in [\Delta_1, \Delta_2] \end{cases}. \tag{S7.15}$$

Given this investment plan, the capital accumulation equation is given by

$$\dot{k} = \begin{cases} -\delta k, & \text{for } t \in [0, \Delta_1] \\ \underline{k} - \delta k, & \text{for } t \in [\Delta_1, \Delta_2] \end{cases}. \tag{S7.16}$$

We next claim that there exists $\Delta_2 \in \left[\Delta_1, \Delta_1 \frac{\underline{k}}{\underline{k} - \delta k^*}\right]$ such that

$$k(\Delta_2) = k(0) = k^*. \tag{S7.17}$$

To prove this claim, suppose the contrary, that $k(t) < k^*$ for all $t \in \left[\Delta_1, \Delta_1 \frac{k}{\underline{k}-\delta k^*}\right]$ in the system described in Eq. (S7.16). Upon integrating Eq. (S7.16), we have

$$
\begin{aligned}
k(t) &= k(0) + (t - \Delta_1)\underline{k} - \int_0^t \delta k(t')\, dt' \\
&> k^* + (t - \Delta_1)\underline{k} - t\delta k^*,
\end{aligned} \tag{S7.18}
$$

where the second line follows since $k(0) = k^*$ and $k(t) < k^*$ for all $t \in (0, \Delta_1 \frac{k}{\underline{k}-\delta k^*}]$ by assumption. For $t = \Delta_1 \frac{k}{\underline{k}-\delta k^*}$, we have

$$
\frac{t - \Delta_1}{t} = \frac{\delta k^*}{\underline{k}}.
$$

Eq. (S7.18) therefore implies that $k\left(t = \Delta_1 \frac{k}{\underline{k}-\delta k^*}\right) > k^*$, providing a contradiction. Hence, there exists $\Delta_2 \in \left[\Delta_1, \Delta_1 \frac{k}{\underline{k}-\delta k^*}\right]$ satisfying Eq. (S7.17) as claimed. Let

$$
\Delta_2(\Delta_1) \equiv \inf\left\{ t' \in \left[\Delta_1, \Delta_1 \frac{k}{\underline{k} - \delta k^*}\right] \mid k(t') = k^* \right\}
$$

be the first time at which capital comes back up to k^* and note that $\lim_{\Delta_1 \to 0} \Delta_2(\Delta_1) = 0$. Intuitively, the capital stock gets depreciated for a period Δ_1, but we are "over-investing" (since $\underline{k} > \delta k^*$) after that, hence, if we over-invest for sufficiently long, then we will get the capital level back at exactly k^*. Moreover, the amount of time necessary to replenish the capital back to k^* is going to 0 as Δ_1 goes to 0. For the rest of the analysis, we use Δ_2 to represent $\Delta_2(\Delta_1)$ for notational simplicity.

We next extend the investment plan over $[0, \Delta_2]$ given in Eq. (S7.15) to $\mathbb{R}_+$ by repeating it periodically as follows

$$
i(t) = \begin{cases} 0, & \text{for } t \in [0, \Delta_1) \\ \underline{k}, & \text{for } t \in [\Delta_1, \Delta_2) \\ i(t - \Delta_2) & \text{for all } t \geq \Delta_2. \end{cases}
$$

Note that this investment plan and the resulting path for the capital stock is well defined for any given $\Delta_1 > 0$. We next claim that

$$
\lim_{\Delta_1 \to 0} k(t) = k^*, \quad \text{for all } t \tag{S7.19}
$$

that is, the capital stock limits pointwise to k^*. To see this, note that using (S7.16) and $i(t) = 0$ for $t \in [0, \Delta_1]$, we have

$$
k(\Delta_1) = k^* (1 - \exp(-\delta \Delta_1)). \tag{S7.20}
$$

Note also that, by construction, $k(\Delta_1)$ is the lower bound of capital, that is, $k(t) \in [k(\Delta_1), k^*]$ for all t. Since, $\lim_{\Delta_1 \to 0} k(\Delta_1) = k^*$ by Eq. (S7.20), it follows that Eq. (S7.19) holds.

Next, we claim that average consumption over $[0, \Delta_2]$ limits to c^*, that is

$$
\lim_{\Delta_1 \to 0} \frac{\int_0^{\Delta_2} c(t)\, dt}{\Delta_2} = c^*. \tag{S7.21}
$$

To see this, rewrite consumption as the residual of output net of investment, that is

$$
\frac{\int_0^{\Delta_2} c(t)\, dt}{\Delta_2} = \frac{\int_0^{\Delta_2} (f(k(t)) - i(t))\, dt}{\Delta_2}. \tag{S7.22}
$$

By Eq. (S7.16), we have

$$k\left(\Delta_2\right) = k\left(0\right) + \int_0^{\Delta_2} i\left(t\right) dt - \int_0^{\Delta_2} \delta k\left(t\right) dt,$$

and since $k\left(\Delta_2\right) = k\left(0\right) = k^*$, this implies $\int_0^{\Delta_2} i\left(t\right) dt = \int_0^{\Delta_2} \delta k\left(t\right) dt$, that is, total investment over $[0, \Delta_2]$ is just enough to replenish the depreciated capital. Using this in Eq. (S7.22), we have

$$\frac{\int_0^{\Delta_2} c\left(t\right) dt}{\Delta_2} = \frac{\int_0^{\Delta_2} \left[f\left(k\left(t\right)\right) - \delta k\left(t\right)\right] dt}{\Delta_2}$$

Since $k\left(t\right)$ pointwise limits to k^* (as $\Delta_1 \to 0$), the right hand side limits to $f\left(k^*\right) - \delta k^* = c^*$ as $\Delta_1 \to 0$, proving Eq. (S7.21).

We next claim that the utility implied by this path limits (but never attains) the unconstrained optimum as $\Delta_1 \to 0$, that is

$$\lim_{\Delta_1 \to \infty} \int_0^\infty \exp\left(-\rho t\right) c\left(t\right) dt = \int_0^\infty \exp\left(-\rho t\right) c^* dt = c^*/\rho. \qquad (S7.23)$$

To see this, note that $[k\left(t\right), c\left(t\right)]_{t=0}^\infty$ constructed here is feasible in the unconstrained problem. Hence it always attains a weakly lower value than the unconstrained optimum (k^*, c^*), that is

$$\int_0^\infty \exp\left(-\rho t\right) c\left(t\right) dt \leq \int_0^\infty \exp\left(-\rho t\right) c^* dt = c^*/\rho. \qquad (S7.24)$$

On the other hand, we have

$$\int_0^\infty \exp\left(-\rho t\right) c\left(t\right) dt = \sum_{n=0}^\infty \int_{n\Delta_2}^{(n+1)\Delta_2} \exp\left(-\rho t\right) c\left(t\right) dt$$

$$= \sum_{n=0}^\infty \exp\left(-\rho n \Delta_2\right) \int_0^{\Delta_2} \exp\left(-\rho t\right) c\left(t\right) dt$$

$$\geq \sum_{n=0}^\infty \exp\left(-\rho\left(n+1\right)\Delta_2\right) \int_0^{\Delta_2} c\left(t\right) dt$$

$$= \int_0^{\Delta_2} \frac{c\left(t\right)}{\Delta_2} dt \times \sum_{n=0}^\infty \exp\left(-\rho\left(n+1\right)\Delta_2\right) \Delta_2, \qquad (S7.25)$$

where the second line uses $c\left(n\Delta_2 + t\right) = c\left(t\right)$ for all n and $t \in [0, \Delta_2]$, and the inequality in the third line follows since $\exp\left(-\rho t\right) \geq \exp\left(-\rho \Delta_2\right)$ for $t \in [0, \Delta_2]$. Using $\lim_{\Delta_1 \to 0} \Delta_2\left(\Delta_1\right) = 0$, we get

$$\lim_{\Delta_1 \to 0} \sum_{n=0}^\infty \exp\left(-\rho\left(n+1\right)\Delta_2\right) \Delta_2 = \int_0^\infty \exp\left(-\rho t\right) dt = 1/\rho.$$

As the limit of the first term in Eq. (S7.25) is c^* (cf. Eq. (S7.21)), we have

$$\lim_{\Delta_1 \to 0} \inf \int_0^\infty \exp\left(-\rho t\right) c\left(t\right) dt \geq c^*/\rho.$$

The last equation and Eq. (S7.24) jointly imply Eq. (S7.23) as desired.

Thus we have constructed feasible paths that attain an objective value which is arbitrarily close to the unconstrained maximum c^*/ρ. As the final step, we claim that there does not exist a solution to the constrained optimization problem, that is, there does not exist a feasible path $[k\left(t\right), c\left(t\right)]_{t=0}^\infty$ that attains the optimum value c^*/ρ. Suppose, to reach a contradiction, there is. We have that $[k\left(t\right), c\left(t\right)]_{t=0}^\infty \neq [k\left(t'\right) = k^*, c\left(t'\right) = c^*]_{t'=0}^\infty$, since the latter is not feasible in the constrained problem. Moreover, if $[k(t), c(t)]_{t=0}^{\infty}$ is optimal, then it is also feasible in the unconstrained problem (see our discussion in the third point above). Then both $[k(t), c(t)]_{t=0}^{\infty}$ and $[k(t') = k^*, c(t') = c^*]_{t'=0}^{\infty}$ are feasible in the unconstrained problem and both attain the maximum value c^*/ρ for the problem. But this is a contradiction since the unconstrained problem is strictly concave and by Arrow's sufficiency theorem $(k(t') = k^*, c(t') = c^*)_{t'=0}^{\infty}$ is its unique optimum.

We conclude that the value of the constrained problem is c^*/ρ, this value can be arbitrarily approximated, but cannot be attained by any sequences of feasible paths. It is instructive to think about the limit of the paths we have constructed as $\Delta_1 \to 0$. The limiting path of consumption does not exist since consumption jumps infinitely often in any given interval and it does not have a piecewise continuous limit. The limiting path of capital exists and is equal to $k(t) = k^*$ for all t, but is not feasible. The optimum is not attained essentially because the limiting path either does not exist and/or is not feasible. Theorem 7.15 in Section 7.6 makes assumptions on the optimization problem which guarantee that when we (carefully) pick a sequence of paths that arbitrarily approximate the value function, those paths converge to a path within the feasible set. As long as the limiting path is well defined and feasible, it would also be optimal and the optimum would be attained.

Exercise 7.25

Exercise 7.25, Part (a). For any $M > 0$, there exists $c \in (0, 1/M)$ such that $f_y(x, y) = u_c(c) = 1/c > M$, which proves that part (iii) of Assumption 7.1 is violated.

Exercise 7.25, Part (b). Consider the constrained problem in which $c(t)$ is restricted to lie in $[\varepsilon, +\infty)$ and suppose $[c(t), k(t)]_t$ is an optimal path for this problem which satisfies $c(t) > \varepsilon$ for all t. Note that the constrained problem satisfies Assumption 7.1, hence Theorem 7.13 applies to this problem and shows that the interior solution $[c(t), k(t)]_t$ satisfies the necessary conditions

$$\hat{H}_c(c(t), k(t), \mu(t)) = 0 \implies u'(c(t)) = \mu(t),$$

$$\hat{H}_k(c(t), k(t), \mu(t)) = \rho\mu(t) - \dot{\mu}(t) \implies \frac{\dot{\mu}(t)}{\mu(t)} = -\left(f'(k(t)) - \delta - \rho\right),$$

$$\dot{k}(t) = f(k(t)) - \delta k(t) - c(t), \ k(t) \geq 0 \text{ for all } t,$$

along with the strong form of the transversality condition

$$\lim_{t \to \infty} \exp(-\rho t) k(t) \mu(t) = 0.$$

Note that these conditions are also the first-order conditions for an interior solution of the unconstrained problem. Since the current value Hamiltonian $H(c, k, \mu(t)) = \log(c) + \mu(t)(f(k) - \delta k - c)$ is strictly concave in c and k, and since any feasible path $\left[\hat{c}(t), \hat{k}(t)\right]_t$ satisfies $\lim_{t \to \infty} \exp(-\rho t) \mu(t) \hat{k}(t) \geq 0$, Theorem 7.14 applies to the unconstrained problem and shows that $[c(t), k(t)]_t$ (which is interior by assumption) is also a solution to the unconstrained optimal growth problem.

Essentially, Theorem 7.14 does not require Assumption 7.1, so the sufficiency theorem continues to apply even though the necessity theorem, Theorem 7.13, does not apply to the optimal control problem with log utility. Hence, as long as we find an interior solution that is optimal for the constrained problem, it will be feasible and optimal for the unconstrained problem since the latter is a concave problem.

Exercise 7.25, Part (c). The analysis in Chapter 8 shows that the saddle path $[c(t), k(t)]_{t=0}^{\infty}$ that converges to (c^*, k^*) satisfies the requirements of Theorem 7.14 and thus is the unique optimal plan. We claim that there exists $\varepsilon > 0$ such that this optimal plan satisfies $c(t) > \varepsilon$ for all t. We prove this in three steps.

We first claim that $c^* > 0$. Recall that the pair (c^*, k^*) is the unique solution to

$$f'(k^*) = \rho + \delta$$
$$c^* = f(k^*) - \delta k^*.$$

Since f is strictly concave, the first equation shows that k^* maximizes $f(k) - (\delta + \rho)k$, and in particular,

$$f(k^*) - (\delta + \rho)k^* > f(0) - (\delta + \rho) \times 0 = f(0) \geq 0.$$

This inequality further implies that $f(k^*) - \delta k^* \geq \rho k^* + f(0) > 0$, proving that $c^* > 0$.

Second, we claim that $c(t) > 0$ for all t. Suppose, to reach a contradiction, that $c(t') = 0$ for some t'. Since the plan $[c(t), k(t)]_{t=0}^{\infty}$ satisfies the Euler equation $\dot{c}(t) = c(t)(f'(k(t)) - \delta - \rho)/\theta$, this implies $c(t) = 0$ for all $t \geq t'$. But this further implies $\lim_{t\to\infty} c(t) = 0 < c^*$, which yields a contradiction and proves that $c(t) > 0$ for all t.

Third, we claim that there exits $\varepsilon > 0$ such that the optimal plan satisfies $c(t) > \varepsilon$ for all t. We have $\lim_{t\to\infty} c(t) = c^*$, thus there exists $T > 0$ such that $c(t) > c^*/2$ for all $t \geq T$. Let $\bar{\varepsilon} = \frac{1}{2}\min_{t\in[0,T]} c(t)$ which is well defined since $c(t)$ is continuous and $[0,T]$ is compact, and which is positive since $c(0) > 0$ for all $t \in [0,T]$. For $\varepsilon = \min(c^*/2, \bar{\varepsilon})$ we have that the optimal plan satisfies $c(t) > \varepsilon$ for all t, completing the proof.

Exercise 7.28

Exercise 7.28, Part (a). Integrating the condition $\phi''(I) = 0$, we have $\phi(I) = \gamma I + \eta$ for some constants γ and η. Consider the parameterized optimization problem in which the firm's cost function is given by $\phi_n(I) = \gamma I + \eta + aI^2/(2n)$, that is

$$P(n) : \max_{[K(t),I(t)]_{t=0}^{\infty}} \int_0^{\infty} \exp(-rt)\left[f(K(t)) - (1+\gamma)I(t) - \eta - \frac{aI(t)^2}{2n}\right] dt \quad (S7.26)$$

s.t. $\dot{K}(t) = I(t) - \delta K(t).$

Denote the value of this problem with $V(n)$. We are interested in the problem $P(\infty)$, but $P(\infty)$ does not necessarily fit into the optimal control framework of Chapter 7, hence we instead analyze $\lim_{n\to\infty} P(n)$.

For any $P(n)$ with finite n, note that the investment function is strictly convex therefore the results in Section 7.8 apply. In particular, the solution $[K_n(t), I_n(t)]_t$ satisfies the first-order conditions and the feasibility condition

$$\dot{I}_n(t) = \frac{n}{a}\left[(r+\delta)\left(1+\gamma+\frac{a}{n}I_n(t)\right) - f'(K_n(t))\right] \quad (S7.27)$$
$$\dot{K}_n(t) = I_n(t) - \delta K_n(t),$$

and converges to the steady state with $I_n^* = \delta K_n^*$ where K_n^* is defined as the unique positive solution to

$$f'(K_n^*) = (r+\delta)\left(1+\gamma+\frac{1}{n}\delta K_n^*\right).$$

Taking the limit of this condition, we have that $\lim_{n\to\infty} K_n^* = K^*$, where K^* is defined as the solution to

$$f'(K^*) = (r+\delta)(1+\gamma).$$

Then, taking the limit of Eq. (S7.27) at $t = 0$ and noting that $K_n(0) = K(0)$ for all n, we have

$$\lim_{n \to \infty} \dot{I}_n(0) = \begin{cases} \infty \text{ if } K(0) < K^* \\ -\infty \text{ if } K(0) > K^*. \end{cases}$$

It follows that as n goes to ∞, $K_n(t)$ converges to K^* immediately. More specifically, for a given $t' > 0$, we have $\lim_{n \to \infty} K_n(t') = K^*$. Next, note that since the objective function in (S7.26) is continuous in n, we have $\lim_{n \to \infty} V(n) = V(\infty)$ and the optimal plans that attain K_n^* approximate $V(\infty)$ arbitrarily closely. In fact, $P(\infty)$ does not have a continuous optimal solution, but the optimal solution is approximated arbitrarily closely by $[K_n(t), I_n(t)]_t$ as n increases. It follows that the optimal investment plan for $P(\infty)$ is such that the capital level jumps to the steady state value K^* immediately and remains there forever.

Exercise 7.28, Part (b). Recall that the dynamic system is

$$\begin{bmatrix} \dot{K} \\ \dot{I} \end{bmatrix} = G\left(\begin{bmatrix} K \\ I \end{bmatrix} \right) = \begin{bmatrix} I - \delta K \\ \frac{1}{\phi''(I)} \left((r + \delta)\left(1 + \phi'(I)\right) - f'(K) \right) \end{bmatrix}. \quad (S7.28)$$

The steady state is (I^*, K^*) that solves

$$I^* = \delta K^* \text{ and } f'(K^*) = (r + \delta)\left(1 + \phi'(I^*)\right). \quad (S7.29)$$

The curve for (7.88) plotted in Figure 7.1 is characterized by $I(K)$ that solves

$$(r + \delta)\left(1 + \phi'(I(K))\right) - f'(K) = 0. \quad (S7.30)$$

Note that since ϕ' is increasing, this equation has a unique solution for all $K < f'^{-1}(r + \delta)$ hence $I(K)$ is well defined in this range. It follows that $I(K)$ is well defined around the steady state K^* as $K^* < (f')^{-1}(r + \delta)$ (see Eq. (S7.29)). We claim that $I(K)$ is decreasing over the range it is defined (and in particular at $K = K^*$). To see this, we use the implicit function theorem and differentiate Eq. (S7.30) with respect to K, which gives,

$$\frac{dI(K)}{dK} = \frac{1}{r + \delta} \cdot \frac{f''(K)}{\phi''(I(K))} < 0,$$

where the inequality follows since $\phi'' > 0$ and $f'' < 0$. Hence, $I(K)$ is indeed decreasing over the range it is defined and its plot in Figure 7.1 is downward sloping.

Exercise 7.28, Part (c). We first claim that the system in (S7.28) is locally saddle path stable. To study the local behavior, we linearize the system around this steady state. The Jacobian of G is given by

$$\nabla G(K, I) = \begin{bmatrix} -\delta & 1 \\ -\frac{f''(K)}{\phi''(I)} & \left[\left(d\left(\frac{1}{\phi''(I)} \right) / dI \right) \left((r + \delta)\left(1 + \phi'(I)\right) - f'(K) \right) + r + \delta \right] \end{bmatrix}.$$

The Jacobian evaluated at the steady state is

$$\nabla G|_{(K^*, I^*)} = \begin{bmatrix} -\delta & 1 \\ -\frac{f''(K^*)}{\phi''(I^*)} & (r + \delta) \end{bmatrix}.$$

Hence, the linearized system around the steady state is

$$\begin{bmatrix} \dot{K} \\ \dot{I} \end{bmatrix} = \nabla G|_{(K^*, I^*)} \begin{bmatrix} K - K^* \\ I - I^* \end{bmatrix}. \quad (S7.31)$$

By Theorem 7.19, the stability of the system is characterized by the eigenvalues of $\nabla G|_{(K^*,I^*)}$. The eigenvalues are found by solving

$$\det\left(\nabla G|_{(K^*,I^*)} - \lambda I\right) = \det\left(\begin{bmatrix} -\delta - \lambda & 1 \\ -\frac{f''(K^*)}{\phi''(I^*)} & (r+\delta) - \lambda \end{bmatrix}\right) = 0.$$

Hence, the eigenvalues are the roots of the following polynomial:

$$P(\lambda) = (\lambda + \delta)(\lambda - r - \delta) + f''(K^*)/\phi''(I^*).$$

Note that $P(0) < 0$ (since f is concave and ϕ is convex) and $\lim_{\lambda \to -\infty} P(\lambda) = \lim_{\lambda \to \infty} P(\lambda) = \infty$, which implies that P has two real roots (λ_1, λ_2) that satisfy $\lambda_1 < 0 < \lambda_2$. Since only one eigenvalue is negative, Theorem (7.19) implies that there exists a one dimensional manifold M in a neighborhood of (K^*, I^*) such that starting from $(K(0), I(0))$ on M, the solution to the differential equation in (S7.28), $[K(t), I(t)]_t$, converges to (K^*, I^*). This proves our claim that the system in (S7.28) is locally saddle path stable.

We next claim that the saddle path plan $[K(t), I(t)]_t$ is the unique optimal plan, which in turn shows that the optimal investment plan will converge to the steady state. To show this, we verify that the conditions of Theorem 7.14 are satisfied. The first-order and feasibility conditions are satisfied by construction. This plan also satisfies the transversality condition since

$$\lim_{t \to \infty} \exp(-rt) q(t) k(t) = \lim_{t \to \infty} \exp(-rt) \left(1 + \phi'(I^*)\right) K^* = 0.$$

The concavity condition is satisfied since

$$M(K, q) = \max_I f(K) - I - \phi(I) + q(I - \delta K)$$

is strictly concave in K. Finally, for any feasible plan $\left(\tilde{K}(t), \tilde{I}(t)\right)$, we have

$$\lim_{t \to \infty} \exp(-rt) q(t) \tilde{K}(t) \geq 0$$

since $q = 1 + \phi'(I) \geq 0$ and $\tilde{K} \geq 0$. Then, we invoke Theorem 7.14 which proves that the saddle path plan is the unique optimal investment plan.

Exercise 7.28, Part (d). We have shown that the optimal plan is the saddle path stable plan, hence the statement in this exercise follows if we show the saddle path is downward sloping.

We first claim that the linearized system in (S7.31) has a downward sloping saddle path. This amounts to showing that any eigenvector $v_1 \equiv \left(v_1^1, v_1^2\right)$ corresponding to the negative eigenvalue $\lambda_1 < 0$ of the system (S7.31) has the property that v_1^1 and v_1^2 have opposite signs. Note that the eigenvector $\left(v_1^1, v_1^2\right)$ satisfies $\nabla G|_{(K^*,I^*)} v_1 = \lambda_1 v_1$, that is

$$\begin{bmatrix} -\delta & 1 \\ -\frac{f''(k^*)}{\phi''(i^*)} & (r+\delta) \end{bmatrix} \begin{bmatrix} v_1^1 \\ v_1^2 \end{bmatrix} = \lambda_1 \begin{bmatrix} v_1^1 \\ v_1^2 \end{bmatrix}.$$

Suppose, to reach a contradiction, that v_1^1, v_1^2 have the same signs, and suppose that they are both positive (the proof for the negative case is symmetric). The second equation in the previous displayed matrix equation implies

$$0 < -\frac{f''(k^*)}{\phi''(i^*)} v_1^1 + (r+\delta) v_1^2 = \lambda_1 v_1^2 < 0,$$

where the first inequality follows since $-\frac{f''(k^*)}{\phi''(i^*)} > 0$ and the last since $\lambda_1 < 0$. This yields the desired contradiction, proving that the eigenvector has components with different signs and the saddle path for the linearized system is downward sloping.

It then follows that, in a neighborhood of K^*, when $K(0)$ is strictly less than K^*, $I(0)$ is greater than I^* and gradually decreases towards I^*. The statement is generalized to all $K(0) < K^*$ by analyzing the saddle path for the nonlinear system in Figure 7.1.

Exercise 7.28, Part (e). We assume that the adjustment cost of installing capital I when the current capital is K is given by $I\phi(I/K)$, so the total cost of installing I is $I(1 + \phi(I/K))$. Let us define the investment rate $i \equiv I/K$ since it is easier to derive the first-order conditions in terms of i and K. The Hamiltonian is given by

$$\hat{H}(K, i, q) = f(K) - iK - \phi(i) + q(iK - \delta K).$$

The first-order conditions are

$$\hat{H}_i = 0 \implies \phi'(i) = K(q - 1)$$
$$\hat{H}_K = rq - \dot{q} \implies f'(K) - i + q(i - \delta) = rq - \dot{q}$$

Combining these equations, we get the equivalent of Eq. (7.88), given by

$$
\begin{aligned}
f'(K) &= i + (r + \delta - i)\left(\frac{\phi'(i)}{K} + 1\right) - \frac{\phi''(i)}{K}\frac{di}{dt} + \frac{\phi'(i)\dot{K}}{K^2} \\
&= r + \delta + \left(r + \delta - i + \frac{\dot{K}}{K}\right)\frac{\phi'(i)}{K} - \frac{\phi''(i)}{K}\frac{di}{dt}.
\end{aligned}
$$

Substituting for $\dot{K}$ from the feasibility equation

$$\dot{K} = iK - \delta K,$$

we can solve for di/dt as

$$\frac{di}{dt} = \frac{K}{\phi''(i)}\left(r + \delta + r\frac{\phi'(i)}{K} - f'(K)\right).$$

Hence, any optimal plan solves the previous two differential equations. The steady state is the unique (i^*, K^*) which solves

$$i^* = \delta \text{ and } f'(K^*) = r + \delta + r\frac{\phi'(\delta)}{K^*}. \tag{S7.32}$$

It can be checked that the system is saddle path stable, that is, for any $K(0)$, there exists a unique $i(0)$ such that $[i(t), K(t)]_t$ converges to (i^*, K^*) along the saddle path. Moreover, Theorem 7.14 also applies to this problem and shows that the saddle path plan is the optimal plan.

We next compare the steady state characterized by Eq. (S7.32) with the steady state of the problem analyzed in Section 7.8. Rewriting Eq. (S7.32), we have that the marginal product of capital satisfies

$$
\begin{aligned}
f'(K^*) &= r + \delta + r\frac{\phi'(I/K)}{K^*} = r + \delta + r\frac{d}{dI}\phi\left(\frac{I}{K}\right) \\
&< (r + \delta) + (r + \delta)\frac{d}{dI}\phi\left(\frac{I}{K}\right) \\
&= (r + \delta)\left(1 + \frac{d}{dI}\phi\left(\frac{I}{K}\right)\right),
\end{aligned}
$$

where the last line is the analogue of the marginal cost of installing capital in Section 7.8. Intuitively, the marginal product of capital is lower in this case and hence the capital level is higher, since investment has the additional benefit of lowering future investment costs in view of the functional form $\phi(I/K)$.

Exercise 7.28, Part (f). As we have shown in Exercise 7.10, the optimality conditions in this case are the same as the baseline case except for the condition $\hat{H}_I = 0$, which is now replaced by the complementary slackness condition. Hence the optimality conditions can be written as

$$q(t) \leq 1 + \phi'(I(t)), \text{ with equality if } I(t) > 0, \tag{S7.33}$$
$$f'(K(t)) = (r + \delta) q(t) - \dot{q}(t)$$
$$\lim_{t \to \infty} \exp(-rt) q(t) K(t) = 0.$$

We next construct a plan $[K(t), I(t)]_t$ that satisfies these conditions along with the feasibility constraints

$$\dot{K}(t) = I(t) - \delta K(t), \; K(0) \text{ given, and } I(t) \geq 0 \text{ for all } t, \tag{S7.34}$$

which will be the optimal plan using the version of Arrow's sufficiency theorem (analogue of Theorem 7.14) for constrained problems.

For $K(0) < K^*$ where K^* is the steady state capital level, the unconstrained problem has $I(t)$ decreasing towards $I^* = \delta K^*$. Hence, the constraint $I(t) \geq 0$ never binds along the unconstrained optimum. Then the plan $[K(t), I(t)]_t$ that solves the unconstrained problem satisfies the above conditions and is also the solution for the constrained problem.

For $K(0) > K^*$, consider the saddle path for the unconstrained problem and let $\hat{K} > K^*$ be the capital level at which this saddle path intersects the $I = 0$ axis. Recall that the unconstrained optimum is such that $[K(t), I(t)]_t$ starts at the saddle path and converges to (K^*, I^*), that is, $I(t)$ increases towards $I^* = \delta K^*$. Hence for $K(0) \leq \hat{K}$, the same reasoning above implies that the constraint $I(t) \geq 0$ does not bind and the solution to the unconstrained problem is therefore also the solution to the constrained problem.

When $K(0) > \hat{K}$, the unconstrained optimum features $I(0) < 0$ and violates the irreversibility constraint. In this case, we construct a plan $\left[\tilde{K}(t), \tilde{I}(t)\right]_t$ as follows. Let $\tilde{I}(t) = 0$ for all $t \in [0, \tilde{t}]$ where $\tilde{t}$ is the unique positive value that satisfies $\tilde{K}(\tilde{t}) = K(0) \exp(-\tilde{t}\delta) = \hat{K}$. For all $t > \tilde{t}$, let $\left(\tilde{K}(t), \tilde{I}(t)\right) = \left(\underline{K}(t - \tilde{t}), \underline{I}(t - \tilde{t})\right)$ where $[\underline{K}(t), \underline{I}(t)]_t$ is the solution to the unconstrained problem starting at $K(0) = \hat{K}$. We claim that the plan $\left[\tilde{K}(t), \tilde{I}(t)\right]_t$ is optimal. First note that this plan satisfies all the feasibility constraints in (S7.34). Second, note that it also satisfies all of the optimality conditions in (S7.33) for $t \geq \tilde{t}$, since in this region, the plan is the solution to the unconstrained problem. Moreover, note also that the complementary slackness condition in (S7.33) is satisfied with equality in this region, hence $q(\tilde{t}) = 1 + \phi'\left(\tilde{I}(\tilde{t})\right) = 1 + \phi'(\underline{I}(0))$. Then, the second equation in (S7.33) and the end-value constraint $q(\tilde{t}) = 1 + \phi'(\underline{I}(0))$ uniquely solves for $q(t)$ in the range $[0, \tilde{t}]$. We only need to show that this solution $(q(t))_{t \in [0, \tilde{t}]}$ satisfies the complementary slackness condition in (S7.33), that is,

$$q(t) \leq 1 + \phi'(\underline{I}(0)) = q(\tilde{t}), \text{ for all } t \in [0, \tilde{t}]. \tag{S7.35}$$

Intuitively, this condition holds since $q(t)$, which measures the marginal value of installed capital, must increase as capital decreases (i.e. as $K(t)$ falls towards $\hat{K}$). To see this formally, first note that in a neighborhood $t \in [\tilde{t}, \tilde{t} + \varepsilon)$, we have $q(t) = 1 + \phi'\left(\underline{I}\left(t - \tilde{t}\right)\right)$ and $\phi'\left(\underline{I}(t)\right)$ is an increasing function of t, which implies $\dot{q}\left(\tilde{t}\right) > 0$. Second, note that

$$\dot{q}(t) = (r + \delta) q(t) - f'(K(t)) \text{ for } t \in \left[0, \tilde{t}\right], \tag{S7.36}$$

which can be integrated backwards and gives

$$q(t) = q\left(\tilde{t}\right) \exp\left(-(\dot{r} + \delta)\left(\tilde{t} - t\right)\right) + \int_t^{\tilde{t}} f'(K(s)) \exp\left(-(r + \delta)(s - t)\right) ds.$$

Third note that $K(s) > K\left(\tilde{t}\right)$ for all $s \in \left[0, \tilde{t}\right]$, thus $f'(K(s)) < f'\left(K\left(\tilde{t}\right)\right)$, which implies

$$
\begin{aligned}
q(t) &\leq q\left(\tilde{t}\right) \exp\left(-(r + \delta)\left(\tilde{t} - t\right)\right) + f'\left(K\left(\tilde{t}\right)\right) \int_t^{\tilde{t}} \exp\left(-(r + \delta)(s - t)\right) ds \\
&= q\left(\tilde{t}\right) \exp\left(-(r + \delta)\left(\tilde{t} - t\right)\right) + \frac{f'\left(K\left(\tilde{t}\right)\right)}{r + \delta} \left(1 - \exp\left(-(r + \delta)\left(\tilde{t} - t\right)\right)\right) \\
&= q\left(\tilde{t}\right) - \frac{\dot{q}\left(\tilde{t}\right)}{r + \delta} \left(1 - \exp\left(-(r + \delta)\left(\tilde{t} - t\right)\right)\right) \\
&< q\left(\tilde{t}\right),
\end{aligned}
$$

where the third line substitutes for $f'\left(K\left(\tilde{t}\right)\right)$ from Eq. (S7.36) and the last line uses the fact that $\dot{q}\left(\tilde{t}\right) > 0$. It follows that the complementary slackness condition in Eq. (S7.35) holds. This in turn proves that the plan $\left[\tilde{K}(t), \tilde{I}(t)\right]_t$ which we have constructed satisfies the optimality and the feasibility conditions and hence is the optimal investment plan.

Chapter 8: The Neoclassical Growth Model

Exercise 8.2

Exercise 8.2, Part (a). The maximization problem the representative household solves is given by

$$\max_{[c(t)]_{t=0}^{\infty}} \int_0^{\infty} \exp(-(\rho - n)t)u(c(t))dt$$

$$\text{s.t.} \quad \dot{a}(t) = (r(t) - n)a(t) + w(t) - c(t). \tag{S8.1}$$

The household takes the sequence of wages $[w(t)]_{t=0}^{\infty}$ and asset returns $[r(t)]_{t=0}^{\infty}$ as given. Let $a(0)$ be given and consider the consumption plan $[c(t)]_{t=0}^{\infty}$. Together with (S8.1), this consumption plan induces a sequence of asset holdings $[a(t)]_{t=0}^{\infty}$. Now consider the consumption plan $[c'(t)]_{t=0}^{\infty}$ where $c'(t) = c(t) + \Delta$. Again use (S8.1) to *define* the sequence of asset holding $[a'(t)]_{t=0}^{\infty}$ which correspond to $[c'(t)]_{t=0}^{\infty}$, define $[a'(t)]_{t=0}^{\infty}$ by $a'(0) = a_0$ and

$$\dot{a}'(t) = (r(t) - n)a'(t) + w(t) - c'(t).$$

As $c'(t) > c(t)$ for all t, it is clear that $[c'(t)]_{t=0}^{\infty}$ yields a higher level of utility than $[c(t)]_{t=0}^{\infty}$. Furthermore, the resource flow constraint (S8.1) is satisfied by construction. Hence, $[c(t)]_{t=0}^{\infty}$ could not have been optimal. As $[c(t)]_{t=0}^{\infty}$ was arbitrary, it follows that for any candidate consumption sequence $[c(t)]_{t=0}^{\infty}$ we can find $[c'(t)]_{t=0}^{\infty}$ which yields higher utility, satisfies the resource constraint and involves $c'(t) > c(t)$ for all t.

Exercise 8.2, Part (b). We prove this result by contradiction. Let $[c(t)]_{t=0}^{\infty}$ and the corresponding asset sequence $[a(t)]_{t=0}^{\infty}$ satisfying (S8.1) be given and suppose that there exists some $\bar{t}$ for which per capita assets are finite, i.e. $a(\bar{t}) > -\infty$. Integrating (S8.1) and using the initial condition $a(0)$, yields

$$a(\bar{t}) = \int_0^{\bar{t}} w(t) \exp\left(\int_t^{\bar{t}} (r(s) - n)ds\right) dt + a(0) \exp\left(\int_0^{\bar{t}} (r(s) - n)ds\right) \tag{S8.2}$$

$$- \int_0^{\bar{t}} c(t) \exp\left(\int_t^{\bar{t}} (r(s) - n)ds\right) dt.$$

Now consider again the consumption and induced asset sequence $[c'(t)]_{t=0}^{\infty}$ and $[a'(t)]_{t=0}^{\infty}$ characterized in Part (a). Substituting into (S8.2) yields

$$a'(\bar{t}) = a(\bar{t}) - \Delta \int_0^{\bar{t}} \exp\left(\int_t^{\bar{t}} (r(s) - n)ds\right) dt.$$

By construction this plan satisfies (S8.1) for all Δ. As $u(c)$ is assumed to be strictly increasing, lifetime utility is strictly increasing in Δ. Hence, for any $a(\bar{t}) > -\infty$ there is a $\Delta > 0$ such that lifetime utility will be higher and $a'(\bar{t}) < a(\bar{t})$. This shows that the household will choose a consumption plan where the corresponding asset holdings are arbitrarily negative for all t.

Exercise 8.2, Part (c). In order to show that such an allocation will violate feasibility, we have to analyze what effects such a behavior would have in equilibrium (recall that the analysis above was entirely from the household's point of view taking wages and interest rates as given and acting as if assets were in infinite supply). In equilibrium, per capita assets have to be equal to the economy's per capita capital stock, i.e. $a(t) = k(t)$ for all t (see (8.9)). Hence, an allocation as in Part (b) would require that the economy's capital stock will be arbitrarily negative. Feasibility however requires that $k(t) \geq 0$.

Exercise 8.11

Recall that the household's problem in the neoclassical growth model is

$$\max_{[c(t),a(t)]_t} W\left([a(t),c(t)]_t\right) \equiv \int_0^\infty \exp(-\rho t)\, u(c(t))\, dt \tag{S8.3}$$

$$\text{s.t.} \quad \dot{a}(t) = r(t)\, a(t) + w(t) - c(t) \quad \text{and} \quad \lim_{t\to\infty} a(t) \exp\left(-\int_0^t r(s)\, ds\right) \geq 0. \tag{S8.4}$$

Denote the Hamiltonian with $H(t,c,a,\lambda)$ and note that the maximized Hamiltonian is given by

$$
\begin{aligned}
M(t,a,\lambda) &= \max_c \exp(-\rho t)\, u(c) + \lambda\left(r(t)\, a(t) + w(t) - c(t)\right) \\
&= \exp(-\rho t)\, u\left(c^*(t,\lambda,r(t))\right) + \lambda\left[r(t)\, a + w(t) - c^*(t,\lambda,r(t))\right],
\end{aligned} \tag{S8.5}
$$

where

$$c^*(t,\lambda,r) \in \arg\max_{c\geq 0} \exp(-\rho t)\, u(c) - \lambda c. \tag{S8.6}$$

Note that $M(t,a,\lambda)$ is linear in a and hence is weakly but not strictly concave in a. Therefore, even though Theorem 7.14 can be used to show that a path $[a(t),c(t)]_t$ that satisfies the first-order conditions and the transversality condition is an optimum of the household problem, it cannot be used to show that this path is the unique optimum. We claim however that a slight modification of Arrow's theorem can be used to establish uniqueness for the household problem (S8.3).

To prove the claim, consider a path $[\hat{a}(t), \hat{c}(t), \lambda(t)]_{t=0}^\infty$ that satisfies the first-order conditions and the transversality condition, and hence is optimal from Theorem 7.14. Consider any admissible path $[a(t),c(t)]_t$ that attains the optimal value for the representative household. We will show that this path must be the same as $[\hat{a}(t), \hat{c}(t)]_t$, proving uniqueness. To see this, note that since $M(t,a,\lambda)$ is linear in a, we have

$$
\begin{aligned}
M(t,a(t),\lambda(t)) &= M(t,\hat{a}(t),\lambda(t)) + M_a(t,\hat{a}(t),\lambda(t))\left(a(t) - \hat{a}(t)\right) \\
&= M(t,\hat{a}(t),\lambda(t)) + \lambda(t)\, r(t)\left(a(t) - \hat{a}(t)\right).
\end{aligned}
$$

Integrating this expression, we have

$$\int_0^\infty M(t,a(t),\lambda(t))\, dt = \int_0^\infty M(t,\hat{a}(t),\lambda(t)) + \int_0^\infty \lambda(t)\, r(t)\left(a(t) - \hat{a}(t)\right) dt. \tag{S8.7}$$

Recall that $[\hat{a}(t), \hat{c}(t), \lambda(t)]_t$ satisfies the first-order conditions, and in particular, we have

$$H_a = -\dot{\lambda}(t) \implies r(t)\,\lambda(t) = -\dot{\lambda}(t),$$

which, after plugging in Eq. (S8.7) implies

$$\int_0^\infty M(t,a(t),\lambda(t))\, dt = \int_0^\infty M(t,\hat{a}(t),\lambda(t)) - \int_0^\infty \dot{\lambda}(t)\left(a(t) - \hat{a}(t)\right) dt. \tag{S8.8}$$

Next using the definition of the maximized Hamiltonian in Eq. (S8.5), we have

$$\int_0^\infty M\left(t, a\left(t\right), \lambda\left(t\right)\right) dt \;\geq\; \int_0^\infty \exp\left(-\rho t\right) u\left(c\left(t\right)\right) + \lambda\left(t\right) \dot{a}\left(t\right) dt \qquad \text{(S8.9)}$$

$$\int_0^\infty M\left(t, \hat{a}\left(t\right), \lambda\left(t\right)\right) dt \;=\; \int_0^\infty \exp\left(-\rho t\right) u\left(\hat{c}\left(t\right)\right) + \lambda\left(t\right) d\hat{a}/dt$$

Here, the inequality in the first line follows since M takes its maximum value for $c^*\left(t, \lambda\left(t\right), r\left(t\right)\right)$ defined in Eq. (S8.6) and $c\left(t\right)$ is not necessarily equal to $c^*\left(t, \lambda\left(t\right), r\left(t\right)\right)$. The corresponding inequality for $M\left(t, \hat{a}\left(t\right), \lambda\left(t\right)\right)$ (the second line) is satisfied with equality since $\left(\hat{c}\left(t\right), \hat{a}\left(t\right), \lambda\left(t\right)\right)$ satisfies the first-order condition $\hat{H}_c = 0$ so we have $\hat{c}\left(t\right) = c^*\left(t, \lambda\left(t\right), r\left(t\right)\right)$. Moreover, since the Hamiltonian is strictly concave in c, the first line is satisfied with equality if and only if $c\left(t\right) = c^*\left(t, \lambda\left(t\right), r\left(t\right)\right) = \hat{c}\left(t\right)$ for all t. Then, using Eqs. (S8.8) and (S8.9), we have

$$\int_0^\infty \exp\left(-\rho t\right) u\left(c\left(t\right)\right) dt \;\leq\; \int_0^\infty \exp\left(-\rho t\right) u\left(\hat{c}\left(t\right)\right) dt +$$
$$\int_0^\infty \lambda\left(t\right)\left(d\hat{a}/dt - \dot{a}\left(t\right)\right) dt - \int_0^\infty \dot{\lambda}\left(t\right)\left(a\left(t\right) - \hat{a}\left(t\right)\right) dt,$$

with equality if and only if $c\left(t\right) = \hat{c}\left(t\right)$ for all t. Using integration by parts and the fact that $a\left(0\right) = \hat{a}\left(0\right) = a_0$ (initial asset level is given), this equality can be rewritten as

$$\int_0^\infty \exp\left(-\rho t\right) u\left(c\left(t\right)\right) dt \;\leq\; \int_0^\infty \exp\left(-\rho t\right) u\left(\hat{c}\left(t\right)\right) dt + \lim_{t\to\infty} \lambda\left(t\right)\left(\hat{a}\left(t\right) - a\left(t\right)\right)$$
$$- \int_0^\infty \dot{\lambda}\left(t\right)\left(\hat{a}\left(t\right) - a\left(t\right)\right) dt - \int_0^\infty \dot{\lambda}\left(t\right)\left(a\left(t\right) - \hat{a}\left(t\right)\right) dt$$
$$= \int_0^\infty \exp\left(-\rho t\right) u\left(\hat{c}\left(t\right)\right) dt + \lim_{t\to\infty}\left(\lambda\left(t\right)\hat{a}\left(t\right) - \lambda\left(t\right) a\left(t\right)\right),$$

with equality if and only if $c\left(t\right) = \hat{c}\left(t\right)$. Since $\hat{a}\left(t\right)$ satisfies the strong form of the transversality condition, we have $\lim_{t\to\infty} \int_0^t \lambda\left(t\right)\hat{a}\left(t\right) = 0$. Since $a\left(t\right)$ satisfies the no-Ponzi scheme condition in (S8.4) and since $\lambda\left(t\right) = \lambda\left(0\right)\exp\left(\int_0^t -r\left(s\right) ds\right)$, we have $\lim_{t\to\infty} a\left(t\right)\lambda\left(t\right) \geq 0$. Using these, the previous displayed inequality can be rewritten as

$$\int_0^\infty \exp\left(-\rho t\right) u\left(c\left(t\right)\right) dt \leq \int_0^\infty \exp\left(-\rho t\right) u\left(\hat{c}\left(t\right)\right) dt,$$

with equality if and only if $c\left(t\right) = \hat{c}\left(t\right)$ for all t and $\left[a\left(t\right), c\left(t\right)\right]_t$ satisfies the no-Ponzi scheme condition in Eq. (S8.4) with equality. Since the path $\left[a\left(t\right), c\left(t\right)\right]_t$ attains the same value as $\left[\hat{a}\left(t\right), \hat{c}\left(t\right)\right]_t$, it follows that $c\left(t\right) = \hat{c}\left(t\right)$ for all t. Note that the differential equations for the evolution of a and $\hat{a}$ are identical and are given by

$$da\left(t\right)/dt = r\left(t\right) a\left(t\right) + w\left(t\right) - c\left(t\right) \text{ with initial condition } a\left(0\right) = \hat{a}\left(0\right) = a_0.$$

Then, the fact that $c\left(t\right) = \hat{c}\left(t\right)$ for all t also implies that $a\left(t\right) = \hat{a}\left(t\right)$ for all t, proving uniqueness.

The critical step of the proof is the observation in Eq. (S8.9) that, due to the separability of the Hamiltonian in c and a and due to the concavity of the Hamiltonian in c, the Hamiltonian is maximized at the same c regardless of the asset level, that is, the optimal choice of c only depends on current asset level indirectly through $\lambda\left(t\right)$ but does depend on a once $\lambda\left(t\right)$ is controlled for. This leads to the uniqueness of the optimal path as established above.

Exercise 8.15

Exercise 8.15, Part (a). Recall that the equilibrium path of $[c(t), k(t)]_t$ in the neo-classical model is characterized by the differential equation system

$$\begin{bmatrix} \dot{c} \\ \dot{k} \end{bmatrix} = F(c, k) \equiv \begin{bmatrix} \frac{c(t)}{\epsilon_{u_c}(c)} (f'(k) - \delta - \rho) \\ f(k) - (\delta + n)k - c \end{bmatrix}, \tag{S8.10}$$

where $F(c, k)$ is a vector valued function, and the strong form of the transversality condition $\lim_{t \to \infty} \exp(-\rho t) \mu(t) k(t) = 0$. The steady state (c^*, k^*) is given by

$$\begin{aligned} f'(k^*) &= \delta + \rho \\ c^* &= f(k^*) - (\delta + n)k^*. \end{aligned}$$

In this exercise, we linearize the system in (S8.10) around the steady state (c^*, k^*) and show that locally there is a one-dimensional stable subspace which approximates the saddle path.

A first-order approximation of the system in Eq. (S8.10) around steady state gives

$$\frac{d}{dt}\begin{pmatrix} c - c^* \\ k - k^* \end{pmatrix} \approx \nabla F(c^*, k^*)\begin{pmatrix} c - c^* \\ k - k^* \end{pmatrix} \tag{S8.11}$$

where $\nabla F(c^*, k^*)$ is the derivative of F evaluated at (c^*, k^*). Hence the local behavior of system (S8.10) is characterized by the matrix $\nabla F(c^*, k^*)$. Let ξ_1 and ξ_2 denote the eigenvalues of $\nabla F(c^*, k^*)$ with corresponding eigenvectors $v_1 = (v_{1c}\ v_{1k})$ and $v_2 = (v_{2c}\ v_{2k})$. Then, the solution to the linearized system (S8.11) is given by

$$\begin{bmatrix} c(t) - c^* \\ k(t) - k^* \end{bmatrix} \approx a_1 \exp(\xi_1 t)\begin{bmatrix} v_{1c} \\ v_{1k} \end{bmatrix} + a_2 \exp(\xi_2 t)\begin{bmatrix} v_{2c} \\ v_{2k} \end{bmatrix}, \tag{S8.12}$$

for some constants a_1 and a_2 which are determined by the initial condition $(c(0), k(0))$. Considering the equation for $k(t)$, we have

$$k(t) - k^* \approx a_1 v_{1k} \exp(\xi_1 t) + a_2 v_{2k} \exp(\xi_2 t).$$

Hence, if we define $\eta_1 = a_1 v_{1k}$ and $\eta_2 = a_2 v_{2k}$, the previous displayed equation gives the desired expression

$$k(t) \approx k^* + \eta_1 \exp(\xi_1 t) + \eta_2 \exp(\xi_2 t). \tag{S8.13}$$

Exercise 8.15, Part (b). Note that the derivative of F (the Jacobian) is given by

$$\nabla F(c, k) = \begin{bmatrix} \frac{d\frac{c}{\epsilon_{u_c}(c)}}{dc}(f'(k) - \delta - \rho) & \frac{c}{\epsilon_{u_c}(c)}f''(k) \\ -1 & f'(k) - \delta - n \end{bmatrix}.$$

Evaluated at steady state, this expression reduces to

$$\nabla F(c^*, k^*) = \begin{bmatrix} 0 & \frac{c^*}{\epsilon_{u_c}(c^*)}f''(k^*) \\ -1 & \rho - n \end{bmatrix},$$

The eigenvalues of $\nabla F(c^*, k^*)$ are found as the roots of the polynomial $P(\xi)$ given by

$$\begin{aligned} P(\xi) &= \det\left(\begin{bmatrix} -\xi & \frac{c^*}{\epsilon_{u_c}(c^*)}f''(k^*) \\ -1 & \rho - n - \xi \end{bmatrix}\right) \\ &= (\xi + n - \rho)\xi + \frac{c^*}{\epsilon_{u_c}(c^*)}f''(k^*). \end{aligned}$$

Note that, $P(\xi)$ is a quadratic with positive coefficient on ξ^2 which also satisfies

$$P(0) = \frac{c^*}{\epsilon_{u_c}(c^*)} f''(k^*) < 0,$$

hence $P(\xi)$ has one negative and one positive root. Without loss of generality, we assume $\xi_1 < 0 < \xi_2$ for the eigenvalues. This establishes that one of the eigenvalues, ξ_1 is negative and the other one, ξ_2, is positive.

Exercise 8.15, Part (c). The analysis in Chapter 8 establishes that the equilibrium path $[k(t), c(t)]_t$ in the neoclassical model starts on the saddle path and converges to (k^*, c^*). Hence, had the linear approximation in Eq. (S8.13) been exact, we would have required $\eta_2 = 0$, since otherwise $k(t)$ would diverge away from k^* due to the fact that $\xi^2 > 0$. Hence, the fact that the equilibrium path is stable implies that η_2 corresponding to the equilibrium path must be close to zero, that is $\eta_2 \approx 0$. For this value of η_2, we can verify that the capital stock indeed converges to k^*, that is

$$
\begin{aligned}
\lim_{t \to \infty} k(t) &\approx \lim_{t \to \infty} k^* + \eta_1 \exp(\xi_1 t) + \eta_2 \exp(\xi_2 t) \\
&= \lim_{t \to \infty} k^* + \eta_1 \exp(\xi_1 t) = k^*,
\end{aligned}
$$

where the last equality follows since $\xi_1 < 0$.

Exercise 8.15, Part (d). We now assume that Eq. (S8.13) is exact.[1] Recall that $k(0)$ is given, hence the expression in (S8.13) must satisfy

$$
\begin{aligned}
k(0) &= k^* + \eta_1 \exp(\xi_1 0) + \eta_2 \exp(\xi_2 0) \\
&= k^* + \eta_1
\end{aligned}
$$

where the last line used our observation that $\eta_2 = 0$ for the equilibrium path. Then, the last equation solves η_1 uniquely as

$$\eta_1 = k(0) - k^*.$$

Hence η_1 is uniquely determined from the initial value of capital.

From Parts 3 and 4, we note that the solution is uniquely pinned down from the joint facts that the system is saddle path stable (that is, it converges to some k^*) and that the initial value of capital $k(0)$ is given. Intuitively, given $k(0)$, the household must choose $c(0)$ such that $(k(0), c(0))$ is exactly on the saddle path, which is a one dimensional linear sub-space in this example, and once $(c(t), k(t))$ is on the saddle path, it converges to (c^*, k^*) at the exponential rate ξ_1 as given by Eq. (S8.12).

Exercise 8.15, Part (e). From Parts 3 and 4, we have

$$k(t) \approx k^* + (k(0) - k^*) \exp(\xi_1 t),$$

hence $k(t)$ adjusts to its steady state value k^* at rate ξ_1, where ξ_1 is the negative eigenvalue of $\nabla F(c^*, k^*)$. We next explicitly calculate ξ_1 and see how it responds to the exogenous parameters. Recall that ξ_1 is the negative solution to

$$\xi^2 - (\rho - n)\xi + \frac{c^*}{\epsilon_{u_c}(c^*)} f''(k^*) = 0.$$

---

[1] This would not be the case for realistic production functions but we make the assumption to demonstrate how to solve linear systems with one initial condition and one end value constraint (i.e. the transversality condition). The intuition generalizes to solving non-linear systems with one initial and one end value constraint.

The solutions are given by the quadratic formula

$$\xi_{1,2} = \frac{1}{2}\left(\rho - n \pm \sqrt{(\rho - n)^2 - 4\frac{c^* f''(k^*)}{\epsilon_{u_c}(c^*)}}\right).$$

The smaller (and the negative) real root, ξ_1, is given by

$$\xi_1 = \frac{1}{2}\left(\rho - n - \sqrt{(\rho - n)^2 + 4\frac{c^*|f''(k^*)|}{\epsilon_{u_c}(c^*)}}\right)$$

$$= \frac{1}{2}(\rho - n)\left(1 - \sqrt{1 + 4\frac{c^*|f''(k^*)|}{(\rho - n)\epsilon_{u_c}(c^*)}}\right),$$

This expression establishes a number of comparative statics for the rate of convergence, $|\xi_1| = -\xi_1$. Recall that the higher $|\xi_1|$, the faster the convergence.[2]

(1) The higher $|f''(k^*)|$, the higher the rate of convergence $|\xi_1|$. Intuitively, the more inelastic the substitution between capital and labor, the faster the economy faces diminishing returns and the faster the convergence to steady state (note that this effect is also present in the Solow model).

(2) The higher $\epsilon_{u_c}(c^*)$, the lower the rate of convergence $|\xi_1|$. Recall that, $\epsilon_{u_c}(c^*)$ is elasticity of marginal utility and the inverse elasticity of intertemporal substitution. Hence, the higher $\epsilon_{u_c}(c^*)$, the less elastic intertemporal substitution, the less willing are people to give up consumption now to invest, hence the slower the economy converges to steady state level of k^* (say from some $k(0) < k^*$).

Exercise 8.19

Exercise 8.19, Part (a). The steady state saving rate s^* is given by

$$s^* = \frac{\delta k^*}{f(k^*)}.$$

The steady state capital-labor ratio k^* is of course a function of the underlying parameters (see Proposition 8.3). Hence,

$$\frac{ds^*}{d\rho} = \frac{\partial s^*}{\partial k^*}\frac{dk^*}{d\rho} = \delta\frac{f(k^*) - k^* f'(k^*)}{(f(k^*))^2}\frac{dk^*}{d\rho}.$$

That $\frac{dk^*}{d\rho} < 0$ was shown in Proposition 8.3 and that $f(k^*) - k^* f'(k^*) > 0$ follows from the concavity of f. To see this, note that $f(k^*) - k^* f'(k^*) = k^*\left(\frac{f(k^*)}{k^*} - f'(k^*)\right) > 0$ as the average product is higher than the marginal product or from the fact that we assumed $F(K(t), L(t))$ to have CRS, so that $f(k^*) - k^* f'(k^*)$ is just equal to the marginal product of labor (i.e. the wage rate, see (8.6)) which is positive. Hence

$$\frac{ds^*}{d\rho} = \frac{\partial s^*}{\partial k^*}\frac{dk^*}{d\rho} = \delta\frac{f(k^*) - k^* f'(k^*)}{(f(k^*))^2}\frac{dk^*}{d\rho} < 0,$$

i.e. a lower discount rate will increase the steady state saving rate.

---

[2]Note that, if we were to change the parameters of the model, in general the steady state values (k^*, c^*) would also change. So the comparative statics we note here apply keeping (k^*, c^*) constant, that is they compare two economies with identical (k^*, c^*) that differ in $|f''(k^*)|, \epsilon_{u_c}(c^*)$, or $\rho - n$. But to keep $(k^* c^*)$ constant after changing one of these variables, we typically need to change other things in this economy, so what other things we change might affect convergence to steady state. Therefore we should take these comparative statics as suggestive.

Exercise 8.19, Part (b). The per capita consumption level in the steady state is given by (see (8.37))

$$c^* = f(k^*) - (n + \delta)k^*.$$

Differentiating this with respect to the discount rate ρ yields

$$\frac{dc^*}{d\rho} = (f'(k^*) - (n + \delta))\frac{dk^*}{d\rho}. \tag{S8.14}$$

Again we have $\frac{dk^*}{d\rho} < 0$. In the steady state, the marginal product of capital has to be such that there is no consumption growth (see (8.35)), i.e.

$$f'(k^*) = \rho + \delta$$

Substituting this into (S8.14) yields

$$\frac{dc^*}{d\rho} = (\rho + \delta - (n + \delta))\frac{dk^*}{d\rho} = (\rho - n)\frac{dk^*}{d\rho}.$$

But from Assumption 4' we know that $\rho > n$, so that

$$\frac{dc^*}{d\rho} = (\rho - n)\frac{dk^*}{d\rho} < 0.$$

This shows that the steady state level of consumption will always be decreasing in the discount rate. The reason why there cannot be "oversaving" in the neoclassical growth model (in contrast to the Solow model) is simply that equilibrium has to be consistent with consumer maximization. But any plan which would have had the property that by saving less, consumption could be increased could not have been optimal in the first place as such a plan was clearly available by simply consuming more to begin with.

Exercise 8.23

Exercise 8.23, Part (a). In this exercise we consider a neoclassical economy where technological progress is not Harrod neutral, but capital-augmenting. The production function is given by

$$Y(t) = F(A(t)K(t), L(t)).$$

Besides that, everything is standard, in particular preferences are given by

$$\int_0^\infty \exp(-\rho t)\frac{c(t)^{1-\theta} - 1}{1 - \theta}dt,$$

and the budget constraint is the usual flow constraint

$$\dot{a}(t) = r(t)a(t) + w(t) - c(t), \tag{S8.15}$$

augmented by the no-Ponzi condition

$$\lim_{t \to \infty} a(t)\exp\left(-\int_0^t r(s)ds\right) \geq 0. \tag{S8.16}$$

Note that there is no population growth. Besides the different technology, this is just the standard economy with technological progress described in Chapter 8. Hence the competitive equilibrium is defined as in Definition 8.2, i.e. as paths of per capita consumption, capital-labor ratios, wage rates and rental rates of capital, $[c(t), k(t), w(t), R(t)]_{t=0}^\infty$, such that firms maximize profits, the representative household maximizes utility subject to the budget constraint (S8.15) and the no-Ponzi condition (S8.16) and markets clear.

Exercise 8.23, Part (b). The household maximization problem follows exactly along the same lines as in Chapter 8. In particular, the Euler equation will be given by

$$\frac{\dot{c}(t)}{c(t)} = \frac{1}{\theta}(r(t) - \rho) = \frac{1}{\theta}(A(t)f'(A(t)k(t)) - \delta - \rho), \tag{S8.17}$$

where the second equality uses the equilibrium condition $r(t) = R(t) - \delta = A(t)f'(A(t)k(t)) - \delta$ and the definition of per capita production

$$y(t) = \frac{Y(t)}{L} = \frac{F(A(t)K(t), L)}{L} = F\left(\frac{A(t)K(t)}{L}, 1\right) \equiv f(A(t)k(t)).$$

Note that capital-augmenting technological progress introduces the technology term $A(t)$ in front of $f'(A(t)k(t))$. Hence the competitive equilibrium is characterized by the capital accumulation equation

$$\dot{k}(t) = f(A(t)k(t)) - \delta k(t) - c(t)) \tag{S8.18}$$

the Euler equation (S8.17) and the transversality condition

$$\lim_{t \to \infty}\left[\exp\left(-\int_0^t \rho ds\right)\mu(t)k(t)\right] = 0,$$

where $\mu(t)$ is the costate variable of the consumer's maximization problem.

Let us now look for a steady state equilibrium where $A(t) = A(0)$ for all t, i.e. there is no technological progress. In the steady state, consumption has to be constant, so that from (S8.17) we get that the steady state capital stock k^* is implicitly defined by

$$A(0)f'(A(0)k^*) = \delta + \rho. \tag{S8.19}$$

The steady state level of consumption is given from (S8.18) as

$$c^* = f(A(0)k^*) - \delta k^*.$$

As (S8.19) determines the steady state capital-labor ratio k^* in this economy and does not depend on θ, it is clear that k^* is independent of θ. The reason is the following: θ is the inverse of the intertemporal elasticity of substitution, i.e. it regulates the willingness of individuals to substitute between consumption today and consumption in the future. But this economy does not experience growth in the steady state as the technology is constant. Hence, consumption is constant over time so the consumer's preferences about intertemporal substitution do not matter once the steady state is reached. Note that θ matters of course for the transitional dynamics, in particular for the speed of convergence.

Exercise 8.23, Part (c). Let us now allow for technological progress, i.e. $A(t) = A(0)\exp(gt)$. It is clear that this economy will not have a steady state where consumption and output are constant. Hence we are looking for a balanced growth path (BGP) where both consumption growth and the capital share in national income $k(t)/f(A(t)k(t))$ is constant (i.e. capital and output grow at the same rate). For consumption growth to be constant, (S8.17) implies that $A(t)f'(A(t)k(t))$ has to be constant. Hence, for a BGP to exist we need that

$$A(t)f'(A(t)k(t)) = c_1 \tag{S8.20}$$
$$\frac{k(t)}{f(A(t)k(t))} = c_2,$$

where c_1 and c_2 are constants. Let us define $z(t) \equiv A(t)k(t)$ and combine the two equations above to get

$$\frac{z(t)f'(z(t))}{f(z(t))} = c_1 c_2 \equiv \alpha. \qquad \text{(S8.21)}$$

Note that $z(t)$ has to be increasing along the BGP. This can be seen from (S8.20), which implies

$$z(t) = f'^{-1}\left[\frac{c_1}{A(t)}\right]. \qquad \text{(S8.22)}$$

As f is neoclassical, $f'(z(t))$ is decreasing in $z(t)$. And as $A(t)$ grows at an exponential rate, $z(t)$ also has to increase over time for (S8.22) to be satisfied. As $z(t)$ is not constant, (S8.21) defines a differential equation which we can solve to recover f. Rearranging terms yields the differential equation

$$z(t)f'(z(t)) - \alpha f(z(t)) = 0. \qquad \text{(S8.23)}$$

The solution to (S8.23) is given by

$$f(z(t)) = Cz(t)^\alpha,$$

where C is the constant of integration. Using $z(t) = A(t)k(t)$ we get that

$$Y(t) = L(t)f(A(t)k(t)) = L(t)\left(CA(t)\frac{K(t)}{L(t)}\right)^\alpha = \tilde{C}(A(t)K(t))^\alpha L(t)^{1-\alpha},$$

where $\tilde{C} \equiv C^\alpha$. Hence, this economy does only admit a BGP equilibrium if the production function indeed takes the Cobb-Douglas form.

Exercise 8.23, Part (d). Let us now characterize the BGP if the production function is of the Cobb-Douglas form (and where we normalized $\tilde{C} = 1$), i.e.

$$y(t) = f(A(t)k(t)) = (A(t)k(t))^\alpha.$$

Let us denote the growth rate of variable W by g_W. The growth rate of output per capita is given by

$$g_y = \frac{\dot{y}(t)}{y(t)} = \frac{d\log(f(t))}{dt} = \alpha\left(\frac{\dot{A}(t)}{A(t)} + \frac{\dot{k}(t)}{k(t)}\right) = \alpha(g + g_k).$$

Along the BGP, $k(t)$ grows at the same rate as output, i.e. $g_k = g_y$. Hence,

$$g_y = g_k = \frac{\alpha}{1-\alpha}g. \qquad \text{(S8.24)}$$

To determine the capital-labor ratio along the BGP, we have to go back to the Euler equation. As consumption also grows at g_k[3] we get that

$$g_k = \frac{\dot{c}(t)}{c(t)} = \frac{1}{\theta}(A(t)f'(A(t)k(t)) - \delta - \rho) = \frac{1}{\theta}(\alpha A(t)^\alpha k(t)^{\alpha-1} - \delta - \rho). \qquad \text{(S8.25)}$$

---

[3]This can be easily seen from the resource constraint. The resource constraint is given by

$$\dot{k}(t) = y(t) - c(t) + (1-\delta)k(t).$$

Dividing by $k(t)$ and rearranging terms yields

$$\frac{c(t)}{k(t)} = 1 - \delta + \frac{y(t)}{k(t)} - \frac{\dot{k}(t)}{k(t)} = 1 - \delta - g_k + \frac{y(t)}{k(t)}.$$

As $y(t)$ and $k(t)$ grow at the same rate, $\frac{y(t)}{k(t)}$ is constant. Hence the RHS of the equation above is constant along the BGP so that $\frac{c(t)}{k(t)}$ has to be constant too. This shows that consumption grows at rate g_k along the BGP.

As both the capital-labor ratio $k(t)$ and the technology term $A(t)$ are growing, let us define the normalized capital-labor ratio

$$\chi(t) = \frac{k(t)}{A(t)^{\alpha/(1-\alpha)}},$$

so that (S8.25) reads

$$g_k = \frac{1}{\theta}(\alpha\chi(t)^{\alpha-1} - \delta - \rho). \tag{S8.26}$$

From (S8.26) it is seen that the BGP level of $\chi(t)$ is given by

$$\chi(t) = \chi^* = \left(\frac{\alpha}{\theta g_y + \delta + \rho}\right)^{1/(1-\alpha)}, \tag{S8.27}$$

i.e. the BGP, which refers to the equilibrium path where $k(t), y(t)$ and $c(t)$ grow at the common rate g_k (given in (S8.24)), is a steady state of the transformed variable $\chi(t)$. The capital-labor ratio along the BGP can then be found as

$$k(t) = A(t)^{\alpha/(1-\alpha)}\chi^*.$$

First of all note that indeed

$$\frac{\dot{k}(t)}{k(t)} = \frac{\alpha}{1-\alpha}\frac{d\log(A(t))}{dt} = \frac{\alpha}{1-\alpha}g = g_k$$

as required on the BGP (see (S8.24)). Secondly note that now θ does matter as it determines χ^* (see (S8.27)). The reason is that now there is consumption growth on the BGP so that consumers' preferences about substituting consumption intertemporally do matter. Note however, that θ only matters for levels but not for the growth rate of the economy as $g_k = g_y = g_c = \frac{\alpha}{1-\alpha}g$ is independent of θ. In particular, note that (S8.27) shows that

$$\frac{\partial\chi^*}{\partial\theta} < 0,$$

i.e. the lower the elasticity of substitution (recall that θ is the inverse of the elasticity of substitution), the lower the normalized capital-labor ratio along the BGP. To understand this result, note that per capita consumption grows at rate g_y so that (S8.25) implies that

$$g_y = \frac{\alpha}{1-\alpha}g = \frac{1}{\theta}(r^* - \rho),$$

where r^* denotes the BPG interest rate. The level of θ governs the consumers' willingness to intertemporally substitute consumption. In particular, the lower the elasticity of substitution, the higher the utility cost of having a non-flat consumption profile, so that the BGP interest rates r^* are increasing in θ. Intuitively, if θ is higher, interest rates also have to be higher to convince consumers to have consumption growing at rate g_y. But as interest rates equal the (net of depreciation) marginal product of capital and f has decreasing returns, the normalized level of the capital-labor ratio $\chi(t)$ will have to be lower.

From (S8.27) we can also get some more basic comparative static results. An increase in the discount rate ρ and an increase in the depreciation rate δ will both reduce the economy's (normalized per capita) capital stock. This is also intuitive. If consumers discount the future more, there will be less capital accumulation so that the capital stock will be lower. Similarly, if the depreciation rate is higher, more savings are needed to preserve a given capital stock. This will also reduce capital accumulation.

Exercise 8.27

Exercise 8.27, Part (a). Consider the discrete version of the neoclassical growth model with labor-augmenting technological progress $A(t+1) = (1+g)A(t)$. This means that the production function is given by

$$Y(t) = F(K(t), A(t)L(t)).$$

As there is no population growth, we can normalize the labor force to $L(t) = \bar{L} = 1$. The preferences of the representative consumer are given by

$$U_0 = \sum_{t=0}^{\infty} \beta^t u(c(t)). \tag{S8.28}$$

We need to show that balanced growth requires u in (S8.28) to take the CRRA form. The necessary condition of maximizing (S8.28) subject to the capital accumulation equation

$$K(t+1) = F(K(t), A(t)) - c(t) + (1-\delta)K(t), \tag{S8.29}$$

is the Euler equation

$$u'(c(t)) = u'(c(t+1))\beta(1 + F_K(K(t+1), A(t+1)) - \delta). \tag{S8.30}$$

Along the balanced growth path we require that the capital output ratio $Y(t)/K(t)$ is constant. As the production function is assumed to be neoclassical, it is clear that

$$\frac{Y(t)}{K(t)} = F\left(1, \frac{A(t)}{K(t)}\right),$$

so that $A(t)/K(t)$ has to be constant along the BGP. Hence, the capital stock has to grow at rate g. Using (S8.29) we get that

$$\frac{K(t+1)}{A(t)} = F\left(\frac{K(t)}{A(t)}, 1\right) - \frac{c(t)}{A(t)} + (1-\delta)\frac{K(t)}{A(t)}.$$

Along the BGP we have that $k(t) = \frac{K(t)}{A(t)} = k^*$ is constant, so that

$$k^*(1+g) = F(k^*, 1) - \frac{c(t)}{A(t)} + (1-\delta)k^*.$$

Hence, $\frac{c(t)}{A(t)}$ is constant too, i.e. consumption $c(t)$ also has to grow at rate g. The Euler equation (S8.30) implies that

$$\frac{u'(c(t))}{u'(c(t+1))} = \beta(1 + F_K(K(t+1), A(t+1)) - \delta). \tag{S8.31}$$

As $F_K(K(t), A(t)) = F_K\left(\frac{K(t)}{A(t)}, 1\right)$ (recall that the marginal products are homogenous of degree zero) is constant along the BGP, (S8.31) implies that the ratio of marginal utilities is constant, i.e.

$$\frac{u'(c(t))}{u'(c(t+1))} = \beta(1 + F_K(k^*, 1) - \delta) = \beta R^*, \tag{S8.32}$$

where R^* is constant. As (S8.32) has to hold for all t and consumption grows at rate g, it follows that

$$\frac{u'(c(t))}{u'(c(t+1))} = \frac{u'(c(t))}{u'((1+g)c(t))} = \beta R^*. \tag{S8.33}$$

Additionally, (S8.33) also has to hold for any level of consumption $c(t)$. Differentiating (S8.33) with respect to $c(t)$ yields

$$\frac{u''(c(t))u'((1+g)c(t)) - u'(c(t))u''((1+g)c(t))(1+g)}{(u'((1+g)c(t)))^2} = 0.$$

Rearranging terms and resubstituting $c(t)(1+g) = c(t+1)$ gives

$$\frac{u''(c(t))}{u'(c(t))} = \frac{u''(c(t)(1+g))(1+g)}{u'(c(t)(1+g))} = \frac{u''(c(t+1))(1+g)}{u'(c(t+1))}. \tag{S8.34}$$

Multiplying both sides by $c(t)$ shows that (S8.34) implies that

$$\frac{u''(c(t))c(t)}{u'(c(t))} = \frac{u''(c(t+1))c(t+1)}{u'(c(t+1))},$$

so that the inverse of the intertemporal elasticity of substitution

$$\frac{1}{\varepsilon_u(c(t))} = -\frac{u'(c(t))}{u''(c(t))c(t)} \tag{S8.35}$$

has to be constant, say equal to $\theta = \frac{1}{\varepsilon_u(c(t))}$. As $c(t)$ is growing along the BGP (in particular consumption is growing at rate g), we can rewrite (S8.35) as the differential equation

$$-\theta u'(c(t)) - u''(c(t))c(t) = 0$$

which has the solution $u'(c(t)) = Bc(t)^{-\theta}$, where B is the constant of integration. Integrating again, we recover the required utility function

$$u(c(t)) = \begin{cases} \frac{c(t)^{1-\theta}-1}{1-\theta} & \text{if } \theta \neq 1 \\ \ln(c(t)) & \text{if } \theta = 1 \end{cases} \tag{S8.36}$$

up to the constant of integration. Hence, utility of the CRRA form is the only utility function which is consistent with balanced growth if technological progress is labor-augmenting.

Exercise 8.27, Part (b). Let us now assume that preferences do take the CRRA form given in (S8.36). A competitive equilibrium in this economy consists of allocations of consumption and capital $\{c(t), K(t)\}_{t=0}^{\infty}$ and of sequences of wages and rental rates $\{R(t), w(t)\}_{t=0}^{\infty}$ such that consumers maximize utility, firms maximize profits and markets clear. Profit maximization of firms implies that the rental rate is given by

$$R(t) = 1 + F_K(K(t), A(t)) - \delta = 1 + f'(k(t)) - \delta, \tag{S8.37}$$

where we defined $k(t) = K(t)/A(t)$ as the effective capital-labor ratio and $f(k) = F(k, 1)$. The necessary first-order condition for utility maximization is given by

$$c(t)^{-\theta} = c(t+1)^{-\theta}\beta R(t+1) = c(t+1)^{-\theta}\beta(1 + f'(k(t+1)) - \delta), \tag{S8.38}$$

where the second equality uses (S8.37). That we recover the Euler equation is not surprising - it is just a consequence of the First Welfare Theorem. Additionally we have the resource constraint (S8.29) which is implied by all markets clearing.[4] Normalizing all variables by the

---

[4]To see this, simply note that we always implicitly assumed that the labor market cleared as consumers supply labor inelastically. The consumers' budget constraint is given by

$$c(t) + K(t+1) = w(t) + K(t)R(t), \tag{S8.39}$$

as consumers earn wage income for their one unit of labor and receive the gross interest $R(t)$ for their capital holdings. But as firms are perfectly competitive we get that $w(t) = F_L(K(t), A(t))A(t)$. Using the definition technology level $A(t)$ or $A(t+1)$ respectively, this can be written as

$$k(t+1)(1+g) = f(k(t)) - \frac{c(t)}{A(t)} + (1-\delta)k(t). \qquad \text{(S8.40)}$$

Now consider the BGP equilibrium where the effective capital-labor ratio is constant, say equal to k^*. From (S8.40) it is clear that in such a steady state we need

$$\frac{c(t)}{A(t)} = f(k^*) - (g+\delta)k^*,$$

so that consumption per efficiency unit $c(t)/A(t)$ is constant. Hence, consumption grows at rate g. But then we can use (S8.38) to arrive at

$$\left(\frac{c(t+1)}{c(t)}\right)^\theta = \left(\frac{c(t+1)/A(t+1)}{c(t)/(A(t)(1+g))}\right)^\theta = (1+g)^\theta = \beta(1+f'(k^*)-\delta). \qquad \text{(S8.41)}$$

As (S8.41) defines k^* uniquely as a function of parameters, there is a BGP equilibrium where the effective capital-labor ratio is constant. To ensure that such an equilibrium is well defined, we finally need to make appropriate parametric assumptions to satisfy the transversality condition. As usual the transversality condition is given by

$$\lim_{t\to\infty} \beta^t \lambda(t)K(t+1) = \lim_{t\to\infty} \beta^t c(t)^{-\theta} k(t+1)A(t+1) = 0. \qquad \text{(S8.42)}$$

Along the BGP $k(t)$ is constant and equal to k^* and $\tilde{c}(t) = \frac{c(t)}{A(t)}$ is also constant (and equal to $\tilde{c}^*$) as consumption grows at rate g. Hence the transversality condition in (S8.42) can be written as

$$\lim_{t\to\infty} \beta^t (A(t)\tilde{c}^*)^{-\theta} A(t+1)k^* = k^* (\tilde{c}^*)^{-\theta} A(0)^{1-\theta}(1+g) \lim_{t\to\infty} \beta^t (1+g)^{(1-\theta)t} = 0,$$

so that a steady state equilibrium exists if

$$\beta(1+g)^{(1-\theta)} < 1. \qquad \text{(S8.43)}$$

Whereas the growth rate of the economy g is exogenous.

Exercise 8.27, Part (c). To prove global stability and monotone convergence, we have to show that the sequence of effective capital-labor ratios $\{k(t)\}_{t=0}^\infty$ converges to k^* starting from any $k(0)$ and that $k(t+1) > k(t)$ if and only if $k(0) < k^*$. To prove these properties in this economy we will show that we can transform the problem so that it coincides with the optimal growth problem of the neoclassical growth model without technological progress. First of all note that the First Welfare Theorem applies to the economy of this exercise. Hence, the equilibrium is Pareto efficient and the solution $\{c(t), k(t)\}_{t=0}^\infty$ can be characterized as the

---

of the gross interest rate in (S8.37) it then follows that

$$\begin{aligned} w(t) + K(t)R(t) &= F_L(K(t),A(t))A(t) + (1 + F_K(K(t),A(t)) - \delta)K(t) \\ &= F_L(K(t),A(t))A(t) + F_K(K(t),A(t))K(t) + (1-\delta)K(t) \\ &= F(K(t),A(t)) + (1-\delta)K(t) \end{aligned}$$

where the last equality followed from F being CRS. Substituting this into (S8.39) yields the economy wide resource constraint.

solution to the maximization problem faced by the social planner.

$$\max_{\{c(t),k(t)\}_{t=0}^\infty} \sum_{t=0}^\infty \beta^t \frac{c(t)^{1-\theta}-1}{1-\theta} \tag{S8.44}$$

$$\text{s.t.} \quad k(t)(1+g) = f(k(t)) - \tilde{c}(t) + (1-\delta)k(t) \tag{S8.45}$$

$$\tilde{c}(t) = \frac{c(t)}{A(t)}. \tag{S8.46}$$

where again $k(t)$ denotes capital in efficiency units and $\tilde{c}(t)$ refers to normalized consumption. To make this problem isomorphic to the canonical optimal growth problem without technological progress, note that (S8.44) can be rewritten as

$$\sum_{t=0}^\infty \beta^t \frac{c(t)^{1-\theta}-1}{1-\theta} = \sum_{t=0}^\infty \beta^t \frac{\tilde{c}(t)^{1-\theta}A(t)^{1-\theta}-1}{1-\theta}$$

$$= A(0)^{1-\theta} \sum_{t=0}^\infty [\beta(1+g)^{1-\theta}]^t \frac{\tilde{c}(t)^{1-\theta}}{1-\theta} - \frac{1}{(1-\theta)(1-\beta)},$$

where we used that $A(t) = A(0)(1+g)^t$. As $A(0)^{1-\theta}$ and the last term are just positive transformations which do not affect the maximization, we can drop those terms. Let us also define $\tilde{\beta} = \beta(1+g)^{1-\theta}$ to conclude that if $\{\tilde{c}(t), k(t)\}_{t=0}^\infty$ solves (S8.44) subject to (S8.45) and (S8.46), it also solves

$$\max_{\{\tilde{c}(t),k(t)\}_{t=0}^\infty} \sum_{t=0}^\infty \tilde{\beta}^t \frac{\tilde{c}(t)^{1-\theta}-1}{1-\theta} \tag{S8.47}$$

$$\text{s.t.} \quad k(t)(1+g) = f(k(t)) - \tilde{c}(t) + (1-\delta)k(t).$$

Note that we dropped the second constraint (S8.46) as $c(t)$ does not appear anywhere any longer. But the problem in transformed variables contained in (S8.47) is just the optimal growth problem, where global stability and monotonicity of convergence was shown in Chapter 6 (see especially Proposition 6.3). The only thing we have to ensure is, that the problem is well defined, i.e. that $\tilde{\beta} < 1$. But this is the case as $\tilde{\beta} = \beta(1+g)^{1-\theta} < 1$ by (S8.43) above. This proves global stability and monotone convergence of the economy in normalized variables $k(t)$ and $\tilde{c}(t)$. Having characterized the time path $\{\tilde{c}(t), k(t)\}_{t=0}^\infty$ we can then simply calculate the implied behavior of the capital-labor ratio and per capita consumption from

$$\frac{K(t)}{L(t)} = k(t)A(t) \text{ and } c(t) = \tilde{c}(t)A(t).$$

A steady state in the system of normalized variables refers to a BGP for $c(t)$ and the capital-labor ratio (and both variables grow at the rate of technological progress g) and the transitional dynamics are similar to the canonical neoclassical growth model as both consumption and capital per capita are simple transformations of $k(t)$ and $\tilde{c}(t)$ (in fact they are just "scaled" versions of those variables where the scaling factor $A(t)$ grows at a constant rate).

Exercise 8.31

Exercise 8.31, Part (a). Consider an economy populated by a representative household whose preferences are given by

$$U(0) = \int_0^\infty \exp(-\rho t) \frac{(c(t)-\gamma)^{1-\theta}-1}{1-\theta} dt$$

with $\gamma > 0$. The production function $Y(t) = F(K(t), A(t)L(t))$ is neoclassical, there is no population growth and technology grows exponentially, i.e. $A(t) = \exp(gt)A(0)$. The utility function $u(c) = \frac{(c-\gamma)^{1-\theta}-1}{1-\theta}$ is meant to capture that there is a minimum level of consumption γ the consumer has to consume every period, i.e. γ can be seen as a subsistence level of consumption.

Exercise 8.31, Part (b). Changing the utility function does not change anything in the definition of an equilibrium. Hence, a competitive equilibrium in this economy consists of allocations of consumption and effective capital-labor ratios $[c(t), k(t)]_{t=0}^{\infty}$ and of sequences of wages and interest rates $[r(t), w(t)]_{t=0}^{\infty}$ such that consumers maximize utility taking prices as given, firms maximize profits taking prices as given and markets clear. As this economy features labor-augmenting technological change, we use the effective capital-labor ratio $k(t) = \frac{K(t)}{A(t)L(t)} = \frac{K(t)}{A(t)L}$ instead of the usual capital-labor ratio $\frac{K(t)}{L}$.

Exercise 8.31, Part (c). As shown in the definition above, the central object of the equilibrium are the time paths of consumption and capital-labor ratios $[c(t), k(t)]_{t=0}^{\infty}$. Hence, to characterize the equilibrium in this economy we have to derive the system of differential equations characterizing the entire evolution of these two variables. From the consumer's maximization problem we get the usual Euler equation

$$\frac{\dot{c}(t)}{c(t)} = \frac{1}{\varepsilon_u(c(t))}(r(t) - \rho), \tag{S8.48}$$

where $\varepsilon_u(c(t))$ is the inverse of the intertemporal elasticity of substitution and in our case given by

$$\varepsilon_u(c(t)) = -\frac{u''(c(t))c(t)}{u'(c(t))} = \theta \frac{c(t)}{c(t) - \gamma}. \tag{S8.49}$$

In the case of standard CRRA preferences with $\gamma = 0$, (S8.49) shows that $\varepsilon_u(c(t))$ is just given by the constant θ. In this exercise this term is *not* constant but depends on the level of consumption $c(t)$. Profit maximization by competitive firms implies that the marginal product of capital net of depreciation is equal to the real interest rate, i.e.

$$r(t) = F_K(K(t), A(t)L(t)) - \delta \equiv f'(k(t)) - \delta, \tag{S8.50}$$

where $k(t) = \frac{K(t)}{A(t)L}$ and $f(k) \equiv F(\frac{K}{AL}, 1)$ as the production function is neoclassical. From (S8.48) and (S8.50) we therefore get

$$\frac{\dot{c}(t)}{c(t)} = \frac{1}{\varepsilon_u(c(t))}(f'(k(t)) - \delta - \rho). \tag{S8.51}$$

The economy wide resource constraint

$$\dot{K}(t) = F(K(t), L(t)A(t)) - C(t) - \delta K(t)$$

implies that the effective capital-labor ratio accumulates according to

$$\dot{k}(t) = f(k(t)) - \frac{c(t)}{A(t)} - (\delta + g)k(t). \tag{S8.52}$$

In contrast to the analysis contained in Chapter 8, we cannot exclude the technology term $A(t)$ from the analysis. Even if we would analyze the system using normalized consumption $\tilde{c}(t) = \frac{c(t)}{A(t)}$, (S8.52) would not explicitly depend on $A(t)$ anymore, but this transformation would cause (S8.51) to feature an explicit dependence on $A(t)$. Hence we have to analyze the system in all three variables $k(t), c(t)$ and $A(t)$. As the technology term grows exponentially, its law of motion is simply given by

$$\dot{A}(t) = gA(t). \tag{S8.53}$$

This being said, we have now derived the equations characterizing the evolution of the entire system. The three equations contained in (S8.51), (S8.52) and (S8.53) are three differential equations in the three variables $k(t), c(t)$ and $A(t)$. Additionally we have two initial conditions for $k(t)$ and $A(t)$ as $k(0)$ and $A(0)$ are given. To pin down the exact path for the evolution of per capita consumption $c(t)$, we get a terminal condition from the transversality condition

$$\lim_{t \to \infty} \exp\left(-\rho t\right) \mu\left(t\right) k\left(t\right) = 0, \tag{S8.54}$$

where $\mu(t)$ is the multiplier of the corresponding current value Hamiltonian. Hence we have three differential equations in three variables and three terminal conditions so that the analysis above pins down the entire path $[c(t), k(t), A(t)]_{t=0}^{\infty}$. The implied path for per capita consumption and the effective capital-labor ratio is the desired equilibrium path for these variables. Equilibrium prices can then be recovered as

$$\begin{aligned} r(t) &= f'(k(t)) - \delta \\ w(t) &= f(k(t)) - k(t)f'(k(t)). \end{aligned}$$

This concludes the characterization of the equilibrium.

We will now show that this economy does not admit a BGP equilibrium. To see why, recall that along the BGP the capital-output ratio is constant. But now note that

$$\frac{K(t)}{Y(t)} = \frac{K(t)/(A(t)L(t))}{Y(t)/(A(t)L(t))} = \frac{k(t)}{f(k(t))},$$

so that $\frac{K(t)}{Y(t)}$ can only be constant when $k(t)$ is constant, as f is strictly concave. Hence along the BGP we need $k(t) = k^*$ for some constant k^*. From (S8.52) it then follows that

$$\frac{c(t)}{A(t)} = f(k^*) - (\delta + g)k^*.$$

Hence $\frac{c(t)}{A(t)}$ has to be constant along the BGP, i.e. consumption per capita grows at the constant rate g. Using (S8.51) and (S8.49) we therefore get that along the BGP we need that

$$g = \frac{1}{\theta}\frac{c(t) - \gamma}{c(t)}(f'(k^*) - \delta - \rho).$$

This however is a contradiction as the LHS is constant, whereas the RHS changes over time as $c(t)$ grows at rate g. This proves that this economy does not admit a BGP with a positive growth rate. The reason is that the consumer's intertemporal elasticity of substitution is not constant but decreasing in $c(t)$ as

$$\frac{\partial \varepsilon_u(c(t))}{\partial c(t)} = -\theta\frac{\gamma}{(c(t) - \gamma)^2}.$$

For given interest rates $r > \rho$, consumption growth will therefore be increasing in the level of consumption. Intuitively, the higher the level of consumption, the more willing the consumer to tilt his consumption schedule as the subsistence level γ loses in importance. Along the BGP with a positive growth rate however, interest rates are constant (as $k(t) = k^*$) and per capita consumption is growing. Hence, the growth rate of consumption will be a function of the level of consumption and consumption growth is not constant. This is inconsistent with balanced growth. We will show below however, that this economy will feature balanced growth asymptotically.

Exercise 8.31, Part (d). The transversality condition was given in (S8.54) as

$$\lim_{t \to \infty} \exp(-\rho t)\mu(t)k(t) = 0, \tag{S8.55}$$

where recall $\mu(t)$ is the multiplier in the corresponding current value Hamiltonian. From the necessary condition

$$\mu(t)[f'(k(t)) - \delta - g] = \rho\mu(t) - \dot{\mu}(t)$$

we can solve for $\mu(t)$ as

$$\mu(t) = \mu(0) \exp\left(-\int_0^t (f'(k(s) - \delta - \rho - g)ds\right).$$

Substituting this into (S8.55) yields

$$\lim_{t \to \infty} \mu(0) \exp\left(-\int_0^t (f'(k(s) - \delta - g)ds\right) k(t)L = 0. \tag{S8.56}$$

Although we saw that this economy does not admit a BGP, we will show below that growth will be balanced asymptotically. In particular we show that asymptotically per capita consumption will grow at the constant rate g and that the effective capital-labor ratio will be constant. Using the Euler equation (S8.51) we therefore know that (asymptotically)

$$\lim_{t \to \infty} k(t) = k^* \text{ and } \lim_{t \to \infty} \frac{\dot{c}(t)}{c(t)} = g = \frac{1}{\theta}\left(f'(k^*) - \delta - \rho\right),$$

where we used (and will argue below) that

$$\lim_{t \to \infty} \varepsilon_u(c(t)) = \theta \lim_{t \to \infty} \frac{c(t)}{c(t) - \gamma} = \theta.$$

Substituting this in (S8.56) yields

$$\lim_{t \to \infty} \exp\left(-(\theta g + \rho - g)t\right) = \lim_{t \to \infty} \exp\left((1 - \theta)g - \rho)t\right) = 0.$$

This can only be satisfied if

$$\rho > (1 - \theta)g \tag{S8.57}$$

which is the required parametric condition for the transversality condition to be satisfied.

Exercise 8.31, Part (e). Now let us think about the transitional dynamics of this economy. To do so and to show the relationship between this economy and the canonical neoclassical economy let us consider the transformation

$$x(t) = c(t) - \gamma.$$

From (S8.51) we therefore get that

$$\frac{\dot{x}(t)}{x(t)} = \frac{1}{\theta}(f'(k(t)) - \delta - \rho),$$

and the accumulation equation of the effective capital-labor ratio (S8.52) changes to

$$\dot{k}(t) = f(k(t)) - \frac{x(t)}{A(t)} - (\delta + g)k(t) - A(t)^{-1}\gamma.$$

To stress the similarity between this economy and the baseline model with labor-augmenting technological progress analyzed in Section 8.7, let us consider the normalized variable $\tilde{x}(t) = x(t)/A(t)$. Doing so yields the two differential equations

$$\frac{d\tilde{x}(t)dt}{\tilde{x}(t)} = \frac{1}{\theta}(f'(k(t)) - \delta - \rho - \theta g) \tag{S8.58}$$

$$\dot{k}(t) = f(k(t)) - \tilde{x}(t) - (\delta + g)k(t) - A(t)^{-1}\gamma.$$

Together with the initial conditions $k(0)$ and the terminal condition given by the transversality condition (see (S8.56))

$$\lim_{t\to\infty} \exp\left(-\int_0^t \left(f'\left(k\left(s\right)\right) - \delta - g\right) ds\right) k\left(s\right) = 0,$$

this economy looks exactly the same as the baseline model except for the $A(t)^{-1}\gamma$ term in the capital accumulation equation. So if this term was absent, this economy (in normalized variables $\tilde{x}$ and k) would have a steady state $(\tilde{x}^*, k^*)$ given by

$$f'(k^*) = \delta + \rho + \theta g \text{ and } \tilde{x}^* = f(k^*) - (\delta + g)k(t). \tag{S8.59}$$

Furthermore, the system was saddle path stable such that $x(0)$ would be chosen to ensure that the solution would be on the stable arm of the system and converge to the steady state.

Now consider the original economy where $A(t)^{-1}\gamma$ is not absent. As this term will vanish in the limit as $\lim_{t\to\infty} A(t)^{-1}\gamma = 0$, the steady state of the original economy will also be given by (S8.59). In particular, the economy will also be saddle path stable so that there is one stable arm and the solution will be on this arm and converges to the steady state. In particular (S8.59) shows that $k(t)$ will be constant in the steady state and $x(t)$ will be proportional to $A(t)$ (as $\tilde{x}(t)$ is constant). Hence, $x(t)$ asymptotically grows at rate g so that

$$g = \lim_{t\to\infty} \frac{\dot{x}(t)}{x(t)} = \lim_{t\to\infty} \frac{\dot{c}(t)}{c(t) - \gamma} = \lim_{t\to\infty} \frac{\dot{c}(t)}{c(t)} \frac{c(t)}{c(t) - \gamma} = \lim_{t\to\infty} \frac{\dot{c}(t)}{c(t)}$$

as $\lim_{t\to\infty} \frac{\dot{c}(t)}{c(t)} > 0$. This shows that growth will be balanced asymptotically as claimed in the analysis in Part (d) above.

Although the steady state of the system is the same as in the economy where the $A(t)^{-1}\gamma$ term is absent, the transitional dynamics are different. If we consider the phase diagram in the $(k, \tilde{x})$ space, it is apparent from (S8.58) that the $d\tilde{x}(t)dt = 0$ locus has exactly the same form as in the baseline model. The $\dot{k}(t) = 0$-locus however is different. This locus is given by the equation

$$\tilde{x}(t) = f(k(t)) - (\delta + g)k(t) - A(t)^{-1}\gamma.$$

Hence in the $(k, \tilde{x})$ space, this locus shift up over time (as $A(t)^{-1}\gamma$ decreases over time) and converges to the $\dot{k}(t) = 0$-locus of the baseline model. Hence asymptotically as t tends to infinity, this economy is characterized by exactly the same equations as the baseline model. Therefore it is also intuitive that the required parametric restriction in (S8.57) is the same as in the baseline model (see Assumption 4). Note in particular that the saddle path will also be a function of time. Hence, together with the $\dot{k}(t) = 0$-locus, the saddle path will also shift as time progresses. The system however will still be saddle path stable, i.e. in each period the solution will be on the respective period's saddle path and converge to the unique steady state.

Exercise 8.31, Part (f). With the alternative preferences, the Euler equation is still given by

$$\frac{\dot{c}(t)}{c(t)} = \frac{1}{\varepsilon_u(c(t))}(r(t) - \rho),$$

where now $\varepsilon_u(c(t))$ is given by

$$\varepsilon_u(c(t)) = -\frac{u''(c(t))c(t)}{u'(c(t))} = \theta\frac{c(t)}{c(t) - \gamma(t)}.$$

The rest of the analysis is exactly analogous to the case considered above. In particular there will not exist a BGP as $\varepsilon_u(c(t))$ is not constant. Asymptotically however, we have that

$$\lim_{t\to\infty}\varepsilon_u(c(t)) = \lim_{t\to\infty}\theta\frac{c(t)}{c(t) - \gamma(t)} = \lim_{t\to\infty}\theta\frac{c(t)}{c(t) - \gamma} = \theta,$$

as $\gamma(t)$ converges to a constant and $c(t)$ grows over time. Hence, the economy will again have a BGP asymptotically and this BGP is exactly the same as the one characterized above (and therefore also the same as in the baseline model). Note however that if the dynamics of $\gamma(t)$ are unrestricted, we cannot conclude anything about the behavior of the $k(t) = 0-$locus over time. Although we know that this locus will converge to its counterpart of the baseline model, there is no reason why it should shift up over time as in Part (e) above.

Exercise 8.33

Exercise 8.33, Part (a). A (symmetric) competitive equilibrium (in which all households choose the same per capita variables) is a path of allocations $[c(t), l(t), a(t), k(t)]_t$ and prices $[r(t), w(t)]_t$ such that each household solves

$$\max_{[c(t), l(t)\in[0,1], a(t)]_t} U(0) = \int_0^\infty \exp(-\rho t) u(c(t), 1 - l(t)), \tag{S8.60}$$

$$\text{s.t.} \quad \dot{a}(t) = r(t)a(t) + w(t)l(t) - c(t), \tag{S8.61}$$

$$\text{and} \quad \lim_{t\to\infty} a(t)\exp\left(-\int_0^t r(s)\,ds\right) \geq 0,$$

firms maximize profits which gives

$$r(t) = F_K(k(t), A(t)l(t)) - \delta, \; w(t) = A(t)F_L(k(t), A(t)l(t)), \tag{S8.62}$$

and all markets clear, in particular, $a(t) = k(t)$ for all t.

Exercise 8.33, Part (b). Note that Problem (S8.60) is a problem with one state variable, a, and two control variables, c and l. The current value Hamiltonian is

$$\hat{H}(t, a, c, l, \mu) = u(c, 1 - l) + \mu(r(t)a + w(t)l - c).$$

The first-order conditions are

$$
\begin{aligned}
\hat{H}_c &= 0, \text{ which gives } u_c(c, 1 - l) = \mu \\
\hat{H}_l &= 0, \text{ which gives } u_2(c, 1 - l) = \mu w(t) \\
\hat{H}_a &= \rho\mu - \dot{\mu}, \text{ which gives } \frac{\dot{\mu}}{\mu} = \rho - r(t).
\end{aligned}
$$

(here, $u_2(c, 1-l) = \partial u_l(c, 1-l)/\partial(1-l)$ denotes the partial derivative of u with respect to leisure choice $1-l$) The first-order conditions can be simplified to

$$\epsilon_u(c, 1-l)\frac{\dot{c}}{c} - \frac{u_{c2}(c, 1-l)\dot{l}}{u_c(c, 1-l)} = r(t) - \rho \qquad (S8.63)$$

$$u_2(c, 1-l) = u_c(c, 1-l)w(t), \qquad (S8.64)$$

where

$$\epsilon_u(c, 1-l) = -\frac{u_{cc}(c, 1-l)c}{u_c(c, 1-l)}$$

is the elasticity of the marginal utility u_c with respect to c. Note that the first condition (S8.63) is the intertemporal condition, i.e. the Euler equation, and the second condition (S8.74) is the intratemporal condition, i.e. the labor-leisure trade-off. The strong form of the transversality condition is also necessary in this problem, that is $\lim_{t\to\infty} \exp(-\rho t)\mu(t)a(t) = 0$. As in the baseline case, the transversality condition can be rewritten as

$$\lim_{t\to\infty} a(t)\exp\left(-\int_0^t r(s)\,ds\right) = 0. \qquad (S8.65)$$

Note that the maximized Hamiltonian $M(t, a, \mu) = \max_{c,l} \hat{H}(t, a, c, l, \mu)$ is linear and hence concave in a. Note also that for each feasible $\left[\tilde{a}(t), \tilde{c}(t), \tilde{l}(t)\right]_t$, by the no-Ponzi condition, we have $\lim_{t\to\infty} \exp(-\rho t)\mu(t)\tilde{a}(t) \geq 0$. Then Theorem 7.14 applies and shows that these conditions are sufficient for optimality.

Exercise 8.33, Part (c). The social planner solves

$$\max_{[c(t),l(t)\in[0,1],k(t)]_t} U(0) = \int_0^\infty \exp(-\rho t)u(c(t), 1-l(t)),$$

$$\text{s.t. } \dot{k}(t) = F(k(t), A(t)l(t)) - \delta k(t) - c(t) \text{ and } k(t) \geq 0. \quad (S8.66)$$

Note that this problem is also an optimal control problem with one state variable $k(t)$ and two control variables $\{c(t), l(t)\}$. The current value Hamiltonian is

$$\hat{H}(t, k, c, l, \mu) = u(c, 1-l) + \mu(F(k, A(t)l) - \delta k - c).$$

The first-order conditions are

$$\hat{H}_c = 0, \text{ which gives } u_c(c, 1-l) = \mu$$

$$\hat{H}_l = 0, \text{ which gives } u_2(c, 1-l) = \mu A(t)F_L(k, A(t)l)$$

$$\hat{H}_k = \rho\mu - \dot{\mu}, \text{ which gives } \frac{\dot{\mu}}{\mu} = \rho + \delta - F_K(k, A(t)l).$$

The first-order conditions can once again be simplified to

$$\epsilon_u(c, 1-l)\frac{\dot{c}}{c} - \frac{u_{c2}(c, 1-l)\dot{l}}{u_c(c, 1-l)} = F_K(k, A(t)l) - \delta - \rho \qquad (S8.67)$$

$$u_2(c, 1-l) = u_c(c, 1-l)A(t)F_L(k, A(t)l). \qquad (S8.68)$$

The transversality condition can be written as

$$\lim_{t\to\infty} \exp(-\rho t)k(t)\int_0^t -(F_K(k(s), A(s)l(s)) - \delta)\,ds = 0. \qquad (S8.69)$$

Under the parametric restriction $g(1-\theta) < \rho$, there is a unique path that satisfies all of Eqs. (S8.66) − (S8.69).

Assuming that u is jointly concave in c and l, the current value Hamiltonian $\hat{H}(t, k, c, l, \mu)$ is concave and we have $\lim_{t \to \infty} \exp(-\rho t) \mu(t) \tilde{k}(t) \geq 0$ for all feasible paths since $\tilde{k}(t) \geq 0$. Then Theorem 7.14 applies and shows that these conditions are sufficient for optimality, that is, the path described above is the unique solution to the social planner's problem.

Exercise 8.33, Part (d). Note that, after substituting the competitive market prices for $r(t)$ and $w(t)$ from Eq. (S8.62), the household resource constraints (S8.61), first-order conditions (S8.63) $-$ (S8.64), and the transversality condition (S8.65) become equivalent to respectively to their counterparts in the social planner's problem, Eqs. (S8.66),(S8.67) $-$ (S8.68) and (S8.69).

It follows that given any equilibrium allocation $[a(t) \equiv k(t), k(t), c(t), r(t), w(t)]_t$, the allocation $[c(t), k(t)]_t$ solves the social planner's problem. Conversely, consider a solution $[c(t), k(t)]_t$ to the social planner's problem and define the competitive prices $r(t)$ and $w(t)$ as in Eq. (S8.62). From the correspondence that we have noted above, the allocation

$$a^h(t) = k(t), \ c^h(t) = c(t), \ l^h(t) = l(t)$$

solves the household's problem given the path of prices $[r(t), w(t)]_t$ (where we use the superscript h to distinguish between the household's and the social planner's allocations). It follows that the allocation $[a(t) \equiv k(t), k(t), c(t), r(t), w(t)]_t$ is a competitive equilibrium, proving that the two problems are equivalent when the prices are given by Eq. (S8.62).

Exercise 8.33, Part (e). Suppose that the equilibrium we have described in Part (d) has constant and equal rates of consumption and output growth, and a constant level of labor supply $l^* \in [0, 1]$. From the resource constraints, we have

$$\dot{k}(t) = F(k(t), A(t) l^*) - \delta k(t) - c(t).$$

This equation implies that, $k(t)$ grows at the same constant rate as output and consumption, and that this constant rate must be equal to g, the growth rate of $A(t)$, since F is constant returns to scale. Moreover, in any such BGP, the interest rate is constant since

$$\begin{aligned} r(t) &= F_K(k(t), A(t) l^*) - \delta \\ &= F_K\left(\frac{k(t)}{A(t)}, l^*\right) - \delta = r^*, \end{aligned}$$

where the second line uses the fact that F_K is homogenous of degree 0 and the equality follows from the fact that $k(t)$ and $A(t)$ grow at the same rate g on a BGP. Further, the wages grow at the constant rate g since

$$\begin{aligned} w(t) &= A(t) F_L(k(t), A(t) l^*) & \text{(S8.70)} \\ &= A(t) F_L(k(t)/A(t), l^*) = A(t) w^*, \end{aligned}$$

where the second line uses linear homogeneity and the last line uses the fact that $k(t)/A(t)$ is constant.

Next, note that substituting $l(t) = l^*$, the $\dot{l}$ term in Eq. (S8.63) drops out and the Euler equation can be rewritten as

$$\epsilon_u(c(t), 1 - l^*) \frac{\dot{c}(t)}{c(t)} = r^* - \rho$$

Since $\dot{c}(t)/c(t)$ is constant on the BGP, it follows that $\epsilon_u(c(t), 1 - l^*)$ should be independent of $c(t)$. Since we assume (in the exercise statement) that the function $\epsilon_u(c, 1 - l)$ does not depend on l, it follows that it should be a constant function, that is

$$\epsilon_u(c, 1 - l) = -\frac{u_{cc}(c, 1 - l) c}{u_c(c, 1 - l)} = \theta \tag{S8.71}$$

for all $c \geq c(0)$ and l, where $\theta \in \mathbb{R}_+$ is some constant. Rewriting Eq. (S8.71) as

$$\frac{\partial \log[u_c(c, 1 - l)]}{\partial \log(c)} = -\theta$$

and partially integrating this expression with respect to c, we get

$$\log[u_c(c, 1 - l)] = -\theta \log(c) + X(1 - l),$$

where $X(1 - l)$ is a constant of (partial) integration that could depend on l but not c. Rewriting the previous expression, we have

$$u_c(c, 1 - l) = X(1 - l) c^{-\theta}. \tag{S8.72}$$

Let us now distinguish between two cases.

Case 1, $\theta \neq 1$. Integrating Eq. (S8.72) with respect to c once more, we have

$$u(c, 1 - l) = X(1 - l)\frac{c^{1-\theta}}{1 - \theta} + Y(1 - l), \tag{S8.73}$$

where $Y(1 - l)$ is a constant of partial integration that could depend on l. Note that the intratemporal first-order condition in Eq. (S8.64) must also hold on a BGP, which, after substituting $w(t) = w^* A(t)$ from Eq. (S8.70), implies

$$u_2(c(t), 1 - l^*) = A(t) w^* u_c(c(t), 1 - l^*). \tag{S8.74}$$

Plugging in the functional form in Eq. (S8.73), the previous equation can be rewritten as

$$X'(1 - l^*)\frac{c(t)^{1-\theta}}{1 - \theta} + Y'(1 - l^*) = X(1 - l^*) A(t) w^* c(t)^{-\theta}.$$

Recall that $c(t)$ and $A(t)$ grow at the same constant rate g. Then, the left hand side and the right hand side grow at the same constant rate only if

$$Y'(1 - l^*) = 0. \tag{S8.75}$$

In particular, we have

$$Y(1 - l) = Y$$

for some constant Y.[5] We define $h(1 - l) = X(1 - l)$ and take $Y = 0$ (which is without loss of generality since it only normalizes the utility function) and conclude that, when $\theta \neq 1$, the only functional form for $u(c, 1 - l)$ that is consistent with a BGP is

$$u(c(t), 1 - l(t)) = h(1 - l(t))\frac{c(t)^{1-\theta}}{1 - \theta}. \tag{S8.76}$$

Note also that we should have $h(.) > 0$ since otherwise the marginal utility, u_c, would be negative.[6]

---

[5]This assumes that the restriction in Eq. (S8.75) holds not just for l^* but for any l. This is not entirely correct. Actually, the only restriction we will get will be Eq. (S8.75), since, given l is constant at l^*, we do not really have any information on functional forms away from the BGP value $l = l^*$.

[6]It turns out that the condition $h'(.) > 0$ is not necessary in this case. Note that we have

$$u_2(c(t), 1 - l(t)) = h'(1 - l(t))\frac{c(t)^{1-\theta}}{1 - \theta}.$$

Hence, to ensure that $u_2 > 0$ so that the individual enjoys leisure, we need $h'(.) > 0$ when $\theta < 0$ and $h'(.) < 0$ when $\theta > 1$.

Case 2, $\theta = 1$. In this case, integrating Eq. (S8.72) gives

$$u\left(c, 1 - l\right) = X\left(1 - l\right)\log\left(c\right) + Y\left(1 - l\right).$$

Substituting this in the intratemporal condition, we have

$$X'\left(1 - l^*\right)\log\left(c\left(t\right)\right) + Y'\left(1 - l^*\right) = X\left(1 - l^*\right)\frac{A\left(t\right)}{c\left(t\right)}w^*.$$

This time, since $A\left(t\right)/c\left(t\right)$ is constant on a BGP, this can be satisfied only if

$$X'\left(1 - l^*\right) = 0, \text{ and } Y'\left(1 - l^*\right)/X\left(1 - l^*\right) > 0. \tag{S8.77}$$

In particular, we have[7]

$$X\left(1 - l\right) = X$$

for some X. This time we define $h\left(1 - l\right) = Y\left(1 - l\right)$, normalize $X = 1$, and conclude that the only functional form for $u\left(c, 1 - l\right)$ that is consistent with a BGP is

$$u\left(c\left(t\right), 1 - l\left(t\right)\right) = \log c\left(t\right) + h\left(1 - l\left(t\right)\right), \tag{S8.78}$$

where $h\left(.\right)$ is some function with $h'\left(.\right) > 0$ as desired.

Intuitively, the interest rate is constant only if the intertemporal elasticity of substitution remains constant as c grows, which explains why the utility function must be CES when viewed as a function of c. For the intratemporal trade-off, there are three economic forces. First, income and hence consumption is growing at rate g hence the marginal utility of consumption is shrinking at rate $-\theta g$, which creates a force towards more leisure (the income effect). Second, wages are growing at rate g hence the marginal return to labor is growing at rate g, which creates a force towards more labor (the substitution effect). Third, marginal benefit to leisure might also be changing as consumption grows, depending on whether consumption or leisure are complements or substitutes. To have a constant labor choice l^* on a BGP, we must have the functional form such that the third force exactly balances the first two forces. In particular, when $\theta > 1$, we need the leisure and consumption to be substitutes with the functional form in (S8.76) so that with more consumption marginal value for leisure decreases just enough that the individual keeps leisure choice constant. When $\theta < 1$, we need the leisure and consumption to be complements with exactly the functional form in (S8.76) so that with more consumption marginal value for leisure increases just enough that the individual keeps leisure choice constant. With $\theta = 1$, the first two effects (income and substitution) cancel so we want consumption and labor to be separable (neither substitutes nor complements) as in Eq. (S8.78).

---

[7]The same caveat above applies here as well. The only restriction we get is Eq. (S8.77). Given that l is constant at l^* on a BGP, we do not have any information on the shape of the function away from the BGP level $l = l^*$.

Chapter 9: Growth with Overlapping Generations

Exercise 9.1

Exercise 9.1, Part (a). We claim that an allocation $\left(c_i^i, c_i^{i+1}, p_i\right)$ is an equilibrium if and only $c_i^i = 1, c_i^{i+1} = 0$ for all i and the price sequence $(p_i)_{i=0}^{\infty}$ is weakly increasing in i and satisfies $p_i > 0$ for all i. We first show that the consumption allocations are uniquely characterized. Note that household i solves

$$P(i) \quad : \quad \max_{\{c_i^i, c_i^{i+1}\}} \quad c_i^i + c_i^{i+1}$$

$$\text{s.t.} \quad c_i^i p_i + c_i^{i+1} p_{i+1} \leq p_i.$$

Hence we have $p_i > 0$ for all i, otherwise household i would demand infinite amount of good i, violating market clearing. Next note that household 0 is the only household that can consume period 0 goods. So the market clearing in period 0 goods along with the fact that $p_0 > 0$ implies that $c_0^0 = 1$, which also implies $c_0^1 = 0$ from her budget constraint. Hence household 0 consumes her own endowment in any equilibrium. Since $c_0^1 = 0$, we have that household 1 is the only household that can consume period 1 goods. The same reasoning shows that household 1 consumes her own endowment, that is $c_1^1 = 1$. By induction, we have that $c_i^i = 1$ for all i. Hence, the consumption of households are uniquely characterized with $c_i^i = 1, c_i^{i+1} = 0$ for all i.

We next characterize the price sequences $(p_i)_{i=0}^{\infty}$ that support this consumption allocation as an equilibrium. Note that when $p_i \leq p_{i+1}$, $c_i^i = 1$ solves problem $P(i)$ for each i. Hence any weakly increasing price sequence $(p_i)_{i=0}^{\infty}$ along with the allocation $(c_i^i = 1)_{i=0}^{\infty}$ is an equilibrium. Conversely, consider a price sequence $(p_i)_{i=0}^{\infty}$ that is not weakly increasing. Let $i \geq 0$ be the smallest index such that $p_i > p_{i+1}$. Then, $c_i^i = 1$ does not solve problem $P(i)$ since household i would rather choose $\tilde{c}_i^{i+1} = p_i/p_{i+1} > 1$ and $\tilde{c}_i^i = 0$. This proves that $(p_i)_{i=0}^{\infty}$ that is not weakly increasing cannot be part of an equilibrium and completes the characterization of the equilibria.

Exercise 9.1, Part (b). Let $\delta = 1/(i_2 + 1 - i_1)$. Consider the allocation $\tilde{\mathbf{x}}_{i_1, i_2}$ defined as follows:

$$\begin{aligned}
c_i^i &= 1, \ c_i^{i+1} = 0 \text{ for all } i < i_1, \\
c_i^i &= 1 - \delta(i - i_1), \ c_i^{i+1} = \delta(i - i_1 + 1) \ \text{ for all } i \in [i_1, i_2] \\
c_i^i &= 0, \ c_i^{i+1} = 1 \text{ for all } i > i_2.
\end{aligned}$$

That is, each old household $i \in [i_1, i_2]$ receives δ more than the amount she gives when she is young. This allocation satisfies the resource constraints since

$$c_i^i + c_{i-1}^i = \begin{cases} 1 + 0 = 1 \text{ if } i \leq i_1, \\ 1 - \delta(i - i_1) + \delta(i - 1 - i_1 + 1) = 1 \text{ if } i \in (i_1, i_2], \\ 0 + \delta(i_2 + 1 - i_1) = 1 \text{ if } i = i_2 + 1, \\ 0 + 1 = 1 \text{ if } i > i_2 + 1, \end{cases}$$

where the third line follows since δ is chosen to be $1/(i_2 + 1 - i_1)$. Moreover, each household $i \in [i_1, i_2]$ is strictly better off since she receives a utility $1 + \delta$ which is greater than 1. Finally, all other households receive utility 1 and are as well off as in equilibrium. This proves that, in the simple overlapping generations economy introduced by Shell (1971), a reallocation of resources can make an arbitrary number of generations better off while making no other generation worse off.

Exercise 9.6

Rearranging Eq. (9.17), we have

$$g(k(t+1)) \equiv \left(\frac{1+n}{1-\alpha} \left[k(t+1) + \beta^{-1/\theta} \alpha^{-(1-\theta)/\theta} k(t+1)^{(1-\alpha)/\theta+\alpha} \right] \right)^{1/\alpha} = k(t). \qquad (S9.1)$$

Note that the function $g(.)$ is increasing in $k(t+1)$ and hence has an inverse $g^{-1}(.)$. Moreover $g(0) = 0$ and $\lim_{k \to \infty} g(k) = \infty$, hence for a given level of $k(t)$, the next period capital-labor ratio is uniquely defined by $k(t+1) = g^{-1}(k(t))$.

We first claim that the system characterized by (S9.1) has a unique steady state with positive capital-labor ratio, k^*. Plugging $k(t) = k(t+1) = k^*$ in Eq. (S9.1), using $k^* > 0$ and rewriting the equation in terms of the rental rate of capital $R^* = \alpha(k^*)^{\alpha-1}$, we obtain Eq. (9.16), which can be rearranged as

$$h(R^*) \equiv 1 + \beta^{-1/\theta} (R^*)^{(\theta-1)/\theta} - \frac{1-\alpha}{(1+n)\alpha} R^* = 0.$$

Note that $\lim_{R^* \to 0} h(R^*) > 0$ and $\lim_{R^* \to \infty} h(R^*) < 0$ (since R^* grows faster than $R^{*1-1/\theta}$ for any $\theta > 0$), hence the previous equation always has a solution. Note also that the derivative of $h(R^*)$ is given by

$$h'(R^*) = \beta^{-1/\theta} \frac{\theta-1}{\theta} (R^*)^{-1/\theta} - \frac{1-\alpha}{(1+n)\alpha}. \qquad (S9.2)$$

For $\theta \leq 1$, $h'(R^*) < 0$ and $h(R^*)$ is everywhere decreasing which in turn shows $h(R^*) = 0$ has a unique solution. For $\theta > 0$, $h(R^*)$ is increasing for sufficiently small R^*, however this does not overturn the uniqueness result. In particular, when $\theta > 1$, we claim that h is decreasing at all crossing points, that is, $h'(R^*) < 0$ for all R^* such that $h(R^*) = 0$, which in turn shows that there exists exactly one crossing point. To see this, note that $h(R^*) = 0$ implies $\beta^{-1/\theta} (R^*)^{-1/\theta} = \frac{1-\alpha}{(1+n)\alpha} - \frac{1}{R^*}$, which, after plugging in Eq. (S9.2) gives

$$\begin{aligned} h'(R^*)|_{h(R^*)=0, \theta>1} &= \frac{\theta-1}{\theta} \left(\frac{1-\alpha}{(1+n)\alpha} - \frac{1}{R^*} \right) - \frac{1-\alpha}{(1+n)\alpha} \\ &= -\frac{1}{\theta} \frac{1-\alpha}{(1+n)\alpha} - \frac{\theta-1}{\theta} \frac{1}{R^*} < 0, \end{aligned}$$

proving our claim. Hence, for any $\theta > 0$, there exists a unique R^* that solves $h(R^*) = 0$. It follows that there exists a unique (non-zero) steady state for the system in (S9.1), given by $k^* = (R^*/\alpha)^{1/(\alpha-1)}$.

We next claim that the system $k(t+1) = g^{-1}(k(t))$ is globally stable, so that the economy converges to the unique steady state capital-labor ratio k^* starting at any $k(0) > 0$. The above analysis has established that the function $g^{-1}(k(t))$ crosses the 45 degree line exactly once. We next claim that

$$\frac{dg^{-1}(k(t))}{dk(t)}\Big|_{k(t)=k^*} < 1 \tag{S9.3}$$

so that $g^{-1}(k(t))$ crosses the 45 degree line from above. This claim implies that the plot of $k(t+1) = g^{-1}(k(t))$ starts above the 45 degree line, crosses it once and goes below the 45 degree line (as displayed in Figure 9.2) and thus the system is globally stable. To show the claim in Eq. (S9.3), we first take the derivative of the inverse function to obtain

$$\frac{dg^{-1}(k(t))}{dk(t)}\Big|_{k(t)=k^*} = \left(g'(k(t+1))|_{k(t+1)=g^{-1}(k^*)=k^*}\right)^{-1} = \tag{S9.4}$$

$$\left(\frac{k(t)^{1-\alpha}}{\alpha}\frac{1}{k(t+1)}\frac{1+n}{1-\alpha}\left(\frac{[k(t+1)]+}{\beta^{\frac{-1}{\theta}}\alpha^{\frac{-(1-\theta)}{\theta}}\left[\frac{1-\alpha}{\theta}+\alpha\right]k(t+1)^{\frac{1-\alpha}{\theta}+\alpha}}\right)\right)^{-1}\Bigg|_{\substack{k(t)= \\ k(t+1)=k^*}}.$$

We consider the cases $\theta \leq 1$ and $\theta > 1$ separately. If $\theta \leq 1$, then $\frac{1-\alpha}{\theta} + \alpha \geq 1$ and replacing the bracketed term $\left[\frac{1-\alpha}{\theta} + \alpha\right]$ in Eq. (S9.4) with 1 and using Eq. (S9.1), we have

$$\frac{dg^{-1}(k(t))}{dk(t)}\Big|_{k(t)=k^*} \leq \left(\frac{1}{\alpha}k(t)^{1-\alpha}\frac{1}{k(t+1)}k(t)^\alpha\right)^{-1}\Big|_{k(t)=k(t+1)=k^*} = \alpha < 1,$$

proving Eq. (S9.3). Else if $\theta > 1$, then $\frac{1-\alpha}{\theta} + \alpha \leq 1$ and replacing the bracketed term $[k(t+1)]$ in Eq. (S9.4) with $\left(\frac{1-\alpha}{\theta} + \alpha\right)k(t+1)$ and using Eq. (S9.1), we have

$$\frac{dg^{-1}(k(t))}{dk(t)}\Big|_{k(t)=k^*} \leq \left(\frac{1}{\alpha}k(t)^{1-\alpha}\frac{\frac{1-\alpha}{\theta}+\alpha}{k(t+1)}k(t)^\alpha\right)^{-1}\Big|_{k(t)=k(t+1)=k^*}$$

$$= \left(\frac{1-\alpha}{\alpha\theta}+1\right)^{-1} < 1.$$

This proves Eq. (S9.3) also for the case $\theta > 0$ and shows that the system $k(t+1) = g^{-1}(k(t))$ is globally stable for any $\theta > 0$.

The economic intuition for global stability can be given as follows. When $\theta \leq 1$, the substitution effect dominates the income effect so households save a higher fraction of their wage income (i.e. the saving rate is higher) when the interest rate is higher. When the capital-labor ratio in the economy is lower than the steady state level, the interest rate is higher, which induces households to save more and increases the capital-labor ratio towards the steady state. A second stabilizing force, which applies for all $\theta > 0$, comes from diminishing returns in the aggregate production function. When the capital-labor ratio is lower than the steady state level, the marginal product of capital is higher and the ratio of income to capital $f(k)/k$ is higher, which tends to increase capital accumulation controlling for the saving rate (i.e. controlling for the first effect). Thus, when $\theta < 1$, both forces help to stabilize the system. When $\theta > 1$, the two forces go in opposing directions, but our analysis shows that the second (diminishing returns) force dominates the first force and the system is globally stable.

Exercise 9.7

Exercise 9.7, Part (a). Let $L(t)$ denote the population of the young at time t and $k(t) \equiv K(t)/L(t)$ denote capital-labor ratio in this economy. A competitive equilibrium is a sequence of capital-labor ratios, household consumption and savings, and prices $\{k(t), c_1(t), s(t), c_2(t), R(t), w(t)\}_{t=0}^{\infty}$ such that the household consumption solves

$$\max_{\{c_1(t), c_2(t), s(t) \geq 0\}} \log(c_1(t)) + \beta \log(c_2(t+1)) \tag{S9.5}$$

$$c_1(t) + s(t) \leq w(t)$$

$$c_2(t+1) \leq s(t) R(t+1),$$

competitive firms maximize, that is,

$$\begin{aligned} R(t) &= \alpha A(t)(k(t))^{\alpha-1} \\ w(t) &= (1-\alpha) A(t)(k(t))^{\alpha}, \end{aligned} \tag{S9.6}$$

and markets clear,

$$k(t+1) = \frac{s(t)}{1+n} \text{ for all } t. \tag{S9.7}$$

We can define a steady state equilibrium as an equilibrium in which capital-labor ratio, $k(t)$, and output per labor $y(t) = F(k(t), A(t))$ grow at constant rates.

Exercise 9.7, Part (b). With log preferences, the solution to the household's Problem (S9.5) is given by

$$c_1(t) = \frac{1}{1+\beta} w(t) \text{ and } s(t) = \frac{\beta}{1+\beta} w(t). \tag{S9.8}$$

Since income and substitution effects exactly cancel, interest rates have no effect on the saving decision of the households. Using Eqs. (S9.7), (S9.8) and (S9.6), we have

$$k(t+1) = \frac{\beta}{(\beta+1)(1+n)}(1-\alpha) A(t)(k(t))^{\alpha}, \tag{S9.9}$$

which describes the evolution of $k(t)$. Note that this expression takes the form $k(t+1) = SA(t)k(t)^{\alpha}$ for some positive constant S, hence the behavior of capital in this model is very similar to the Solow model. From the analysis in Chapter 2, we predict that $k(t)$ grows by a factor of $(1+g)^{1/(1-\alpha)}$ in steady state, hence we define

$$\hat{k}(t) = \frac{k(t)}{A(t)^{1/(1-\alpha)}}$$

as the normalized capital-labor ratio. By Eq. (S9.9), normalized capital-labor ratio evolves according to

$$\hat{k}(t+1) = g\left(\hat{k}(t)\right) \equiv \frac{\beta(1-\alpha)}{(\beta+1)(1+n)(1+g)^{1/(1-\alpha)}}\left(\hat{k}(t)\right)^{\alpha}.$$

This is a stable system and starting from any $\hat{k}(0) = k(0)$, $\hat{k}(t)$ converges to

$$\hat{k}^* = \left[\frac{\beta(1-\alpha)}{(\beta+1)(1+n)(1+g)^{1/(1-\alpha)}}\right]^{1/(1-\alpha)}. \tag{S9.10}$$

To prove stability, note that $g\left(\hat{k}\right)/\hat{k}$ is decreasing for all t and is equal to 1 for $\hat{k}=\hat{k}^*$, thus

$$\frac{\hat{k}\left(t+1\right)-\hat{k}\left(t\right)}{\hat{k}\left(t\right)}=\frac{g\left(\hat{k}\left(t\right)\right)}{\hat{k}\left(t\right)}-1\left\{\begin{array}{l}>0 \text{ if } \hat{k}\left(t\right)<\hat{k}^* \\ <0 \text{ if } \hat{k}\left(t\right)<\hat{k}^* \end{array}\right.,$$

which shows that $\hat{k}\left(t\right)$ moves towards $\hat{k}^*$. Note also that $g\left(\hat{k}\right)$ is increasing in $\hat{k}$, thus if $\hat{k}\left(t\right)<\hat{k}^*$, then $\hat{k}\left(t+1\right)=g\left(\hat{k}\left(t\right)\right)<g\left(\hat{k}^*\right)=\hat{k}^*$ so $\hat{k}\left(t\right)$ does not overshoot $\hat{k}^*$, hence it converges to $\hat{k}^*$. This characterizes the steady state and proves that the steady state is asymptotically stable. On the steady state, capital-labor ratio grows by a factor of $(1+g)^{1/(1-\alpha)}$.

We next calculate the interest rate, wages, and the growth rates of output and consumption on steady state. Using Eq. (S9.6) and (S9.10), we have

$$R^*=\alpha\hat{k}^{*\alpha-1}=\frac{\alpha\left(1+\beta\right)\left(1+n\right)\left(1+g\right)^{1/(1-\alpha)}}{\left(1-\alpha\right)\beta} \tag{S9.11}$$

hence the interest rate is constant on the steady state. Using Eq. (S9.6)), we have

$$w\left(t\right)=\left(1-\alpha\right)\hat{k}^{*\alpha}A\left(t\right)^{1/(1-\alpha)}, \tag{S9.12}$$

so wages grow by the same factor as capital-labor ratio $(1+g)^{1/(1-\alpha)}$ on the steady state. Similarly, for consumption of each generation, we have,

$$\begin{aligned} c_1\left(t\right) &= \frac{1}{1+\beta}w\left(t\right) \\ c_2\left(t\right) &= \frac{\beta}{1+\beta}w\left(t\right)R\left(t+1\right)=\frac{\beta}{1+\beta}w\left(t\right)R^*, \end{aligned} \tag{S9.13}$$

hence, consumption also grows by the same factor $(1+g)^{1/(1-\alpha)}$ on the steady state. Finally, output per labor is given by

$$y\left(t\right)=A\left(t\right)k\left(t\right)^{\alpha}=\hat{k}^{*\alpha}A\left(t\right)^{1/(1-\alpha)},$$

which also grows by a factor of $(1+g)^{1/(1-\alpha)}$ on steady state. We conclude that, capital, output, consumption, and wages grow by the same factor $(1+g)^{1/(1-\alpha)}$ on the steady state and interest rate remains constant at R^* given by Eq. (S9.11).

Exercise 9.7, Part (c). By the capital accumulation equation (S9.9), an increase in g increases $A\left(t\right)$ at all points and hence increases $k\left(t\right)$ at all times t (except for the initial time $t=1$ at which $k\left(t\right)$ will be constant). To prove this rigorously, let us compare two economies that start with $k\left(0\right)=k'\left(0\right)$ and $A\left(0\right)=A'\left(0\right)$ in which $A\left(t\right)$ grows at rates $g'>g$. By Eq. (S9.9), we have $k'\left(1\right)\geq k\left(1\right)$. Suppose that $k'\left(t\right)\geq k\left(t\right)$ for some $t\geq 1$. Then, since $A'\left(t\right)>A\left(t\right)$ and $k'\left(t\right)\geq k\left(t\right)$, by Eq. (S9.9), we have $k'\left(t+1\right)>k'\left(t\right)$. This proves by induction that for each time $t\geq 2$, we have $k'\left(t\right)>k\left(t\right)$ as desired. Note also that, from Eq. (S9.10), an increase in g reduces the effective steady state capital-labor ratio $\hat{k}^*$ (in fact, reduces $\hat{k}\left(t\right)$ at all times), but as our analysis shows it increases capital-labor ratio $k\left(t\right)$ at all times.

By Eq. (S9.12), wages are an increasing function of both $A\left(t\right)$ and $k\left(t\right)$, which shows that an increase in g increases wages at all times $t\geq 2$. By Eq. (S9.11), an increase in g also increases the interest rate at all times t since the effective capital-labor ratio, $\hat{k}\left(t\right)$, is lower at all times. Finally, using Eq. (S9.13) and the fact that $w(t)$ and $R(t)$ are higher, $c_1(t)$ and $c_2(t)$ are also higher for all t.

Exercise 9.7, Part (d). We claim that an increase in β at time $t = 1$ increases $k(t)$ at all $t \geq 2$. Consider two otherwise identical economies with $\beta' > \beta$, and denote their capital-labor ratios with $k'(.)$ and $k(.)$. We have $k'(1) = k(1)$. Suppose $k'(t) \geq k(t)$ for some $t \geq 1$. Then, by Eq. (S9.9), we have

$$
\begin{aligned}
k(t+1) &= \frac{\beta}{(\beta+1)(1+n)}(1-\alpha)A(t)(k(t))^{\alpha} \\
&< \frac{\beta'}{(\beta'+1)(1+n)}(1-\alpha)A(t)(k'(t))^{\alpha} = k'(t+1),
\end{aligned}
$$

where the inequality follows since $k(t) \leq k'(t)$ and $\beta/(\beta+1) < \beta'/(\beta'+1)$. This proves by induction that $k'(t) > k(t)$ for each $t \geq 2$, showing our claim. Note that capital-labor ratio increases at all periods, and consequently, the steady state capital-labor ratio with $\beta' > \beta$ is also higher, as can be seen from Eq. (S9.10). Intuitively, a higher β induces households to save more and increases the capital-labor ratio at all periods, including the steady state. Note that this model resembles the Solow model and β acts as a proxy for the savings rate in the Solow model, hence the qualitative implications of an increase in β is identical to the implications of an increase in the savings rate in the Solow model.

Next, we characterize the effect of β on steady state consumption, $c_1(t)$ and $c_2(t)$. Using (S9.13) and (S9.6), we have

$$
\begin{aligned}
c_1(t) &= \frac{1}{1+\beta}(1-\alpha)A(t)^{1/(1-\alpha)}\left(\hat{k}^*\right)^{\alpha} \\
&= A(t)^{1/(1-\alpha)}\frac{1-\alpha}{1+\beta}\left[\frac{\beta(1-\alpha)}{(\beta+1)(1+n)(1+g)^{1/(1-\alpha)}}\right]^{\alpha/(1-\alpha)} \\
&= A(t)^{1/(1-\alpha)} \times S \times \beta^{\alpha/(1-\alpha)}(1+\beta)^{-1/(1-\alpha)},
\end{aligned}
$$

where the second line substitutes for $\hat{k}^*$ from Eq. (S9.10) and the last line defines a constant S that doesn't depend on β. It follows that the effect of an increase on $c_1(t)$ is ambiguous. In particular, when α is not too large, for low levels of β, increasing β increases $c_1(t)$, while for high levels of β it decreases $c_1(t)$. On the one hand, a higher β induces individuals to save more, which directly reduces consumption at young age. On the other hand, higher savings increase the capital stock in the economy and the wages at steady state, which increases consumption at young age.

For $c_2(t)$, a similar analysis gives

$$
\begin{aligned}
c_2(t) &= \frac{\beta}{1+\beta}(1-\alpha)A(t)^{1/(1-\alpha)}\left(\hat{k}^*\right)^{\alpha}\alpha\left(\hat{k}^*\right)^{\alpha-1} \\
&= A(t)^{1/(1-\alpha)}\frac{\beta}{1+\beta}(1-\alpha)\alpha\left[\frac{\beta(1-\alpha)}{(\beta+1)(1+n)(1+g)^{1/(1-\alpha)}}\right]^{(2\alpha-1)/(1-\alpha)} \\
&= A(t)^{1/(1-\alpha)} \times S \times \left(\frac{\beta}{1+\beta}\right)^{\alpha/(1-\alpha)},
\end{aligned}
$$

where S is a constant that doesn't depend on β. This expression shows that $c_2(t)$ unambiguously increases. An increase in β increases the saving rate which creates a direct effect towards increasing $c_2(t)$. It also generates price effects (an increase in $w(t)$ and a decrease in $R(t+1)$) but our analysis shows that these price effects do not overturn the direct effect.

Therefore, for low levels of β, increasing β increases the steady state consumption both at young and old age. However, for high levels of β, it may decrease the first period consumption while increasing the second period consumption. This is related to overaccumulation of capital and the dynamic inefficiency in the OLG model. From the expression for the steady state interest rate (S9.11), we have $R^* < 1+n$ when

$$\frac{\beta}{1+\beta} > \frac{\alpha(1+g)^{1/(1-\alpha)}}{1-\alpha}.$$

Then, if g and α are such that the expression on the right hand side is less than 1, there exists a level $\bar{\beta} \in (0,1)$ such that increasing β beyond $\bar{\beta}$ will create dynamic inefficiency. When there is dynamic inefficiency, total resources available for consumption is reduced so the steady state consumption cannot increase both at young and old age, providing a different perspective for our results regarding $c_1(t)$ and $c_2(t)$.

Exercise 9.15

Suppose that the economy is initially on a steady state equilibrium, $\{c_1^*, c_2^*, k^*, R^*, w^*\}$. Assume that the steady state equilibrium is dynamically inefficient, that is, $r^* \equiv R^* - 1 < n$, or equivalently, $k^* > k_{gold} \equiv f'^{-1}(1+n)$. Similar to Diamond (1965), suppose that at time 0, the government issues new debt $D(0) = \bar{D} > 0$ and keeps debt to labor ratio $D(t)$ constant at $\bar{D}$ for all subsequent periods.[1] In equilibrium, the government bonds must pay interest rate $r(t+1)$, otherwise there would be no demand for these bonds. The new debt issued at any time $t+1$ is used to settle the debt at time t, and any residual government revenue is distributed to the old generation at time $t+1$ as lump sum transfers (or taxes, if this amount is negative). With a constant debt to labor ratio, the lump sum transfers to the old generation at time $t+1$ is given by

$$D(t+1)(1+n) - D(t)(1+r(t+1)) = \bar{D}(1+n-R(t+1)).$$

Let $s(t)$ denote the savings of a young individual, which includes investment in both capital and government bonds. A young individual at time $t \geq 0$ chooses $s(t)$ that solves

$$\max_{s(t),c_1(t),c_2(t)} u(c_1(t)) + \beta u(c_2(t+1)) \tag{S9.14}$$

$$\text{s.t.} \quad c_1(t) + s(t) \leq w(t)$$
$$c_2(t) \leq R(t+1)s(t) + \bar{D}(1+n-R(t+1)).$$

An equilibrium in this economy with constant debt to labor ratio $\bar{D}$ and initial capital $k(0) = k^*$ is a sequence $[c_1(t), c_2(t), k(t), R(t), w(t)]_{t=0}^{\infty}$ such that young individuals at all $t \geq 0$ solve Eq. (S9.14), factor prices are competitive, and factor and goods markets clear.

First, we note that capital market clearing in this economy requires

$$k(t+1) = \frac{s(t) - \bar{D}}{1+n} \text{ for all } t, \tag{S9.15}$$

that is, government debt substitutes capital investment, which creates a direct effect towards decreasing the capital-labor ratio in this economy. Second, we also claim that, in the dynamically inefficient region, the lump-sum transfers $\bar{D}(1+n-R(t+1))$ create an income effect which increases the household's period consumption and reduces savings $s(t)$, further

---

[1]We use capital letters $D(t)$ for debt to labor ratio since we reserve $d(t)$ for the social security policy analyzed in the next exercise.

decreasing the capital-labor ratio. To prove this claim, note that the first-order condition for Problem (S9.14) is

$$u'\left(w\left(t\right)-s\left(t\right)\right)=\beta R\left(t+1\right)u'\left(R\left(t+1\right)s\left(t\right)+\bar{D}\left(1+n-R\left(t+1\right)\right)\right).$$

Define the savings function $s\left(w\left(t\right),R\left(t+1\right),\bar{D}\right)$ as the solution to this equation and note that when $r\left(t+1\right)<n$ (i.e. when there is dynamic inefficiency) the function $s\left(w\left(t\right),R\left(t+1\right),\bar{D}\right)$ is decreasing in $\bar{D}$, that is

$$\frac{\partial s\left(w\left(t\right),R\left(t+1\right),\bar{D}\right)}{\partial\bar{D}}<0,\tag{S9.16}$$

proving our claim. Hence, government debt creates a direct effect and an indirect income effect both of which decrease capital accumulation when the economy is in the dynamically inefficient region (keeping prices $w\left(t\right)$ and $R\left(t+1\right)$ constant).

We next show that these effects are not overturned by general equilibrium price effects caused by the reduction in the capital-labor ratio. More specifically, we claim that, by appropriately choosing $\bar{D}$, the government can reduce the long run capital stock towards k_{gold}. Note that the equilibrium prices are given by $w\left(t\right)=f\left(k\left(t\right)\right)-k\left(t\right)f'\left(k\left(t\right)\right)$ and $R\left(t+1\right)=f'\left(k\left(t+1\right)\right)$, hence using the savings function $s\left(w\left(t\right),R\left(t+1\right),\bar{D}\right)$ defined above, Eq. (S9.15) can be rewritten as

$$k\left(t+1\right)=\frac{s\left(f\left(k\left(t\right)\right)-k\left(t\right)f'\left(k\left(t\right)\right),f'\left(k\left(t+1\right)\right),\bar{D}\right)-\bar{D}}{1+n},\tag{S9.17}$$

which is the analogue of Eq. (9.8) with government debt. This equation implicitly defines $k\left(t+1\right)$ in terms of $k\left(t\right)$, that is, there exists a function $g\left(k\left(t\right),\bar{D}\right)$ such that the capital-labor ratio dynamics are given by $k\left(t+1\right)=g\left(k\left(t\right),\bar{D}\right)$. Note also that $k\left(t+1\right)=g\left(k\left(t\right),\bar{D}=0\right)$ captures the dynamics for the baseline economy without national debt. Implicitly differentiating Eq. (S9.17) with respect to $\bar{D}$, we have

$$\frac{\partial g\left(k\left(t\right),\bar{D}\right)}{\partial\bar{D}}=\frac{\frac{\partial s\left(w(t),R(t+1),\bar{D}\right)}{\partial\bar{D}}-1}{1+n-\frac{\partial s\left(w(t),R(t+1),\bar{D}\right)}{\partial R(t+1)}f''\left(k\left(t+1\right)\right)}.$$

Using Eq. (S9.16), this expression is negative at $\bar{D}=0$ under the regularity assumption $\frac{\partial s(w^{*},R^{*},0)}{\partial R(t+1)}f''\left(k^{*}\right)<1+n,$[2] which implies that increasing $\bar{D}$ shifts the $g\left(k\left(t\right),\bar{D}\right)$ function down and lowers the steady state capital-labor ratio (see Figure S9.1). Starting from $\bar{D}=0$ and the corresponding steady state $k^{*}>k_{gold}$, the social planner can introduce a constant level of national debt $\bar{D}>0$ and reduce the capital-labor ratio to a new steady state $\bar{k}\in[k_{gold},k^{*})$. Moreover, the capital stock $k\left(t\right)$ monotonically declines from $k\left(0\right)=k^{*}$ to $\bar{k}\in[k_{gold},k^{*})$ so we have $k\left(t\right)\in[k_{gold},k^{*}]$ for all t.

We next claim that this path of capital-labor ratio increases net resources at every period. To see this, note that the resource constraints at time t are given by

$$\frac{c_{2}\left(t\right)}{1+n}+c_{1}\left(t\right)\leq f\left(k\left(t\right)\right)-\left(1+n\right)k\left(t+1\right)\text{ for all }t\geq0,\tag{S9.18}$$

---

[2]See Exercise 9.16, which works out the details of this argument in a related economy with social security (instead of national debt).

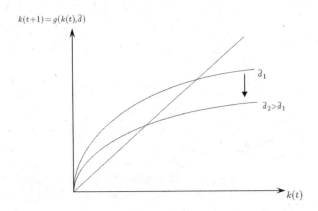

FIGURE S9.1. Introducing government debt (Exercise 9.15) or an unfunded social security system (Exercise 9.16) lowers the steady state capital-labor ratio in the OLG economy. Starting from the old steady state, the capital-labor ratio monotonically converges to the new steady state.

where the right hand side of this expression constitutes the net output at time t. We have

$$
\begin{aligned}
f\left(k\left(t\right)\right)-\left(1+n\right)k\left(t+1\right) &= f\left(k\left(t\right)\right)-\left(1+n\right)k\left(t\right)+\left(1+n\right)\left(k\left(t\right)-k\left(t+1\right)\right) \\
&\geq f\left(k\left(t\right)\right)-\left(1+n\right)k\left(t\right) \\
&> f\left(k^{*}\right)-\left(1+n\right)k^{*},
\end{aligned}
$$

where the first inequality follows since $k\left(t\right)$ is weakly decreasing (so $k\left(t\right)\geq k\left(t+1\right)$), and the second inequality follows since $k\left(t\right)\in\left[k_{gold},k^{*}\right]$ for all t and $f\left(k\right)-\left(1+n\right)k$ is a concave function maximized at $k=k_{gold}$. It follows that the right hand side of (S9.18) is increased for all periods, hence by issuing national debt the government increases net resources for all periods.

This result is in contrast with the Ricardian equivalence result for the neoclassical economy (cf. Exercise 8.35). Note that the government in this economy borrows at competitive interest rates and transfers the net borrowing back to the public, thus it does not change the lifetime budget of the representative household. According to the Ricardian equivalence reasoning, government actions (tax, transfer, debt/repayment etc.) that do not change the lifetime budget of the representative household should have no effect on consumption. The reasoning does not apply to the OLG economy since there is no representative household and the government's debt/repayment plans redistribute resources between current and future generations, which have potentially different consumption patterns. When there is dynamic inefficiency, the government debt may increase the consumption of all generations by slowing down capital accumulation.

Exercise 9.16

Consider a steady state equilibrium denoted by $\{c_{1}^{*},c_{2}^{*},k^{*},R^{*},w^{*}\}$. Assume that the steady state equilibrium is dynamically inefficient, that is, $r^{*}\equiv R^{*}-1<n$, or equivalently, $k^{*}>k_{gold}\equiv f^{\prime-1}\left(1+n\right)$. We provide two different proofs for the proposition. The first proof is based on the Second Welfare Theorem and highlights the efficiency properties of the OLG model, while the second proof is more constructive and is similar to the original analysis in Samuelson (1975).

Proof 1, the less constructive proof based on the Second Welfare Theorem.
The proof has three steps. First, we show that the government can improve the net output
(i.e. the part of output that is consumed) in every period by reducing the capital stock
at all $t \geq 1$ to k_{gold}. Second, we use the finding in step one to show that there exists an
allocation $[c_1(t), c_2(t), k(t)]_{t=0}^{\infty}$ that (i) Pareto dominates the equilibrium allocation, (ii) is
Pareto efficient, that is, no further improvements are possible without making some generation
worse off. As the third and the final step, we show that the Pareto efficient allocation
$[c_1(t), c_2(t), k(t)]_{t=0}^{\infty}$ that Pareto dominates the equilibrium allocation can be decentralized
using an unfunded social security system.

As the first step, we claim that the plan $k(t) = k_{gold}$ for all $t \geq 1$ increases net output in every period relative to the equilibrium plan, $k(t) = k^*$. Note that the allocation
$[c_1(t), c_2(t), k(t)]_{t=0}^{\infty}$ is feasible if it satisfies Eq. (S9.18). Consider a plan in which capital-
labor ratio allocations $k(t) = \tilde{k}$ are constant for all $t \geq 1$. Note that both the equilibrium
plan $k(t) = k^*$ and the proposed plan with $k(t) = k_{gold}$ for all $t \geq 1$ fall in the category of
such plans. The period $t \geq 1$ feasibility condition (S9.18) for these plans is given by

$$\frac{c_2(t)}{1+n} + c_1(t) \leq f\left(\tilde{k}\right) - (1+n)\,\tilde{k} \text{ for all } t \geq 1. \tag{S9.19}$$

Since $f(k_{gold}) - (1+n)\,k_{gold} > f(k^*) - (1+n)\,k^*$, the feasibility condition (S9.19) is strictly
relaxed with the plan $k(t) = k_{gold}$ for all $t \geq 1$. The period $t = 0$ feasibility condition for
the proposed plan is

$$\frac{c_2(0)}{1+n} + c_1(0) \leq f(k^*) - (1+n)\,k_{gold},$$

which is also relaxed with respect to the equilibrium period 0 constraint since $f(k^*) -
(1+n)\,k^* < f(k^*) - (1+n)\,k_{gold}$. Hence, the proposed plan with $k(t) = k_{gold}$ for all $t \geq 1$
relaxes the feasibility condition and increases net output at all times.

As the second step, we show that there exists an allocation $[c_1(t), c_2(t), k(t)]_{t=0}^{\infty}$ that
Pareto dominates the equilibrium allocation and that is Pareto efficient. To see this, consider
the Pareto problem that maximizes the welfare of the old generation at time 0 without making
future generations worse off

$$P(0) \quad : \quad \max_{\{c_1(t), c_2(t), k(t)\}_{t=0}^{\infty}} u(c_2(0))$$

$$\text{s.t.} \quad \frac{c_2(t)}{1+n} + c_1(t) \leq f(k(t)) - (1+n)\,k(t+1) \text{ for all } t \geq 1,$$

$$u(c_1(t)) + \beta u(c_2(t+1)) \geq u(c_1^*) + \beta u(c_2^*) \text{ for all } t \geq 0.$$

By step one, the allocation with capital-labor ratio $k(t) = k_{gold}$ for all $t \geq 1$ and consumption
given by

$$[c_1(t) = c_1^*, c_2(t) = c_2^*]_{t=0}^{\infty}, c_1(0) = c_1^*, c_2(0) = c_2^* + \epsilon$$

is feasible for sufficiently small ϵ. Hence the constraint set of $P(0)$ is non-empty and its
value is greater than the equilibrium utility $u(c_2^*)$. It follows that there exists a solution
$[c_1(t), c_2(t), k(t)]_{t=0}^{\infty}$ to the Pareto problem $P(0)$ that Pareto dominates the equilibrium
allocation, and the solution is Pareto efficient by construction. For future reference (to be
used in step three), note also that any solution to Problem $P(0)$ satisfies the first-order
condition

$$u'(c_1(t)) = \beta f'(k(t+1))\,u'(c_2(t+1)), \text{ for all } t \geq 0. \tag{S9.20}$$

As the third step, we show that there exists an unfunded social security allocation
$[d(t), b(t) = (1+n)\,d(t)]_{t=0}^{\infty}$, where $d(t)$ represents the social security payments of young

and $b(t) = (1 + n) d(t)$ the benefits received by old at time t, which decentralizes the plan $[c_1(t), c_2(t), k(t)]_{t=0}^{\infty}$ constructed in step two. This step essentially follows since the Second Welfare Theorem applies to the OLG economy, hence any Pareto efficient allocation can be decentralized. We provide a direct proof by constructing the social security payments $[d(t)]_{t=0}^{\infty}$ such that the resulting decentralized allocation is identical to the Pareto efficient allocation $[c_1(t), c_2(t), k(t)]_{t=0}^{\infty}$. We define

$$R(t) = f'(k(t)), \text{ and } w(t) = f(k(t)) - k(t) f'(k(t)), \qquad (S9.21)$$
$$s(t-1) = k(t)(1+n), \text{ for all } t \geq 0,$$

as the prices and the amount of per capita savings consistent with the allocation $[c_1(t), c_2(t), k(t)]_{t=0}^{\infty}$. We also define

$$d(t) = c_1(t) + s(t) - w(t), \text{ for all } t \geq 0,$$

so after making the social security payment the young at time t has just enough to consume $c_1(t)$ and save $s(t)$. Finally, we define

$$b(t) = c_2(t) - R(t) s(t-1), \text{ for all } t \geq 0$$

so after the social security transfer $b(t)$, the old generation at time t has just enough to consume $c_2(t)$.

We claim that the constructed endowments $[d(t), b(t)]_{t=0}^{\infty}$ constitute an unfunded social security system, that is, the payments by young at time t are just enough to cover the benefits received by the old. To see this, note that

$$
\begin{aligned}
b(t) + (1+n) d(t) &= c_2(t) - R(t) s(t-1) + (1+n)(c_1(t) + s(t) - w(t)) \\
&= c_2(t) + (1+n) c_1(t) + (1+n)^2 k(t+1) \\
&\quad - (1+n) f'(k(t)) k(t) - (1+n)(f(k(t)) - k'(t) f'(k(t))) \\
&= c_2(t) + (1+n) c_1(t) + (1+n)^2 k(t+1) - (1+n) f(k(t)) \\
&= 0,
\end{aligned}
$$

where the second line follows from Eq. (S9.21), the third line from algebra, and the last line from the fact that the Pareto efficient allocation $[c_1(t), c_2(t), k(t)]_{t=0}^{\infty}$ satisfies the resource constraints with equality. This proves that the constructed allocations $[d(t), b(t)]_{t=0}^{\infty}$ represent an unfunded social security system.[3]

We next claim that the allocations and prices $[c_1(t), c_2(t), s(t), k(t), R(t), w(t)]_{t=0}^{\infty}$ constitute a competitive equilibrium with endowments $[d(t), b(t)]_{t=0}^{\infty}$. From our construction of $[d(t), b(t)]_{t=0}^{\infty}$, all we need to check is that generation $t \geq 0$ chooses $c_1(t), c_2(t+1)$ and $s(t)$ when they are entitled to the endowments $d(t), b(t+1)$ and when they face prices $R(t), w(t)$. Note that generation t solves

$$\max_{\tilde{c}_1(t), \tilde{c}_2(t+1), \tilde{s}(t)} u(\tilde{c}_1(t)) + \beta u(\tilde{c}_2(t+1)) \qquad (S9.22)$$

$$\text{s.t.} \quad \tilde{c}_1(t) + \tilde{s}(t) \leq w(t) + d(t)$$
$$\tilde{c}_2(t) \leq \tilde{s}(t) R(t+1) + b(t+1).$$

Since the consumption plan $(c_1(t), c_2(t+1))$ satisfies the first-order condition (S9.20) for problem $P(0)$, it follows that

$$u'(c_1(t)) = \beta R(t+1) u'(c_2(t+1)),$$

---

[3]Note, however, that this is not necessarily a fair unfunded social security system, in the sense that $d(t)$ is not necessarily equal to $d(t+1)$ so generations are not necessarily treated equally.

which is the first-order condition for Problem (S9.22). Since the allocation $(c_1(t), c_2(t+1), s(t))$ satisfies the budget constraints in Problem (S9.22) with equality by construction, it follows that $(c_1(t), c_2(t+1), s(t))$ solves Problem (S9.22). This further shows that the path of allocations and prices $[c_1(t), c_2(t), s(t), k(t), R(t), w(t)]_{t=0}^{\infty}$ is an equilibrium with unfunded social security endowments $[d(t), b(t)]_{t=0}^{\infty}$, completing the proof of step 3 and the proof of Proposition 9.8.

Proof 2, the more constructive proof. In this proof, we consider the new equilibrium path $[c_1(t), c_2(t), s(t), k(t), R(t), w(t)]_{t=0}^{\infty}$ corresponding to a social security scheme that treats all generations the same, that is $d(t) = \bar{d} > 0$ for all t so $b(t) = \bar{d}(1+n)$. We claim that there exists $\bar{d}$ sufficiently small such that the new equilibrium is a Pareto improvement over the old equilibrium (i.e. the equilibrium with $\bar{d} = 0$). We prove this claim in two steps. First, similar to Exercise 9.15, we show that there exists a sufficiently small $\bar{d} > 0$ such that the steady state capital-labor ratio in the new equilibrium, $\bar{k}$, lies in $[k^{gold}, k^*)$ and $k(t)$ monotonically converges to $\bar{k}$ starting from k^*, that is

$$k(t) \downarrow \bar{k} \in [k^{gold}, k^*). \tag{S9.23}$$

Second, we show that every generation (including the generations along the transition path) is better off in the new equilibrium than in the old equilibrium.

Step one, showing that the capital-labor ratio declines. Note that the consumer solves Problem (S9.22) with $d(t) = \bar{d}$ and $b(t+1) = \bar{d}(1+n)$, which leads to the first-order condition

$$u'(w(t) - s(t) - \bar{d}) = \beta R(t+1) u'(s(t) R(t+1) + \bar{d}(1+n)). \tag{S9.24}$$

We define the savings function $s(w(t), R(t+1), \bar{d})$ as the solution to this equation. Using the competitive prices for $w(t)$ and $R(t+1)$, the capital-labor ratio at time $t+1$ is found as the solution to the following fixed point equation.

$$k(t+1) = \frac{1}{1+n} s(f(k(t)) - k(t) f'(k(t)), f'(k(t+1)), \bar{d}). \tag{S9.25}$$

We denote the solution to this equation by $k(t+1) = g(k(t), \bar{d})$. Note that when $\bar{d} = 0$, $k(t+1) = g(k(t), 0)$ describes the dynamics in the original economy without transfers. We make the following regularity assumption which ensures that the function $g(k, 0)$ is increasing in a neighborhood of the steady state capital (so that the equilibrium in the original economy is stable and well behaved).

ASSUMPTION 1. *The function $g(k, 0)$ is increasing in k in a neighborhood of $k = k^*$, or equivalently,* $\frac{\partial s(w^*, R^*, 0)}{\partial R(t+1)} f''(k^*) < 1 + n$.[4]

---

[4]This conditions ensures $g_k(k^*, 0) > 0$. To see this, differentiate Eq. (S9.25) with respect to $k(t)$ and evaluate at the steady state $(k(t) = k^*, \bar{d} = 0)$ to get

$$g_k(k^*, 0) = \frac{1}{1+n} \left(s_w(w^*, R^*, 0) \frac{\partial(f(k) - kf'(k))}{\partial k}\Big|_{k=k^*} + s_R(w^*, R^*, 0) f''(k^*) g_k(k^*, 0) \right),$$

which implies

$$g_k(k^*, 0) = s_w(w^*, R^*, 0) \frac{\partial(f(k) - kf'(k))}{\partial k}\Big|_{k=k^*} \frac{1}{1+n - s_R(w^*, R^*, 0) f''(k^*)}.$$

We have $s_w(w^*, R^*, 0) > 0$ since increasing the wage income always increases $c_2(t) = s(t) R^*$ (while keeping the interest rate constant). We also have $\frac{\partial(f(k) - kf'(k))}{\partial k}\Big|_{k=k^*} > 0$ hence $g_k(k^*, 0) > 0$ iff $s_R(w^*, R^*, 0) f''(k^*) < 1 + n$.

Under this regularity assumption, we claim that the function $g\left(k\left(t\right),\bar{d}\right)$ is decreasing in $\bar{d}$ in a neighborhood of $k\left(t\right)=k^{*}$ and $\bar{d}=0$, that is

$$\frac{\partial g\left(k^{*},0\right)}{\partial\bar{d}}<0. \tag{S9.26}$$

To prove the claim, first we show

$$\frac{\partial s\left(w^{*},R^{*},0\right)}{\partial\bar{d}}<-1, \tag{S9.27}$$

that is, keeping equilibrium prices constant, a unit increase in $\bar{d}$ reduces savings by more than one unit. To see this partially differentiate the first-order condition Eq. (S9.24) with respect to $\bar{d}$ and evaluate at $w\left(t\right)=w^{*}$, $R\left(t+1\right)=R^{*}$, $\bar{d}=0$ to get

$$\left(-\frac{\partial s\left(w^{*},R^{*},0\right)}{\partial\bar{d}}-1\right)u^{''}\left(c_{1}^{*}\right)=\beta R^{*}u^{''}\left(c_{2}^{*}\right)\left[\frac{\partial s\left(w^{*},R^{*},0\right)}{\partial\bar{d}}R^{*}+1+n\right]$$

From here, we solve

$$\frac{\partial s\left(w^{*},R^{*},0\right)}{\partial\bar{d}}=-\frac{u^{''}\left(c_{1}^{*}\right)+\beta\left(1+n\right)\left(R^{*}\right)u^{''}\left(c_{2}^{*}\right)}{u^{''}\left(c_{1}^{*}\right)+\beta\left(R^{*}\right)^{2}u^{''}\left(c_{2}^{*}\right)}<-1,$$

where the inequality follows from the fact that $1+n>R^{*}$, i.e. the original economy is in the dynamically inefficient region, proving Eq. (S9.27). Next, to show Eq. (S9.26), partially differentiate Eq. (S9.25) with respect to $\bar{d}$ and evaluate at $k\left(t\right)=k^{*}$ and $\bar{d}=0$ (and $k\left(t+1\right)=g\left(k^{*},0\right)=k^{*}$) to get

$$\frac{\partial g\left(k^{*},0\right)}{\partial\bar{d}}=\frac{1}{1+n}\left(\frac{\partial s\left(w^{*},R^{*},0\right)}{\partial R\left(t+1\right)}f^{''}\left(k^{*}\right)\frac{\partial g\left(k^{*},0\right)}{\partial\bar{d}}+\frac{\partial s\left(w^{*},R^{*},0\right)}{\partial\bar{d}}\right).$$

Solving for $\frac{\partial g(k^{*},0)}{\partial\bar{d}}$ from this expression, we have

$$g_{d}\left(k^{*},0\right)=\frac{\frac{\partial s(w^{*},R^{*},0)}{\partial\bar{d}}}{1+n-\frac{\partial s(w^{*},R^{*},0)}{\partial R(t+1)}f^{''}\left(k^{*}\right)}.$$

Since $\frac{\partial s(w^{*},R^{*},0)}{\partial\bar{d}}<-1<0$, this expression is negative when Assumption 1 holds, proving the claim in (S9.26).

By Eq. (S9.26), increasing $\bar{d}$ shifts the function $g\left(k\left(t\right),\bar{d}\right)$ downwards (in a neighborhood of $\bar{d}=0$) as in Figure S9.1. Then there exists a sufficiently small $\bar{d}$ which leads to a new steady state capital-labor ratio $\bar{k}<k^{*}$. We can also choose $\bar{d}$ sufficiently small to ensure $\bar{k}\geq k^{gold}$, that is, we do not overshoot the golden rule capital-labor ratio. Moreover, Figure S9.1 shows that capital-labor ratio monotonically declines to the new steady state level $\bar{k}$, proving Eq. (S9.23).

Intuitively, the social security policy reduces capital accumulation through two channels. First, the social security payments can be thought of as coming from the savings account of the young generation, directly reducing their savings and slowing down capital accumulation. Second, the social security system creates an income effect for the young (since the returns from social security are higher than R^{*}) which increases $c_{1}\left(t\right)$ and further decreases $s\left(t\right)$, leading to Eq. (S9.27). Consequently one unit of the social security payment reduces savings by more than one unit. Eq. (S9.26) shows that at the margin, these effects are not overturned by general equilibrium price effects and the social security system slows down capital accumulation.

Step two, showing that the welfare of all generations increase. We consider the equilibrium corresponding to the capital-labor ratio constructed in step one and we claim that the old equilibrium consumption is in the lifetime budget of generation t for Problem (S9.22), that is

$$c_1^* + \frac{c_2^*}{R(t+1)} < w(t) + \bar{d}\frac{1+n}{R(t+1)} - \bar{d} \text{ for all } t. \tag{S9.28}$$

If this claim holds, then by revealed preference and non-satiation, generation t must be strictly better off consuming $(c_1(t), c_2(t))$ than (c_1^*, c_2^*). To prove Eq. (S9.28), we use

$$c_1^* = w^* - s^* = w^* - k^*(1+n) = f(k^*) - R^*k^* - k^*(1+n)$$
$$\text{and } c_2^* = s^*R^* = k^*(1+n)R^*$$

to get

$$c_1^* + \frac{c_2^*}{R(t+1)} = f(k^*) - R^*k^* - k^*(1+n) + \frac{k^*(1+n)R^*}{R(t+1)}. \tag{S9.29}$$

Since $f(k^*)$ is concave, we have

$$f(k^*) < f(k(t)) + f'(k(t))(k^* - k(t)) = f(k(t)) + R(t)(k^* - k(t)).$$

Using this in Eq. (S9.29), we have

$$c_1^* + \frac{c_2^*}{R(t+1)} < f(k(t)) - k(t)R(t) + k^*(R(t) - R^*) - k^*(1+n) + \frac{k^*(1+n)R^*}{R(t+1)}$$
$$< f(k(t)) - k(t)R(t) + k^*(R(t+1) - R^*) + \frac{k^*(1+n)(R^* - R(t+1))}{R(t+1)}$$
$$= w(t) + k^*(R(t+1) - R^*)\left[1 - \frac{1+n}{R(t+1)}\right]$$
$$< w(t), \tag{S9.30}$$

where the second line uses $R(t) < R(t+1)$ (which holds since $k(t+1) < k(t)$) and the last inequality follows since $R(t+1) < 1+n$. Eq. (S9.28) then follows from Eq. (S9.30) and the fact that $R(t+1) < 1+n$, completing the proof. Intuitively, step one shows that the new equilibrium has lower capital-labor ratio and hence higher net resources at every period (due to dynamic inefficiency), while step two ensures that these greater resources are divided between generations so that all generations are better off.

Exercise 9.17

We will show, more generally, that the equilibrium in this case is Pareto optimal. Hence, any allocation that increases the welfare of the current old generation (in particular, the unfunded social security system) must necessarily reduce the welfare of some future generation. To show that the equilibrium is Pareto optimal, recall that the equilibrium path in this economy is unique $[c_1(t), c_2(t), K(t), L(t), R(t), w(t), r(t)]_{t=0}^{\infty}$ and satisfies $\lim_{t\to\infty}\{R(t+1) = 1 + r(t+1)\} \to 1 + r^*$. Our goal is to map this economy into an Arrow-Debreu economy with production and apply Theorem 5.6 for the equilibrium path. Let $[p_c(t)]_{t=0}^{\infty}$ denote the sequence of Arrow-Debreu prices for the final good and normalize $p_c(0) = 1$. For any $t \geq 1$, $p_c(t)$ can be determined from the interest rate sequence $[r(t)]_{t=1}^{\infty}$ as

$$p_c(t) = \frac{1}{\prod_{t'=1}^{t} 1 + r(t')}$$

Next note that the endowments in this economy are the labor supply of each young generation at t, $[L(t)]_{t=0}^{\infty}$, and the initial capital stock $K(0)$ held by the old generation at time 0 (there are Arrow-Debreu production firms that convert these endowments to consumption and capital in subsequent periods). Then, this is a standard Arrow-Debreu economy with production and Theorem 5.6 applies for the equilibrium path as long as the sum of the value of all households' endowments,

$$K(0)R(0) + \sum_{t=0}^{\infty} L(t)w(t)p_c(t) = K(0)R(0) + L(0)w(0) + \sum_{t=1}^{\infty} L(0) \prod_{t'=1}^{t} \left(\frac{1+n}{1+r(t')} \right),$$
(S9.31)

is finite. Since $1 + r(t') \to 1 + r^* > 1 + n$, there exists some $\varepsilon > 0$ and T sufficiently large such that $(1+n)/(1+r(t')) < 1 - \varepsilon$ for all $t' > T$. Then the endowment sum is smaller than

$$K(0)R(0) + L(0)w(0) + \sum_{t=1}^{T-1} L(0) \prod_{t'=1}^{t} \left(\frac{1+n}{1+r(t')} \right) + \prod_{t'=1}^{T} \left(\frac{1+n}{1+r(t')} \right) \sum_{k=0}^{\infty} L(0)(1-\varepsilon)^k$$

$$= K(0)R(0) + L(0)w(0) + \sum_{t=1}^{T} L(0) \prod_{t'=1}^{t} \left(\frac{1+n}{1+r(t')} \right) + \prod_{t'=1}^{T} \left(\frac{1+n}{1+r(t')} \right) \frac{L(0)}{\varepsilon}$$

$$< \infty,$$

which is finite, proving that Theorem 5.6 applies and the equilibrium allocation is Pareto optimal.

We next consider the role of the finiteness of endowments in ensuring Pareto optimality. Intuitively, the standard proof of the First Welfare Theorem (Theorem 5.6) compares the budget sum of a Pareto improving allocation to the budget sum of the equilibrium allocation and obtains a contradiction. This logic applies as long as the relevant budget sums (which is equal to the endowment sum) is finite. But the logic breaks down and does not yield a contradiction when the sums are infinite, since an inequality between two infinite sums is not a rigorous mathematical statement. For example, consider the infinite sums

$$A = 1 + 2 + 1 + 2 + \dots$$
$$B = 2 + 1 + 2 + 1 + \dots$$

There is a sense in which B is greater than A, since $B = 2 + A$. But also, there is a sense in which A is greater than B, since $A = 1 + B$. The problem is that A and B are infinite and hence cannot be compared. In the OLG economy, the endowment sum in Eq. (S9.31) is finite if and only if $r^* > n$, so the standard proof of the First Welfare Theorem only applies in this case. Moreover, when $r^* < n$, not only the standard proof fails but also the equilibrium is Pareto inefficient as we have seen in Exercises 9.15 and 9.16.

Exercise 9.21

Recall from Section 9.6 that the equilibrium dynamics for the bequests are characterized by

$$b_i(t) = \frac{\beta}{1+\beta} [w(t) + R(t)b_i(t-1)]$$
(S9.32)

where $R(t) = \alpha A k(t)^{\alpha-1}$ and $w(t) = (1-\alpha)Ak(t)^{\alpha}$, and aggregate capital-labor ratio evolves according to

$$k(t+1) = \frac{\beta}{1+\beta} f(k(t)).$$

Since all individuals earn the same wage, a natural measure of wealth distribution for generation t is is a distribution of initial assets $b_i(t-1)$, or equivalently, bequests left from the parents. To derive the result in the exercise, we need a measure of inequality given this wealth distribution. We consider the variance of the distribution as a natural measure of inequality and we claim that the inequality can increase away from steady state.

To construct a simple example, suppose initially that there are two bequest levels, that is, $b_i(-1) = \bar{b}_l$ for $i \in \mathcal{H}_l$ and $b_i(-1) = \bar{b}_h = 2\bar{b}_l$ for $i \in \mathcal{H}_h$. Let $\mathcal{H}_l$ and $\mathcal{H}_h$ each have measure $1/2$. The initial level of capital-labor ratio is $k(0) = 3\bar{b}_l/2$. Note that the sequence of bequests will be identical for all $i \in \mathcal{H}_l$, which we denote by $b_l(t)$, and will be identical for all $i \in \mathcal{H}_h$, which we denote by $b_h(t)$. By Eq. (S9.32), we have

$$
\begin{aligned}
b_j(1) &= \frac{\beta}{1+\beta}\left[(1-\alpha)Ak(0)^\alpha + \alpha Ak(0)^{\alpha-1}\bar{b}_j\right] & \text{(S9.33)} \\
&= \frac{\beta Ak(0)^{\alpha-1}}{1+\beta}\left[(1-\alpha)k(0) + \alpha\bar{b}_j\right] \\
&= \frac{\beta Ak(0)^{\alpha-1}}{1+\beta}\left[(1-\alpha)\frac{3\bar{b}_l}{2} + \alpha\bar{b}_j\right] \quad \text{for } j \in \{l,h\}.
\end{aligned}
$$

The variance of $[b_i(t)]_{i\in\mathcal{H}}$ is given by

$$
\begin{aligned}
var(t) &\equiv \frac{1}{2}\left(b_h(t) - \frac{b_h(t)+b_l(t)}{2}\right)^2 + \frac{1}{2}\left(b_l(t) - \frac{b_h(t)+b_l(t)}{2}\right)^2 \\
&= \left(\frac{b_h(t)-b_l(t)}{2}\right)^2
\end{aligned}
$$

Note that by Eq. (S9.33), we have

$$
var(0) = \frac{1}{4}\left(\bar{b}_h - \bar{b}_l\right)^2 \text{ and } var(1) = \frac{\beta Ak(0)^{\alpha-1}}{1+\beta}\frac{\alpha^2}{4}\left(\bar{b}_h - \bar{b}_l\right)^2,
$$

thus $var(1) > var(0)$ if and only if

$$
\beta Ak(0)^{\alpha-1}\alpha^2 > 1+\beta. \qquad \text{(S9.34)}
$$

Since $\alpha < 1$, the preceding inequality holds for sufficiently small $k(0) = 3\bar{b}_l/2$, i.e. for a sufficiently small choice of $\bar{b}_l$. Hence, the variance of the bequests may increase away from the steady state. Eq. (S9.34) shows that this is more likely for low levels of capital-labor ratio.

The economic intuition for this result is as follows. For low levels of capital-labor ratio, wages are relatively low, which implies that bequests constitute a relatively large portion of household wealth. Moreover, the interest rate is relatively high, which implies that even small bequest differences get amplified through asset returns (cf. Eq. (S9.32)). In view of these effects, wealth inequality may increase for low levels of capital-labor ratio.

Exercise 9.24*

We first derive an Euler-like equation in terms of the per capita consumption and the consumption of the newborn cohort. With log preferences, the Euler equation (9.36) of an individual of cohort τ at time t is

$$
\frac{c(t+1\mid\tau)}{c(t\mid\tau)} = \beta\left[(1+r(t+1))(1-\nu)+\nu\right], \qquad \text{(S9.35)}
$$

where recall that $r(t+1) = f'(k(t)) - 1$. Recall that at any time the share of the people aged $j \geq 0$ in the population is given by $\frac{n}{1+n-\nu}\left(\frac{1-\nu}{1+n-\nu}\right)^j$. Hence, we have

$$c(t) = \sum_{j=0}^{\infty} \frac{n}{1+n-\nu}\left(\frac{1-\nu}{1+n-\nu}\right)^j c(t \mid t-j),$$

where $c(t)$ denotes the per capita consumption t. Considering the same equation for $c(t+1)$ and using the Euler equation (S9.35) to write $c(t+1 \mid t-j)$ in terms of $c(t \mid t-j)$, we obtain an Euler-like equation

$$c(t+1) = \frac{n}{1+n-\nu}c(t+1 \mid t+1) + \frac{1-\nu}{1+n-\nu}\beta\left[(1+r(t+1))(1-\nu)+\nu\right]c(t). \quad \text{(S9.36)}$$

Next, we characterize the consumption of the newborn cohort $c(t \mid \tau)$ in terms of the per capita variables and obtain an Euler-like equation only in per capita variables. As usual log preferences imply that each cohort consumes a constant fraction of its lifetime wealth, in particular we have[5]

$$c(t \mid \tau) = (1 - \beta(1-\nu))\left[\omega(t) + (1+r(t))a(t \mid \tau)\right] \quad \text{(S9.37)}$$

where $\omega(t) = \sum_{t'=t}^{\infty} \frac{w(t')}{\prod_{s=t+1}^{t'} 1+r(s)+\frac{\nu}{1-\nu}}$ is the present discounted value of the future income of an individual. Aggregating Eq. (S9.37) over all cohorts $\tau \leq t+1$ that are alive at time $t+1$, we have

$$c(t+1) = (1 - \beta(1-\nu))\left[\omega(t+1) + (1+r(t+1))a(t+1)\right]. \quad \text{(S9.38)}$$

Using Eq. (S9.37) for the newborn cohort $t = \tau = t+1$ and noting that $a(t+1 \mid t+1) = 0$, we have

$$\begin{aligned}
c(t+1 \mid t+1) &= (1 - \beta(1-\nu))\omega(t+1) \\
&= c(t+1) - (1 - \beta(1-\nu))(1+r(t+1))a(t+1),
\end{aligned}$$

where the second line uses Eq. (S9.38). Note that the individuals in the newborn cohort consume less than average since they have no accumulated assets. Plugging the expression for $c(t+1 \mid t+1)$ in Eq. (S9.36), we have

$$\frac{c(t+1)}{c(t)} = \beta\left[(1+r(t+1))(1-\nu)+\nu\right] - \frac{n(1-\beta(1-\nu))}{1-\nu}(1+r(t+1))\frac{a(t+1)}{c(t)}, \quad \text{(S9.39)}$$

which is an Euler-like equation that contains only aggregated variables. Intuitively, consumption per capita grows at a slower rate than than what would be in a representative consumer economy due to the fact that newborns consume less than old cohorts, captured by the second term in Eq. (S9.39).

---

[5]To derive this expression, first note that the Euler equation (S9.35) implies

$$c(t' \mid \tau) = c(t \mid \tau)\beta^{t'-t}\prod_{s=t+1}^{t'}\left[(1+r(s))(1-\nu)+\nu\right]$$

for all $t' > t$. Second, note that summing the budget constraints (9.35) and using the transversality condition leads to the lifetime budget constraint for cohort τ at time t

$$\sum_{t'=t}^{\infty} \frac{c(t' \mid \tau)}{\prod_{s=t+1}^{t'} 1+r(s)+\frac{\nu}{1-\nu}} = \sum_{t'=t}^{\infty} \frac{w(t')}{\prod_{s=t+1}^{t'} 1+r(s)+\frac{\nu}{1-\nu}} + (1+r(t))a(t \mid \tau).$$

Plugging the above expression for $c(t' \mid \tau)$ in this budget constraint and solving for $c(t \mid \tau)$ leads to Eq. (S9.37).

Next, we characterize the equilibrium path in per capita variables, $[c(t), k(t)]_{t=0}^{\infty}$. Plugging in $r(t+1) = f'(k(t)) - 1$ and $a(t+1) = k(t+1)$, the previous displayed equation can be rewritten as

$$\frac{c(t+1)}{c(t)} = \beta\left[(f'(k(t)))(1-\nu) + \nu\right] - \frac{n(1-\beta(1-\nu))}{1-\nu}f'(k(t))\frac{k(t+1)}{c(t)}.$$

Note also that we have the resource constraint

$$c(t) + \frac{k(t+1)}{1+n-\nu} = f(k(t)) - k(t).$$

The last two equations and a transversality condition uniquely characterizes the path $[c(t), k(t)]_{t=0}^{\infty}$. Starting with any $k(t) \geq 0$, the equilibrium $[c(t), k(t)]_{t=0}^{\infty}$ converges to the steady state (c^*, k^*) solved from

$$\beta\left[(f'(k^*))(1-\nu) + \nu\right] - \frac{n(1-\beta(1-\nu))}{1-\nu}f'(k^*)\frac{k^*}{c^*} = 1$$

and $\qquad c^* + \dfrac{k^*}{1+n-\nu} = f(k^*) - k^*.$

Exercise 9.32*

Exercise 9.32, Part (b). We first obtain the analogue of the Euler-like equation (9.48) in aggregated variables for the case in which the labor income declines at rate $\zeta > 0$. We do this in two steps. First, we derive an equation that relates consumption growth $\dot{c}(t)$ to consumption per capita $c(t)$ and the consumption of the newborn cohort $c(t \mid t)$. Second, we characterize $c(t \mid t)$ in terms of the average per capita variables and obtain the analogue of Eq. (9.48).

To show the first step, note that the usual Euler equation applies for every cohort τ and gives

$$\dot{c}(t \mid \tau) = (r(t) - \rho) c(t \mid \tau). \tag{S9.40}$$

Moreover, we have

$$
\begin{aligned}
c(t) &= \int_{-\infty}^{t} c(t \mid \tau) \frac{L(t \mid \tau)}{L(t)} d\tau \\
&= \int_{-\infty}^{t} c(t \mid \tau) \lim_{t_{init} \to -\infty} \frac{n\exp(-\nu(t-\tau) + (n-\nu)(\tau - t_{init}))}{\exp((n-\nu)(t - t_{init}))} d\tau \\
&= \int_{-\infty}^{t} c(t \mid \tau) n\exp\left[-n(t-\tau)\right] d\tau, \tag{S9.41}
\end{aligned}
$$

where the second and third lines derive that the relative population of cohort τ, $L(t \mid \tau)/L(t)$, is equal to $n\exp\left[-n(t-\tau)\right]$. Differentiating Eq. (S9.41) with respect to t, and using the Leibniz' and the chain rules, we have

$$
\begin{aligned}
\dot{c}(t) &= nc(t \mid t) + \int_{-\infty}^{t} \dot{c}(t \mid \tau) n\exp(-n(t-\tau)) - nc(t \mid \tau)n\exp(-n(t-\tau)) d\tau. \\
&= n(c(t \mid t) - c(t)) + \int_{-\infty}^{t} \dot{c}(t \mid \tau) n\exp(-n(t-\tau)) d\tau \\
&= n(c(t \mid t) - c(t)) + \int_{-\infty}^{t} (r(t) - \rho) c(t \mid \tau) n\exp(-n(t-\tau)) d\tau \\
&= n(c(t \mid t) - c(t)) + (r(t) - \rho) c(t), \tag{S9.42}
\end{aligned}
$$

where the second and the fourth lines use Eq. (S9.41) and the third line uses Eq. (S9.40). Eq. (S9.42) characterizes the evolution of consumption per capita, $c(t)$, in terms of the consumption of the newborn cohort, $c(t \mid t)$, completing our step one. The usual Euler equation is distorted in Eq. (S9.42) by the term $(c(t \mid t) - c(t))$, which takes into account the fact the newborn cohort may consume differently than the average cohort.

As our second step, we characterize $c(t \mid t)$ in terms of aggregated (per capita) variables. Let

$$\underline{w}(t) = \int_t^\infty w(s) \exp\left(-\int_t^s \left(r(t') + \nu + \zeta\right) dt'\right) ds,$$

denote the net present discounted value of the newborn cohort, taking into account that the wages are declining at rate ζ. Note that the net present discounted value of the wages of cohort $\tau \le t$ is

$$\exp\left(-\zeta(t - \tau)\right) \underline{w}(t)$$

since the wages are declining at an exponential rate. The same arguments that leads to Eq. (9.45) (in particular, combining log utility, the Euler equation and the lifetime budget constraints) in this case imply

$$c(t \mid \tau) = (\rho + \nu)\left(a(t) + \exp\left(-\zeta(t - \tau)\right)\underline{w}(t)\right), \tag{S9.43}$$

that is, the individuals of cohort τ consume a constant fraction of their lifetime wealth. Aggregating the previous displayed equation over all cohorts $\tau \le t$ and using $L(t \mid \tau)/L(t) = n \exp\left[-n(t - \tau)\right]$, we have

$$\begin{aligned} c(t) &= (\rho + \nu)\left(a(t) + \left[\int_{-\infty}^t n \exp\left[-n(t-\tau)\right] \exp\left(-\zeta(t-\tau)\right) d\tau\right]\underline{w}(t)\right) \\ &= (\rho + \nu)\left(a(t) + \frac{n}{n+\zeta}\underline{w}(t)\right). \end{aligned} \tag{S9.44}$$

Considering Eq. (S9.43) for $\tau = t$, we have

$$\begin{aligned} c(t \mid t) &= (\rho + \nu)\underline{w}(t) \\ &= \left[c(t) - (\rho + \nu)a(t)\right]\frac{n+\zeta}{n}, \end{aligned} \tag{S9.45}$$

where the last line uses Eq. (S9.44). Eq. (S9.45) characterizes $c(t \mid t)$ in terms of aggregated variables, completing our step two. Note that in contrast with the text (and Exercise 9.24) the comparison between $c(t \mid t)$ and $c(t)$ is ambiguous. On the one hand, the newborn cohort has less accumulated wealth which tends to reduce $c(t \mid t)$. On the other hand, the newborn cohort has a higher present value of wage income (captured by ζ in Eq. (S9.45)) which tends to increase $c(t \mid t)$.

We next combine our findings in steps one and two to obtain an Euler-like equation in aggregated variables. Plugging this expression for $c(t \mid t)$ in Eq. (S9.42) and substituting $a(t) = k(t)$, we obtain

$$\frac{\dot{c}(t)}{c(t)} = f'(k(t)) - \delta - \rho + \zeta - (n + \zeta)(\rho + \nu)\frac{k(t)}{c(t)}, \tag{S9.46}$$

which is the analogue of Eq. (9.48) as desired. The intuition behind Eq. (S9.46) is similar to the intuition for Eq. (9.48) provided in the text. The term with $k(t)/c(t)$ on the right hand side captures the decline in consumption growth due to the arrival of new cohorts that have below-average asset holdings. The present model also features a counter force (captured by ζ) which pushes up consumption growth.

The equilibrium path of $(c(t), k(t))_{t=0}^{\infty}$ in this model is characterized by Eq. (S9.46), the capital accumulation equation (9.42), and the transversality condition (9.44). A steady state equilibrium (c^*, k^*) is found by solving $\dot{c}(t) = 0$ and $\dot{k}(t) = 0$, hence it satisfies

$$\frac{f(k^*)}{k^*} - (n + \delta - \nu) - \frac{(n + \zeta)(\rho + \nu)}{f'(k^*) - \delta - \rho + \zeta} = 0, \qquad \text{(S9.47)}$$

which is a generalization of Eq. (9.50). Next, we claim that there exists $\zeta > 0$ sufficiently high such that $k^* > k_{gold}$, that is, overaccumulation of capital is possible in this model. Note that we have $f'(k^*) > \delta + \rho - \zeta$, which shows $k^* < k_{mgr}$ when $\zeta = 0$. However, when $\zeta > 0$ it is possible to have $k_{mgr} < k^*$. More strongly, we claim that it is possible to have $k^* > k_{gold} > k_{mgr}$. To see this, let the production function take the Cobb-Douglas form $f(k) = k^{\alpha}$ and consider the parameters

$$\alpha = 1/5, \ n = 0.01, \nu = 0, \zeta = 10, \rho = 0.02, \delta = 0.01.$$

The solution to Eq. (S9.47) gives $k^* = 54.38$, while we have $k_{gold} = f'^{-1}(\delta + n - \nu) = 17.78, k_{mgr} = f'^{-1}(\delta + \rho) = 10.71$, hence k^* is larger than both the golden rule and the modified golden rule capital-labor ratios.

The economic intuition is as follows. With a large ζ, each household has a declining income stream and thus a strong motive for saving. More specifically, an increase in the interest rate reduces the lifetime wealth of the household which in turn (given the log utility) reduces their consumption and increases their savings. With a strong motive to save and overlapping generations, the equilibrium capital-labor ratio may increase beyond the dynamically efficient level. This exercise then emphasizes that, in the baseline OLG model, the assumption that individuals work only when they are young plays an important role in generating dynamic inefficiency (see also Blanchard (1985) and Blanchard and Fischer (1989)).

Chapter 10: Human Capital and Economic Growth

Exercise 10.2

Exercise 10.2, Part (a). The basic tension in the case of credit market imperfections is that the individual may have high wage payments in the future which she cannot borrow against. The desire to smooth consumption can therefore affect an individual's schooling choice. Hence, to provide a counterexample we have to find a solution to the individual's problem with credit constraints which does not maximize the lifetime budget set. Let us again assume that the individual takes the process of wages $[w(t)]_{t=0}^T$ as given. Furthermore assume for simplicity that there is no non-human capital labor supply, i.e. $\omega(t) = 0$ for all t. The problem the individual has to solve is the following:

$$\max_{\{[c(t)]_{t=0}^T, [s(t)]_{t=0}^T\}} \int_0^T \exp(-(\rho + \nu)t)u(c(t))dt$$

$$\begin{aligned}
\text{s.t.} \quad \dot{h}(t) &= G(t, h(t), s(t)) \\
s(t) &\in [0, 1] \\
\dot{a}(t) &= ra(t) - c(t) + w(t)h(t)(1 - s(t)) \\
a(t) &\geq 0.
\end{aligned}$$

Let us assume that the accumulation equation of human capital takes the form of the Ben-Porath model, i.e.

$$\dot{h}(t) = \phi(h(t)s(t)) - \delta_h h(t). \tag{S10.1}$$

We can characterize the solution by studying the current value Hamiltonian

$$\begin{aligned}
\hat{H}^U(h, s, c, \mu, \eta) = {}& u(c(t)) + \eta(t)(\phi(h(t)s(t)) - \delta_h h(t)) + \\
& \mu(t)(ra(t) - c(t) + w(t)h(t)(1 - s(t))) + \chi(t)a(t) + \xi(t)(1 - s(t)),
\end{aligned}$$

where we for simplicity ignored the $s(t) \geq 0$ constraint on schooling expenditures (by imposing some Inada-type conditions on ϕ this will be satisfied automatically). Furthermore, $\mu(t)$ and $\eta(t)$ are the multipliers on the two accumulation equations and $\chi(t)$ and $\xi(t)$ are the multiplier on the borrowing constraint and the remaining constraint on schooling expenditures. The necessary conditions for this problem are given by

$$\begin{aligned}
\hat{H}_c^U &= u'(c(t)) - \mu(t) = 0 && \text{(S10.2)} \\
\hat{H}_s^U &= \eta(t)\phi'(h(t)s(t))h(t) = \mu(t)w(t)h(t) + \xi(t) && \text{(S10.3)} \\
\hat{H}_a^U &= r\mu(t) + \chi(t) = -\dot{\mu}(t) + (\rho + \nu)\mu(t) && \text{(S10.4)} \\
\hat{H}_h^U &= \eta(t)(\phi'(h(t)s(t))s(t) - \delta_h) + w(t)(1 - s(t)) = -\dot{\eta}(t) + (\rho + \nu)\eta(t). && \text{(S10.5)}
\end{aligned}$$

107

Now consider the problem of maximizing life time earnings. This problem is given by

$$\max_{\{[s(t)]_{t=0}^{T}\}} \int_0^T \exp(-rt)w(t)h(t)(1-s(t))dt$$

$$\text{s.t. } \dot{h}(t) = \phi(h(t)s(t)) - \delta_h h(t)$$
$$s(t) \in [0,1],$$

and the corresponding current value Hamiltonian

$$\hat{H}^{LTI}(h,s,\eta) = w(t)h(t)(1-s(t)) + \eta_L(t)(\phi(h(t)s(t)) - \delta_h h(t)) + \xi_L(t)(1-s(t)),$$

where the superscript LTI indicates that this current value Hamiltonian refers to the problem of maximizing life-time earnings (instead of utility). Again we neglected the $s(t) \geq 0$ constraint for simplicity. The two multipliers $\eta_L(t)$ and $\xi_L(t)$ are the multipliers on the accumulation equation and the constraint $s(t) \leq 0$ and the subscript L indicates that they refer to the problem of maximizing life-time earning. The necessary conditions for this problem are

$$\hat{H}_s^{LTI} = -w(t)h(t) + \eta_L(t)\phi'(h(t)s(t))h(t) - \xi_L(t) = 0 \tag{S10.6}$$
$$\hat{H}_h^{LTI} = \eta_L(t)(\phi'(h(t)s(t))s(t) - \delta_h) + w(t)(1-s(t)) = -\dot{\eta}_L(t) + r\eta_L(t). \tag{S10.7}$$

To show that Theorem 10.1 does not necessarily hold in the case of credit constraints, suppose to arrive at a contradiction that it does, i.e. that the two problems have the same solution $[\hat{s}(t)]_{t=0}^{T}$. Let us furthermore suppose that $r = \rho + n$ and that ϕ is such that $\hat{s}(t) < 1$ so that $\xi_L(t) = \xi(t) = 0$. Note that given $h(0)$ and $[\hat{s}(t)]_{t=0}^{T}$ the entire path $[h(t)]_{t=0}^{T}$ is determined by (S10.1). Then it follows from (S10.7) and (S10.5) that $\eta(t) = \eta_L(t)$, i.e. the multipliers on the human capital accumulation constraints are the same. From and (S10.3) and (S10.6) we get that

$$\mu(t) = \frac{\eta(t)\phi'(h(t)\hat{s}(t))h(t)}{w(t)h(t)} = \frac{\eta_L(t)\phi'(h(t)\hat{s}(t))h(t)}{w(t)h(t)} = 1,$$

so that consumption will be constant (see (S10.2)) and credit constraint will never bind, i.e. $\chi(t) = 0$ (from (S10.4)). Note that this solution made no reference to the initial asset level $a(0)$.

But now suppose that wages are increasing over time. For consumption to be constant and the budget constraint to be satisfied, we then need that

$$c(0) > w(0).$$

In particular consider a solution where $c(0) > w(0)h(0)$. This is clearly possible if $h(0)$ and $w(0)$ are small enough. Assuming that initial assets are zero, the capital accumulation equation implies that

$$\dot{a}(0) = w(0)h(0)(1-\hat{s}(0)) - c(0) < w(0)h(0) - c(0) < 0,$$

so that the borrowing constraint is violated. This yields a contradiction and shows that the conclusion of Theorem 10.1 does not apply in this example.

To see that this result does not hinge on the *inability* to borrow, let us now suppose that credit market imperfections are such that the borrowing rate r' exceeds the lending rate r. In this case, the capital accumulation equation for the individual is given by

$$\dot{a}(t) = ra(t) - c(t) + w(t)h(t)(1-s(t)) + (r'-r)a(t)\mathbf{1}\{a(t)<0\},$$

where $\mathbf{1}\{.\}$ is an indicator variable. Using this constraint in the current value Hamiltonian above, the corresponding first-order condition (S10.4) is now given by

$$\left(r + (r' - r)\mathbf{1}\{a(t) < 0\}\right)\mu(t) = -\dot{\mu}(t) + (\rho + \nu)\mu(t).$$

Using the parametric assumption $r = \rho + \nu$, this can be written as

$$(r' - r)\mathbf{1}\{a(t) < 0\}\mu(t) = -\dot{\mu}(t). \tag{S10.8}$$

But this yields a similar contradiction. By the same argument as above, if the solution is the same and involves $0 < \hat{s}(t) < 1$, the multiplier on the asset accumulation $\mu(t)$ should be constant and non-zero. This however is inconsistent with (S10.8) as long as there exits some t where along the solution the consumer needs to acquire debt. Hence, the example above shows that Theorem 10.1 does not apply in case the lending rate does not equal the borrowing rate.

Exercise 10.2, Part (b). To find an example where a nontrivial leisure choice violates Theorem 10.1 is relatively easy. Let us denote leisure by $l(t)$. Note first, that the solution to the problem of maximizing life-time earnings will involve $l(t) = 0$, i.e. leisure "expenses" will be set to zero throughout. But now suppose for concreteness that the instantaneous utility function $u(c(t), l(t))$ takes the Cobb-Douglas form

$$u_2(c, l) = c^{\alpha}l^{1-\alpha}.$$

To arrive at the contradiction that the solution for schooling $s(t)$ will be the same, note that the necessary conditions for the problem to maximize lifetime earnings are still given by (S10.6) and (S10.7), whereas for the consumer's problem we now have the additional intratemporal necessary condition, i.e. consumption and leisure are chosen to satisfy

$$u_c(c(t), l(t)) = \mu(t) \tag{S10.9}$$
$$u_l(c(t), l(t)) = \mu(t)w(t)h(t)\left(1 - s(t)\right). \tag{S10.10}$$

By the same argument as above, if the solutions to those problems are the same, $\mu(t)$ needs to be constant over time, i.e. $\mu(t) = \mu^*$. From (S10.9) this implies that

$$\mu(t) = \mu^* = u_c(c(t), l(t)) = \alpha\left(\frac{l(t)}{c(t)}\right)^{1-\alpha},$$

so that $\frac{l(t)}{c(t)}$ needs be constant. But (S10.10) requires that

$$u_l(c(t), l(t)) = (1 - \alpha)\left(\frac{c(t)}{l(t)}\right)^{\alpha} = \mu(t)w(t)h(t)\left(1 - s(t)\right) = \mu^*w(t)h(t)\left(1 - s(t)\right),$$

so that so that $w(t)h(t)\left(1 - s(t)\right)$ has to be constant. However, wages are exogenous so that there is no reason why this should be true in general, i.e. irrespective of $[w(t)]_{t=0}^T$ and the functional form ϕ. This yields the required contradiction and shows that Theorem 10.1 will not be true once we allow for a nontrivial leisure choice.

Exercise 10.6

We are going to prove this result with a constructive proof, that is we are going to show that the path conjectured in the exercise statement will indeed solve the necessary and sufficient conditions of the problem. So let us first derive those conditions. The current value Hamiltonian for this problem is given by

$$\hat{H}(s, h, \mu) = (1 - s(t))h(t) + \mu(t)[\phi(h(t))s(t) - \delta_h h(t)] + \xi_0(t)s(t) + \xi_1(t)(1 - s(t)),$$

where $\xi_0(t)$ and $\xi_1(t)$ are the multipliers on the constraints $0 \le s(t) \le 1$. The necessary conditions are then given by

$$\hat{H}_s(s, h, \mu) = -h(t) + \mu(t)\phi(h(t)) + \xi_0(t) - \xi_1(t) = 0 \qquad \text{(S10.11)}$$

$$\hat{H}_h(s, h, \mu) = 1 - s(t) + \mu(t)(s(t)\phi'(h(t)) - \delta_h) = (r + v)\mu(t) - \dot{\mu}(t), \quad \text{(S10.12)}$$

and the complementary slackness conditions

$$0 = \xi_0(t)s(t) = \xi_1(t)(1 - s(t)) \text{ and } \xi_0(t), \xi_1(t), s(t), (1 - s(t)) \ge 0. \qquad \text{(S10.13)}$$

Together with the transversality condition

$$\lim_{T \to \infty} [\exp(-(r + v)T)\mu(T)h(T)] = 0$$

those conditions are also sufficient to characterize the solution.

Hence let us conjecture there exists $T > 0$ such that $s(t) \in (0, 1)$ for all $t \ge T$, i.e. starting at T the schooling choice will be interior. Along such a solution (S10.13) implies that

$$\xi_0(t) = \xi_1(t) \quad \text{for all } t \ge T$$

so that (S10.11) yields

$$h(t) = \mu(t)\phi(h(t)) \quad \text{for all } t \ge T. \qquad \text{(S10.14)}$$

Differentiating this condition with respect to time and using the law of motion

$$\dot{h}(t) = s(t)\phi(h(t)) - \delta_h h(t) \qquad \text{(S10.15)}$$

we get that for all $t \ge T$

$$\begin{aligned}
\frac{\dot{\mu}(t)}{\mu(t)} &= \frac{\dot{h}(t)}{h(t)}\left(1 - \frac{\phi'(h(t))h(t)}{\phi(h(t))}\right) \\
&= \frac{s(t)\phi(h(t)) - \delta_h h(t)}{h(t)}\left(1 - \frac{\phi'(h(t))h(t)}{\phi(h(t))}\right) \\
&= \frac{s(t)\phi(h(t))}{h(t)} - s(t)\phi'(h(t)) - \delta_h + \delta_h \frac{\phi'(h(t))h(t)}{\phi(h(t))}.
\end{aligned} \qquad \text{(S10.16)}$$

Furthermore, (S10.12) implies that

$$\begin{aligned}
\frac{\dot{\mu}(t)}{\mu(t)} &= \delta_h + r + v - \frac{1 - s(t)}{\mu(t)} - s(t)\phi'(h(t)) \\
&= \delta_h + r + v - \frac{(1 - s(t))\phi(h(t))}{h(t)} - s(t)\phi'(h(t)),
\end{aligned} \qquad \text{(S10.17)}$$

where the second lines used (S10.14). From (S10.16) and (S10.17) we therefore get

$$\delta_h\left(1 - \frac{\phi'(h(t))h(t)}{\phi(h(t))}\right) = \frac{\phi(h(t))}{h(t)} - (\delta_h + r + v) \quad \text{for all } t \ge T. \qquad \text{(S10.18)}$$

Note that any *interior* solution of $s(t)$ has to satisfy the relationship contained in (S10.18). Obviously, the above does not depend on $s(t)$ directly. And as (S10.18) has to hold for all $t \ge T$, under regularity conditions on $h(.)$ there exists a unique $h(t) = h^*$, i.e. $h(t)$ is constant for all $t \ge T$. Using $\dot{h}(t) = 0$ however, we can directly pin down the level of schooling expenditures $s(t)$ from the law of motion. Using (S10.15), it is given by

$$s(t) = \frac{\delta_h h(t)}{\phi(h(t))} = \frac{\delta_h h^*}{\phi(h^*)} = s^*, \qquad \text{(S10.19)}$$

where we assume that δ_h and the function ϕ are such that $s^* < 1$. This shows that whenever $s(t)$ is interior it actually has to be constant and equal to s^*.

Let us now turn to the behavior of the system for $t \in [0, T)$. We conjecture the following solution. Starting from $h(0) < h^*$ the path $[h(t), \mu(t), s(t)]_{t=0}^T$ satisfies the necessary conditions above and satisfies $h(T) = h^*$ and $\mu(T) = \mu^*$, where h^* solves (S10.18) and μ^* is given by (see (S10.14))

$$\mu^* = \frac{h^*}{\phi(h^*)} \qquad (S10.20)$$

and has $s(t) = 1$ for all $t \in [0, T)$. Using (S10.11), (S10.12), (S10.13) and (S10.15) this path is characterized by

$$0 = -h(t) + \mu(t)\phi(h(t)) - \xi_1(t) < -h(t) + \mu(t)\phi(h(t)) \qquad (S10.21)$$

$$\frac{\dot{\mu}(t)}{\mu(t)} = \delta_h + r + v - \phi'(h(t)) \qquad (S10.22)$$

$$\dot{h}(t) = \phi(h(t)) - \delta_h h(t). \qquad (S10.23)$$

So what is the joint evolution of $h(t)$ and $\mu(t)$ as implied by (S10.21)-(S10.23)? Let us suppose that $h(0) = h_0 < h^*$ and consider first (S10.23) which determines the evolution of $h(t)$ irrespective of $[\mu(t)]_{t=0}^T$. Note especially that (S10.23) has exactly the same structure as the capital accumulation equation of the Solow growth model. Hence $[h(t)]_{t=0}^\infty$ as implied by (S10.23) will be monotonically increasing towards its steady state value $\tilde{h}$, where $\tilde{h}$ is implicitly defined by

$$\frac{\phi(\tilde{h})}{\tilde{h}} = \delta_h. \qquad (S10.24)$$

We now claim that $\tilde{h} > h^*$. To see this, simply observe from (S10.19) and (S10.24) that

$$\frac{\phi(h^*)}{h^*} = \frac{\delta_h}{s^*} = \frac{1}{s^*} \frac{\phi(\tilde{h})}{\tilde{h}} > \frac{\phi(\tilde{h})}{\tilde{h}},$$

where the last inequality follows from the fact that $s^* < 1$. But as $\phi(.)$ is concave, it is clear that $\frac{\phi(h)}{h}$ is decreasing in h so that $h^* < \tilde{h}$ as required. It then follows that we can choose T such that $[h(t)]_{t=0}^T$ is governed by (S10.23) and satisfies

$$h(T) = h^*.$$

Note in particular that $h(t)$ increases over time.

Let us now turn to the behavior of $[\mu(t)]_{t=0}^\infty$ as governed by (S10.22). First of all observe that we can solve for $\mu(t)$ as

$$\mu(t) = \mu(0) \exp\left(\int_0^t [\delta_h + r + v - \phi'(h(s))] \, ds\right).$$

This shows that $\mu(t)$ is a decreasing function of the initial starting value $\mu(0)$, which is a free variable. Hence for any $[h(t)]_{t=0}^T$, there exists a unique $\mu(0)$ such that $\mu(T) = \mu^*$. In particular, this $\mu(0)$ is given by

$$\mu(0) = \mu^* \exp\left(-\int_0^T [\delta_h + r + v - \phi'(h(s))] \, ds\right).$$

The two paths $[h(t), \mu(t)]_{t=0}^T$ therefore satisfy $h(T) = h^*$ and $\mu(T) = \mu^*$ and the initial condition $h(0) = h_0$. We therefore just have to establish that $[h(t), \mu(t)]_{t=0}^T$ also satisfy the first-order condition (S10.21), i.e. satisfy

$$-h(t) + \mu(t)\phi(h(t)) = h(t)\left(\frac{\phi(h(t))}{h(t)}\mu(t) - 1\right) \geq 0.$$

First of all note that

$$\mu(T)\frac{\phi(h(T))}{h(T)} = \mu^*\frac{\phi(h^*)}{h^*} = 1 \qquad (\text{S10.25})$$

as seen in (S10.20). But now note that using (S10.22) and (S10.23) we get that

$$\frac{d}{dt}\left[\mu(t)\frac{\phi(h(t))}{h(t)}\right] = \dot{\mu}(t)\frac{\phi(h(t))}{h(t)} + \mu(t)\frac{\phi'(h(t))h(t) - \phi(h(t))}{h(t)^2}\dot{h}(t)$$

$$= \mu(t)\frac{\phi(h(t))}{h(t)}\left[\frac{\dot{\mu}(t)}{\mu(t)} + \frac{\phi'(h(t))h(t) - \phi(h(t))}{\phi(h(t))}\frac{\dot{h}(t)}{h(t)}\right]$$

$$= \mu(t)\frac{\phi(h(t))}{h(t)}\left[\delta_h + r + v - \frac{\phi(h(t))}{h(t)} + \delta_h\left(1 - \frac{\phi'(h(t))h(t)}{\phi(h(t))}\right)\right].$$

From (S10.18) we know that

$$\delta_h + r + v = \frac{\phi(h^*)}{h^*} - \delta_h\left(1 - \frac{\phi'(h^*)h^*}{\phi(h^*)}\right).$$

Substituting this above yields

$$\frac{d}{dt}\left[\mu(t)\frac{\phi(h(t))}{h(t)}\right] = \mu(t)\frac{\phi(h(t))}{h(t)}\left[\frac{\phi(h^*)}{h^*} - \frac{\phi(h(t))}{h(t)} + \delta_h\left(\frac{\phi'(h^*)h^*}{\phi(h^*)} - \frac{\phi'(h(t))h(t)}{\phi(h(t))}\right)\right].$$
$$(\text{S10.26})$$

Now note that

$$\frac{\phi(h^*)}{h^*} < \frac{\phi(h(t))}{h(t)}$$

as $\frac{\phi(h)}{h}$ is decreasing in h and $h(t) \leq h^*$ for all $t \leq T$. Additionally let us assume that $\frac{\phi'(h)h}{\phi(h)}$ is also nonincreasing in h. Note that this does not follow from concavity of ϕ, but is for example satisfied if $\phi(h) = h^\gamma$. Under this assumption (S10.26) implies that

$$\frac{d}{dt}\left[\mu(t)\frac{\phi(h(t))}{h(t)}\right] \leq 0,$$

i.e. for all $t \leq T$

$$\mu(t)\frac{\phi(h(t))}{h(t)} \geq \mu^*\frac{\phi(h^*)}{h^*} = 1,$$

where the last equality uses (S10.25). This shows that the paths $[h(t), \mu(t)]_{t=0}^T$ also satisfies the first-order condition in (S10.21).

These two characterizations also describe the entire solution. We found paths $[h(t), \mu(t), s(t)]_{t=0}^\infty$ with the following properties. $h(t)$ is increasing for $t \in [0, T]$, satisfies $h(T) = h^*$ and stays constant at h^* thereafter. $\mu(t)$ is decreasing for $t \in [0, T]$, satisfies $\mu(T) = \mu^*$ and stays constant thereafter. And $s(t)$ is given by

$$s(t) = \begin{cases} 1 & \text{if } t < T \\ s^* & \text{if } t \geq T \end{cases}.$$

We showed that this part satisfied all the necessary conditions of the problem. Additionally we have that

$$\lim_{T\to\infty}[\exp(-(r+v)T)\mu(T)h(T)] = \mu^*h^*\lim_{T\to\infty}[\exp(-(r+v)T)] = 0$$

so that the transversality condition is also satisfied along the conjectured path. Hence the conjectured path satisfies the necessary and sufficient conditions for this problem and therefore is a solution as required.

Note we made the assumption (which seems natural in this context) that $h(0) < h^*$. The case $h(0) > h^*$ would be similar in the sense that the optimal plan would involve some period $[0, T]$ where no schooling investment would be conducted so that human capital $h(t)$ would depreciate over time. Once the critical level of human capital h^* is reached, schooling investment would again be constant. In the context of human capital accumulation however, this seems to be a counterfactual case (as you would have been able to solve this problem in elementary school but then decided to let your optimal control skills depreciate to make grad school a more thrilling experience).

Exercise 10.7

Exercise 10.7, Part (a). If we modify the Ben-Porath (1967) model along the lines suggested in the exercise, the maximization problem is given by

$$\max_{[s(t)]_{t=0}^T} \int_0^T \exp(-(r+\nu)t)(1-s(t))h(t)dt \qquad (S10.27)$$

$$\text{s.t. } \dot{h}(t) = \phi(s(t)h(t)) - \delta_h h(t)$$
$$s(t) \in [0,1].$$

To characterize the solution of this problem, we can directly apply the Maximum Principle, which we encountered in Chapter 7. In Theorem 7.4 we saw that the necessary conditions could be derived from the Hamiltonian, which in this example takes the form

$$H(t, s(t), h(t), \lambda(t)) = \exp(-(r+\nu)t)(1-s(t))h(t) + \lambda(t)(\phi(s(t)h(t)) - \delta_h h(t))$$
$$+ \xi_0(t)s(t) + \xi_1(t)(1-s(t))$$

where $\xi_0(t)$ and $\xi_1(t)$ are the respective multipliers on the constraint $s(t) \in [0,1]$. As $s(t)$ refers to the control and $h(t)$ to the state variable, the necessary conditions are given by

$$H_s = -\exp(-(r+\nu)t)h(t) + \lambda(t)\phi'(s(t)h(t))h(t) + \xi_0(t) - \xi_1(t) = 0 \quad (S10.28)$$
$$H_h = \exp(-(r+\nu)t)(1-s(t)) + \lambda(t)(\phi'(s(t)h(t))s(t) - \delta_h) = -\dot{\lambda}(t), \quad (S10.29)$$

and the complementary slackness condition

$$0 = \xi_0(t)s(t) = \xi_1(t)(1-s(t)) \text{ and } \xi_0(t), \xi_1(t), s(t), (1-s(t)) \geq 0.$$

Together with the boundary condition

$$\lambda(T)h(T) = 0 \qquad (S10.30)$$

these conditions are necessary and sufficient. An interior solution $0 < s(t) < 1$ is then characterized by (S10.28) and (S10.29) with $\xi_0(t) = \xi_1(t) = 0$.

Exercise 10.7, Part (b). In contrast to formally introduce such multiplier and solve the problem explicitly we will take another route that turns out to be convenient in many economic problems. In order to characterize the behavior of the solution we will show that assuming an interior solution throughout will lead to a contradiction. Another way would be to consider a constructive proof, i.e. to show that there exists a plan with the required properties that would satisfy the necessary and sufficient conditions for an optimum. For a formal analysis along that route we refer to Exercise 10.6.

To achieve the desired contradiction, suppose there was an interior solution. If so, then the conditions provided above would be satisfied with $\xi_0(t) = \xi_1(t) = 0$. The first necessary condition (S10.28) can then be solved for

$$\exp(-(r+\nu)t) = \lambda(t)\phi'(s(t)h(t)).$$ (S10.31)

Substituting this into the second one (S10.29), we get that

$$
\begin{aligned}
\dot{\lambda}(t) &= -\exp(-(r+\nu)t)(1-s(t)) - \lambda(t)(\phi'(s(t)h(t))s(t) - \delta_h) \\
&= -\exp(-(r+\nu)t)(1-s(t)) - \lambda(t)(\frac{\exp(-(r+\nu)t)}{\lambda(t)}s(t) - \delta_h) \\
&= -\exp(-(r+\nu)t) + \lambda(t)\delta_h.
\end{aligned}
$$ (S10.32)

Solving the differential equation yields

$$\exp(-\delta_h T)\lambda(T) - \lambda(0) = \frac{1}{\delta_h + r + \nu}\left[\exp(-(\delta_h + r + \nu)T) - 1\right].$$

Using the boundary condition $\lambda(T) = 0$ (which follows from (S10.30)) we get that

$$\lambda(0) = \frac{1}{\delta_h + r + \nu}\left[1 - \exp(-(\delta_h + r + \nu)T)\right].$$ (S10.33)

Note however that the set of necessary conditions has to hold at all t, in particular at $t = 0$. Hence, (S10.33) and (S10.31) together imply that

$$\frac{1}{\delta_h + r + \nu}\left[1 - \exp(-(\delta_h + r + \nu)T)\right]\phi'(s(0)h(0))) = 1,$$

which yields

$$\phi'(s(0)h(0))) = \frac{\delta_h + r + \nu}{[1 - \exp(-(\delta_h + r + \nu)T)]}.$$ (S10.34)

Now note that ϕ is concave so that (S10.34) implies that

$$\frac{\delta_h + r + \nu}{[1 - \exp(-(\delta_h + r + \nu)T)]} = \phi'(s(0)h(0))) > \phi'(h(0))),$$

which contradicts the parametric assumption[1]

$$\phi'(h(0))) > \frac{\delta_h + r + \nu}{[1 - \exp(-(\delta_h + r + \nu)T)]}.$$ (S10.35)

The necessary condition for an interior solution is therefore not satisfied at $t = 0$ contradicting our assumption that $s(t)$ is interior throughout. To argue that schooling expenditures $s(t)$ will actually be zero for some time *before* T, suppose that this is not the case. This implies that the necessary condition (S10.28) holds at $T - \Delta$, i.e.

$$\lambda(T - \Delta) = \frac{\exp(-(r+\nu)(T - \Delta))}{\phi'(s(T - \Delta)h(T - \Delta))} > 0,$$

which follows from our assumption that $\phi'(s(T-\Delta)h(T-\Delta)) < \infty$. As this inequality holds for Δ and λ is continuous, this also implies that

$$\lim_{\Delta \to 0} \lambda(T - \Delta) = \lambda(T) = \lim_{\Delta \to 0} \frac{\exp(-(r+\nu)(T - \Delta))}{\phi'(s(T - \Delta)h(T - \Delta))} = \frac{\exp(-(r+\nu)T)}{\phi'(0)} > 0,$$

which violates the boundary condition in (S10.30). Hence there exists some $\varepsilon > 0$ such that $s(t) = 0$ for all $t \in (T - \varepsilon, T]$. Up to now we have shown that schooling will necessarily be set

---

[1]Note that there is a little typo in the exercise statement. The appropriate discount rate is given by $\delta_h + r + v$ and not δ_h so that the right parametric condition is given in (S10.35).

at a corner solution at the beginning of life and at the end. Now it only remains to be shown the $s(t)$ takes intermediate values in some time interval $[t_1, t_2]$. From (S10.28) we know that

$$-\exp(-(r+\nu)t)h(t) + \lambda(t)\phi'(s(t)h(t))h(t) + \xi_0(t) - \xi_1(t) = 0.$$

Now suppose $s(t)$ is always chosen to be at a corner. In that case there is some t_0 such that $s(t) = 1$ for $t \le t_0$ and $s(t) = 0$ for $t > t_0$. The respective multipliers are strictly positive in case the constraint binds and zero otherwise. Hence this implies

$$0 \; < \; -\exp(-(r+\nu)t_0)h(t_0) + \lambda(t_0)\phi'(h(t_0))h(t_0)$$
$$0 \; > \; -\exp(-(r+\nu)(t_0+\Delta))h((t_0+\Delta)) + \lambda((t_0+\Delta))\phi'(0)h((t_0+\Delta))$$

Taking the limit $\Delta \to 0$, these two conditions yield

$$\phi'(h(t_0))h(t_0) > \phi'(0)h(t_0).$$

This however is a contradiction as $h(t_0) > 0$ so that

$$\phi'(0) > \phi'(h(t_0))$$

by the concavity of ϕ. Hence there is some interval $[t_1, t_2]$ where schooling $s(t)$ is interior.

Exercise 10.7, Part (c). As wages are normalized to $w = 1$, per period earnings are given by $y(t) = (1 - s(t))h(t)$. The law of motion of earnings is therefore given by

$$
\begin{aligned}
\dot{y}(t) &= (1 - s(t))\dot{h}(t) - \dot{s}(t)h(t) \\
&= (1 - s(t))\phi(s(t)h(t)) - (1 - s(t))\delta_h h(t) - \dot{s}(t)h(t),
\end{aligned}
$$

where $s(t)$ is the solution of the consumer's problem. We showed above that there are three cases to consider. In the beginning of life, the individual will invest her entire time endowment into her schooling choice so that $s(t) = 1$ for all $t \in [0, t')$. Hence it is clear that $y(t) = 0$ for all $t \in [0, t')$. Secondly we showed that there is some $\varepsilon > 0$ such that $s(t) = 0$ for all $t \in (T - \varepsilon, T]$ so that the above yields $y(t) = h(t)$ for all $t \in (T - \varepsilon, T]$ Hence,

$$\dot{y}(t) = \dot{h}(t) = \phi(0) - \delta_h h(t) \qquad \text{for all } t \in (T - \varepsilon, T],$$

i.e. during this last time interval $(T - \varepsilon, T]$, earnings (and human capital) depreciate. If we assume that $\phi(0) = 0$ (i.e. you need some schooling or training to accumulate human capital), earnings depreciate geometrically at the rate δ_h. So what about the middle interval $[t', T - \varepsilon]$ where the schooling choice is interior? Clearly for all $t \in [t', T - \varepsilon]$, the two necessary conditions (S10.28) and (S10.29) have to hold. From (S10.32) we can again solve the differential equation for λ to arrive at

$$\lambda(t) = \frac{1}{\delta_h + r + \nu}\exp(-(r+\nu)(t - t')) + \exp(\delta_h(t - t'))\left[\lambda(t') - \frac{1}{\delta_h + r + \nu}\right],$$

whenever $t \in [t', T - \varepsilon]$. By using (S10.28) again, an interior solution satisfies

$$1 = \left(\frac{1}{\delta_h + r + \nu} + \exp((r+\nu+\delta_h)(t - t'))\left[\lambda(t') - \frac{1}{\delta_h + r + \nu}\right]\right)\phi'(s(t)h(t)). \quad \text{(S10.36)}$$

To simplify the notation, let us define $x(t) = s(t)h(t)$. As (S10.36) has to hold for all $t \in [t', T - \varepsilon]$ we can differentiate with respect to time to get

$$\dot{x}(t) = -\frac{\phi'(x(t))\exp(\kappa(t - t'))\kappa}{\phi''(x(t))}\frac{\lambda(t') - \kappa^{-1}}{\kappa^{-1} + \exp(\kappa(t - t'))(\lambda(t') - \kappa^{-1})}, \quad \text{(S10.37)}$$

where $\kappa \equiv r + \nu + \delta_h$. We are now going to show that $\dot{x}(t) < 0$ for all $t \in [t', T - \varepsilon]$. To see this, note first that ϕ is assumed to be concave and we therefore have

$$-\frac{\phi'(x(t)) \exp(\kappa(t - t'))\kappa}{\phi''(x(t))} > 0 \quad \text{for all } t \in [t', T - \varepsilon].$$

Furthermore we will now argue that

$$\lambda(t') - \kappa^{-1} = \lambda(t') - \frac{1}{\delta_h + r + \nu} < 0.$$

To see this, suppose this is not the case. This implies that

$$\frac{\lambda(t') - \kappa^{-1}}{\kappa^{-1} + \exp(\kappa(t - t')) \left(\lambda(t') - \kappa^{-1}\right)} > 0 \quad \text{for all } t \in [t', T - \varepsilon]$$

so that

$$\dot{x}(t) > 0 \quad \text{for all } t \in [t', T - \varepsilon].$$

This however cannot be the case as $s(t)$ is continuous and satisfies

$$\lim_{t \to T - \varepsilon} s(t) = 0 \tag{S10.38}$$

so that $x(t)$ goes to zero too. With $\lambda(t') - \kappa^{-1} < 0$ however, (S10.37) shows that $x(t)$ declines over time.[2], i.e.

$$\dot{x}(t) < 0 \quad \text{for all } t \in [t', T - \varepsilon].$$

But now note that we can write personal income as

$$y(t) = (1 - s(t))h(t) = h(t) - x(t)$$

so that

$$\dot{y}(t) = \dot{h}(t) - \dot{x}(t).$$

As $\dot{h}(t) = \phi(h(t)s(t)) - \delta_h h(t) = \phi(x(t)) - \delta_h h(t)$ it will typically be the case that $h(t)$ will first increase for a while and then decrease. Note that individuals continue their training while already starting working, i.e. $s(t) \in (0, 1)$ in $t \in [t', T - \varepsilon]$. Earnings have therefore a similar shape. In the beginning we have that $\dot{h}(t) > 0$ and $-\dot{x}(t) > 0$ so that earning increase. This is a time where the individual still spends substantial time resources on training on the job. Over time, schooling expenditures are reduced so that the stock of human capital deteriorates. This puts downward pressure on income growth as $\dot{h}(t) < 0$. At $T - \varepsilon$, no resources are spent on training (or schooling) so that $x(t) = \dot{x}(t) = 0$ and earnings decrease over time.

Exercise 10.7, Part (d). In order to think about an empirical analysis of the testable implications of this model, it is important to be precise about which aspect of theory one is interested in testing. There are two broad directions one could go for. On the one hand there is the connection between wages and the stock of an individual's human capital, on the other hand there are the implications on individual earning dynamics. Whereas clearly both are very important, the center of interest in Ben-Porath's model of human capital accumulation is the second one. The major implication of this approach to understand human capital is that its accumulation is an ongoing process which has the flavor of investment. Hence it is this aspect that offers the most fruitful chance to test its implications.

---

[2]Note that $t', T - \varepsilon$ and $\lambda(t')$ will be such that $\kappa^{-1} + \exp(\kappa(t - t')) \left(\lambda(t') - \kappa^{-1}\right) > 0$. This follows from the following argument. Suppose there was $\hat{t} < T - \varepsilon$ such that $\kappa^{-1} + \exp(\kappa(\hat{t} - t')) \left(\lambda(t') - \kappa^{-1}\right) < 0$. Then this would imply that $\kappa^{-1} + \exp(\kappa(\hat{t} - t')) \left(\lambda(t') - \kappa^{-1}\right) < 0$ for all $t \in [\hat{t}, T - \varepsilon]$, i.e. $x(t)$ would be increasing towards the end of the working life. This however contradicts (S10.38).

One important determinant in the maximization problem above is the time horizon t. Especially it is clear that human capital investment (i.e. schooling or rather training $s(t)$) should decrease as T comes closer. To empirically investigate this property one could either try to exploit regional variations in retirement laws (or the execution thereof) or focus on changes in such laws over time. E.g. the change in the minimum age of retirement could be exploited in a regression-discontinuity design if there is a well-defined group of people affected by the change of the law. There is also the casual observation that, both historically and across countries, schooling is longer when life expectancy increases. This could however be driven by many other mechanisms. If, for example, schooling and human capital accumulation fosters economic growth which in turn increases the average life expectancy we would see that countries where life expectancy is higher have also higher schooling expenditures. The Ben-Porath model however posits a causal effect of the time horizon on individual schooling expenditures.

Another potential candidate to test this model of human capital accumulation is the return to human capital, i.e. the wage rate. Note however that the *level* of the wage rate will not influence the accumulation decision - the solution to the individuals' problem (S10.27) is invariant with respect to a different scale (i.e. multiplying wages by a constant). The time-profile of wages however will matter a great deal for the investment decision as it determines the marginal costs of doing so. So if we hypothetically had two different life-cycle wage profiles (as a function of time!) for two identical individuals, this model would predict that their human capital accumulation decision would be responsive to those differences. It is far from clear however, how this should be tested in practice. The reason is that wage changes occur mostly together with promotions or job changes that are likely to be correlated with prior investments in human capital. The higher wage would therefore be caused by the human capital investment itself. Furthermore - and this is probably the biggest challenge in examining this model empirically - note that the assumption of individuals *either* investing in human capital *or* earning wages is highly questionable once we are trying to analyze the part of the interior solution of the model, i.e. the case of non-formal schooling. In reality such a distinction is mostly unclear and very hard to observe.

Chapter 11: First-Generation Models of Endogenous Growth

Exercise 11.4

Exercise 11.4, Part (a). A competitive equilibrium is a path of allocations and prices $[k(t), c(t), a(t), r(t), w(t)]_{t=0}^{\infty}$ such that the representative consumer solves

$$\max_{[c(t),a(t)]_t} \int_0^{\infty} \exp\left(-(\rho - n)t\right) \frac{c(t)^{1-\theta} - 1}{1-\theta} dt,$$

s.t. $\dot{a}(t) = (r(t) - n)a(t) + w(t) - c(t)$, and $\lim_{t \to \infty} a(t) \exp\left(-\int_0^t r(s) ds\right) \geq 0$,

competitive firms maximize profits, that is

$$r(t) = f'(k(t)) - \delta, \ w(t) = f(k(t)) - k(t) f'(k(t)), \tag{S11.1}$$

where

$$f(k(t)) = F(k(t), 1) = A\left[k(t)^{\frac{\sigma-1}{\sigma}} + 1\right]^{\frac{\sigma}{\sigma-1}},$$

and asset and final good markets clear.

We next characterize the competitive equilibrium. The factor prices in (S11.1) can be calculated as

$$r(t) = Ak(t)^{-1/\sigma}\left(\left[1 + k(t)^{(\sigma-1)/\sigma}\right]^{\sigma/(\sigma-1)}\right)^{1/\sigma} - \delta, \tag{S11.2}$$

$$w(t) = A\left(\left[1 + k(t)^{(\sigma-1)/\sigma}\right]^{\sigma/(\sigma-1)}\right)^{1/\sigma}.$$

The current value Hamiltonian for the consumer optimization is

$$\hat{H}(t, a, c, \mu) = \frac{c^{1-\theta} - 1}{1-\theta} + \mu\left((r(t) - n)a + w(t) - c\right)$$

and the necessary conditions are

$$\hat{H}_c = 0 \implies c^{-\theta} = \mu$$

$$\hat{H}_a = (\rho - n)\mu - \dot{\mu} \implies \frac{\dot{\mu}}{\mu} = -(r(t) - \rho).$$

Combining these conditions, we get the Euler equation

$$\frac{\dot{c}(t)}{c(t)} = \frac{1}{\theta}(r(t) - \rho)$$

$$= \frac{1}{\theta}\left(Ak(t)^{-1/\sigma}\left(\left[1 + k(t)^{(\sigma-1)/\sigma}\right]^{\sigma/(\sigma-1)}\right)^{1/\sigma} - \delta - \rho\right), \tag{S11.3}$$

where the second line substitutes for $r(t)$ from Eq. (S11.2). The strong form of the transversality condition $\lim_{t \to \infty} \exp\left(-(\rho - n)t\right)\mu(t) a(t) = 0$ is also necessary for this problem.

119

Solving the differential equation $\frac{\dot{\mu}(t)}{\mu(t)} = -(r(t) - \rho)$ and substituting for $r(t)$ from Eq. (S11.2), this condition can be written as

$$\lim_{t \to \infty} \exp\left(\int_0^t -(f'(k(s)) - \delta - n)\, ds\right) k(t) = 0. \tag{S11.4}$$

Finally, using the asset market clearing condition $a(t) = k(t)$ and substituting factor prices from Eq. (S11.2), the agent's budget constraint gives the resource constraints

$$\dot{k}(t) = f(k(t)) - (\delta + n)\, k(t) - c(t). \tag{S11.5}$$

The differential equations (S11.3) and (S11.5), along with the transversality condition (S11.4) and the initial condition $k(0)$ uniquely characterize the equilibrium allocation $[k(t), c(t)]_{t=0}^{\infty}$. Note also that every plan that satisfies these conditions is optimal by Theorem 7.14.

Exercise 11.4, Part (b). The social planner solves the following optimal growth problem

$$\max_{(c,k)} \int_0^\infty \exp\left(-(\rho - n)\, t\right) \frac{c(t)^{1-\theta} - 1}{1 - \theta}\, dt, \tag{S11.6}$$

$$\text{s.t. } \dot{k}(t) = f(k(t)) - (\delta + n)\, k(t) - c(t), \text{ and } k(t) \geq 0.$$

The current value Hamiltonian of this problem is

$$\hat{H}(k, c, \mu) = \frac{c^{1-\theta} - 1}{1 - \theta} + \mu\, (f(k) - (\delta + n)\, k - c)$$

and the first-order conditions yield the Euler equation (S11.3). Since the maximized Hamiltonian is strictly concave, the path that satisfies the resource constraints Eq. (S11.5), the Euler equation (S11.3), and the transversality condition Eq. (S11.4) is the unique solution to Problem (S11.6). Hence the per capita variables $[k(t), c(t)]_{t=0}^{\infty}$ chosen by the planner are identical to the corresponding equilibrium values, proving that the equilibrium is Pareto optimal.

Exercise 11.4, Part (c). First, we consider the case $\sigma = 1$. In this case, the production function takes the Cobb-Douglas form $f(k) = Ak^{1/2}$, which satisfies Assumption 2 and fits the framework studied in Chapter 8. Hence the equilibrium $[k(t), c(t)]_t$ converges to a steady state (k^*, c^*) and there is no sustained growth.

Second, we consider the case $\sigma < 1$. In this case, using the expression in (S11.2) for the marginal product of capital, we have that $f'(k(t))$ is decreasing and

$$\lim_{k(t) \to 0} f'(k(t)) = A \text{ and } \lim_{k(t) \to \infty} f'(k(t)) = 0. \tag{S11.7}$$

In particular, Assumption 2 is violated for $k(t) \to 0$. There are two subcases to consider. First suppose

$$A < \delta + \rho. \tag{S11.8}$$

Then, we have $f'(k(t)) - \delta - n < 0$ regardless of the level of the capital-labor ratio, and the Euler equation implies $\dot{c}(t)/c(t) < 0$ for all t and thus $\lim_{t \to \infty} c(t) = 0$. From Eq. (S11.5), it follows that $\lim_{t \to \infty} k(t) = 0$, since otherwise $k(t)$ would grow at ever increasing rates and would violate the transversality condition (S11.4). Hence, in this case both the capital-labor ratio and consumption per capita asymptotically converge to 0. In particular, there is no sustained growth. As the second subcase, suppose Condition (S11.8) is not satisfied, that is $A \geq \delta + \rho$. In this case, there exists a steady state equilibrium (k^*, c^*) characterized by

$$k^* = f'^{-1}(\delta + \rho) \text{ and } c^* = f(k^*) - (\delta + n)\, k^*.$$

Moreover, as in the baseline case analyzed in Chapter 8, given $k(0)$ there exists a unique path $[k(t), c(t)]_{t=0}^{\infty}$ that converges to (k^*, c^*) along the stable arm, which is the equilibrium path. In particular, the capital-labor ratio is constant in the limit and sustained growth is not possible. Intuitively, sustained growth is not possible in this case since the Inada condition as $k(t) \to \infty$ is satisfied (cf. (S11.7)). As the capital-labor ratio increases, the economy runs into diminishing returns and growth cannot be sustained by capital accumulation alone.

Exercise 11.4, Part (d). Next suppose $\sigma > 1$. Using the expression in (S11.2) for the marginal product of capital, we have

$$\lim_{k(t)\to 0} f'(k(t)) = \infty \text{ and } \lim_{k(t)\to\infty} f'(k(t)) = A. \tag{S11.9}$$

In particular, Assumption 2 (the Inada condition) is violated as $k(t) \to \infty$ so there is a possibility of sustained growth. Once again, we distinguish between two cases. First, suppose that Condition (S11.8) is satisfied. Then, since $f'(k(t))$ is a decreasing function, there exists a unique steady state equilibrium (k^*, c^*) given as the solution to

$$f'(k^*) = \delta + \rho \text{ and } c^* = f(k^*) - (\delta + n)k^*.$$

Moreover, it can be seen in the phase diagram that the steady state equilibrium in this case is saddle path stable just like in the baseline neoclassical economy. Hence, the equilibrium path $[k(t), c(t)]_t$ converges to the steady state (k^*, c^*) along the stable arm. In particular, sustained growth is not possible since capital-labor ratio limits to a constant.

Next, suppose Condition (S11.8) is not satisfied, that is $A \geq \delta + \rho$. In this case, from the Euler equation we have $\dot{c}(t)/c(t) > 0$ for any $k(t) > 0$. It follows that $\lim_{t\to\infty} c(t) = \infty$. By the resource constraint (S11.5), this can only hold if $\lim_{t\to\infty} k(t) = \infty$. Given that the capital-labor ratio limits to infinity, the Euler equation further implies that

$$\lim_{t\to\infty} \frac{\dot{c}(t)}{c(t)} = \frac{1}{\theta}\left(\lim_{k(t)\to\infty} f'(k(t)) - \delta - \rho\right)$$
$$= \frac{1}{\theta}(A - \delta - \rho).$$

Hence, consumption per capita and the capital-labor ratio limit to infinity, and consumption per capita asymptotically grows at rate $(A - \delta - \rho)/\theta$, proving that the model generates asymptotically sustained growth. In Part (e), we will characterize the transitional dynamics and we will also show that $\lim_{t\to\infty} \dot{k}(t)/k(t) = (A - \delta - \rho)/\theta$.

Intuitively, there is sustained growth since the Inada condition is violated [cf. Eq. (S11.9)] so that the returns to capital does not run into strong diminishing returns, that is, the marginal product of capital remains bounded away from zero even with abundant levels of capital. With a sufficiently large marginal product of capital (i.e. if $A \geq \delta + \rho$), the interest rate is always higher than the discount rate and the representative consumer chooses to save some of her wealth rather than consume immediately, generating sustained growth.

Exercise 11.4, Part (e). In this part, we consider the case $A \geq \delta + \rho$ and $\sigma > 1$, since we have completely characterized the equilibrium path in all of the remaining cases. Since the variables in this economy grow, we will analyze the equilibrium in normalized variables. To come up with the appropriate normalization, we rewrite the system in Eqs. (S11.3) and

(S11.5) as

$$\frac{\dot{c}(t)}{c(t)} = \frac{1}{\theta}\left(A^{(\sigma-1)/\sigma}\left(\frac{k(t)}{f(k(t))}\right)^{-1/\sigma} - \delta - \rho\right) \qquad (S11.10)$$

$$\frac{\dot{k}(t)}{k(t)} = \frac{f(k)}{k(t)} - \delta - n - \frac{c(t)}{k(t)}, \ k(0) \text{ given.}$$

These expressions show that the growth rate of consumption and capital only depends on the normalized variables $z \equiv f(k)/k$ and $\chi \equiv c/k$ and suggests that we consider the system in these variables.

Note that, in normalized variables (χ, z), we have the differential equation system

$$\frac{\dot{\chi}}{\chi} = \frac{\dot{c}}{c} - \frac{\dot{k}}{k} = \frac{1}{\theta}\left(A\left(\frac{z}{A}\right)^{1/\sigma} - \delta - \rho\right) - z + \chi + \delta + n \qquad (S11.11)$$

$$\frac{\dot{z}}{z} = \left(\frac{f'(k)k}{f(k)} - 1\right)\frac{\dot{k}}{k} = \left[\left(\frac{A}{z}\right)^{(\sigma-1)/\sigma} - 1\right](z - \chi - \delta - n),$$

$$z(0) = f(k(0))/k(0) > A \text{ given and } z(t) > A \text{ for all } t.$$

Here, the first differential equation follows by substituting for $\dot{c}/c$ and $\dot{k}/k$ from Eq. (S11.10). The second differential equation substitutes for $\dot{k}/k$ and uses

$$f'(k) = A^{(\sigma-1)/\sigma}z^{1/\sigma}. \qquad (S11.12)$$

The inequality $z(t) > A$ follows since

$$f(k) = A\left(1 + k^{(\sigma-1)/\sigma}\right)^{\sigma/(\sigma-1)} > A\left(k^{(\sigma-1)/\sigma}\right)^{\sigma/(\sigma-1)} = Ak.$$

We have added the restriction $z(t) > A$ to the normalized system since the normalized system might have some solutions with $z(t) < A$ that do not correspond to a solution in the original system. Note also that $\lim_{k\to\infty} f(k)/k = A$ thus the equilibrium will feature $\lim_{t\to\infty} z(t) = A$ even though $z(t) > A$ for all t.

Conversely, note that for any given path $[\chi(t), z(t)]_{t=0}^\infty$ that satisfies the system in (S11.11) and satisfies $z(t) > A$ for all t, we can construct a path of $[k(t), c(t)]_{t=0}^\infty$ that satisfies our original system in Eq. (S11.10). To see this, note that $z(t) = f(k(t))/k(t)$ is one-to-one in the range $z(t) \in (A, \infty)$ since $f(k(t))/k(t)$ is decreasing and satisfies $\lim_{k(t)\to 0} f(k(t))/k(t) = \infty$ and $\lim_{k(t)\to\infty} f(k(t))/k(t) = A$. Then, given $[z(t), \chi(t)]_t$ that solves the normalized system, $k(t)$ is uniquely solved from the previous displayed equation and $c(t)$ is given by $\chi(t)k(t)$. It follows that the normalized system in (S11.11) is equivalent to the original system.

Note also that the normalized system in (S11.11) [in the relevant range $z \geq A$] has a unique steady state given by $z^* = A$ and $\chi^* = A - \delta - n - \frac{1}{\theta}(A - \delta - \rho)$. As we will show below, this system is saddle path stable, that is, for any given $z(0)$, there exists a unique $\chi(0)$ such that the path $[z(t), \chi(t)]_t$ starts on the saddle path and converges to the steady state (z^*, χ^*). Then, the corresponding path $[k(t), c(t)]_t$ is an equilibrium whenever the parametric restriction

$$(1 - \theta)(A - \delta) < \rho$$

which ensures that the transversality condition holds, since $[k(t), c(t)]_t$ constructed in this way satisfy all the equilibrium conditions (S11.3) − (S11.4).

We next analyze the phase diagram in the (χ, z) space. First, note that the $\dot{z} = 0$ locus is the union of the line $z = A$ and the line $z - \chi = \delta + n$. These lines and the arrows that

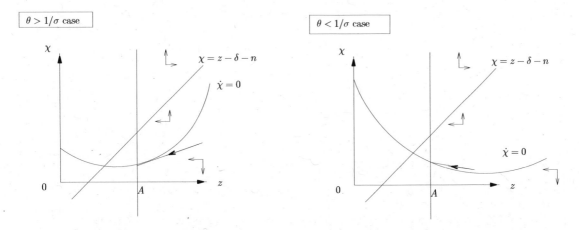

FIGURE S11.1. Transitional dynamics for the normalized variables $z(t) = f(k(t))/k(t)$ and $\chi(t) = c(t)/k(t)$. The left hand side corresponds to the sub-case $\theta > 1/\sigma$ and the right hand side to $\theta < 1/\sigma$.

represent the behavior of z are drawn in Figure S11.1. Second, to analyze the $\dot{\chi} = 0$ locus, we define

$$g(z) = z - \frac{1}{\theta}\left(A\left(\frac{z}{A}\right)^{1/\sigma} - \delta - \rho\right) - \delta - n,$$

and note that $\dot{\chi}/\chi = \chi - g(z)$. Note that

$$g'(z) = 1 - \frac{1}{\theta\sigma}\left(\frac{A}{z}\right)^{(\sigma-1)/\sigma}$$

is decreasing in z (since we are analyzing the $\sigma > 1$ case) and $g'(z) = 0$ for $z = A(\theta\sigma)^{-\sigma/(\sigma-1)}$. Hence, the $\dot{\chi} = 0$ locus is U shaped and there are two cases to distinguish depending on whether the minimum is to the left or to the right of the $z = A$ locus. When $\theta > 1/\sigma$, the minimum of the $\dot{\chi} = 0$ locus is to the left of $z = A$. As shown in Figure S11.1, in this case, there is a stable arm in which $(z(t), \chi(t)) \to (z^*, \chi^*)$ and $z(t)$ and $\chi(t)$ are both decreasing on the stable arm. When $\theta < 1/\sigma$, the minimum of $\dot{\chi} = 0$ locus is to the right of $z = A$. As shown in Figure S11.1, in this case, there is a stable arm on which $(z(t), \chi(t)) \to (z^*, \chi^*)$ and $z(t)$ is decreasing along the transitional path while $\chi(t)$ is increasing. Combining the two cases, the capital output ratio $k(t)/f(k(t)) = 1/z(t)$ is always increasing along the transition path (i.e. there is always capital deepening) while the consumption capital ratio $c(t)/k(t) = \chi(t)$ is increasing (resp. decreasing) if $\theta < 1/\sigma$ (resp. if $\theta > 1/\sigma$).

Exercise 11.4, Part (f). The share of capital in this economy is

$$\frac{kr}{y} = \frac{kf'(k)}{f(k)} = \frac{kf'(k)}{f(k)} = \left(\frac{A}{z}\right)^{(\sigma-1)/\sigma},$$

where we have used Eq. (S11.12). Since z is decreasing towards A, the capital's share is increasing towards 1 and limits to 1. Consequently, the share of labor is decreasing and limits to 0. This is not plausible since it is not consistent with the Kaldor facts, which suggest that the share of labor roughly remains constant around 2/3.

We can modify the model by introducing different production functions for consumption and capital goods as in Rebelo (1991). Consider the variant of the model in which investment goods are produced with the CES technology given in the problem

$$I = A \left[L_I^{(\sigma-1)/\sigma} + K_I^{(\sigma-1)/\sigma} \right]^{\sigma/(\sigma-1)}$$

and consumption goods are produced with the technology

$$C = BK_C^\alpha L_C^{1-\alpha}. \tag{S11.13}$$

The capital accumulation technology is given by

$$\dot{K} = I - \delta K.$$

For simplicity, suppose that there is no population growth. Aside from the two sector structure, this model is very similar to the model we have analyzed in this exercise. A similar analysis as above shows that the equilibrium in this economy will approximate a BGP as in the baseline model in Rebelo (1991), so we have

$$L_I(t) \;\; \to \;\; 0, \; L_C(t) \to L, \; \kappa(t) \equiv \frac{K_I(t)}{K(t)} \to \kappa^*,$$

$$\frac{\dot{K}}{K} \;\; \to \;\; g_K, \; \frac{\dot{C}}{C} = \alpha g_K, \; \frac{\dot{p}_I}{p_I} = -(1-\alpha)\, g_K.$$

More importantly, in this version of the model, we have that the share of labor limits to a constant in $(0,1)$, which is in line with the Kaldor facts. Intuitively, the necessary ingredient to generate sustained growth is a linear production technology in the accumulating factor (which is capital in this model). This implies that the share of labor in the capital sector must go to zero, but the share of labor in aggregate output need not necessarily go to zero. In particular, as long as labor is essential for the consumption sector [which is ensured by the functional form in (S11.13)], the share of labor in aggregate output remains bounded away from zero as the economy develops.

Another way to modify the model is to add human capital into the production of the final good and allow for human capital to accumulate also with a linear technology. As shown in Section 11.2, this model generates AK-like growth that is driven by factor accumulation, but it also keeps the share of labor and capital constant. Intuitively, both factors accumulate in balance and remain equally important in production.

Exercise 11.4, Part (g). We assume that the returns from assets are taxed at rate τ and redistributed to consumers as lump sum transfers (alternatively, without any qualitative change in results, we can assume that the collected taxes are wasted). In this case, the Euler equation takes the form

$$\frac{\dot{c}}{c} = \frac{1}{\theta} \left((1-\tau)\, r - \rho \right)$$

which, after substituting competitive prices, implies

$$\frac{\dot{c}}{c} = \frac{1}{\theta} \left((1-\tau) \left(Ak^{-1/\sigma} \left[1 + k^{(\sigma-1)/\sigma} \right]^{1/(\sigma-1)} - \delta \right) - \rho \right).$$

The same analysis as above now establishes the following:

- If $\sigma < 1$ or $(1-\tau)(A-\delta) < \rho$, the economy converges to a steady state and there is no sustained growth.

- If $\sigma > 1$ and $(1-\tau)(A-\delta) > \rho$, (under the parametric restriction $(1-\tau)(A-\delta)(1-\theta) < \rho$), the equilibrium features sustained growth for c and k at rate $\frac{1}{\theta}((1-\tau)(A-\delta)-\rho)$.

We conclude that, in the case of sustained growth, taxes reduce the growth rate of the economy.

Exercise 11.14

Exercise 11.14, Part (a). As in the baseline model, we use $p_C(t)$ and $p_I(t)$ to denote the prices of the consumption and the investment good in this economy. A competitive equilibrium is a sequence of aggregate allocations $[C(t), I(t), K(t), L_C(t), L_I(t), K_C(t), K_I(t)]_t$ and prices $[p_I(t), p_C(t), r_C(t), r_I(t), R(t), w(t)]_t$ such that the representative consumer maximizes (11.1) subject to the budget constraints (with interest rate $r_C(t)$), consumption and investment good producers choose inputs $[L_C(t), L_I(t), K_C(t), K_I(t)]_t$ to maximize profits given prices $[p_I(t), p_C(t), w(t), R(t)]_t$, and factor and goods markets clear.

Exercise 11.14, Part (b). We normalize $p_C(t) = 1$ for all t without loss of generality. First we claim that the steady state equilibrium does not involve sustained growth. Suppose, to reach a contradiction, that there is a BGP equilibrium in which $K(t)$ grows at a constant rate $g_K > 0$. Note that

$$\dot{K}(t) = I(t) - \delta K(t), \qquad (S11.14)$$

which implies that $I(t)$ must also grow at the constant rate g_K. Let

$$\kappa(t) = K_I(t)/K(t) \text{ and } \lambda(t) = L_I(t)/L(t)$$

denote the share of capital and labor employed in the investment sector. Then, considering the growth of the terms in the production of the investment good

$$I(t) = A(K_I(t))^\beta (L_I(t))^{1-\beta},$$

we have

$$g_K = g_I = \beta(g_K + g_\kappa(t)) + (1-\beta)g_\lambda(t),$$

which implies

$$(1-\beta)g_K = \beta g_\kappa(t) + (1-\beta)g_\lambda(t). \qquad (S11.15)$$

Note that the right hand side is the growth rate of $\kappa(t)^\beta \lambda(t)^{1-\beta}$. Hence the previously displayed equation suggests that this term should be growing at the constant rate $(1-\beta)g_K > 0$. In particular, it eventually exceeds 1, which yields a contradiction since $\lambda(t) \in [0,1]$ and $\kappa(t) \in [0,1]$. This proves our claim that there is no steady state equilibrium in which $K(t)$ grows at a constant rate. Intuitively, since the investment sector has diminishing returns to capital, the economy runs into diminishing returns and cannot sustain growth by only capital accumulation.

We next claim that there exists a steady state equilibrium in which capital and consumption remain at constant levels K^* and C^*, and the price of the investment good $p_I(t) = p_I^*$ is constant. First, note that since the relative price of the investment and the capital good remains constant, the no arbitrage condition implies that

$$
\begin{aligned}
r_C(t) = r_I(t) &= \frac{d}{dK_I(t)}\left(A(K_I(t))^\beta (L_I(t))^{1-\beta}\right) - \delta \\
&= \frac{\beta I(t)}{K_I(t)} - \delta.
\end{aligned}
$$

Second, note that in a steady state, Eq. (S11.14) satisfies $I(t) = \delta K(t)$. From the previous equation, this implies

$$r_C(t) = \frac{\beta\delta}{\kappa(t)} - \delta. \tag{S11.16}$$

Third, note that since consumption is constant, the Euler equation implies $r_C(t) = \rho$. Using this in the previous equation, we have

$$\kappa(t) = \kappa^* = \frac{\beta\delta}{\rho + \delta}, \tag{S11.17}$$

that is, the steady state allocation of capital to the investment sector is also constant. Note that a higher depreciation rate, a lower discount rate, and a higher share of capital in the accumulation technology increase the allocation of resources to the accumulation sector, which is intuitive.

Next, we characterize the allocation of labor between the two sectors. Optimization by investment and consumption good producers implies

$$p_I(t) A\beta \left(\frac{\kappa(t)}{\lambda(t)}\frac{K(t)}{L}\right)^{\beta-1} = B\alpha \left(\frac{1-\kappa(t)}{1-\lambda(t)}\frac{K(t)}{L}\right)^{\alpha-1} = R(t) \tag{S11.18}$$

$$p_I(t) A(1-\beta) \left(\frac{\kappa(t)}{\lambda(t)}\frac{K(t)}{L}\right)^{\beta} = B(1-\alpha) \left(\frac{1-\kappa(t)}{1-\lambda(t)}\frac{K(t)}{L}\right)^{\alpha} = w(t).$$

Dividing these two equations, we get

$$\frac{1-\beta}{\beta}\frac{\kappa(t)}{\lambda(t)} = \frac{1-\alpha}{\alpha}\frac{1-\kappa(t)}{1-\lambda(t)}, \tag{S11.19}$$

which defines λ as a function of κ

$$\lambda(\kappa) = \frac{\kappa}{\kappa + (1-\kappa)\frac{1-\alpha}{\alpha}\frac{\beta}{1-\beta}}. \tag{S11.20}$$

Note that $\lambda(\kappa)$ is increasing in κ, that is, resources are allocated together in the sense that relatively more capital is allocated to the investment sector if and only if relatively more labor is also allocated to that sector. Given the level of κ^* in Eq. (S11.17), the previous equation determines λ^* and the allocation of labor between sectors.

Next, we characterize the steady state level of capital, K^*. Using $\delta K^* = I(t)$, we have

$$\delta K^* = A(\kappa^* K^*)^{\beta} (\lambda(\kappa^*) L)^{1-\beta}.$$

Solving for K^* and plugging in Eq. (S11.20), we have

$$K^* = \left(\frac{A}{\delta}\right)^{1/(1-\beta)} L\lambda(\kappa^*)(\kappa^*)^{\beta/(1-\beta)} \tag{S11.21}$$

$$= \left(\frac{A}{\delta}\right)^{1/(1-\beta)} L\frac{(\kappa^*)^{1/(1-\beta)}}{\frac{1-\alpha}{\alpha}\frac{\beta}{1-\beta} - \kappa^*\left(\frac{1-\alpha}{\alpha}\frac{\beta}{1-\beta} - 1\right)}. \tag{S11.22}$$

Note that K^* is unambiguously increasing in κ^*. This is intuitive: if more resources are allocated to the investment sector, investment is greater and the steady state level of capital is greater.

Next, we characterize the level of p_I^* that is consistent with this allocation of resources between sectors. Combining Eq. (S11.19) with Eq. (S11.18), we have

$$p_I^* A\beta \left(\frac{\kappa^*}{\lambda^*}\frac{K^*}{L}\right)^{\beta-\alpha} = B\alpha \left(\frac{1-\beta}{\beta}\frac{\alpha}{1-\alpha}\right)^{\alpha-1}, \tag{S11.23}$$

which solves for the level of p_I^*. The prices R^* and w^* are also uniquely determines from Eq. (S11.18). Finally, the equilibrium level of consumption can be solved from (11.27) as

$$C^* = B \left((1 - \kappa^*) K^* \right)^\alpha \left((1 - \lambda(\kappa^*)) L \right)^{1-\alpha}. \tag{S11.24}$$

It then follows that the allocation $(K^*, I^*, C^*, \kappa^*, \lambda(\kappa^*))$ along with prices $(p_I^*, r_I^* = r_C^* = \rho, R^*, w^*)$ constitutes a steady state equilibrium.

Exercise 11.14, Part (c). We have shown that, in this case, the only BGP equilibrium is a steady state equilibrium, that is, different from the baseline case with $\beta = 1$, there is no growth and the equilibrium converges to a steady state. The analysis in this exercise emphasizes the role of $\beta = 1$ in generating sustained growth. Without a linear accumulation technology, the economy runs into diminishing returns for sufficiently large levels of capital and growth cannot be sustained forever (cf. Eq. (S11.15)).

Exercise 11.14, Part (d). Suppose that the government taxes the returns from assets at rate τ and redistributes the returns lump-sum to the consumer (without changing any of the qualitative results, we could also assume that the government consumes the returns). Then, the after-tax return on assets is given by $r_C(t)(1 - \tau)$. The steady state equilibrium is solved as in Part 2. In particular, Eq. (S11.16) continues to apply for before-tax returns $r_C(t)$ but the Euler equation in this case implies $r_C(t)(1-\tau) = \rho$, which yields

$$\kappa^*(\tau) = \frac{\beta\delta}{\frac{\rho}{1-\tau} + \delta}. \tag{S11.25}$$

Moreover, conditional on κ^*, the allocation of the remaining variables are characterized as before, that is, Eqs. (S11.20), (S11.22), (S11.23) and (S11.24) continue to apply in this case, characterizing the equilibrium.

Note that $\kappa^*(\tau)$ is decreasing in τ. Since K^* given in Eq. (S11.22) is increasing in κ^*, it follows that the steady state level of capital is decreasing in the tax rate. These results are intuitive: taxing capital income reduces the share of resources allocated to the investment sector and reduces the steady state level of capital.

We next claim that taxing capital income also reduces the steady state level of consumption, C^*. Note that K^* decreases with taxes, but the share of resources allocated to the consumption sector increases. Thus, from Eq. (S11.24), it seems at first glance unclear which effect dominates. However, we know, a priori, that the steady state consumption level with taxes must be lower than without taxes, since the first welfare theorem applies to the economy.[1] This suggests that the reduction in K^* should dominate the increased resource allocation to the consumption sector and C^* should also decrease in response to taxes. With some algebra, we can indeed prove that this is the case. To see this, note that

---

[1]To see this more formally, suppose, to reach a contradiction, that $C^*(\tau) > C^*(0)$ for some $\tau > 0$. Then, a social planner could reallocate the production and consumption decisions in the original economy to move the economy immediately to the steady state of the economy with $\tau > 0$, and she would have leftover capital at time 0 since $K^*(\tau) < K^*(0)$. Hence, consumers would strictly prefer the latter allocation, which provides a contradiction to the fact that the economy with $\tau = 0$ is Pareto optimal. It follows that $C^*(\tau)$ is decreasing in τ in a neighborhood of $\tau = 0$.

$$
\begin{aligned}
C^{*}\left(\kappa^{*}\right) &= B\left(\frac{A}{\delta}\right)^{\alpha/(1-\beta)} L\left(1-\kappa^{*}\right)^{\alpha}\left(\kappa^{*}\right)^{\alpha\beta/(1-\beta)} \lambda\left(\kappa^{*}\right)^{\alpha}\left(1-\lambda\left(\kappa^{*}\right)\right)^{1-\alpha} \\
&= B\left(\frac{A}{\delta}\right)^{\alpha/(1-\beta)} L\left(1-\kappa^{*}\right)^{\alpha}\left(\kappa^{*}\right)^{\alpha\beta/(1-\beta)} \frac{\left(\kappa^{*}\right)^{\alpha}\left(1-\kappa^{*}\right)^{1-\alpha}}{\kappa^{*}+\left(1-\kappa^{*}\right)\frac{1-\alpha}{\alpha}\frac{\beta}{1-\beta}}\left(\frac{1-\alpha}{\alpha}\frac{\beta}{1-\beta}\right)^{1-\alpha} \\
&= B\left(\frac{A}{\delta}\right)^{\alpha/(1-\beta)}\left(\frac{1-\alpha}{\alpha}\frac{\beta}{1-\beta}\right)^{1-\alpha} Lg\left(\kappa^{*}\right),
\end{aligned}
$$

where the first line plugs Eq. (S11.21) into Eq. (S11.24), the second line uses Eq. (S11.20) and the third line defines the function

$$
g\left(\kappa^{*}\right) = \frac{\left(\kappa^{*}\right)^{\alpha/(1-\beta)}}{\frac{\kappa^{*}}{1-\kappa^{*}}+\frac{1-\alpha}{\alpha}\frac{\beta}{1-\beta}}.
$$

Next note that

$$
\begin{aligned}
\frac{\partial}{\partial\kappa^{*}}\left(g\left(\kappa^{*}\right)\right) &= \frac{\frac{\alpha}{1-\beta}\left(\kappa^{*}\right)^{\alpha/(1-\beta)-1}}{\left(\frac{\kappa^{*}}{1-\kappa^{*}}+\frac{1-\alpha}{\alpha}\frac{\beta}{1-\beta}\right)^{2}}\left(\frac{\kappa^{*}}{1-\kappa^{*}}+\frac{1-\alpha}{\alpha}\frac{\beta}{1-\beta}-\frac{1-\beta}{\alpha}\frac{\kappa^{*}}{\left(1-\kappa^{*}\right)^{2}}\right) \\
&= \frac{\frac{\alpha}{1-\beta}\left(\kappa^{*}\right)^{\alpha/(1-\beta)-1}}{\left(\frac{\kappa^{*}}{1-\kappa^{*}}+\frac{1-\alpha}{\alpha}\frac{\beta}{1-\beta}\right)^{2}}\left(\frac{\kappa^{*}}{1-\kappa^{*}}\left(1-\frac{1-\beta}{\alpha\left(1-\kappa^{*}\right)}\right)+\frac{1-\alpha}{\alpha}\frac{\beta}{1-\beta}\right) \\
&> \frac{\frac{\alpha}{1-\beta}\left(\kappa^{*}\right)^{\alpha/(1-\beta)-1}}{\left(\frac{\kappa^{*}}{1-\kappa^{*}}+\frac{1-\alpha}{\alpha}\frac{\beta}{1-\beta}\right)^{2}}\left(\frac{\kappa^{*}}{1-\kappa^{*}}\frac{\alpha-1}{\alpha}+\frac{1-\alpha}{\alpha}\frac{\beta}{1-\beta}\right) > 0,
\end{aligned}
$$

where the last two inequalities follow using $\kappa^{*} < \beta$ from Eq. (S11.25). Hence, we have $\partial C^{*}\left(\kappa^{*}\right)/\partial\kappa^{*} > 0$. Since $\kappa^{*}\left(\tau\right)$ is decreasing in τ, this proves our claim that $C^{*}\left(\tau\right)$ is decreasing in τ.

This analysis establishes that taxing capital income reduces relative resources allocated to the accumulation sector and consequently reduces the capital stock and consumption levels in equilibrium. From Eqs. (S11.25) and (S11.22), note that the magnitude of the effect of τ on $\kappa^{*}\left(\tau\right)$ and $K^{*}\left(\tau\right)$ is mostly determined by β while α playing a minor role through the allocation of labor force between the sectors. In particular, with higher β capital declines more in response to taxes. Intuitively, the investment and capital falls in response to taxes, and with a high β (which recall denotes the share of capital in the production of the investment good) the output of the investment sector is more sensitive to the level of capital in the economy, which reduces investment and slows down capital accumulation further. In contrast, α mostly controls how a decline in K^{*} affects the steady state level of consumption C^{*}. Intuitively (ignoring the resource reallocation), the larger the share of capital in the consumption sector, the more consumption will fall in response to capital income taxes (cf. Eq. (S11.24)).

Note also that the implied magnitudes for income differences are different than in one-sector neoclassical growth model. The one sector neoclassical model essentially corresponds to the case $\alpha = \beta$ in the present model. Since α and β play different roles in generating income differences, the implied magnitudes will be different as long as $\alpha < \beta$. The magnitudes differ since, as argued above it is mostly the production technology of the investment sector (and hence β) that determines the response of the capital stock to taxes and other distortions to investment. One puzzle of the neoclassical model is that $\alpha = 1/3$, which is the common estimate for the share of capital in output, is too low to generate the observed differences in income levels in response to distortions. If we calibrate the present model with a relatively low α (say $\alpha \approx 1/3$) while allowing β to be larger (say $\beta \approx 2/3$), then this model could generate larger differences in capital stock and income, while still being consistent with the estimates for the share of capital in output.

Exercise 11.17

The representative household's problem in this economy can be written as

$$\max_{[c(t),a(t)]_{t=0}^{\infty}} \int_0^{\infty} \exp\left(-\rho t\right) \frac{c\left(t\right)^{1-\theta} - 1}{1 - \theta} dt$$

s.t. $\dot{a}\left(t\right) = r\left(t\right) a\left(t\right) + w\left(t\right) - c\left(t\right)$ and $\lim_{t\to\infty} \exp\left(-\int_0^t r\left(s\right) ds\right) a\left(t\right) = 0$,

where $a\left(t\right)$ denotes the level of per capita assets, which is equal to $k\left(t\right)$ in equilibrium. Since the representative consumer's problem is identical to the one in the standard neoclassical model, the analysis in Chapter 8 shows that Theorems 7.13 and 7.14 apply and the optimal path satisfies the Euler equation (11.39).

The social planner's problem can be written as

$$\max_{[c(t),k(t)\geq 0]_{t=0}^{\infty}} \int_0^{\infty} \exp\left(-\rho t\right) \frac{c\left(t\right)^{1-\theta} - 1}{1 - \theta} dt \qquad (S11.26)$$

s.t. $\dot{k}\left(t\right) = \tilde{f}\left(L\right) k\left(t\right) - c\left(t\right) - \delta k\left(t\right).$

To show that Theorem 7.13 applies to this problem, we verify that Assumption 7.1 holds. First, note that $f\left(c\right) \equiv \left(c^{1-\theta} - 1\right) / \left(1 - \theta\right)$ and $g\left(k, c\right) = \tilde{f}\left(L\right) k - c - \delta k$ are weakly monotone in c and k, hence Part 1 of Assumption 7.1 is satisfied. Second, note that $|g_c| = 1 > 0$, hence Part 2 of Assumption 7.1 is satisfied. Third, since $\lim_{c\to 0} c^{-\theta} = \infty$, Part 3 of Assumption 7.1 is not satisfied, but an analysis similar to Exercise 7.25 shows that the choice of consumption can be restricted to $c\left(t\right) \geq \varepsilon$ for sufficiently small $\varepsilon > 0$ without loss of generality, and Part 3 of Assumption 7.1 is also satisfied for this restricted problem. Hence Theorem 7.13 applies and shows that the following first-order conditions and the strong form of the transversality condition are necessary

$$\hat{H}_c\left(k, c, \mu\right) = c\left(t\right)^{-\theta} - \mu\left(t\right) = 0 \qquad (S11.27)$$
$$\hat{H}_k\left(k, c, \mu\right) = \mu\left(t\right)\left[\tilde{f}\left(L\right) - \delta\right] = -\dot{\mu}\left(t\right) + \rho\mu\left(t\right),$$
$$\lim_{t\to\infty}\left[\exp\left(-\rho t\right) \mu\left(t\right) k\left(t\right)\right] = 0.$$

When the parametric conditions $(1 - \theta)\left(\tilde{f}\left(L\right) - \delta\right) < \rho$ and $\tilde{f}\left(L\right) - \delta > \rho$ are satisfied, there exists a unique path $[k\left(t\right), c\left(t\right)]_{t=0}^{\infty}$ that satisfies the first-order conditions in (S11.27) and the constraints of Problem (S11.26). We next claim that Theorem 7.14 applies and shows that this path is optimal. To see this, first note that the current value Hamiltonian

$$\hat{H}\left(t, k, c, \mu\left(t\right)\right) = \frac{c^{1-\theta} - 1}{1 - \theta} + \mu\left(t\right)\left[\tilde{f}\left(L\right) k - c - \delta k\right]$$

is jointly concave in c and k since $\mu(t) = c(t)^{-\theta} > 0$. Note also that, for any feasible path $\left[\tilde{k}(t), \tilde{c}(t)\right]_{t=0}^{\infty}$, we have $\lim_{t \to \infty} \exp(-\rho t)\mu(t)\tilde{k}(t) \geq 0$ since $\tilde{k}(t) \geq 0$, hence the path $[k(t), c(t)]_{t=0}^{\infty}$ that is feasible and satisfies (S11.27) is optimal by Theorem 7.14.

Exercise 11.18

The labor market clearing condition now takes the form $\int L_i(t)\,di = L(t)$. As in the baseline Romer (1987) model, firms choose the same capital-labor ratio (although the scale of each firm is indeterminate), thus we have

$$
\begin{aligned}
Y(t) = \int_0^1 Y_i(t)\,di &= \int_0^1 F(K_i(t), A(t)L_i(t))\,di \\
&= F(K(t), A(t)L(t)) \\
&= F(K(t), BK(t)L(t)) \\
&= K(t)\tilde{f}(L(t)),
\end{aligned}
$$

where the second line uses $A(t) = BK(t)$ and the last line defines $\tilde{f}(L(t)) = F(1, BL(t))$. Wages and the rental rate of capital are given by

$$
\begin{aligned}
w(t) &= K(t)\tilde{f}'(L(t)) \\
R(t) &= \tilde{f}(L(t)) - L(t)\tilde{f}'(L(t)).
\end{aligned}
$$

Note that $R(t)$ is an increasing function of $L(t)$ with $\lim_{L(t) \to \infty} R(t) = \infty$.

On the consumer side, we assume dynastic preferences as in Section 11.1. Hence the consumer maximizes (11.1) subject to (11.2). Any interior solution to this problem satisfies the Euler equation

$$
\frac{\dot{c}(t)}{c(t)} = \frac{1}{\theta}(r(t) - n - (\rho - n)) = \frac{1}{\theta}(R(t) - \delta - \rho).
$$

As $L(t)$ increases, $R(t)$ grows unbounded and thus consumption grows at an ever increasing rate. If $c(0) \neq 0$, after some T consumption will grow faster than $\rho - n$ which implies that the representative household's utility $\int_0^\infty \exp(-(\rho-n)t)c(t)^{1-\theta}/(1-\theta)$ limits to infinity. That is, in this economy any interior solution to the consumer's problem results in infinite utility. Then, the analysis in Chapter 7 does not apply, in particular Theorem 7.13 and Theorem 7.14 cannot be used to characterize the solution to the consumer's problem since the value function is infinite. Intuitively, the knowledge externalities in the Romer (1987) economy are too potent and there are increasing returns to capital accumulation. Hence output per capita and consumption per capita increase at ever increasing rates, violating the finiteness of utility and the transversality condition.

Chapter 12: Modeling Technological Change

Exercise 12.2

Exercise 12.2, Part (a). Suppose first that the innovation is drastic enough so that $p^M < \psi$. The unique equilibrium then involves $p_1 = p^M$ and the innovator makes profits of $\hat{\pi}_1^I = D\left(p^M\right)\left(p^M - \lambda^{-1}\psi\right) - \mu$ as given in (12.3). Note first that this is an equilibrium. Setting $q_j = 0$ is a best response for the other firms as their marginal costs exceed the market price $p_1 = p^M < \psi$. And that given the other firms do not produce, the maximizing price for the innovator is the monopolistic price $p_1 = p^M$. Hence the allocation above is an equilibrium. To show that it is also unique, suppose there was another equilibrium involving $q_j > 0$ for some $j > 1$. For this to be an equilibrium, we need that the prevailing market price p is weakly greater than the marginal costs ψ. This however cannot be an equilibrium as the innovator could set the monopolistic price p^M and increase his profits. Hence, the allocation above is the unique equilibrium. To see that this is also true in the case of $p^M = \psi$, first note that the proposed allocation still *is* an equilibrium as the other firms $j > 1$ are indifferent between selling and not selling at $p^M = \psi$. To see that the equilibrium is still unique, note that there is a profitable deviation for the innovator in case $q_j > 0$ for some $j > 1$. The profits for the innovator at market prices of $p^M = \psi$ are given by

$$\pi_1(p^M) = ([D\left(p^M\right) - \sum_{j>1} q_j]\left(p^M - \lambda^{-1}\psi\right) - \mu,$$

where $\sum_{j>1} q_j > 0$. The profits from offering a slightly smaller price $p = \psi - \varepsilon$ are given by

$$\pi_1(p^M - \varepsilon) = [D\left(p^M - \varepsilon\right)]\left(p^M - \varepsilon - \lambda^{-1}\psi\right) - \mu,$$

where we already used that $q_j = 0$ for all $j > 1$ as $p < \psi$. Hence, the gain from lowering the price is given by

$$\Delta = \pi_1(p^M - \varepsilon) - \pi_1(p^M) = (D\left(\psi - \varepsilon\right) - D\left(\psi\right))\psi\frac{\lambda - 1}{\lambda} - D\left(\psi - \varepsilon\right)\varepsilon + \psi\frac{\lambda - 1}{\lambda}\sum_{j>1} q_j.$$

As the last term $\psi\frac{\lambda-1}{\lambda}\sum_{j>1} q_j$ is positive by hypothesis and the demand function D is continuous, there exists some ε small enough to make $\Delta > 0$. This shows that there is no equilibrium with $p^M = \psi$ and $q_j > 0$ for some $j > 1$. But there is no equilibrium involving $p = \psi - \varepsilon$ either. To achieve a contradiction, suppose there is. Now consider setting $\tilde{p} = \psi - \frac{\varepsilon}{2}$. This will clearly increase firm 1's profits as it will still get the whole market demand but the profit function is increasing in p at $\tilde{p}$. As ε is arbitrary, this shows that there is no equilibrium involving $p = \psi - \varepsilon$. Hence, even in the case of $p^M = \psi$, the unique equilibrium involves the innovator capturing the whole market.

Exercise 12.2, Part (b). Let us now assume that $p^M > \psi$. To see that the unique equilibrium involves $p_1 = \psi$ and $q_j = 0$ for all $j > 1$, let us suppose this is not the case. By the same argument as given in Part (a), it is clear that any price $p_1 < \psi$ cannot be profit maximizing. As $p^M > \psi > p_1$, the monopolistic objective function is increasing in p at $p = p_1$. Hence, $p_1 < \psi$ cannot be optimal as $\tilde{p} \in (p_1, \psi)$ yields a higher profit. But $p_1 > \psi$ cannot be an equilibrium either. If $q_j > 0$ for some $j > 1$, then the argument is exactly the same as in Part (a) - undercutting the price slightly and catering to the whole market will always be a profitable. But $q_j = 0$ for all $j > 1$ will of course not be an equilibrium either, as firm j would make positive profits by setting $q_j > 0$ as market prices exceed their marginal costs. Hence, the unique equilibrium price will involve $p_1 = \psi$. That the unique equilibrium allocation will also involve $q_j = 0$ for all $j > 1$ can again be shown by exactly the same argument as in Part (a). If not, offering a lower price close enough to ψ will always be profitable for the innovator. This proves this part of the proposition.

Exercise 12.2, Part (c). To show that $\hat{\pi}_1^I > \pi_1^I$ it is important to note that these two cases refer to different values of the productivity gain from innovation λ. Hence let us denote $\lambda_1 \geq \lambda^* > \lambda_2$ where the unconstrained monopoly price $p_1 = p^M$ refers to the case of λ_1 and the constrained case, i.e. $p_1 = \psi \leq p^M$, refers to the case of λ_2. Note that p^M also depends on λ (see (12.2)), so that the monopoly prices p^M are different in the two cases. To finally compare the two profit levels, note that

$$
\begin{aligned}
\hat{\pi}_1^I &= D\left(p^M\right)\left(p^M - \lambda_1^{-1}\psi\right) - \mu \\
&\geq D\left(\psi\right)\left(\psi - \lambda_1^{-1}\psi\right) - \mu \\
&= D\left(\psi\right)\frac{\lambda_1 - 1}{\lambda_1}\psi - \mu \\
&= D\left(\psi\right)\frac{\lambda_2 - 1}{\lambda_2}\psi - \mu + D(\psi)\left(\frac{\lambda_1 - 1}{\lambda_1} - \frac{\lambda_2 - 1}{\lambda_2}\right) \\
&= \pi_1^I + D(\psi)\frac{\lambda_1 - \lambda_2}{\lambda_1\lambda_2} > \pi_1^I,
\end{aligned}
$$

where the first inequality follows from a revealed preference type argument that p^M is the profit maximizing price (so it must give a higher profit than ψ) and the last inequality follows from the fact that $\lambda_1 > \lambda_2$. Even though this is an intuitive result, it is nevertheless important: the innovator would always prefer his innovation to be drastic.

Exercise 12.11

The maximization problem in (12.14) is given by

$$
\max_{p_i \geq 0}\left(\left(\frac{p_i}{P}\right)^{-\varepsilon} C\right)(p_i - \psi), \tag{S12.1}
$$

where the price index P is given in (12.11) by

$$
P \equiv \left(\sum_{i=1}^N p_i^{1-\varepsilon}\right)^{\frac{1}{1-\varepsilon}} \tag{S12.2}
$$

and the consumption index is given in (12.8) as

$$
C \equiv \left(\sum_{i=1}^N c_i^{\frac{\varepsilon-1}{\varepsilon}}\right)^{\frac{\varepsilon}{\varepsilon-1}}.
$$

As the maximizing argument of a function is invariant with respect to positive transformations of this function, it is convenient to first take the logarithm of the objective function in (S12.1).

In many models using the Dixit-Stiglitz (1977) framework, this simplifies the math. Hence, the objective function is given by

$$\max_{p_i \geq 0} -\varepsilon \log p_i + \frac{\varepsilon}{1-\varepsilon} \log \left(\sum_{i=1}^{N} p_i^{1-\varepsilon} \right) + \log C + \log (p_i - \psi),$$

so that the first-order condition results in

$$-\varepsilon \frac{1}{p_i} + \frac{\varepsilon}{1-\varepsilon} \frac{1}{\sum_{i=1}^{N} p_i^{1-\varepsilon}} (1-\varepsilon) p_i^{-\varepsilon} + \frac{1}{p_i - \psi} = 0. \tag{S12.3}$$

Since the first-order condition is the same for all monopolists i, we have that $p_i = p_j = p(N)$ (where the argument N stresses the dependence of the equilibrium price on the number of firms). Hence we get that $\sum_{i=1}^{N} p_i^{1-\varepsilon} = Np(N)^{1-\varepsilon}$ so that (S12.3) yields

$$p(N) = \frac{(N-1)\varepsilon}{(N-1)\varepsilon - N} \psi = \frac{\varepsilon}{\varepsilon - \frac{N}{N-1}} \psi.$$

As $\lim_{N \to \infty} \frac{(N-1)\varepsilon}{(N-1)\varepsilon - N} = \frac{\varepsilon}{\varepsilon - 1}$ we find that

$$\lim_{N \to \infty} p(N) = \frac{\varepsilon}{\varepsilon - 1} \psi,$$

which is the also the required solution given in (12.15). Note that $p(N) > \frac{\varepsilon}{\varepsilon-1} \psi$ and that $p(N)$ is monotonically decreasing in N. The reason is the following: if firms internalize their influence on the price aggregator P, optimal prices will be higher as P is increasing in p_i and firms i's demand is increasing in P for given p_i (see (S12.1)). Intuitively, each firm cares about its price relative to the price index P. So if firms internalize their influence, they realize that their relative increase by less as P adjusts too. If only a small number of firms is in the market (i.e. N is low), each firms' price has a large share in the determination of P so that this effect will be important in each firm's pricing decision.

Another way to see this, is the following. The elasticity of demand if P is taken as given, is

$$\varepsilon_D(p_i)|_P = -\left. \frac{p_i D'(p_i)}{D(p)} \right|_P = \varepsilon.$$

In contrast, the demand elasticity when the influence on P is internalized, is given by

$$\varepsilon_D(p_i) = -\frac{p_i \left[\frac{\partial D(p_i)}{\partial p_i} + \frac{\partial D(p_i)}{\partial P} \frac{\partial P}{\partial p_i} \right]}{D(p)} = \varepsilon - \varepsilon P^{-1} \frac{\partial P}{\partial p_i} < \varepsilon_D(p_i)|_P.$$

Hence, by recognizing their influence on P, firms perceive consumers' demand as less elastic and will therefore set higher prices. From (S12.2) we see that

$$\frac{\partial P}{\partial p_i} = P^\varepsilon p_i^{-\varepsilon} = \left(Np_i^{1-\varepsilon} \right)^{\frac{\varepsilon}{1-\varepsilon}} p_i^{-\varepsilon} = N^{\frac{\varepsilon}{1-\varepsilon}},$$

where the second equality follows from the symmetry $p_i = p_j$. In the limit where N goes to infinity, each firm's influence on P vanishes (i.e. $\lim_{N \to \infty} \frac{\partial P}{\partial p_i} = 0$) so that P is effectively taken as given and equilibrium prices are lower.

Exercise 12.13

Exercise 12.13, Part (a). As the social planner wants to maximize social surplus, there will not be any monopolistic distortions like they are present in the pricing decision of monopolists. Hence, he will set each varieties' price equal to its (common) marginal costs ψ. Using this, we get from the consumer's optimality condition

$$\left(\frac{c_i}{c_{i'}}\right)^{-\frac{1}{\varepsilon}} = \frac{p_i}{p_{i'}} = \frac{\psi}{\psi} = 1,$$

i.e. all varieties will be consumed in the same amount $c_i = c_{i'} = c$. Note that this is also true in the equilibrium. For a given number of varieties N the social planner will therefore chose a consumption aggregator

$$C \equiv \left(\sum_{i=1}^{N} c_i^{\frac{\varepsilon-1}{\varepsilon}}\right)^{\frac{\varepsilon}{\varepsilon-1}} = \left(Nc^{\frac{\varepsilon-1}{\varepsilon}}\right)^{\frac{\varepsilon}{\varepsilon-1}} = cN^{\frac{\varepsilon}{\varepsilon-1}}, \tag{S12.4}$$

where c is the consumption level of each variety. To allocate resources between the consumption goods c and the $y-$good and to decide about the number of varieties N, the social planner solves the problem

$$\max_{y,c,N} cN^{\frac{\varepsilon}{\varepsilon-1}} + y^{1-\alpha}(1-\alpha) \tag{S12.5}$$

$$\text{s.t.} \quad m = Nc\psi + y + N\mu, \tag{S12.6}$$

where the resource constraint stems from the fact that each good is produced in quantity c and costs ψ. Another way to see this (which is more in line with the exposition in the book) is that the ideal price index is equal to $P \equiv \left(\sum_{i=1}^{N} \psi^{1-\varepsilon}\right)^{\frac{1}{1-\varepsilon}} = \psi N^{1/(1-\varepsilon)}$. Note that P also denotes the unit costs of producing the aggregate good C. As c units of each variety are bought, the social planner buys $N^{\frac{\varepsilon}{\varepsilon-1}}c = C$ units of differentiated varieties (see (S12.4)) so that we can also express (S12.5) as

$$\max_{y,C,N} C + y^{1-\alpha}/(1-\alpha)$$

$$\text{s.t.} \quad m = CP + y + N\mu,$$

where the constraint follows from the fact that

$$Nc\psi = N^{\frac{\varepsilon}{\varepsilon-1}}N^{\frac{-1}{\varepsilon-1}}c\psi = N^{\frac{\varepsilon}{\varepsilon-1}}cN^{\frac{1}{1-\varepsilon}}\psi = CP.$$

This is exactly the form given in the book (using the specific utility function given here). Solving the constraint in (S12.6) for the consumption level $c = \frac{m-y-N\mu}{N\psi}$ and substituting this into (S12.5), we arrive at the unconstrained maximization problem

$$\max_{y,N} \frac{m-y-N\mu}{\psi}N^{\frac{1}{\varepsilon-1}} + y^{1-\alpha}/(1-\alpha).$$

The corresponding first-order conditions are

$$y^{-\alpha} = \frac{1}{\psi}N^{\frac{1}{\varepsilon-1}} \tag{S12.7}$$

$$m - y = \mu\varepsilon N. \tag{S12.8}$$

Using that from (S12.7) we get that $y = \psi^{1/\alpha} N^{-\frac{1}{\alpha(\varepsilon-1)}}$, (S12.8) determines the optimal number of varieties of the social planner N^{SP} by

$$m - \psi^{1/\alpha} \left(N^{SP}\right)^{-\frac{1}{\alpha(\varepsilon-1)}} = \mu\varepsilon N^{SP}. \tag{S12.9}$$

Exercise 12.13, Part (b). Let us now suppose that the social planner is not able to control prices, i.e. he has to take the monopolistic prices $p = \frac{\varepsilon}{\varepsilon-1}\psi$ as given. The ideal price index in this case is given by $P = \frac{\varepsilon}{\varepsilon-1}\psi N^{1/(1-\varepsilon)}$. Hence, the only difference from the problem solved in Part (a) is, that the consumption good is now more expensive (relative to the y-good), as the monopolistic pricing decision involves the mark-up $\frac{\varepsilon}{\varepsilon-1}$. Hence the social planer solves the problem

$$\max_{y,N} \frac{m - y - N\mu}{\frac{\varepsilon}{\varepsilon-1}\psi} N^{\frac{1}{\varepsilon-1}} + y^{1-\alpha}/(1-\alpha),$$

which has the first-order conditions

$$y^{-\alpha} = \frac{1}{\frac{\varepsilon}{\varepsilon-1}\psi} N^{\frac{1}{\varepsilon-1}}$$

$$m - y = \mu\varepsilon N.$$

Note especially that the second condition $m - y = \mu\varepsilon N$ is not affected by the different pricing. Similarly to (S12.9), the optimal number of varieties N^C (with the constraint that prices cannot be changed) solves the equation

$$m - \left(\frac{\varepsilon}{\varepsilon-1}\psi\right)^{1/\alpha} \left(N^C\right)^{\frac{-1}{\alpha(\varepsilon-1)}} = \mu\varepsilon N^C. \tag{S12.10}$$

Exercise 12.13, Part (c). Consider finally the equilibrium number of varieties, which is determined by free entry. To do so we have to find the expression for monopolistic profits. From the consumers' first-order condition we get that for each variety i

$$C^{1/\varepsilon}c_i^{-1/\varepsilon} = p_i y^{-\alpha}. \tag{S12.11}$$

Since the monopolist of variety i faces an isoelastic demand function, the monopolistic price is given by

$$p_i = p_j = \frac{\varepsilon}{\varepsilon-1}\psi, \tag{S12.12}$$

which immediately implies that $c_i = c_j = c$, i.e. all varieties are consumed by the same amount. From the definition of C we therefore get that

$$C = \left(\sum_{i=1}^{N} c_i^{\frac{\varepsilon-1}{\varepsilon}}\right)^{\frac{\varepsilon}{\varepsilon-1}} = cN^{\frac{\varepsilon}{\varepsilon-1}}. \tag{S12.13}$$

Substituting (S12.12) and (S12.13) into (S12.11), we arrive at

$$C^{1/\varepsilon}c^{-1/\varepsilon} = N^{1/(\varepsilon-1)} = \frac{\varepsilon}{\varepsilon-1}\psi y^{-\alpha}. \tag{S12.14}$$

Together with the budget constraint[1]

$$m = y + \sum_{i=1}^{N} p_i c_i = y + \frac{\varepsilon}{\varepsilon - 1} \psi N c = y + \frac{\varepsilon}{\varepsilon - 1} \psi N^{\frac{-1}{\varepsilon - 1}} C \qquad (S12.15)$$

we get two equations in two unknowns (C and y) which we can solve. Substituting y from (S12.14) into (S12.15) yields

$$C = \frac{\varepsilon - 1}{\varepsilon \psi} N^{\frac{1}{\varepsilon - 1}} \left(m - \left(\frac{\varepsilon}{\varepsilon - 1} \psi \right)^{1/\alpha} N^{\frac{-1}{\alpha(\varepsilon - 1)}} \right) \qquad (S12.16)$$

as a function of N and parameters.

To solve for the equilibrium number of firms N^{EQ}, we have to derive the monopolistic profits in this economy. These are given by

$$
\begin{aligned}
\pi &= (p_i - \psi)c_i = \frac{1}{\varepsilon - 1} \psi C N^{\frac{-\varepsilon}{\varepsilon - 1}} \\
&= \frac{1}{\varepsilon} N^{-1} \left(m - \left(\frac{\varepsilon}{\varepsilon - 1} \psi \right)^{1/\alpha} N^{\frac{-1}{\alpha(\varepsilon - 1)}} \right),
\end{aligned}
$$

where the second line followed upon substituting (S12.16). Hence, the equilibrium number of firms N^{EQ} is given by the zero profit condition $\pi = \mu$, which in this example is given by

$$m - \left(\frac{\varepsilon}{\varepsilon - 1} \psi \right)^{1/\alpha} \left(N^{EQ} \right)^{\frac{-1}{\alpha(\varepsilon - 1)}} = \mu \varepsilon N^{EQ}. \qquad (S12.17)$$

When we compare the respective conditions (S12.9), (S12.10) and (S12.17) we see that the structure is really similar and that we can learn about the sources of the differences between those allocations. Consider first the equilibrium number of varieties N^{EQ} determined in (S12.17). This condition is exactly the same as for the number of varieties N^C the social planner would choose if he would have to take monopolistic prices as given (determined in (S12.10)). In fact this result is relatively general in this kind of model. Dixit and Stiglitz (1977) work with the more general utility function

$$U \left(y, \left(\sum_{i=1}^{N} c_i^{\frac{\varepsilon - 1}{\varepsilon}} \right)^{\frac{\varepsilon}{\varepsilon - 1}} \right) \qquad (S12.18)$$

and show that a social planner who is choosing p_i, N and c_i subject to the constraint that each monopolist has to break even will in fact set $p_i = \frac{\varepsilon}{\varepsilon - 1} \psi$. Furthermore they show that even in this more general case the social planner will choose the same number of firms as in the equilibrium allocation.

When we compare (S12.10) or (S12.17) to (S12.9), we see that the difference between the optimal and the equilibrium number of varieties comes from the fact that the social planner internalizes that the marginal rate of transformation between a new variety and the y-good is equal to the marginal costs ψ and not equal to $\frac{\varepsilon}{\varepsilon - 1} \psi$ as in either (S12.10) or (S12.17). Hence, the only source of distortions in the equilibrium number of varieties comes from the fact that prices are set monopolistically. Conditional on equilibrium prices, the zero-profit

---

[1]Note that $m = y + \sum_{i=1}^{N} p_i c_i$ is the correct budget constraint for the respresentative consumer. Even though the consumer is the owner of the N firms in the market and will therefore receive the profits $\sum_{i=1}^{N} \pi_i = N\pi$, those profits are exactly spent on the entry costs $N\mu$. Hence, the consumer has only his initial income m, which he can spend on the two consumption goods C and y.

condition determines the number of varieties at exactly the number the social planner would also have chosen.

To see that the unconstrained social planner will in fact provide strictly more varieties, i.e. $N^{SP} > N^{EQ}$, consider the following argument. Although this could also be shown from the first-order conditions, we think the proof below is instructive as it illustrates various important properties of the Dixit-Stiglitz model. It is also closely related to the original argument provided in Dixit and Stiglitz (1977). We showed above that the consumers' problem can be thought of as choosing the two goods C and y with prices $p_C = P$ and $p_y = 1$. Hence, in both the equilibrium and the social planners solution the marginal condition $\frac{\partial U/\partial C}{\partial U/\partial y} = \frac{p_C}{p_y} = P$ will hold true. With the utility function assumed above this yields

$$P = \frac{\partial U/\partial C}{\partial U/\partial y} = \frac{1}{y^{-\alpha}} = y^{\alpha}. \tag{S12.19}$$

Hence, y is increasing in P. Above we showed that $P^{SP} = \psi N^{1/(1-\varepsilon)} < \frac{\varepsilon}{\varepsilon-1}\psi N^{1/(1-\varepsilon)} = P^{EQ}$, i.e. due to the monopolistic distortions, the equilibrium price index will be higher. (S12.19) then implies that $y^{EQ} > y^{SP}$, i.e. in equilibrium a higher quantity of the y-good will be consumed. But now note that we will have $U(C^{SP}, y^{SP}) > U(C^{EQ}, y^{EQ})$. This follows simply from the fact that the social planner could have chosen to set the monopolistic prices $p = \frac{\varepsilon}{\varepsilon-1}\psi$ but decided not to. As U is increasing in both arguments and $y^{EQ} > y^{SP}$, it will necessarily be the case that $C^{SP} > C^{EQ}$, i.e. given that less of the y-good will be consumed, the social planner will provide more of the consumption aggregate C. Intuitively, this could either be achieved by $c^{SP} > c^{EQ}$ or $N^{SP} > N^{EQ}$. Economically speaking, the social planner could either increase the scale of each firm and save the fixed costs expenses or he could exploit the aggregate demand externality and chose a higher number of firms.

To see that he will decide to use the latter channel, we are going to show that the social planner will in fact choose the same consumption level of each variety as the equilibrium allocation, i.e. $c^{SP} = c^{EQ}$. To see this, note that from the budget constraint we have that

$$m = p^{SP}c^{SP}N^{SP} + y^{SP} + N^{SP}\mu.$$

Hence,

$$c^{SP} = \frac{m - y^{SP} - N^{SP}\mu}{\psi N^{SP}}, \tag{S12.20}$$

where we substituted $p^{SP} = \psi$. Now note that the first-order condition of the social planner (see (S12.8)) is given by $m - y^{SP} = \mu\varepsilon N^{SP}$, so that (S12.20) implies that

$$c^{SP} = \frac{\mu\varepsilon N^{SP} + N^{SP}\mu}{\psi N^{SP}} = \frac{\mu\varepsilon - \mu}{\psi} = \frac{\varepsilon-1}{\psi}\mu. \tag{S12.21}$$

This determines the variety-specific consumption level in the social planner's allocation as a function of parameters only.

Now consider the equilibrium. The profit of each firm producing one variety is given by

$$\pi = \left(p^{EQ} - \psi\right)c^{EQ} = \frac{1}{\varepsilon-1}\psi c^{EQ}$$

where the second equality uses (S12.12). In equilibrium, firms make zero profits, i.e. we will have $\pi = \mu$. This however implies that

$$c^{EQ} = \frac{\varepsilon-1}{\psi}\mu. \tag{S12.22}$$

Hence, (S12.21) and (S12.22) show that $c^{EQ} = c^{SP}$, i.e. in both the equilibrium and the optimal allocation the consumption level of each variety is exactly the same. Using this and the definition of the consumption aggregate C (see (S12.4)), we therefore get that

$$C^{SP} = c^{SP} \left(N^{SP}\right)^{\frac{\varepsilon}{\varepsilon-1}} = c^{EQ} \left(N^{EQ}\right)^{\frac{\varepsilon}{\varepsilon-1}} \left(\frac{N^{SP}}{N^{EQ}}\right)^{\frac{\varepsilon}{\varepsilon-1}} = C^{EQ} \left(\frac{N^{SP}}{N^{EQ}}\right)^{\frac{\varepsilon}{\varepsilon-1}},$$

which from $C^{SP} > C^{EQ}$ directly implies that $N^{SP} > N^{EQ}$. Hence, the social planner will provide the same amount of each variety as in the equilibrium but will provide a larger number of varieties. Again, this result is not a consequence of the special structure of the preferences assumed in this exercise. Dixit and Stiglitz (1977) show that the same result is true for general preferences of the form given in (S12.18).

Chapter 13: Expanding Variety Models

Exercise 13.1

Exercise 13.1, Part (a). First of all note that we can rewrite (13.7) as

$$
\begin{aligned}
V(\nu, t) &= \int_t^\infty \exp\left[-\int_t^s r(s')ds'\right] \pi(\nu, s)ds \\
&= \int_t^{t+\Delta t} \exp\left[-\int_t^s r(s')ds'\right] (p^x(\nu, s) - \psi)x(\nu, s)ds \\
&\quad + \int_{t+\Delta t}^\infty \exp\left[-\int_t^s r(s')ds'\right] (p^x(\nu, s) - \psi)x(\nu, s)ds, \qquad \text{(S13.1)}
\end{aligned}
$$

where we used that per period profits are given by $\pi(\nu, s) = (p^x(\nu, t) - \psi)x(\nu, t)$. Intuitively, (S13.1) shows that the total value of a firm owning a patent can be decomposed into the flow profits of the present (i.e. in the arbitrary small time interval Δt) and the discounted "sum" of all future profits. This is closely related to the Principle of Optimality encountered in Chapter 6 and also discussed in detail by Stokey, Lucas and Prescott (1989), which concerns the equivalence of the sequence formulation and the recursive formulation and also decomposes the criterion function into current payoffs and the future discounted value.

Exercise 13.1, Part (b). To arrive at the required formulation consider the first term in (S13.1) and define the function $m(s)$ as

$$
m(s) = \exp\left[-\int_t^s r(s')ds'\right] \pi(\nu, s).
$$

By the mean value theorem we can find $\tilde{s}(s)$ for any s so that

$$
m(s) = m(t) + m'(\tilde{s}(s))(s - t),
$$

i.e.

$$
\exp\left[-\int_t^s r(s')ds'\right] \pi(\nu, s) = \pi(\nu, t) + m'(\tilde{s}(s))(s - t), \qquad \text{(S13.2)}
$$

where

$$
m'(\tilde{s}(s)) = \left. \frac{d\exp\left[-\int_t^s r(s')ds'\right]\pi(\nu, s)}{ds} \right|_{s=\tilde{s}(s)}.
$$

Substituting (S13.2) into the first term of (S13.1) yields

$$\int_t^{t+\Delta t} \exp\left[-\int_t^s r(s')ds'\right]\pi(\nu,s)ds$$

$$= \int_t^{t+\Delta t}\left[\pi(\nu,t)ds + \int_t^{t+\Delta t} m'(\tilde{s}(s))(s-t)\right]ds$$

$$\leq \pi(\nu,t)\Delta t + \int_t^{t+\Delta t} \max_{s\in[t,t+\Delta t]}\left|m'(\tilde{s}(s))\right|(s-t)ds$$

$$= \pi(\nu,t)\Delta t + \max_{s\in[t,t+\Delta t]}\left|m'(\tilde{s}(s))\right|\int_0^{\Delta t} zdz$$

$$= \pi(\nu,t)\Delta t + \max_{s\in[t,t+\Delta t]}\left|m'(\tilde{s}(s))\right|\frac{1}{2}(\Delta t)^2$$

$$= (p^x(\nu,t)-\psi)x(\nu,t)\Delta t + o(\Delta t), \tag{S13.3}$$

where we used the definition of per-period profits $\pi(\nu,t)$ and the fact that the second term is of order $o(\Delta t)$ (i.e. satisfies $\lim_{\Delta t\to 0}\frac{o(\Delta t)}{\Delta t}=0$). Also note that by definition we have

$$V(\nu,t+\Delta t) = \int_{t+\Delta t}^{\infty}\exp\left[-\int_{t+\Delta t}^s r(s')ds'\right]\pi(\nu,s)ds$$

$$= \exp\left[\int_t^{t+\Delta t} r(s')ds'\right]\int_{t+\Delta t}^{\infty}\exp\left[-\int_t^s r(s')ds'\right]\pi(\nu,s)ds. \tag{S13.4}$$

Using again the mean value theorem yields

$$\exp\left[\int_t^{t+\Delta t} r(s')ds'\right] = \exp\left[\int_t^{t+\Delta t}\left[r(t)+r'(\tilde{s}(s'))(s'-t)\right]ds'\right]$$

$$= \exp\left[r(t)\Delta t + \max_{s\in[t,t+\Delta t]}\left|r'(s)\right|\frac{1}{2}(\Delta t)^2\right]$$

$$= \exp\left[r(t)\Delta t + o(\Delta t)\right].$$

From (S13.4) we therefore know that

$$\int_{t+\Delta t}^{\infty}\exp\left[-\int_t^s r(s')ds'\right]\pi(\nu,s)ds = \exp\left[-\int_t^{t+\Delta t} r(s')ds'\right]V(\nu,t+\Delta t)$$

$$= \exp\left[-r(t)\Delta t\right]\exp\left[-o(\Delta t)\right]V(\nu,t+\Delta t)$$

$$= \exp\left[-r(t)\Delta t\right]V(\nu,t+\Delta t) + o(\Delta t). \tag{S13.5}$$

Substituting (S13.3) and (S13.5) into (S13.1) yields[1]

$$V(\nu,t) = (p^x(\nu,t)-\psi)x(\nu,t)\Delta t + \exp\left[-r(t)\Delta t\right]V(\nu,t+\Delta t) + o(\Delta t). \tag{S13.6}$$

The intuition for this equation is, that the difference between the value of owning a machine at t and the discounted value of owning a machine at $t+\Delta t$ is - up to first-order - only given by the fact that owning the blueprint earlier provides the owner already with flow profits of $\pi(\nu,t)\Delta t$. All second order terms are subsumed in $o(\Delta t)$. From the approximations above, however, we exactly know where those second order differences come from. First of all we could potentially have time varying interest rates, i.e. $\dot{r}(t)\neq 0$, so that the linear

---

[1]Note that there is a small typo in the exercise statement. Instead of $\exp\left[r(t)\Delta t\right]V(\nu,t+\Delta t)$ we should have $\exp\left[-r(t)\Delta t\right]V(\nu,t+\Delta t)$ in the equation given in part (b). Hence the equation derived in (S13.6) is in fact the correct one.

approximation to the discounting might not be exact. Secondly, the profit function $\pi(\nu,t)$ might vary over time. This would also introduce terms of second order.

Exercise 13.1, Part (c). Rearranging (S13.6), dividing by Δt and taking the limit $\Delta t \to 0$ yields

$$(p^x(\nu,t) - \psi)x(\nu,t) + \lim_{\Delta t \to 0} \frac{\exp\left[-r(t)\Delta t\right] V(\nu,t+\Delta t) - V(\nu,t)}{\Delta t} = 0, \qquad \text{(S13.7)}$$

as $\lim_{\Delta t \to 0} \frac{o(\Delta t)}{\Delta t} = 0$. But now note that the second term in the equation above is just the definition of the derivative of the function $\exp\left[-r(t)(\tau - t)\right] V(\nu,\tau)$ with respect to τ evaluated at $\tau = t$, i.e.

$$\lim_{\Delta t \to 0} \frac{\exp\left[-r(t)\Delta t\right] V(\nu,t+\Delta t) - V(\nu,t)}{\Delta t} = \left. \frac{d\exp\left[-r(t)(\tau - t)\right] V(\nu,\tau)}{d\tau}\right|_{\tau=t}$$

$$= -r(t)V(\nu,t) + \dot{V}(\nu,t).$$

Substituting this into (S13.7) and rearranging terms yields

$$r(t)V(\nu,t) - \dot{V}(\nu,t) = (p^x(\nu,t) - \psi)x(\nu,t) = \pi(\nu,t),$$

which is exactly the Hamilton-Bellman-Jacobi equation given in (13.8). The most intuitive economic interpretation of the Hamilton-Bellman-Jacobi equation comes from an asset pricing perspective. The return of holding the asset (i.e. holding a fully-enforced perpetual patent on the discovered blueprint) is given by $r(t)V(\nu,t)$. As with every asset this return is generated by both dividends, i.e. current payoffs represented by $\pi(\nu,t)$ and capital gains, i.e. the change in the asset's value over time $\dot{V}(\nu,t)$. Hence, the Hamilton-Bellman-Jacobi equation can be interpreted as the an asset pricing relationship to "price" the ownership of a patent.

Exercise 13.6

Exercise 13.6, Part (a). To see that $g_C^* > g^*$ is not feasible, recall that the derived production function for the final good is given by

$$Y(t) = \frac{1}{1-\beta}N(t)L,$$

so that

$$g^* = \frac{\dot{Y}(t)}{Y(t)} = \frac{\dot{N}(t)}{N(t)}.$$

But feasibility requires that $C(t) \leq Y(t)$, which directly implies that

$$g_C \leq g_Y = g^*.$$

Exercise 13.6, Part (b). Now suppose $g_C^* < g^*$. The appropriate transversality condition for this economy is given by

$$\lim_{t \to \infty}\left[\exp\left(-\int_0^t r(s)ds\right) N(t)V(t)\right] = 0. \qquad \text{(S13.8)}$$

With growth being balanced, the Euler equation requires that interest rates are constant and given by $r(t) = r^*$. Along the BGP we also have that $V(t) = V^* = \frac{\beta L}{r^*}$. Additionally we can write $N(t) = N(0)\exp[g^*t]$. Using these relationships, (S13.8) can be written as

$$
\lim_{t\to\infty}\left[\exp\left(-\int_0^t r(s)ds\right)N(t)V(t)\right] = \frac{\beta L}{r^*}N(0)\lim_{t\to\infty}[\exp(-r^*t)\exp[g^*t]]
$$
$$
= \frac{\beta L}{r^*}N(0)\lim_{t\to\infty}[\exp((g^*-r^*)t] = 0,
$$

or equivalently

$$
g^* - r^* < 0. \tag{S13.9}
$$

From the free entry condition into research we know that

$$
1 = \eta V^* = \eta\frac{\beta L}{r^*}
$$

so that interest rates are given by $r^* = \eta\beta L$. Hence (S13.9) implies

$$
g^* - \eta\beta L < 0. \tag{S13.10}
$$

Now consider the resource constraint

$$
Y(t) - X(t) = Z(t) + C(t). \tag{S13.11}
$$

As $Y(t) = \frac{1}{1-\beta}N(t)L$, $X(t) = (1-\beta)N(t)L$ and $Z(t) = \frac{1}{\eta}\dot{N}(t)$, (S13.11) can be written as

$$
\frac{\beta(2-\beta)}{1-\beta}L = \frac{1}{\eta}\frac{\dot{N}(t)}{N(t)} + \frac{C(t)}{N(t)}.
$$

So suppose that consumption grows at a slower rate. In that case we have that asymptotically

$$
\lim_{t\to\infty}\frac{C(t)}{N(t)} = 0,
$$

so that the asymptotic growth rate of $N(t)$ is given by

$$
g^* = \frac{\dot{N}(t)}{N(t)} = \eta\frac{\beta(2-\beta)}{1-\beta}L.
$$

This however implies that

$$
g^* - \eta\beta L = \eta\frac{\beta(2-\beta)}{1-\beta}L - \eta\beta L = \frac{1}{1-\beta}\eta\beta L > 0,
$$

which violates the transversality condition in (S13.10). This shows that consumption cannot grow slower than the number of varieties. Together with the result derived in Part (a), this proves that if the number of varieties and consumption grow at a constant rate, this rate has to be equal.

Exercise 13.7

Exercise 13.7, Part (a). The world equilibrium is a path of allocations and prices for each country $\left\{\left[\begin{array}{c} Y_j(t), C_j(t), Z_j(t), X_j(t), N_j(t), \\ \left(p_j^x(\nu,t), x_j(\nu,t)\right)|_{\nu\in N(t)}, r_j(t), w_j(t) \end{array}\right]_{t=0}^{\infty}\right\}_{j\in\{1,..,M\}}$ such that in each country j, all monopolists choose $\left[p_j^x(\nu,t), x_j(\nu,t)\right]_{\nu\in[0,N_j(t)],t=0}^{\infty}$ to maximize the discounted value of profits, the evolution of $[N_j(t)]_{t=0}^{\infty}$ is determined by free entry, the paths of interest rates and wage rates $[r_j(t), w_j(t)]_{t=0}^{\infty}$ clear capital and labor markets, and the paths of aggregate allocations $[C(t), X(t), Z(t)]_{t=0}^{\infty}$ are consistent with household maximization.

Exercise 13.7, Part (b). Since there are no interactions between countries, each country equilibrium is characterized separately as a closed economy. The characterization of the closed economy equilibrium for each country j is very similar to the characterization provided in Section 13.1. The only difference of the present model from the one analyzed in Section 13.1 is the presence of the ζ_j parameter, which controls the costs of R&D expenditure. Since ζ_j units of the final good spent on R&D generates a flow rate of η_j new blueprints, 1 unit of final good spent on R&D generates a flow rate of η_j/ζ_j blueprints. Hence, defining $\bar{\eta}_j \equiv \eta_j/\zeta_j$ as the unit productivity of R&D, the model for each country j becomes identical to the one analyzed in Section 13.1. It follows that, if Condition (13.21) holds for the parameters of country j, then Theorem 13.2 applies to country j and shows that $N_j(t), Y_j(t)$ and $C_j(t)$ all grow at the constant rate

$$g_j = \frac{1}{\theta}\left(\beta L_j \bar{\eta}_j - \rho_j\right) = \frac{1}{\theta}\left(\beta L_j \frac{\eta_j}{\zeta_j} - \rho_j\right). \tag{S13.12}$$

Moreover, country j variables grow at this rate starting at time $t = 0$, that is, there are no transitional dynamics.

Exercise 13.7, Part (c). From the expression for the growth rate of each country in Eq. (S13.12), it follows that different countries grow at different rates except for knife-edge cases. Therefore, according to this model, small changes in preferences, population, or R&D technology of economies would lead to large differences in levels of output and consumption in the long run.

Exercise 13.7, Part (d). We now incorporate taxes into the framework studied in Section 13.1. There are various ways the government could tax the economy. We consider a few variants in our analysis.

First suppose that the government of country j taxes returns on assets (i.e. capital income taxation) linearly at rate τ_j^A and distributes the proceeds back to the consumers in a lump sum fashion. In this case, the consumer Euler equation is

$$\frac{\dot{C}_j(t)}{C_j(t)} = \frac{1}{\theta}\left(r_j(t)\left(1 - \tau_j^A\right) - \rho_j\right).$$

The monopolist's per-period profits are still given by $\pi_j(\nu, t) = \beta L_j$ (cf. Eq. (13.11)) and the value function along the BGP is given by $V_j(\nu, t) = \beta L_j/r_j^*$. From the free entry condition, the BGP interest rate is pinned down as $r_j^* = \eta_j \beta L_j/\zeta_j$. Using this in the Euler equation above, the BGP growth rate is given by

$$g_j = \frac{1}{\theta}\left(\frac{\eta_j \beta L_j}{\zeta_j}\left(1 - \tau_j^A\right) - \rho_j\right).$$

This allocation corresponds to an equilibrium if Condition (13.21) is satisfied. Moreover, output, technology and consumption grow at this rate starting at time $t = 0$, i.e. there are no transitional dynamics. Note that a linear tax on capital reduces growth since it reduces the incentives for the representative consumer to save. R&D investments in this model are financed by savings of the representative household, thus a reduction in savings slows down innovation and growth.

Second, suppose instead that the government taxes profits of the monopolists (machine producers) at a constant linear rate τ_j^π and redistributes the revenues to the consumers in a lump sum fashion. This time, per-period profits and the value function on a BGP are given by

$$\pi_j(\nu,t) = \beta L_j\left(1 - \tau_j^\pi\right) \text{ and } V_j(\nu,t) = \frac{\beta L_j\left(1 - \tau_j^\pi\right)}{r^*}.$$

From the free entry condition, the BGP interest rate is pinned down as $r_j^* = \beta L_j\left(1 - \tau_j^\pi\right)\eta_j/\zeta_j$, and from the Euler equation, the growth rate is given by

$$g_j = \frac{1}{\theta}\left(\frac{\beta L_j \eta_j}{\zeta_j}\left(1 - \tau_j^\pi\right) - \rho_j\right).$$

Note that taxing profits of the machine producers reduces the value of innovated varieties, which in turn reduces innovation and growth.

Third, consider the case in which the government taxes (or subsidizes) R&D investment linearly at rate τ^R and redistributes (finances) in a lump-sum fashion. This will change the R&D arbitrage equation as

$$\eta_j V_j(\nu,t) = \frac{\zeta_j}{\left(1 - \tau^R\right)},$$

and consequently, the BGP interest rate is pinned down by $r_j(t) = \beta L_j \eta_j \left(1 - \tau_j^R\right)/\zeta_j$ and the growth rate is given by

$$g_j = \frac{1}{\theta}\left(\frac{\beta L_j \eta_j}{\zeta_j}\left(1 - \tau_j^R\right) - \rho_j\right).$$

We note that, the same amount of linear tax applied in various different forms yield the same growth rate (and equilibrium path) in this economy. In particular, taxes that discourage savings, private sector profits or innovation all reduce the growth rate in this economy. Note also that, if two countries have different tax policies or different discount factors, they will have different growth rates and their income per capita levels will rapidly diverge. Then, according to this model, small differences in policy distortions can explain large income differences, suggesting that endogenizing the growth rate may help resolve some of the empirical challenges discussed in Chapters 3 and 8. Note, however, that the present model is too simplistic since it ignores all cross-country interactions. As analyzed in the Chapters 18 and 19, introducing cross-country interactions in goods, financial or R&D markets create stabilizing effects that make the countries grow at rates closer to each other.

Exercise 13.13*

Exercise 13.13, Part (a). An equilibrium is a collection of time paths of aggregate resource allocations, the set of machine varieties whose patents haven't expired (denoted by $N_1(t)$), the set of machine varieties whose patents expired (denoted by $N_2(t)$), quantities, prices and the value function for each machine, and interest rates and wages

$$\left[\begin{array}{c} Y(t), C(t), Z(t), X(t), N_1(t), N_2(t), \\ (p^x(\nu,t), x(\nu,t), V(\nu,t))|_{\nu\in N_1(t)}, [p^x(\nu,t), x(\nu,t)]_{\nu\in N_2(t)}, r(t), w(t) \end{array}\right]_{t=0}^{\infty} \text{ such that con-}$$

sumers choose consumption and asset holdings optimally, the evolution of patented machines is determined by free entry in R&D and the expiration of patents, machine producers with patents set prices to maximize profits, machines with expired patents are produced competitively, the final good is produced competitively, and asset and the final good markets clear.

We first characterize the static equilibrium allocations for given $N_1(t)$ and $N_2(t)$. The demand for machines from the final good producers is given by $x(\nu, t) = p^x(\nu, t)^{-1/\beta} L$. The machine producers with patents set the monopoly prices. Thus given the isoelastic demand, we have[2]

$$p^x(\nu, t) = \psi/(1 - \beta) \text{ and } x(\nu, t) = \left(\frac{\psi}{1 - \beta}\right)^{-1/\beta} L \text{ for } \nu \in N_1(t).$$

The monopolists' per period profits are

$$\pi(\nu, t) = \left(\frac{\psi}{1 - \beta}\right)^{-(1-\beta)/\beta} \beta L. \qquad (S13.13)$$

The machines with expired patents are priced at marginal cost, hence we have

$$p^x(\nu, t) = \psi \text{ and } x(\nu, t) = \psi^{-1/\beta} L \text{ for } \nu \in N_2(t).$$

Total output is therefore given by

$$Y(t) = \frac{1}{1 - \beta} L \psi^{-(1-\beta)/\beta} \left(N_1(t)(1 - \beta)^{(1-\beta)/\beta} + N_2(t)\right), \qquad (S13.14)$$

and equilibrium wages by

$$w(t) = \frac{\beta}{1 - \beta} \psi^{-(1-\beta)/\beta} \left(N_1(t)(1 - \beta)^{(1-\beta)/\beta} + N_2(t)\right).$$

Note also that the aggregate machine expenditure is given by

$$X(t) = L \psi^{-(1-\beta)/\beta} \left(N_1(t)(1 - \beta)^{1/\beta} + N_2(t)\right). \qquad (S13.15)$$

We next turn to the dynamic trade-offs in this economy. The value function $V(\nu, t)$ for machine producers with patents satisfies the HJB equation

$$r(t) V(\nu, t) = \pi(\nu, t) + \dot{V}(\nu, t) - \iota V(\nu, t), \qquad (S13.16)$$

where the last term captures the fact that with a flow rate of ι, the firm loses the patent and its monopoly power at which point the value drops to 0. We are interested in equilibria in which $Z(t) > 0$ for all t, which implies that the value function is uniquely pinned down from free entry in R&D as

$$\eta V(\nu, t) = 1.$$

Using this and the expression for $\pi(\nu, t)$ in Eq. (S13.13) to solve Eq. (S13.16), we have that $r(t)$ is constant at all t and given by

$$r(t) = \left(\frac{\psi}{1 - \beta}\right)^{-(1-\beta)/\beta} \eta \beta L - \iota.$$

Consumer optimization gives the Euler equation

$$\frac{\dot{C}(t)}{C(t)} = \frac{1}{\theta}(r(t) - \rho),$$

hence the growth rate of consumption is also constant and given by

$$g = \frac{1}{\theta}\left[\left(\frac{\psi}{1 - \beta}\right)^{-(1-\beta)/\beta} \eta \beta L - \iota - \rho\right]. \qquad (S13.17)$$

---

[2]In this exercise, we do not impose the normalization assumption $\psi = 1 - \beta$ to provide a slightly more general solution.

Since consumption grows at a constant rate, we have

$$C(t) = C(0) \exp(gt). \tag{S13.18}$$

Next note that the evolution of $N_1(t)$ and $N_2(t)$ are given by

$$
\begin{aligned}
\dot{N}_1(t) &= \eta Z(t) - \iota N_1(t), \text{ with } N_1(0) \text{ given} \tag{S13.19}\\
\dot{N}_2(t) &= \iota N_1(t), \text{ with } N_2(0) \text{ given},
\end{aligned}
$$

where the expression $\iota N_1(t)$ in both equations capture the fact that the patent for each machine expires at a flow rate of ι. Now, using Eqs. (S13.14), (S13.15), (S13.18), and market clearing in the final good, we have

$$Z(t) = \frac{1}{1-\beta} L\psi^{-(1-\beta)/\beta}\left(N_1(t)(1-\beta)^{1/\beta}\left[\frac{1}{1-\beta}-(1-\beta)\right]+\beta N_2(t)\right) - C(0)\exp(gt). \tag{S13.20}$$

Plugging this in (S13.19) gives us a set of differential equations with two variables $N_1(t)$ and $N_2(t)$ and two initial conditions, which can be solved for a given $C(0)$. Among the possible choices for $C(0)$, only one gives a stable solution for $N_1(t)$ and $N_2(t)$ where N_1 and N_2 asymptotically grow at rate g, and this solution satisfies all equilibrium requirements (the unstable solutions either violate the transversality condition or the resource constraints). Hence, the equilibrium is saddle path stable and is uniquely characterized by the two differential equations for N_1 and N_2.

We are interested in the BGP equilibrium, so we conjecture that N_1 and N_2 grow at the same constant rate as g. From the differential equation system in (S13.19), we have that the BGP values of N_1 and N_2 must satisfy

$$\frac{N_1}{N_2} = \frac{g}{\iota} \tag{S13.21}$$

Note also that from Eq. (S13.19), we have

$$
\begin{aligned}
Z(t) &= \left(\dot{N}_1(t) + \iota N_1(t)\right)/\eta\\
&= N_1(t)(g+\iota)/\eta,
\end{aligned}
$$

where the second line uses our BGP conjecture that $N_1(t)$ grows at the constant rate g. Then, on our conjectured BGP, Eq. (S13.20) can be rewritten

$$
N_1(0)\exp(gt)\frac{g+\iota}{\eta}
$$
$$
= \left\{\frac{1}{1-\beta}L\psi^{-(1-\beta)/\beta}\left(N_1(0)(1-\beta)^{1/\beta}\left[\frac{1}{1-\beta}-(1-\beta)\right]+\beta N_1(0)\frac{\iota}{g}\right) - C(0)\right\}\exp(gt).
$$

Canceling the growing terms $\exp(gt)$ from each side and collecting the $N_1(0)$ terms, we have

$$C(0) = N_1(0)\left\{\frac{1}{1-\beta}L\psi^{-(1-\beta)/\beta}\left((1-\beta)^{1/\beta}\left[\frac{1}{1-\beta}-(1-\beta)\right]+\beta\frac{\iota}{g}\right) - \frac{g+\iota}{\eta}\right\},$$

which characterizes the initial level of consumption. We assume

$$\left(\left(\frac{\psi}{1-\beta}\right)^{-(1-\beta)/\beta}\eta\beta L - \iota\right)(1-\theta) < \rho, \tag{S13.22}$$

so that the described path also satisfies the transversality condition, and

$$\left(\frac{\psi}{1-\beta}\right)^{-(1-\beta)/\beta}\eta\beta L - \iota > \rho, \tag{S13.23}$$

so that there is positive growth (which we need to verify our assumption that there is positive R&D investment in equilibrium).

It follows that when the parametric restrictions in Eqs. (S13.22) and (S13.23) are satisfied and the initial values of the technology, $N_1(0)$ and $N_2(0)$, satisfy Condition (S13.21), there exists a BGP equilibrium in which $N_1(t), N_2(t), C(t), Y(t), w(t)$ all grow at the constant rate g given by Eq. (S13.17). Note also that if the initial levels of $N_1(0), N_2(0)$ do not satisfy Condition (S13.21), then there will be transitional dynamics in this economy: $N_1(0)/N_2(0)$ ratio will monotonically converge to g/ι and the aggregate variables will asymptotically grow at rate g.

Exercise 13.13, Part (b). We have shown that the BGP growth rate is given by the expression in (S13.17) hence the value of ι that maximizes the growth rate is $\iota^* = 0$. When patents expire faster, incentives for innovation are lower, that is, firms' expected profits are lower for a given interest rate. To have entry in the R&D sector, the interest rates will have to decline. With lower interest rates, consumers demand a flatter consumption profile and reduce their savings, which leads to lower investment in R&D and lower growth.

Exercise 13.13, Part (c). We first make a couple of observations about the nature of the distortions in this economy. Note that there are static monopoly distortions in this economy which reduce net output for a given level of machines $N(t)$. Note also that, as in the baseline expanding varieties model analyzed in Section 13.1, there are dynamic distortions since the marginal value of a new technology is higher for the social planner for two reasons. First, the social planner takes into account the effect of new technologies on both wages and profits while the equilibrium firms only care about profits, and second, the social planner produces a higher net output for a given level of machines (since it avoids the monopoly distortions). Since the marginal value of a new technology is higher for the planner, the growth rate in the socially planned economy is also higher than the equilibrium growth rate.

Next, in view of these observations, we note that the effect of patents are two-fold. On the one hand, increasing ι increases the rate at which products become competitive and increases the static output for a given level of machines. This is best seen in Eq. (S13.14): there is a coefficient $(1-\beta)^{1/\beta} < 1$ in front of $N_1(t)$, so for a given level of $N(t) = N_1(t) + N_2(t)$, total output is increasing in $N_2(t)$. The effect through this channel is welfare improving since it alleviates some of the static monopoly distortions. On the other hand, as we have seen in Part (b), increasing ι decreases the growth rate in this economy. Since the growth rate in the economy is less than optimal to begin with (as we have noted in the previous paragraph), increasing ι reduces welfare through this channel.

Depending on consumer preferences one or the other effect may dominate and increasing ι may be welfare improving or welfare reducing. The less patient the consumers are (the higher the discount rate ρ) and the lower the intertemporal substitution (the higher θ), the more likely it is that the first effect will dominate and increasing ι will be welfare enhancing. In this case, consumers care relatively more about consumption today and they dislike a growing consumption profile, hence they may prefer immediate benefits of a more competitive market to delayed benefits of the monopolistic market.

Viewed differently, increasing ι is not the best policy to cure the inefficiencies in this economy. This argument is also forcefully made by Romer (1990). To achieve efficiency, we need to reduce the distortions through the monopolistic mark-ups but we also need to give sufficient surpluses to the monopolists so they have the right incentives to innovate. When $\iota = 0$, a linear subsidy on the monopolist output (just enough to get the production to competitive levels) financed by a lump-sum tax on the consumers can decentralize the social planner's solution.[3] However, increasing ι is only an imperfect solution and may or may not be welfare improving. For a discussion along those lines, see also Romer (1987).

Exercise 13.15

Exercise 13.15, Part (a). The equilibrium in this economy is a sequence of aggregate allocations, aggregate prices, pricing and production decisions for intermediate monopolists and value functions $\left[\begin{array}{c} Y\left(t\right),C\left(t\right),Z\left(t\right),X\left(t\right),A\left(t\right),N\left(t\right),r\left(t\right),w\left(t\right), \\ \left[p^{x}\left(\nu,t\right),x\left(\nu,t\right),V\left(\nu,t\right)\right]_{\nu\in N(t)} \end{array} \right]_{t=0}^{\infty}$ such that the representative consumer maximizes utility, the competitive final good producers maximize profits taking prices given, the intermediate good monopolists set prices to maximize profits, the expenditure on R&D and the evolution of the number of varieties is determined by free entry, and the asset and the final good markets clear. We can define a BGP equilibrium as an equilibrium on which consumption and output grows at a constant rate.

We next state some of these requirements in more detail to highlight their differences with the baseline continuous time model. Note that the representative consumer now solves the discrete time problem

$$\max_{\{C(t),A(t)\}_t} \sum_{t=0}^{\infty} \beta^t \frac{C\left(t\right)^{1-\theta}-1}{1-\theta}$$

$$\text{s.t.} \quad A\left(t+1\right)=\left(1+r\left(t\right)\right)A\left(t\right)+w\left(t\right)-C\left(t\right) \text{ for all } t,$$

$$\text{and} \quad \lim_{t\to\infty} A\left(t\right) \prod_{t'=1}^{t} \frac{1}{1+r\left(t'\right)} \geq 0.$$

Here $r\left(t\right)$ denotes the net rate of return on assets. The asset evolution equation and the no-Ponzi condition are slightly different due to the discrete time formulation. The solution is still characterized by the Euler equation and the transversality condition condition, which now take the form

$$C\left(t\right)^{-\theta} = \beta\left(1+r\left(t\right)\right)C\left(t+1\right)^{-\theta} \text{ and} \tag{S13.24}$$

$$\lim_{t\to\infty} A\left(t\right) \prod_{t'=1}^{t} \frac{1}{1+r\left(t'\right)} = 0.$$

Next, note that the evolution of $N\left(t\right)$ is given by the R&D technology evolution equation in discrete time

$$N\left(t+1\right)-N\left(t\right) = \eta Z\left(t\right).$$

Note that we assume the timing convention that investment in R&D at time t generates blueprints at time $t+1$. With this convention, the free entry condition can be written as

$$\eta \frac{V\left(\nu,t+1\right)}{1+r\left(t+1\right)} \leq 1 \text{ with equality if } Z\left(t\right) > 0.$$

Note also that with this timing convention the asset market clearing condition takes the form

$$A\left(t\right) = \int_{0}^{N(t)} V\left(\nu,t\right)d\nu.$$

---

[3]Even though this policy is Pareto optimal in the model, in reality it would be difficult to implement and it may also be undesirable. If we add heterogeneity to the model and assume that the firms' shares are held by a small fraction of the population, this policy would most likely increase wealth inequality and may therefore be undesirable if the social planner has a preference for lower inequality.

Finally, note that the value function of the monopolist, $V(\nu, t)$, is the discounted sum of future profits, i.e.

$$V(\nu, t) = \sum_{t'=t}^{\infty} \pi(\nu, t) \prod_{s=t}^{t'} \left(\frac{1}{1 + r(s)} \right). \tag{S13.25}$$

In the next part, we analyze these conditions in more detail and characterize the equilibrium path. To avoid notational conflict, we denote the inverse elasticity of substitution between intermediate goods as α rather than β, since β refers to the discount factor in this model. We continue to make the normalization $\psi = 1 - \alpha$ for the marginal cost of producing a machine.

Exercise 13.15, Part (b). First, we characterize the static equilibrium allocation given the number of varieties $N(t)$. Intermediate good monopolists choose $p^x(\nu, t)$ to maximize profits given the isoelastic demand from the final good sector, which implies

$$p^x(\nu, t) = 1, x(\nu, t) = L, \text{ and } \pi(\nu, t) = \alpha L. \tag{S13.26}$$

This shows that the final output and the equilibrium wages are given by

$$Y(t) = \frac{1}{1 - \alpha} N(t) L, \text{ and } w(t) = \frac{\alpha}{1 - \alpha} N(t).$$

The expenditures on machines is given by

$$X(t) = (1 - \alpha) L N(t).$$

Note that the static equilibrium allocations are identical to those in the continuous time model.

We next turn to the dynamic trade-offs in this economy. We characterize a BGP equilibrium in which the interest rate $r(t) \equiv r^*$ is constant and there is positive growth. From Eqs. (S13.25) and (S13.26), we calculate $V(\nu, t)$ as

$$V(\nu, t) = \sum_{t'=0}^{\infty} \frac{\alpha L}{(1 + r^*)^{t'}} = \alpha L \frac{1 + r^*}{r^*}.$$

Since there is positive growth, there is positive investment in R&D and the free entry condition implies that

$$\frac{V(\nu, t)}{1 + r^*} = 1/\eta.$$

Putting the last two expressions together, we can solve for the BGP interest rate as $r^* = \eta \alpha L$. Using this in the Euler equation (S13.24), we arrive at

$$C(t+1) = (\beta(1 + r^*))^{1/\theta} C(t).$$

Since consumption grows by a factor of $(\beta(1 + r^*))^{1/\theta}$, we define

$$1 + g_c \equiv (\beta(1 + r^*))^{1/\theta} \equiv (\beta(1 + \eta \alpha L))^{1/\theta},$$

hence g_c is the one period growth rate of consumption. Note that this implies $C(t) = C(0)(1 + g_c)^t$. Plugging the equilibrium values for $Y(t), C(t), X(t)$ and $Z(t)$ in the resource constraint $Y(t) = C(t) + X(t) + Z(t)$, we have

$$\frac{1}{1 - \alpha} L = \frac{C(0)(1 + g_c)^t}{N(t)} + (1 - \alpha) L + \frac{N(t+1)/N(t) - 1}{\eta}.$$

We conjecture a path for $N(t)$ in which $N(t+1) = N(t)(1+g_c)$ for all t, that is, $N(t)$ grows by the same factor as $C(t)$. Plugging the conjectured path into the previous displayed equation yields

$$\frac{1}{1-\alpha}L = \frac{C(0)}{N(0)} + (1-\alpha)L + \frac{g_c}{\eta}.$$

Hence for the initial value of consumption

$$C(0) = \left(\left[\frac{1}{1-\alpha} - (1-\alpha) \right] L - \frac{g_c}{\eta} \right) N(0),$$

the paths $[C(t), N(t)]_t$ in which both $C(t)$ and $N(t)$ grow at the same rate g_c satisfy the resource constraints for all t. Finally, we make the following parametric restrictions so that the transversality condition is satisfied and there is positive growth

$$(1+r)^{-1}(1+g_c) \quad < \quad 1 \ (\text{or equivalently } \beta(1+\eta\alpha L)^{1-\theta} < 1),$$
$$1 + g_c \quad > \quad 0 \ (\text{equivalently, } \beta(1+\eta\alpha L) > 1).$$

Under these parametric restrictions, the path $[C(t), N(t)]_{t=0}^{\infty}$ that we describe corresponds to an equilibrium.

Exercise 13.15, Part (c). The equilibrium we have characterized in Part (b) features constant growth starting at $t = 0$ which also shows that there are no transitional dynamics. Starting at any $N(0)$, all variables grow at constant rates and the interest rate is constant at every point in equilibrium.

Exercise 13.19

Exercise 13.19, Part (a). In order to characterize the transitional dynamics let us first gather the equations which determine the equilibrium allocation. From the consumer side we know that the evolution of per capita consumption $c(t)$ has to satisfy the Euler equation

$$\frac{\dot{c}(t)}{c(t)} = \frac{1}{\theta}(r(t) - \rho) \tag{S13.27}$$

and that the transversality condition

$$\lim_{t \to \infty} \left[\exp\left(-\int_0^t r(s)ds \right) \int_0^{N(t)} V(\nu, t)d\nu \right] = 0 \tag{S13.28}$$

has to be satisfied. The evolution of the economy's product varieties is given by the innovation possibility frontier

$$\dot{N}(t) = \eta N(t)^{\phi} L_R(t).$$

Equilibrium on the labor market requires that wages are given by the marginal product of labor

$$w(t) = \frac{\partial Y(t)}{\partial L_E} = \frac{\beta}{1-\beta} \int_0^{N(t)} x(\nu, t)^{1-\beta} d\nu L_E^{\beta-1} = \frac{\beta}{1-\beta} N(t),$$

as in equilibrium $x(\nu, t) = L_E(t)$ for all ν. By the same argument, the derived production function for the final good is given by

$$Y(t) = \frac{1}{1-\beta} N(t) L_E(t) \tag{S13.29}$$

and the resources spent on intermediary production are given by

$$X(t) = \int_0^{N(t)} \psi x(\nu, t)d\nu = (1-\beta)L_E(t)N(t). \tag{S13.30}$$

The resource constraint is therefore given by

$$Y(t) - X(t) = \frac{(2-\beta)\beta}{1-\beta}L_E(t)N(t) = C(t) = L(t)c(t). \tag{S13.31}$$

Given that only labor is needed in the R&D-process, the free entry condition for the research sector is given by

$$\eta N(t)^\phi V(\nu, t) \leq w(t) \text{ with equality if } L_R(\nu, t) \geq 0. \tag{S13.32}$$

This condition reflects the fact that a researcher employed in research sector ν costs the labor cost given by the current wage rate $w(t)$ and and generates a flow rate of $\eta N(t)^\phi$ innovations which have a value of $V(\nu, t)$ each. The value function is again implicitly defined by the Hamilton-Jacobi-Bellman equation

$$r(t)V(\nu, t) - \dot{V}(\nu, t) = \pi(\nu, t) = \beta L_E(t), \tag{S13.33}$$

where $L_E(t)$ denotes the labor force employed in the production of the final good.

Let us now consider an equilibrium where the research sectors are active. We will argue below that this is without loss of generality in this model. With positive research expenditures, the free entry condition contained in (S13.32) has to hold with equality, i.e. we need that

$$\eta N(t)^\phi V(\nu, t) = w(t) = \frac{\beta}{1-\beta}N(t) \text{ for all } t. \tag{S13.34}$$

As (S13.34) has to hold in all periods, we can differentiate this condition to arrive at

$$\frac{\dot{V}(t)}{V(t)} = (1-\phi)\frac{\dot{N}(t)}{N(t)}.$$

Substituting this into (S13.33) and rearranging terms, it follows that the equilibrium value function is given by

$$V(\nu, t) = \frac{\beta L_E(t)}{r(t) - (1-\phi)\frac{\dot{N}(t)}{N(t)}}. \tag{S13.35}$$

Substituting this back into the free entry condition (S13.34) yields

$$\frac{1}{\eta}\frac{\beta}{1-\beta} = \frac{V(\nu, t)}{N(t)^{1-\theta}} = \frac{\beta}{r(t) - (1-\phi)\frac{\dot{N}(t)}{N(t)}}\frac{L_E(t)}{N(t)^{1-\theta}}. \tag{S13.36}$$

From (S13.31) and (S13.27) we furthermore get that

$$\frac{\dot{L}_E(t)}{L_E(t)} + \frac{\dot{N}(t)}{N(t)} = \frac{\dot{L}(t)}{L(t)} + \frac{\dot{c}(t)}{c(t)} = n + \frac{1}{\theta}(r(t) - \rho). \tag{S13.37}$$

Solving this for the equilibrium interest rate $r(t) = \theta\left(\frac{\dot{L}_E(t)}{L_E(t)} + \frac{\dot{N}(t)}{N(t)}\right) + \rho$ and substituting into (S13.36) yields

$$\frac{\beta}{\theta\left(\frac{\dot{L}_E(t)}{L_E(t)} + \frac{\dot{N}(t)}{N(t)}\right) + \rho - (1-\phi)\frac{\dot{N}(t)}{N(t)}}\frac{L_E(t)}{N(t)^{1-\theta}} = \frac{1}{\eta}\frac{\beta}{1-\beta}. \tag{S13.38}$$

The growth rate of technological progress is determined by the innovation possibilities frontier, i.e. is given by

$$\frac{\dot{N}(t)}{N(t)} = \eta\frac{L_R(t)}{N(t)^{1-\phi}} = \eta\frac{L(t) - L_E(t)}{N(t)^{1-\phi}}, \tag{S13.39}$$

where the last equality uses the market clearing condition on the labor market. (S13.38) and (S13.39) are two differential equations in the two unknowns $N(t)$ and $L_E(t)$, which (together with the initial condition $N(0)$ and the transversality condition (S13.28)) we can solve for $[N(t), L_E(t)]_{t=0}^{\infty}$. With these two paths at hand, interest rates are found from (S13.37), (S13.31) determines the evolution of consumption and the value function can be calculated from (S13.34). This concludes the characterization of the equilibrium in this economy.

Let us now consider the BGP. Along the BGP the number of varieties $N(t)$ grows at a constant rate g^*. (S13.39) then implies that

$$\frac{\dot{L}_R(t)}{L_R(t)} = (1-\phi)g^*,\qquad\qquad\text{(S13.40)}$$

which in turn implies that

$$\frac{\dot{L}_R(t)}{L_R(t)} = \frac{\dot{L}_E(t)}{L_E(t)} = \frac{\dot{L}(t)}{L(t)} = n.$$

From (S13.40) we can therefore determine the BGP growth rate of varieties as

$$g^* = \frac{n}{1-\phi}.\qquad\qquad\text{(S13.41)}$$

Furthermore we get from (S13.31) that aggregate consumption grows at rate

$$\frac{\dot{C}(t)}{C(t)} = \frac{\dot{L}_E(t)}{L_E(t)} + \frac{\dot{N}(t)}{N(t)} = n + g^*,$$

so that per capita consumption grows at $g^* = \frac{n}{1-\phi}$. The Euler equation hence determines equilibrium interest rates as

$$r^* = \theta g^* + \rho = \theta\frac{n}{1-\phi} + \rho.\qquad\qquad\text{(S13.42)}$$

Finally we have to make sure that the transversality condition (S13.28) is satisfied. From (S13.35) we know that $V(t)$ grows at rate n. Hence,

$$\lim_{t\to\infty}\left[\exp\left(-\int_0^t r(s)ds\right)\int_0^{N(t)} V(\nu,t)d\nu\right] = \lim_{t\to\infty}\exp\left[(-r^* + n + g^*)t\right] = 0$$

which (using (S13.42)) requires that

$$(1-\theta)g^* + n = \frac{2-\theta-\phi}{1-\phi}n < \rho.\qquad\qquad\text{(S13.43)}$$

This concludes the characterization of the BGP equilibrium.

Let us now turn to the transitional dynamics. First of all we will show that this economy does feature transitional dynamics. To prove this, suppose by contradiction this is not the case, i.e. growth is always balanced. First of all note that the innovation possibilities frontier (S13.39) and the BGP growth rate (S13.41) imply that

$$g^* = \frac{n}{1-\phi} = \eta\frac{L_R(t)}{N(t)^{1-\phi}},$$

so that along the BGP we have

$$\frac{N(t)^{1-\phi}}{L_R(t)} = \left(\frac{N^{1-\phi}}{L_R}\right)^{BGP} = \frac{1-\phi}{n}\eta\qquad\qquad\text{(S13.44)}$$

i.e. $\frac{N(t)^{1-\phi}}{L_R(t)}$ is constant along the BGP.

On the other hand however, the free entry condition (S13.36) needs to be satisfied, i.e.

$$\frac{1}{\eta}\frac{\beta}{1-\beta} = \frac{\beta}{r^* - (1-\phi)g^*}\frac{L_E(t)}{N(t)^{1-\theta}} = \frac{\beta}{r^* - (1-\phi)g^*}\frac{L(t) - L_R(t)}{N(t)^{1-\theta}},$$

so that

$$\left(\frac{L_R}{N^{1-\phi}}\right)^{BGP} = \left(\frac{L}{N^{1-\theta}}\right)^{BGP} - \frac{1}{\eta}\frac{r^* - (1-\phi)g^*}{1-\beta}. \tag{S13.45}$$

Using (S13.44) and (S13.45) we can solve for $\left(\frac{L}{N^{1-\theta}}\right)^{BGP}$ as

$$\left(\frac{L}{N^{1-\theta}}\right)^{BGP} = \frac{1}{\eta}\left[\frac{n}{1-\phi} + \frac{(\theta+\phi-1)\frac{n}{1-\phi}+\rho}{1-\beta}\right], \tag{S13.46}$$

where we used (S13.41) and (S13.42) to solve for g^* and r^*. Hence, as long as the initial conditions $L(0)$ and $N(0)$ do not start at their BGP ratio given in (S13.46), there will be transitional dynamics.

To finally characterize the transitional dynamics, we will just present the intuition. Suppose that $\frac{N(0)^{1-\phi}}{L(0)} > \left(\frac{N^{1-\phi}}{L}\right)^{BGP}$. From (S13.44) we know that the share of researchers $\frac{L_R}{L}$ to generate a growth rate of g^* is increasing in $\frac{N(0)^{1-\phi}}{L(0)}$. So consider a path where $\frac{L_R}{L}$ is constant but larger than $\left(\frac{L_R}{L}\right)^{BGP}$ in order to generate a growth rate of g^*. Labor market clearing requires that $\frac{L_E}{L}$ is also constant and smaller than $\left(\frac{L_E}{L}\right)^{BGP}$. Along such a path, consumption grows at a constant rate as both $N(t)$ and $L_E(t)$ grow at rates g^* and n^* respectively. This however shows that interest rates are still given by r^* so that the free entry condition is violated (i.e. it is slack) as per-period profits are decreasing in $L_E(t)$. Hence, this cannot occur in equilibrium. To satisfy both the free entry condition and to clear the labor market we will therefore have that the share of researchers will be smaller and the share of production workers will be higher. This increases the value of a patent via the market size effect until the free entry condition is satisfied. As $N(t)$ initially grows slower than g^*, $\frac{N(t)^{1-\phi}}{L(t)}$ decreases over time. Hence, $\frac{N(t)^{1-\phi}}{L(t)}$ will converge to its BGP level $\left(\frac{N^{1-\phi}}{L}\right)^{BGP}$. Once this level is reached, the economy will be on the balanced growth path characterized above. Economically, the transitional dynamics are as follows. At $t = 0$, the economy is characterized by technology abundance in the sense that $N(0)$ is relatively big (compared to $L(0)$). In equilibrium the research sector will therefore be relatively small compared to the production sector. Over time, the technology level deteriorates (compared to $L(t)$) so that the share of production workers will be decreasing along the transition path. Once the BGP is reached, labor shares will be constant across the two sectors and the economy will grow at a constant rate.

To conclude the characterization of the equilibrium in this economy we finally have to show that it is without loss of generality to assume that the research sector will be active. In particular we will show that there cannot be an equilibrium where the research sector will always be inactive. So suppose there is such an equilibrium. Then it is the case that $L_R(t) = 0$ and $\dot{N}(t) = 0$ for all t. By (S13.29) output grows at rate n as $L_E(t) = L(t)$. As the final good market has to clear, per capita consumption is constant as aggregate consumption also has to grow at rate n (see (S13.31)). Hence, the Euler equation in (S13.27) requires that $r(t) = \rho$, i.e. interest rates are constant. From (S13.33) we know that the value function is given by

$$\rho V(\nu, t) - \dot{V}(\nu, t) = \beta L_E(t) = \beta L(t),$$

i.e. $V(v,t)$ also grows at rate n. Hence, $\dot{V}(v,t) = nV(v,t)$ so that

$$V(v,t) = \frac{\beta}{\rho - n} L_E(t) = \frac{\beta}{\rho - n} L(0) \exp(nt). \tag{S13.47}$$

In the proposed equilibrium with no research, the free entry condition has to be slack in all periods, i.e.

$$V(v,t) \leq \frac{1}{\eta} \frac{\beta}{1 - \beta} N(t)^{1-\phi} = \frac{1}{\eta} \frac{\beta}{1 - \beta} N(0)^{1-\phi}, \tag{S13.48}$$

where the last equality uses that $\dot{N}(t) = 0$ for all t. This however is a contradiction as (S13.47) shows that $V(v,t)$ grows at rate n so that there will be $\tilde{t}$ such that (S13.48) will be violated and research becomes profitable. This shows that there is no equilibrium where there will never be research.

Note however that in contrast to the baseline model of expanding varieties it is possible that there will not be research at $t = 0$. Intuitively, if $N(0)$ is very high and $L(0)$ is very low, there are only little incentives to employ researchers as the innovation flow rates are low (stemming from the high $N(0)$) and the returns of the patent are low as $L_E(0) \leq L(0)$ so that the size of the market is small. The profitability of patents however improves over time so that at some point research will start to be profitable. Hence it is without loss of generality to simply assume that $N(0)$ and $L(0)$ are such that there will be research in equilibrium.

Exercise 13.19, Part (b). Let us now consider the Pareto optimal allocation. That the equilibrium is not necessarily Pareto optimal follows from the fact that (a) the producers of machines are not competitive and (b) that the model with knowledge spillovers features an externality in that firms do not internalize the effect of their research on the economies' future innovation possibilities. The problem of the social planner is given by

$$\max_{[c(t),L_R(t),L_E(t),[x(v,t)]_{v=1}^{N(t)},N(t)]_{t=1}^{\infty}} \int_0^{\infty} \exp(-(\rho - n)t) \frac{c(t)^{1-\theta} - 1}{1 - \theta}$$

subject to the constraints

$$
\begin{aligned}
Y(t) &= X(t) + c(t)L(t) \\
Y(t) &= \frac{1}{1-\beta} \int_0^{N(t)} x(v,t)^{1-\beta} dv \, L_E(t)^{\beta} \\
X(t) &= \int_0^{N(t)} \psi x(v,t) dv \\
\dot{N}(t) &= \eta N(t)^{\phi} L_R(t) \\
L(t) &= L_E(t) + L_R(t).
\end{aligned}
$$

Again we can simplify the problem by first solving for the optimal allocation of machines $[x(v,t)]_{v=1}^{N(t)}$ for a given $N(t)$ and $L_E(t)$. This subproblem is just given by

$$\max_{[x(v,t)]_{v=1}^{N(t)}} \frac{1}{1-\beta} \int_0^{N(t)} x(v,t)^{1-\beta} dv \, L_E(t)^{\beta} - \int_0^{N(t)} \psi x(v,t) dv,$$

i.e. the social planner allocates $[x(v,t)]_{v=1}^{N(t)}$ to maximize net output. The solution is given by

$$x^S(v,t) = \psi^{-\frac{1}{\beta}} L_E(t) \equiv (1-\beta)^{-\frac{1}{\beta}} L_E(t),$$

so that

$$Y(t) - X(t) = (1-\beta)^{-1/\beta} \beta N(t) L_E(t).$$

Substituting this into the program above, the social planner's problem reduces to

$$\max_{[c(t),L_E(t),N(t)]_{t=1}^{\infty}} \int_0^{\infty} \exp(-(\rho-n)t) \frac{c(t)^{1-\theta}-1}{1-\theta}$$

$$\text{s.t.} \quad c(t)L(t) = (1-\beta)^{-1/\beta}\beta N(t)L_E(t)$$

$$\dot{N}(t) = \eta N(t)^{\phi}(L(t)-L_E(t))$$

Defining the share of people employed in the production sector by $s_E(t) \equiv \frac{L_E(t)}{L(t)}$ and substituting the expression for $c(t)$, the current value Hamiltonian is given by

$$\hat{H}(N(t),s_E(t),\mu(t)) = \frac{((1-\beta)^{-1/\beta}\beta N(t)s_E(t))^{1-\theta}-1}{1-\theta} + \mu(t)\eta N(t)^{\phi}L(t)(1-s_E(t))$$

where $s_E(t)$ is the control and $N(t)$ the state variable. The sufficient conditions for a maximum are the first-order conditions and the transversality condition where the former are given by

$$\hat{H}_{s_E} = [(1-\beta)^{-1/\beta}\beta N(t)]^{1-\theta}s_E(t)^{-\theta} - \mu(t)\eta N(t)^{\phi}L(t) = 0 \qquad (S13.49)$$

$$\hat{H}_N = [(1-\beta)^{-1/\beta}\beta s_E(t)]^{1-\theta}N(t)^{-\theta} + \phi\eta\mu(t)N(t)^{\phi-1}L(t)(1-s_E(t)) \quad (S13.50)$$

$$= (\rho-n)\mu(t) - \dot{\mu}(t).$$

Substituting (S13.49) into (S13.50) and rearranging terms yields

$$\eta\frac{L(t)}{N(t)^{1-\phi}}[(1-\phi)s_E(t)+\phi] - (\rho-n) = -\frac{\dot{\mu}(t)}{\mu(t)}. \qquad (S13.51)$$

In order to compare the Pareto optimal allocation with the equilibrium allocation it is convenient to derive an equation akin to the consumer's Euler equation. Substituting the definition of per capita consumption into (S13.49) yields

$$(1-\beta)^{-1/\beta}\beta c(t)^{-\theta} = \mu(t)\eta N(t)^{\phi-1}L(t).$$

Differentiating this expression with respect to time yields the Euler equation of the social planner's problem as

$$\frac{\dot{c}(t)}{c(t)} = \frac{1}{\theta}(-\frac{\dot{\mu}(t)}{\mu(t)} + (1-\phi)\frac{\dot{N}(t)}{N(t)} - n)$$

$$= \frac{1}{\theta}(\eta\frac{L(t)}{N(t)^{1-\phi}}[(1-\phi)s_E(t)+\phi] - \rho + (1-\phi)\frac{\dot{N}(t)}{N(t)}),$$

where the second line substituted (S13.51). From the innovation possibilities frontier we know that

$$\frac{\dot{N}(t)}{N(t)} = \eta\frac{L_R(t)}{N(t)^{1-\phi}} = \eta\frac{L(t)}{N(t)^{1-\phi}}(1-s_E(t)), \qquad (S13.52)$$

so that the Euler equation simplifies to

$$\frac{\dot{c}(t)}{c(t)} = \frac{1}{\theta}(\eta\frac{L(t)}{N(t)^{1-\phi}}[(1-\phi)s_E(t)+\phi] - \rho + (1-\phi)\eta\frac{L(t)}{N(t)^{1-\phi}}(1-s_E(t)))$$

$$= \frac{1}{\theta}(\eta\frac{L(t)}{N(t)^{1-\phi}} - \rho). \qquad (S13.53)$$

Let us also consider a solution with balanced growth, i.e. where consumption grows at a constant rate. Like in the analysis for the equilibrium above, the solution to the problem will converge to the BGP. From (S13.53) this also implies that $\frac{L(t)}{N(t)^{1-\phi}}$ is constant, so that the growth rate of technology g^S is the same as in the equilibrium allocation, namely

$$g^S = \frac{n}{1-\phi}.$$

From the innovation possibilities frontier (S13.52) this implies that $s_E(t)$ is constant, i.e. $s_E(t) = s_E^S$, so that (using the resource constraint)

$$c^S(t) = (1-\beta)^{-1/\beta}\beta N(t)s_E(t) = (1-\beta)^{-1/\beta}\beta s_E^S N(t).$$

This shows that per capita consumption in the planner's problem $c^S(t)$ also grows at the rate of technological progress g^S on the BGP.

This however does not imply that the equilibrium is Pareto efficient. First of all, the growth rate along the transition path will typically differ between the social planner's solution and the equilibrium. More importantly though, we can show that the equilibrium normalized technology level $\left(\frac{N^{1-\phi}}{L}\right)^{BGP}$ is always lower than the technology level $\left(\frac{N^{1-\phi}}{L}\right)^{SP}$ chosen by the social planner. To see this claim, note that Eqs. (S13.53) and (S13.46) imply

$$\left(\frac{N^{1-\phi}}{L}\right)^{SP} = \frac{\eta}{\theta\frac{n}{1-\phi} + \rho}$$

$$\left(\frac{N^{1-\phi}}{L}\right)^{BGP} = \frac{\eta}{\frac{n}{1-\phi} + \frac{(\theta+\phi-1)\frac{n}{1-\phi}+\rho}{1-\beta}},$$

which already shows that the equilibrium allocation does not coincide with the social planner's solution. Comparing $\left(\frac{N^{1-\phi}}{L}\right)^{SP}$ with $\left(\frac{N^{1-\phi}}{L}\right)^{BGP}$, we furthermore see that the social planner's normalized technology level is higher whenever

$$\theta\frac{n}{1-\phi} + \rho < \frac{n}{1-\phi} + \frac{(\theta+\phi-1)\frac{n}{1-\phi}+\rho}{1-\beta}.$$

Simple algebra establishes that this is the case whenever

$$(1-\theta)\frac{n}{1-\phi} < \rho + \frac{1}{\beta}\frac{n}{1-\phi}\phi.$$

Recall that the parametric restriction for the transversality condition (S13.43) requires $(1-\theta)\frac{n}{1-\phi} < \rho - n$, which implies that the previous displayed equality is always satisfied. This proves our claim the the steady state level of normalized technology, $\left(\frac{N^{1-\phi}}{L}\right)$, is always higher in the social planner's solution. Intuitively, similar to the baseline expanding varieties model, the social planner avoids the static monopoly distortions and internalizes the benefits of innovation on future workers, which induces her to employ more labor in R&D. In this model this leads to a higher level of technology (instead of a higher growth rate). Additionally, the social planner also internalizes the positive knowledge spillovers (the $N(t)^\phi$ term in the R&D technology equation), which works in the same direction. Hence, the equilibrium level of technology (relative to the labor force) on the BGP is inefficiently low. The distortions in this economy are the same as the distortions in the original Romer (1990) model. Here they imply that the equilibrium level of technology is lower than optimal, while in the Romer (1990) model they imply that the equilibrium growth rate is lower. The reason why the distortions have growth consequences in the Romer (1990) model and only level differences in this specification is, that this model assumes decreasing returns to current technology in the research process (i.e. $\phi < 1$), whereas Romer (1990) considers the case constant returns $\phi = 1$. For an interesting discussion about the growth effects of different specifications of the innovation possibilities frontier, we also refer to Rivera-Batiz and Romer (1991).

Exercise 13.19, Part (c). Let us now analyze the effect of policy on the equilibrium allocation. As both policy interventions only affect the research firms, we can directly focus on their decision problem. Consider first a subsidy to research. In particular, suppose that the government subsidizes research by paying each research firm a fraction ϑ of the wage bill they would have to pay. Hence, the effective wage research firms have to pay is given by

$$w^R(t) = (1 - \vartheta)w(t).$$

The free entry condition into research then reads

$$\eta N(t)^\phi V(\nu, t) = w^R(t) = (1 - \vartheta)w(t) = (1 - \vartheta)\frac{\beta}{1 - \beta}N(t), \qquad (S13.54)$$

where the value function is still given by

$$V(\nu, t) = \frac{\beta L_E(t)}{r(t) - (1 - \phi)g(t)}. \qquad (S13.55)$$

Along the BGP, interest rates are constant and the number of varieties grows at a constant rate g, so that from (S13.54) and (S13.55) we get that

$$\frac{\beta L_E(t)}{r - (1 - \phi)g}\eta N(t)^\phi = (1 - \vartheta)\frac{\beta}{1 - \beta}N(t),$$

so that (as along the BGP, $L_E(t)$ still grows at rate n) the subsidy does not have an effect on the economy's growth rate, which is still given by

$$\frac{\dot{N}(t)}{N(t)} = g^* = \frac{n}{1 - \phi}.$$

Equilibrium interest rates are not affected by the subsidy either, as the Euler equation still requires that

$$r^* = \theta g^* + \rho = \theta \frac{n}{1 - \phi} + \rho.$$

By again denoting $L_E(t) = s_E L(t)$ (where s_E and $s_R = 1 - s_E$ are constant along the BGP), the crucial two equations to determine the BGP are the free entry condition (S13.54) and the innovation possibilities frontier

$$\frac{\beta}{r^* - n}\frac{L}{N^{1-\phi}}s_E = \frac{1}{\eta}(1 - \vartheta)\frac{\beta}{1 - \beta} \qquad (S13.56)$$

$$\eta\frac{L}{N^{1-\phi}}s_R = g^* = \frac{n}{1 - \phi}, \qquad (S13.57)$$

where we omitted the time arguments in the $\frac{L}{N^{1-\phi}}$ term to stress that this ratio is constant along the BGP. As $s_R = 1 - s_E$, (S13.56) and (S13.57) are two equations in the two unknowns s_E and $\frac{L}{N^{1-\phi}}$. Substituting for $\frac{L}{N^{1-\phi}}$ yields

$$\frac{\beta}{r^* - n}\frac{n}{1 - \phi}\frac{1}{\eta}\frac{s_E}{s_R} = \frac{1}{\eta}(1 - \vartheta)\frac{\beta}{1 - \beta}$$

which we can solve for

$$\frac{s_E}{1 - s_E} = \frac{(1 - \vartheta)(1 - \phi)}{n}\frac{r^* - n}{1 - \beta}.$$

Hence we get that

$$\frac{\partial s_E}{\partial \vartheta} = -\frac{(1-\phi)}{n}\frac{r^* - n}{1-\beta}(1-s_E)^2 < 0,$$

i.e. the BGP share of production workers is decreasing in the subsidy. This immediately implies that the fraction of researchers s_R is increasing in the subsidy. Somewhat more interestingly however, (S13.57) shows that $\frac{L}{N^{1-\phi}}s_R$ is constant along the BGP so that an increase in the BGP share of researchers s_R decreases the BGP ratio $\frac{L}{N^{1-\phi}}$, i.e. after the subsidy is implemented and the economy will have reached the new BGP, the (normalized) technology level $\frac{N(t)^{1-\phi}}{L(t)}$ will be relatively higher (compared to the old steady state). This also informs us about the transitional dynamics. Suppose the economy settled in a BGP and the government implements the wage subsidy for researchers. For the free entry condition to be satisfied, the share of production workers will decrease. With a higher share of researchers being employed in the research sector, the growth rate of $N(t)$ will be higher than the BGP growth rate g^* and $\frac{L(t)}{N(t)^{1-\phi}}$ declines over time. After a while, the economy reaches its new BGP ratio $\frac{L(t)}{N(t)^{1-\phi}}$, which is lower than before. To make sure that the growth rate of the economy is still given by g^*, the share of researchers will be higher. Hence the subsidy induces a temporary increase in the growth rate of technology and causes a long-run reallocation between workers and researchers in the labor force.

Consider now the policy of patent expiration. With patents expiring at some constant rate ι, the value function will solve the new HJB equation

$$r(t)V(v,t) - \dot{V}(t) = \beta L_E(t) - \iota V(v,t), \tag{S13.58}$$

where the new term on the RHS accounts for the fact that with a flow rate of ι, the patent is lost and competition will reduce the value of the blueprint to zero. Along the BGP, the value function from (S13.58) is given by

$$V(v,t) = \frac{\beta L_E(t)}{r + \iota - n},$$

so that the free entry condition into research reads

$$\eta N(t)^\phi V(\nu, t) = \eta N(t)^\phi \frac{\beta L_E(t)}{r + \iota - n} = w(t) = \frac{\beta}{1-\beta}N(t).$$

This again shows that the growth rate of varieties will be given by $g = \frac{n}{1-\phi}$ and the free entry condition and innovation possibilities frontier reduce to

$$\frac{\beta}{r + \iota - n}s_E\frac{L}{N^{1-\phi}} = \frac{1}{\eta}\frac{\beta}{1-\beta}$$

$$\eta\frac{L}{N^{1-\phi}}s_R = g^* = \frac{n}{1-\phi}.$$

An analysis similar to above establishes that

$$\frac{\partial s_E}{\partial \iota} > 0$$

i.e. the higher the rate at which patens expire, the lower the share of workers employed in the research sector. As this implies that s_R will decrease, the new BGP technology ratio $\frac{L}{N^{1-\phi}}$ will be higher, i.e. the technology level $N(t)$ will relatively decline. This is again an intuitive results. Owning a patent that expires is of course less valuable. At a given wage rate $w(t)$, there will therefore be less incentives to do research. To induce research activity, the value of the patent conditional on survival has to increase. This is achieved by allocating a larger share of workers in the production sector, which increases the demand for machines and therefore monopolistic profits.

Hence, in contrast to the baseline endogenous growth model, policy does not affect the growth rate of the economy. The reason is the difference in the innovation possibilities frontier. By introducing limited technological spillovers, the growth rate of the economy along the BGP is entirely determined by the population growth rate and the degree of decreasing returns to current knowledge $N(t)$. Policy then only affects the allocation of researchers and workers in the labor market and the BGP value of technology $N^{1-\phi}/L$. The BGP growth rate however is independent of policy variables. Again, Romer (1990) shows these policy considerations have similar effect on the growth rate if $\phi = 1$.

Exercise 13.22

Exercise 13.22, Part (a). An equilibrium in this economy are consumption levels, machine expenditures and research expenses $[C(t), X(t), Z(t)]_{t=0}^{\infty}$, wages, prices for intermediary products and value functions $[w(t), [p^x(\nu,t)]_{\nu=1}^{N(t)}, [V(\nu,t)]_{\nu=1}^{N(t)}]_{t=0}^{\infty}$ and interest rates $[r(t)]_{t=0}^{\infty}$ such that markets clear, the allocation is consistent with utility maximization of the representative household, firms maximize profits, the evolution of $N(t)$ is consistent with the innovation possibilities frontier

$$\dot{N}(t) = \eta N(t)^{-\phi} Z(t), \tag{S13.59}$$

and the value function is consistent with free entry.

Note that there are negative externalities in innovation, that is, the greater the number of machines, the more costly it is to innovate a new machine. This specification for the R&D technology corresponds to a view where innovation ideas are driven from a common pool and innovation today creates a fishing out effect and makes future innovations more difficult. Except for the innovation possibilities frontier the structure of this economy is entirely analogous to the baseline model of endogenous growth. As machine demand will be isoelastic, the monopolistic price of intermediaries is again given by

$$p^x(\nu,t) = \frac{\psi}{1-\beta} = 1,$$

where the last equality follows from our normalization $\psi = 1 - \beta$. The labor market is competitive so that wages are given by the marginal product of labor which is just

$$\frac{\partial Y(t)}{\partial L} = \frac{\beta}{1-\beta} \int_0^{N(t)} x(\nu,t)^{1-\beta} d\nu L^{\beta-1} = \frac{\beta}{1-\beta} N(t),$$

where we used that $x(\nu,t) = L(t)$ for all ν. To derive the free entry condition in this economy we again have to derive the value function. As per period profits of research firms are still given by

$$\pi(\nu,t) = \beta L(t) \tag{S13.60}$$

and the value function solves the Hamilton-Jacobi-Bellman equation

$$r(t)V(\nu,t) - \dot{V}(\nu,t) = \pi(\nu,t), \tag{S13.61}$$

we get that along the BGP (where interest rates are constant and equal to r^*) the value function is given by

$$V(\nu,t) = \frac{\pi(t)}{r^* - g_\pi} = \frac{\beta L(t)}{r^* - n},$$

where the last equality follows since profits grow at the same rate n as $L(t)$ (see (S13.60)).

Using (S13.59) the free entry condition in this economy is given by

$$\eta N(t)^{-\phi} V(\nu, t) = \eta N(t)^{-\phi} \frac{\beta L(t)}{r^* - n} \leq 1 \text{ with equality if } Z(t) > 0. \tag{S13.62}$$

To understand (S13.62), note that one unit of the final good invested in research yields a flow rate of innovation equal to $\eta N(t)^{-\phi}$ and each innovation has a value of $V(\nu, t)$.

Exercise 13.22, Part (b). Now consider the case where population is constant, i.e. $n = 0$ and $L(t) = L$. In that case, the free entry condition (S13.62) requires that on the BGP we have

$$\eta N(t)^{-\phi} \frac{\beta L}{r^*} \leq 1 \text{ with equality if } Z(t) > 0. \tag{S13.63}$$

If this condition is satisfied with strict inequality, then we have $Z(t) = 0$ and $N(t)$ remains constant. If it is satisfied with equality, then $N(t)$ is also constant at the level $(\eta \beta L / r^*)^{1/\phi}$. This shows that along the BGP we have

$$N(t) = N^* \geq \left(\eta \frac{\beta L}{r^*}\right)^{1/\phi}. \tag{S13.64}$$

Hence, there will be no growth and total output is constant. From the consumer's Euler equation we then get that $r^* = \rho$ as consumption has to be constant too. That consumption is constant follows from the fact that (S13.59) implies that $Z(t) = 0$ once $N(t)$ reaches its long-run level determined by (S13.64), so that from the resource constraint, consumption is given by

$$Y(t) - X(t) = \frac{\beta(2 - \beta)}{1 - \beta} N(t) L = C(t).$$

Hence, as long as there is no population growth, the economy will not be able to generate sustained growth. The reason is the following: with population being constant, the profits from intermediary producers are constant over time. However, R&D gets more and more expensive as the flow rate of innovation is decreasing in the current level of varieties. Hence, there is no endogenous growth in this model as long as the population is constant.

Note that when $N(0) < N^*$, $N(t)$ will *converge to* N^*, as in contrast to the baseline model of the lab equipment formulation, this economy will have transitional dynamics. Along the transition path, $N(t)$ will gradually increase to N^*, while the interest rate will gradually decline to $r^* = \rho$. Note also that when $N(0) > N^*$, the free entry condition in (S13.63) will be slack. However, since there is no depreciation of machines, $N(t)$ will remain at the higher level and thus this economy has a continuum of steady states.

Exercise 13.22, Part (c). Consider now the case where the population grows over time at rate n. Again we can use the free entry condition to determine the joint evolution of $N(t)$ and $L(t)$. On an equilibrium with positive R&D, the free entry condition (S13.62) will be satisfied with equality, so that

$$1 = \eta N(t)^{-\phi} V(\nu, t). \tag{S13.65}$$

Differentiating this condition with respect to time yields

$$\frac{\dot{V}(\nu, t)}{V(\nu, t)} = \phi \frac{\dot{N}(t)}{N(t)} = \phi g_N(t). \tag{S13.66}$$

From the HJB equation (S13.61) we therefore get that

$$V(\nu, t) = \frac{\pi(\nu, t)}{r(t) - \frac{\dot{V}(\nu, t)}{V(\nu, t)}} = \frac{\beta L(t)}{r(t) - \phi g_N(t)}.$$

Along the BGP interest rates are constant and $N(t)$ grows at a constant rate g_N. Hence, $V(\nu, t)$ is given by $V(\nu, t) = \frac{\beta L(t)}{r - \phi g_N}$, so that

$$\frac{\dot{V}(\nu, t)}{V(\nu, t)} = \frac{\dot{L}(t)}{L(t)} = n.$$

Hence, (S13.66) implies that

$$\frac{\dot{N}(t)}{N(t)} = g_N(t) = \frac{n}{\phi} > 0. \tag{S13.67}$$

The reason why the economy now generates sustained growth is precisely that research becomes more valuable over time as population growth increases per period profits (by the usual market size effect). This counteracts the fact that research becomes more costly due to the congestion effects $N(t)^{-\phi}$. It is still the case that total output is given by

$$Y(t) = \frac{1}{1 - \beta} \int_0^{N(t)} x(\nu, t)^{1-\beta} d\nu \, L(t)^\beta = \frac{1}{1 - \beta} N(t) L(t),$$

so that

$$g_Y = \frac{\dot{Y}(t)}{Y(t)} = \frac{\dot{N}(t)}{N(t)} + \frac{\dot{L}(t)}{L(t)} = \frac{1 + \phi}{\phi} n.$$

Similarly we can show that research expenditures $Z(t)$ and total consumption expenditures $C(t) = c(t) L(t)$ grow at the same rate. To see this, note that from from the innovation possibilities frontier (S13.59) and Eq. (S13.67) we have

$$\frac{\dot{N}(t)}{N(t)} = \frac{n}{\phi} = \eta \frac{Z(t)}{N(t)^{1+\phi}}.$$

Hence, $\frac{Z(t)}{N(t)^{1+\phi}}$ has to be constant, so that

$$\frac{\dot{Z}(t)}{Z(t)} = (1 + \phi) \frac{\dot{N}(t)}{N(t)} = (1 + \phi) \frac{n}{\phi} = g_Y,$$

i.e. $Z(t)$ is proportional to $Y(t)$. Therefore we can write $Z(t) = zY(t) = z\frac{1}{1-\beta} N(t) L(t)$, so that the resource constraint implies

$$\begin{aligned} C(t) &= Y(t) - X(t) - Z(t) \\ &= \left[\frac{\beta(2 - \beta) - z}{1 - \beta} \right] N(t) L(t). \end{aligned}$$

This shows that aggregate consumption is also proportional to $N(t)L(t)$, i.e. grows at rate

$$g_C = \frac{\dot{N}(t)}{N(t)} + \frac{\dot{L}(t)}{L(t)} = \frac{n}{\phi} + n = \frac{1 + \phi}{\phi} n,$$

and per capita consumption grows at the same rate as the number of varieties $N(t)$, that is

$$g_c = \frac{n}{\phi} = \frac{1}{\theta}(r^* - \rho), \tag{S13.68}$$

where the last equality is simply the Euler equation. Note that the described path will correspond to a BGP equilibrium with positive growth if

$$0 < \frac{n(1 - \theta)}{\phi} < \rho - n,$$

where the second inequality ensures that the transversality condition holds.

Note that there are transitional dynamics in this economy. In particular, (S13.65) and (S13.68) imply that on a BGP, we have

$$\frac{N(t)^{\phi}}{L(t)} = \frac{\eta\beta}{r^{*} - n} = \frac{\eta\beta}{\theta g_c + \rho - n} = \frac{\eta\beta}{n\left(\frac{\theta}{\phi} - 1\right) + \rho - n} = \left(\frac{N^{\phi}}{L}\right)^{BGP}. \tag{S13.69}$$

Hence, if $N(0)^{\phi}/L(0)$ ratio is below this level, that is, the economy starts with a low level of technology relative to its population, then $N(t)$ will initially grow faster than n/ϕ and $N(t)^{\phi}/L(t)$ will gradually increase towards its BGP value given in (S13.69). Intuitively, the economy initially has higher incentives to innovate (since the diminishing returns to innovation, $N(t)^{-\phi}$, have not kicked in yet) and grows faster along the transition path.

Finally, note that the equilibrium is not Pareto optimal, but the socially planned economy does not always feature higher growth than the equilibrium allocation. In this model, there are both monopoly distortions and negative technological externalities in innovation. Without the technology externalities, monopoly distortions would make the equilibrium grow at a slower rate, because entrants do not capture the entire surplus of the innovation. However, the technological externalities create an opposing force, since each innovating firm fails to take into account the fact that it is making innovation for future firms more difficult. A social planner will internalize this effect and thus may want to slow down innovation and growth.[4]

---

[4]Analyzing the social planner's problem shows that the number of varieties in the social planner's allocation asymptotically grows at the same constant rate n/ϕ, but it may grow slower than the equilibrium allocation along the transition path to the BGP.

Chapter 14: Models of Schumpeterian Growth

Exercise 14.2

Exercise 14.2, Part (a). Let us explicitly allow for a choice of R&D expenditures z to prove that incumbents will never invest in R&D. Consider an incumbent with current quality q. By (14.8) per period profits are equal to

$$\pi(\nu, t \mid q) = \beta q(\nu, t) L.$$

In equilibrium, the value of owning a patent will be given by the value function $V(\nu, t|q)$, which now solves the HJB equation

$$r(t) V(\nu, t|q) - \dot{V}(\nu, t|q) = \qquad\qquad\qquad\qquad\qquad\qquad\qquad (S14.1)$$

$$\max_{\hat{z}} \left\{ \pi(\nu, t|q) - \hat{z} + \frac{\eta \hat{z}}{q}(V(\nu, t|\lambda q) - V(\nu, t|q)) - z(\nu, t|q) V(\nu, t|q) \right\}.$$

To understand (S14.1), note that by spending $\hat{z}$ units of resources, the incumbent generates a flow rate of innovation $\frac{\eta \hat{z}}{q}$ which gives him an additional payoff of $V(\nu, t|\lambda q) - V(\nu, t|q)$. The incumbent takes the flow rate of replacement $z(\nu, t|q)$ as given. The optimality condition for incumbents' research expenditures is given by

$$\frac{\eta}{q}(V(\nu, t|\lambda q) - V(\nu, t|q)) \leq 1 \text{ and } \left[-1 + \frac{\eta}{q}(V(\nu, t|\lambda q) - V(\nu, t|q)) \right] \hat{z} = 0 \text{ and } \hat{z} \geq 0.$$

$$\qquad\qquad\qquad\qquad\qquad\qquad\qquad\qquad\qquad\qquad\qquad\qquad (S14.2)$$

Let us focus on an equilibrium, where there are potential entrants, i.e. $z(\nu, t \mid q) > 0$. Free entry implies that

$$\eta V(\nu, t \mid q) = \lambda^{-1} q(\nu, t)$$

as derived in (14.14). Substituting this in (S14.2) yields

$$\left[-1 + \frac{\eta}{q}(V(\nu, t \mid \lambda q) - V(\nu, t \mid q)) \right] \hat{z} = \left[-1 + \frac{\eta}{q}\left(\frac{1}{\eta}q - \frac{1}{\eta}\frac{q}{\lambda} \right) \right] \hat{z} = -\frac{1}{\lambda}\hat{z},$$

so that (S14.2) implies that

$$\hat{z} = 0.$$

This shows that incumbents would not want to engage in research if entrants are willing to do so. The intuition is as follows: as incumbents make positive profits from the existing machine, their benefits from innovation are lower as they replace themselves. As entrants do not earn profits before innovating, their benefits from innovation are strictly higher than for the incumbents. If entrants want to engage in research, equilibrium (in particular the free entry condition) requires that they are indifferent to do so. But if this is the case, incumbents are strictly better off to not invest in research. This proves that Arrow's replacement effect is at work in the baseline model of Schumpeterian growth.

Exercise 14.2, Part (b). To prove this result, suppose there was an equilibrium where incumbents do not incur any research efforts. From the analysis in Section 14.1 we know that in such an equilibrium the value function has to satisfy the entrants' free entry condition

$$V(q) = \frac{q}{\lambda \eta},$$

where we explicitly noted that V does not depend on time t or on the sector ν. Now consider the decision problem of an incumbent. By spending one unit of the final good, he creates a flow rate of innovation $\frac{\phi \eta}{q}$ which has a value of $V(\lambda q) - V(q)$ as he replaces himself. Hence, the above allocation is an equilibrium if the incumbent would not want to spend those resources, i.e. if

$$1 \geq \frac{\phi \eta}{q}(V(\lambda q) - V(q)) = \frac{\phi \eta}{q} \frac{q}{\eta}\left(1 - \frac{1}{\lambda}\right) = \phi \frac{\lambda - 1}{\lambda}. \tag{S14.3}$$

For (S14.3) to be satisfied we need that

$$\phi \leq \frac{\lambda}{\lambda - 1},$$

which is the required condition. The intuition is similar to the one given in Part (a). Given that entrants are indifferent between doing research or not, incumbents strictly prefer to not do research if they use the same technology. Hence, they need an advantage of doing research to be willing to do so. To generate the same flow rate of innovation as entrants do, incumbents only have to spend a fraction ϕ^{-1} of resources. Note however that $\frac{\lambda}{\lambda - 1} > 1$ so that even if incumbents do have an advantage of doing research (i.e. $\phi^{-1} < 1$) they might still not want to do it. Only if the advantage is substantial, i.e. if they pay at most a fraction $\phi^{-1} = \frac{\lambda - 1}{\lambda}$, incumbents would want to invest in research themselves as the cost advantage dominates Arrow's replacement effect.

Exercise 14.7*

The equilibrium in this economy is a collection of time paths of aggregate allocations and prices, a stochastic process for the quality of machine lines, and a collection of R&D expenditures, quantities, prices and value functions for machine lines (as a function of quality) $\left[\begin{array}{l} C(t), Z(t), X(t), A(t), r(t), w(t), [q(\nu,t)]_{\nu \in N(t)}, \\ [Z(\nu,t \mid q), p^x(\nu,t \mid q), x(\nu,t \mid q), V(\nu,t \mid q)]_{\nu \in N(t)} \end{array} \right]_{t=0}^{\infty}$ such that the representative consumer maximizes utility, the final good sector is competitive, the quality of a machine line evolves according to the R&D technology given the investment on the line, the R&D investment on each line is determined by free entry, the machine producers set prices to maximize profits and all markets clear.

To characterize the equilibrium, we first look at the pricing decision of machine producers. The demand from final good producers is

$$x(\nu,t \mid q) = \left(\frac{q(\nu,t)^{\zeta_1}}{p^x(\nu,t \mid q)}\right)^{1/\beta} L,$$

and the marginal cost of producing a quality $q(\nu,t)$ good is $\psi q(\nu,t)^{\zeta_2}$. Thus, the unconstrained profit maximizing price (that, is, the price a monopolist would charge) is given by $p^x(\nu,t \mid q) = \psi q^{\zeta_2}/(1-\beta)$, which after the usual normalization $\psi = (1-\beta)$ implies $p^x(\nu,t \mid q) = q^{\zeta_2}$. Since the higher quality machine producer faces competition from lower quality machine producers, this price will be the profit maximizing price only if λ is sufficiently large, that is, only if the new technology is sufficiently advanced that a lower quality machine producer would have to suffer a loss to undercut the more advanced producer even when the latter charges the unconstrained monopoly price. In the present model, this will be the case if

$$\lambda \geq \left(\frac{1}{1-\beta}\right)^{\frac{1-\beta}{\zeta_1 - (1-\beta)\zeta_2}}. \tag{S14.4}$$

Otherwise, the higher quality machine producers will be forced to charge a limit price. Suppose the parameters are such that (S14.4) holds and producers charge the unconstrained price. Then the production is given by

$$x(\nu, t \mid q) = q^{(\zeta_1 - \zeta_2)/\beta} L, \tag{S14.5}$$

and profits by

$$\pi(\nu, t \mid q) = \beta q^{\zeta_2} q^{(\zeta_1 - \zeta_2)/\beta} L. \tag{S14.6}$$

We next look at the value function of a machine producer. Let

$$z(\nu, t \mid q) = Z(\nu, t) \eta / q^{\zeta_3} \tag{S14.7}$$

denote the flow rate of innovation on machine line ν with current quality q when the level of investment is given by $Z(\nu, t)$. By Arrow's replacement effect, only outsiders invest in R&D in this model and thus $z(\nu, t \mid q)$ is also the replacement rate of the incumbent. It follows that the HJB equation for the value function of a machine producer is given by

$$r(t) V(\nu, t \mid q) = \pi(\nu, t \mid q) + \dot{V}(\nu, t \mid q) - z(\nu, t \mid q) V(\nu, t \mid q). \tag{S14.8}$$

We are interested in BGP equilibria in which the interest rate, $r(t) = r^*$, is constant and the replacement probability $z(\nu, t \mid q)$ is constant across ν and over time, i.e. $z(\nu, t) = z^* > 0$. Since there is positive innovation on each line ($z^* > 0$), the free entry condition implies

$$\frac{\eta}{(\lambda^{-1} q)^{\zeta_3}} V(\nu, t \mid q) = 1, \ \forall \, \nu, t, \tag{S14.9}$$

where the λ^{-1} term captures the fact that an innovation on an old machine leads to the value function for the new machine. This further implies $\dot{V} = 0$. Using this and Eq. (S14.6) in Eq. (S14.8), we can solve for the value function on the BGP equilibrium as

$$V(\nu, t \mid q) = \frac{\beta q^{\zeta_2} q^{(\zeta_1 - \zeta_2)/\beta} L}{r^* + z^*}.$$

Using this in Eq. (S14.9), we obtain that the following condition should hold for all q

$$\frac{\lambda \eta}{q^{\zeta_3}} \frac{\beta q^{\zeta_2} q^{(\zeta_1 - \zeta_2)/\beta} L}{r^* + z^*} = 1. \tag{S14.10}$$

In words, to have positive and balanced research on each line, the benefits and costs of research on each line should be equated, which leads to Eq. (S14.10). This can be satisfied for all q only if

$$\zeta_2 + (\zeta_1 - \zeta_2)/\beta - \zeta_3 = 0. \tag{S14.11}$$

If this condition is not satisfied, there will only be investment in a subset of the machines and the economy would not feature balanced growth. Under the restriction (S14.11) for the parameters, Eq. (S14.10) will be satisfied for all q if

$$r^* + z^* = \lambda \eta \beta L. \tag{S14.12}$$

From the consumption Euler equation, we have

$$\frac{\dot{C}(t)}{C(t)} = \frac{1}{\theta}(r^* - \rho) \equiv g_C, \tag{S14.13}$$

where the last line defines g_C.

The last two displayed equations constitute 2 equations in 3 unknowns, r^*, z^* and g_C. To solve for the endogenous variables, we need one more relation, which we obtain by relating the growth rate, g_C, to the rate of innovation, z^*. Using Eq. (S14.5), aggregate output is given by

$$Y(t) = \frac{1}{1-\beta} \int_0^1 q(\nu, t)^{\zeta_1 + (\zeta_1 - \zeta_2)(1-\beta)/\beta} \, d\nu L,$$

which further gives

$$\dot{Y}(t) = \frac{1}{1-\beta} \int_0^1 z^* \left(\lambda^{\zeta_1 + (\zeta_1 - \zeta_2)(1-\beta)/\beta} - 1 \right) q(\nu, t)^{\zeta_1 + (\zeta_1 - \zeta_2)(1-\beta)/\beta} \, d\nu L.$$

Intuitively, at every time, a share z^* of the sectors have an innovation and the ones that have an innovation increase their scale by a factor of $\lambda - 1 > 0$. The last displayed equation further implies

$$g_Y = \frac{\dot{Y}(t)}{Y(t)} = z^* \left(\lambda^{\zeta_1 + (\zeta_1 - \zeta_2)(1-\beta)/\beta} - 1 \right). \tag{S14.14}$$

Similarly, total expenditures on machines are given by

$$X(t) = (1-\beta) \int_0^1 q(\nu, t)^{\zeta_2 + (\zeta_1 - \zeta_2)(1-\beta)/\beta} \, d\nu L,$$

which leads to

$$g_X = \frac{\dot{X}(t)}{X(t)} = z^* \left(\lambda^{\zeta_2 + (\zeta_1 - \zeta_2)(1-\beta)/\beta} - 1 \right). \tag{S14.15}$$

Finally, using Eq. (S14.7), aggregate spending on R&D is given by

$$Z(t) = \frac{z^*}{\eta} \int_0^1 q(\nu, t)^{\zeta_3} \, d\nu,$$

which leads to

$$g_Z = \frac{\dot{Z}(t)}{Z(t)} = z^* \left(\lambda^{\zeta_3} - 1 \right). \tag{S14.16}$$

Eqs. (S14.13), (S14.14), (S14.15), (S14.16) above show that the variables $C(t), Y(t), X(t)$ and $Z(t)$ grow at constant rates g_C, g_Y, g_X and g_Z. Market clearing in final good then implies

$$\exp(g_Y t) Y(0) = \exp(g_X t) X(0) + \exp(g_Z t) Z(0) + \exp(g_C t) C(0),$$

which holds only if

$$g_C = g_X = g_Y = g_Z \equiv g^*,$$

where the last equality defines the common growth rate g^*. The parametric restriction that we impose in Eq. (S14.11) already ensures $g_Z = g_Y$ (cf. Eqs. (S14.16) and (S14.14)). To ensure $g_X = g_Y$ from Eqs. (S14.15) and (S14.14), we also require

$$\zeta_2 = \zeta_1. \tag{S14.17}$$

Under this requirement, using $g_C = g_Z$ and Eq. (S14.16) gives us the desired relationship between the growth rate and the rate of innovation as

$$g^* = g_C = z^* \left(\lambda^{\zeta_3} - 1 \right). \tag{S14.18}$$

Next, solving Eqs. (S14.12),(S14.13) and (S14.18) yields

$$z^* = \frac{(\lambda \beta L \eta - \rho)}{\theta \left(\lambda^{\zeta_3} - 1 \right) + 1}$$

$$r^* = \frac{\theta \left(\lambda^{\zeta_3} - 1 \right) \lambda \beta L \eta + \rho}{\theta \left(\lambda^{\zeta_3} - 1 \right) + 1}$$

and the growth rate

$$g^* = \frac{\lambda \beta L \eta - \rho}{1 + \left(\lambda^{\zeta_3} - 1 \right)^{-1}}. \tag{S14.19}$$

The path we have described also satisfies the transversality condition if $g^* < r^*$ and leads to a positive growth rate $g^* > 0$ if the parameters satisfy

$$\lambda \beta L \eta > \rho > (1 - \theta) \frac{\lambda \beta L \eta - \rho}{1 + \left(\lambda^{\zeta_3} - 1 \right)^{-1}} \tag{S14.20}$$

It follows that the parametric restrictions on $(\zeta_1, \zeta_2, \zeta_3)$ in (S14.11) and (S14.17) are necessary for a BGP equilibrium. Moreover, these restrictions are satisfied if and only if

$$\zeta_1 = \zeta_2 = \zeta_3.$$

It also follows that, when this condition on $(\zeta_1, \zeta_2, \zeta_3)$ holds and when the remaining parameters satisfy Eq.(S14.20), there exists a BGP equilibrium in which the aggregate variables $Y(t), X(t), Z(t), C(t)$ grow at the constant and positive rate given in (S14.19).

Exercise 14.13

Exercise 14.13, Part (a). The equilibrium is defined as a sequence of aggregate allocations, aggregate prices, innovation levels in each sector, and intermediate good quantities and prices, $\left(\begin{array}{c} Y(t), C(t), X(t), A(t), r(t), w(t), \\ [Z(\nu, t \mid MC)]_{\nu=0}^{1}, [p(\nu, t \mid MC), x(\nu, t \mid MC), V(\nu, t \mid MC)]_{\nu=0}^{1} \end{array} \right)$ such that consumers maximize utility, competitive final good producers choose quantities to maximize profits taking prices given, intermediate good monopolists set prices to maximize profits, there is free entry in the R&D sector, the technology (the distribution of the marginal costs) evolves according to the R&D process that we describe below. The BGP equilibrium can be defined as an equilibrium in which $Y(t)$ and $C(t)$ grow at the same rate, $r(t) = r^*$ is constant and innovations on each machine line occur at a constant flow rate, $z(\nu, t \mid MC) = z^*$.

Exercise 14.13, Part (b). We partially solve for the equilibrium before we specify the form of the innovation possibilities frontier, in particular, we calculate the value function for the intermediate good monopolists. To calculate the value function, we first characterize the profits of a monopolist with marginal cost MC. The monopolist faces an isoelastic demand schedule $x = p^{-1/\beta} L$ and would therefore set $p^u = \frac{1}{1-\beta} MC$. The monopolist can set this price only if innovations are sufficiently drastic. Since she is facing competition from a firm with marginal costs $MC \times \lambda$, she will have to charge a limit price whenever $p^u > MC \times \lambda$. It follows that the monopolist sets the price

$$p(\nu, t \mid MC) = \min \left(\frac{1}{1 - \beta}, \lambda \right) MC = \mu \, MC,$$

where $\mu = \min \left(\frac{1}{1-\beta}, \lambda \right)$ is the markup. The current monopolist produces

$$x(\nu, t \mid MC) = p(\nu, t \mid MC)^{-1/\beta} L = (\mu \, MC)^{-1/\beta} L \tag{S14.21}$$

and makes profits of

$$\pi\left(\nu,t\mid MC\right)=(\mu-1)\,\mu^{-1/\beta}MC^{-(1-\beta)/\beta}L.$$

We next calculate the value function of the monopolist. On a BGP on which the interest rate is constant at r^* and the flow rate of innovation (and hence the replacement rate) is constant at z^*, the value function is given by

$$V\left(\nu,t\mid MC\right)=\frac{\pi\left(\nu,t\mid MC\right)}{r^*+z^*}=\frac{(\mu-1)\,\mu^{-1/\beta}L}{r^*+z^*}MC^{-(1-\beta)/\beta}.$$

In particular, the value function is higher on lines with lower marginal costs.

We next consider an innovation possibilities frontier that allows for positive innovation on each machine line. Since the value function is higher on lines with lower marginal costs, ceteris paribus, there would be more innovation on lines that have lower marginal cost. Hence, to have balanced innovation on all lines, the cost of innovation must be higher on lines with lower marginal cost (i.e. more advanced lines). In other words, defining $f\left(MC\right)$ as the flow rate of innovation on a line with marginal cost MC from a unit R&D investment, we have that $f\left(MC\right)$ must be increasing. To specify the exact functional form for $f\left(MC\right)$ that is consistent with a BGP, consider the free entry condition, $f\left(MC\right)V\left(\lambda^{-1}MC\right)=1$, which leads to

$$f\left(MC\right)\frac{(\mu-1)\,\mu^{-1/\beta}L}{r^*+z^*}\left(\lambda^{-1}MC\right)^{-(1-\beta)/\beta}=1. \tag{S14.22}$$

It follows that there can be balanced innovation only if

$$f\left(MC\right)=\eta MC^{(1-\beta)/\beta} \tag{S14.23}$$

for some constant η.

Exercise 14.13, Part (c). Using Eq. (S14.21) in the final good sector, we have

$$\begin{aligned}Y\left(t\right)&=\frac{1}{1-\beta}\int_0^1\left[(\mu MC)^{-1/\beta}L\right]^{1-\beta}d\nu L^\beta\\&=\frac{\mu^{-(1-\beta)/\beta}L}{1-\beta}\int_0^1 MC^{-(1-\beta)/\beta}d\nu.\end{aligned}$$

This expression suggests to define the following aggregate of marginal costs

$$A\left(t\right)=\int_0^1 MC^{-(1-\beta)/\beta}d\nu, \tag{S14.24}$$

which we can loosely interpret as the average productivity in this economy. In terms of average productivity, output is given by

$$Y\left(t\right)=\frac{\mu^{-(1-\beta)/\beta}L}{1-\beta}A\left(t\right), \tag{S14.25}$$

and wages are given by $w\left(t\right)=\beta Y\left(t\right)/L$. To calculate the growth rate of $A\left(t\right)$, note that

$$\begin{aligned}A\left(t+\Delta t\right)-A\left(t\right)&=\int_0^1 z^*\Delta t\left(\left(\frac{MC}{\lambda}\right)^{-(1-\beta)/\beta}-MC^{-(1-\beta)/\beta}\right)d\nu\\&=z^*\Delta t\left(\lambda^{(1-\beta)/\beta}-1\right)\int_0^1 MC^{-(1-\beta)/\beta}d\nu\\&=z^*\Delta t\left(\lambda^{(1-\beta)/\beta}-1\right)A\left(t\right)\end{aligned}$$

Hence, at the limit as Δt goes to 0, we have

$$g = \frac{\dot{A}(t)}{A(t)} = z^* \left(\lambda^{(1-\beta)/\beta} - 1 \right), \tag{S14.26}$$

where the growth rate g is also the growth rate of consumption and output since $A(t)$ and $Y(t)$ grow at the same rate (see Eq. (S14.25)).

Next note that the Euler equation implies

$$g = \frac{1}{\theta} \left(r^* - \rho \right), \tag{S14.27}$$

and with our choice of $f(MC)$ in Eq. (S14.23), the free entry condition (S14.22) gives

$$\eta \lambda^{(1-\beta)/\beta} (\mu - 1) \mu^{-1/\beta} L = r^* + z^*. \tag{S14.28}$$

Eqs. (S14.26), (S14.27) and (S14.28) are three equations in three unknowns r^*, g, and z^*. Solving these equations, we get the growth rate

$$g = \frac{\eta \lambda^{(1-\beta)/\beta} (\mu - 1) \mu^{-1/\beta} L - \rho}{\theta + \left(\lambda^{(1-\beta)/\beta} - 1 \right)^{-1}}. \tag{S14.29}$$

To ensure that the growth rate is positive and the transversality condition holds, we assume

$$(1 - \theta) \frac{\eta \lambda^{(1-\beta)/\beta} (\mu - 1) \mu^{-1/\beta} L - \rho}{\theta + \left(\lambda^{(1-\beta)/\beta} - 1 \right)^{-1}} < \rho < \eta \lambda^{(1-\beta)/\beta} (\mu - 1) \mu^{-1/\beta} L. \tag{S14.30}$$

We next solve for consumption from the resource equation $Y(t) = C(t) + X(t) + Z(t)$ and show that the path we have described is an equilibrium. Note that the expenditure on machines is given by

$$
\begin{aligned}
X(t) &= \int_0^1 x(\nu, t \mid MC) \, MC d\nu \\
&= \int_0^1 (\mu \, MC)^{-1/\beta} LMC d\nu = \mu^{-1/\beta} LA(t),
\end{aligned}
$$

where the last equality follows from Eq. (S14.24). Note also that the total R&D expenditure is given by

$$
\begin{aligned}
Z(t) = \int_0^1 Z(\nu, t) \, d\nu = \int_0^1 \frac{z^*}{f(MC)} d\nu &= \int_0^1 \frac{g}{\left(\lambda^{(1-\beta)/\beta} - 1 \right) \eta} MC^{-(1-\beta)/\beta} d\nu \\
&= \frac{g}{\left(\lambda^{(1-\beta)/\beta} - 1 \right) \eta} A(t),
\end{aligned}
$$

where the third equality uses Eq. (S14.26). Plugging these expressions for $X(t)$ and $Z(t)$ and the expression for $Y(t)$ from (S14.25) into the aggregate resource constraints, we have

$$
\begin{aligned}
C(t) &= \frac{\mu^{-(1-\beta)/\beta} L}{1 - \beta} A(t) - \mu^{-1/\beta} LA(t) - \frac{g}{\left(\lambda^{(1-\beta)/\beta} - 1 \right) \eta} A(t) \\
&= A(t) \left[\frac{\mu^{-(1-\beta)/\beta} L}{1 - \beta} - \mu^{-1/\beta} L - \frac{g}{\left(\lambda^{(1-\beta)/\beta} - 1 \right) \eta} \right].
\end{aligned}
$$

Hence consumption also grows at the constant rate g. This completes the characterization and shows that, given the R&D technology in (S14.23) and the parametric restriction (S14.30), there exists a BGP equilibrium in which consumption and output grow at the same constant rate and there is innovation at the same constant rate on each machine line. Moreover, the path we have described is an equilibrium starting with any initial distribution of marginal costs, $[MC(\nu, 0)]_{\nu \in [0,1]}$, hence there are no transitional dynamics.

Exercise 14.13, Part (d). We first characterize the social planner's allocation of resources for a given distribution of marginal costs $[MC(\nu, t)]_{\nu \in [0,1]}$. The social planner will set $p(\nu, t \mid MC) = MC$ and produce

$$x(\nu, t \mid MC) = p(\nu, t \mid MC)^{-1/\beta} L = MC^{-1/\beta} L$$

units of each intermediate good. Hence the aggregate output will be

$$
\begin{aligned}
Y(t) &= \frac{1}{1-\beta} \int_0^1 \left[MC^{-1/\beta} L \right]^{1-\beta} d\nu L^\beta \\
&= \frac{1}{1-\beta} A(t) L,
\end{aligned}
$$

where $A(t)$, given by (S14.24), denotes the average productivity in the economy. Comparing this expression with Eq. (S14.25), we note that the social planner produces more output for a given level of average productivity since she corrects for the monopoly distortions. Note also that the social planner's expenditures on machines are given by

$$X(t) = \int_0^1 MC \times MC^{-1/\beta} L d\nu = A(t) L.$$

Using the last two displayed equations and the final resource allocation, we have

$$C(t) = Y(t) - X(t) - Z(t) = \frac{\beta}{1-\beta} A(t) L - Z(t),$$

where $Z(t)$ denotes the aggregate investment in R&D.

Next, we consider the social planner's dynamic trade-off. Note that the social planner's unit investment in a machine line with marginal cost MC, generates $f(MC)$ new machines and increases the contribution of the line to average productivity by

$$f(MC) \left((MC/\lambda)^{-(1-\beta)/\beta} - MC^{-(1-\beta)/\beta} \right) = \eta \left(\lambda^{(1-\beta)/\beta} - 1 \right).$$

In particular, the social planner is indifferent between investing in various machine lines. Moreover, by investing an aggregate amount of $Z(\nu, t)$ on R&D, she increases average productivity by $Z(t) \eta \left(\lambda^{(1-\beta)/\beta} - 1 \right)$. It follows that the social planner's problem can be written as

$$\max_{[Z(t),C(t),A(t)]_t} \int_0^\infty \exp(-\rho t) \frac{C(t)^{1-\theta} - 1}{1-\theta} dt$$

$$\text{s.t.} \quad C(t) = \frac{\beta}{1-\beta} A(t) L - Z(t)$$

$$\dot{A}(t) = Z(t) \eta \left(\lambda^{(1-\beta)/\beta} - 1 \right).$$

After substituting the first constraint into the second to eliminate $Z(t)$, the current value Hamiltonian is given by

$$\hat{H}(t, C, A, \mu) = \frac{C^{1-\theta} - 1}{1 - \theta} + \mu \left(\left(\frac{\beta}{1 - \beta} AL - C \right) \eta \left(\lambda^{(1-\beta)/\beta} - 1 \right) \right).$$

The first-order conditions lead to the consumption growth equation

$$g^S \equiv \frac{\dot{C}}{C} = \frac{1}{\theta} \left(\frac{\beta}{1 - \beta} \eta \left(\lambda^{(1-\beta)/\beta} - 1 \right) L - \rho \right).$$

We next compare this growth expression with the equilibrium growth rate (S14.29) when the markup μ is equal to $(1 - \beta)^{-1}$ (so that machine producers can charge the unconstrained monopoly price), given by

$$g^{Eq} \left(\mu \equiv (1 - \beta)^{-1} \right) = \frac{1}{\theta + \left(\lambda^{(1-\beta)/\beta} - 1 \right)^{-1}} \left(\frac{\beta}{1 - \beta} \eta \lambda^{(1-\beta)/\beta} (1 - \beta)^{1/\beta} L - \rho \right).$$

First, note that the social planner internalizes the static monopoly distortions and produces more output for a given number of machines (captured by the $(1 - \beta)^{1/\beta}$ term in g^{Eq} compared to 1 in g^S) which creates a force that tends to increase the social planner's growth rate relative to the equilibrium growth rate. Second, in equilibrium, firms do not internalize the fact that they are replacing an existing producer (the business stealing effect, captured by the $\lambda^{(1-\beta)/\beta}$ term in g^{Eq} compared to $\left(\lambda^{(1-\beta)/\beta} - 1 \right)$ in g^S) while the social planner does, which creates a force that tends to decrease the social planner's relative growth rate. Third, in equilibrium, firms are concerned about the fact that they are going to be replaced by another producer in the future while the social planner is not (the replacement effect captured by the $\theta + \left(\lambda^{(1-\beta)/\beta} - 1 \right)^{-1}$ term in g^{Eq} compared to θ in g^S), which creates a force that tends to increase the social planner's relative growth rate. The net comparison between g^S and g^{Eq} depends on which of these forces dominate. If the second force (business stealing effect) dominates, then the social planner's growth rate will be lower than the equilibrium growth rate. Therefore, it is possible to have excessive innovations in this model.

Exercise 14.15

Exercise 14.15, Part (a). Given that the structure of the economy is exactly the same as the one characterized in section 14.1, the definition of the equilibrium also takes the same form. Hence, an equilibrium in this economy consists of time paths of consumption levels, aggregate spending on machines, and aggregate R&D expenditure, $[C(t), X(t), Z(t)]_{t=0}^{\infty}$, time paths of the qualities of leading-edge machines $[q(\nu, t)]_{\nu \in [0,1], t=0}^{\infty}$, time paths of prices and quantities of each machine and the net present discounted value of profits from that machine, $[p^x(\nu, t \mid q), x(\nu, t \mid q), V(\nu, t \mid q)]_{\nu \in [0,1], t=0}^{\infty}$, and time paths of interest rates and wage rates, $[r(t), w(t)]_{t=0}^{\infty}$ such that consumers maximize utility, entry into research is determined by free entry, both final food and intermediary producers maximize profits and all markets clear. Furthermore we again define a BGP equilibrium as an equilibrium where output and consumption grow at a common rate g^*.

Let us now turn to the characterization of the BGP. As the production side is identical to the one in section 14.1 in the book we refer to the exposition there. There it is shown that equilibrium profits for an intermediary producer with quality $q(\nu, t)$ are given by $\pi(\nu, t|q) = \beta q L$ and that the value function solves the HJB equation

$$r(t)V(t, \nu|q) - \dot{V}(t, \nu|q) = \pi(\nu, t|q) - z(\nu, t|q)V(t, \nu|q). \tag{S14.31}$$

Along the BGP, both interest rates $r(t)$ and innovation rates $z(\nu, t|q)$ are constant over time, i.e. $r(t) = r^*$ and $z(\nu, t|q) = z^*$. Hence the differential equation above has the stable solution

$$V(t, \nu|q) = V(q) = \frac{\beta L q}{r^* + z^*}, \tag{S14.32}$$

where we already explicitly noted that the value of having a patent does neither depend on time, nor on the sector ν. Let us now turn to the free entry condition of the research sector. The innovation possibilities frontier still posits that by spending one unit of the final good one generates a flow rate of innovation equal to $\frac{\eta}{q}$, where q is the current quality of the sector one tries to improve upon. Now however, the quality improvement is random and so are the benefits of innovation. As the representative agent holds a balanced portfolio of the firms in this economy, the appropriate objective of potential entrants in the research sector is the maximization of their expected value. To arrive at this expression, simply note that having an innovation of quality λ in a sector with current quality q, has a value of $V(\lambda q)$. As the support of possible values of λ is given by $[(1-\beta)^{(1-\beta)/\beta}, \bar{\lambda}]$, and the distribution function of λ is given by H, the expected value of a firm conditional on having a successful innovation is equal to

$$\int_{(1-\beta)^{-(1-\beta)/\beta}}^{\bar{\lambda}} V(\lambda q) dH(\lambda).$$

Using this, the free entry condition into research reads

$$1 = \frac{\eta}{q} \int_{(1-\beta)^{-(1-\beta)/\beta}}^{\bar{\lambda}} V(\lambda q) dH(\lambda) = \frac{\eta}{q} \int_{(1-\beta)^{-(1-\beta)/\beta}}^{\bar{\lambda}} \frac{\beta L \lambda q}{r^* + z^*} dH(\lambda), \tag{S14.33}$$

where the second equality uses the expression for the value function given in (S14.32). Let us define the average quality improvement as

$$\mu_\lambda \equiv \int_{(1-\beta)^{-(1-\beta)/\beta}}^{\bar{\lambda}} \lambda dH(\lambda).$$

Then we can rewrite the free entry condition (S14.33) as

$$1 = \frac{\eta \beta L}{r^* + z^*} \mu_\lambda, \tag{S14.34}$$

which determines the equilibrium replacement adjusted discount rate $r^* + z^*$ in terms of exogenous parameters.

From the consumer's problem we again get the Euler equation

$$\frac{\dot{C}(t)}{C(t)} = g^* = \frac{1}{\theta}(r^* - \rho). \tag{S14.35}$$

Additionally we can express the economy's growth rate g^* directly via the entrants research expenditures. Following the analysis from section 14.1 in the book we get that aggregate output $Y(t)$ is proportional to average quality

$$Q(t) = \int q(\nu, t) d\nu.$$

Hence we need to determine the growth of the average quality in the economy. To derive this expression we can again make use of the law of large numbers. Above we denoted the (endogenous) innovation probability by z^*. Hence, in a (small) time interval Δt, there will be a measure $z^* \Delta t$ of entrants which will experience an innovation. Let us call this random set of sectors that experiences an innovation by $\Lambda \subset [0,1]$. Consequently, all sectors in Λ^C will not experience an innovation. Hence

$$
\begin{aligned}
Q(t + \Delta t) &= \int q(\nu, t + \Delta t) d\nu = \int_\Lambda q(\nu, t + \Delta t) d\nu + \int_{\Lambda^C} q(\nu, t + \Delta t) d\nu \\
&= \int_\Lambda q(\nu, t + \Delta t) d\nu + \int_{\Lambda^C} q(\nu, t) d\nu \\
&= \int_\Lambda q(\nu, t + \Delta t) d\nu + (1 - z^* \Delta t) Q(t) + o(\Delta t).
\end{aligned}
$$

But then note that

$$
\begin{aligned}
\int_\Lambda q(\nu, t + \Delta t) d\nu &= \mathbb{E}[\lambda q(\nu, t) | Innovate] = \mathbb{E}[\mathbb{E}[\lambda | q(\nu, t), Innovate] q(\nu, t) | Innovate] \\
&= \mu_\lambda Q(t) z^* \Delta t,
\end{aligned}
$$

where we used that both the improvement conditional on innovating and innovating itself is random, i.e. independent of the current quality so that $\mathbb{E}[\lambda | q(\nu, t), Innovate] = \mu_\lambda$ and $\mathbb{E}[q(\nu, t) | Innovate] = \int_\Lambda q(\nu, t) d\nu = Q(t) z^* \Delta t$. Using these results, we get that

$$
Q(t + \Delta t) = (1 - z^* \Delta t) Q(t) + \mu_\lambda Q(t) z^* \Delta t + o(\Delta t),
$$

which yields

$$
\begin{aligned}
g^* &= \frac{\dot{Q}(t)}{Q(t)} = \lim_{\Delta t \to 0} \frac{Q(t + \Delta t) - Q(t)}{\Delta t} \frac{1}{Q(t)} = (\mu_\lambda - 1) z^* + \lim_{\Delta t \to 0} \frac{o(\Delta t)}{\Delta t} \frac{1}{Q(t)} \\
&= (\mu_\lambda - 1) z^*. \tag{S14.36}
\end{aligned}
$$

Using (S14.34), (S14.35) and (S14.36), we get that

$$
\begin{aligned}
g^* &= \frac{1}{\theta}(r^* - \rho) = \frac{1}{\theta}(\mu_\lambda \eta \beta L - z^* - \rho) = \frac{1}{\theta}\left(\mu_\lambda \eta \beta L - \rho - \frac{g^*}{(\mu_\lambda - 1)}\right) \\
&= \frac{\mu_\lambda \eta \beta L - \rho}{\theta + \frac{1}{\mu_\lambda - 1}}, \tag{S14.37}
\end{aligned}
$$

so that this economy has positive growth as long as

$$
\mu_\lambda \eta \beta L > \rho.
$$

Note that the growth rate in (S14.37) is very similar to growth rate of the baseline model (see (14.23)). In particular, the only difference is that λ is replaced by its expected value μ_λ. Hence, the restriction to constant quality improvements in the baseline version of the model is for convenience only.

For the transversality condition to hold we need the usual condition that the growth rate of the economy does not exceed the interest rate, i.e. that $g^* < r^*$. Using (S14.35) and (S14.37) we therefore need that

$$
\rho > (1 - \theta) g^* = (1 - \theta) \frac{\mu_\lambda \eta \beta L - \rho}{\theta + \frac{1}{\mu_\lambda - 1}},
$$

which can be simplified to

$$
\rho > (1 - \theta)(\mu_\lambda - 1) \eta \beta L.
$$

Hence, there exists a BGP equilibrium with positive growth if

$$\mu_\lambda \eta \beta L > \rho > (1-\theta)(\mu_\lambda - 1)\eta\beta L. \tag{S14.38}$$

Exercise 14.15, Part (b). The importance of the lower support of the distribution of λ is, that this is precisely the threshold that makes the innovation drastic, i.e. the quality improvement is big enough such that the entrant can charge the unconstrained monopoly price (see (14.5) and the discussion there). Hence, by assuming that $\lambda > (1-\beta)^{-(1-\beta)/\beta}$ we make sure that whatever the realization of λ, the innovator will be able to charge the unconstrained monopoly price. If this assumption was relaxed, we would have to consider two different regimes with two different value functions. The value function in (S14.32) used the result that equilibrium profits are given by $\pi(\nu,t|q) = \beta q L$. This in turn relied on the entrant's ability to charge the unconstrained monopoly price. However, if $\lambda < (1-\beta)^{-(1-\beta)/\beta}$ this can not occur in equilibrium, as the old incumbent with quality $\lambda^{-1}q(\nu,t)$ can set a price low enough such that final good producers would prefer the old quality at this lower price. Hence, the new entrant has to resort to limit pricing, i.e. he will set a price $p^L(\nu,t|q)$ such that final good producers are indifferent between buying quality q at $p^L(\nu,t|q)$ and buying quality $\lambda^{-1}q$ at price $\psi\lambda^{-1}q$ (which are the marginal costs of the old incumbent). Hence, spending one unit on an intermediary of quality $\lambda^{-1}q$, yields $x(\nu,t|\lambda^{-1}q) = (\psi\lambda^{-1}q)^{-1}$ many intermediaries of variety ν, whose value in the production function (see (14.3)) is given by

$$\lambda^{-1}q x(\nu,t|\lambda^{-1}q)^{1-\beta} = \lambda^{-1}q \left(\psi\lambda^{-1}q\right)^{-(1-\beta)}.$$

Similarly, spending the unit on the better quality product yields an input level of

$$q x(\nu,t|q)^{1-\beta} = q \left(p^L(\nu,t|q)\right)^{-(1-\beta)}.$$

The limit price $p^L(\nu,t|q)$ will be set to ensure that final good producers are exactly indifferent between spending the unit on the new or the old vintage in the respective machine line. This requires that

$$\lambda^{-1}q \left(\psi\lambda^{-1}q\right)^{-(1-\beta)} = q \left(p^L(\nu,t|q)\right)^{-(1-\beta)},$$

which shows that

$$p^L(\nu,t|q) = \lambda^{\beta/(1-\beta)}\psi q = \lambda^{\beta/(1-\beta)}(1-\beta)q. \tag{S14.39}$$

Note that it is from the limit price formula in (S14.39) that the lower bound on λ in (14.5) can be derived. In particular, this bound ensures that the unconstrained monopoly price $p^x(\nu,t|q)$ satisfies

$$p^x(\nu,t|q) = q(\nu,t) \le p^L(\nu,t|q).$$

For an extensive discussion of the importance of limit pricing see Chapter 12, especially Proposition 12.1 and the discussion thereafter. This being said, the unique equilibrium price of intermediary goods is equal to

$$p^x(\nu,t|q) = \begin{cases} q & \text{if } \lambda \ge (1-\beta)^{-(1-\beta)/\beta} \\ (1-\beta)\lambda^{(1-\beta)/\beta}q & \text{if } \lambda < (1-\beta)^{-(1-\beta)/\beta} \end{cases}. \tag{S14.40}$$

Note especially that the unique equilibrium has the entrant being the only producer in the market (but not necessarily being able to charge the unconstrained monopoly price). Profits of the intermediary producer are still given by

$$\pi(\nu,t|q) = (p^x(\nu,t|q) - \psi q)\left(\frac{q}{p^x(\nu,t|q)}\right)^{1/\beta}L,$$

so that with (S14.40) we get

$$\pi(\nu,t|q) = \begin{cases} \pi^M(\nu,t|q) = & q\beta L & \text{if } \lambda \geq (1-\beta)^{-(1-\beta)/\beta} \\ \pi^L(\nu,t|q) = & (\frac{1}{1-\beta})^{\frac{1-\beta}{\beta}}(\lambda^{(1-\beta)/\beta}-1)\lambda^{-(1-\beta)/\beta^2}qL & \text{if } \lambda < (1-\beta)^{-(1-\beta)/\beta} \end{cases}.$$

Using this we also get that the value function $V(\lambda q)$ depends on the particular value of λ drawn, i.e.

$$V(\lambda q) = \begin{cases} \pi^M(\nu,t|\lambda q)/(r^*+z^*) & \text{if } \lambda \geq (1-\beta)^{-(1-\beta)/\beta} \\ \pi^L(\nu,t|\lambda q)/(r^*+z^*) & \text{if } \lambda < (1-\beta)^{-(1-\beta)/\beta} \end{cases}. \qquad (S14.41)$$

Having derived this expression of the value function, the free entry condition has to be changed accordingly. Using (S14.41) we get from (S14.33) that free entry requires

$$\begin{aligned} 1 &= \frac{\eta}{q}\int_{\underline{\lambda}}^{\bar{\lambda}} V(\lambda q)dH(\lambda) \\ &= \frac{\eta}{q}\int_{\underline{\lambda}}^{(1-\beta)^{-(1-\beta)/\beta}} \pi^L(\nu,t|\lambda q)/(r^*+z^*)dH(\lambda) \\ &\quad + \frac{\eta}{q}\int_{(1-\beta)^{-(1-\beta)/\beta}}^{\bar{\lambda}} \pi^M(\nu,t|\lambda q)/(r^*+z^*)dH(\lambda) \\ &= \frac{\eta L}{(r^*+z^*)}\left[\int_{\underline{\lambda}}^{\lambda^*}(\frac{1}{1-\beta})^{\frac{1-\beta}{\beta}}(\lambda^{(1-\beta)/\beta}-1)\lambda^{-(1-\beta)/\beta^2}\lambda dH(\lambda) + \beta\int_{\lambda^*}^{\bar{\lambda}}\lambda dH(\lambda)\right], \end{aligned}$$

where $\lambda^* = (1-\beta)^{-(1-\beta)/\beta}$. Although the expression in parenthesis looks daunting, note that it is only a function of exogenous parameters. Hence, the analysis stays in principle unchanged (of course we have to change the parametric restrictions accordingly to ensure that the transversality condition is satisfied).

Exercise 14.15, Part (c). To analyze the transitional dynamics (or absence thereof) in this economy, let us again focus on the equilibrium conditions which have to hold at every point in time. We consider an equilibrium where there are positive research expenditures in some sector ν. Whereas per period profits are always given by $\pi(\nu,t|q) = q\beta L$, the value function is in principle only defined implicitly by the HJB equation (S14.31) as the particular form in (S14.32) was only derived as the solution along the BGP. Now we have to show that this will always be the case, i.e. that the only equilibrium is characterized by balanced growth. If the equilibrium features positive research efforts in sector ν at period t, the free entry condition has to hold, i.e. it will have to be true that

$$1 = \frac{\eta}{q(\nu,t)}\int_{(1-\beta)^{-(1-\beta)/\beta}}^{\bar{\lambda}} V(\nu,t|\lambda q(\nu,t))dH(\lambda). \qquad (S14.42)$$

Note that in contrast to (S14.33), (S14.42) potentially allows for the value function to depend on the sector ν and the time t. Then however, (S14.42) shows that conditional on the current quality $q(\nu,t)$, the free entry condition implies that the value function V can neither depend on time nor on the sector, i.e. $V(\nu,t|q) = V(q)$ and $\dot{V}(\nu,t|q) = 0$. Consequently, the HJB equation simplifies to

$$r(t)V(q) = \pi(q) - z(\nu,t|q)V(q).$$

This however shows that $z(\nu,t|q)$ will be independent of the sector ν too, i.e. $z(\nu,t|q) = z(t|q)$. Substituting the expression for $\pi(q)$, we get

$$(r(t) + z(t|q))V(q) = \pi(q) = q\beta L, \tag{S14.43}$$

so that $r(t) + z(t|q)$ will be independent of time (as $\frac{q\beta L}{V(q)}$ does not depend on t). Substituting (S14.43) in (S14.42) yields

$$1 = \frac{\eta}{q(\nu,t)} \int_{(1-\beta)^{-(1-\beta)/\beta}}^{\bar\lambda} \frac{\lambda q(\nu,t)\beta L}{r(t) + z(t|\lambda q(\nu,t))} dH(\lambda)$$

$$= \eta\beta L \int_{(1-\beta)^{-(1-\beta)/\beta}}^{\bar\lambda} \frac{\lambda}{r(t) + z(t|\lambda q(\nu,t))} dH(\lambda). \tag{S14.44}$$

As this has to hold for all $q(\nu,t)$, (S14.44) implies that the replacement rates $z(t|q(\nu,t))$ are not only independent of the specific sector ν, but also constant across qualities, i.e. $z(t|q(\nu,t)) = z(t)$ for all $q(\nu,t)$. Hence in equilibrium we will need to have

$$r(t) + z(t) = s, \tag{S14.45}$$

where s is some constant. In fact we can use (S14.44) to explicitly solve for s. Rearranging terms, we get

$$r(t) + z(t) = \eta\beta L \int_{(1-\beta)^{-(1-\beta)/\beta}}^{\bar\lambda} \lambda dH(\lambda) = \eta\beta L\mu_\lambda, \tag{S14.46}$$

where we again defined the average quality improvement $\mu_\lambda = \int_{(1-\beta)^{-(1-\beta)/\beta}}^{\bar\lambda} \lambda dH(\lambda)$. All that remains to be shown for the proof that the unique equilibrium features balanced growth is that (S14.45) implies that both $r(t)$ and $z(t)$ individually are constant. To do so, note first that the resource constraint in this economy is given by

$$Y(t) - X(t) = C(t) + Z(t) = C(t) + \frac{1}{\eta} \int_0^1 z(t|q(\nu,t))q(\nu,t)d\nu. \tag{S14.47}$$

As in section 14.1, equilibrium output is given by $Y(t) = \frac{1}{1-\beta}Q(t)L$ and expenditures on machines are given by $X(t) = (1-\beta)Q(t)L$. Additionally we showed above that $z(t|q(\nu,t)) = z(t)$ so that $Z(t) = \frac{1}{\eta}z(t)Q(t)$. Hence, we can rewrite (S14.47) as

$$\left(\frac{1}{1-\beta} - (1-\beta)\right)Q(t)L - \frac{1}{\eta}z(t)Q(t) = C(t),$$

or rather

$$\left(\frac{1}{1-\beta} - (1-\beta)\right)L - \frac{1}{\eta}z(t) = \frac{C(t)}{Q(t)}. \tag{S14.48}$$

Differentiating (S14.48) with respect to time yields

$$\frac{\frac{1}{\eta}z(t)}{\left(\frac{1}{1-\beta} - (1-\beta)\right)L - \frac{1}{\eta}z(t)} \frac{\dot z(t)}{z(t)} = \frac{\dot C(t)}{C(t)} - \frac{\dot Q(t)}{Q(t)}. \tag{S14.49}$$

As consumption growth is determined by the Euler equation, the growth rate of average quality $Q(t)$ is still given by $\frac{\dot Q(t)}{Q(t)} = (\mu_\lambda - 1)z(t)$ and (S14.45) provides a relation between $r(t)$

and $z(t)$, we can express (S14.49) as

$$\frac{\frac{1}{\eta}z(t)}{\left(\frac{1}{1-\beta}-(1-\beta)\right)L-\frac{1}{\eta}z(t)}\frac{\dot{z}(t)}{z(t)}=\frac{1}{\theta}(s-z(t)-\rho)-(\mu_\lambda-1)z(t). \qquad \text{(S14.50)}$$

This is a differential equation in a single variable $z(t)$. Hence to show that growth is always balanced, we only have to show that the only stable solution of (S14.50) is given by $z(t)=z^*$, where z^* is BGP replacement rate. First of all, note that $z(t)=z^*$ indeed solves (S14.50), as this would imply that consumption grows at the same rate as average quality (which is the case on the BGP). To see that this is the only stable solution, suppose that $z(t)<z^*$. Rewriting the RHS of (S14.50) as

$$\frac{1}{\theta}(s-z(t)-\rho)-(\mu_\lambda-1)z(t)=\frac{(s-\rho)}{\theta}-(\frac{1}{\theta}+\mu_\lambda-1)z(t)$$

shows that this term is strictly decreasing in $z(t)$. As

$$\frac{1}{\theta}(s-z^*-\rho)-(\mu_\lambda-1)z^*=0$$

this implies that the RHS of (S14.50) is negative whenever $z(t)<z^*$. To determine the evolution of $z(t)$ from (S14.50) the sign of the term $\left(\frac{1}{1-\beta}-(1-\beta)\right)L-\frac{1}{\eta}z(t)$ is crucial. So suppose first that

$$\eta\left(\frac{1}{1-\beta}-(1-\beta)\right)L=\eta\beta\frac{2-\beta}{1-\beta}L>z(t). \qquad \text{(S14.51)}$$

Then we get from (S14.50) that

$$\dot{z}(t)=\left(\frac{(s-\rho)}{\theta}-(\frac{1}{\theta}+\mu_\lambda-1)z(t)\right)\left(\eta\beta\frac{2-\beta}{1-\beta}L-z(t)\right)<0.$$

But with $z(t)$ decreasing at t, we will have that $z(t)<z^*$ in the next instance and (S14.51) will still be satisfied. Hence, whenever $z(t)<z^*$ and (S14.51) holds true, $z(t)$ will be strictly decreasing and hence will converge to $z(t)=0$. This however violates that resource constraint in (S14.48) as $z(t)=0$ implies that average quality $Q(t)$ is constant so that consumption also has to be constant asymptotically. However (S14.46) implies that interest rates would asymptotically be given by

$$r(t)=\eta\beta L\mu_\lambda>\rho,$$

where the inequality follows from (S14.38). Hence, the Euler equation requires that consumption will still be increasing asymptotically, which is a contradiction. Now suppose that (S14.51) is not satisfied. Then we get that

$$z(t)<z^* \text{ implies } \dot{z}(t)>0$$

so that $z(t)$ converges to the BGP level z^*. We will now show that this is impossible as the transversality condition will be violated. If (S14.51) is violated and $z(t)$ is increasing towards z^*, it implies that

$$z^*>\eta\beta\frac{2-\beta}{1-\beta}L. \qquad \text{(S14.52)}$$

Now note that from (S14.46), the Euler equation and (S14.36) we get

$$\begin{aligned}z^* &= \eta\beta L\mu_\lambda-r^*=\eta\beta L\mu_\lambda-\theta g^*-\rho=\eta\beta L\mu_\lambda-\theta z^*(\mu_\lambda-1)-\rho\\ &= \frac{\eta\beta L\mu_\lambda-\rho}{1+\theta(\mu_\lambda-1)},\end{aligned}$$

so that it follows from (S14.52) that

$$\eta\beta L\mu_\lambda - (1 + \theta(\mu_\lambda - 1))\eta\beta\frac{2-\beta}{1-\beta}L > \rho.$$

From (S14.38) we need for the transversality condition to be satisfied that

$$\rho > (1 - \theta)(\mu_\lambda - 1)\eta\beta L.$$

These two inequalities imply that

$$\eta\beta L\mu_\lambda - (1 + \theta(\mu_\lambda - 1))\eta\beta\frac{2-\beta}{1-\beta}L > (1 - \theta)(\mu_\lambda - 1)\eta\beta L.$$

This however is a contradiction, as $\frac{2-\beta}{1-\beta} > 1$. This shows that we can never have $z(t) < z^*$.

Now suppose that $z(t) > z^*$. Consider first the case where (S14.51) is satisfied. Then it is clear that $z(t)$ increases over time. To see that $z(t)$ will converge towards to $\eta\beta\frac{2-\beta}{1-\beta}L$, note that (S14.50) implies that

$$\lim_{z(t)\to\eta\beta\frac{2-\beta}{1-\beta}L} \dot{z}(t) = 0,$$

as the RHS of (S14.50) is finite. Hence, $z(t) = \eta\beta\frac{2-\beta}{1-\beta}L$ at the BGP equilibrium. However, the same steps as above show that this violates the transversality condition. Finally suppose that $z(t) > z^*$ and (S14.51) is violated. As $z(t)$ decreases over time, there will be some $\bar{t}$ such that $z(\bar{t}) = z^*$ or $z(\bar{t}) = \eta\beta\frac{2-\beta}{1-\beta}L$. Either way this implies that $z(t)$ is converging to a constant that satisfies $z(t) = z \geq \eta\beta\frac{2-\beta}{1-\beta}L$. As shown above, this is a contradiction as the transversality condition is violated. Hence the differential equation in (S14.50) has a unique solution which satisfies the transversality condition and has positive research expenditures on the entire equilibrium path. This solution is given by $z(t) = z^*$. This proves that this economy does not have transitional dynamics and that growth is always balanced.

The economics of this result are intuitive. As in most models featuring endogenous growth, the only technology to save for the future are resources spent on research. Hence, the current interest rates and the amount of resources spent on research are closely related. If interest rates decline over time, consumers - taking those interest rates as given - postpone their consumption to the future as savings get less attractive over time. However, for a given level of average quality $Q(t)$ (which is the appropriate state variable in this economy) we cannot have both higher consumption and higher investment into research in the future. Hence, interest and replacement rates have to go hand in hand which - from (S14.45) - is only possible if both are constant over time, i.e. if growth is balanced. This shows that the general equilibrium effects are a crucial force towards balanced growth.

Exercise 14.15, Part (d). Let us now focus on the social planner's problem to derive the Pareto optimal growth rate. As the production side is identical to the one studied in the book, we refer to the analysis there to show that net output which can be distributed between consumption and research expenditures is given by (see (14.25))

$$Y^S(t) - X^S(t) = (1-\beta)^{-1/\beta}\beta Q^S(t)L = Z^S(t) + C^S(t), \tag{S14.53}$$

where again the superscript denotes the social planner's allocation. This already shows that the social planner's appropriate state variable is also average quality $Q(t)$. The law of motion of aggregate quality is given by

$$\dot{Q}(t) = \eta(\mu_\lambda - 1)Z^S(t).$$

Substituting for $Z^S(t)$ from (S14.53), the social planner solves the problem

$$\max_{[C^S(t),Q(t)]_{t=0}^{\infty}} \int \exp(-\rho t) \frac{C^S(t)^{1-\theta}-1}{1-\theta} dt$$

$$\text{s.t.} \quad \dot{Q}(t) = \eta(\mu_\lambda - 1)\left[(1-\beta)^{-1/\beta}\beta Q^S(t)L - C^S(t)\right].$$

The current value Hamiltonian for this problem is given by

$$\hat{H}(Q^S, C^S, \mu^S) = \frac{C^S(t)^{1-\theta}-1}{1-\theta} + \mu^S(t)[\eta(\mu_\lambda-1)((1-\beta)^{-1/\beta}\beta Q^S(t)L - C^S(t))].$$

The sufficient conditions for a maximum are the two first-order conditions and the transversality condition

$$\hat{H}_C(Q^S, C^S, \mu^S) = C^S(t)^{-\theta} - \mu^S(t)\eta(\mu_\lambda-1) = 0 \tag{S14.54}$$

$$\hat{H}_Q(Q^S, C^S, \mu^S) = \mu^S(t)\eta(\mu_\lambda-1)(1-\beta)^{-1/\beta}\beta L = \rho\mu^S(t) - \dot{\mu}^S(t) \tag{S14.55}$$

$$0 = \lim_{t\to\infty}[\exp(-\rho t)\mu^S(t)Q^S(t)]. $$

From (S14.55) we get that

$$-\frac{\dot{\mu}^S(t)}{\mu^S(t)} = \eta(\mu_\lambda-1)(1-\beta)^{-1/\beta}\beta L - \rho,$$

so that - using (S14.54) - we arrive at

$$\frac{\dot{C}^S(t)}{C^S(t)} = -\frac{1}{\theta}\frac{\dot{\mu}^S(t)}{\mu^S(t)} = \frac{1}{\theta}(\eta(\mu_\lambda-1)(1-\beta)^{-1/\beta}\beta L - \rho). \tag{S14.56}$$

In the decentralized equilibrium, interest rates were given by

$$r^* = \frac{\eta(\mu_\lambda-1)\beta L\mu_\lambda\theta + \rho}{1 + \theta(\mu_\lambda-1)^{-1}}. \tag{S14.57}$$

In order to judge if the social planner would want to induce faster or slower growth compared to the equilibrium allocation, we need to compare (S14.57) with the analogous expression in (S14.56), i.e.

$$\eta(\mu_\lambda-1)(1-\beta)^{-1/\beta}\beta L \lesseqgtr \frac{\eta(\mu_\lambda-1)\beta L\mu_\lambda\theta + \rho}{1 + \theta(\mu_\lambda-1)^{-1}}.$$

From here it is seen that the comparison is ambiguous, i.e. the equilibrium growth rate can be too small or too big. The reason is that we still have the two effects always present in the Schumpeterian models of creative destructions. The appropriability effect (i.e. monopolistic intermediaries do not capture the whole benefits of the innovation) tends to reduce equilibrium growth, the business-stealing effect (i.e. new entrants do not take account of the effect that they are replacing an old incumbent) tends to make growth excessive. Hence, as in the baseline version of the model no unambiguous comparison can be made.

Exercise 14.18

Exercise 14.18, Part (a). An equilibrium in this economy is a collection of time paths of allocations and prices $\left\{ \begin{matrix} Y(t\mid q), C(t\mid q), \dot{x}(t\mid q), L_E(t\mid q), L_R(t\mid q), \\ p^x(t\mid q), r(t\mid q), w(t\mid q) \end{matrix} \right\}_{t=0}^{\infty}$ given the current quality and a deterministic path for quality $[q(t)]_t$ such that the representative consumer maximizes utility, the final good sector maximizes profits given prices, the machine producer chooses quantities and prices to maximize profits, the R&D sector hires scientists to maximize profits and all markets clear.

The representative consumer's optimization gives the Euler equation

$$C\left(t \mid q\right)^{-\theta} = \left(1+r\right)\exp\left(-\rho\right)C\left(t+1\right)^{-\theta}$$

and the transversality condition

$$\lim_{t\to\infty}\exp\left(-\rho t\right)C\left(t\right)^{-\theta}V\left(t \mid q\right) = 0.$$

Since the consumer is risk neutral, we have $\theta = 0$, hence the Euler equation is satisfied if and only if the interest rate is the inverse of the time discount rate, i.e.

$$1 + r\left(t \mid q\right) = \exp\left(\rho\right), \tag{S14.58}$$

hence the interest rate is constant in equilibrium.

The final good producers' maximization yields the following demand for machines

$$x\left(t \mid q\right) = q\left(t\right)L_E\left(t\right)p^x\left(t \mid q\right)^{-1/\beta}.$$

To reduce the number of cases we need to study, we assume that once a new technology is invented, the old vintage gets destroyed so the new monopolist can price at unconstrained monopoly prices. Since the machine producer faces isoelastic demand, its pricing decision is given by

$$p^x\left(t \mid q\right) = \frac{1}{1-\beta}\psi = 1,$$

which also gives $x\left(t \mid q\right) = qL_E\left(t\right)$ and per-period profits

$$\pi\left(q\right) = \beta q L_E\left(t\right).$$

Wages are then also given by

$$\begin{aligned}
w\left(t \mid q\right) &= \frac{\beta}{1-\beta}\frac{x\left(t \mid q\right)^{1-\beta}\left(q\left(t\right)L_E\left(t\right)\right)^{\beta}}{L_E\left(t\right)} \tag{S14.59}\\
&= \frac{\beta}{1-\beta}q.
\end{aligned}$$

The output of the final good sector is given by

$$Y\left(t \mid q\right) = \frac{1}{1-\beta}qL_E\left(t \mid q\right). \tag{S14.60}$$

Since the monopolist gets replaced in the next period with certainty, its value function is only the period profits, that is

$$V\left(t \mid q\right) = \pi\left(t \mid q\right) = \beta q L_E\left(t \mid q\right).$$

Given current quality q, the R&D sector solves

$$\begin{aligned}
\Pi_R\left(t \mid q\right) &= \max_{L_R}\frac{1}{1+r}V\left(t+1 \mid \Lambda\left(L_R\right)q\right) - L_R w\left(t \mid q\right)\\
&= \max_{L_R}\frac{1}{1+r}\beta\Lambda\left(L_R\right)qL_E\left(t+1 \mid q\right) - L_R w\left(t \mid q\right)
\end{aligned}$$

which yields the first-order condition

$$w\left(t \mid q\right) \geq \frac{1}{1+r}\beta\Lambda'\left(L_R\left(t \mid q\right)\right)qL_E\left(t+1 \mid q\right) \text{ with equality if } L_R\left(t \mid q\right) > 0. \tag{S14.61}$$

Note that, different than in the version in the book (where R&D was characterized by free entry), in this case the R&D sector makes profits in equilibrium. We assume that shares of R&D firms are held equally across households, so profits accrue to the representative consumer and the presence of R&D profits changes nothing significant in the analysis.

We next consider a BGP equilibrium on which the allocation of labor is constant over time, that is $L_E \equiv L_E(t)$ and $L_R \equiv L_R(t)$ for all t. Since $\Lambda(L_R)$ satisfies the Inada conditions, Eq. (S14.61) always has an interior solution, which leads to

$$(1 - \beta) \Lambda'(L_R) (L - L_R) = \exp(\rho), \qquad \text{(S14.62)}$$

where we have used Eq. (S14.58), Eq. (S14.59) and the labor market clearing condition $L_E + L_R = L$. The preceding expression shows that, in this economy, the BGP allocation of L_R only depends on the monopoly markups, the discount rate, and the R&D technology. In particular, it does not depend on the quality of the existing machine, since, on the one hand higher quality machines yield more profits but on the other hand, higher quality machines raise wages and make further innovations costlier.

The equilibrium is completely characterized by (S14.62). Once we determine L_R and L_E, output is given by (S14.60) and consumption is given by the net output

$$
\begin{aligned}
C(t \mid q) &= Y(t \mid q) - (1 - \beta) x(t \mid q) \\
&= \left[\frac{1}{1-\beta} - (1 - \beta) \right] q L_E.
\end{aligned}
$$

Each period the quality, and hence output, consumption and wages, all grow by a factor of $\Lambda(L_R)$. We also need to check the transversality condition, which will be satisfied if

$$\lim_{t \to \infty} \exp(-\rho t) C(0) \Lambda(L_R)^t = 0.$$

It follows that the constant growth path we have described is an equilibrium with positive growth whenever the following parametric restriction is satisfied

$$0 < \ln(\Lambda(L_R)) < \rho.$$

Exercise 14.18, Part (b). We first calculate the optimal choice of machine production by the social planner, given the quality of the machine line q and employment in production $L_E(t)$. For this static problem, the social planner solves

$$\max_x C(t \mid q) = \frac{1}{1-\beta} x^{1-\beta} (q L_E(t))^\beta - (1 - \beta) x,$$

which implies

$$x(t \mid q) = q L_E(t) (1 - \beta)^{-1/\beta}$$

and

$$C(t \mid q) = \beta (1 - \beta)^{-1/\beta} q L_E(t).$$

Next, we consider the dynamic trade-off for the social planner and determine the allocation of labor between the R&D and the employment sectors. The social planner's dynamic problem is

$$\max_{\{L_R(t), L_E(t)\}_{t=0}^{\infty}} \sum_{t=0}^{\infty} \exp(-\rho t) C(t)$$

$$\text{s.t.} \quad C(t) = \beta (1 - \beta)^{-1/\beta} q(t) L_E(t),$$
$$q(t+1) = q(t) \Lambda(L_R(t)),$$
$$L_R(t) + L_E(t) = L \text{ for all } t \geq 0.$$

The first-order condition for $L_R(t)$ yields

$$\beta (1 - \beta)^{-1/\beta} q(t) = \Lambda'(L_R(t)) q(t) \exp(-\rho) \beta (1 - \beta)^{-1/\beta} L_E(t+1), \text{ for all } t \geq 0$$

We conjecture a solution to the first-order conditions such that $L_E \equiv L_E(t)$ and $L_R \equiv L_R(t)$ is constant for all t. Under this conjecture the previously displayed first-order condition simplifies to

$$\Lambda'(L_R)(L - L_R) = \exp(\rho), \tag{S14.63}$$

which has a unique intermediate solution, verifying our conjecture. Since the social planner's problem is weakly concave, it follows that the conjectured path that satisfies the first-order conditions is optimal if the transversality condition $\ln \Lambda(L_R) < \rho$ also holds. Then, the social planner's allocation of employment in the R&D sector is also constant and given as the solution to Eq. (S14.63). Quality, output and consumption grow by a factor of $\Lambda(L_R)$.

Comparing (S14.62) and (S14.63), since Λ' is a decreasing function, we have

$$L_R^S > L_R^{Eq},$$

and consequently $\Lambda\left(L_R^S\right) > \Lambda\left(L_R^{Eq}\right)$. The social planner always employs more labor in R&D, achieves a larger size of innovation and a higher growth rate. The reason is the following. The social planner's static allocation is not affected by monopoly distortions, captured by the $(1 - \beta)$ term in (S14.62) that is absent from (S14.63). Hence the social planner produces more machines for a given quality level. Consequently, every unit of quality innovated is more valuable to the social planner than an to equilibrium firm which implies that social planner innovates more and achieves a higher growth rate.

Note that in the variants of this model with stochastic innovations, there is a counteracting replacement effect: in equilibrium, innovation is only done by outsiders which do not take into account that they are replacing an existing producer. With stochastic replacement, with some probability there is no innovation and the incumbent continues to operate. The social planner takes this into account and tends to innovate less than the market (controlling for the monopoly distortion effect above). However, with deterministic innovations, the incumbent is replaced for sure so that the replacement effect is absent. Also, in some other variants of this model, there is a counteracting externality effect: when the outside R&D market is competitive and when there are aggregate negative externalities in the R&D technology, the social planner tends to innovate less than the market since each firm fails to take its negative effect on the innovation possibilities frontier of future entrants into account. Here, the R&D technology requires a single firm to do the innovation, hence the R&D market internalizes the externalities in R&D technology. Since both counteracting forces are absent from the model, the only remaining force is the monopoly distortion effect and consequently the equilibrium unambiguously involves less innovation than in the Pareto optimal allocation. Aghion and Howitt (1992) also discuss these issues in their seminal contribution on models of Schumpeterian growth.

Exercise 14.21*

Exercise 14.21, Part (a). The crucial equilibrium condition to determine the allocation of labor between research and the final good sector is the free entry condition into research. In (14.32) this equilibrium condition was given as

$$1 = \eta\left(L_R^1\right) \frac{\lambda(1 - \beta)\left(L - L_R^2\right)}{\rho + \eta\left(L_R^2\right)L_R^2} = \eta\left(L_R^2\right) \frac{\lambda(1 - \beta)\left(L - L_R^1\right)}{\rho + \eta\left(L_R^1\right)L_R^1}. \tag{S14.64}$$

From (S14.64) we get that L_R^1 and L_R^2 have to solve

$$\eta\left(L_R^1\right) \frac{(1 - \theta_2)}{\rho + \eta\left(L_R^2\right)\theta_2 L} = \eta\left(L_R^2\right) \frac{(1 - \theta_1)}{\rho + \eta\left(L_R^1\right)\theta_1 L},$$

where we defined θ_i as the labor share working in the research sector in the respective period i, i.e. $\theta_i = \frac{L_R^i}{L}$. Now suppose for simplicity that $\eta(.)$ is given by

$$\eta(L) = \kappa L^{-1}. \tag{S14.65}$$

Note that $\eta(.)$ is decreasing as required if $\eta(.)$ is supposed to represent some negative externality in the research process. Using (S14.65), the first term of (S14.64) simplifies to

$$1 = \frac{\kappa}{\theta_1 L} \frac{\lambda(1-\beta)(1-\theta_2)L}{\rho+\kappa} = \frac{\kappa\lambda(1-\beta)}{\rho+\kappa} \frac{1-\theta_2}{\theta_1}.$$

The second one is analogously given by

$$1 = \frac{\kappa}{\theta_1 L} \frac{\lambda(1-\beta)(1-\theta_2)L}{\rho+\kappa} = \frac{\kappa\lambda(1-\beta)}{\rho+\kappa} \frac{1-\theta_1}{\theta_2}.$$

Now let κ be given by

$$\kappa = \frac{\rho}{\lambda(1-\beta)-1},$$

which is positive as long as innovations are drastic enough, i.e. $\lambda(1-\beta) > 1$. Then we get that equilibrium requires that

$$1 = \frac{1-\theta_2}{\theta_1} = \frac{1-\theta_1}{\theta_2},$$

which has the symmetric solution $\theta_1 = \theta_2 = 1/2$ and the asymmetric solution $\theta_1 = 3/4 > 1/4 = \theta_2$ (and of course the analogous one where $\theta_2 = 3/4 > 1/4 = \theta_1$). Hence in this economy there is an equilibrium with endogenous cycles.

The intuition for such an equilibrium is as follows: as both the costs of engaging in research $w(q)$ and the value of having a patent $V^i(q)$ are proportional to current quality q, the basic force of generating endogenous cycles is that "winning" a patent when it is hard to get should have bigger benefits (and vice versa). Hence consider the case where $\theta_1 = 3/4 > 1/4 = \theta_2$. This means that there are many R&D workers for even numbered innovations (i.e. many research firms compete to improve upon an odd numbered technology). As there are congestion effects in the research technology (i.e. $\eta(.)$ is decreasing), ceteris paribus it will be less profitable to do research for odd numbered innovations. Hence, doing so can only be an equilibrium if the benefits of receiving a patent with an odd numbered innovation are higher. This however is exactly satisfied when $\theta_2 < \theta_1$ as this implies that there are more workers employed in the production sector if an even numbered innovation is in place. And as the amount of intermediaries produced is increasing in the employed labor force, monopolistic profits will be higher, the higher the labor force. In particular, profits are given by $\pi(t,q) = \beta q L_E(t)$ (see the analysis in Section 14.2). Hence, in the proposed equilibrium it is harder to win the competition for an even numbered innovation but the prize of doing so is also higher. In equilibrium these effect balance out so that firms are exactly indifferent between entering the research market in odd or even times.

Exercise 14.21, Part (b). That there is always an equilibrium with constant research in case an equilibrium featuring cycles exists follows from the free entry condition given in (S14.64). The equilibrium requirement is that firms should be indifferent between engaging in R&D or not in every period. Using the free entry condition

$$1 = \eta(L_R) \frac{\lambda(1-\beta)(L-L_R)}{\rho+\eta(L_R)L_R},$$

we have to establish that the equation

$$0 = \eta(L_R)[\lambda(1-\beta)(L-L_R)-L_R]-\rho \equiv h(L_R), \tag{S14.66}$$

has some solution L_R. To see that this is the case, note first that

$$h(L) = -\eta(L)L - \rho < 0, \tag{S14.67}$$

so that research is not profitable in case everyone is employed in the research sector. Now suppose there was no solution to (S14.66). As h is continuous and negative for $L_R = L$ (see (S14.67)), this is only possible if

$$h(L_R) = \eta(L_R)\left[\lambda\left(1 - \beta\right)\left(L - L_R\right) - L_R\right] - \rho < 0 \quad \forall L_R \in [0, L].$$

But this is a contradiction. Suppose for example that $L^1 > L^2$. Using (S14.64) we then know that

$$
\begin{aligned}
0 &= \eta(L_R^1)\lambda\left(1 - \beta\right)\left(L - L_R^2\right) - \eta(L_R^2)L_R^2 - \rho \\
&= h(L_R^2) + \left[\eta(L_R^1) - \eta(L_R^2)\right]\lambda\left(1 - \beta\right)\left(L - L^2\right) \\
&< h(L_R^2),
\end{aligned}
$$

as under assumption that $L_R^1 > L_R^2$ we get that $\eta(L_R^1) - \eta(L_R^2) < 0$. This contradicts the hypothesis that there is no solution to (S14.66) and proves that there exists an equilibrium with constant research whenever there exist equilibria with endogenous cycles. Note that this also proves that the solution L_R satisfies $L_R \in (L_R^2, L_R^1)$ when $L_R^2 < L_R^1$.

Exercise 14.21, Part (c). Now suppose that there are no numbers L_R^1 and L_R^2, such that

$$1 = \eta\left(L_R^1\right)\frac{\lambda\left(1 - \beta\right)\left(L - L_R^2\right)}{\rho + \eta\left(L_R^2\right)L_R^2} = \eta\left(L_R^2\right)\frac{\lambda\left(1 - \beta\right)\left(L - L_R^1\right)}{\rho + \eta\left(L_R^1\right)L_R^1}. \tag{S14.68}$$

To show that there exists an equilibrium with oscillatory dynamics which converges to the steady state L_R^*, let us first define the function $g(.)$ implicitly via

$$1 = \eta\left(x\right)\frac{\lambda\left(1 - \beta\right)\left(L - g(x)\right)}{\rho + \eta\left(g(x)\right)g(x)}.$$

Intuitively, if the current number of researchers is equal to x, the free entry condition is satisfied when there are $g(x)$ researchers in the next period. Note that by definition of the steady state solution L_R^* we have

$$L_R^* = g(L_R^*). \tag{S14.69}$$

Furthermore we have that

$$g'(x) < 0, \tag{S14.70}$$

i.e. the more researchers are employed in the current period (and hence, the harder it is to win the patent), the less researchers have to be employed in the future as this increases the profitability of the innovation. Now consider a sequence of equilibrium research allocations $\{L_R(t)\}_{t=1}^{\infty}$. We are going to show that this sequence features oscillatory dynamics and that it converges to the steady state equilibrium allocation L_R^*. Note that by construction, $\{L_R(t)\}_{t=1}^{\infty}$ has to satisfy

$$L_R(t + 1) = g(L_R(t)),$$

as otherwise the free entry condition would not be satisfied. So suppose that $L_R(1) < L_R^*$. Using (S14.69) and (S14.70) we get that

$$L_R(2) = g(L_R(1)) > g(L_R^*) = L_R^*.$$

Similarly we get that

$$L_R(3) = g(L_R(2)) < g(L_R^*) = L_R^*.$$

We are now going to show that in fact

$$L_R(1) < L_R(3) < L_R^*,$$

i.e. there is no overshooting in the sense that $L_R(3) < L_R(1)$. Note first that

$$L_R(3) \neq L_R(1)$$

as otherwise $L_R(1)$ and $L_R(2)$ would be two solutions as in Part (a), i.e. there would be a two-period endogenous cycle. However, we assumed that those solutions do not exist. Hence, let us suppose that

$$L_R(1) - L_R(3) = L_R(1) - g(g(L_R(1))) \equiv m(L_R(1)) > 0. \qquad (S14.71)$$

First of all note that feasibility requires that

$$m(0) = -g(g(0)) \leq 0. \qquad (S14.72)$$

However we cannot have $g(g(0)) = 0$ as otherwise there was a two-period endogenous cycle $(0, g(0), 0, g(0), ...)$. Hence,

$$m(0) = -g(g(0)) < 0.$$

As $m(.)$ is continuous, (S14.71) and (S14.72) imply that there exists some $\tilde{L}$ such that $m(\tilde{L}) = 0$, i.e.

$$\exists \tilde{L} \in [0, L_R(1)) : \tilde{L} = g(g(\tilde{L})).$$

This however just says that the sequence $\{\tilde{L}, g(\tilde{L}), \tilde{L}, g(\tilde{L})...\}$ is an equilibrium so that the economy would have a two-period endogenous cycle, which we assumed would not exist. This shows that

$$L_R(3) > L_R(1).$$

With a similar argument we can show that

$$L_R(4) < L_R(2).$$

Hence, the equilibrium allocation $\{L_R(t)\}_{t=1}^{\infty}$ can be characterized by the two sequences $\{L_R(1+2i)\}_{i=0}^{\infty}$ and $\{L_R(2+2i)\}_{i=0}^{\infty}$, where the former is strictly increasing and the latter is strictly decreasing. As $L_R(t) \in [0, L]$, i.e. those are sequences on a compact set, and

$$L_R(2+2i) = g(L_R(1+2i)) \geq g(L_R^*) = L_R^* \geq L_R(1+2i)$$

those sequences will converge to some limit

$$\lim_{i \to \infty} L_R(1+2i) = L_R^O$$
$$\lim_{i \to \infty} L_R(2+2i) = L_R^E,$$

where

$$L_R^O \leq L_R^E.$$

To argue that $L_R^O = L_R^E = L_R^*$, simply observe that if this was not the case, we would have found $L_1 = L_R^O$ and $L_2 = L_R^E$ which would solve the two equations in (S14.68) contradicting our assumption that such solutions did not exist. Hence, this oscillatory equilibrium indeed converges to the one characterized in Part (b).

To see the intuition for such oscillatory dynamics, consider the incentives for research firms if they expect that there will be a lot of research in the future. This has two effects on the value of a patent. First of all, profits will be low, as demand of intermediaries is proportional to employment. Secondly, the probability of losing the patent is higher. Hence, both effect cause patents to be less valuable. So when would research firms be willing to spend resources trying to improve upon the existing technology? Only when doing so is cheap in the sense that workers generate a high flow rate. But this is only the case when few research firms are active. Similarly, when there will be only little research in the future, the new technology will be worth a lot and research firms compete for researchers until the flow rate is low enough to satisfy the free entry condition. Hence, there is a natural tendency that in an equilibrium where the number of researchers is not constant, the dynamics will be oscillatory.

Exercise 14.26

Exercise 14.26, Part (a). As the new assumption about the incumbents' research technology does only affect the research side of the model, the static equilibrium for given qualities $[q(\nu,t)]_{\nu=0}^{1}$ is unchanged. In particular it will still be true that monopolistic profits are given by

$$\pi(\nu,t|q) = \pi(q) = \beta L q,$$

where we explicitly noted that profits do neither depend on ν nor t once current quality q is controlled for. The value of owning a perpetual patent is still given by the HJB equation. This however is dependent on incumbents' optimal research effort, i.e. is given by

$$r(t)V(\nu,t\mid q) - \dot{V}(\nu,t\mid q) = \pi + \max_{z}\{\phi(z)(V(\nu,t\mid \lambda q) - V(\nu,t\mid q)) - zq\} - \hat{z}\eta(\hat{z})V(\nu,t\mid q),$$

where $\hat{z}$ is the entrants' research effort which incumbents take as given. Incumbents' research efforts z^{*} are implicitly defined by

$$z^{*} = \arg\max_{z}\{\phi(z)(V(\nu,t\mid \lambda q) - V(\nu,t\mid q)) - zq\}. \tag{S14.73}$$

Let us furthermore assume that $\hat{z} > 0$, i.e. in equilibrium entrants will chose positive effort. We will show below that this will indeed be the case. In such an equilibrium, the free entry condition for entrants has to be satisfied with equality. As spending an amount of q yields a flow rate of innovation of $\eta(\hat{z})$ (where each entrant takes $\hat{z}$ as given) and this innovation increases the current quality to κq, the free entry condition is given by

$$\eta(\hat{z})V(\nu,t\mid \kappa q) = q. \tag{S14.74}$$

Let us now conjecture that the value function V is not dependent on the specific sector and linear in q, i.e. $V(\nu,t|q) = V(t|q) = v(t)q$. We will show that in equilibrium $v(t)$ will in fact be constant. But for now let us not assume that a priori. Then (S14.73) implies that

$$z^{*}(t) = \arg\max_{z}\{\phi(z)(\lambda - 1)v(t) - z\}.$$

The necessary condition for an interior solution reads

$$\phi'(z^{*}(t))(\lambda - 1)v(t) = 1. \tag{S14.75}$$

That this condition is also sufficient follows from the fact that we assume $\phi(.)$ to be strictly concave. Let us now show that there exists a unique BGP. We first show that there exists a BGP and then that it is in fact unique. So suppose a BGP exists. Along the BGP interest rates are constant and all variables grow at constant rates. Let us call g_{W} the growth rate of variable W. As we still have that $x(\nu,t|q) = L$, aggregate output is

$$Y(t) = \frac{1}{1-\beta}\left(\int_{0}^{1} q(\nu,t)x(\nu,t|q)^{1-\beta}d\nu\right)L^{\beta} = \frac{1}{1-\beta}LQ(t)$$

and aggregate expenditures on machines $X(t)$ are still given by

$$X(t) = \int_{0}^{1} \psi q(\nu,t)x(t,\nu|q)d\nu = (1-\beta)LQ(t),$$

where

$$Q(t) = \int_0^1 q(\nu, t)d\nu.$$

Hence, $Y(t)$ and $X(t)$ are proportional to $Q(t)$, so that $g_Y = g_X = g_Q$. That this also implies that consumption and research expenditures have to grow at this rate follows from the economies resource constraint which is given by

$$C(t) + Z(t) = Y(t) - X(t) = \frac{(2-\beta)\beta}{1-\beta}LQ(t).$$

Differentiating this with respect to time and noting that g_C and g_Z are constant along the BGP, we get that

$$
\begin{aligned}
g_Y &= \frac{\dot{C}(t)}{C(t)+Z(t)} + \frac{\dot{Z}(t)}{C(t)+Z(t)} \\
&= g_C \frac{C(t)}{C(t)+Z(t)} + g_Z \frac{Z(t)}{C(t)+Z(t)} \\
&= g_C + (g_Z - g_C)\frac{Z(t)}{C(t)+Z(t)}.
\end{aligned}
\tag{S14.76}
$$

As g_Y, g_Z and g_C are constant along the BGP and (S14.76) has to hold for all t, $\frac{Z(t)}{C(t)+Z(t)}$ is also constant along the BGP. Hence $Z(t)$ and $C(t)$ grow at the same rate so that (S14.76) shows that

$$g^* = g_Y = g_C = g_Z = g_Q.$$

From the consumer's Euler equation we know that interest rates have to be constant whenever consumption grows at a constant rate. Additionally, note that aggregate research expenditures are given by

$$Z(t) = z^*(t)Q(t) + \hat{z}(t)Q(t).$$

As $Z(t)$ and $Q(t)$ are growing at the same rate, this implies that $z^*(t) + \hat{z}(t)$ is constant. We now show that the optimality conditions for research firms in fact imply that both $z^*(t)$ and $\hat{z}(t)$ are individually constant. From the entrants' free entry condition (S14.74) we get that

$$\eta(\hat{z}(t))V(\nu, t \mid \kappa q) = \eta(\hat{z}(t))v(t)\kappa q = q,$$

so that

$$\eta(\hat{z}(t))v(t)\kappa = 1. \tag{S14.77}$$

Combining this with the incumbents' optimality condition in (S14.75) we get that

$$\eta(\hat{z}(t))v(t)\kappa = \phi'(z^*(t))(\lambda - 1)v(t),$$

so that

$$\frac{\partial \hat{z}(t)}{\partial z^*(t)} = \frac{\phi''(z^*(t))(\lambda - 1)}{\eta'(\hat{z}(t))\kappa} > 0, \tag{S14.78}$$

i.e. incumbents' and entrants' research expenditures are "aligned" in that they are positively correlated. The mechanism is of course the function $v(t)$. The only reason for either incumbents' or entrants' research efforts to increase is an increase in $v(t)$. Hence, whenever incumbents increase their research efforts, entrants do so too. We saw however that $z^*(t) + \hat{z}(t)$ has to be constant along the BGP. Together with (S14.78) this implies that both $z^*(t)$ and $\hat{z}(t)$ have to be constant, i.e. $z^*(t) = z^*$ and $\hat{z}(t) = \hat{z}$. This however implies from (S14.77) that $v(t) = v$ is constant so that $V(\nu, t|q) = qv(t) = qv$, i.e. the value function is only a function of quality q. Another way to see that $v(t)$ cannot depend on time is the HJB equation. Along the BGP, the HJB equation is given by

$$r^* v(t)q - \dot{v}(t)q = \beta L q - z^* q + v(t)q(\phi(z^*)(\lambda - 1) - \hat{z}\eta(\hat{z})),$$

where we already used that along the BGP $z^*(t) = z^*$ and $\hat{z}(t) = z$. This differential equation has a unique stable solution which is given by[1]

$$v(t) = v = \frac{\beta L - z^*}{r^* + \hat{z}\eta(\hat{z}) - \phi(z^*)(\lambda - 1)}. \tag{S14.79}$$

This is an intuitive equation. The (per unit of quality) cash flows net of research expenditures are given by

$$\beta L - z^*.$$

The effective discount rate has two parts. The first part $r^* + \hat{z}\eta(\hat{z})$ captures the risk-adjusted discounting caused be the probability of replacement and the interest rate. The last part $-\phi(z^*)(\lambda - 1)$ captures the "option value" of being an incumbent as incumbents can improve upon themselves by having access to the innovation technology $\phi(z^*)$. Hence, the BGP is characterized by the system of equations

$$v = \frac{\beta L - z^*}{r^* + \hat{z}\eta(\hat{z}) - \phi(z^*)(\lambda - 1)}$$

$$g^* = \frac{\dot{c}(t)}{c(t)} = \frac{1}{\theta}(r^* - \rho)$$

$$1 \geq \phi'(z^*)(\lambda - 1)v \text{ with equality if } z^* > 0$$

$$1 \geq \kappa\eta(\hat{z})v \text{ with equality if } \hat{z} > 0$$

$$g^* = \frac{\dot{Q}(t)}{Q(t)} = (\kappa - 1)\hat{z}\eta(\hat{z}) + (\lambda - 1)\phi(z^*).$$

These are five equations in the five unknowns $z^*, \hat{z}, r^*, v, g^*$. Hence, provided parameters are such that the transversality condition holds, there exists a BGP where all variables grow at a constant rate, where our conjecture for the value function is true and where both incumbents' and entrants' research efforts are constant.

Let us now characterize this BGP further. First of all note that (S14.75) and (S14.77) imply that $\hat{z}$ and z^* will actually be interior. This follows from the Inada-type conditions

$$\lim_{z \to 0} \eta(z) = \infty \text{ and } \lim_{z \to 0} \phi'(z) = \infty. \tag{S14.80}$$

Using this, the system above can be simplified to

$$1 = \frac{\phi'(z^*)(\lambda - 1)}{\kappa\eta(\hat{z})} \tag{S14.81}$$

$$1 = \frac{\phi'(z^*)(\lambda - 1)(\beta L - z^*)}{[\theta(\kappa - 1) + 1]\hat{z}\eta(\hat{z}) + [\theta - 1]\phi'(z^*)(\lambda - 1) + \rho}. \tag{S14.82}$$

These are two equations in $\hat{z}$ and z^*. Having solved for these two research variables, we can then determine g^*, r^* and v from the remaining equations above. From (S14.81) we again get (S14.78), which showed that we can define a function

$$\hat{z} = h(z^*),$$

---

[1]This solution is the unique solution which is stable in the sense that any other solution would either violate the transversality condition or had $v(t)$ converging to zero, both if which cannot happen along the BGP.

which is strictly increasing and continuous. Additionally h satisfies

$$\lim_{z^*\to 0} h(z^*) = 0 \text{ and } \lim_{z^*\to\infty} h(z^*) = \infty$$

from the Inada-type conditions (S14.80) and

$$\lim_{z\to\infty} \eta(z) = 0 \text{ and } \lim_{z\to\infty} \phi'(z) = 0.$$

Let us now turn to (S14.82). Totally differentiating this equality, we get that

$$\frac{d\hat{z}}{dz^*} = \frac{(\lambda-1)\left[\phi''(z^*)(\beta L - z^*) - \theta\phi'(z^*)\right]}{(\theta(\kappa-1)+1)\left.\frac{\partial\eta(z)z}{\partial z}\right|_{z=\hat{z}}} < 0,$$

where the inequality follows from the fact that $\eta(z)z$ is assumed to be increasing and that $\phi(.)$ is a concave function so that $\phi''(.) < 0$. Hence, (S14.82) defines another function

$$\hat{z} = m(z^*),$$

which is strictly decreasing. Additionally, the Inada conditions imply that

$$\lim_{z^*\to 0} m(z^*) = m(0) > 0.$$

As $m(.)$ and $h(.)$ are continuous function, this shows that there exists a unique

$$\hat{z} = m(z^*) = h(z^*).$$

As given z^* and $\hat{z}$, the interest rate r^*, the growth rate g^* and the value function v^* is uniquely determined, the BGP is unique.

To relate this model to the model analyzed in the chapter, note that we can express the growth rate of the economy as

$$\begin{aligned}
g^* &= (\kappa-1)\hat{z}\eta(\hat{z}) + (\lambda-1)\phi(z^*) \\
&= \phi'(z^*)(\lambda-1) + (\lambda-1)\phi(z^*) - \hat{z}\eta(\hat{z}). \quad\quad \text{(S14.83)}
\end{aligned}$$

Now recall that for the model in the book we assumed that $\phi'(.) = 0$ and $\phi(z^*(t)) = \phi$. Substituting this into (S14.83) yields

$$g = g_C = \frac{\dot{C}(t)}{C(t)} = \frac{1}{\theta}\left(\phi(\lambda-1) - \hat{z}\eta(\hat{z}) - \rho\right),$$

which is exactly the growth rate found in the exposition in the Chapter.

Exercise 14.26, Part (b). Incumbents' optimal level of research expenditures is determined by (S14.75). But (S14.75) determines z^* only as a function of v and λ and (S14.79) shows that v is not a function of q. Hence, incumbents' research expenditures are independent of q. Note that this result follows from our conjecture that the value function is linear in q. We showed above that there is unique BGP where our conjecture turns out to be correct, i.e. that there is a unique BGP where the value function actually turns out to be linear in q. However, if there is an equilibrium where the value function is not linear in q (and we did not prove that such an equilibrium does not exist), we would not expect that the research intensities of incumbents are independent of q. The optimality condition for incumbents' research expenditures was given by

$$z^* = \arg\max_z\{\phi(z)(V(\nu,t\mid\lambda q) - V(\nu,t\mid q)) - zq\}.$$

Even if we assume that V is not a function of the specific sector ν, the general solution is still given by

$$z^*(t,q) = \phi'^{-1}\left(\frac{q}{V(t|\lambda q) - V(t|q)}\right),$$

i.e. is a function of q and t. Hence, as long as $\frac{q}{V(t|\lambda q) - V(t|q)}$ is not independent of the quality q, incumbents with different quality machines will also have different levels of research expenditures. This however cannot occur along the BGP.

Exercise 14.26, Part (c). Once we consider the limiting case where $\phi'(.) = 0$, i.e. where the incumbents' flow rate of innovation is constant, the incumbents' problem is linear in z^* so that in equilibrium the value function has to be such that incumbents are indifferent between all levels of z^*. Hence, there is no reason to believe that all incumbents chose the same level of z^*. In the exposition in the chapter we considered an equilibrium where z^* was constant across "qualities". From the analysis above this seems to be the interesting case, because once we introduce a little curvature into $\phi(.)$ the research efforts will indeed be pinned down uniquely. In Exercise 14.27 we show that even in the case where $\phi'(.) = 0$ the research expenditures of incumbents are not entirely unrestricted along the BGP. In fact even though the distribution of z^* across incumbents is not determined, the BGP implies that aggregate expenditures of incumbents are proportional to $Q(t)$. Hence, the restriction that z^* is the same across all incumbents is without loss of generality (in the class of equilibria we look at here, but recall our discussion in Part (c)) and the natural limiting case of the equilibrium considered above.

Exercise 14.26, Part (d). Let us first consider the entrants and suppose that equilibrium research expenditures are zero. From the Inada condition

$$\lim_{z \to 0} \eta(z) = \infty$$

we get that any unit of research expenditures invested will generate a flow rate of infinity if no other potential entrant is active. Hence, not exerting research efforts cannot be optimal. This shows that in equilibrium entrants will exert positive research efforts, i.e. $\hat{z} > 0$.

Let us now turn to the incumbents. Research expenditures are determined by

$$\phi'(z^*(t))(\lambda - 1)v(t) = 1, \tag{S14.84}$$

as shown in (S14.75). As $v(t) > 0$ because owning a patent has a positive value, $z^* > 0$, as

$$\lim_{z \to 0} \phi'(z) = \infty,$$

which does not satisfy the optimality condition (S14.84). Hence, incumbents' research expenditures are also positive.

Exercise 14.26, Part (e). Introducing taxes on research changes the research decision of incumbents and entrants. In terms of the final good every unit of research invested now costs $1 + \tau$, where τ is the respective tax rate. As the rest of the analysis is unchanged, research expenditures are set according to

$$\phi'(z^*)(\lambda - 1)v(t) = 1 + \tau_I$$
$$\eta(\hat{z})v(t)\kappa = 1 + \tau_E. \tag{S14.85}$$

Those equations reflect the fact that spending one unit of the final good on research, costs $1 + \tau_I$ or $1 + \tau_E$ units respectively. The value function $v(t)$ is now implicitly defined by

$$r^* v(t) = \beta L - z^*(1 + \tau_I) + v(t)\left(\phi(z^*)(\lambda - 1) - \hat{z}\eta(\hat{z})\right),$$

so that

$$v(t) = v = \frac{\beta L - z^*(1 + \tau_I)}{r^* + \hat{z}\eta(\hat{z}) - \phi(z^*)(\lambda - 1)}. \tag{S14.86}$$

Whereas v does not explicitly depend on τ_E (other than via z^* and $\hat{z}$), τ_I of course matters because it affects the net cash flows when being an incumbent. The BGP with taxes is characterized by the analogous system of equations as above. In particular we can still determine z^* and $\hat{z}$ from the two equations

$$\frac{1 + \tau_E}{1 + \tau_I} \frac{\phi'(z^*)(\lambda - 1)}{\eta(\hat{z})\kappa} = 1 \tag{S14.87}$$

$$\frac{\phi'(z^*)(\lambda - 1)\left(\beta L - z^*(1 + \tau_I)\right)}{[\theta(\kappa - 1) + 1]\hat{z}\eta(\hat{z}) + [\theta - 1](\lambda - 1)\phi(z^*) + \rho} = 1 + \tau_I \tag{S14.88}$$

Once we have solved for z^* and $\hat{z}$, we can then back out the equilibrium interest rates and the BGP growth rate from the Euler equation and the definition of the growth rate (e.g. (S14.83)). By the same argument as above, (S14.87) defines a function $\hat{z} = h(z^*; \tau_I, \tau_E)$ which is strictly increasing and (S14.88) defines a function $\hat{z} = m(z^*; \tau_I)$ which is strictly decreasing. As we are interested in the comparative statics results with respect to the R&D tax rates τ_E and τ_I, we explicitly denoted the dependence of $h(.)$ and $m(.)$ on those tax rates. Again there will be be a unique intersection for any tax policy (τ_E, τ_I), i.e. there is a unique BGP equilibrium with taxes.

Let us now look at the comparative statics. Consider first an increase of entrants' taxes τ_E. As $m(z^*; \tau_I)$ does not depend on τ_E, the decreasing locus remains unchanged. The function $h(., \tau_I, \tau_E)$ however depends in taxes. In particular, (S14.87) shows that for a given level of entrants' research expenditures $\hat{z}$, the research activity of incumbents z^* has to increase as

$$\left. \frac{dz^*}{d\tau_E} \right|_{\hat{z}} = -\frac{\phi'(z^*)}{\phi''(z^*)(1 + \tau_E)} > 0.$$

Hence, the $h(., \tau_I, \tau_E)$ locus shifts to the right. This shows that the equilibrium response of research expenditures is given by

$$\frac{dz^*}{d\tau_E} > 0 \text{ and } \frac{d\hat{z}}{d\tau_E} < 0,$$

i.e. entrants will spent less on research and incumbents' research expenditures will increase. The effect on the BGP growth rate is given by

$$\frac{dg^*}{d\tau_E} = (\kappa - 1)\frac{\partial \hat{z}\eta(\hat{z})}{\partial z}\frac{d\hat{z}}{d\tau_E} + (\lambda - 1)\phi'(z^*)\frac{dz^*}{d\tau_E}.$$

As the first effect term is negative (the entrants' contribution to economic growth is reduced) and the second terms is positive (incumbents' increase their R&D expenditures), the overall effect on economic growth is ambiguous.

The analysis of an increase in the tax rate of incumbents is a little more involved as both loci characterized in (S14.87) and (S14.88) are affected. From (S14.87) we get that

$$\left. \frac{dz^*}{d\tau_I} \right|_{\hat{z}} = \frac{\phi'(z^*)}{\phi''(z^*)(1 + \tau_I)} < 0,$$

i.e. for a given level of entrants' research efforts $\hat{z}$, incumbents reduce their R&D expenditure, i.e. the upward sloping curve shifts to the left. Totally differentiating the downward sloping locus characterized in (S14.88) yields

$$\left.\frac{dz^*}{d\tau_I}\right|_{\hat{z}} = \frac{1 + \phi'(z^*)(\lambda - 1)z^*}{\frac{\partial}{\partial z^*}\left[\frac{\phi'(z^*)(\lambda-1)(\beta L - z^*(1+\tau_I))}{M(z^*,\hat{z})}\right]} M(z^*, \hat{z}),$$

where

$$M(z^*, \hat{z}) = [\theta(\kappa - 1) + 1]\,\hat{z}\eta(\hat{z}) + [\theta - 1](\lambda - 1)\phi(z^*) + \rho.$$

As the $m(.,\tau_I)$ is downward sloping, we know that

$$\frac{\partial}{\partial z^*}\left[\frac{\phi'(z^*)(\lambda - 1)(\beta L - z^*(1 + \tau_I))}{M(z^*, \hat{z})}\right] < 0,$$

so that (S14.88) implies that for a given level of $\hat{z}$, z^* is decreasing in the incumbents' tax rate $\frac{dz^*}{d\tau_I}|_{\hat{z}} < 0$, i.e. the downward loping locus also shifts to the left. Hence, the overall effect on entrants' research efforts is ambiguous. This shows that the equilibrium responses of R&D expenditures are given by

$$\frac{dz^*}{d\tau_I} < 0 \text{ and } \frac{d\hat{z}}{d\tau_I} \lessgtr 0.$$

The intuition why the effect on entrants is ambiguous is the following. For a given level of $\hat{z}$, lower research expenditures by incumbents will reduce the growth rate of the economy (see (S14.83)) which (from the Euler equation) will cause interest rates to decline. But lower interest rates will of course make innovations more attractive as future profits are discounted less. This effect tends to increase $\hat{z}$. On the other hand, entrants only incur R&D expenses in order to be incumbents in the future. The value of being an incumbent however is reduced by taxing incumbents more heavily. This tends to discourage research expenditures by entrants. The overall effect is ambiguous.

From here it seems that the overall effect on the equilibrium growth rate is also ambiguous. This however turns out to be not true.[2] In fact we will now show that the growth rate necessarily declines if taxes on incumbents' research expenditures are increased. We will prove this by contradiction and provide the intuition below. Consider again the value function given in (S14.86) and let us explicitly denote its dependence on the endogenous variables r^*, z^* and $\hat{z}$ and the exogenous tax rate τ_I. Doing so allows us to write

$$v(z^*, \hat{z}, r^*; \tau_I) = \frac{\beta L - z^*(1 + \tau_I)}{r^* + \hat{z}\eta(\hat{z}) - \phi(z^*)(\lambda - 1)}.$$

Equivalently we can use the Euler equation to substitute the equilibrium growth rate g^* for the interest rate r^* and write the v-function along the BGP as

$$v(z^*, \hat{z}, g^*; \tau_I) = \frac{\beta L - z^*(1 + \tau_I)}{\theta g^* + \rho + \hat{z}\eta(\hat{z}) - \phi(z^*)(\lambda - 1)}. \tag{S14.89}$$

The total derivative of this function is given by

$$\frac{dv(z^*, \hat{z}, g^*; \tau_I)}{d\tau_I} = \frac{\partial v}{\partial \tau_I} + \frac{\partial v}{\partial z^*}\frac{\partial z^*}{\partial \tau_I} + \frac{\partial v}{\partial \hat{z}}\frac{\partial \hat{z}}{\partial \tau_I} + \frac{\partial v}{\partial g^*}\frac{\partial g^*}{\partial \tau_I}. \tag{S14.90}$$

From (S14.89) it is apparent that $\frac{\partial v}{\partial \tau_I} < 0$. Furthermore note that incumbents' innovation expenditures z^* are set optimally, so that the Envelope Theorem implies that $\frac{\partial v}{\partial z^*} = 0$.

Now suppose to arrive at a contradiction that the equilibrium growth rate g^* is increasing. As the growth rate g^* is a linear combination of z^* and $\hat{z}$, and as we showed above that

---

[2]So, although the exercise asks you to show that the effect is ambiguous, we can in fact show that taxing incumbents will necessarily reduce growth.

$\frac{\partial z^*}{\partial \tau_I} < 0$, g^* can only increase when entrants increase their research expenditures $\hat{z}$ sufficiently strong. Formally,

$$\frac{\partial g^*}{\partial \tau_I} > 0 \implies \frac{\partial \hat{z}}{\partial \tau_I} > 0. \tag{S14.91}$$

However, (S14.89) shows that

$$\frac{\partial v}{\partial g^*} < 0 \text{ and } \frac{\partial v}{\partial \hat{z}} < 0,$$

as $\eta(z)z$ is assumed to be increasing in z. (S14.91) and (S14.90) therefore imply that if g^* increases, we have

$$\frac{dv(z^*, \hat{z}, g^*; \tau_I)}{d\tau_I} = \frac{\partial v}{\partial \tau_I} + \frac{\partial v}{\partial \hat{z}} \frac{d\hat{z}}{d\tau_I} + \frac{\partial v}{\partial g^*} \frac{dg^*}{d\tau_I} < 0. \tag{S14.92}$$

Let us now go back to the entrants' free entry condition contained in (S14.85), i.e.

$$\eta(\hat{z})v(z^*, \hat{z}, g^*; \tau_I)\kappa = 1 + \tau_E.$$

Totally differentiating this condition yields that

$$\eta'(\hat{z})v(z^*, \hat{z}, g^*; \tau_I)\kappa \frac{d\hat{z}}{d\tau_I} + \eta(\hat{z}) \frac{dv(z^*, \hat{z}, g^*; \tau_I)}{d\tau_I} \kappa = 0,$$

which can be solved for

$$\frac{dv(z^*, \hat{z}, g^*; \tau_I)/d\tau_I}{d\hat{z}/d\tau_I} = -\frac{\eta'(\hat{z})v(z^*, \hat{z}, g^*; \tau_I)}{\eta(\hat{z})} > 0 \tag{S14.93}$$

as $\eta'(\hat{z}) < 0$. This however provides the desired contradiction as (S14.91) and (S14.92) show that

$$\frac{dv(z^*, \hat{z}, g^*; \tau_I)/d\tau_I}{d\hat{z}/d\tau_I} < 0.$$

This concludes the proof that

$$\frac{dg^*}{d\tau_I} < 0.$$

The derivation of this result is instructive because it uses exactly the economic intuition why the growth rate cannot increase. As incumbents spent less on research, higher growth will have to be "financed" by entrants. Entrants however will only want to do so, if the value of being an incumbent in the future also increases. This is exactly what (S14.93), which is an implication of the entrants' free entry condition, requires: $\hat{z}$ will only increase if v also increases. But now suppose that the equilibrium value function v does increase. The value function measures the value of being an incumbent. From their point of view, both higher interest rates and higher replacement rates are bad as they increase the appropriate discount rate. Hence, in equilibrium a higher value function can only coexist with higher growth and replacement rates if the cash flows of incumbents are also higher. Higher taxes however represent exactly the opposite in that they reduce the per-period cash flows. Hence, entrants' research efforts cannot increase sufficiently for the growth rate of the economy to increase. This shows that in contrast to the case of taxing entrants' R&D efforts, taxing incumbents is always detrimental to economic growth.

Let us now consider the case where there are no negative externalities of entrants' R&D, i.e. $\eta(z) = \bar{\eta}$ is constant. We will see that this simplifies the analysis. The crucial equations characterizing the BGP with taxes are then given by

$$
\begin{aligned}
\phi'(z^*)(\lambda - 1)v(t) &= 1 + \tau_I \\
\bar{\eta}v(t)\kappa &= 1 + \tau_E \\
v(t) &= v = \frac{\beta L - z^*(1 + \tau_I)}{r^* + \hat{z}\bar{\eta} - \phi(z^*)(\lambda - 1)},
\end{aligned}
$$

where additionally r^* has to be consistent with the Euler equation and the equilibrium growth rate g^* is now given by

$$
g^* = (\kappa - 1)\hat{z}\bar{\eta} + (\lambda - 1)\phi(z^*). \tag{S14.94}
$$

To analyze the equilibrium level of $(z^*, \hat{z})$ and the comparative statics, let us rewrite the system above as

$$
1 + \tau_I = \phi'(z^*)(\lambda - 1)\frac{1 + \tau_E}{\bar{\eta}\kappa} \tag{S14.95}
$$

$$
v = \frac{1 + \tau_E}{\bar{\eta}\kappa} = \frac{\beta L - z^*(1 + \tau_I)}{(\theta(\kappa - 1) + 1)\hat{z}\bar{\eta} + (\theta - 1)(\lambda - 1)\phi(z^*) + \rho}, \tag{S14.96}
$$

where the denominator of the RHS in (S14.96) follows again by substituting the Euler equation $r^* = \theta g^* + \rho$ and using the definition of the growth rate contained in (S14.94). Again, (S14.95) and (S14.96) is a system of two equations in the two unknowns z^* and $\hat{z}$. Now however the solution is easier. In particular note that (S14.95) now determines z^* just in terms of exogenous parameters, i.e. we can solve for z^* using (S14.95). Then we can go to (S14.96), to solve for $\hat{z}$ given z^*. Hence, we can solve the system recursively.

To characterize the comparative statics, note that (S14.95) immediately implies that

$$
\frac{dz^*}{d\tau_I} = \frac{\bar{\eta}\kappa}{1 + \tau_E}\frac{1}{(\lambda - 1)\phi''(z^*)} < 0 \tag{S14.97}
$$

$$
\frac{dz^*}{d\tau_E} = -\frac{1}{1 + \tau_E}\frac{\phi'(z^*)}{\phi''(z^*)} > 0.
$$

To see the comparative statics of entrants' R&D, consider first the change in τ_E. As z^* increases, (S14.96) shows that for given $\hat{z}$, the LHS increases and the RHS decreases. Hence, $\hat{z}$ has to go down to keep (S14.96) satisfied, i.e.

$$
\frac{d\hat{z}}{d\tau_E} < 0.
$$

The comparative statics with respect to τ_I also simplify slightly. From (S14.96) we get that

$$
v\left(\theta(\kappa - 1) + 1\right)\bar{\eta}d\hat{z} + v(\theta - 1)(\lambda - 1)\phi'(z^*)dz^* = -(1 + \tau_I)dz^* - z^*d\tau_I.
$$

Substituting (S14.95) and (S14.97) yields

$$
\begin{aligned}
v\left(\theta(\kappa - 1) + 1\right)\bar{\eta}d\hat{z} &= -\theta(1 + \tau_I)dz^* - z^*d\tau_I \\
&= -\left[\frac{\bar{\eta}\kappa\theta(1 + \tau_I)}{(\lambda - 1)(1 + \tau_E)}\frac{1}{\phi''(z^*)} + z^*\right]d\tau_I \\
&= -\left[\theta\frac{\phi'(z^*)}{\phi''(z^*)} + z^*\right]d\tau_I.
\end{aligned}
$$

As we cannot sign the term $\theta\frac{\phi'(z^*)}{\phi''(z^*)} + z^*$ without further restrictions on the function ϕ, the effect on $\hat{z}$ is still ambiguous. The proof given above that the equilibrium growth rate will be decreasing in τ_I however still applies. This shows that assuming $\eta(z) = \bar{\eta}$ does not change any of the qualitative results of the analysis.

The most important lesson from this part of the exercise is the fundamental asymmetry of policy interventions. Whereas a tax on incumbents will always decrease the growth rate, taxing entrants might have positive effects on growth. The intuition is the following. Entrants' R&D expenditures are good for growth as the process of creative destruction increases the growth rate for a given level of incumbents' research efforts z^*. However, higher replacement rates will reduce the value of being a monopolist and will therefore diminish research incentives of the incumbents. Depending on which effect dominates, taxing entrants' might be good or bad for growth. Taxing incumbents however is always bad for growth as explained above. This shows that the growth implications of innovation policy are very sensitive to which agents they are directed to. Policies which make incumbents' research more costly might increase market entry but will reduce the economy's growth rate. Policies which represent barriers to innovation from entrants' might foster economic growth if incumbents' R&D expenditures are sufficiently responsive.

Chapter 15: Directed Technological Change

Exercise 15.6

The optimal growth problem the social planner solves is given by

$$\max_{[C(t),[x_L(\nu,t),x_H(\nu,t)]_\nu,Z_L(t),Z_H(t)]_{t=0}^\infty} \int_0^\infty \exp(-\rho t) \frac{C(t)^{1-\theta}-1}{1-\theta} dt \qquad \text{(S15.1)}$$

subject to the constraints

$$Y(t) = C(t) + X(t) + Z_L(t) + Z_H(t)$$

$$Y(t) = \left[\gamma_L Y_L(t)^{\frac{\varepsilon-1}{\varepsilon}} + \gamma_H Y_H(t)^{\frac{\varepsilon-1}{\varepsilon}}\right]^{\frac{\varepsilon}{\varepsilon-1}}$$

$$Y_L(t) = \frac{1}{1-\beta}\left(\int_0^{N_L(t)} x_L(\nu,t)^{1-\beta} d\nu\right) L^\beta$$

$$Y_H(t) = \frac{1}{1-\beta}\left(\int_0^{N_H(t)} x_H(\nu,t)^{1-\beta} d\nu\right) H^\beta$$

$$X(t) = (1-\beta)\left(\int_0^{N_L(t)} x_L(\nu,t)\, d\nu + \int_0^{N_H(t)} x_H(\nu,t)\, d\nu\right)$$

$$\dot{N}_L(t) = \eta_L Z_L(t) \text{ and } \dot{N}_H(t) = \eta_H Z_H(t).$$

To simplify this problem, note that we can solve it sequentially. In particular we can first study the optimal allocation of resources across sectors ν. The solution to (S15.1) will maximize net output, i.e. the allocation of machines across sectors has to solve the problem

$$\max_{\{[x_L(\nu,t)]_{\nu=0}^{N_L(t)},[x_H(\nu,t)]_{\nu=0}^{N_H(t)}\}} Y(t) - X(t),$$

where $Y(t)$ and $X(t)$ are defined as above. The necessary conditions are given by

$$\gamma_L Y(t)^{1/\varepsilon} Y_L(t)^{-1/\varepsilon} L^\beta x_L(\nu,t)^{-\beta} = (1-\beta) \quad \forall \nu \in [0, N_L(t)] \qquad \text{(S15.2)}$$

$$\gamma_H Y(t)^{1/\varepsilon} Y_H(t)^{-1/\varepsilon} H^\beta x_H(\nu,t)^{-\beta} = (1-\beta) \quad \forall \nu \in [0, N_H(t)], \qquad \text{(S15.3)}$$

which simply state that the marginal revenue of each machine has to equal its marginal costs. These conditions imply that

$$x_L(\nu',t) = x_L(\nu'',t) = x_L(t) \quad \forall \nu',\nu'' \in [0, N_L(t)]$$

$$x_H(\nu',t) = x_H(\nu'',t) = x_H(t) \quad \forall \nu',\nu'' \in [0, N_H(t)]$$

$$\gamma_L x_L(t)^{-\beta} L^\beta Y_L(t)^{-1/\varepsilon} = \gamma_H x_H(t)^{-\beta} H^\beta Y_H(t)^{-1/\varepsilon}.$$

197

To express the allocations of machines in the required form, let us define the competitive prices of intermediaries of sector $j = H, L$ as

$$p_j(t) \equiv \frac{\partial Y(t)}{\partial Y_j(t)} = \gamma_j Y_j(t)^{-1/\varepsilon} Y(t)^{1/\varepsilon}, \qquad (\text{S15.4})$$

so that (S15.2) and (S15.3) can be written as

$$\begin{aligned} x_L(t) &= (1-\beta)^{-1/\beta} p_L(t)^{1/\beta} L \\ x_H(t) &= (1-\beta)^{-1/\beta} p_H(t)^{1/\beta} H \end{aligned} \qquad (\text{S15.5})$$

as required. Substituting (S15.5) into the production function of L-intermediaries, we get

$$Y_L(t) = \frac{1}{1-\beta} \left(\int_0^{N_L(t)} x_L(\nu,t)^{1-\beta}\, d\nu \right) L^\beta = (1-\beta)^{-1/\beta} L N_L(t) p_L(t)^{\frac{1-\beta}{\beta}}.$$

Let us again denote the derived elasticity of substitution by

$$\sigma \equiv \varepsilon - (\varepsilon-1)(1-\beta) = 1 + (\varepsilon-1)\beta.$$

Using the expression for competitive prices in (S15.4), we arrive at

$$\begin{aligned} Y_L(t) &= (1-\beta)^{-1/\beta} L N_L(t) \gamma_L^{\frac{1-\beta}{\beta}} Y_L(t)^{-\frac{1-\beta}{\beta\varepsilon}} Y(t)^{\frac{1-\beta}{\beta\varepsilon}} \\ &= (1-\beta)^{\frac{-\varepsilon}{\sigma}} (L N_L(t))^{\frac{\varepsilon\beta}{\sigma}} \gamma_L^{\frac{1-\beta}{\sigma}\varepsilon} Y(t)^{\frac{1-\beta}{\sigma}} \end{aligned}$$

and hence

$$\begin{aligned} \gamma_L Y_L(t)^{\frac{\varepsilon-1}{\varepsilon}} &= (1-\beta)^{\frac{-(\varepsilon-1)}{\sigma}} (L N_L(t))^{\frac{(\varepsilon-1)\beta}{\sigma}} \gamma_L^{\frac{\varepsilon}{\sigma}} Y(t)^{\frac{1-\beta}{\sigma}\frac{\varepsilon-1}{\varepsilon}} \\ &= (1-\beta)^{\frac{-(\varepsilon-1)}{\sigma}} Y(t)^{\frac{1-\beta}{\sigma}\frac{\varepsilon-1}{\varepsilon}} (L N_L(t))^{\frac{\sigma-1}{\sigma}} \gamma_L^{\frac{\varepsilon}{\sigma}}. \end{aligned}$$

The expression for $\gamma_H Y_H(t)^{\frac{\varepsilon-1}{\varepsilon}}$ is analogous. Substituting this into the production function of final good yields

$$\begin{aligned} Y(t) &= \left[\gamma_L Y_L(t)^{\frac{\varepsilon-1}{\varepsilon}} + \gamma_H Y_H(t)^{\frac{\varepsilon-1}{\varepsilon}} \right]^{\frac{\varepsilon}{\varepsilon-1}} \\ &= (1-\beta)^{-1/\beta} \left[(L N_L(t))^{\frac{\sigma-1}{\sigma}} \gamma_L^{\frac{\varepsilon}{\sigma}} + (H N_H(t))^{\frac{\sigma-1}{\sigma}} \gamma_H^{\frac{\varepsilon}{\sigma}} \right]^{\frac{\sigma}{\sigma-1}}. \end{aligned}$$

Additionally we can multiply (S15.2) by $x_L(\nu,t) = x_L(t)$ and integrate over all sectors $\nu \in [0, N_L(t)]$ to get

$$\int_0^{N_L(t)} x_L(t)\, d\nu = x_L(t) N_L(t) = \gamma_L \left(\frac{Y_L(t)}{Y(t)} \right)^{-\frac{1}{\varepsilon}} \frac{N_L(t) L^\beta x_L(t)^{1-\beta}}{1-\beta} = \gamma_L Y(t)^{\frac{1}{\varepsilon}} Y_L(t)^{\frac{\varepsilon-1}{\varepsilon}}.$$

Using the same relationship for the skilled sector, the total amount of resources spent on intermediaries is given by

$$\begin{aligned} X(t) &= (1-\beta)(x_L N_L(t) + x_H N_H(t)) = (1-\beta)\left(\gamma_L Y(t)^{1/\varepsilon} Y_L(t)^{\frac{\varepsilon-1}{\varepsilon}} + \gamma_H Y(t)^{1/\varepsilon} Y_H(t)^{\frac{\varepsilon-1}{\varepsilon}} \right) \\ &= (1-\beta) Y(t). \end{aligned}$$

Net output, which can be allocated to either consumption or research, is therefore given by

$$Y(t) - X(t) = \beta Y(t) = \beta (1-\beta)^{-1/\beta} \left[(L N_L(t))^{\frac{\sigma-1}{\sigma}} \gamma_L^{\frac{\varepsilon}{\sigma}} + (H N_H(t))^{\frac{\sigma-1}{\sigma}} \gamma_H^{\frac{\varepsilon}{\sigma}} \right]^{\frac{\sigma}{\sigma-1}}.$$

Using these results, we can write the maximization problem in (S15.1) as

$$\max_{[C(t),Z_L(t),Z_H(t)]_{t=0}^\infty} \int_0^\infty \exp\left(-\rho t\right)\frac{C\left(t\right)^{1-\theta}-1}{1-\theta}dt \tag{S15.6}$$

$$\text{s.t. } C\left(t\right) = (1-\beta)^{-1/\beta}\beta\left[(LN_L(t))^{\frac{\sigma-1}{\sigma}}\gamma_L^{\frac{\varepsilon}{\sigma}}+(HN_H(t))^{\frac{\sigma-1}{\sigma}}\gamma_H^{\frac{\varepsilon}{\sigma}}\right]^{\frac{\sigma}{\sigma-1}}-Z_L\left(t\right)-Z_H(t) \tag{S15.7}$$

$$\dot{N}_L\left(t\right) = \eta_L Z_L\left(t\right)$$
$$\dot{N}_H\left(t\right) = \eta_H Z_H\left(t\right).$$

The simplified problem in (S15.6) is a standard problem in the optimal control framework, the only difference being that it features two state variables $N_H(t)$ and $N_L(t)$ and three control variables $C(t)$, $Z_L\left(t\right)$ and $Z_H\left(t\right)$. Hence, we can characterize the solution by studying the current value Hamiltonian which is given by

$$\hat{H}\left(N_L,N_H,Z_L,Z_H,C,\mu_L,\mu_H\right) = \frac{C\left(t\right)^{1-\theta}-1}{1-\theta}+\mu_L\left(t\right)\eta_L Z_L^S\left(t\right)+\mu_H\left(t\right)\eta_H Z_H^S\left(t\right),$$

where $C(t)$ is given in (S15.7). This is the required expression.

The first-order conditions for the two control variables Z_L and Z_H are given by

$$\hat{H}_{Z_L} = -C(t)^{-\theta}+\mu_L\left(t\right)\eta_L = 0 \tag{S15.8}$$
$$\hat{H}_{Z_H} = -C(t)^{-\theta}+\mu_H\left(t\right)\eta_H = 0.$$

These immediately imply that

$$\frac{\mu_H(t)}{\mu_L(t)} = \frac{\eta_L}{\eta_H}, \tag{S15.9}$$

so that

$$\frac{\dot\mu_H(t)}{\mu_H(t)} = \frac{\dot\mu_L(t)}{\mu_L(t)} = \frac{\dot\mu(t)}{\mu(t)}. \tag{S15.10}$$

Taking the first-order conditions for the two state variables yields

$$\hat{H}_{N_L} = C(t)^{-\theta}\Psi(t)\gamma_L^{\frac{\varepsilon}{\sigma}}L^{\frac{\sigma-1}{\sigma}}N_L(t)^{-\frac{1}{\sigma}} = \rho\mu_L(t)-\dot\mu_L(t) \tag{S15.11}$$
$$\hat{H}_{N_H} = C(t)^{-\theta}\Psi(t)\gamma_H^{\frac{\varepsilon}{\sigma}}H^{\frac{\sigma-1}{\sigma}}N_H(t)^{-\frac{1}{\sigma}} = \rho\mu_H(t)-\dot\mu_H(t), \tag{S15.12}$$

where we defined $\Psi(t)$ as

$$\Psi(t) = (1-\beta)^{-1/\beta}\beta\left[(LN_L(t))^{\frac{\sigma-1}{\sigma}}\gamma_L^{\frac{\varepsilon}{\sigma}}+(HN_H(t))^{\frac{\sigma-1}{\sigma}}\gamma_H^{\frac{\varepsilon}{\sigma}}\right]^{\frac{1}{\sigma-1}}$$

to save on notation. From (S15.11), (S15.12) and (S15.10) we get that

$$1 = \frac{\rho-\frac{\dot\mu_L(t)}{\mu_L(t)}}{\rho-\frac{\dot\mu_H(t)}{\mu_H(t)}} = \frac{\frac{1}{\mu_L(t)}C(t)^{-\theta}\Psi(t)\gamma_L^{\frac{\varepsilon}{\sigma}}L^{\frac{\sigma-1}{\sigma}}N_L(t)^{-\frac{1}{\sigma}}}{\frac{1}{\mu_H(t)}C(t)^{-\theta}\Psi(t)\gamma_H^{\frac{\varepsilon}{\sigma}}H^{\frac{\sigma-1}{\sigma}}N_H(t)^{-\frac{1}{\sigma}}}$$

$$= \frac{\eta_L}{\eta_H}\left(\frac{\gamma_L}{\gamma_H}\right)^{\varepsilon/\sigma}\left(\frac{L}{H}\right)^{\frac{\sigma-1}{\sigma}}\left(\frac{N_L(t)}{N_H(t)}\right)^{-\frac{1}{\sigma}},$$

where we used (S15.9) to get the second equality. Hence, the social planner chooses a technology ratio of

$$\frac{N_L(t)}{N_H(t)} = \left(\frac{\eta_L}{\eta_H}\right)^\sigma\left(\frac{\gamma_L}{\gamma_H}\right)^\varepsilon\left(\frac{L}{H}\right)^{\sigma-1}. \tag{S15.13}$$

From Eq. (S15.8) we get that

$$\frac{\dot{C}(t)}{C(t)} = -\frac{1}{\theta}\frac{\dot{\mu}_L}{\mu_L}.$$

Furthermore (S15.11) and (S15.8) imply that

$$
\begin{aligned}
-\frac{\dot{\mu}_L}{\mu_L} &= \frac{1}{\mu_L}C(t)^{-\theta}\Psi(t)\gamma_L^{\frac{\varepsilon}{\sigma}}L^{\frac{\sigma-1}{\sigma}}N_L(t)^{-\frac{1}{\sigma}} - \rho \\
&= \eta_L(1-\beta)^{-1/\beta}\beta[\gamma_L^{\frac{\varepsilon}{\sigma}}(N_L L)^{\frac{\sigma-1}{\sigma}} + \gamma_H^{\frac{\varepsilon}{\sigma}}(N_H H)^{\frac{\sigma-1}{\sigma}}]^{\frac{1}{\sigma-1}}\gamma_L^{\frac{\varepsilon}{\sigma}}L^{\frac{\sigma-1}{\sigma}}N_L^{-\frac{1}{\sigma}} - \rho.
\end{aligned}
$$

Using (S15.13) we find that

$$[\gamma_L^{\frac{\varepsilon}{\sigma}}(N_L L)^{\frac{\sigma-1}{\sigma}} + \gamma_H^{\frac{\varepsilon}{\sigma}}(N_H H)^{\frac{\sigma-1}{\sigma}}]^{\frac{1}{\sigma-1}} = [\gamma_L^{\varepsilon}(\eta_L L)^{1-\sigma} + \gamma_H^{\varepsilon}(\eta_H H)^{1-\sigma}]^{\frac{1}{\sigma-1}}\frac{1}{\eta_L}N_L^{\frac{1}{\sigma}}L^{-\frac{\sigma-1}{\sigma}}\gamma_L^{-\frac{\varepsilon}{\sigma}},$$

so that

$$-\frac{\dot{\mu}_L}{\mu_L} = (1-\beta)^{-\frac{1}{\beta}}\beta[\gamma_L^{\varepsilon}(\eta_L L)^{1-\sigma} + \gamma_H^{\varepsilon}(\eta_H H)^{1-\sigma}]^{\frac{1}{\sigma-1}} - \rho.$$

Plugging this in Eq. (S15.8) gives the desired growth rate

$$\frac{\dot{C}(t)}{C(t)} = g^S = \frac{1}{\theta}((1-\beta)^{-\frac{1}{\beta}}\beta[\gamma_L^{\varepsilon}(\eta_L L)^{1-\sigma} + \gamma_H^{\varepsilon}(\eta_H H)^{1-\sigma}]^{\frac{1}{\sigma-1}} - \rho)$$

in terms of exogenous parameters. That it is bigger than the equilibrium growth rate (given in (15.29)) follows from the fact that $\beta < 1$ so that $((1-\beta)^{-\frac{1}{\beta}} > 1$.

Let us now turn to the equivalents of weak and strong equilibrium bias. Factor prices are given by

$$
\begin{aligned}
w_L(t) &= p_L(t)\frac{\partial Y_L(t)}{\partial L} = \frac{\beta}{1-\beta}\left(\int_0^{N_L(t)} x_L(\nu,t)^{1-\beta}\,d\nu\right)L^{\beta-1} \\
&= p_L(t)^{1/\beta}\beta(1-\beta)^{-1/\beta}N_L(t),
\end{aligned}
$$

so that

$$\omega(t) = \frac{w_H(t)}{w_L(t)} = \left(\frac{p_H(t)}{p_L(t)}\right)^{1/\beta}\frac{N_H(t)}{N_L(t)} = \left(\frac{\gamma_H}{\gamma_L}\right)^{\frac{\varepsilon}{\sigma}}\left(\frac{H}{L}\right)^{\frac{-1}{\sigma}}\left(\frac{N_H(t)}{N_L(t)}\right)^{\frac{\sigma-1}{\sigma}}, \qquad (S15.15)$$

where we used that

$$
\begin{aligned}
\frac{p_H(t)}{p_L(t)} &= \frac{\gamma_H Y_H(t)^{-1/\varepsilon}Y(t)^{1/\varepsilon}}{\gamma_L Y_L(t)^{-1/\varepsilon}Y(t)^{1/\varepsilon}} = \frac{\gamma_H}{\gamma_L}\left(\frac{Y_H(t)}{Y_L(t)}\right)^{-1/\varepsilon} = \frac{\gamma_H}{\gamma_L}\left(\frac{H}{L}\frac{N_H(t)}{N_L(t)}\right)^{-1/\varepsilon}\left(\frac{p_H(t)}{p_L(t)}\right)^{-\frac{1-\beta}{\beta\varepsilon}} \\
&= \left(\frac{\gamma_H}{\gamma_L}\right)^{\frac{\beta\varepsilon}{\sigma}}\left(\frac{H}{L}\frac{N_H(t)}{N_L(t)}\right)^{-\frac{\beta}{\sigma}}.
\end{aligned}
$$

To see that the result concerning the weak equilibrium bias is also present in the social planner's solution, let us consider the effect of an increase in the relative skill supply on the wage premium holding the relative factor supply in (S15.15) fixed. Clearly,

$$\frac{\partial \omega(t)}{\partial \frac{N_H(t)}{N_L(t)}} = \frac{\sigma-1}{\sigma}\frac{\omega(t)}{\frac{N_H(t)}{N_L(t)}}.$$

Additionally we have from (S15.13) that

$$\frac{\partial \frac{N_H(t)}{N_L(t)}}{\partial \frac{H}{L}} = (\sigma-1)\frac{\frac{N_H(t)}{N_L(t)}}{\frac{H}{L}},$$

so that

$$\frac{\partial \omega(t)}{\partial \frac{N_H(t)}{N_L(t)}} \frac{\partial \frac{N_H(t)}{N_L(t)}}{\partial \frac{H}{L}} = \frac{(\sigma-1)^2}{\sigma} \frac{\omega(t)}{H/L} \geq 0.$$

Hence, the result about weak equilibrium bias is also present in the social planner's solution. To see that we can also reproduce the result about strong equilibrium bias, use (S15.15) and (S15.13) to solve for the BGP skill premium as

$$\begin{aligned}
\omega(t) &= \left(\frac{\gamma_H}{\gamma_L}\right)^{\frac{\varepsilon}{\sigma}} \left(\frac{H}{L}\right)^{\frac{-1}{\sigma}} \left(\left(\frac{\eta_H}{\eta_L}\right)^{\sigma} \left(\frac{\gamma_H}{\gamma_L}\right)^{\varepsilon} \left(\frac{H}{L}\right)^{\sigma-1}\right)^{\frac{\sigma-1}{\sigma}} \\
&= \left(\frac{\gamma_H}{\gamma_L}\right)^{\varepsilon} \left(\frac{\eta_H}{\eta_L}\right)^{\sigma-1} \left(\frac{H}{L}\right)^{\frac{(\sigma-1)^2-1}{\sigma}} \\
&= \left(\frac{\gamma_H}{\gamma_L}\right)^{\varepsilon} \left(\frac{\eta_H}{\eta_L}\right)^{\sigma-1} \left(\frac{H}{L}\right)^{\sigma-2}.
\end{aligned}$$

Hence,

$$\frac{d\omega(t)}{d\frac{H}{L}} = (\sigma-2)\frac{\omega(t)}{H/L},$$

which shows the possibility of strong equilibrium bias if $\sigma > 2$, i.e. if $\sigma > 2$, an increase in the relative supply of skilled labor will increase the relative price of skilled labor, once the process of technological change is endogenized.

Exercise 15.18

Exercise 15.18, Part (a). The change in the production function of intermediary producers does not affect the definition of an equilibrium. Hence, an equilibrium in this economy consists of paths of factor prices and interest rates $[w_L(t), r(t), w_H(t)]_{t=0}^{\infty}$, prices for machines $[p_H^x(\nu, t|q), p_L^x(\nu, t|q)]_{t=0, \nu \in [0,1]}^{\infty}$, prices for the two intermediary goods $[p_L(t), p_H(t)]_{t=0}^{\infty}$, quantities of machines $[x_H(\nu, t|q), x_L(\nu, t|q)]_{t=0, \nu \in [0,1]}^{\infty}$, sequences of value functions $[V_H(\nu, t|q), V_L(\nu, t|q)]_{t=0, \nu \in [0,1]}^{\infty}$, sequences of qualities $[q_H(\nu, t), q_L(\nu, t)]_{t=0, \nu \in [0,1]}^{\infty}$ and consumption levels $[C(t)]_{t=0}^{\infty}$ such that consumers maximize utility, intermediary producers set profit maximizing prices $p_H^x(\nu, t|q)$ and $p_L^x(\nu, t|q)$ monopolistically, final good producers maximize profits taking intermediary prices and wages as given, the wage rate clears the labor market, the value functions $V_H(\nu, t|q)$ and $V_L(\nu, t|q)$ and quality levels $q_L(t, \nu)$ and $q_H(t, \nu)$ are consistent with free entry and consumption levels, expenditures for machines and research spending are consistent with the resource constraint. A BGP equilibrium is an equilibrium where aggregate output grows at a constant rate and where interest and replacement rates are constant.

Let us now characterize the BGP equilibrium in this economy. Consider first the static equilibrium, i.e. the equilibrium for a given distribution of qualities $[q_H(\nu, t), q_L(\nu, t)]_{\nu=0}^{1}$. Monopolistic machine producers set their prices $p_H(\nu, t|q)$ and $p_L(\nu, t|q)$ to maximize profits. The demand for L-complementary machines in sector ν with current quality q is given by

$$x_L(\nu, t \mid q) = \left(\frac{q_L(\nu, t) p_L(t)}{p_L(\nu, t|q)}\right)^{\frac{1}{\beta}} L, \tag{S15.16}$$

where recall $p_L(t)$ is the price of L-intermediaries in terms of the final good. With this isoelastic demand function, monopolistic prices $p_L(\nu, t|q)$ are again given by

$$p_L(\nu, t \mid q) = \frac{\psi}{1 - \beta} q_L(\nu, t) = q_L(\nu, t).$$

From (S15.16) we therefore get that

$$x_L(\nu, t \mid q) = p_L(t)^{\frac{1}{\beta}} L,$$

so that monopolistic profits are

$$\pi_L(\nu, t|q) = (1 - \psi)q(\nu, t)x_L(\nu, t \mid q) = \beta q(\nu, t)p_L(t)^{\frac{1}{\beta}} L = \pi_L(t|q).$$

This again shows that profits are not dependent on the sector ν, once quality is controlled for (and with a slight abuse of notation we just denote the function again by π). Note however that the dependence on L-intermediary prices $p_L(t)$ (potentially) introduces a dependence on time. To make some progress, let us solve for $p_L(t)$. As the market for intermediaries is competitive, $p_L(t)$ will be given by the marginal product of L intermediates, i.e.

$$p_L(t) = Y(t)^{\frac{1}{\varepsilon}} \gamma_L Y_L(t)^{-\frac{1}{\varepsilon}} = \gamma \left(\frac{Y_L(t)}{Y(t)} \right)^{-\frac{1}{\varepsilon}}. \tag{S15.17}$$

Let us conjecture that along the BGP $Y_L(t)$ and $Y(t)$ will grow at the same rate so that $p_L(t)$ will be constant. We will show below that this is actually the case. Hence, along the BGP, $p_L(t)$ will be constant so that profits are also constant (conditional on q), i.e. $\pi_L(t|q) = \pi_L(q)$.

To characterize the research decisions, we have to derive the value of owning a patent (which is now not perpetual due to the process of creative destruction). The value function is characterized by the HJB equation

$$r(t)V_L(\nu, t \mid q) - \dot{V}_L(\nu, t \mid q) = \pi_L(t, q) - z_L(\nu, t \mid q)V_L(\nu, t \mid q). \tag{S15.18}$$

Along the BGP, interest rates and replacement rates will be constant, i.e. $r(t) = r^*$ and $z_L(\nu, t|q) = z_L^*$. As profits are also constant as argued above, (S15.18) reduces to

$$r^*V_L(t|q) - \dot{V}_L(t|q) = \pi_L(q) - z_L^*V_L(t|q), \tag{S15.19}$$

where we already imposed that V will not be dependent on ν as neither profits nor replacement rates are. The differential equation in (S15.19) has the solution

$$V_L(t|q) = \frac{\pi_L(q)}{r^* + z_L^*} + \left[V_L(0|q) - \frac{\pi_L(q)}{r^* + z_L^*} \right] \exp\left((r^* + z_L^*)t\right).$$

Along the BGP we therefore have to have $\frac{\pi_L(q)}{r^* + z_L^*} = V_L(0|q) = V_L(t|q)$. If $V_L(0|q) > \frac{\pi_L(q)}{r^* + z_L^*}$, then $V_L(t|q) \xrightarrow{t} \infty$, which violates the transversality condition. If $V_L(0|q) < \frac{\pi_L(q)}{r^* + z_L^*}$, then $V_L(t|q)$ will be negative in finite time. This cannot occur in equilibrium either. Hence, the value function is given by

$$V_L(t|q) = V_L(q) = \frac{\pi_L(q)}{r^* + z_L^*} = \frac{\beta q p_L^{\frac{1}{\beta}} L}{r^* + z_L^*},$$

where we explicitly noted that p_L will be constant along the BGP. The case of H-complementary machines is analogous. With the value function at hand we can characterize the decisions of research firms. Along the BGP there will be positive research activity across all sectors ν for both machine types L and H. Hence the free entry conditions will hold with equality, i.e.

$$\eta_L V_L(q) = \lambda^{-1} q \tag{S15.20}$$

$$\eta_H V_H(q) = \lambda^{-1} q. \tag{S15.21}$$

Combining (S15.20) and (S15.21), we can solve for the intermediary prices $p_L(t)$ and $p_H(t)$. Doing so yields

$$1 = \frac{\eta_L V_L(q)}{\eta_H V_H(q)} = \frac{\eta_L \beta q p_L^{1/\beta} L}{\eta_H \beta q p_H^{1/\beta} H}$$

so that

$$\frac{p_H}{p_L} = \left(\frac{\eta_L}{\eta_H} \frac{L}{H} \right)^{\beta}. \tag{S15.22}$$

As we normalized the final good to be the numeraire, we also have that

$$\gamma^{\varepsilon} p_L^{1-\varepsilon} + (1-\gamma)^{\varepsilon} p_H^{1-\varepsilon} = 1,$$

so that (using (S15.22)) we get

$$p_H = H^{-\beta} \eta_H^{-\beta} [(L\eta_L)^{\sigma-1} \gamma^{\varepsilon} + (1-\gamma)^{\varepsilon} (H\eta_H)^{\sigma-1}]^{\frac{1}{\varepsilon-1}}. \tag{S15.23}$$

Until now we only used the two free entry conditions to make sure that research firms are indifferent where to direct their research efforts to. Additionally we also need that research firms do not make profits. From (S15.21) we therefore get that

$$\lambda^{-1} q = \eta_H V_H(q) = \frac{\beta q p_H^{\frac{1}{\beta}} H}{r^* + z_H^*},$$

so that the effective discount rate $r^* + z_H^*$ is given by

$$r^* + z_H^* = \beta \lambda \eta_H H p_H^{\frac{1}{\beta}} = \beta \lambda [(L\eta_L)^{\sigma-1} \gamma^{\varepsilon} + (1-\gamma)^{\varepsilon} (H\eta_H)^{\sigma-1}]^{\frac{1}{\sigma-1}}, \tag{S15.24}$$

where the second equality uses (S15.23) and we defined $\sigma = \varepsilon - (\varepsilon - 1)(1-\beta)$. Note however that both r^* and z_H^* are endogenous.

To derive the equilibrium growth rate, let us derive the expression for aggregate output. Equilibrium intermediary productions are given by

$$\begin{aligned} Y_H(t) &= \frac{1}{1-\beta} \left[\int_0^1 q_H(\nu,t) x_H(\nu,t \mid q)^{1-\beta} d\nu \right] H^{\beta} = \frac{1}{1-\beta} \left[\int_0^1 q_H(\nu,t) p_H^{\frac{1-\beta}{\beta}} d\nu \right] H \\ &= \frac{1}{1-\beta} H p_H^{(1-\beta)/\beta} Q_H(t). \end{aligned} \tag{S15.25}$$

The expression for $Y_L(t)$ is of course analogous. Aggregate output is therefore given by

$$\begin{aligned} Y(t) &= \left(\gamma_L Y_L(t)^{\frac{\varepsilon-1}{\varepsilon}} + \gamma_H Y_L(t)^{\frac{\varepsilon-1}{\varepsilon}} \right)^{\frac{\varepsilon}{\varepsilon-1}} \\ &= \frac{1}{1-\beta} \left(\gamma_L (p_L^{\frac{1-\beta}{\beta}} Q_L(t) L)^{\frac{\varepsilon-1}{\varepsilon}} + \gamma_H (p_H^{\frac{1-\beta}{\beta}} Q_H(t) H)^{\frac{\varepsilon-1}{\varepsilon}} \right)^{\frac{\varepsilon}{\varepsilon-1}}. \end{aligned} \tag{S15.26}$$

To derive the BGP growth rate of $Q_L(t)$, consider a small time interval Δt. In this time interval the probability for entrants to have an innovation is $z_L^* \Delta t$ (recall that innovation rates are constant along the BGP) and the probability for two or more innovations is of order $o(\Delta t)$. Hence

$$Q_L(t + \Delta t) = \lambda Q_L(t) z_L^* \Delta t + (1 - z_L^* \Delta t) Q_L(t) + o(\Delta t)$$

so that

$$\frac{Q_L(t+\Delta t) - Q_L(t)}{\Delta t} = (\lambda - 1)Q_L(t)z_L^* + \frac{o(\Delta t)}{\Delta t}.$$

Taking the limit where Δt goes to zero, we get that

$$g_L^* = \frac{\dot{Q}_L(t)}{Q_L(t)} = (\lambda - 1)z_L^*.$$

Now note that (S15.26) implies that

$$\frac{\dot{Y}(t)}{Y(t)} = \frac{\gamma_L \left(p_L^{\frac{1-\beta}{\beta}} Q_L(t)L \right)^{\frac{\varepsilon-1}{\varepsilon}} \frac{\dot{Q}_L(t)}{Q_L(t)} + \gamma_H \left(p_H^{\frac{1-\beta}{\beta}} Q_H(t)H \right)^{\frac{\varepsilon-1}{\varepsilon}} \frac{\dot{Q}_H(t)}{Q_h(t)}}{\gamma_L \left(p_L^{\frac{1-\beta}{\beta}} Q_L(t)L \right)^{\frac{\varepsilon-1}{\varepsilon}} + \gamma_H \left(p_H^{\frac{1-\beta}{\beta}} Q_H(t)H \right)^{\frac{\varepsilon-1}{\varepsilon}}}$$

$$= g_L^* + \frac{\gamma_H \left(p_H^{\frac{1-\beta}{\beta}} Q_H(t)H \right)^{\frac{\varepsilon-1}{\varepsilon}}}{\gamma_L \left(p_L^{\frac{1-\beta}{\beta}} Q_L(t)L \right)^{\frac{\varepsilon-1}{\varepsilon}} + \gamma_H \left(p_H^{\frac{1-\beta}{\beta}} Q_H(t)H \right)^{\frac{\varepsilon-1}{\varepsilon}}} (g_H^* - g_L^*). \quad \text{(S15.27)}$$

Along the BGP, aggregate output grows at a constant rate, i.e. $\frac{\dot{Y}(t)}{Y(t)} = g^*$, so that (S15.27) implies that

$$g^* = g_L^* = g_H^* = (\lambda - 1)z_L^* = (\lambda - 1)z_H^* = (\lambda - 1)z^*.$$

This also verifies that intermediary prices are indeed constant along the BGP (see (S15.17)). Now we are in the position to disentangle r^* and z^*. From the consumer's Euler equation we have that

$$g_C = \frac{1}{\theta}(r^* - \rho).$$

Along the BGP consumption will be growing at rate $g^* = (\lambda - 1)z^*$. Hence we get that

$$r^* = \theta g^* + \rho = \theta(\lambda - 1)z^* + \rho,$$

so that the effective discount rate is given by

$$r^* + z^* = r^* + \frac{r^* - \rho}{\theta(\lambda - 1)} = r^* \frac{1 + \theta(\lambda - 1)}{\theta(\lambda - 1)} - \frac{\rho}{\theta(\lambda - 1)}.$$

Using (S15.24), equilibrium interest rates are therefore given by

$$r^* = \frac{\theta(\lambda - 1)}{1 + \theta(\lambda - 1)} \left[r^* + z^* + \frac{\rho}{\theta(\lambda - 1)} \right]$$

$$= \frac{\theta(\lambda - 1) \left[\beta\lambda[(L\eta_L)^{\sigma-1}\gamma_L^\varepsilon + \gamma_H^\varepsilon(H\eta_H)^{\sigma-1}]^{\frac{1}{\sigma-1}} \right] + \rho}{1 + \theta(\lambda - 1)}.$$

This determines the interest rate as a function of exogenous parameters only, so that the equilibrium growth rate is given by

$$g^* = \frac{1}{\theta}(r^* - \rho) = \frac{(\lambda - 1)}{\theta(\lambda - 1) + 1} (\beta\lambda[(L\eta_L)^{\sigma-1}\gamma_L^\varepsilon + \gamma_H^\varepsilon(H\eta_H)^{\sigma-1}]^{\frac{1}{\sigma-1}} - \rho). \quad \text{(S15.28)}$$

Finally we have to make parametric restrictions such that the economy is actually growing and that the transversality condition is satisfied. The economy has positive growth if

$$\beta\lambda[(L\eta_L)^{\sigma-1}\gamma_L^\varepsilon + \gamma_H^\varepsilon(H\eta_H)^{\sigma-1}]^{\frac{1}{\sigma-1}} > \rho.$$

The transversality condition is satisfied if

$$(1 - \theta)g^* < \rho.$$

Substituting the expression for the equilibrium growth rate in (S15.28), the transversality condition requires that

$$\rho > (1 - \theta)\frac{\lambda - 1}{\lambda}\beta\lambda[(L\eta_L)^{\sigma-1}\gamma_L^{\varepsilon} + \gamma_H{}^{\varepsilon}(H\eta_H)^{\sigma-1}]^{\frac{1}{\sigma-1}}.$$

Hence the allocation characterized above is a BGP equilibrium in this economy if

$$\Theta > \rho > (1 - \theta)\frac{\lambda - 1}{\lambda}\Theta,$$

where

$$\Theta = \beta\lambda[(L\eta_L)^{\sigma-1}\gamma_L^{\varepsilon} + \gamma_H{}^{\varepsilon}(H\eta_H)^{\sigma-1}]^{\frac{1}{\sigma-1}}.$$

Exercise 15.18, Part (b). To derive the equilibrium technology ratio, note that the technologies in this economy are just given by the aggregate qualities $Q_H(t)$ and $Q_L(t)$. Using (S15.22) we get that

$$\frac{Y_H}{Y_L} = \frac{Q_H(t)}{Q_L(t)}\frac{H}{L}\left(\frac{p_H}{p_L}\right)^{\frac{1-\beta}{\beta}} = \frac{Q_H(t)}{Q_L(t)}\frac{H}{L}\gamma^{\frac{1-\beta}{\beta}}\left(\frac{p_H}{p_L}\right)^{\frac{-(1-\beta)}{\varepsilon\beta}}.$$

Additionally, (S15.25) implies that

$$\frac{Y_H}{Y_L} = \frac{\frac{1}{1-\beta}Hp_H^{(1-\beta)/\beta}Q_H(t)}{\frac{1}{1-\beta}Lp_L^{(1-\beta)/\beta}Q_L(t)} = \frac{HQ_H(t)}{LQ_L(t)}\left(\frac{\eta_L}{\eta_H}\frac{L}{H}\right)^{1-\beta},$$

where we again used (S15.22). Combining these two equation determines the equilibrium level of qualities as

$$\frac{Q_H(t)}{Q_L(t)} = \gamma^{\varepsilon}\left(\frac{\eta_H}{\eta_L}\right)^{\sigma}\left(\frac{H}{L}\right)^{\sigma-1}, \tag{S15.29}$$

which is exactly the same equation as in the baseline model of directed technological change.

Exercise 15.18, Part (c). Let us now show that this economy also features weak equilibrium bias and that there is the possibility of strong equilibrium bias. The derived production function of the final good is given in (S15.26) as

$$Y(t) = \frac{1}{1-\beta}\left(\gamma_L\left(p_L^{\frac{1-\beta}{\beta}}Q_L(t)L\right)^{\frac{\varepsilon-1}{\varepsilon}} + \gamma_H\left(p_H^{\frac{1-\beta}{\beta}}Q_H(t)H\right)^{\frac{\varepsilon-1}{\varepsilon}}\right)^{\frac{\varepsilon}{\varepsilon-1}}. \tag{S15.30}$$

To see that an increase in $\frac{H}{L}$ always induces H biased technological change, recall that we called technological change H-biased, if

$$\frac{\partial MP_H(t)/MP_L(t)}{\partial Q_H/Q_H} \geq 0,$$

where $MP_W(t)$ denotes the marginal product of factor W. We said that the economy features weak equilibrium bias if

$$\frac{\partial MP_H(t)/MP_L(t)}{\partial Q_H(t)/Q_L(t)}\frac{\partial Q_H(t)/Q_L(t)}{\partial H/L} \geq 0.$$

In this economy we have from (S15.30) that

$$\frac{MP_H(t)}{MP_L(t)} = \frac{\gamma_H}{\gamma_L}\left(\frac{H}{L}\right)^{\frac{-1}{\varepsilon}}\left(\frac{p_H}{p_L}\right)^{\frac{1-\beta}{\beta}\frac{\varepsilon-1}{\varepsilon}}\left(\frac{Q_H(t)}{Q_L(t)}\right)^{\frac{\varepsilon-1}{\varepsilon}},$$

where $\frac{p_H}{p_L}$ is given in (S15.22). Hence we get that

$$\frac{\partial MP_H(t)/MP_L(t)}{\partial Q_H(t)/Q_L(t)} = \frac{\sigma-1}{\beta\varepsilon}\frac{MP_H(t)/MP_L(t)}{Q_H(t)/Q_L(t)},$$

where we used that $\sigma - 1 = (\varepsilon - 1)\beta$. Additionally we have from (S15.29) that

$$\frac{\partial Q_H(t)/Q_L(t)}{\partial H/L} = (\sigma-1)\frac{Q_H(t)/Q_L(t)}{H/L},$$

so that

$$\frac{\partial MP_H(t)/MP_L(t)}{\partial Q_H(t)/Q_L(t)}\frac{\partial Q_H(t)/Q_L(t)}{\partial H/L} = \frac{(\sigma-1)^2}{\beta\varepsilon}\frac{MP_H(t)/MP_L(t)}{H/L} \geq 0.$$

Hence, the economy features weak equilibrium bias.

To study the conditions for strong equilibrium bias we need to look at equilibrium wages in his economy. Using that the equilibrium level of qualities satisfies (S15.29) and that equilibrium prices were given in (S15.22) as

$$\frac{p_H}{p_L} = \left(\frac{\eta_L}{\eta_H}\frac{L}{H}\right)^{\beta},$$

it follows that equilibrium wages are given by

$$\begin{aligned}
\frac{w_H(t)}{w_L(t)} &= \frac{p_H\frac{\partial Y_H(t)}{\partial H}}{p_L\frac{\partial Y_L(t)}{\partial L}} = \frac{p_H^{1/\beta}Q_H(t)}{p_L^{1/\beta}Q_L(t)} = \frac{\eta_L}{\eta_H}\frac{L}{H}\frac{Q_H(t)}{Q_L(t)} \\
&= \frac{\eta_L}{\eta_H}\frac{L}{H}\gamma^{\varepsilon}\left(\frac{\eta_L}{\eta_H}\right)^{-\sigma}\left(\frac{H}{L}\right)^{\sigma-1} \\
&= \gamma^{\varepsilon}\left(\frac{\eta_L}{\eta_H}\right)^{1-\sigma}\left(\frac{H}{L}\right)^{\sigma-2}.
\end{aligned}$$

Hence, we get exactly the same result as in the baseline model that there is strong equilibrium bias if

$$\sigma - 2 > 0.$$

Exercise 15.18, Part (d). Let us now turn to the transitional dynamics. We showed in (S15.29) that along the BGP the relative qualities in the two sectors have to satisfy

$$\frac{Q_H(t)}{Q_L(t)} = \gamma^{\varepsilon}\left(\frac{\eta_L}{\eta_H}\right)^{-\sigma}\left(\frac{H}{L}\right)^{\sigma-1} = Q^{BGP}. \tag{S15.31}$$

As $Q_L(0)$ and $Q_H(0)$ are exogenously given, there is no reason why (S15.31) has to hold at $t = 0$. We showed above that the BGP is unique and that (S15.31) has to hold at the BGP. Although the BGP of this model is very similar to the baseline model, the transitional dynamics are a little more difficult. In the baseline model, the transitional dynamics are such that off the BGP there will never be both sectors innovating at the same time. This is not necessarily the case here. What we will show is that the system will be globally stable such that if $Q_H(t)/Q_L(t) > Q^{BGP}$, there will be faster innovation in the L sector and vice versa. To show this, let us assume that even off the BGP we have

$$z_H(\nu, t|q) = z_H(t) > 0 \text{ and } z_L(\nu, t|q) = z_L(t) > 0$$

but not necessarily $z_H(t) = z_L(t)$. With positive research expenditures we still get that the free entry condition holds with equality so that

$$\eta_H V_H(t, \nu \mid q) = \lambda^{-1} q_H(\nu, t) \text{ and } \eta_L V_L(t, \nu \mid q) = \lambda^{-1} q_L(\nu, t). \tag{S15.32}$$

Integrating (S15.32) over all sectors yields

$$\int V_H(\nu, t | q) d\nu = \frac{1}{\lambda \eta_H} Q_H(t) \text{ and } \int V_L(\nu, t | q) d\nu = \frac{1}{\lambda \eta_L} Q_L(t).$$

Hence, we have that

$$\frac{\int V_H(\nu, t) d\nu}{\int V_L(\nu, t) d\nu} = \frac{\eta_L}{\eta_H} \frac{Q_H(t)}{Q_L(t)}. \tag{S15.33}$$

But now note that (S15.32) still implies that $\dot{V}_S(t, \nu) = 0$ so that the HJB equation reads

$$(r(t) + z_H(t)) V_H(\nu, t) = \beta p_H(t)^{\frac{1}{\beta}} H q_H(\nu, t).$$

Hence we get that

$$\frac{(r(t) + z_H(t)) \int V_H(\nu, t) d\nu}{(r(t) + z_L(t)) \int V_L(\nu, t) d\nu} = \left(\frac{p_H(t)}{p_L(t)} \right)^{\frac{1}{\beta}} \frac{Q_H(t)}{Q_L(t)} \frac{H}{L}. \tag{S15.34}$$

As $\frac{p_H(t)}{p_L(t)}$ is determined by competition in the final good sector, we have that

$$
\begin{aligned}
\frac{p_H(t)}{p_L(t)} &= \gamma \left(\frac{Y_H(t)}{Y_L(t)} \right)^{\frac{-1}{\varepsilon}} \\
&= \gamma \left(\frac{Q_H(t)H}{Q_L(t)H} \right)^{\frac{-1}{\varepsilon}} \left(\frac{p_H(t)}{p_L(t)} \right)^{\frac{-(1-\beta)}{\beta \varepsilon}} \\
&= \gamma^{\frac{\beta \varepsilon}{\beta \varepsilon + (1-\beta)}} \left(\frac{Q_H(t)H}{Q_L(t)L} \right)^{\frac{-\beta}{\beta \varepsilon + (1-\beta)}}.
\end{aligned}
$$

Substituting this and (S15.33) into (S15.34), we get that

$$\frac{(r(t) + z_H(t))}{(r(t) + z_L(t))} \frac{\eta_L}{\eta_H} \frac{Q_H(t)}{Q_L(t)} = \left(\frac{p_H}{p_L} \right)^{\frac{1}{\beta}} \frac{Q_H(t)}{Q_L(t)} \frac{H}{L} = \gamma^{\frac{\varepsilon}{\sigma}} \left(\frac{Q_H(t)H}{Q_L(t)L} \right)^{\frac{\sigma-1}{\sigma}},$$

which we can write (using (S15.31)) as

$$\frac{(r(t) + z_H(t))}{(r(t) + z_L(t))} = \frac{\eta_H}{\eta_L} \left(\frac{1-\gamma}{\gamma} \right)^{\frac{\varepsilon}{\sigma}} \left(\frac{Q_H(t)}{Q_L(t)} \right)^{\frac{-1}{\sigma}} \left(\frac{H}{L} \right)^{\frac{\sigma-1}{\sigma}} = \left(\frac{Q^{BGP}}{Q_H(t)/Q_L(t)} \right)^{\frac{1}{\sigma}}. \tag{S15.35}$$

From here it is then easy to characterize the transitional dynamics, as (S15.35) implies that

$$z_H(t) > z_L(t) \Leftrightarrow \frac{Q_H(t)}{Q_L(t)} < Q^{BGP},$$

i.e. whenever H-complementary technology is too low (relative to the BGP level), research directed towards H-technologies will be more intense than research directed towards L-technologies. Hence, $\frac{Q_H(t)}{Q_L(t)}$ will grow over time until the qualities reach their BGP ratio Q^{BGP}. Then (S15.35) shows that

$$z_H(t) = z_L(t) = z^*$$

as required along the BGP. As we made no reference to the specific initial conditions, this analysis showed that the system will be globally stable.

Exercise 15.18, Part (e). Let us now consider the Pareto optimal allocation. The social planner solves the following maximization problem

$$\max_{[C(t),[x_H(\nu,t),x_L(\nu,t),z_L(\nu,t),z_H(\nu,t)]_\nu]_{t=0}^\infty} \int_0^\infty \exp\left(-\rho\right) \frac{C(t)^{1-\theta}-1}{1-\theta}dt$$

subject to the constraints

$$Y(t) = X(t)+Z(t)+C(t)$$

$$Y(t) = \left(\gamma Y_L^{\frac{\varepsilon-1}{\varepsilon}}(t)+(1-\gamma)Y_H^{\frac{\varepsilon-1}{\varepsilon}}(t)\right)^{\frac{\varepsilon}{\varepsilon-1}}$$

$$Y_L(t) = \frac{1}{1-\beta}\left(\int_0^1 q_L(\nu,t)x_L(\nu,t\mid q)^{1-\beta}d\nu\right)L^\beta$$

$$Y_H(t) = \frac{1}{1-\beta}\left(\int_0^1 q_H(\nu,t)x_H(\nu,t\mid q)^{1-\beta}d\nu\right)H^\beta$$

$$X(t) = X_H(t)+X_L(t) = \psi\int_0^1 x_H(\nu,t)q_H(\nu,t)d\nu + \psi\int_0^1 x_L(\nu,t)q_L(\nu,t)d\nu$$

$$Z(t) = \int_0^1 z_H(\nu,t)d\nu + \int_0^1 z_L(\nu,t)d\nu$$

Additionally, the quality innovations have to satisfy the restrictions imposed by the R&D technology (we will make that formal later). Let us first eliminate some constraints to make the problem more tractable. Consider first the problem for the intermediary sectors. The social planner will allocate $[x_H(\nu,t),x_L(\nu,t)]_{\nu=0}^1$ to maximize net output. Formally, $[x_H(\nu,t),x_L(\nu,t)]_{\nu=0}^1$ will solve the problem

$$\max_{[x_H(\nu,t),x_L(\nu,t)]_{\nu=0}^1} Y(t)-X(t),$$

where $Y(t)$ and $X(t)$ are defined above. The necessary conditions are given by

$$\frac{\partial Y(t)}{\partial Y_L(t)}q_L(\nu,t)L^\beta x_L(\nu,t|q)^{-\beta} - \psi q_L(\nu,t) = 0 \qquad (S15.36)$$

$$\frac{\partial Y(t)}{\partial Y_H(t)}q_H(\nu,t)H^\beta x_H(\nu,t|q)^{-\beta} - \psi q_H(\nu,t) = 0.$$

These conditions immediately imply that

$$x_L(\nu,t|q) = x_L(t) \text{ and } x_H(\nu,t|q) = x_H(t),$$

i.e. the allocation of machines is equalized across sectors and independent of q. Using this, we get that

$$\frac{\partial Y(t)}{\partial Y_L(t)} = \left(\gamma Y_L^{\frac{\varepsilon-1}{\varepsilon}}(t)+(1-\gamma)Y_H^{\frac{\varepsilon-1}{\varepsilon}}(t)\right)^{\frac{1}{\varepsilon-1}}\gamma Y_L^{\frac{-1}{\varepsilon}}(t) = \gamma\left(\frac{Y(t)}{Y_L(t)}\right)^{1/\varepsilon}.$$

and

$$Y_L(t) = \frac{1}{1-\beta}\left(\int_0^1 q_L(\nu,t)d\nu\right)x_L(t)^{1-\beta}L^\beta = \frac{1}{1-\beta}x_L(t)^{1-\beta}L^\beta Q_L(t). \qquad (S15.37)$$

As (S15.36) implies that

$$x_L(t)^{1-\beta} = \gamma^{(1-\beta)/\beta}\left(\frac{Y(t)}{Y_L(t)}\right)^{(1-\beta)/(\beta\varepsilon)}L^{1-\beta}\left(\frac{1}{1-\beta}\right)^{(1-\beta)/\beta},$$

(S15.37) can be written as

$$
\begin{aligned}
Y_L(t) &= \left(\frac{1}{1-\beta}\right)^{1/\beta} \gamma^{(1-\beta)/\beta} \left(\frac{Y(t)}{Y_L(t)}\right)^{(1-\beta)/(\beta\varepsilon)} LQ_L(t) \\
&= \left(\frac{1}{1-\beta}\right)^{\varepsilon/\sigma} \gamma^{(1-\beta)\varepsilon/\sigma} Y(t)^{(1-\beta)/\sigma} (LQ_L(t))^{(\beta\varepsilon)/\sigma}, \quad\quad (S15.38)
\end{aligned}
$$

where we again defined

$$
\sigma = 1 + (\varepsilon - 1)\beta.
$$

As the analogous equation to (S15.38) holds also true for $Y_H(t)$, we can write aggregate output $Y(t)$ as

$$
\begin{aligned}
Y(t) &= \left[\gamma Y_L(t)^{\frac{\varepsilon-1}{\varepsilon}} + (1-\gamma) Y_H(t)^{\frac{\varepsilon-1}{\varepsilon}}\right]^{\frac{\varepsilon}{\varepsilon-1}} \\
&= \left(\frac{1}{1-\beta}\right)^{\varepsilon/\sigma} Y(t)^{(1-\beta)/\sigma} \left[\gamma^{\varepsilon/\sigma}(LQ_L(t))^{(\sigma-1)/\sigma} + (1-\gamma)^{\varepsilon/\sigma}(HQ_H(t))^{(\sigma-1)/\sigma}\right]^{\frac{\varepsilon}{\varepsilon-1}} \\
&= \left(\frac{1}{1-\beta}\right)^{1/\beta} \left[\gamma^{\varepsilon/\sigma}(LQ_L(t))^{(\sigma-1)/\sigma} + (1-\gamma)^{\varepsilon/\sigma}(HQ_H(t))^{(\sigma-1)/\sigma}\right]^{\frac{\sigma}{\sigma-1}}.
\end{aligned}
$$

Additionally we can use (S15.36) to get

$$
\begin{aligned}
X_L(t) &= \int_0^1 \psi q_L(\nu,t) x_L(t) d\nu = \int_0^1 \gamma \left(\frac{Y(t)}{Y_L(t)}\right)^{1/\varepsilon} q_L(\nu,t) L^\beta x_L(t)^{1-\beta} d\nu \\
&= (1-\beta)\gamma Y(t)^{1/\varepsilon} Y_L(t)^{(\varepsilon-1)/\varepsilon}.
\end{aligned}
$$

As the same relation holds true for the H-machines, aggregate machine expenditures are given by

$$
X(t) = X_L(t) + X_H(t) = (1-\beta)Y(t)^{1/\varepsilon}\left[\gamma Y_L(t)^{(\varepsilon-1)/\varepsilon} + (1-\gamma)Y_H(t)^{(\varepsilon-1)/\varepsilon}\right] = (1-\beta)Y(t).
$$

Using those results, we can write the maximization problem as

$$
\max_{[C(t),Z_H(t),Z_L(t)]_{t=0}^\infty} \int_0^\infty \exp(-\rho)\frac{C(t)^{1-\theta}-1}{1-\theta}dt
$$

$$
\text{s.t.}\quad \beta Y(t) = C(t) + Z_L(t) + Z_H(t)
$$

$$
Y(t) = \left(\frac{1}{1-\beta}\right)^{1/\beta}\left[\gamma^{\varepsilon/\sigma}(LQ_L(t))^{(\sigma-1)/\sigma} + (1-\gamma)^{\varepsilon/\sigma}(HQ_H(t))^{(\sigma-1)/\sigma}\right]^{\frac{\sigma}{\sigma-1}},
$$

where $Q_L(t)$ and $Q_H(t)$ evolve according to the innovation possibilities frontier. As the social planner takes $Q_H(t)$ and $Q_L(t)$ as the two appropriate state variables, he is indifferent between the sectoral allocation of research expenditures $[z_L(\nu,t), z_H(\nu,t)]$ but cares only about the evolution of aggregate qualities $Q_L(t)$ and $Q_H(t)$. Therefore we already used the two control variables $Z_H(t)$ and $Z_L(t)$ as the aggregate research expenditures directed towards H and L technologies respectively. Using this notation, the innovation possibilities frontier is given by

$$
\dot{Q}_L(t) = (\lambda-1)\eta_L Z_L(t) \quad \text{and} \quad \dot{Q}_H(t) = (\lambda-1)\eta_H Z_H(t).
$$

Hence, the Pareto optimal allocation is the solution to the problem

$$\max_{[C(t),Z_L(t),Z_H(t)]_{t=0}^{\infty}} \int_0^\infty \exp(-\rho) \frac{C(t)^{1-\theta} - 1}{1-\theta} dt$$

$$
\begin{aligned}
\text{s.t.} \quad \beta Y(t) &= C(t) + Z_H(t) + Z_L(t) \\
\dot{Q}_L(t) &= (\lambda - 1)\eta_L Z_L(t) \\
\dot{Q}_H(t) &= (\lambda - 1)\eta_H Z_H(t) \\
Y(t) &= \left(\frac{1}{1-\beta}\right)^{1/\beta} \left[\gamma^{\varepsilon/\sigma}(LQ_L(t))^{(\sigma-1)/\sigma} + (1-\gamma)^{\varepsilon/\sigma}(HQ_H(t))^{(\sigma-1)/\sigma}\right]^{\frac{\sigma}{\sigma-1}}.
\end{aligned}
$$

This however is just a standard problem of optimal control with (once we solve the resource constraint for $C(t)$) two control variables $(Z_H(t), Z_L(t))$ and two state variables $(Q_L(t), Q_H(t))$. The current value Hamiltonian for this problem is given by

$$
\begin{aligned}
\hat{H}(Z_H, Z_L, Q_H, Q_L, \mu_H, \mu_L) &= \frac{[\beta Y(t) - Z_H(t) - Z_L(t)]^{1-\theta} - 1}{1-\theta} \\
&\quad + \mu_H(t)(\lambda - 1)\eta_H Z_H(t) + \mu_L(t)(\lambda - 1)\eta_L Z_L(t).
\end{aligned}
$$

The necessary first-order conditions with respect to the two control variables are given by

$$
\begin{aligned}
\hat{H}_{Z_H(t)} &= -C(t)^{-\theta} - \mu_H(t)(\lambda - 1)\eta_H = 0 \quad &\text{(S15.39)} \\
\hat{H}_{Z_L(t)} &= -C(t)^{-\theta} - \mu_L(t)(\lambda - 1)\eta_L = 0.
\end{aligned}
$$

Combining these, we get

$$1 = \frac{-C(t)^{-\theta}}{-C(t)^{-\theta}} = \frac{\mu_H(t)(\lambda - 1)\eta_H}{\mu_L(t)(\lambda - 1)\eta_L},$$

so that

$$\frac{\mu_H(t)}{\mu_L(t)} = \frac{\eta_L}{\eta_H}. \quad \text{(S15.40)}$$

Note that this also implies that

$$\frac{\dot{\mu}_H(t)}{\mu_H(t)} = \frac{\dot{\mu}_L(t)}{\mu_L(t)} = \frac{\dot{\mu}(t)}{\mu(t)}.$$

The first-order conditions with respect to the two state variables are given by

$$
\begin{aligned}
\hat{H}_{Q_H} &= -C(t)^{-\theta}\beta \frac{\partial Y(t)}{\partial Q_H(t)} = \rho\mu_H(t) - \dot{\mu}_H(t) \quad &\text{(S15.41)} \\
\hat{H}_{Q_L} &= -C(t)^{-\theta}\beta \frac{\partial Y(t)}{\partial Q_L(t)} = \rho\mu_L(t) - \dot{\mu}_L(t). \quad &\text{(S15.42)}
\end{aligned}
$$

As

$$
\begin{aligned}
\frac{\partial Y(t)}{\partial Q_H(t)} &= \left(\frac{1}{1-\beta}\right)^{(1-\beta)/\beta} \left[\gamma^{\varepsilon/\sigma}(LQ_L(t))^{(\sigma-1)/\sigma} + (1-\gamma)^{\varepsilon/\sigma}(HQ_H(t))^{(\sigma-1)/\sigma}\right]^{\frac{1}{\sigma-1}} \times \\
&\quad (1-\gamma)^{\varepsilon/\sigma} H^{(\sigma-1)/\sigma} Q_H(t)^{-1/\sigma}, \quad &\text{(S15.43)}
\end{aligned}
$$

(S15.41) and (S15.42) imply that

$$1 = \frac{\frac{\dot{\mu}_H(t)}{\mu_H(t)}}{\frac{\dot{\mu}_L(t)}{\mu_L(t)}} = \frac{\mu_H(t)^{-1}(1-\gamma)^{\varepsilon/\sigma} H^{(\sigma-1)/\sigma} Q_H(t)^{-1/\sigma} - \rho}{\mu_L(t)^{-1}\gamma^{\varepsilon/\sigma} L^{(\sigma-1)/\sigma} Q_L(t)^{-1/\sigma} - \rho},$$

so that

$$\mu_H(t)^{-1}(1-\gamma)^{\varepsilon/\sigma}H^{(\sigma-1)/\sigma}Q_H(t)^{-1/\sigma} = \mu_L(t)^{-1}\gamma^{\varepsilon/\sigma}L^{(\sigma-1)/\sigma}Q_L(t)^{-1/\sigma}.$$

Using (S15.40), the relative technology ratio in the Pareto optimal solution is given by

$$\frac{Q_H(t)}{Q_L(t)} = \left(\frac{\eta_H}{\eta_L}\right)^\sigma \left(\frac{1-\gamma}{\gamma}\right)^\varepsilon \left(\frac{H}{L}\right)^{(\sigma-1)}. \tag{S15.44}$$

Note that this coincides with the equilibrium technology ratio given in (S15.29). Hence, despite there being monopolistic distortions in the intermediary sectors, relative equilibrium technologies are chosen efficiently. This however does *not* imply that the equilibrium is efficient. To see this, let us derive the Pareto optimal growth rate. From the first-order condition in (S15.39) we know that

$$\frac{\dot{C}(t)}{C(t)} = -\frac{1}{\theta}\frac{\dot{\mu}_H(t)}{\mu_H(t)} = -\frac{1}{\theta}\frac{\dot{\mu}(t)}{\mu(t)}.$$

The growth rate of the costate $\mu_H(t)$ however is given in (S15.41) as

$$\begin{aligned}\frac{\dot{\mu}_H(t)}{\mu_H(t)} &= \frac{1}{\mu_H(t)}C(t)^{-\theta}\beta\frac{\partial Y(t)}{\partial Q_H(t)} + \rho \\ &= -(\lambda-1)\eta_H\beta\frac{\partial Y(t)}{\partial Q_H(t)} + \rho,\end{aligned} \tag{S15.45}$$

where the second equality uses (S15.39). But now note that (S15.44) implies that

$$(LQ_L(t))^{(\sigma-1)/\sigma} = (HQ_H(t))^{(\sigma-1)/\sigma}\left(\frac{\eta_L}{\eta_H}\right)^{\sigma-1}\left(\frac{\gamma}{1-\gamma}\right)^{\varepsilon(\sigma-1)/\sigma}\left(\frac{L}{H}\right)^{\sigma-1},$$

so that (S15.43) reduces to

$$\frac{\partial Y(t)}{\partial Q_H(t)} = \left(\frac{1}{1-\beta}\right)^{1/\beta}\left[\gamma^\varepsilon(\eta_L L)^{\sigma-1} + (1-\gamma)^\varepsilon(\eta_H H)^{\sigma-1}\right]^{\frac{1}{\sigma-1}}\eta_H^{-1}.$$

Hence (S15.45) gives us

$$\frac{\dot{\mu}_H(t)}{\mu_H(t)} = -(\lambda-1)\beta\left(\frac{1}{1-\beta}\right)^{1/\beta}\left[\gamma^\varepsilon(\eta_L L)^{\sigma-1} + (1-\gamma)^\varepsilon(\eta_H H)^{\sigma-1}\right]^{\frac{1}{\sigma-1}} + \rho.$$

The Pareto optimal growth rate is therefore given by (S15.39) as

$$g^S = \frac{\dot{C}(t)}{C(t)} = \frac{1}{\theta}\left((\lambda-1)\beta\left(\frac{1}{1-\beta}\right)^{1/\beta}\left[\gamma^\varepsilon(\eta_L L)^{\sigma-1} + (1-\gamma)^\varepsilon(\eta_H H)^{\sigma-1}\right]^{\frac{1}{\sigma-1}} - \rho\right), \tag{S15.46}$$

where we used that in the planner's solution all variables will grow at the same rate. To see if the Pareto optimal allocation features faster growth than the equilibrium, we have to compare (S15.46) with the equilibrium growth rate given in (S15.28). Doing so reveals that no unambiguous comparison can be made. The reason is that - as usual in Schumpeterian models - there are two counteracting effects, each of which can dominate. The distortion caused by monopolistic machine producers tends to make equilibrium growth too low. The business-stealing effect however, tends to make equilibrium growth excessive. Hence, no clear comparison can be made so that we can only conclude that the equilibrium growth rate (generically) does not equal the optimal growth rate.

Exercise 15.18, Part (f). In order to judge the relative merits of different models, it all depends on the topic you want to study. When we are just interested in studying the aggregate implications of directed technological change (for example the strong and weak equilibrium bias), the baseline model of directed technological change is simpler and provides the same economic intuition. However the Schumpeterian extension has some advantages. One concerns the richer transitional dynamics. Whereas in the baseline model, there is only research in one sector if the economy is off the BGP, the ones here seem to have more resemblance with real-world economies: there is an equilibrium where there is research in all sectors, but those sectors that have to catch up will innovate faster on the "stable arm". This seems to be a reasonable prediction. The current model has potentially more testable implications. One of those is, that - as innovation comes only from entrants - on the way to the BGP it will be sectors which are "younger", i.e. where quality is relatively low, where entry is more likely. Hence, there will be more churning in the sectors of the industry which grow faster. This could offer interesting applications in both political economy and when thinking about industrial policy and could not have been analyzed in the baseline model of directed technological change. Note however, that the last aspect is not specific to the Schumpeterian version of the directed technological change model. It is rather a general difference between Schumpeterian models and models of expanding varieties. Hence, for the specific aspect of directed technological change the simpler baseline model seems to be more appropriate.

Exercise 15.19

Exercise 15.19, Part (a). In a neoclassical-type model, each firm solves the problem

$$\max_{A,L} F(A, L) - wL - \Gamma(A).$$

Hence, the optimal technology and labor choices satisfy

$$F_L(A^*, L^*) = w \tag{S15.47}$$
$$F_A(A^*, L^*) = \Gamma'(A^*). \tag{S15.48}$$

Now suppose that w increases. From (S15.47) we know that the endogenous variables A^* and L^* change according to

$$dw = dF_L(A^*, L^*) = F_{LA}(A^*, L^*)dA^* + F_{LL}(A^*, L^*)dL^*. \tag{S15.49}$$

Additionally we can totally differentiate (S15.48). This yields

$$F_{AA}(A^*, L^*)dA^* + F_{AL}(A^*, L^*)dL^* = \Gamma''(A^*)dA^*,$$

which we can solve for

$$dL^* = \frac{\Gamma''(A^*) - F_{AA}(A^*, L^*)}{F_{AL}(A^*, L^*)}dA^*.$$

Substituting this in (S15.49) yields

$$dw = \left[F_{LA}(A^*, L^*) + F_{LL}(A^*, L^*)\frac{\Gamma''(A^*) - F_{AA}(A^*, L^*)}{F_{AL}(A^*, L^*)}\right]dA^*,$$

so that the implied change of the optimal technology level is given by

$$\frac{dA^*}{dw} = \frac{F_{AL}(A^*, L^*)}{F_{LL}(A^*, L^*)}\left(\Gamma''(A^*) - F_{AA}(A^*, L^*) + \frac{F_{LA}^2(A^*, L^*)}{F_{LL}(A^*, L^*)}\right)$$

$$= \frac{F_{AL}(A^*, L^*)}{F_{LL}(A^*, L^*)}\left(\Gamma''(A^*) - \frac{F_{LL}(A^*, L^*)F_{AA}(A^*, L^*) - F_{LA}^2(A^*, L^*)}{F_{LL}(A^*, L^*)}\right).$$

Now note that the last term $F_{LL}F_{AA} - F_{LA}^2$ is negative by the second order condition, that $F_{AL} > 0$ and $F_{LL} < 0$ as the production function is neoclassical and that $\Gamma'' \geq 0$ as the cost function is convex. Hence, $\frac{dA^*}{dw} < 0$ as required. The intuition is as follows: for a given level of technology A, a higher wage will reduce labor demand. This however will decrease the marginal returns of the technology level A (recall that $F_{AL} > 0$) so that a lower level of technology will be used.

Exercise 15.19, Part (b). Now consider the directed technological change model. As the only change vis-a-vis the model laid out in the book concerns the process of technological progress, the static equilibrium for given levels $N_L(t)$ and $N_H(t)$ is exactly the same as in the baseline model of directed technological change. First of all note, that this economy will not feature balanced growth. To see this, note that we can write the growth rate of output as

$$\frac{\dot{Y}(t)}{Y(t)} = \frac{\gamma_L Y_L(t)^{\frac{\varepsilon-1}{\varepsilon}} \frac{\dot{Y}_L(t)}{Y_L(t)} + \gamma_H Y_H(t)^{\frac{\varepsilon-1}{\varepsilon}} \frac{\dot{Y}_H(t)}{Y_H(t)}}{\gamma_L Y_L(t)^{\frac{\varepsilon-1}{\varepsilon}} + \gamma_H Y_H(t)^{\frac{\varepsilon-1}{\varepsilon}}},$$

so that growth is balanced if

$$\frac{\dot{Y}_L(t)}{Y_L(t)} = \frac{\dot{Y}_H(t)}{Y_H(t)} = \frac{\dot{Y}(t)}{Y(t)}.$$

In equilibrium, intermediary production levels are given by

$$Y_L(t) = \frac{1}{1-\beta} p_L(t)^{\frac{1-\beta}{\beta}} N_L(t)L \text{ and } Y_H(t) = \frac{1}{1-\beta} p_H(t)^{\frac{1-\beta}{\beta}} N_H(t)L$$

so that

$$\frac{\dot{Y}_L(t)}{Y_L(t)} = \frac{1-\beta}{\beta} \frac{\dot{p}_L(t)}{p_L(t)} + \frac{\dot{N}_L(t)}{N_L(t)} \text{ and } \frac{\dot{Y}_H(t)}{Y_H(t)} = \frac{1-\beta}{\beta} \frac{\dot{p}_H(t)}{p_H(t)} + \frac{\dot{N}_H(t)}{N_H(t)}.$$

Hence, growth is balanced if

$$\frac{\dot{N}_L(t)}{N_L(t)} - \frac{\dot{N}_H(t)}{N_H(t)} = \frac{\dot{N}_L(t)}{N_L(t)} = \frac{1-\beta}{\beta} \left[\frac{\dot{p}_H(t)}{p_H(t)} - \frac{\dot{p}_L(t)}{p_L(t)} \right], \tag{S15.50}$$

where we used that $\dot{N}_H(t) = 0$. Along the BGP interest rates $r(t)$ would need to be constant. From the free entry condition into research, the analysis in Chapter 15 established that this also requires that

$$1 = \eta_L V_L(t) = \frac{\eta_L \beta p_L(t) L}{r^*},$$

which immediately shows that $p_L(t)$ would need to be constant, i.e. $\frac{\dot{p}_L(t)}{p_L(t)} = 0$. But as we normalized the price of the final good to be one and this normalization is equivalent to setting

$$\gamma_L^\varepsilon p_L(t)^{1-\varepsilon} + \gamma_H^\varepsilon p_H(t)^{1-\varepsilon} = 1, \tag{S15.51}$$

it is clear that whenever $p_L(t)$ is constant, $p_H(t)$ also has to be constant. This however is only consistent with $\dot{N}_L(t) = 0$ as shown in (S15.50). Hence, all equilibria in this economy will either have no growth or will be unbalanced.

Let us focus on the first case. So suppose there was a steady state equilibrium where

$$\dot{N}_L(t) = 0,$$

i.e. $N_L(t)$ is constant at a level N_L^*. The equilibrium intermediary prices in the steady state of this economy are given by

$$\frac{p_H(t)}{p_L(t)} = \frac{\partial Y(t)/\partial Y_H(t)}{\partial Y(t)/\partial Y_L(t)} = \left(\frac{\gamma_H}{\gamma_L} \right)^{\frac{\varepsilon\beta}{\sigma}} \left(\frac{N_H H}{N_L^* L} \right)^{\frac{-\beta}{\sigma}}, \tag{S15.52}$$

which together with (S15.51) implies that intermediary prices are constant in the steady state. In the steady state final output is constant over time so that the consumer's Euler equation implies that

$$r(t) = \rho,$$

as consumption also has to be constant for product markets to clear. The value function of machine producers is still implicitly defined by the HJB equation

$$r(t)V_L(t) - \dot{V}_L(t) = \pi(t) = \beta p_L(t)^{1/\beta} L.$$

In the steady state we have that $r(t) = \rho$ and $p_L(t) = p_L$, so that $V_L(t)$ will be constant over time. In particular, the stable solution of the differential equation above is given by

$$V_L(t) = V_L = \frac{\beta p_L^{1/\beta} L}{\rho}. \tag{S15.53}$$

Hence, for this conjectured allocation to be an equilibrium, research firms' free entry condition has to be satisfied, i.e.

$$1 \geq \eta_L V_L = \eta_L \frac{\beta p_L^{1/\beta} L}{\rho}. \tag{S15.54}$$

Let us focus on the case, where this condition holds with equality. Prices p_L however are of course endogenous. Hence we have to use the price normalization and the equilibrium condition for intermediary prices (S15.52) to solve for p_L in terms of exogenous parameters. These two conditions are given by

$$1 = \gamma_L^\varepsilon p_L^{1-\varepsilon} + \gamma_H^\varepsilon p_H^{1-\varepsilon} \tag{S15.55}$$

$$\frac{p_H}{p_L} = \left(\frac{\gamma_H}{\gamma_L}\right)^{\frac{\varepsilon\beta}{\sigma}} \left(\frac{N_H H}{N_L^* L}\right)^{\frac{-\beta}{\sigma}}. \tag{S15.56}$$

Clearly (S15.55) and (S15.56) give us two equations in two unknowns (p_L and p_H) which we can solve for p_L. Doing so yields

$$
\begin{aligned}
1 &= \gamma_L^\varepsilon p_L^{1-\varepsilon} + \gamma_H^\varepsilon p_H^{1-\varepsilon} \\
&= \gamma_L^\varepsilon p_L^{1-\varepsilon} + \gamma_H^\varepsilon \left(\left(\frac{\gamma_H}{\gamma_L}\right)^{\frac{\varepsilon\beta}{\sigma}} \left(\frac{N_H}{N_L^*} \frac{H}{L}\right)^{\frac{-\beta}{\sigma}} p_L\right)^{1-\varepsilon} \\
&= p_L^{1-\varepsilon} \left(\gamma_L^{\frac{\varepsilon\beta(\varepsilon-1)}{\sigma}} (LN_L^*)^{-\frac{\sigma-1}{\sigma}}\right) \left[\gamma_L^{\varepsilon/\sigma} (LN_L^*)^{(\sigma-1)/\sigma} + \gamma_H^{\varepsilon/\sigma} (HN_H)^{(\sigma-1)/\sigma}\right],
\end{aligned}
$$

where we again made use of our definition of the derived elasticity of substitution $\sigma = 1 + (\varepsilon - 1)\beta$. Solving for p_L we get that

$$
\begin{aligned}
p_L &= \left[\frac{\gamma_L^{\varepsilon/\sigma} (LN_L^*)^{(\sigma-1)/\sigma} + \gamma_H^{\frac{\varepsilon}{\sigma}} (HN_H)^{\frac{\sigma-1}{\sigma}}}{\gamma_L^{-\frac{\varepsilon\beta(\varepsilon-1)}{\sigma}} (LN_L^*)^{\frac{\sigma-1}{\sigma}}}\right]^{1/(\varepsilon-1)} \\
&= \left[\gamma_L^{\frac{\varepsilon(\sigma-1)}{\sigma}} + \gamma_H^{\frac{\varepsilon}{\sigma}} \gamma_L^{\frac{\varepsilon\beta(\varepsilon-1)}{\sigma}} \left(\frac{HN_H}{LN_L^*}\right)^{\frac{\sigma-1}{\sigma}}\right]^{\beta/(\varepsilon-1)}. \tag{S15.57}
\end{aligned}
$$

Substituting this in (S15.54) shows that the steady state level of labor-augmenting technology N_L^* solves

$$\rho = \eta_L L \beta p_L^{1/\beta} = \eta_L \beta \left[L^{\sigma-1} \gamma_L^{-\frac{\varepsilon(\sigma-1)}{\sigma}} + \gamma_H^{\frac{\varepsilon}{\sigma}} \gamma_L^{-\frac{\varepsilon\beta(\varepsilon-1)}{\sigma}} \left(\frac{HN_H}{N_L^*} \right)^{\frac{\sigma-1}{\sigma}} L^{\frac{(\sigma-1)^2}{\sigma}} \right]^{\frac{1}{\sigma-1}}. \qquad (S15.58)$$

Using this we can now analyze the Habakkuk hypothesis which is developed in Habakkuk (1962). First of all note that (S15.58) implies that

$$\frac{\partial N_L^*}{\partial H} > 0, \qquad (S15.59)$$

i.e. the more land there is in a country (for a given level of labor), the higher the steady state level of labor-augmenting technology will be. To see this simply note that (S15.58) requires $\frac{H}{N_L^*}$ to be constant, so that (S15.59) immediately follows. If we think of the US being characterized by a larger supply of land, this shows that the Habakkuk hypothesis is confirmed by the directed technological change model, i.e. a larger supply of land triggers labor-augmenting technological progress.

However we could of course also consider the comparative statics of the steady state level of technology N_L^* with respect to L. From (S15.58) we find that

$$\frac{\partial N_L^*}{\partial L} > 0 \text{ if } \sigma > 1 \text{ and } \frac{\partial N_L^*}{\partial L} < 0 \text{ if } \sigma \text{ sufficiently low.}$$

For $\sigma > 1$, the RHS of (S15.58) is increasing in L. Hence, for (S15.58) to be satisfied at the higher level of L, the term $\left(\frac{HN_H}{N_L^*} \right)^{\frac{\sigma-1}{\sigma}}$ has to decrease, which (as $\sigma > 1$) requires N_L^* to increase. For the second case, note that (S15.58) requires (after cancelling L on both sides)

$$(N_L^*)^{-\frac{(\sigma-1)}{\sigma}} L^{\frac{(\sigma-1)(2\sigma-1)}{\sigma}}$$

to be constant. Hence,

$$\frac{\partial N_L^*}{\partial L} \propto 2\sigma - 1,$$

so that $\frac{\partial N_L^*}{\partial L} < 0$ if $\sigma < 1/2$.

The intuition for this ambiguous result is again rooted in the two counteracting forces of the market size and the price effect. Everything else equal, an increase in L makes the development of L-technologies more attractive (see (S15.53) which shows that the value of L-patents is increasing in L for given prices and interest rates). Hence, the price of L-intermediaries has to decrease in order for the free entry condition to be satisfied. From (S15.57) we see that p_L is decreasing in LN_L^*. Hence, LN_L^* has to increase. If σ is very small however, price are very responsive to such changes. To see this note that

$$\lim_{\sigma \to 0} \frac{d}{LN_L^*} \left(\frac{HN_H}{LN_L^*} \right)^{\frac{\sigma-1}{\sigma}} = \lim_{\sigma \to 0} \frac{1-\sigma}{\sigma} \left(\frac{HN_H}{LN_L^*} \right)^{\frac{\sigma-1}{\sigma}} \frac{1}{LN_L^*} = \infty.$$

This of course just revisits the special case of the production function being Leontief if the elasticity of substitution goes to zero. Hence, the price effect induced by an increase in the labor force would be so strong that it would dominate the market size effect and hence violate the free entry condition. If that is the case, N_L^* will decrease to add upward pressure to intermediary prices. If $\sigma > 1/2$, the price effect is sufficiently weak such that if the technology level would not adjust, the market size effect would dominate and research would be profitable (which is inconsistent with being at a steady state).

The Habakkuk hypothesis conjectures that countries which are labor scarce have a higher technology level to respond to high wages. Hence, this hypothesis requires that

$$\frac{\partial N_L^*}{\partial L} < 0.$$

The discussion above then established that the directed technological model is consistent with the Habakkuk hypothesis if the elasticity of substitution σ is sufficiently small. For a more detailed discussion of the Habakkuk hypothesis in the context of models of directed technological change, see also Acemoglu (2002).

Exercise 15.24*

Let us first show that the model has a BGP with constant interest rates (and consumption and income growth) and then show that it is indeed the only one. To reduce notation, let us drop the time indices. Recall first that equilibrium intermediate prices are given by

$$\frac{p_K}{p_L} = \left(\frac{\gamma_K}{\gamma_L}\right)^{\frac{\varepsilon\beta}{\sigma}} \left(\frac{N_K}{N_L}\right)^{\frac{-\beta}{\sigma}} \left(\frac{K}{L}\right)^{\frac{-\beta}{\sigma}}. \tag{S15.60}$$

Equilibrium factor payments are given by

$$\frac{w_K}{w_L} = \frac{r}{w} = \left(\frac{\gamma_K}{\gamma_L}\right)^{\frac{\varepsilon}{\sigma}} \left(\frac{N_K}{N_L}\right)^{\frac{\sigma-1}{\sigma}} \left(\frac{K}{L}\right)^{\frac{-1}{\sigma}},$$

so that

$$\frac{rK}{wL} = \left(\frac{\gamma_K}{\gamma_L}\right)^{\frac{\varepsilon}{\sigma}} \left(\frac{N_K}{N_L}\right)^{\frac{\sigma-1}{\sigma}} \left(\frac{K}{L}\right)^{\frac{\sigma-1}{\sigma}}. \tag{S15.61}$$

The innovation possibilities frontier featuring extreme state dependence reads

$$\dot{N}_L = N_L \eta_L S_L \text{ and } \dot{N}_K = N_K \eta_K S_K$$

so that equilibrium on the technology market requires that

$$w_S(t) = \eta_L N_L V_L = \eta_K N_K V_K. \tag{S15.62}$$

Along the BGP interest rates are constant so that the value functions are given by $V_L = \frac{\pi_L}{r}$ and $V_K = \frac{\pi_K}{r}$ so that (S15.62) implies that

$$\frac{N_K}{N_L} = \left(\frac{\eta_K}{\eta_L}\right)^{-1} \frac{\pi_L}{\pi_K} = \left(\frac{\eta_K}{\eta_L}\right)^{-1} \left(\frac{p_L}{p_K}\right)^{\frac{1}{\beta}} \frac{L}{K},$$

where we used the usual expression of equilibrium profits $\pi^L = \beta p_L^{1/\beta} L$. From (S15.60) we then get that along the BGP technologies are given by

$$\left(\frac{N_K}{N_L}\right)^{\frac{\sigma-1}{\sigma}} = \left(\frac{\eta_K}{\eta_L}\right)^{-1} \left(\frac{K}{L}\right)^{-\frac{\sigma-1}{\sigma}} \left(\frac{\gamma_K}{\gamma_L}\right)^{-\frac{\varepsilon}{\sigma}}. \tag{S15.63}$$

From (S15.61) and (S15.63) we therefore get that along the BGP factor shares are constant, i.e.

$$\frac{rK}{wL} = \left(\frac{\eta_K}{\eta_L}\right)^{-1}. $$

Now note that (S15.61) and (S15.63) imply that $\frac{N_K}{N_L}\frac{K}{L}$ is constant, as

$$\frac{N_K}{N_L}\frac{K}{L} = \left(\frac{rK}{wL}\right)^{\sigma/(\sigma-1)} \left(\frac{\gamma_K}{\gamma_L}\right)^{-\varepsilon/(\sigma-1)} = \left(\frac{\eta_K}{\eta_L}\right)^{\frac{-\sigma}{\sigma-1}} \left(\frac{\gamma_K}{\gamma_L}\right)^{\frac{-\varepsilon}{\sigma-1}}. \tag{S15.64}$$

Hence,

$$0 = \frac{\dot{N}_K}{N_K} - \frac{\dot{N}_L}{N_L} + \frac{\dot{K}}{K} - \frac{\dot{L}}{L}.$$

And as $\dot{L} = 0$, we get

$$\frac{\dot{N}_L}{N_L} - \frac{\dot{N}_K}{N_K} = \frac{\dot{K}}{K} = s_K. \tag{S15.65}$$

Along the conjectured BGP allocation, interest rates have to be constant. Interest rates are given by

$$r = p_K \frac{\partial Y_K}{\partial K} = p_K \frac{\beta}{1-\beta} N_K p_K^{\frac{1-\beta}{\beta}} = \frac{\beta}{1-\beta} N_K p_K^{\frac{1}{\beta}}.$$

As intermediate prices are equal to

$$p_K = \frac{\partial Y}{\partial Y_K} = [\gamma_L Y_L^{\frac{\varepsilon-1}{\varepsilon}} + \gamma_K Y_K^{\frac{\varepsilon-1}{\varepsilon}}]^{\frac{1}{\varepsilon-1}} \gamma_K Y_K^{-\frac{1}{\varepsilon}},$$

and equilibrium intermediate productions are just

$$Y_L = \frac{1}{1-\beta} p_L^{(1-\beta)/\beta} N_L L \text{ and } Y_L = \frac{1}{1-\beta} p_K^{(1-\beta)/\beta} N_K K,$$

we get

$$\begin{aligned}
p_K &= \left(\gamma_L Y_L^{\frac{\varepsilon-1}{\varepsilon}} + \gamma_K Y_K^{\frac{\varepsilon-1}{\varepsilon}} \right)^{\frac{1}{\varepsilon-1}} \gamma_K Y_K^{-\frac{1}{\varepsilon}} \\
&= \left(\gamma_L \left(\frac{Y_L}{Y_K} \right)^{\frac{\varepsilon-1}{\varepsilon}} + \gamma_K \right)^{\frac{1}{\varepsilon-1}} \gamma_K Y_K^{-\frac{1}{\varepsilon}} Y_K^{\frac{1}{\varepsilon}} \\
&= \left(\gamma_L \left(\left(\frac{p_L}{p_K} \right)^{\frac{1-\beta}{\beta}} \frac{N_L L}{N_K K} \right)^{\frac{\varepsilon-1}{\varepsilon}} + \gamma_K \right)^{\frac{1}{\varepsilon-1}} \gamma_K
\end{aligned}$$

and hence

$$r = \frac{\beta}{1-\beta} N_K \gamma_K^{\frac{1}{\beta}} \left(\gamma_L \left(\left(\frac{p_L}{p_K} \right)^{\frac{1-\beta}{\beta}} \frac{N_L L}{N_K K} \right)^{\frac{\varepsilon-1}{\varepsilon}} + \gamma_K \right)^{\frac{1}{(\varepsilon-1)\beta}}.$$

Substituting from (S15.60) we also know that

$$\begin{aligned}
\left(\left(\frac{p_L}{p_K} \right)^{\frac{1-\beta}{\beta}} \frac{N_L L}{N_K K} \right)^{\frac{\varepsilon-1}{\varepsilon}} &= \left(\left(\left(\frac{\gamma_L}{\gamma_K} \right)^{\frac{\varepsilon\beta}{\sigma}} \left(\frac{N_L L}{N_K K} \right)^{\frac{-\beta}{\sigma}} \right)^{\frac{1-\beta}{\beta}} \frac{N_L L}{N_K K} \right)^{\frac{\varepsilon-1}{\varepsilon}} \\
&= \left(\frac{\gamma_L}{\gamma_K} \right)^{\frac{(\varepsilon-1)(1-\beta)}{\sigma}} \left(\frac{N_L L}{N_K K} \right)^{\frac{\sigma-(1-\beta)}{\sigma} \frac{\varepsilon-1}{\varepsilon}}.
\end{aligned}$$

Now observe that

$$\frac{\sigma - (1-\beta)}{\sigma} \frac{\varepsilon-1}{\varepsilon} = \frac{1 + (\varepsilon-1)\beta - (1-\beta)}{\sigma} \frac{\sigma-1}{\beta\varepsilon} = \frac{\sigma-1}{\sigma}$$

and

$$\frac{(\varepsilon-1)(1-\beta)}{\sigma} = \frac{\varepsilon-1-(\varepsilon-1)\beta}{\sigma} = \frac{\varepsilon-\sigma}{\sigma}.$$

to finally arrive at equilibrium interest rates, which are given by

$$
\begin{aligned}
r &= \frac{\beta}{1-\beta} N_K \gamma_K^{\frac{1}{\beta}} \left(\gamma_L \left(\frac{\gamma_L}{\gamma_K} \right)^{\frac{\varepsilon-\sigma}{\sigma}} \left(\frac{N_L L}{N_K K} \right)^{\frac{\sigma-1}{\sigma}} + \gamma_K \right)^{\frac{1}{(\varepsilon-1)\beta}} \\
&= \frac{\beta}{1-\beta} N_K \gamma_K^{\frac{\varepsilon}{\sigma}} \left(\gamma_L^{\frac{\varepsilon}{\sigma}} \left(\frac{N_L L}{N_K K} \right)^{\frac{\sigma-1}{\sigma}} + \gamma_K^{\frac{\varepsilon}{\sigma}} \right)^{\frac{1}{\varepsilon-1}}.
\end{aligned}
\tag{S15.66}
$$

As $\frac{N_L L}{N_K K}$ is constant (see (S15.64)), (S15.66) implies that interest rates are constant, whenever N_K is constant. Using (S15.65), this implies that

$$
\frac{\dot{N}_L}{N_L} = \frac{\dot{K}}{K} = s_K,
$$

i.e. there is a BGP, where interest rates are constant and technological progress is purely labor-augmenting. This proves existence of a BGP.

Let us now turn to uniqueness. Given the results above, this is also easily verified. For a BGP we need that interest rates are constant. In such a BGP interest rates are given in (S15.66). From the equilibrium on the innovation market we also know that $\frac{N_L L}{N_K K}$ is constant (see (S15.64)). But then it is immediately clear that there is no capital-augmenting progress, i.e. $\dot{N}_K = 0$ as otherwise interest rates could not be constant. Then it follows from (S15.65) that in any BGP equilibrium, technological progress is purely labor-augmenting.

Exercise 15.27

Exercise 15.27, Part (a). To show the required result, we have to determine the value of having skills and confront this with the costs of acquiring those. To derive the value of being skilled, let us use the HJB equation. We denote the value of being skilled at time t for an individual x by $V_{HS}(x,t)$. The HJB equation defines $V_{HS}(x,t)$ implicitly by

$$
r(t)V_{HS}(x,t) - \dot{V}_{HS}(x,t) = w_H(t) - v V_{HS}(x,t).
\tag{S15.67}
$$

To understand (S15.67) consider the asset-pricing interpretation of the HJB equation. The return to the asset of being skilled consist of three parts. First of all we have the current dividends $w_H(t)$. Secondly we have the equilibrium appreciation of the asset $\dot{V}_{HS}(x,t)$. And finally the asset could lose its value if the individual dies. In equilibrium the assets must be "priced" such that those returns are equal to $r(t)V_{HS}(x,t)$. Note we appeal here to a separation theorem (see Section 10.1). $V_{HS}(x,t)$ only measures the value of acquiring skills in monetary terms. By assuming that individuals chose their schooling decisions to maximize $V_{HS}(x,t)$, we implicitly assume that individuals maximize their lifetime wealth and then chose consumption expenditures given this wealth. See the discussion following Theorem 10.1 and the solution to exercise 10.2 for an analysis when this approach is appropriate.

Along the BGP interest rates are constant and equal to r^*. This however is not true for wages. Equilibrium wages are given by

$$
w_H(t) = \frac{\partial p_H(t)Y_H(t)}{\partial H} = \frac{\beta}{1-\beta} p_H(t)^{1/\beta} N_H(t).
$$

The analysis in the Chapter established that along the BGP intermediary prices $p_H(t)$ and $p_L(t)$ are constant so that wages grow at the rate of technological progress (which is also equal to the growth rate of the economy), say g. As neither wages, nor interest rates depend on x, $V_{HS}(x,t)$ will also be independent of x. Hence, let us denote the value of being skilled by $V_{HS}(t)$. Using those results, (S15.67) simplifies to

$$r^* V_{HS}(t) - \dot{V}_{HS}(t) = \frac{\beta}{1-\beta} p_H^{1/\beta} N_H(t) - v V_{HS}(t).$$

The stable solution of this differential equation is given by

$$V_{HS}(t) = \frac{w_H(t)}{r^* + v - g} = \frac{\frac{\beta}{1-\beta} p_H^{1/\beta}}{r^* + v - g} N_H(t).$$

The same reasoning holds true for the value of not having skills $V_{LS}(t)$. Hence it is clear that

$$\frac{V_{HS}(t)}{V_{LS}(t)} = \frac{w_H(t)}{w_L(t)} \equiv \omega(t). \tag{S15.68}$$

Now let us determine the costs of acquiring skills $\zeta(t,x)$. The costs are just the discounted value of foregone earnings (priced at the low wage). As individual x starting education at time t foregoes wages in the interval $[t, t+K_x]$, $\zeta(t,x)$ is given by

$$
\begin{aligned}
\zeta(t,x) &= \int_t^{t+K_x} \exp\left(-(r^*+v)(\tau-t)\right) w_L(\tau) d\tau \\
&= w_L(t) \int_t^{t+K_x} \exp\left(-(r^*+v-g)(\tau-t)\right) d\tau \\
&= \frac{w_L(t)}{r^*+v-g}(1 - \exp\left(-(r^*+v-g)K_x\right)) \\
&= V_{LS}(t)(1 - \exp\left(-(r^*+v-g)K_x\right)),
\end{aligned}
$$

where we used that $w_L(\tau) = w_L(t)\exp(g(\tau-t))$ as wages grow at the (constant) rate g. As the benefits of having acquired skills only accrue in the future, the net value of skill acquisition of individual x is given by

$$
\begin{aligned}
\mathcal{U}_S(t,x) &= \exp[-(r^*+v)K_x] (V_{HS}(t+K_x) - V_{LS}(t+K_x)) - \zeta(t,x) \\
&= \exp[-(r^*+v-g)K_x] (V_{HS}(t) - V_{LS}(t)) - V_{LS}(t)(1 - \exp[-(r^*+v-g)K_x]) \\
&= \exp[-(r^*+v-g)K_x]V_{HS}(t) - V_{LS}(t).
\end{aligned}
$$

This is an intuitive expression: you could either start earning high wages in K_x periods or you could start earning low skilled wages today. In case the former exceed the latter, the net value of acquiring skills is positive and the individual will join the skilled workforce. Now consider two individuals $x' < x$ (where we "order" the individuals such that $K_{x'} < K_x$). From above we get that

$$\mathcal{U}_S(t,x') - \mathcal{U}_S(t,x) = (\exp[-(r^*+v-g)K_{x'}] - \exp[-(r^*+v-g)K_x]) V_{HS}(t) > 0$$

as $V_{HS}(t) > 0$ and $K_{x'} < K_x$. Hence, whenever it is worthwhile for x to acquire skills, all individuals $x' < x$ will also acquire skills as their net value of acquiring skills is strictly higher.

To prove the cutoff-form of the equilibrium, i.e. that there exits some $\bar{x}$ such that x acquires skills if and only if $x \leq \bar{x}$, consider again $\mathcal{U}_S(t,x)$. As

$$\lim_{K_x \to 0} \mathcal{U}_S(t,x) = V_{HS}(t) - V_{LS}(t) > 0 \text{ and } \lim_{K_x \to \infty} \mathcal{U}_S(t,x) = -V_{LS}(t) < 0,$$

and

$$\frac{\partial \mathcal{U}_S(t,x)}{\partial x} = -(r^*+v-g)\exp[-(r^*+v-g)K_x]V_{HS}(t)\frac{\partial K_x}{\partial x} < 0,$$

as $\frac{\partial K_x}{\partial x} > 0$ and $\mathcal{U}_S(t,x)$ is continuous by the continuity of K_x, there exists $\bar{x}$ such that

$$\mathcal{U}_S(t,\bar{x}) = \exp[-(r^* + v - g)K_{\bar{x}}]V_{HS}(t) - V_{LS}(t) = 0.$$

And as $\bar{x}$ is indifferent between acquiring skills or not, all individuals $x < \bar{x}$ strictly prefer acquiring skills, whereas all $x > \bar{x}$ are better off staying unskilled.

Exercise 15.27, Part (b). Let us now derive the equilibrium supply of skilled and unskilled workers. Note that at every point in time, people can be in three possible states - they could either be skilled or unskilled workers or they could be in school. Hence let us denote these states by $L(t), S(t)$ and $H(t)$ respectively. Let us first start to characterize $L(t)$. The dynamics of $L(t)$ are given by

$$\dot{L}(t) = -vL(t) + v(1 - \Gamma(K_{\bar{x}})), \qquad (S15.69)$$

as each period there is a flow rate of death of v in the population of low skilled workers and each period v people are born and a fraction $1 - \Gamma(K_{\bar{x}})$ (namely those with $x > \bar{x}$) enter the labor force immediately. Now consider the skilled workforce. Let us define the density of Γ by γ. Using this, the set of people $H(t)$ evolves according to

$$\dot{H}(t) = -vH(t) + \int_0^{\bar{K}} v\gamma(k)\exp(-vk)dk. \qquad (S15.70)$$

To understand (S15.70) note that each period a fraction v of skilled people dies. This is captured by the first term. Additionally, the skilled workforce accumulates by individuals graduating. Consider the set of individuals characterized by having a schooling requirement of k periods. At $t - k$ periods ago, this set had a measure $v\gamma(k)$ because the entire new born population has a size v and each population is drawn randomly from Γ. However, from this set each period a fraction v dies. Hence, from all those individuals who need k periods of schooling and were born k periods ago, only $\exp(-vk)$ survive. Putting this together shows that $v\gamma(k)\exp(-vk)$ denotes exactly the size of graduates in t who need k periods of schooling. Aggregating this over all schooling requirements $k = [0, \bar{K}]$ which actually decide to go to school yields the number of graduates in t.

The number of people at school $S(t)$ can then simply be derived using the accounting identity

$$S(t) = 1 - L(t) - H(t). \qquad (S15.71)$$

Let us first consider the case of $v > 0$. Along the BGP, $L(t), S(t)$ and $H(t)$ are constant and equal to its respective BGP values L^*, S^* and H^*. Using (S15.69), (S15.70) and (S15.71) we get that

$$\dot{L}(t) = 0 \Rightarrow L^* = 1 - \Gamma(K_{\bar{x}}) \qquad (S15.72)$$
$$\dot{S}(t) = 0 \Rightarrow S^* = 1 - L^* - H^*$$
$$\dot{H}(t) = 0 \Rightarrow H^* = \int_0^{\bar{K}} \gamma(k)\exp(-vk)dk. \qquad (S15.73)$$

Using those BGP values from (S15.72) and (S15.73) we therefore find that

$$\frac{H^*}{L^*} = \frac{\int_0^{\bar{K}} \gamma(k)\exp(-vk)dk}{1 - \Gamma(K_{\bar{x}})}.$$

Let us now consider the limiting case, where the population stays the same, i.e. $v \to 0$. As

$$\lim_{v \to 0} \int_0^{\bar{K}} \gamma(k)\exp(-vk)dk = \int_0^{\bar{K}} \gamma(k)dk = \Gamma(\bar{K})$$

we get that

$$\lim_{v \to 0} \frac{H^*}{L^*} = \frac{\Gamma(\bar{K})}{1 - \Gamma(\bar{K})},$$

where we used that $\Gamma(K_{\bar{x}}) = \Gamma(\bar{K})$. This indeed shows that

$$\frac{H^*}{L^*} \approx \frac{\Gamma(\bar{K})}{1 - \Gamma(\bar{K})} \tag{S15.74}$$

if v is small. The intuition for this result is, that if there is no replacement in the population, at some point everyone who decided to acquire skills (i.e. a measure $\Gamma(\bar{K})$ of the population) will have graduated and hence will have joined the skilled work force.

Exercise 15.27, Part (c). Up to now we have characterized the economy for a given value of the cutoff $K_{\hat{x}} \equiv \bar{K}$. But $\bar{K}$ is of course endogenous as it is implicitly defined by.

$$\mathcal{U}_S(t, \bar{x}) = \exp[-(r^* + v - g)\bar{K}]V_{HS}(t) - V_{LS}(t) = 0.$$

Solving this for $\bar{K}$ yields

$$\bar{K} = \frac{1}{r^* + v - g} \log\left(\frac{V_{HS}(t)}{V_{LS}(t)}\right),$$

which - upon substituting (S15.68) - gives us the required equation

$$\bar{K} = \frac{\log \omega}{r^* + v - g}.$$

Note that we explicitly noted that along the BGP the skill premium will be constant. Using this in (S15.74), we can express the relative skill supply as a function of the skill-premium $\omega(t)$ as

$$\frac{H^{SS}}{L^{SS}} = \frac{\Gamma\left(\frac{\log \omega}{r^* + v - g}\right)}{1 - \Gamma\left(\frac{\log \omega}{r^* + v - g}\right)}. \tag{S15.75}$$

Exercise 15.27, Part (d). In equilibrium, the relative demand for skills has to be equal to the relative supply. In the baseline model of directed technological change, the labor demand curve was given in (15.30) as

$$\omega = \eta^\sigma \gamma^\varepsilon \left(\frac{H}{L}\right)^{\sigma - 2}.$$

Combining this with the supply curve in (S15.75), we get that the equilibrium level of relative skills solves the equation

$$\frac{H}{L} = \frac{\Gamma\left(\frac{\log(\eta^\sigma \gamma^\varepsilon) + (\sigma - 2)\log\left(\frac{H}{L}\right)}{r^* + v - g}\right)}{1 - \Gamma\left(\frac{\log(\eta^\sigma \gamma^\varepsilon) + (\sigma - 2)\log\left(\frac{H}{L}\right)}{r^* + v - g}\right)}. \tag{S15.76}$$

Hence, this economy has a unique equilibrium if and only if (S15.76) has a unique solution. To show that this is not necessarily the case, note that the RHS of (S15.76) is not necessarily decreasing in $\frac{H}{L}$. This is seen as

$$\frac{\partial}{\partial \frac{H}{L}} \left[\frac{\Gamma\left(\frac{\log(\eta^\sigma \gamma^\varepsilon) + (\sigma - 2)\log\left(\frac{H}{L}\right)}{r^* + v - g}\right)}{1 - \Gamma\left(\frac{\log(\eta^\sigma \gamma^\varepsilon) + (\sigma - 2)\log\left(\frac{H}{L}\right)}{r^* + v - g}\right)} \right] = \frac{\frac{1}{r^* + v - g}\left(\frac{H}{L}\right)^{-1}\gamma\left(\frac{\log(\eta^\sigma \gamma^\varepsilon) + (\sigma - 2)\log\left(\frac{H}{L}\right)}{r^* + v - g}\right)}{\left(1 - \Gamma\left(\frac{\log(\eta^\sigma \gamma^\varepsilon) + (\sigma - 2)\log\left(\frac{H}{L}\right)}{r^* + v - g}\right)\right)^2} (\sigma - 2),$$

where again $\gamma(.)$ denotes the pdf of Γ. Note in particular that

$$sgn\left(\frac{\partial}{\partial \frac{H}{L}}\left[\frac{\Gamma(\frac{\log(\eta^\sigma\gamma^\varepsilon)+(\sigma-2)\log(\frac{H}{L})}{r^*+v-g})}{1-\Gamma(\frac{\log(\eta^\sigma\gamma^\varepsilon)+(\sigma-2)\log(\frac{H}{L})}{r^*+v-g})}\right]\right) = sgn\left(\sigma - 2\right).$$

So the RHS of (S15.76) is increasing if there is strong equilibrium bias. Hence, the existence of strong equilibrium bias is a necessary condition for there to exist multiple equilibria. If (in case $\sigma > 2$) this economy will have multiple equilibria is then dependent on the functional form of Γ and other parameters (determining r^* and g). The economic intuition is as follows. If ω is low, not many people acquire skill and research firms respond to this by only directing little research efforts towards $N_H(t)$. As this in turn implies that ω is indeed low, this is one equilibrium. But suppose ω is high. Then many people acquire skills. The market size effect induces directed technological change, i.e. firm invest in technology which is biased towards high skilled labor. This increases their relative marginal product ceteris paribus and if $\sigma > 2$ this effect is strong enough to make the demand curve upward sloping so that ω is indeed high and this can also be an equilibrium. Hence, the reason why multiple equilibria can exist, is exactly the complementarity (on the aggregate level) between individuals' skill decision and research firms' innovation decision. For further discussions we also refer to Acemoglu (2003).

Chapter 16: Stochastic Dynamic Programming

Exercise 16.4*

Consider the mapping

$$Tf(x,z) = \max_{y \in G(x,z)} \left\{ U(x,y,z) + \beta \int f(y,z') Q(z,dz') \right\}. \qquad \text{(S16.1)}$$

Note that when f is continuous and bounded, Tf is also continuous from Berge's Maximum Theorem (cf. Theorem A.16) and bounded. We also claim that when $f(x,z)$ is concave in x for all $z \in \mathcal{Z}$, $Tf(x,z)$ is strictly concave in x for all $z \in \mathcal{Z}$. To see this, let $z \in \mathcal{Z}$, $x', x'' \in X$ such that $x' \neq x''$ and $\alpha \in (0,1)$, and define $x_\alpha \equiv \alpha x' + (1-\alpha)x''$. Let $y' \in G(x',z)$ and $y'' \in G(x'',z)$ be solutions to Problem (S16.1) with vectors x' and x'', so that

$$Tf(x',z) = U(x',y',z) + \beta \int f(y',z') Q(z,dz') \qquad \text{(S16.2)}$$

$$Tf(x'',z) = U(x'',y'',z) + \beta \int f(y'',z') Q(z,dz').$$

By Assumption 16.3, $G(x,z)$ is convex in x, hence $y_\alpha \equiv \alpha y' + (1-\alpha)y'' \in G(x_\alpha,z)$, moreover

$$
\begin{aligned}
Tf(x_\alpha,z) &\geq U(x_\alpha,y_\alpha,z) + \beta \int f(y_\alpha,z') Q(z,dz') \\
&> \alpha \left[U(x',y',z) + \beta \int f(y',z') Q(z,dz') \right] \\
&\quad + (1-\alpha) \left[U(x'',y'',z) + \beta \int f(y'',z') Q(z,dz') \right] \\
&= \alpha Tf(x',z) + (1-\alpha) Tf(x'',z)
\end{aligned}
$$

where the first line follows since Tf is the solution to Problem (S16.1), the second line since U is strictly concave from Assumption 16.3 and f is assumed to be concave, and the last line from Eq. (S16.2). This proves our claim that Tf is strictly concave.

Let $\mathbf{C}'(X \times \mathcal{Z})$ be the set of continuous, bounded functions that are concave in x for all z, and $\mathbf{C}''(X \times \mathcal{Z})$ the set of continuous, bounded functions that are strictly concave in x for all z. We have shown that for all $f \in \mathbf{C}'(X \times \mathcal{Z})$, Tf lies in $\mathbf{C}''(X \times \mathcal{Z})$. Note that the set $\mathbf{C}'(X \times \mathcal{Z})$ is complete in the sup norm. Moreover, the operator T satisfies Blackwell's (1965) sufficient conditions and hence is a contraction mapping over $\mathbf{C}'(X \times \mathcal{Z})$. Hence, by Theorem 6.7, there exists $V \in \mathbf{C}'(X \times \mathcal{Z})$ such that $TV = V$, that is, the unique solution to Problem 16.2 is concave in x for all z. Moreover, since T maps $\mathbf{C}'(X \times \mathcal{Z})$ to $\mathbf{C}''(X \times \mathcal{Z})$, we also have that $V = TV$ is strictly concave in x for all z, as desired.

Since V is strictly concave and continuous, Problem 16.2 has a unique solution for each z, which we denote by the policy function $\pi(x,z)$. By Berge's Maximum Theorem (cf. Theorem A.16), the policy function is continuous, as desired.

Exercise 16.8

Let us consider CRRA preferences for simplicity, i.e. let $u(c) = \left(c^{1-\theta} - 1\right)/1 - \theta$ for $\theta > 0$. Then, the stochastic Euler equation implies

$$\mathbb{E}_t \left[\left(\frac{c(t+1)}{c(t)} \right)^{-\theta} \right] = \frac{1}{\beta(1+r)}. \tag{S16.3}$$

An excess sensitivity test regresses consumption growth $c(t+1)/c(t)$ on current income $w(t)$ and some control variables $\mathbf{x}(t) \equiv [x(1),..,x(n)]$ to see whether current income predicts future consumption growth, that is it runs a regression along the lines

$$\frac{c(t+1)}{c(t)} = \gamma_0 + w(t)\gamma_w + \mathbf{x}(t)\gamma_x + \varepsilon(t), \text{ for } t = 0, ..., T.$$

A positive coefficient on current income is interpreted as excess sensitivity. In general, for a stochastic income stream, Eq. (S16.3) does not rule out excess sensitivity for any θ other than $\theta = -1$ which corresponds to the case of quadratic utility. To see this formally, note that when $\theta = -1$, Eq. (S16.3) implies $E_t[c(t+1)/c(t)] = 1/\beta(1+r)$, thus if the data is generated by the model, the plim of the OLS estimate $\hat{\gamma} = (\hat{\gamma}_0, \hat{\gamma}_w, \hat{\gamma}_x)$ will be given by

$$\hat{\gamma}_0 = \frac{1}{\beta(1+r)}, \hat{\gamma}_w = 0, \hat{\gamma}_x = \mathbf{0}.$$

Hence if $\theta = -1$, the coefficient on $w(t)$ will be asymptotically 0. However, this is not necessarily the case if $\theta \neq 1$ and the regression coefficient on $w(t)$ could be significant even if the data is generated by the above model. Zeldes (1989) provides numerical solutions when $\theta > 0$ and shows that consumption will typically display excess sensitivity, especially when consumption is close to zero. Caballero (1990) analyzes the behavior of consumption with CARA utility and shows that the precautionary savings motive can generate excess sensitivity.

Exercise 16.10

In this case, the consumer's value function equation is still given by

$$V(a, w) = \max_{a' \in [-b_1, (1+r)a+w]} u\left(a(1+r) + w - a'\right) + \beta E\left[V\left(a', w'\right) \mid w\right].$$

A similar analysis as in Section 16.5.1 yields the Euler equation

$$u'(c(t)) = \beta(1+r) E\left[u'(c(t+1)) \mid \Omega_t\right],$$

where Ω_t denotes the information set of the household at time t, which includes the wages $w(t)$ and the current asset level $a(t)$. With quadratic utility, this Euler equation implies

$$c(t) = \phi(1 - \beta(1+r)) + \beta(1+r) E[c(t+1) \mid \Omega_t]. \tag{S16.4}$$

Let $\Omega_t' = \{\omega \mid c(t \mid \omega) = c(t)\}$ be the set of events over which the consumption at time t is equal to $c(t)$. Note that $\Omega_t \subset \Omega_t'$ but Ω_t' potentially has some events $\omega' \notin \Omega_t$ such that $w(t \mid \omega') \neq w(t)$ and $a(t \mid \omega') \neq a(t)$, that is, other income and current asset level pairs that yield a current consumption $c(t)$. Taking expectations of Eq. (S16.4) conditional on Ω_t', we have

$$\begin{aligned} c(t) &= \phi(1 - \beta(1+r)) + \beta(1+r) E\left[E[c(t+1) \mid \Omega_t] \mid \Omega_t'\right] \\ &= \phi(1 - \beta(1+r)) + \beta(1+r) E\left[c(t+1) \mid \Omega_t'\right], \end{aligned} \tag{S16.5}$$

where the second line uses the law of iterated expectations. In words, when the excess sensitivity test holds for an information set, it also holds for coarser information sets in which the current level of consumption is held constant at $c(t)$.

Note that an econometrician who believes that w is independently distributed will not control for $w(t)$ even if he observes it. Hence, he will run a regression identical to the one that an econometrician who does not observe $w(t)$ would run. Eq. (S16.5) shows that this regression should also find a zero coefficient on current income as long as the econometrician conditions on $c(t)$. Thus, the excess sensitivity test will not reject simply because the econometrician incorrectly believes that $w(t)$ is independently distributed.

Exercise 16.11*

Exercise 16.11, Part (a). Recall that the consumer chooses a stochastic process for consumption $\{c(t)\}_{t=0}^{\infty}$ to maximize utility subject to budget constraints, that is she solves

$$V^*(a(0), w(0)) = \max_{\{c(t)\}_{t=0}^{\infty}} \mathbb{E}_0\left[\sum_{t=0}^{\infty} \beta^t u(c(t))\right] \tag{S16.6}$$

$$\sum_{t=0}^{\infty} \frac{1}{(1+r)^t} c(t) \le \sum_{t=0}^{\infty} \frac{1}{(1+r)^t} w(t) + a(0), \text{ a.s.}$$

Suppose, to get a contradiction, that $c(t)$ converges to some $\bar{c}$, that is $c(t) \to^{a.s.} \bar{c}$ for some $\bar{c}$. Consider any $\delta > 0$ and note that there exists $\bar{t}_\delta > 0$ such that

$$|c(t) - \bar{c}| < \delta \text{ for all } t \ge \bar{t}_\delta, \text{ a.s.} \tag{S16.7}$$

Consider any history up to $\bar{t}_\delta$, $w^{\bar{t}_\delta-1} = (w(0), .., w(\bar{t}_\delta - 1))$, denote the level of assets at this history with $a(\bar{t}_\delta)$ and note that the lifetime budget constraint at time $\bar{t}_\delta$ following this history can be written as

$$\sum_{t=0}^{\infty} \frac{1}{(1+r)^t} c(\bar{t}_\delta + t) = \sum_{t=0}^{\infty} \frac{1}{(1+r)^t} w(\bar{t}_\delta + t) + a(\bar{t}_\delta), \text{ a.s.} \tag{S16.8}$$

We have used the fact that the lifetime budget constraint at this history must hold with equality except for a measure zero of events, since otherwise the consumer could increase consumption in the events in which this condition is violated and thus increase the objective value for Problem S16.6.

Next, for any positive integer T we define the event

$$E_{\min}(T) = \left\{ w \in \mathcal{W}^{\infty} \mid w^{\bar{t}_\delta+T-1} = \left(w^{\bar{t}_\delta}, w(\bar{t}_\delta) = w_{\min}, ..., w(\bar{t}_\delta + T - 1) = w_{\min}\right) \right\}$$

in which the agent receives the lowest wage shock $w_{\min} \equiv \min_{w \in \mathcal{W}} w$ for T periods following history $w^{\bar{t}_\delta-1}$. Since $E_{\min}(T)$ has positive probability and since Eqs. (S16.7) and (S16.8) hold a.s., there exists $w^{\infty} \in E_{\min}(T)$ for which both of these conditions hold, which implies

$$\sum_{t=0}^{T-1} \frac{1}{(1+r)^t} w_{\min} + \sum_{t=T}^{\infty} \frac{1}{(1+r)^t} w(\bar{t}_\delta + t) + a(\bar{t}_\delta) \ge \sum_{t=0}^{\infty} \frac{1}{(1+r)^t} c(\bar{t}_\delta + t)$$

$$\ge \frac{1+r}{r}(\bar{c} - \delta).$$

Since T is arbitrary, we can take the limit of the previous inequality over T to obtain

$$\frac{1+r}{r} w_{\min} + a(\bar{t}_\delta) \ge \frac{1+r}{r}(\bar{c} - \delta). \tag{S16.9}$$

In words, the agent's accumulated assets at time $\bar{t}_\delta$ should be sufficiently large that she can consume at least $\bar{c} - \delta$ in every period even after long spells of low income.

Similarly, for any positive integer T we define the event

$$E_{\max}(T) = \left\{ w \in \mathcal{W}^\infty \mid w^{\bar{t}_\delta + T - 1} = \left(w^{\bar{t}_\delta}, w\left(\bar{t}_\delta\right) = w_{\max}, ..., w\left(\bar{t}_\delta + T - 1\right) = w_{\max} \right) \right\},$$

that is, $E_{\max}(T)$ denotes the event in which the agent receives the highest wage shock $w_{\max} = \max_{w \in \mathcal{W}} w$ for T periods following history $w^{\bar{t}_\delta - 1}$. Since $E_{\max}(T)$ has a positive probability and since Eqs. (S16.7) and (S16.8) hold a.s., there exists $w^\infty \in E_{\min}(T)$ for which both of these conditions are satisfied, which implies

$$\sum_{t=0}^{T-1} \frac{1}{(1+r)^t} w_{\max} + \sum_{t=T}^{\infty} \frac{1}{(1+r)^t} w\left(\bar{t}_\delta + t\right) + a\left(\bar{t}_\delta\right) = \sum_{t=0}^{\infty} \frac{1}{(1+r)^t} c\left(\bar{t}_\delta + t\right)$$

$$\leq \frac{1+r}{r}\left(\bar{c} + \delta\right).$$

As $T \to \infty$, the previous inequality implies

$$\frac{1+r}{r} w_{\max} + a\left(\bar{t}_\delta\right) \leq \frac{1+r}{r}\left(\bar{c} + \delta\right). \tag{S16.10}$$

In words, the agent's accumulated assets at time $\bar{t}_\delta$ should be sufficiently small that her budget constraint is not slack even at very lucky histories at which she receives the highest income for many periods (given that she consumes at most $\bar{c} + \delta$ in every period).

Next, we note that Eqs. (S16.9) and (S16.10) together imply $w_{\max} - w_{\min} \leq 2\delta$. The analysis so far can be repeated for any $\delta > 0$, in particular, it also applies for $\delta < (w_{\max} - w_{\min})/2$, which yields a contradiction and proves that consumption cannot converge to a constant level. Intuitively, when the income stream is stochastic, the consumption stream must necessarily also be stochastic, otherwise, for long enough spells of good or bad shocks, either the budget constraint would be violated, or it would be slack, which means that the agent is sub-optimally leaving resources unconsumed.

Exercise 16.11, Part (b). To prove this result, we consider the recursive formulation of the problem. Recall that $w(t)$ is distributed independently over time, thus the functional equation corresponding to Problem (S16.6) is

$$V(a, w) = \max_{a'} u\left(a + w - \frac{a'}{1+r}\right) + \beta E_{w'}\left[V\left(a', w'\right)\right] \tag{S16.11}$$

$$\text{s.t.} \qquad a' \geq \sum_{s=0}^{\infty} \frac{1}{(1+r)^s} w_{\min} = 0,$$

where we have used the fact that the budget constraint $\frac{a'}{1+r} + c \leq a + w$ holds with equality and we have noted the natural borrowing constraint. Recall that the natural borrowing constraint holds since otherwise the consumer cannot pay her debt off after a very long spell of minimum wage shocks (which is zero in this problem since the exercise states that the lower support of the wage distribution is zero).

Since the operator in (S16.29) is a contraction mapping, there exists a unique continuous V that satisfies Eq. (S16.11). Moreover, since u is strictly concave, continuously differentiable and increasing (cf. Section 16.5), V is strictly concave in a and strictly increasing in a and w, which also implies that the solution to Problem (S16.11) (the policy function) is single valued. Note also that the only payoff relevant state variable for Problem (S16.11) is the current wealth $a + w$ (since the wage shocks are i.i.d.) thus without loss of generality we can denote the optimal policy as a function of current wealth, i.e. by $A(a+w)$. Finally, note that $V(a, w)$ is differentiable in a whenever $a > 0$ and $A(a+w) > 0$, with derivative

$$\frac{\partial V(a, w)}{\partial a} = u'(c(a+w)), \tag{S16.12}$$

where we have defined $c(a+w) = a + w - \frac{A(a+w)}{1+r}$ as the current consumption given the optimal policy. Note that the derivative in Eq. (S16.12) is continuous thus it can also be extended to the boundary cases $a = 0$ and $A(a+w) = 0$.

Next note that the first-order condition for Problem (S16.11) is

$$u'(c(a+w)) \geq \beta(1+r) E_{w'}\left[\frac{\partial V(A(a+w), w')}{\partial a}\right] \text{ with equality if } A(a+w) > 0, \tag{S16.13}$$

which, after combining with Eq. (S16.12), yields the Euler equation

$$u'(c(a+w)) \geq \beta(1+r) E_{w'}\left[u'(c(A(a+w)+w'))\right] \text{ with equality if } A(a+w) > 0. \tag{S16.14}$$

Note that with CRRA utility and a possibility of a wage shock of $w' = 0$, the consumer would never choose $A(a+w) = 0$. Suppose that she did, then with positive probability her consumption would drop to 0 and this would violate Eq. (S16.14) in view of $u'(0) = \infty$. Therefore, as long as $a > 0$, we have $A(a+w) > 0$ and Eqs. (S16.13) and (S16.14) hold with equality. Moreover, since V and u are strictly concave and since the budget constraint

$$\frac{A(a+w)}{1+r} + c(a+w) = a + w$$

holds with equality, Eq. (S16.13) implies that $A'(x) > 0$ and $c'(x) \in (0,1)$ (where we use x to denote the total wealth $x = a + w$), that is, the consumer splits an additional unit of wealth between consumption and investment.

We next claim that there exists some $\tilde{a}$ such that,

$$\text{if } a(t) > \tilde{a} \text{ then } A(a(t)+w) < a(t) \text{ for any } w \in \mathcal{W}, \tag{S16.15}$$

that is, if the level of assets is above $\tilde{a}$ then the consumer necessarily lowers the level of assets in the following period. Note that this claim implies that the asset levels in this economy will always be bounded by $\bar{a} = \max(a(0), \tilde{a})$, completing the proof for this part of the exercise. Note that if the function $A(x)$ is bounded above by K, the claim trivially holds by taking $\tilde{a} = K$, thus suppose

$$\lim_{x \to \infty} A(x) = \infty.$$

Under this assumption, we prove the claim in (S16.15) in three steps.

As the first step, we show that consumption is unbounded as a function of wealth, that is[1]

$$\lim_{x \to \infty} c(x) = \infty. \tag{S16.16}$$

Suppose, to reach a contradiction, that $\lim_{x \to \infty} c(x) < \bar{c}$ for some $\bar{c}$. By the intertemporal condition (S16.12), for any $(a \in \mathbb{R}_+, w \in \mathcal{W})$ we have

$$V'(a, w) > u'(\bar{c}).$$

---

[1]Our approach in this exercise closely follows Aiyagari (1993). However, the proof for Eq. (S16.16) in Aiyagari (1993) is not entirely correct since it posits that the value function $V(a, w)$ is bounded, which is not necessarily the case since we have to allow assets to take values in $\mathbb{R}_+$ to avoid circular reasoning. We provide an alternative analysis here.

Integrating the previous inequality over $a \in \mathbb{R}_+$ (for a given $w \in \mathcal{W}$), we have

$$V(a, w) > V(0, w) + u'(\bar{c}) a, \qquad (S16.17)$$

i.e. $V(., w)$ is bounded below by a linear function with positive slope. Next, let $w^{\max} \equiv (w(t) = w_{\max}, t \in \{0, 1, ..\})$ denote the best possible history in the sense that the highest income shock is realized in every period. Since $V(., w)$ solves the sequence problem (S16.6), it is equal to $\mathbb{E}_0 \left[\sum_{t=0}^{\infty} \beta^t u(c(t)) \right]$ and this expectation is less than the realization for the best possible history $w^{\max}$. This implies

$$
\begin{aligned}
V(a, w) \quad &\leq \quad \sum_{t=0}^{\infty} \beta^t u\left(c\left(t \mid w^{\max}\right)\right) \\
&\leq \quad u\left(\sum_{t=0}^{\infty} \beta^t c\left(t \mid w^{\max}\right)\right) \\
&\leq \quad u\left(\sum_{t=0}^{\infty} \frac{c\left(t \mid w^{\max}\right)}{(1+r)^t}\right) \\
&\leq \quad u\left(\sum_{t=0}^{\infty} \frac{w_{\max}}{(1+r)^t} + a\right) = \frac{\left(\frac{1+r}{r} w_{\max} + a\right)^{1-\theta} - 1}{1 - \theta},
\end{aligned}
\qquad (S16.18)
$$

where the first line follows from Jensen's inequality and the concavity of the utility function $u(.)$, the second line uses $\beta(1+r) < 1$ and the last line follows since the lifetime budget constraint holds for history $w^{\max}$. Combining Eqs. (S16.17) and (S16.18), we have for all $a \in \mathbb{R}_+$

$$V(0, w) + u'(\bar{c}) a < V(a, w) < \frac{\left(\frac{1+r}{r} w_{\max} + a\right)^{1-\theta} - 1}{1 - \theta}.$$

Note, however that since $1 - \theta < 1$ the difference between the left and the right hand side terms satisfy

$$\lim_{a \to \infty} \left(V(0, w) + u'(\bar{c}) a - \frac{\left(\frac{1+r}{r} w_{\max} + a\right)^{1-\theta} - 1}{1 - \theta} \right) = \infty,$$

in particular, this difference is positive for sufficiently large $a \in \mathbb{R}_+$, providing a contradiction. Intuitively, Eq. (S16.17) bounds $V(a, w)$ below by a linear function and Eq. (S16.18) bounds it above by a strictly concave function that satisfies the Inada condition, which yields a contradiction for sufficiently large levels of assets. This shows (S16.16) and completes the first step.

As the second step, we claim

$$\frac{c(A(x))}{c(x)} \leq (\beta(1+r))^{1/\theta} < 1 \text{ for all } x \in \mathbb{R}_+. \qquad (S16.19)$$

To prove this step, note that the Euler equation (S16.13) implies

$$1 = \frac{u'(c(x))}{\beta(1+r) \mathbb{E}_{w'}[u'(c(A(x) + w'))]} \geq \frac{u'(c(x))}{\beta(1+r) u'(c(A(x)))},$$

where the inequality follows by replacing w' with the worst possible shock $w_{\min} = 0$ and using the fact that $c(.)$ is an increasing function (and $u'(.)$ is a decreasing function). Using the CRRA utility $u(c) = (c^{1-\theta} - 1)/(1 - \theta)$ in the previous displayed inequality proves Eq. (S16.19) and completes the second step.

As the third and the final step, we combine Eqs. (S16.16) and (S16.19) to prove the claim in (S16.15). Suppose, to reach a contradiction, that the claim does not hold. Then, for any $\tilde{a}$ there exists $a > \tilde{a}$ and $w \in \mathcal{W}$ such that $A(a + w) > a > \tilde{a}$. We then have

$$
\begin{aligned}
c(A(a+w)) &\geq c(A(a+w)+w) - w \\
&\geq c(a+w) - w \\
&\geq c(a+w) - w_{\max},
\end{aligned}
$$

where the first inequality uses the fact that $c'(x) < 1$, the second inequality uses the assumption that $A(a+w) > a$ and the last inequality uses $w \leq w_{\max}$. The last displayed inequality further implies

$$
\frac{c(A(a+w))}{c(a+w)} + \frac{w_{\max}}{c(a+w)} > 1.
$$

Taking the limit as $\tilde{a} \to \infty$ and using Eq. (S16.16) from step 1, we have $\lim_{\tilde{a} \to \infty} c(a+w) = \infty$ (since $a > \tilde{a}$ goes to ∞ and $w \in \mathcal{W}$ is bounded), which implies $\lim_{\tilde{a} \to \infty} \frac{c(A(a+w))}{c(a+w)} \geq 1$. This further implies that Eq. (S16.19) from Step 2 is violated for sufficiently large levels of wealth, providing a contradiction and proving the claim in Eq. (S16.15).

The intuition for this result is as follows: with CRRA utility, as the consumer accumulates wealth, the coefficient of absolute risk aversion declines and the elasticity of intertemporal substitution increases. As the consumer becomes less risk averse, the precautionary savings motive weakens and consumer is tempted to save less. As the intertemporal substitution becomes more elastic, low interest rates (recall that $\beta(1+r) < 1$) induce the consumer to consume immediately. Since both effects work in the same direction, a sufficiently wealthy consumer would decumulate assets (cf. Eq. (S16.15)) and the level of assets would remain bounded.

Exercise 16.11, Part (c). We claim that, with CARA utility, $u(c) = -\exp(-\gamma c)$, the assets may grow arbitrarily large. To prove the result, we will derive a closed form solution for the asset policy $A(a+w)$ and will use the expression to show that the level of assets grow arbitrarily large after a long spell of favorable wage shocks. To simplify the analysis, we allow for negative consumption and negative levels of wealth, that is, the consumption policy function $c(x)$ is a mapping from $\mathbb{R}$ to $\mathbb{R}$. We first show that consumption is linear in wealth, in particular

$$
c(x) = c(0) + \frac{xr}{1+r}. \tag{S16.20}
$$

We can see this directly from the sequence problem (S16.6). Let $w(0) \in \mathcal{W}$ and $a(0) = -w(0)$ so that the initial level of wealth is zero and consider any $x \in \mathbb{R}$. A stochastic process $[c(t)]_{t=0}^{\infty}$ is feasible starting with aggregate wealth 0 if and only if the process $[c(t) + xr/(1+r)]_{t=0}^{\infty}$ is feasible starting with aggregate wealth x. Moreover, the CARA assumption implies that the expected utility from the process $[c(t) + xr/(1+r)]_{t=0}^{\infty}$ is a constant multiple of the expected utility from the process $[c(t)]_{t=0}^{\infty}$, that is

$$
\mathbb{E}_0 \left[\sum_{t=0}^{\infty} \beta^t u \left(c(t) + \frac{xr}{1+r} \right) \right] = -\exp\left(-\gamma \frac{xr}{1+r} \right) \mathbb{E}_0 \left[\sum_{t=0}^{\infty} \beta^t u(c(t)) \right].
$$

It then follows that the stochastic process $[c(t)]_{t=0}^{\infty}$ is optimal starting with wealth 0 if and only if the stochastic process $[c(t) + xr/(1+r)]_{t=0}^{\infty}$ is optimal starting with wealth x. Since the optimal process is unique, we have $c(x) = c(0) + xr/(1+r)$, proving Eq. (S16.20). From

(S16.20), we also have

$$A(x) = (1+r)[x - c(x)]$$ (S16.21)
$$= x - (1+r)c(0),$$

which gives the asset policy in terms of $c(0)$

To calculate $c(0)$, note that the Euler equation (S16.14) in this case holds with equality since we do not have the restriction $c(0) > 0$. Plugging $a + w = 0$ and $u(c) = -\exp(-\gamma c)$ in this equation, we have

$$\gamma \exp(-\gamma c(0)) = \beta(1+r) E_{w'}\left[\gamma \exp\left(-\gamma c\left(A(0) + w'\right)\right)\right]$$
$$= \beta(1+r)\gamma \exp(-\gamma c(0)) \exp\left(-\gamma A(0)\frac{r}{1+r}\right) E_{w'}\left[\exp\left(-\gamma w'\frac{r}{1+r}\right)\right],$$

where the second line uses Eq. (S16.20). Combining this with the budget constraint $A(0) = -(1+r)c(0)$, we calculate $c(0)$ as

$$c(0) = \frac{1}{r\gamma}\left[-\log\beta(1+r) - \log E_{w'}\left[\exp\left(-\gamma w'\frac{r}{1+r}\right)\right]\right].$$

Plugging this in Eq. (S16.21) gives

$$A(x) = x + \frac{1+r}{r\gamma}\left(\log\beta(1+r) + \log E_{w'}\left[\exp\left(-\gamma w'\frac{r}{1+r}\right)\right]\right).$$

Letting $x = a + w$ and rearranging terms, for all $a \in \mathbb{R}$ and $w \in \mathcal{W}$ we obtain the asset policy

$$A(a+w) - a = w - \overline{w} + \left(\frac{1+r}{r\gamma}\log\beta(1+r)\right)$$ (S16.22)
$$+ \frac{1+r}{r\gamma}\log E_{w'}\left[\exp\left(-\gamma(w' - \overline{w})\frac{r}{1+r}\right)\right],$$

where $\overline{w} = E_{w'}[w']$ denotes the expected wage. Eq. (S16.22) is an intuitive expression. The left hand side shows the increase in the consumer's asset holdings after receiving wage shock w. The $w - \overline{w}$ term on the right hand side captures the fact that the consumer tends to increase asset holdings in response to more than expected wage shocks to smooth consumption over time. The second term on the first line captures the fact that, when $\beta(1+r) < 1$ the consumer tends to decrease asset level with a drift term which captures the desire of the agent to consume sooner than later. Finally, the term on the second line captures the fact that the consumer tends to increase savings due to the precautionary motive. It can be checked that this term is positive since the CARA utility satisfies $u''' > 0$ and features the precautionary savings motive.

The expression for asset policy in Eq. (S16.22) implies that the asset level may increase after a more than expected wage shock. First suppose $\beta(1+r) = 1$. In this case, the drift term is zero and the asset level always increases when $w > \overline{w}$. In particular, if the agent receives the shock $w' = w_{\max} > \overline{w}$ for T periods in a row, then the asset level will increase at least by $T(w_{\max} - \overline{w})$, which limits to ∞ as T increases. Thus the asset level cannot be bounded from above. The same intuition generalizes to the case in which $\beta(1+r) < 1$. In this case, even though there is a downward drift in the asset policy, the asset level will breach any bound with positive probability if $w_{\max} - \overline{w}$ is sufficiently large, in particular if

$$w_{\max} - \overline{w} > -\frac{1+r}{r\gamma}\log\beta(1+r).$$

The intuition for this result is as follows. As the consumer with CARA utility accumulates wealth, she has the same coefficient of absolute risk aversion and the same elasticity of intertemporal substitution. Consequently, no matter how rich she is, when she gets a favorable wage shock she would like to save some of it for consumption smoothing and precautionary saving purposes (cf. Eq. (S16.22)). Consequently, after a long spell of good wage shocks, the consumer's asset levels will get arbitrarily large.

Exercise 16.11, Part (d). Multiplying both sides of the Euler equation (S16.14) with $(\beta(1+r))^t$, we have

$$(\beta(1+r))^t u'(c(t)) \geq (\beta(1+r))^{t+1} E_t \left[u'(c(t+1)) \right],$$

which shows that the random variable $(\beta(1+r))^t u'(c(t))$ is a non-negative supermartingale. Then, the martingale convergence theorem implies that $(\beta(1+r))^t u'(c(t))$ converges almost surely to a nonnegative and finite random variable m. First consider the case $\beta(1+r) > 1$ and note that in this case $(\beta(1+r))^t u'(c(t)) \to^{a.s.} m$ can only hold if $u'(c(t)) \to^{a.s.} 0$. This further implies $c(t) \to^{a.s.} \infty$, proving the result. Next suppose $\beta(1+r) = 1$. The argument is slightly more complicated but Chamberlain-Wilson (2000) show that consumption also diverges to infinity in this case (when the income stream is sufficiently stochastic, which is the case in our setup). Hence, we conclude that $c(t) \to^{a.s.} \infty$ when $\beta(1+r) \geq 1$.

Exercise 16.11, Part (e). Note that in Part (d) we have not used $u''' > 0$. Therefore the same analysis shows that $c(t) \to^{a.s.} \infty$ also in the case in which u''' may sometimes be negative. However, we can prove a stronger result than in Part (d) when $u''' > 0$, that is we claim

$$E_t[c(t+1)] > c(t), \tag{S16.23}$$

whenever $u''' > 0$. To prove the claim, note that the Euler equation (S16.14) implies

$$u'(c(t)) \geq E_t \left[u'(c(t+1)) \right].$$

When $u''' > 0$, $u'(.)$ is a concave function and hence Jensen's inequality implies

$$E_t \left[u'(c(t+1)) \right] > u'(E_t(c(t+1))),$$

where the inequality is strict since $c(t+1)$ does not converge to a constant (see Part (a)). Combining the last two inequalities and using the fact that $u'(.)$ is a decreasing function proves the claim in Eq. (S16.23). Intuitively, when $u''' > 0$, the convergence to ∞ is more orderly in the sense that expected consumption tomorrow is always greater than consumption today. When u''' may sometimes be negative, Eq. (S16.23) does not necessarily apply and expected consumption may be lower than current consumption for some periods, but nevertheless consumption eventually limits to ∞.

Exercise 16.12

Exercise 16.12, Part (a). Let $a^m(t) = \max_{t' \in [0,t]} a(t')$ denote the best technique available to the entrepreneur at time t. The entrepreneur would not accept any technique in $\{a(0), .., a(t)\}$ that is not equal to $a^m(t)$, so $a^m(t)$ is the payoff relevant state variable at time t. Suppose the entrepreneur searches at time t. Then she produces at technique $a^m(t)$ and receives the continuation value $V(a^m(t+1) = a^m(t))$ since she doesn't discover a new technique. Suppose instead the entrepreneur searches at time t. In this case, the entrepreneur doesn't produce at time t but receives the continuation value $V(a^m(t+1) = \max(a^m(t), \tilde{a}))$

where $\tilde{a}$ is the technique discovered at time t. Combining these observations, the recursive problem of the entrepreneur can be formulated as

$$
\begin{aligned}
V\left(a^{m}\right) &= \max\left\{a^{m}+\beta V\left(a^{m}\right),\beta\mathbb{E}\left[V\left(\max\left(a^{m},\tilde{a}\right)\right)\right]\right\} \\
&= \max\left\{a^{m}+\beta V\left(a^{m}\right),\beta\int_{0}^{\bar{a}}V\left(\max\left(a^{m},\tilde{a}\right)\right)dH\left(\tilde{a}\right)\right\}.
\end{aligned}
$$

Note that V is a fixed point of a contraction mapping T over the set of continuous and bounded functions over $[0,\bar{a}]$. Moreover, T takes weakly increasing functions to weakly increasing functions, hence V is weakly increasing.

Exercise 16.12, Part (b). Without loss of any essential generality, assume that the entrepreneur accepts a technique when he is indifferent between accepting and searching more. Suppose, to reach a contradiction, that an entrepreneur who has access to $\mathbf{a}^{t}=(a\left(0\right),..,a',..,a\left(t\right))$ chooses to search at time t and accepts technique a' at time $t+s$ for some $s>0$. Since the entrepreneur decides to search at time t, we have

$$
a^{m}\left(t\right)+\beta V\left(a^{m}\left(t\right)\right)<\beta\int_{0}^{\bar{a}}V\left(\max\left(a^{m}\left(t\right),\tilde{a}\right)\right)dH\left(\tilde{a}\right),
$$

and since he accepts technique a' at time $t+s$, we have $a^{m}\left(t+s\right)=a'$ and thus

$$
a^{m}\left(t+s\right)+\beta V\left(a^{m}\left(t+s\right)\right)\geq\beta\int_{0}^{\bar{a}}V\left(\max\left(a^{m}\left(t+s\right),\tilde{a}\right)\right)dH\left(\tilde{a}\right).
$$

Since $a^{m}\left(t+s\right)\geq a^{m}\left(t\right)$ for any realization of events between t and $t+s$, and since V is weakly increasing, the last two equations imply

$$
a^{m}\left(t+s\right)+\beta V\left(a^{m}\left(t+s\right)\right)>a^{m}\left(t\right)+\beta V\left(a^{m}\left(t\right)\right).
$$

Since V is weakly increasing, this further implies $a^{m}\left(t+s\right)>a^{m}\left(t\right)$. On the other hand, we have $a'=a^{m}\left(t+s\right)$ and $\mathbf{a}^{t}=(a\left(0\right),..,a',..,a\left(t\right))$, which implies $a^{m}\left(t+s\right)=a^{m}\left(t\right)$. This yields a contradiction and proves that the entrepreneur never recalls a technique she has rejected in the past.

Exercise 16.12, Part (c). Suppose the entrepreneur accepts technique a' at time t, that is, $a^{m}\left(t\right)=a'$ and

$$
a'+\beta V\left(a'\right)\geq\beta\int_{0}^{\bar{a}}V\left(\max\left(a',\tilde{a}\right)\right)dH\left(\tilde{a}\right). \tag{S16.24}
$$

Since the entrepreneur does not search at time $t+1$, we have $a^{m}\left(t+1\right)=a^{m}\left(t\right)=a'$. Hence by Eq. (S16.24), the entrepreneur also accepts technique a' at time $t+1$. It follows by induction that the entrepreneur will continue to produce with technique a' for all dates $s\geq t$ and will never go back to searching.

Exercise 16.12, Part (d). Part (b) shows that the entrepreneur never recalls a technique from the past so there is no loss of generality in assuming that the payoff relevant state variable is the latest technique discovered. Part (c) shows that the entrepreneur never goes back to searching after accepting a technique, so the value of accepting technique a is given by $V^{accept}\left(a\right)=a/\left(1-\beta\right)$. Hence, the maximization problem of the entrepreneur can be formulated as in (16.28).

Exercise 16.12, Part (e). We assume $b < \bar{a}$, since otherwise it is never optimal for the entrepreneur to accept any technique and the optimal solution is trivially characterized as always searching. When $b < \bar{a}$, a similar analysis to Parts 2-4 establishes that, without loss of generality, the recursive problem of the entrepreneur can be written as

$$V(a) = \max \left\{ \frac{a}{1-\beta}, b + \beta \int_0^{\bar{a}} V(\tilde{a}) \, dH(\tilde{a}) \right\}.$$

Since V is a maximum of a linear function and a constant function, V is piecewise linear and the optimal policy takes a cutoff rule. The cutoff technology level, which we denote by R, satisfies

$$\frac{R}{1-\beta} = b + \beta \int_0^{\bar{a}} V(\tilde{a}) \, dH(\tilde{a}).$$

Moreover, for $a < R$, we have $V(a) = V(R)$ and for $a > R$, we have $V(a) = a/(1-\beta)$. The previous displayed equation then implies

$$\frac{R}{1-\beta} = b + \frac{\beta R}{1-\beta} H(R) + \beta \int_R^{\bar{a}} \frac{a}{1-\beta} dH(a). \tag{S16.25}$$

Subtracting the identity

$$\frac{\beta R}{1-\beta} = \frac{\beta R}{1-\beta} H(R) + \beta \int_R^{\bar{a}} \frac{R}{1-\beta} dH(a)$$

from both sides of Eq. (S16.25), we have that the cutoff rule R solves

$$R = b + \frac{\beta}{1-\beta} \int_R^{\bar{a}} (a - R) \, dH(a).$$

We denote the right hand side of this expression with $\gamma(b, R)$, which is decreasing in R. Moreover, $\gamma(b, 0) > 0$ and $\gamma(b, \bar{a}) = b < \bar{a}$ by assumption, which implies that the function $\gamma(b, .)$ crosses the 45 degree line. Since it is a decreasing function, it crosses the 45 degree line exactly once, hence the equation $R = \gamma(b, R)$ has a unique solution $R \in (0, \bar{a})$ for any b. Moreover, since $\gamma(b, R)$ is increasing in b, the unique solution R is also increasing in b, which proves that the cutoff threshold increases as b increases. Intuitively, when the entrepreneur receives more benefits while searching, she has more incentives to search and requires a higher threshold to accept a technique.

Exercise 16.14

Exercise 16.14, Part (a). The time t budget constraint of a household with claims $x(t)$ on the tree and with the realization of state, $z(t)$, is given by

$$
\begin{aligned}
c(t) + p(z(t)) x(t+1) &\leq z(t) x(t) + p(z(t)) x(t) \\
&= (z(t) + p(z(t))) x(t).
\end{aligned}
$$

The right hand side of this constraint is the income of the household. The term $z(t) x(t)$ is the amount of consumption goods delivered at time t by the claims on the tree, and $p(z(t)) x(t)$ is the market value of the claims. The left hand side of the same constraint is the expenditure of the household. The household spends $c(t)$ of its time t income on consumption goods and reinvests the remaining to buy $x(t+1)$ claims at the current market price $p(z(t))$ to bring into next period.

Exercise 16.14, Part (b). Given a stationary price function, $p(z)$, the payoff relevant state variables for a household are her current claims on the tree, x, and the current state, z. Given the payoff relevant state, the household's problem can be represented with the following recursive formulation

$$V(x,z) = \sup_{c \geq 0, y \geq 0} \left\{ u(c) + \beta \mathbb{E}\left[V(y, z') \mid z \right] \right\}$$

$$\text{s.t.} \quad c + p(z) y \leq (z + p(z)) x,$$

where the second line is the budget constraint we have derived in Part (a). Since u is increasing in c, any solution to this problem satisfies the budget constraint with equality. Hence we can substitute $c = (z + p(z)) x - p(z) y$ and reduce the problem to one of choosing y, the level of claims for next period. With this substitution, the constraint $c \geq 0$ is equivalent to $y \leq p(z)^{-1} (z + p(z)) x$, hence the recursive problem can be written as

$$V(x,z) = \sup_{y \in \left[0, p(z)^{-1}(z+p(z))x \right]} \left\{ u\left((z + p(z)) x - p(z) y \right) + \beta \mathbb{E}\left[V(y, z') \mid z \right] \right\}. \quad \text{(S16.26)}$$

Exercise 16.14, Part (c). Market clearing in claims ensures that $x = 1$ in equilibrium (see Part (e)), thus without loss of generality we restrict the domain of Problem (S16.26) to the compact set $X = [0,1]$ and the constraint set to $y \in \left[0, p(z)^{-1}(z + p(z)) x \right] \cap X$. The restricted problem satisfies Assumptions 16.1 and 16.2 hence Theorem 16.3 applies and shows that there exists a unique, continuous and bounded solution $V : X \times \mathcal{Z} \to \mathbb{R}$. Since u is strictly concave in x and y, Assumption 16.3 is also satisfied and Theorem 16.4 applies, showing that the solution V is strictly concave and the optimal plan can be expressed with a policy function $\pi(x,z)$. Moreover, since $p(z) \geq 0$, u is strictly increasing in x, hence Assumption 16.4 is satisfied and Theorem 16.5 applies, showing that V is strictly increasing in x. Finally, u is continuously differentiable in x, hence Assumption 16.5 is satisfied and Theorem 16.6 applies, showing that $V(x,z)$ is continuously differentiable in x for $x \in Int\ X$ and $\pi(x,z) \in Int\left(\left[0, p(z)^{-1}(z + p(z)) x \right] \cap X \right)$, with derivative

$$\nabla_x V(x,z) = (z + p(z)) u'\left((z + p(z)) x - p(z) \pi(x,z) \right). \quad \text{(S16.27)}$$

Exercise 16.14, Part (d). We have established that V is continuously differentiable and strictly concave which implies that the objective function for the optimization problem (S16.27) is also continuously differentiable and strictly concave. The first-order conditions for optimality are

$$p(z) u'\left((z + p(z)) x - p(z) y \right) = \beta \mathbb{E}\left[D_y V(y, z') \mid z \right].$$

Substituting Eq. (S16.27) on the right hand side of this expression and using the notation for consumption yields the stochastic Euler equation

$$p(z) u'(c(t)) = \beta \mathbb{E}_t \left[(z' + p(z')) u'(c(t+1)) \right]. \quad \text{(S16.28)}$$

Exercise 16.14, Part (e). The market clearing condition for claims on trees is $x(t) = 1$. This condition is sufficient for market clearing since when each individual holds one unit of the tree at all times the aggregate holding of claims necessarily equates aggregate supply of claims, which is also one unit per individual. To see why this condition is also necessary, note that individuals are symmetric and they face the same shocks, thus the recursive optimization problem (S16.26) has a unique solution as we have established in Part (c). Then, all individuals hold the same amount of claims at all times, showing that market clearing can be satisfied only if they all hold at most 1 claim, that is, $x(t) \leq 1$. Note also that $x(t) < 1$ would imply that the price of claims is 0, which in turn would generate infinite demand for claims from problem (S16.26), creating a contradiction. Hence $x(t) = 1$ is also necessary for market clearing on claims on trees.

Exercise 16.14, Part (f). Using the fact that the flow budget constraint is satisfied with equality and that market clearing implies $x(t) = 1$, we have

$$c(t) = [z(t) + p(z(t))] x(t) - p(z(t)) x(t+1) = z(t). \qquad (S16.29)$$

Using this in the stochastic Euler equation (S16.28), we have

$$
\begin{aligned}
p(z_j) u'(z_j) &= \beta \mathbb{E}_t \left[(z' + p(z')) u'(z') \mid z_j \right] \\
&= \beta \sum_{i=1}^{N} (z_i + p(z_i)) u'(z_i) q_{ji}, \text{ for all } j \in \{1, ..., N\}, \qquad (S16.30)
\end{aligned}
$$

where $q_{ji} = q(z_i \mid z_j)$ denotes the transition probability from state z_j to state z_i. The system in (S16.30) has N equations in N unknown prices, $\{p(z_j)\}_{z_j \in \mathcal{Z}}$. Hence, this system of equations characterizes the price of the tree in each state of the world. Intuitively, as in Lucas (1978), the tree is in fixed supply, thus asset prices adjust so that individuals optimally demand and consume exactly the amount $z(t)$ delivered by the trees at time t. More generally, the dual facts that asset markets clear and consumers choose optimal consumption paths (consistent with Euler equation) determine asset prices in an exchange economy. A large literature on asset pricing is built on this insight.

Exercise 16.14, Part (g). Let $p_B(z(t))$ denote the price of the riskless bond when the current state realization is $z(t)$. The household's first-order condition for bond trades is given by

$$p_B(z(t)) u'(c(t)) = \beta E_t \left[u'(c(t+1)) \right].$$

Since each household is identical and since the riskless bond is in zero net supply, in equilibrium each household holds zero unit of the riskless bond thus the market clearing equation $c(t) = z(t)$ continues to apply (cf. Eq. (S16.29)). Using this in the previous displayed equation, we have

$$p_B(z_j) = \beta \sum_{i=1}^{N} (z_i + p(z_i)) \frac{u'(z_i)}{u'(z_j)} q_{ji} \text{ for all } z,$$

which characterizes the price of the riskless bond at any state z in terms of the price vector for the trees, $\{p(z_j)\}_{z_j \in \mathcal{Z}}$.

Chapter 17: Stochastic Growth Models

Exercise 17.13

To prove that the equilibrium allocation is Pareto optimal (i.e. that the optimal and competitive growth paths coincide), we are going to apply Theorem 16.8 to the social planner's problem. Theorem 16.8 shows that (under Assumptions 16.1-16.5) the solution is completely characterized by the Euler equations and the transversality condition. To be more precise, this theorem shows that a plan is optimal if and only if it satisfied the Euler equations and the transversality condition of the social planner's problem. Then we are going to show that the equilibrium allocation will satisfy the same Euler equations and that the transversality condition will also hold.

Hence let us now verify that Theorem 16.8 applies to the social planner's problem. The recursive formulation of the optimal growth problem is given by

$$V\left(k, z\right) = \max_{k' \in [0, f(k,z)+(1-\delta)k]} \left\{ u\left(f(k,z) + (1-\delta)k - k'\right) + \beta \sum_{z' \in \mathcal{Z}} q\left[z'|z\right] V\left(k', z'\right) \right\}, \tag{S17.1}$$

where we already substituted the resource constraint

$$c = f(k, z) - (1 - \delta)k - k'.$$

Hence, let us now verify that Assumptions 16.1-16.5 are applicable so that Theorem 16.8 can be applied. As

$$f(k, z) + (1 - \delta)k > 0 \text{ for all } k \in \mathbb{R}_+, z \in \mathcal{Z}$$

we get that the constraint correspondence

$$G(k, z) = [0, f(k, z) + (1 - \delta)k] \tag{S17.2}$$

is nonempty-valued for all $k \in \mathbb{R}_+$ and $z \in \mathcal{Z}$. The limit condition on expected utility is satisfied as u is continuous and the support for k is bounded. To see that $k(t)$ is contained in a compact set, note that the resource constraint requires that

$$\begin{aligned} k(t+1) &\leq f(k(t), z) + (1-\delta)k(t) \\ &\leq \max_{z \in \mathcal{Z}} f(k(t), z) + (1-\delta)k(t). \end{aligned}$$

Then define the fixed point

$$\tilde{k}_{\max} = \max_{z \in \mathcal{Z}} f(\tilde{k}_{\max}, z) + (1-\delta)\tilde{k}_{\max}.$$

This fixed point exists as $\tilde{k}_{\max}$ solves

$$\frac{\max_{z \in \mathcal{Z}} f(\tilde{k}_{\max}, z)}{\tilde{k}_{\max}} = \delta$$

237

and $\frac{f(k,z)}{k}$ is decreasing in k for all z. Hence, by construction we have

$$k(t) \leq \tilde{k}_{\max} \implies k(t+1) \leq \tilde{k}_{\max}$$

and

$$k(t) > \tilde{k}_{\max} \implies k(t+1) \leq k(t).$$

To see the last statement, note that

$$\begin{aligned} \frac{k(t+1) - k(t)}{k(t)} &= \frac{f(k(t), z) - \delta k(t)}{k(t)} \leq \frac{\max_{z \in \mathcal{Z}} f(k(t), z)}{k(t)} - \delta \\ &= \frac{\max_{z \in \mathcal{Z}} f(k(t), z)}{k(t)} - \frac{\max_{z \in \mathcal{Z}} f(\tilde{k}_{\max}, z)}{\tilde{k}_{\max}} < 0 \end{aligned}$$

where the last inequality follows from the fact that

$$\frac{\max_{z \in \mathcal{Z}} f(k, z)}{k}$$

is decreasing in k and $k(t) > \tilde{k}_{\max}$. This shows that

$$0 \leq k(t) \leq \max\{\tilde{k}_{\max}, k(0)\},$$

i.e. $k(t)$ is contained in a compact set. Furthermore, G is also continuous and compact-valued (see (S17.2)) and U is continuous by the assumptions made on u. This verifies Assumptions 16.1 and 16.2. Assumptions 16.3 and 16.5. are also satisfied as u is assumed to be strictly concave and differentiable. Furthermore, U is strictly increasing in its first argument as

$$\frac{\partial}{\partial k} U(k, k', z) = u'(c) \left(f'(k, z) + 1 - \delta \right) > 0 \quad \text{for all } k, z,$$

as $u'(c) > 0$ and $f'(k, z) > 0$ for all k, z and $\delta < 1$. This also shows that G is monotone in k for all z and hence verifies Assumption 16.5.

As the social planner's problem satisfies Assumptions 16.1 to 16.5, Theorem 16.8 implies that the Euler equations and the transversality condition are necessary and sufficient for the characterization of the optimal plan. From (S17.1) we find that the necessary condition for the choice of future capital is given by

$$-u'\left(f(k, z) + (1 - \delta)k - k' \right) + \beta \sum_{z' \in \mathcal{Z}} q\left[z' \mid z \right] V'\left(k', z' \right) = 0,$$

and that the Envelope Condition reads

$$V'(k, z) = u'\left(f(k, z) + (1 - \delta)k - k' \right) \left[f'(k, z) + (1 - \delta) \right].$$

Combining these equation and explicitly denoting the dependence on the history z^t gives the Euler equations

$$u'\left(c\left[z^t \right] \right) = \beta \sum_{z(t+1)} q\left[z^{t+1} | z^t \right] u'\left(c\left[z^{t+1} \right] \right) R(z^{t+1}) \tag{S17.3}$$

where

$$R[z^{t+1}] = f'(k\left[z^t \right], z(t+1)) + (1 - \delta). \tag{S17.4}$$

Additionally, the appropriate transversality condition for problem (S17.1) is

$$\lim_{t \to \infty} \beta^t \mathbb{E}\left[u'\left(c\left[z^t \right] \right) R[z^t] k\left[z^{t-1} \right] \mid z(0) \right] = 0. \tag{S17.5}$$

From Theorem 16.8 we know that any plan $\{c[z^t], k[z^t]\}_{z^t}$ which satisfies (S17.3) and (S17.5) will be a solution to the social planner's problem.

Now consider the characterization of the competitive equilibrium. We are going to show that the equilibrium allocation satisfies (S17.3) and (S17.5). The first part, i.e. that the equilibrium satisfies (S17.3) follows directly from (17.22), which is exactly the required Euler equation and was shown to hold in the competitive equilibrium. In order to see that the transversality condition contained in (S17.5) is also satisfied, let us go back to the flow constraint of the consumer. Hence, we have to go to the sequential trading formulation of the equilibrium. Letting $a[z^{t+1}]$ be the claims bought in history z^t for history $(z^t, z(t+1))$ and $\bar{p}[z^{t+1}]$ their price, the flow constraint of the consumer is given by

$$c[z^t] + \sum_{z(t+1)} \bar{p}[z^{t+1}]a[z^{t+1}] = w[z^t] + a[z^t].$$

Hence

$$
\begin{aligned}
a[z^t] &= c[z^t] - w[z^t] + \sum_{z(t+1)} \bar{p}[z^{t+1}]a[z^{t+1}] \\
&= c[z^t] - w[z^t] + \sum_{z(t+1)} \bar{p}[z^{t+1}](c[z^{t+1}] - w[z^{t+1}]) + \sum_{z(t+1)} \bar{p}[z^{t+1}] \sum_{z(t+2)} \bar{p}[z^{t+2}]a[z^{t+2}] \\
&= \dots \\
&= \sum_{s=t}^{T}\left[\sum_{z_t^s} p\left[z^t, z_t^s\right]\left(c[z^t, z_t^s] - w[z^t, z_t^s]\right)\right] + \sum_{z_t^{T+1}} p[z^t, z_t^{T+1}]a[z^t, z_t^{T+1}] \qquad \text{(S17.6)}
\end{aligned}
$$

where we recursively defined

$$p\left[z^t, z(t+1), z(t+2)\right] = \bar{p}[z^{t-1}, z(t+1)]\bar{p}[z^{t-1}, z(t+1), z(t+2)]$$

and let $\sum_{z_t^s}$ denote the summation over all histories of length $(s-t)$ starting at t. At $t=0$ and $z^t = z^0 = z(0)$, (S17.6) reads

$$a[z(0)] = \sum_{s=0}^{T}\left[\sum_{z_0^s} p\left[z(0), z_0^s\right]\left(c[z(0), z_0^s] - w[z(0), z_0^s]\right)\right] + \sum_{z_0^{T+1}} p\left[z(0), z_0^{T+1}\right] a[(0), z_0^{T+1}].$$

Now define $p\left[z(0), z_0^s\right] = p_0\left[z^s\right]$, $[z(0), z_0^s] = [z^s]$, $p\left[z(0), z_0^s\right] w[z(0), z_0^s] = w_0[z^s]$ and reintroduce the index t instead of s. Then we get from above that

$$a[z(0)] + \sum_{t=0}^{T}\sum_{z^t} w_0[z^t] = \sum_{t=0}^{T}\sum_{z^t} p_0\left[z^t\right] c[z^t] + \sum_{z^{T+1}} p_0\left[z_0^{T+1}\right] a[z^{T+1}]. \qquad \text{(S17.7)}$$

Now observe that the lifetime budget constraint in (17.11) requires that

$$\lim_{T\to\infty}\left[a[z(0)] + \sum_{t=0}^{T}\sum_{z^t} w_0[z^t] - \sum_{t=0}^{T}\sum_{z^t} p_0\left[z^t\right] c[z^t]\right] \geq 0,$$

so that (S17.7) implies that

$$\lim_{T\to\infty}\sum_{z_0^{T+1}} p_0\left[z_0^{T+1}\right] a[z^{T+1}] \geq 0.$$

Using that in equilibrium the assets available have to be equal to the capital stock, we arrive at

$$\lim_{T\to\infty}\sum_{z_0^{T+1}} p_0\left[z_0^{T+1}\right] k[z^{T+1}] \geq 0, \qquad \text{(S17.8)}$$

Now observe that (see (17.21) and (17.22))

$$
\begin{aligned}
p_0\left[z_0^{T-1}\right] &= \lambda\beta^{T-1}u'(c[z^{T-1}])q[z^{T-1}|z(0)] \\
&= \lambda\beta^{T-1}q[z^{T-1}|z(0)]\beta\sum_{z_T}q[z^T|z^{T-1}]R[z^T]u'(c[z^T]),
\end{aligned}
$$

where λ is the Lagrange multiplier and where we again used $R(z^T)$ defined in (S17.4). As (S17.8) has to hold with equality, we can substitute the above expression for $p_0\left[z_0^{T-1}\right]$ (and redefine the time indices) to arrive at

$$
\begin{aligned}
0 &= \lim_{T\to\infty}\sum_{z_0^{T-1}}p_0\left[z_0^{T-1}\right]k[z^{T-1}] \\
&= \lambda\lim_{T\to\infty}\sum_{z_0^{T-1}}k[z^{T-1}]\beta^T q[z^{T-1}|z(0)]\sum_{z(T)}q[z^T|z^{T-1}]R[z^T]u'(c[z^T]) \\
&= \lambda\lim_{T\to\infty}\mathbb{E}\left[\beta^T k[z^{T-1}]\mathbb{E}\left[R[z^T]u'(c[z^T])|z^{T-1}\right]|z(0)\right] \\
&= \lambda\lim_{T\to\infty}\mathbb{E}\left[\beta^T k[z^{T-1}]R[z^T]u'(c[z^T])|z(0)\right], \qquad\qquad (S17.9)
\end{aligned}
$$

where the last line follows from the law of iterated expectations. As $\lambda > 0$, (S17.9) is exactly the same condition as (S17.5). This shows that the competitive equilibrium satisfies both the Euler equation and the transversality condition of the social planner's problem. As Theorem 16.8 shows that those conditions are necessary and sufficient to characterize the solution, we conclude that the solution to the optimal growth problem coincides with the equilibrium allocation. This proves Proposition 17.3.

Exercise 17.18

Consider the social planner's problem of the RBC model presented in Section 17.3. Let us directly start with the recursive formulation of the problem. The economy-wide resource constraint is given by

$$
C[z^t] + K[z^t] = F\left(K[z^{t-1}], z^t A(t)L[z^t]\right) + (1-\delta)K[z^{t-1}],
$$

where we explicitly noted that the current capital stock $K[z^{t-1}]$ was decided based on information available in $t-1$. Another problem is of course the apparent nonstationarity of the problem as technology A grows at rate g. This however we can deal with by introducing the current level of technology as a state variable. The recursive formulation of the problem reads

$$
V(K,z,A) = \max_{K',L}\{u(F(K,zAL) + (1-\delta)K - K', L) + \beta\mathbb{E}[V(K',z',A(1+g)) \mid z]\}.
$$

As there are two choice variables K' and L, we also have two necessary conditions. These are

$$
\begin{aligned}
u_C(C,L) &= \beta\mathbb{E}[V'(K',z',A(1+g))|z] &\qquad (S17.10) \\
u_C(C,L)F_L(K,zAL)Az &= -u_L(C,L), &\qquad (S17.11)
\end{aligned}
$$

where (S17.11) is the intratemporal condition to allocate between leisure and consumption. Additionally we have the Envelope Condition

$$
V'(K,z,A) = u_C(C,L)[F_K(K,zAL) + (1-\delta)],
$$

so that - iterating this forward and again using the policy functions π^C, π^K and π^L- we have

$$V'(K', z', A(1+g)) = u_C(\pi^C, \pi^L)[F_K(\pi^K, z'A(1+g)\pi^L) + (1-\delta)], \qquad (S17.12)$$

where we suppressed the arguments of the policy functions to save on notation. Using (S17.12) and (S17.10) we get the Euler equation

$$u_C(C, L) = \beta\mathbb{E}[u_C(\pi^c, \pi^L)[F_K(\pi^K, z'A(1+g)\pi^L) + (1-\delta)]|z], \qquad (S17.13)$$

which together with the intratemporal condition (S17.11) characterizes the solution to the planners problem.

To find restrictions on the preferences to guarantee balanced growth, let us first be precise what we mean by a balanced growth path in this economy. We define a balanced growth allocation as one, where the policy function of $\frac{C}{A}, L$ and $\frac{K}{A}$ have invariant distributions over the state space $\mathcal{K} \times \mathcal{Z}$, where $\mathcal{Z}$ is the set of N states and $\mathcal{K}$ is a compact set $\mathcal{K} = [k_{\min}, k_{\max}]$ where the effective capital stock $k = \frac{K}{A}$ is contained in. Hence along such a conjectured BGP we can write

$$\frac{C}{A} = c(k, z), \quad L = l(k, z), \quad \frac{K'}{A} = k'(k, z). \qquad (S17.14)$$

We have to find restrictions on preferences such that the necessary conditions (S17.11) and (S17.13) are satisfied for policy functions of the form given in (S17.14). Let us start with the Euler equation given in (S17.13). Using the notation of the conjectured policy functions we can write this condition for the current state (k, z) as

$$u_C(cA, l) = \beta\mathbb{E}[u_C(c'A(1+g), l')[F_K(k'A(1+g), z'A(1+g)l') + (1-\delta)]|z] \qquad (S17.15)$$

where

$$c = c(k, z), \ l = l(k, z), \ c' = c(k', z'), \ l' = l(k', z'), \ k' = k'(k, z).$$

Note in particular the appearance of the $A(1+g)$ terms on the RHS. To see where these come from, go back to (S17.13) and observe that

$$\pi^C(K', z', A(1+g)) = C = \frac{C}{A(1+g)}A(1+g) = c(k', z')A(1+g),$$

i.e. the appropriate state variables for RHS of the general problem are given by K', z' and $A(1+g)$. The reasoning for the other $A(1+g)$ terms on the RHS of (S17.15) is similar. Now note that F has constant returns to scale so that

$$F_K(k'A(1+g), z'A(1+g)l') = F_K(k', z'l').$$

Consequently, (S17.15) simplifies to

$$u_C(cA, l) = \beta\mathbb{E}[u_C(c'A(1+g), l')[F_K(k', z'l') + (1-\delta)]|z],$$

or rather

$$1 = \beta\mathbb{E}\left[\frac{u_C(c'A(1+g), l')}{u_C(cA, l)}[F_K(k', z'l') + (1-\delta)]\,\bigg|\, z\right]. \qquad (S17.16)$$

As (S17.16) has to hold for all A, we get that

$$\begin{aligned}
0 &= \frac{d}{dA}\left[\frac{u_C(c'A(1+g), l')}{u_C(cA, l)}\right] \\
&= \frac{u_{CC}(c'A(1+g), l')c'(1+g)u_C(cA, l) - u_C(c'A(1+g), l')u_{CC}(cA, l)c}{u_C(cA, l)^2}.
\end{aligned}$$

In particular, this has to hold for $A = 1$ so that we need that

$$\frac{u_{CC}(c'(1+g), l')c'(1+g)}{u_C(c'(1+g), l')} = \frac{u_{CC}(c, l)c}{u_C(c, l)}.$$

Hence the elasticity of substitution

$$\varepsilon_u(c,l) \equiv -\frac{u_{CC}(c,l)c}{u_C(c,l)}$$

is neither a function of c nor of l. This is only possible if the utility function takes the form of

$$u(C,L) = \frac{C^{1-\theta}}{1-\theta}v(L) + w(L), \tag{S17.17}$$

for some functions v and w, which are only dependent on L.

Let us now go back to the intratemporal condition given in (S17.11). Using the notation of the policy functions in (S17.14) we get that

$$u_C(c(k,z)A, l(k,z))F_L(kA, zAl(k,z))Az = -u_L(c(k,z)A, l(k,z)). \tag{S17.18}$$

By constant returns to scale of F we again know that

$$F_L(kA, zAl(k,z)) = F_L(k, zl(k,z)).$$

If we additionally use the functional form restriction contained in (S17.17), (S17.18) can be written as

$$(Ac)^{-\theta}v(l)F_L(k, zl(k,z))Az = -\frac{(cA)^{1-\theta}}{1-\theta}v'(l) + w'(l), \tag{S17.19}$$

where we again denoted $c = c(k,z)$ and $l = l(k,z)$ for brevity. To see how (S17.19) restricts the function w and v, consider first the case of $\theta \neq 1$. In that case, we can write (S17.19) as

$$c^{-\theta}v(l)F_L(k, zl(k,z))z = -\frac{c^{1-\theta}}{1-\theta}v'(l) + w'(l)A^{\theta-1}. \tag{S17.20}$$

As (S17.20) has to hold for all A, this clearly requires that

$$w'(L) = 0,$$

so that the utility function in (S17.17) reduces to

$$u(C,L) = \frac{C^{1-\theta}}{1-\theta}v(L) + w,$$

where w is some constant.

If on the other hand we have $\theta = 1$, (S17.19) implies that

$$\frac{1}{c}v(l)F_L(k, zl(k,z))z = -\log(cA)v'(l) + w'(l). \tag{S17.21}$$

Again, (S17.21) has to hold for all A, which directly implies that $v'(l) = 0$. With $v(.)$ being a constant, we can write (S17.17) as

$$u(C,L) = v\log(C) + w(L). \tag{S17.22}$$

Now note that we can normalize w to zero in the case of $\theta \neq 1$ and multiply the utility function in (S17.22) by v^{-1} and define $\tilde{w}(L) = v^{-1}w(L)$ in the case of $\theta = 1$. This is possible because those are only affine transformations. We therefore conclude that preferences will have to take to the form

$$u(C,L) = \begin{cases} \frac{C^{1-\theta}}{1-\theta}v(L) & \text{if } \theta \neq 1 \\ \log(C) + \tilde{w}(L) & \text{if } \theta = 1 \end{cases}$$

for growth to be balanced in the sense defined above. So if there exists an invariant distribution of (k,z) on the space $\mathcal{K} \times \mathcal{Z}$, labor supply does not go to zero or infinity (with probability one) as it itself has an invariant distribution on the $K \times \mathcal{Z}$ space. Hence there will be fluctuations in labor supply due to the stochastic behavior of k and z, but it will not converge to zero or infinity (with probability one).

Exercise 17.30 *

Exercise 17.30, Part (a). To get a contradiction, suppose the contrary. First consider the case in which the equilibrium investment price in a sector j is equal to some $p(j) < 1$. In this case, the intermediary j is losing money on her investment in the project, which yields a contradiction. Consider next the case in which $p(j) > 1$. Then, intermediary j is making expected profits. Consider another intermediary that offers the contract which invests in project j at price $p(j) - \varepsilon$ for sufficiently small ε. This intermediary will attract all the consumers of the incumbent intermediary that is currently investing in project j, hence it will attract an investment level at least as high as $K(j)$. Since $K(j) \geq M(j)$, it will indeed be able to invest in project j and promise positive expected returns. Moreover, this new intermediary makes positive profits after entry. Therefore, it will choose to enter and hence equilibrium price cannot be $p(j)$, yielding a contradiction. In essence, Bertrand competition between financial intermediaries drives down their expected profits to 0, which implies that the price of all assets is equal to 1 in equilibrium.

Exercise 17.30, Part (b). To show that the aggregate investment in all open projects is the same, we first claim that each households invests equally in active projects. Let $N^A \subset N$ denote the set of open projects and $n = |N^A|$ denote the level of diversification in this economy. We consider a household and denote her investment in a risky project $j \in N^A$ by $I(j)$ and her investment in the safe technology by X. We denote by $R(j) \in \{0, Q\}$ the random variable corresponding to the return from the risky project j. Given the level of set of active projects N^A, the household chooses an investment portfolio that solves

$$U(N^A) = \max_{c, X, \{I(j)\}_{j=1}^{n} \geq 0} u(c) + \mathbb{E}\left[v\left(qX + \sum_{j \in N^A} R(j)I(j)\right)\right] \quad \text{(S17.23)}$$

$$\text{s.t.} \quad c + X + \sum_{j \in N^A} I(j) = w.$$

Since $u(.)$ and $v(.)$ are strictly concave, the objective value of Problem (S17.23) is strictly concave and the solution is unique. Moreover, since each project has an identical and independent distribution, the only payoff relevant state variable is n, thus we denote the optimal portfolio choice with functions $c(n), X(n)$ and $\{I(j \mid n)\}_{j \in N^A}$ and the optimal value of Problem (S17.23) with $U(n)$. We next claim that $I(j \mid n) = I(j' \mid n)$ for all $j, j' \in N^A$, that is, the household invests equally on all active projects. Suppose, to reach a contradiction, that $I(j \mid n) \neq I(j' \mid n)$ for some j, j'. Consider the alternative allocation $\left[\bar{c}, \bar{X}, \{\bar{I}(j)\}_{j \in N^A}\right]$ which is identical to $\left[c(n), X(n), \{I(j \mid n)\}_{j \in N^A}\right]$ except for $\bar{I}(j), \bar{I}(j')$ which are given by

$$\bar{I}(j) = \bar{I}(j') = \frac{I(j \mid n) + I(j' \mid n)}{2}.$$

Since the projects have identical Bernoulli distributions, this allocation yields the same expected return as the original allocation. Moreover, since the project returns are independently distributed, the random variable $qX + \sum_{j \in N^A} R(j)I(j \mid n)$ is a nondegenerate mean preserving lottery over the random variable $q\bar{X} + \sum_{j \in N^A} R(j)\bar{I}(j)$. Since v is strictly concave, the household strictly prefers the allocation $\left[\bar{c}, \bar{X}, \{\bar{I}(j)\}_{j \in N^A}\right]$ to

$\left[c\left(n\right),X\left(n\right),\left\{I\left(j\mid n\right)\right\}_{j\in N^{A}}\right]$, which yields a contradiction and shows that $I\left(j\mid n\right)=I\left(j'\mid n\right)$ for all j,j'. We denote this common level of investment on active projects with $I\left(n\right)$. Since all households have the same initial wealth, each household invests $I\left(n\right)$ on each active project, which implies

$$K\left(j\right)=K\left(j'\right)=I\left(n\right)\ \text{for all } j,j'\in N^{A},$$

where we have also used the fact that the measure of the households is normalized to 1. Hence the aggregate investment on each risky project is the same.

Exercise 17.30, Part (c). The equilibrium in this economy is a collection of the set of active projects, the investment level and the share price for each active project, and the household's portfolio choice $\left[N^{A},\left\{K\left(j\right),p\left(j\right)\right\}_{j\in N^{A}},\left(c,X,\left\{I\left(j\right)\right\}_{j\in N^{A}}\right)\right]$ such that the portfolio choice $\left(c,X,\left\{I\left(j\right)\right\}_{j\in N^{A}}\right)$ solves the household's optimization Problem (S17.23), the markets for investment in risky projects clear and the levels of investment satisfy the minimum size requirements, that is $K\left(j\right)=I\left(j\right)\geq M\left(j\right)$ for each $j\in N^{A}$, and the share price for each active project is 1, i.e. $p\left(j\right)=1$ for each $j\in N^{A}$. In addition, the set of active projects N^{A} is determined by free entry in the sense that another project $j'\in N\setminus N^{A}$ cannot be opened without violating the minimum size requirement, that is $I\left(j'\mid N^{A}\cup\left\{j'\right\}\right)<M\left(\bar{j}\right)$, where $I\left(j'\mid N^{A}\cup\left\{\bar{j}\right\}\right)$ denotes the level the household would invest in project j' if the set of open projects were $N^{A}\cup\left\{j'\right\}$.

We next characterize the equilibrium allocation. Our analysis in Part (b) shows that the level of investment $I\left(n\right)$ is the same across all sectors and depends only on the level of diversification $n=\left|N^{A}\right|$. Since the minimum size requirement $M\left(j\right)$ is increasing, it follows that a project j is open iff all projects $j'\leq j$ are open, that is $N^{A}=\left\{1,..,n\right\}$. Then the free entry condition which determines the equilibrium level of diversification n can be written as

$$I\left(n^{*}\right)\geq M\left(n^{*}\right)\ \text{and}\ I\left(n^{*}+1\right)<M\left(n^{*}+1\right)).$$

Thus, the equilibrium level of diversification n^{*} can be determined by plotting the function $I\left(n\right)$ and finding an intersection (from above) with the increasing function $M\left(n\right)$. Given the level of diversification n^{*}, the rest of the portfolio allocations are uniquely determined as in Part (b) with $\left(c\left(n^{*}\right),I\left(n^{*}\right),X\left(n^{*}\right)\right)$, completing the characterization of the equilibrium.

Exercise 17.30, Part (d). The social planner chooses the level of diversification n, the investment level in riskless asset X and the investment levels in risky projects $\left\{I\left(j\right)\right\}_{j=1}^{n}$ to maximize the utility of the representative household, that is, she solves

$$U^{P}=\max_{n\in\left\{1,..,N\right\}}\max_{c,X,\left\{I(j)\right\}_{j=1}^{n}\geq0}u\left(c\right)+E\left[v\left(qX+\sum_{j=1}^{n}R\left(j\right)I\left(j\right)\right)\right] \quad \text{(S17.24)}$$

$$\text{s.t.}\quad c+X+\sum_{j\in N^{A}}I\left(j\right)=w.$$

$$\text{and}\quad I\left(j\right)\geq M\left(j\right)\ \text{for all } j\in\left\{1,2,..,n\right\}. \quad \text{(S17.25)}$$

There is no loss of generality in assuming that the set of open projects take the interval form $\left\{1,..,n\right\}$ since whenever a project j is closed and $j'>j$ is open, the project j (which has a lower minimum size requirement) could be opened instead of j' and would yield the same level of utility for the household. Problem (S17.24) is written with two max operators to emphasize that the first optimization problem over $\{1,..,n\}$ is a discrete optimization problem, and conditional on n, the second optimization problem (portfolio choice) over $\left(c, X, \{I(j)\}_{j=1}^n\right)$ is a concave maximization problem. In particular, whenever the feasible set is not empty the inner problem (given n) has a unique solution which we denote by $c^P(n)$, $X^P(n)$, $\left\{I^P(j \mid n)\right\}_{j=1}^n$. Given the characterization for portfolio choice, we denote the level of diversification chosen by the planner (the solution to the outer problem) with n^P.

Problem (S17.24) is the analogue of the household's portfolio choice problem (S17.24) but with the important difference that the social planner endogenizes the choice of the level of diversification n subject to minimum size requirements in (S17.24). Note that the planner always attains a weakly higher welfare, $U^P \geq U(n^*)$, since the equilibrium allocation $\left(n^*, \left(c(n^*), X(n^*), \{I(j) = I(n^*)\}_{j=1}^{n^*}\right)\right)$ is also feasible for the social planner. The following lemma further characterizes the planner's allocation and shows that $U^P = U(n^*)$ whenever $n^* = n^P$, that is, the equilibrium is efficient when the planner chooses to open exactly the same number projects as the equilibrium allocation.

LEMMA S17.1. *(i) The solution to the social planner's problem (S17.24) takes the following form: there exists a $j^P \in \left\{1,..,n^P\right\}$ and $I^P < M(j^p + 1)$ such that*

$$I^P\left(j \mid n^P\right) \equiv \hat{I}^P > M(j) \text{ for all } j \leq j^P,$$
$$I^P\left(j \mid n^P\right) = M(j) \text{ for all } j \in \left\{j^P + 1,..,n^P\right\}.$$

(ii) The social planner opens weakly more projects, that is $n^P \geq n^*$.

(iii) If $n^P = n^*$, then the social planner's portfolio choice coincides with the equilibrium portfolio choice and $U^P = U^*(n^*)$, that is, the equilibrium is efficient.

PROOF. To prove the first part, we first show that for $j, j' \in \{1,..,n\}$ such that the constraint in (S17.25) does not bind, we have $I(j) = I(j')$. Suppose that this does not hold, that is, there exists $j, j' \in \{1,..,n\}$ such that $I^P\left(j \mid n^P\right) > I^P\left(j' \mid n^P\right)$, $I^P\left(j \mid n^P\right) > M(j)$ and $I^P\left(j' \mid n^P\right) > M(j')$. Consider the alternative allocation with

$$\bar{I}(j) = I^P\left(j \mid n^P\right) - \delta,$$
$$\bar{I}(j') = I^P\left(j' \mid n^P\right) + \delta,$$

where $\delta \in \min\left(\frac{I^P(j \mid n^P) - I^P(j' \mid n^P)}{2}, I^P\left(j \mid n^P\right) - M(j)\right)$. The new allocation also satisfies the size requirements. Moreover, it yields the household the same expected return with lower risk hence it increases the household's welfare. This proves that $I(j) = I(j')$ for all $j, j' \in \{1,..,n\}$ such that the constraint in (S17.25) does not bind. Let us call this common level of investment by $\hat{I}^P$.

Next, we claim that the set of projects for which the constraint (S17.25) does not bind is given by some $\{1,..,j^P\}$. Suppose the contrary, i.e. that there exists $j < j'$ such that Constraint (S17.25) binds for j but does not bind not for j'. Then, it follows that $I^P\left(j' \mid n^P\right) > M(j') > M(j) = I^P\left(j \mid n^P\right)$, but a similar argument as above shows that a reallocation $\bar{I}(j') = I^P\left(j' \mid n^P\right) - \delta$, $\bar{I}(j') = I^P\left(j' \mid n^P\right) + \delta$ improves welfare, proving our claim. This also implies that $\hat{I}^P = M(j^p) < M(j^p + 1)$ and concludes the proof of the first part of the lemma.

To prove the second and the third parts, we claim that the consumer could replicate the social planner's portfolio choice whenever the equilibrium level of diversification is weakly greater, i.e. when $n^P \leq n^*$. To see this, note that the consumer could choose $\bar{X} = X^P\left(n^P\right)$,

$\bar{I}(j) = I^P(j \mid n^P)$ for each $j \in \{1, .., n^p\}$ and $\bar{I}(j) = 0$ for each $j \in \{n^P + 1, .., n\}$, which would be feasible for Problem (S17.23). This shows that $U^P \leq U(n^*)$ whenever $n^P \leq n^*$. If $n^P < n^*$, the social planner's allocation and the equilibrium allocation are different which implies $U^P < U(n^*)$ in view of the strict concavity of Problem (S17.23). This proves the second part and shows $n^P \geq n^*$. If $n^P = n^*$, then it must be the case that $U^P = U(n^*)$ and, moreover, the social planner's and the equilibrium allocation must be the same again in view of strict concavity. This completes the proof of the lemma.   □

This lemma suggests that, starting from $n = n^*$ the planner could lower the investment in some risky sectors and perhaps could also reduce the investment in the riskless asset to accumulate enough funds to open a new project. The benefit of this deviation is the reduction of the risk of the portfolio from the additional diversification. At the same time, the cost of this deviation is also related to risk since this deviation necessarily creates level differences in the amounts invested in different projects and increases the risk of the overall portfolio through this channel. In the baseline model, there is a continuum of sectors and some of this deviation is always profitable, which implies that the social planner always chooses to open more projects at the margin. However, in the present model, the social planner's choice of n is a discrete problem and it is possible that opening a new sector will increase overall portfolio risk, that is, we may have $n^P = n^*$ as the optimum level of diversification for the planner. Moreover, Part (iii) of Lemma S17.1) shows that, conditional on the level of diversification, the equilibrium portfolio choice is efficient, thus the decentralized equilibrium may be efficient even when some projects are inactive. Intuitively, the only advantage of the social planner over the equilibrium allocation is her ability to internalize the minimum size constraints and increase the level of diversification. If this advantage is absent due to the discrete nature of the project selection, then the equilibrium allocation will be efficient.

Increasing the level of diversification is more likely to reduce welfare (and hence to be undesirable) when the discrete difference in minimum size requirements is relatively large (in particular, if $M(n^* + 1) - M(n^*)$ is large), since in that case opening a new sector tends to increase portfolio risk relatively more. The following lemma essentially rules out this possibility and provides a condition under which the equilibrium allocation can be strictly improved.

LEMMA S17.2. *Let* $(n^*, (c(n^*), X(n^*), I(n^*)))$ *denote an equilibrium allocation and suppose that*

$$M(n^* + 1) < \min\left((I(n^*) - M(n^*))n^*, \frac{2n}{n+1}I(n^*)\right). \tag{S17.26}$$

Then, the social planner can strictly improve welfare by choosing the level of diversification $\bar{n}^P = n^* + 1$ *and the corresponding portfolio allocation* $\bar{c} = c(n^*)$, $\bar{X} = X^*$, $\bar{I}(j) = I(n^*) - M(n^* + 1)/n^*$ *for all* $j \in \{1, 2, .., n^*\}$ *and* $\bar{I}(n^* + 1) = M(n^* + 1)$. *In particular,* $U^P > U(n^*)$.

PROOF. First note that the condition $M(n^* + 1) < (I(n^*) - M(n^*))n^*$ ensures that $\bar{I}(j) > M(n^*)$ for all $j \in \{1, 2, .., n^*\}$ so the proposed allocation is feasible for the social planner. Second note that the allocations $(n^*, (c(n^*), X(n^*), I(n^*)))$ and $\left(\bar{n}^P, \left(\bar{c}, \bar{X}, \{\bar{I}(j)\}_{j=1}^{\bar{n}^P}\right)\right)$ give the same first period consumption and yield the same expected return in the second period. Hence, between these two allocations, the consumer will choose the one with lower variance for the second period returns. The variance of the equilibrium portfolio is

$$var\left(qX^* + \sum_{j=1}^{n} R(j) I(n^*)\right) = \sum_{j=1}^{n^*} (I(n^*))^2 Q^2 \pi (1-\pi) = n^* (I(n^*))^2 Q^2 \pi (1-\pi),$$

where we have used the fact that the variance of a sum of independent random variables is the sum of the variances and we have noted that the variance corresponding to a Bernoulli distribution with success probability π is $\pi (1-\pi)$. The variance corresponding to the proposed allocation can be similarly calculated as

$$var\left(q\bar{X} + \sum_{j=1}^{n^P} R(j) \bar{I}(j)\right) = \sum_{j=1}^{n^*} (I(n^*) - M(n^*+1)/n^*)^2 Q^2 \pi (1-\pi) + M(n^*+1)^2 Q^2 \pi (1-\pi).$$

Comparing the two displayed equations, we have that $var\left(q\bar{X} + \sum_{j=1}^{n^P} R(j) \bar{I}(j)\right) <$ $var\left(qX^* + \sum_{j=1}^{n} R(j) I(n^*)\right)$ if and only if $M(n^*+1) < \frac{2n}{n+1} I(n^*)$, which is implied by the Condition in (S17.26). Hence, under the condition stated in the lemma, the proposed allocation improves welfare and we have $U^P > U(n^*)$, completing the proof. $\square$

Exercise 17.30, Part (e). We have defined and characterized the efficient allocation in Part (d) (see Problem (S17.24) and Lemma S17.1). In particular, the social planner could reduce investment in some low minimum size requirement projects to cross-subsidize the projects with high minimum size requirements, effectively opening more projects and improving the level of diversification. The equilibrium cannot achieve the same allocation, since each household does not take into account the fact that her investment in a risky project relaxes the minimum size constraint for the project. Consequently, each individual underinvests in the marginal sectors with high minimum size requirements, without internalizing her effect on the diversification possibilities of other household.

Exercise 17.30, Part (f). First consider the case in which the intermediaries must charge linear prices for shares of the projects. In equilibrium, the fixed costs will increase the price of the shares above 1. Moreover, it is no longer the case that each open project has the same price. Note that, the more aggregate investment there is in a sector, the less will be the difference between the price and the marginal cost. Moreover, the less the price of a sector, the more individuals will invest in that sector. These two effects jointly imply that the equilibrium prices satisfy

$$1 < p(j) < p(j') \text{ whenever } M(j) < M(j'), \text{ for } j, j' \in N^A. \tag{S17.27}$$

Since the marginal price of investment $p(j)$ is above its marginal cost 1, there will be additional distortions that make the individuals' portfolio choice sub-optimal. In particular, as Eq. (S17.27) suggests, there will be too little overall investment in the risky sector. As for the allocation of resources within the risky sectors, there will be too little investment in higher fixed cost sectors and too much investment in lower fixed cost sectors. In addition to the distortion that we have noted in the previous parts, a social planner does not face linear prices and thus can improve the portfolio allocation by increasing investment in risky assets and shifting investment towards (already open) high fixed cost assets.

Consider next the case in which the intermediaries are allowed to discriminate prices. Since the average costs are falling in the size of investment, the intermediaries will offer larger bundles at a reduced price-per-share (i.e., using a two-part tariff), which will effectively remove the distortion described in the previous paragraph. With price discrimination, the market will be able to internalize the welfare loss due to fixed costs, but the social planner can still increase savings and open more projects so as to change the market structure and increase welfare.

Chapter 18: Diffusion of Technology

Exercise 18.8

Exercise 18.8, Part (a). The parametric condition $\rho - n_j > (1-\theta)g$ is necessary for the transversality condition to be satisfied. In this economy, the transversality condition in country j takes the form

$$\lim_{t\to\infty} \left[K_j(t) \exp\left(-\int_0^t r_j(s)ds \right) \right] = \lim_{t\to\infty} \left[k_j(t) \exp\left(-\int_0^t \left[f'(k_j(s)) - \delta - g - n_j \right] ds \right) \right] = 0,$$
(S18.1)

where the second equality used $k_j(t) = \frac{K_J(t)}{L_j(t)A_j(t)}$, the fact that interest rates are given by $r_j(s) = f'(k_j(s)) - \delta$ and that $L_j(t)$ and $A_j(t)$ grow exponentially at rates n_j and g respectively. Along the BGP (or in the steady state of the transformed variables k and $\tilde{c}$), $k_j(t)$ is constant and equal to k_j^*. Additionally consumption grows at rate g so that the Euler equation requires that

$$\theta g + \rho = r^* = f'(k_j^*) - \delta.$$
(S18.2)

Substituting (S18.2) into (S18.1) yields

$$\lim_{t\to\infty} \left[\exp\left(-\int_0^t [\theta g + \rho - g - n_j] ds \right) \right] = \lim_{t\to\infty} \left[\exp\left(- \left[(\theta-1)g + \rho - n_j \right] t \right) \right] = 0,$$

which requires that

$$(\theta - 1)g + \rho - n_j > 0.$$

Rearranging terms yields the required condition

$$\rho - n_j > (1-\theta)g.$$

Exercise 18.8, Part (b). To complete the proof of Proposition 18.3 we have to show that the BGP is unique and that the system is globally saddle path stable. The equilibrium in each country is characterized by a system of four differential equations, namely

$$\frac{\frac{d}{dt}\tilde{c}_j(t)}{\tilde{c}_j(t)} = \frac{1}{\theta}\left(f'(k_j(t)) - \delta - \rho \right) - g_j(t)$$
(S18.3)

$$\dot{k}_j(t) = f(k_j(t)) - \tilde{c}_j(t) - (n_j + g_j(t) + \delta)k_j(t)$$
(S18.4)

$$\dot{a}_j(t) = \sigma_j - (\sigma_j + g - \lambda_j)a_j(t)$$
(S18.5)

$$g_j(t) = \frac{\dot{a}_j(t)}{a_j(t)} + g.$$
(S18.6)

The first two differential equations are just the Euler equation (in this case for consumption in efficiency units $\tilde{c}_j(t) = \frac{c_j(t)}{A_j(t)}$) and the law of motion for capital. (S18.5) and (S18.6) describe the behavior of country j's distance to frontier and country j's growth rate of technological progress. Note that we can substitute (S18.6) into (S18.3) and (S18.4). Doing so, (S18.3)-(S18.5) are three differential equations in the three unknowns $[\tilde{c}_j(t), k_j(t), a_j(t)]_{t=0}^{\infty}$. As we

249

have two initial condition $k(0)$ and $a_j(0) = \frac{A_j(0)}{A(0)}$ and the transversality condition (S18.1) as another terminal condition, we can solve the system for $[\tilde{c}_j(t), k_j(t), a_j(t)]_{t=0}^{\infty}$. Having done so we can simply back out $[g_j(t)]_{t=0}^{\infty}$ using $[a_j(t)]_{t=0}^{\infty}$ and (S18.6). To show that this system has a unique steady state, we have to show that there is a unique solution to (S18.3)-(S18.6) where all variables are constant. Using (S18.5) we first find that there is a unique level a_j^* given by

$$a_j^* = \frac{\sigma_j}{\sigma_j + g - \lambda_j}, \tag{S18.7}$$

which satisfies $\dot{a}_j(t) = 0$. (S18.6) immediately shows that

$$g_j(t) = g, \tag{S18.8}$$

whenever $a_j(t) = a_j^*$. (S18.4) then shows that if $k_j(t) = k_j^*$ it will have to be true that

$$\tilde{c}_j(t) = \tilde{c}_j^* = f(k_j^*) - (n_j + g + \delta)k_j^*, \tag{S18.9}$$

i.e. if the capital stock per efficiency unit is constant, normalized consumption also has to be constant. In particular, (S18.9) determines $\tilde{c}_j^*$ uniquely as a function of k_j^*. As $\tilde{c}_j(t)$ has to be constant and in the steady state, (S18.3) finally determines k_j^* via

$$f'(k_j^*) = \delta + \rho + \theta g. \tag{S18.10}$$

As f is strictly concave, (S18.10) has a unique solution. This shows that the steady is unique and is given by (S18.7), (S18.8), (S18.9) and (S18.10). To prove that the system is globally saddle path stable we will show that the dynamics of the equilibrium are very similar to the ones of the neoclassical growth model with exogenous technological progress. To show global stability of this system, note first that (S18.5) and (S18.6) can be solved independently of $k_j(t)$ and $c_j(t)$. In particular, given an initial condition $a_j(0)$, (S18.5) has the solution

$$a_j(t) = \frac{\sigma_j}{\sigma_j + g - \lambda_j} + \left(a_j(0) - \frac{\sigma_j}{\sigma_j + g - \lambda_j}\right)\exp(-(\sigma_j + g - \lambda_j)t).$$

Recall that we assumed that $\lambda_j < g$ so that $\sigma_j + g - \lambda_j > 0$. This shows that independently of $a_j(0)$, $a_j(t)$ will converge to its steady state level as

$$\lim_{t\to\infty}\left(a_j(0) - \frac{\sigma_j}{\sigma_j + g - \lambda_j}\right)\exp(-(\sigma_j + g - \lambda_j)t) = 0.$$

Hence, the differential equation for $a_j(t)$, (S18.5), is globally stable. Additionally, convergence is monotone as

$$\dot{a}_j(t) = -(\sigma_j + g - \lambda_j)\left(a_j(0) - \frac{\sigma_j}{\sigma_j + g - \lambda_j}\right)\exp(-(\sigma_j + g - \lambda_j)t),$$

which shows that

$$\dot{a}_j(t) > 0 \Leftrightarrow a_j(0) < \frac{\sigma_j}{\sigma_j + g - \lambda_j}.$$

Hence, whenever $a_j(t)$ starts below its steady state level, it increases over time and vice versa. Using these results, (S18.6) shows that

$$g_j(t) > g \Leftrightarrow a_j(0) < \frac{\sigma_j}{\sigma_j + g - \lambda_j},$$

i.e. those countries that start below their steady state value grow faster then the world technology frontier and the countries starting above their steady state value grow slower.

Now rewrite (S18.4) as

$$\dot{k}_j(t) = f(k_j(t)) - \hat{c}_j(t)\frac{1}{a_j(t)} - (\delta + n_j + \frac{\dot{a}_j(t)}{a_j(t)} + g)k_j(t), \qquad \text{(S18.11)}$$

where we defined $\hat{c}_j(t) = \frac{c_j(t)}{A(t)}$. As $A(t)$ grows exponentially at rate g, the behavior of consumption per efficiency unit $\hat{c}(t)$ is given by

$$\frac{d\hat{c}(t)}{dt}\frac{1}{\hat{c}(t)} = \frac{\dot{c}(t)}{c(t)} - \frac{\dot{A}(t)}{A(t)} = \frac{1}{\theta}(r_j(t) - \rho_j) - g = \frac{1}{\theta}(f'(k_j(t)) - \delta - \rho_j) - g. \qquad \text{(S18.12)}$$

(S18.11) and (S18.12) are almost the same equations as the ones characterizing the neoclassical growth model with technological progress. And as the differential equation for $a_j(t)$ is globally stable, the extra terms $\frac{\dot{a}_j(t)}{a_j(t)}$ and $\frac{1}{a_j(t)}$ are immaterial as they tend to zero and a constant respectively. Hence, given that the neoclassical growth model with technological progress is a system which is saddle path stable, the steady state equilibrium is saddle path stable in each country. This establishes also saddle path stability for the world equilibrium.

Exercise 18.8, Part (c). Let us now characterize the world equilibrium as the solution to a social planners' problem in each country. As the Second Welfare Theorem holds in each country we know that the solution of this problem can be decentralized as an equilibrium. The problem the social planner in country j solves is given by

$$\max_{[c_j(t),k_j(t)]_{t=0}^{\infty}} \int_0^{\infty} \exp(\rho - n_j)\frac{c_j(t)^{1-\theta} - 1}{1-\theta}dt \qquad \text{(S18.13)}$$

$$\text{s.t.} \quad k_j(t) = f(k_j(t)) - \frac{c_j(t)}{A(t)a_j(t)} - (n_j + g_j(t) + \delta)k_j(t)$$

$$g_j(t) = \frac{\frac{d}{dt}[A(t)a_j(t)]}{A(t)a_j(t)} \qquad \text{(S18.14)}$$

$$\dot{a}_j(t) = \sigma_j - (\sigma_j + g - \lambda_j)a_j(t) \qquad \text{(S18.15)}$$

$$\dot{A}(t) = gA(t), \qquad \text{(S18.16)}$$

where $A(0), k(0)$ and $a_j(0) = \frac{A_j(0)}{A(0)}$ are given. Hence, using this formulation a world equilibrium consists of allocations $\{[c_j(t),k_j(t)]_{t=0}^{\infty}\}_{j=1}^{J}$ and paths of relative technologies $\{[a_j(t)]_{t=0}^{\infty}\}_{j=1}^{J}$ such that $\{[c_j(t),k_j(t)]_{t=0}^{\infty}\}_{j=1}^{J}$ solve the problem contained in (S18.13) for $j = 1, 2, ..., J$ and $\{[a_j(t)]_{t=0}^{\infty}\}_{j=1}^{J}$ evolves according to (S18.15) with the initial conditions $\{a_j(0)\}_{j=1}^{J}$.

So consider the social planner in country j. The current value Hamiltonian is given by

$$\hat{H}^j(c_j, k_j, \mu_j) = \frac{c_j(t)^{1-\theta} - 1}{1-\theta} + \mu_j(t)\left(f(k_j(t)) - \frac{c_j(t)}{A(t)a_j(t)} - (n_j + g_j(t) + \delta)k_j(t)\right) \qquad \text{(S18.17)}$$

where $a_j(t)$ and $A(t)$ evolve exogenously according to (S18.15) and (S18.16). The necessary and sufficient conditions stemming from (S18.17) are given by

$$\hat{H}_c^j(c_j, k_j, \mu_j) = c_j(t)^{-\theta} - \frac{\mu_j(t)}{A(t)a_j(t)} \tag{S18.18}$$

$$\hat{H}_k^j(c_j, k_j, \mu_j) = \mu_j(t)\left(f'(k_j(t)) - (n_j + g_j(t) + \delta)\right) = (\rho - n_j)\mu_j(t) - \frac{\dot{\mu}_j(t)}{\mu_j(t)} \tag{S18.19}$$

$$0 = \lim_{t \to \infty}\left[\exp(-(\rho - n_j)t)\mu_j(t)k_j(t)\right], \tag{S18.20}$$

where (S18.20) are the J transversality conditions. From (S18.19) we get that

$$-\frac{\dot{\mu}_j(t)}{\mu_j(t)} = f'(k_j(t)) - g_j(t) - \delta - \rho. \tag{S18.21}$$

Differentiating (S18.18) with respect to time and using (S18.14) we get that

$$-\theta\frac{\dot{c}_j(t)}{c_j(t)} = \frac{\dot{\mu}_j(t)}{\mu_j(t)} - \frac{\frac{\partial}{\partial t}A(t)a_j(t)}{A(t)a_j(t)} = \frac{\dot{\mu}_j(t)}{\mu_j(t)} - g_j(t). \tag{S18.22}$$

Combining (S18.21) and (S18.22) and defining $\tilde{c}_j(t) = \frac{c_j(t)}{A_j(t)} = \frac{c_j(t)}{a_j(t)A(t)}$ we get that the optimal allocation will satisfy

$$\begin{aligned}
\frac{\frac{d}{dt}\tilde{c}_j(t)}{\tilde{c}_j(t)} &= \frac{\dot{c}_j(t)}{c_j(t)} - g_j(t) = \frac{1}{\theta}\left(g_j(t) - \frac{\dot{\mu}_j(t)}{\mu_j(t)}\right) - g_j(t) \\
&= \frac{1}{\theta}\left(f'(k_j(t)) - \delta - \rho\right) - g_j(t) \\
&= \frac{1}{\theta}\left(f'(k_j(t)) - \delta - \rho\right) - \frac{\dot{a}_j(t)}{a_j(t)} - g,
\end{aligned}$$

where the last line uses that

$$g_j(t) = \frac{\dot{A}_j(t)}{A_j(t)} = \frac{\frac{d}{dt}A(t)a_j(t)}{A(t)a_j(t)} = \frac{\dot{A}(t)}{A(t)} + \frac{\dot{a}_j(t)}{a_j(t)} = g + \frac{\dot{a}_j(t)}{a_j(t)}. \tag{S18.23}$$

Additionally, we can use (S18.21) and (S18.22) to solve for the multiplier $\mu_j(t)$. Doing so shows that

$$\begin{aligned}
\mu_j(t) &= \mu_j(0)\exp\left(-\int_0^t (f'(k_j(s)) - \frac{\dot{a}_j(t)}{a_j(t)} - g - \delta - \rho)ds\right) \\
&= c_j(0)^{-\theta}A(0)a_j(0)\exp\left(-\int_0^t (f'(k_j(s)) - \frac{\dot{a}_j(t)}{a_j(t)} - g - \delta - \rho)ds\right). \tag{S18.24}
\end{aligned}$$

Hence the social planners' allocation satisfies the equations

$$\frac{\frac{d}{dt}\tilde{c}_j(t)}{\tilde{c}_j(t)} = \frac{1}{\theta}\left(f'(k_j(t)) - \delta - \rho\right) - \frac{\dot{a}_j(t)}{a_j(t)} - g \tag{S18.25}$$

$$k_j(t) = f(k_j(t)) - \tilde{c}_j(t) - (n_j + \frac{\dot{a}_j(t)}{a_j(t)} + g + \delta)k_j(t)$$

$$0 = \tilde{c}_j(0)^{-\theta}\lim_{t \to \infty}\left[\exp\left(-\int_0^t (f'(k_j(s)) - \frac{\dot{a}_j(s)}{a_j(s)} - g - n_j)ds\right)k_j(t)\right] \tag{S18.26}$$

$$\dot{a}_j(t) = \sigma_j - (\sigma_j + g - \lambda_j)a_j(t), \tag{S18.27}$$

with $k_j(0)$ and $a_j(0)$ given and (S18.26) follows from (S18.24) and (S18.20). This is a system of three differential equations in the three unknowns $[\tilde{c}_j(t), k_j(t), a_j(t)]_{t=0}^{\infty}$ with two initial conditions $a_j(0)$ and $k_j(0)$ and one terminal condition given by the transversality condition in (S18.26). Any solution to the social planner's problem will have to satisfy the equations (S18.25)-(S18.27). Furthermore, the maximized Hamiltonian is strictly concave so that the results presented in Chapter 7 establish that the solution will actually be unique. This being said, we can conclude with the Second Welfare Theorem that (S18.25)-(S18.27) together with the initial conditions $a_j(0)$ and $k_j(0)$ characterize the equilibrium in this economy.

Exercise 18.8, Part (d). Let us now consider the characterization of the equilibrium allocation. The technological evolution of $[A_1(t), A_2(t), ..., A_J(t), A(t)]_{t=0}^{\infty}$ is given by

$$\dot{A}(t) = gA(t) \tag{S18.28}$$
$$\dot{a}_j(t) = \sigma_j - (\sigma_j + g - \lambda_j)a_j(t), \quad j = 1, ..., J$$
$$A_j(t) = a_j(t)A(t) \tag{S18.29}$$

where $[A_1(t), A_2(t), ..., A_J(t), A(t)]_{t=0}^{\infty}$ satisfies the initial condition $[A_1(0), A_2(0), ..., A_J(0), A(0)]_{t=0}^{\infty}$. Hence a world equilibrium are allocations $\{[c_j(t), k_j(t)]_{t=0}^{\infty}\}_{j=1}^{J}$ and prices $\{[r_j(t), w_j(t)]_{t=0}^{\infty}\}_{j=1}^{J}$ such that $\{[c_j(t)]_{t=0}^{\infty}\}_{j=1}^{J}$ maximizes the utility of the representative household in country j taking prices as given, $\{[k_j(t)]_{t=0}^{\infty}\}_{j=1}^{J}$ is consistent with profit maximization of the representative firm in country j, prices are such that markets clear and technology evolves according to (S18.28)-(S18.29).

Profit maximization of firms in country j implies that

$$r_j(t) = f'(k_j(t)) - \delta. \tag{S18.30}$$

Letting $z_j(t)$ denote the per capita assets of the representative household in country j, the household's maximization problem is given by

$$\max_{[c_j(t), z_j(t)]_{t=0}^{\infty}} \int_0^{\infty} \exp(\rho - n_j) \frac{c_j(t)^{1-\theta} - 1}{1 - \theta} dt$$
$$\text{s.t.} \quad \dot{z}_j(t) = (r_j(t) - n_j) z_j(t) - c_j(t) + w_j(t) \tag{S18.31}$$
$$0 \le \lim_{t \to \infty} \left[z_j(t) \exp\left(-\int_0^t (r(s) - n_j) \, ds \right) \right].$$

Standard arguments (see e.g. the analysis in Chapter 8) establish that this problem has a unique solution which is characterized by

$$\frac{\dot{c}_j(t)}{c_j(t)} = \frac{1}{\theta}(r_j(t) - \rho)$$
$$\lim_{t \to \infty} \left[z_j(t) \exp\left(-\int_0^t (r_j(s) - n) \, ds \right) \right] = 0. \tag{S18.32}$$

In equilibrium markets have to clear. This implies that

$$k_j(t) = \frac{z_j(t)}{A_j(t)} = \frac{z_j(t)}{a_j(t)A(t)}. \tag{S18.33}$$

Additionally we have from f being constant returns to scale that

$$
\begin{aligned}
w_j(t) &= A_j(t)F_L(K_j(t), A_j(t)L_j(t)) \\
&= \frac{1}{L_j(t)}\left[F(K_j(t), A_j(t)L_j(t)) - K_j(t)F_K(K_j(t), A_j(t)L_j(t))\right] \\
&= A_j(t)\left(f(k_j(t) - k_j(t)f'(k_j(t)))\right).
\end{aligned}
$$

From (S18.33) we get that

$$
\dot{z}_j(t) = \dot{k}_j(t)A_j(t) + \dot{A}_j(t)k_j(t)
$$

so that (S18.31), (S18.30) and (S18.33) imply that

$$
\dot{z}_j(t) = \left(f'(k_j(t)) - \delta - n_j\right)k_j(t)A_j(t) - \tilde{c}_j(t)A_j(t) + A_j(t)\left(f(k_j(t) - k_j(t)f'(k_j(t)))\right).
$$

This can be solved for

$$
\dot{k}_j(t) = f(k_j(t) - \left(\delta + n_j - \frac{\dot{a}_j(t)}{a_j(t)} - g\right)k_j(t) - \tilde{c}_j(t),
$$

where we again used (S18.23).

This shows that the equilibrium allocation in country j is characterized by the equations

$$
\begin{aligned}
\frac{\frac{d}{dt}\tilde{c}_j(t)}{\tilde{c}_j(t)} &= \frac{\dot{c}_j(t)}{c_j(t)} - g_j(t) = \frac{1}{\theta}(r_j(t) - \rho) = \frac{1}{\theta}(f'(k_j(t)) - \delta - \rho) \\
\dot{k}_j(t) &= f(k_j(t) - \left(\delta + n_j - \frac{\dot{a}_j(t)}{a_j(t)} - g\right)k_j(t) - \tilde{c}_j(t) \\
\dot{a}_j(t) &= \sigma_j - (\sigma_j + g - \lambda_j)a_j(t) \\
0 &= \lim_{t \to \infty}\left[k_j(t)A_j(0)\exp\left(-\int_0^t\left(r(s) - n_j - \frac{\dot{a}_j(s)}{a_j(s)} - g\right)ds\right)\right],
\end{aligned}
$$

where the last equation stems from (S18.32) after substituting the expression for $r_j(t)$ contained in (S18.30) and using that (S18.33) implies that

$$
z_j(t) = k_j(t)A_j(t) = k_j(t)A_j(0)\exp\left(\int_0^t\frac{\dot{A}_j(t)}{A_j(t)}dt\right) = k_j(t)A_j(0)\exp\left(\int_0^t\left[\frac{\dot{a}_j(s)}{a_j(s)} + g\right]ds\right).
$$

These however are exactly the same equations as (S18.25)-(S18.27) characterizing the social planner's solution (note that $A_j(0) > 0$ and $c_j(0)^{-\theta} > 0$ so the constants in the transversality conditions are immaterial). Hence, the mathematical problem characterizing the equilibrium and the social planner's problem is exactly the same - both problems boil down to solve the system of differential equations given above. See also Lucas (1993) for some thoughts on a similar model with human capital accumulation.

Exercise 18.13*

We are looking for an equilibrium where all countries grow at the same rate. Since there is positive R&D in all countries, the free entry condition in country j holds with equality

$$
\eta_j\left(\frac{N(t)}{N_j(t)}\right)^\phi V_j = \zeta_j.
$$

Since all countries grow at the same rate, the relative level of technology $\mu_j^* \equiv N_j(t)/N(t)$ remains constant over time and the previous equation implies

$$V_j(t) = \left(\mu_j^*\right)^\phi \frac{\zeta_j}{\eta_j},$$

that is, the value function is constant in every country. Note also that the analysis in Chapter 13 implies that profits are constant and given by $\pi_j(t) = \pi_j = \beta L_j$. Then, the HJB equation

$$r_j(t)V_j(t) - \dot{V}_j(t) = \pi_j(t), \tag{S18.34}$$

implies that the interest rate in every country is also constant and given as the solution to

$$\eta_j \left(\mu_j^*\right)^{-\phi} \frac{\beta L_j}{r_j^*} = \zeta_j. \tag{S18.35}$$

Note that (S18.35) has two endogenous variables, the interest rate and μ_j^*. In equilibrium, the interest rate and the growth rate also have to be consistent with the intertemporal optimization of consumers, i.e. with the Euler equation. In particular, interest rates r_j^* will be given by

$$r_j^* = g\theta + \rho_j,$$

where g denotes the growth rate of $N_j(t)$, which is common to all countries. Substituting this in (S18.35) defines the equilibrium relative level of technologies μ_j^* as

$$\mu_j^* = \left(\frac{\eta_j \beta L_j}{(g\theta + \rho_j)\zeta_j}\right)^{1/\phi}.$$

Using the fact that $\sum_{j=1}^J \mu_j^* = 1$, the previous equation implies

$$f(g) \equiv \sum_{j=1}^J \left(\frac{\eta_j \beta L_j}{(g\theta + \rho_j)\zeta_j}\right)^{1/\phi} = 1. \tag{S18.36}$$

Note that $f(g(t))$ is a continuous and strictly decreasing function of $g(t)$ and satisfies $\lim_{g(t)\to\infty} f(g(t)) = 0$. Therefore, if we assume

$$f(0) = \sum_{j=1}^J \left(\frac{\eta_j \beta L_j}{\rho_j \zeta_j}\right)^{1/\phi} > 1,$$

then Eq. (S18.36) has a unique solution g. Hence, under this condition there is an allocation in which the level of technology $N_j(t)$ and consumption $C_j(t)$ in every country grows at the constant rate g. If the following condition holds

$$(1-\theta)g < \rho_j \text{ for each } j \in \{1,..,J\},$$

then the transversality condition is satisfied for every country and the described allocation is a world equilibrium. This analysis establishes that (under the above conditions) there is a unique BGP equilibrium in which all countries grow at the same rate.

Note that countries with a higher discount rate, ρ_j, have a lower relative level of technology, μ_j^* (cf. Eq. (S18.35)). The reason is that a higher degree of impatience requires higher equilibrium interest rates to induce people to save. This is turn reduces the present value of a patent so that research incentives are reduced. In equilibrium $N_j(t)$ has to be sufficiently low so that the degree of backwardness $\frac{N(t)}{N_j(t)}$ is sufficiently high to generate higher innovation rates in country j to compensate for the higher interest rates. Hence, again all countries grow at the same rate but higher saving rates (or a lower value of ρ_j) will cause a higher *level* of GDP per capita.

Let us now consider the transitional dynamics. As $\{N_1(0), N_2(0), ..., N_J(0), N(0)\}$ are initial conditions, there is of course no reason to believe, that all of them satisfy

$$\mu_j^* = \frac{N_j(0)}{N(0)}. \tag{S18.37}$$

Hence, suppose there was some j for which (S18.37) was not satisfied. First we will show that there is no equilibrium where $Z_j(t) = 0$ for all t. If this was the case, then we had $N_j(t) = N_j(0)$. From the resource constraint we then get that

$$Y_j(t) - X_j(t) = \left(\frac{1}{1-\beta} - (1-\beta)\right) L_j N_j(t) = \left(\frac{1}{1-\beta} - (1-\beta)\right) L_j N_j(0) = C_j(t), \tag{S18.38}$$

i.e. consumption will also be constant. To derive (S18.38) we used that fact that $X(t)$ and $Y(t)$ will be proportional to $N(t)$ as shown in Chapter 13. But for consumption not to change, interest rates will be given by $r_j(t) = r_j = \rho_j$. With interest rates and per period profits being constant, the HJB equation for the value function in (S18.34) implies that $V_j(t) = V_j = \frac{\beta L_j}{\rho_j} > 0$. For this allocation to be consistent with free entry into research we need that it is not profitable to engage in research activities, i.e. that for all t

$$\eta_j \left(\frac{N(t)}{N_j(t)}\right)^\phi V_j = \eta_j \left(\frac{N(t)}{N_j(0)}\right)^\phi \frac{\beta L_j}{\rho_j} < \zeta_j. \tag{S18.39}$$

Note that in (S18.39) we already used that $N_j(t) = N_j(0)$ as by hypothesis there will be no research in country j. But (S18.39) cannot hold for all t as $N(t)$ is growing at rate g. Hence, there will be some period $\bar{t}$, where research will start to be profitable, contradicting that there is an equilibrium where $Z(t) = 0$ for all t. Intuitively, the benefits from being backward will at some point be strong enough to make research worthwhile. Once this period is reached, the free entry condition will hold in all periods in the future, i.e.

$$\eta_j \left(\frac{N(t)}{N_j(t)}\right)^\phi V_j(t) = \zeta_j.$$

This shows that the growth rate of the value function will be equal to

$$\frac{\dot{V}_j(t)}{V_j(t)} = \phi \left(\frac{\dot{N}_j(t)}{N_j(t)} - \frac{\dot{N}(t)}{N(t)}\right) = \phi \left(\frac{\dot{N}_j(t)}{N_j(t)} - g\right). \tag{S18.40}$$

Note first that if there is some $\tilde{t}$ where $\frac{\dot{N}_j(t)}{N_j(t)} = g$, the economy reached the balanced growth path, as from then on the equilibrium will be characterized by exactly the conditions we derived on the BGP. Hence, to show that the economy always converges to the BGP equilibrium, it is sufficient to show that we can neither have $\frac{\dot{N}_j(t)}{N_j(t)} > g$ for all $t > \bar{t}$ nor $\frac{\dot{N}_j(t)}{N_j(t)} < g$ for all $t > \bar{t}$. Suppose first that $\frac{\dot{N}_j(t)}{N_j(t)} > g$ for all t. From the innovation possibilities frontier we have

$$\frac{\dot{N}_j(t)}{N_j(t)} = \eta_j \frac{Z_j(t)}{N_j(t)} \left(\frac{N(t)}{N_j(t)}\right)^\phi. \tag{S18.41}$$

From the resource constraint (S18.38) we get that

$$\left(\frac{1}{1-\beta} - (1-\beta)\right) L_j N_j(t) = C_j(t) + \zeta_j Z_j(t).$$

Using (S18.41) we can write this as

$$\left(\frac{1}{1-\beta} - (1-\beta)\right) L_j = \frac{C_j(t)}{N_j(t)} + \frac{\zeta_j}{\eta_j} \frac{\dot{N}_j(t)}{N_j(t)} \left(\frac{N_j(t)}{N(t)}\right)^{\phi}. \tag{S18.42}$$

But now note that $\frac{C_j(t)}{N_j(t)} \geq 0$ and (by hypothesis) $\frac{\dot{N}_j(t)}{N_j(t)} > g$. Hence we get

$$\left(\frac{1}{1-\beta} - (1-\beta)\right) L_j \geq \frac{\zeta_j}{\eta_j} g \left(\frac{N_j(t)}{N(t)}\right)^{\phi}.$$

This however is a contradiction as $\frac{\dot{N}_j(t)}{N_j(t)} > g$ so that $\frac{N_j(t)}{N(t)} \to \infty$. Hence, there is no equilibrium with $\frac{\dot{N}_j(t)}{N_j(t)} > g$. The intuition is as follows: the innovation possibilities frontier features the advantages from backwardness as stressed in the text. These could however also be seen as disadvantages from being ahead, as having a higher technology level than the world level reduces the innovation flow rate. So if one country would try to persistently grow faster than the exogenous frontier, it would have to devote more and more resources to the research sector. This however would violate the resource constraint in finite time, so it cannot occur in equilibrium.

Now consider the other case of $\frac{\dot{N}_j(t)}{N_j(t)} < g$ for all t. Using (S18.40), we know that the growth rate of the value function is negative, i.e. the value of owning a patent will be going to zero. But the value function still solves the HJB equation, which (using (S18.40)) we can now solve as

$$r_j(t)V_j(t) - \dot{V}_j(t) = r_j(t)V_j(t) - \phi\left(\frac{\dot{N}_j(t)}{N_j(t)} - g\right)V_j(t) = \pi_j$$

$$V_j(t) = \frac{\pi_j}{r_j(t) - \phi\left(\frac{\dot{N}_j(t)}{N_j(t)} - g\right)}.$$

We argued above that in such an equilibrium the value function has to go to zero. As $-\phi\left(\frac{\dot{N}_j(t)}{N_j(t)} - g\right) \in (0, g)$, this can only happen when $r(t) \to \infty$. From the Euler equation however we then know that consumption growth will be arbitrarily large. In particular we know that there exits some t such that consumption will grow faster than $N_j(t)$, which is bounded from above by g. Now go back to (S18.42). As consumption growth will exceed the growth of $N_j(t)$ we have that $\frac{C_j(t)}{N_j(t)} \to \infty$. But the last term in (S18.42) $\frac{\zeta_j}{\eta_j} \frac{\dot{N}_j(t)}{N_j(t)} \left(\frac{N_j(t)}{N(t)}\right)^{\phi}$ is weakly positive as $\dot{N}_j(t) \geq 0$, i.e. $N_j(t)$ never shrinks. Hence the RHS of (S18.42) will be arbitrarily large at some t, i.e. the resource constraint will be violated in finite time. This show that there is no equilibrium with $\frac{\dot{N}_j(t)}{N_j(t)} < g$ for all t. The intuition is follows. The spillovers in the innovation possibilities frontier make innovation increasingly easy the farther you are from the frontier. If $\frac{\dot{N}_j(t)}{N_j(t)} < g$, the economy will at some point be arbitrarily far from the frontier so that the flow rate of innovation will tend to infinity. This can only be consistent with free entry, if future patents have lower values. But as flow-profits π_j are constant, this can only be achieved if the future is discounted heavily. In equilibrium however, an increasing interest profile will also trigger an increasing consumption profile which at some point violates feasibility (as the growth of $N_j(t)$ is bounded from above).

Hence, we have shown that in the unique equilibrium all countries will reach the BGP specification at some point. Once this is the case, the equilibrium is the one characterized above. All countries grow at a common rate and the income distribution in the world is stable. As we made no reference to the initial conditions $\{N_1(0), N_2(0), ..., N_J(0), N(0)\}$, this shows that the equilibrium is globally saddle path stable.

Note that this proof of stability referred to the case of exogenous world technology growth. Although the details would be slightly different, a similar argument would also apply to the case with endogenous growth. In particular this world economy would also be globally stable, i.e. for all initial conditions $\{N_1(0), N_2(0), ..., N_J(0)\}$ the world economy would converge the unique BGP characterized in the text.

Exercise 18.16*

Consider the steady state world equilibrium. The crucial two variables whose dynamic we have to analyze are consumption and the evolution of the country's technology level $N_j(t)$. As consumption and $N_j(t)$ are growing over time, let us normalize both these variables by the technology level of the frontier $N(t)$, i.e. let us define $\chi_j(t) = \frac{c_j(t)}{N(t)}$ and $\mu_j(t) = \frac{N_j(t)}{N(t)}$. To prove global stability we will linearize the system around its steady state (χ_j^*, μ_j^*). This will give us an equation of the form

$$\frac{d}{dt} \begin{pmatrix} \chi_j - \chi_j^* \\ \mu_j - \mu_j^* \end{pmatrix} \approx A \begin{pmatrix} \chi_j - \chi_j^* \\ \mu_j - \mu_j^* \end{pmatrix},$$

for some matrix A. Then we will show that A has one negative and one positive eigenvalue which in turn proves local stability. For the argument why this implies local stability we refer to Exercise 8.15, which considers a very similar problem in the framework of the neoclassical growth model.

First of all we have to get an expression for the dynamic system of $\chi_j(t)$ and $\mu_j(t)$. The laws of motion of these variables are given by

$$\dot{\chi}_j(t) = \chi_j(t) \left(\frac{\dot{c}_j(t)}{c_j(t)} - \frac{\dot{N}(t)}{N(t)} \right) = \chi_j(t) \left(\frac{1}{\theta}(r_j(t) - \rho) - g \right) \qquad \text{(S18.43)}$$

$$\dot{\mu}_j(t) = \mu_j(t) \left(\frac{\dot{N}_j(t)}{N_j(t)} - \frac{\dot{N}(t)}{N(t)} \right) = \mu_j(t) \left(\eta_j \frac{Z_j(t)}{N_j(t)} \left(\frac{N(t)}{N_j(t)} \right)^\phi - g \right), \qquad \text{(S18.44)}$$

where $r_j(t)$ and $Z_j(t)$ are determined in equilibrium. Consider first the determination of interest rates. The HJB equation was given by

$$r_j(t)V_j(t) - \dot{V}_j(t) = \beta L_j. \qquad \text{(S18.45)}$$

In an equilibrium where there is positive research, the free entry condition has to hold, i.e. the value function has to satisfy

$$\eta_j \left(\frac{N(t)}{N_j(t)} \right)^\phi V_j(t) = \zeta_j. \qquad \text{(S18.46)}$$

Note that we showed above that this world economy will have transitional dynamics (see exercise 18.13). Around the BGP however, all countries' research expenditures $Z_j(t)$ will be positive so that the free entry condition will hold with equality around the BGP. Combining

(S18.45) and (S18.46) yields

$$
\begin{aligned}
r_j(t) &= \frac{\beta L_j}{V_j(t)} + \frac{\dot{V}_j(t)}{V_j(t)} \\
&= \frac{\eta_j \beta L_j}{\zeta_j} \left(\frac{N(t)}{N_j(t)} \right)^\phi + \phi \frac{\frac{d}{dt}\left(\frac{N_j(t)}{N(t)} \right)}{N_j(t)/N(t)} \\
&= \frac{\eta_j \beta L_j}{\zeta_j} \mu_j(t)^{-\phi} + \phi \frac{\dot{\mu}_j(t)}{\mu_j(t)}.
\end{aligned}
$$
(S18.47)

Additionally we can use resource constraint to get

$$
\begin{aligned}
\frac{Z_j(t)}{N_j(t)} &= \left[\frac{1}{1-\beta} - (1-\beta) \right] L_j - \frac{c_j(t)}{N_j(t)} \\
&= \left[\frac{\beta(2-\beta)}{1-\beta} \right] L_j - \frac{\chi_j(t)}{\mu_j(t)}.
\end{aligned}
$$
(S18.48)

Substituting (S18.47) and (S18.48) into (S18.43) and (S18.44) yields

$$
\begin{aligned}
\frac{\dot{\mu}_j(t)}{\mu_j(t)} &= \eta_j \left(\frac{\beta(2-\beta)}{1-\beta} L_j - \frac{\chi_j(t)}{\mu_j(t)} \right) \mu_j(t)^{-\phi} - g, \\
\frac{\dot{\chi}_j(t)}{\chi_j(t)} - g &= \frac{1}{\theta} \left(\frac{\eta_j \beta L_j}{\zeta_j} \mu_j(t)^{-\phi} + \phi \frac{\dot{\mu}_j(t)}{\mu_j(t)} - \rho \right) \\
&= \frac{1}{\theta} \left(\frac{\eta_j \beta L_j}{\zeta_j} \mu_j(t)^{-\phi} - \rho \right) + \frac{\phi}{\theta} \left[\eta_j \left(\frac{\beta(2-\beta)}{1-\beta} L_j - \frac{\chi_j(t)}{\mu_j(t)} \right) \mu_j(t)^{-\phi} - g \right].
\end{aligned}
$$

Let us now define the function

$$
F(\chi_j(t), \mu_j(t)) = \begin{bmatrix} \eta_j \left(\frac{\beta(2-\beta)}{1-\beta} L_j - \frac{\chi_j(t)}{\mu_j(t)} \right) \mu_j(t)^{-\phi} - g \\ \frac{1}{\theta} \left(\frac{\eta_j \beta L_j}{\zeta_j} \mu_j(t)^{-\phi} - \rho \right) + \frac{\phi}{\theta} \left[\eta_j \left(\frac{\beta(2-\beta)}{1-\beta} L_j - \frac{\chi_j(t)}{\mu_j(t)} \right) \mu_j(t)^{-\phi} - g \right] \end{bmatrix}.
$$

Around the steady state, a first-order approximation around the steady state values χ_j^* and μ_j^* yields

$$
\frac{d}{dt} \begin{pmatrix} \chi_j - \chi_j^* \\ \mu_j - \mu_j^* \end{pmatrix} \approx \nabla F(\chi_j^*, \mu_j^*) \begin{pmatrix} \chi_j - \chi_j^* \\ \mu_j - \mu_j^* \end{pmatrix}.
$$

The crucial condition concerning local stability concerns the matrix of derivatives $\nabla F(\chi_j^*, \mu_j^*)$ evaluated at the steady state. In this model we get that

$$
\nabla F(\chi_j^*, \mu_j^*) = \begin{bmatrix} \frac{\chi_j^*}{\mu_j^*} - \phi \left(\frac{\beta(2-\beta)}{1-\beta} L_j - \frac{\chi_j^*}{\mu_j^*} \right) & -1 \\ -\frac{\phi}{\theta} \frac{\beta L_j}{\zeta_j} + \frac{\phi}{\theta} \left(\frac{\chi_j^*}{\mu_j^*} - \phi \left(\frac{\beta(2-\beta)}{1-\beta} L_j - \frac{\chi_j^*}{\mu_j^*} \right) \right) & -\frac{\phi}{\theta} \end{bmatrix} \eta_j \left(\mu_j^* \right)^{-1-\phi}.
$$

To simplify the notation, let us define

$$
\frac{\chi_j^*}{\mu_j^*} - \phi \left(\frac{\beta(2-\beta)}{1-\beta} L_j - \frac{\chi_j^*}{\mu_j^*} \right) \equiv \psi.
$$

To prove local stability we have to look at the eigenvalues of $\nabla F(\chi_j^*, \mu_j^*)$. These are given by the numbers ξ, which solve the equation

$$
0 = \det \left(\begin{bmatrix} \psi - \xi & -1 \\ -\frac{\phi}{\theta} \frac{\beta L_j}{\zeta_j} + \frac{\phi}{\theta} \psi & -\frac{\phi}{\theta} - \xi \end{bmatrix} \eta_j \left(\mu_j^* \right)^{-1-\phi} \right),
$$

i.e. ξ has to solve the polynomial

$$
\begin{aligned}
0 &= (\psi - \xi)\left(-\frac{\phi}{\theta} - \xi\right) - \frac{\phi}{\theta}\frac{\beta L_j}{\zeta_j} + \frac{\phi}{\theta}\psi \\
&= \xi^2 - \xi(\psi - \frac{\phi}{\theta}) - \frac{\phi}{\theta}\beta L_j.
\end{aligned} \tag{S18.49}
$$

As this is a quadratic in ξ, there will be two roots ξ_1 and ξ_2. The system is locally stable if those roots satisfy

$$ \xi_1 > 0 > \xi_2. \tag{S18.50} $$

From (S18.49) we can solve for the two roots as

$$ \xi_{1,2} = \frac{(\psi - \frac{\phi}{\theta})}{2} \pm \sqrt{\frac{(\psi - \frac{\phi}{\theta})^2}{4} + \frac{\phi}{\theta}\beta L_j}. \tag{S18.51} $$

As

$$ \sqrt{\frac{(\psi - \frac{\phi}{\theta})^2}{4} + \frac{\phi}{\theta}\beta L_j} > \sqrt{\frac{(\psi - \frac{\phi}{\theta})^2}{4}} = \left|\frac{(\psi - \frac{\phi}{\theta})}{2}\right|, $$

we get from (S18.51) that the two solutions ξ_1 and ξ_2 will indeed satisfy (S18.50) so that the system is locally stable.

Exercise 18.21

In order to characterize the labor market equilibrium, i.e. the allocation of low and high skilled workers across sectors $i \in [0,1]$, let us first derive the labor demand for firm i. Let us focus on the demand for low-skilled labor. The demand for high skilled labor can then be derived analogously. Using the production function for intermediate goods as given in equation (18.17) and the fact that labor markets are competitive, labor demand for low skilled labor is characterized by

$$ w_L(t) \geq p(i,t)\frac{\partial y_j(i,t)}{\partial l_j(i,t)} = p(i,t)\frac{\beta}{1-\beta}(1-i)^\beta l_j(i,t)^{\beta-1}\int_0^{N_L(t)} x_L(i,\nu,t)^{1-\beta}d\nu, \tag{S18.52} $$

were (S18.52) holds with equality whenever $l_j(i,t) > 0$. In order to characterize the labor demand function from (S18.52) we have to realize that both sector specific prices $p(i,t)$ and the quantities of machines $[x_L(i,\nu,t)]_{\nu=0}^{N_L(t)}$ are endogenous. Producer i's demand for machines of type ν is given by

$$ x_L(i,\nu,t) = \left(\frac{p(i,t)}{p_L^x(\nu,t)}[(1-i)l_j(i,t)]^\beta\right)^{\frac{1}{\beta}}. \tag{S18.53} $$

As machine producers are monopolists for their variety ν, equilibrium prices $p_L^x(\nu,t)$ are again given by

$$ p_L^x(\nu,t) = \frac{\psi}{1-\beta} = 1. \tag{S18.54} $$

Plugging (S18.53) and (S18.54) into (S18.52), we get that whenever $l_j(i,t) > 0$, low skilled wages are given by

$$ w_L(t) = \frac{\beta}{1-\beta}p(i,t)^{\frac{1}{\beta}}(1-i)N_L(t). \tag{S18.55} $$

Using the same steps, equilibrium labor demand for high-skilled labor is given by

$$ w_H(t) = \frac{\beta}{1-\beta}p(i,t)^{\frac{1}{\beta}}i\omega N_H(t), \tag{S18.56} $$

for all sectors where $h_j(i,t) > 0$. From (S18.55) and (S18.56) we can now see that the labor market equilibrium indeed has a cutoff form in the sense that there exists a threshold $I_j(t)$ such that sectors $i > I_j(t)$ will only employ high skilled labor, whereas sectors $i < I_j(t)$ will only employ low-skilled labor. To see this we first show that there cannot be two sectors $m \neq k$ which employ both skill groups. Suppose this was the case. From (S18.55) and (S18.56) we would need that

$$\frac{w_L(t)}{w_H(t)} = \frac{N_L(t)}{N_H(t)\omega}\frac{1-m}{m} = \frac{N_L(t)}{N_H(t)\omega}\frac{1-k}{k}.$$

For $m \neq k$ this is obviously a contradiction. Hence at any point in time there can only be one sector $I_j(t)$ which employs both high and low skilled labor.

Secondly we show that whenever a sector m employs low skilled labor, all sectors $k < m$ employ low skilled labor too. From sector m's labor demand decision we find that

$$\frac{w_L(t)}{w_H(t)} \leq \frac{N_L(t)}{N_H(t)\omega}\frac{1-m}{m}.$$

And as $k < m$ implies that $\frac{1-k}{k} > \frac{1-m}{m}$ we get that

$$\frac{w_L(t)}{w_H(t)} < \frac{N_L(t)}{N_H(t)\omega}\frac{1-k}{k},$$

so that sector k will also specialize in employing low skilled labor. This is intuitive as sector k is relatively more productive employing low skilled labor instead of high skilled labor as sector m. A similar reasoning shows that if some sector m employs only high skilled labor, all sectors $k > m$ will also employ high skilled labor. Finally it is clear that sector $i = 0$ will only employ low skilled labor and sector $i = 1$ will only employ high skilled labor so that market clearing is assured. This shows that the labor market equilibrium will be characterized by the cutoff $I_j(t) \in (0,1)$.

Let us now explicitly solve for the quantities $l_j(i,t)$ and $h_j(i,t)$. Consider again the case of low skilled labor, i.e. sectors $i \in [0, I_j(t)]$. Using equilibrium machine demand (S18.53), the production function and the fact that $h_j(i,t) = 0$ for $i \in [0, I_j(t)]$, we get that

$$y_j(i,t) = \frac{1}{1-\beta}p_j(i,t)^{\frac{1-\beta}{\beta}}(1-i)l_j(i,t)N_L(t). \qquad \text{(S18.57)}$$

As the market for intermediate goods is competitive, intermediary prices $p_j(i,t)$ will be given by the marginal product, i.e.

$$p_j(i,t) = \frac{\partial Y_j(t)}{\partial y_j(i,t)} = Y_j(t)\frac{1}{y_j(i,t)}, \qquad \text{(S18.58)}$$

where we used the form of the production function of the final good

$$Y_j(t) = \exp\left[\int_0^1 \ln y_j(i,t)di\right]$$

and the fact that the final good is the numeraire. Substituting (S18.57) and (S18.55) we get from (S18.58) that

$$Y_j(t) = p_j(i,t)y_j(i,t) = \frac{1}{1-\beta}p_j(i,t)^{\frac{1}{\beta}}(1-i)l_j(i,t)N_L(t) = \frac{1}{\beta}w_L(t)l_j(i,t). \qquad \text{(S18.59)}$$

As $l_j(i,t) = \beta w_L(t)^{-1} Y_j(t)$ does not depend on i, all sectors $i \in [0, I_j(t)]$ employ the same amount of labor. As labor markets have to clear in equilibrium, this implies that

$$l_j(i,t) = l_j(t) = \frac{L_j}{I_j(t)}, \quad i \in [0, I_j(t)]. \tag{S18.60}$$

Similarly we get that

$$h_j(i,t) = h_j(t) = \frac{H_j}{1 - I_j(t)}, \quad i \in [I_j(t), 1].$$

Using those expressions, we can define the low-skill price index $P_{L,j}(t)$. From (S18.59) and (S18.60) we find that

$$p_j(i,t) = \left((1-\beta) \frac{Y_j(t) I_j(t)}{L_j N_L(t)} \right)^{\beta} (1-i)^{-\beta} \equiv P_{L,j}(t)(1-i)^{-\beta}, \tag{S18.61}$$

where $P_{L,j}(t)$ is constant across *sectors*. As the definition of $P_{H,j}(t)$ is analogous we get

$$\left(\frac{P_{H,j}(t)}{P_{L,j}(t)} \right)^{\frac{1}{\beta}} = \frac{1 - I_j(t)}{I_j(t)} \frac{L_j N_L(t)}{H_j N_H(t) \omega}.$$

Finally we can now solve for the skill premium $\frac{w_{H,j}(t)}{w_{L,j}(t)}$ and the threshold $I_j(t)$. The threshold is characterized by the sector which is indifferent between hiring skilled and unskilled labor, i.e.

$$\frac{w_{H,j}(t)}{w_{L,j}(t)} = \frac{I_j(t)}{1 - I_j(t)} \frac{\omega N_H(t)}{N_L(t)}.$$

Additionally we know the expression for low and high skill wages by using (S18.55) and (S18.56) for the sectors $i = 1$ and $i = 0$ respectively. Together with (S18.61) this yields

$$\frac{w_{H,j}(t)}{w_{L,j}(t)} = \left(\frac{p(1,t)}{p(0,t)} \right)^{\frac{1}{\beta}} \frac{\omega N_H(t)}{N_L(t)} = \left(\frac{P_{H,j}(t)}{P_{L,j}(t)} \right)^{\frac{1}{\beta}} \frac{\omega N_H(t)}{N_L(t)} = \frac{1 - I_j(t)}{I_j(t)} \frac{L_j}{N_j}.$$

Using these two expressions we get that the threshold is characterized by

$$\frac{I_j(t)}{1 - I_j(t)} = \left(\frac{\omega N_H(t)}{N_L(t)} \right)^{-\frac{1}{2}} \left(\frac{H_j}{L_j} \right)^{-\frac{1}{2}}$$

and the skill premium is given by

$$\frac{w_{H,j}(t)}{w_{L,j}(t)} = \left(\frac{\omega N_H(t)}{N_L(t)} \right)^{\frac{1}{2}} \left(\frac{H_j}{L_j} \right)^{-\frac{1}{2}}.$$

Again we see that for given technology levels, the skill-premium is decreasing in the relative supply of skilled labor - this is the usual substitution effect - and that it is increasing in the relative productivity of skilled labor $\frac{\omega N_H(t)}{N_L(t)}$.

Chapter 19: Trade and Growth

Exercise 19.2*

Exercise 19.2, Part (a). The representative household in country j faces the rate of return $r(t)$ from investing in international assets and $f'(k_j(t)) - \delta$ from investing in domestic assets. These two returns must be equal in equilibrium, hence we still have

$$k_j(t) = k(t) = f'^{-1}(r(t) + \delta) \text{ for all } j \in \{1, .., J\},$$

as desired.

Exercise 19.2, Part (b). Suppose that there is a steady state world equilibrium with asymptotic interest rate r^*. Note that the asymptotic effective capital-labor ratios are uniquely determined as $k_j^* = k^* = f'^{-1}(r^* + \delta)$. Note also that, aggregating the country-specific budget constraints

$$\dot{k}_j(t) = f(k_j(t)) - (n + g + \delta)k_j(t) - \tilde{c}_j(t) + b_j(t) \tag{S19.1}$$

over all countries and using the international capital market clearing condition $\sum_{j=1}^{J} A_j(t) L_j(t) b_j(t) = \sum_{j=1}^{J} B_j(t) = 0$ (cf. (19.6)) we obtain the following world resource constraint

$$\sum_{j=1}^{J} A_j(t) L_j(t) \dot{k}_j(t) = \sum_{j=1}^{J} A_j(t) L_j(t) [f(k_j(t)) - (n + g + \delta)k_j(t) - \tilde{c}_j(t)].$$

Using the fact that $L_j(t) = L(t)$ and $A_j(t) = A_j \exp(gt)$ for each country j, and noting that $\dot{k}_j(t) \to 0$ on the asymptotic steady state, the world resource constraint is asymptotically given by

$$\sum_{j=1}^{J} A_j \tilde{c}_j(t) = \sum_{j=1}^{J} A_j \left[f(k_j^*) - (n + g + \delta)k_j^* \right], \tag{S19.2}$$

that is, the weighted sum of normalized consumption over all countries asymptotes to a constant. Next note that the Euler equation for country j implies

$$\frac{d\tilde{c}_j(t)/dt}{\tilde{c}_j(t)} = \frac{r^* - \rho_j - \theta g}{\theta}. \tag{S19.3}$$

Let $j' = \arg\min_j \rho_j$ denote the country with the most patient consumers and suppose, for simplicity, that this country is unique. The previous displayed equation shows that for any $j \neq j'$, the growth rate of $\tilde{c}_j(t)$ is lower than the growth rate of $\tilde{c}_{j'}(t)$ thus $\tilde{c}_j(t)/\tilde{c}_{j'}(t)$ limits to 0. Combining this observation with Eq. (S19.2), we have that

$$\lim_{t \to \infty} \tilde{c}_j(t) = 0 \text{ for each } j \neq j'$$

and $\tilde{c}_{j'}(t)$ converges to a constant positive level $\tilde{c}_{j'}^*$ given by

$$\tilde{c}_{j'}^* = \frac{1}{A_{j'}} \sum_{j=1}^{J} A_j \left[f\left(k_j^*\right) - (n+g+\delta)\, k_j^* \right], \tag{S19.4}$$

that is, asymptotically the normalized consumption per capita is bounded away from zero only in the most patient country.

Next consider some $j \neq j'$ and note that using $\lim_{t\to\infty} \tilde{c}_j(t) = 0$ in the budget constraint (S19.1), we have

$$\lim_{t\to\infty} b_j(t) = -\left(f\left(k^*\right) - (n+\delta+g)\, k^*\right) < 0. \tag{S19.5}$$

Taking the limit of the flow international budget constraint

$$\mathsf{a}_j(t) = (r(t) - g - n)\, \mathsf{a}_j(t) - b_j(t)$$

for the same country j and plugging the value of $\lim_{t\to\infty} b_j(t)$ from Eq. (S19.5), we have that $\mathsf{a}_j(t)$ is also asymptotically constant and is given by

$$\lim_{t\to\infty} \mathsf{a}_j(t) = \mathsf{a}_j^* \equiv \frac{-\left(f\left(k^*\right) - (n+\delta+g)\, k^*\right)}{r^* - n - g} < 0. \tag{S19.6}$$

Note that we have $\mathcal{A}_j(t) = \mathsf{a}_j(t)\, A_j(t)\, L(t)$, hence

$$\lim_{t\to\infty} \dot{\mathcal{A}}_j(t) = \lim_{t\to\infty} \mathsf{a}_j(t)\, A_j(t)\, L(t) + \mathsf{a}_j(t) \frac{d\left(A_j(t)\, L(t)\right)}{dt} = \lim_{t\to\infty} \mathsf{a}_j^* \frac{d\left(A_j(t)\, L(t)\right)}{dt} = -\infty.$$

In words, each country $j \neq j'$ maintains a negative normalized asset position in the limit and runs a perpetual current account deficit (i.e. $\lim_{t\to\infty} \dot{\mathcal{A}}_j(t) < 0$). This proves that there are no steady state equilibria with $\dot{\mathcal{A}}_j(t) = 0$ for all j. Intuitively, a relatively impatient country $j \neq j'$ shifts consumption to earlier dates, accumulates a large debt early on and runs a persistent current account deficit in later dates. This is not a Ponzi scheme since the lending country (in this case, the most patient country) is willing to lend early on and receive the interest payments in the long run. Moreover, even in the long run, the lending country j' (since it is relatively patient) runs a current account surplus by investing some of the interest income that it receives from country j, $-r_j(t)\, \mathcal{A}_j(t)$, back in country j so that asymptotic balance of payments $-B_j(t) = -b_j(t)\, A_j(t)\, L(t)$ is positive but less than $-r_j(t)\, \mathcal{A}_j(t)$.

Exercise 19.2, Part (c). We next characterize the asymptotic equilibrium. Recall that we have established $\tilde{c}_j(t) \to 0$ for all $j \neq j'$ and $\tilde{c}_{j'}(t) \to \tilde{c}_{j'}^*$, where $j' = \arg\min_j \rho_j$ denotes the most patient country. Since $\lim_{t\to\infty} d\tilde{c}_{j'}(t)/dt = 0$ and $\lim_{t\to\infty} \tilde{c}_{j'}(t) = \tilde{c}_{j'}^* > 0$, Eq. (S19.3) for country j' implies that the asymptotic interest rate is given by

$$r^* = \rho_{j'} + \theta g.$$

Given the asymptotic interest rate, the asymptotic effective capital-labor ratio in any country j can be solved from $k_j^* = k^* = f'^{-1}(r^* + \delta)$. Plugging this in Eq. (S19.4), asymptotic normalized consumption in country j', $c_{j'}^*$, can be solved in terms of the parameters. For each $j \neq m$, the asymptotic levels of $b_j(t)$ and $\mathsf{a}_j(t)$ are given respectively in Eqs. (S19.5) and (S19.6). To calculate $\lim_{t\to\infty} b_{j'}(t)$, we take the limit of the capital market clearing condition (19.6) and use the value of $\lim_{t\to\infty} b_j(t)$ from Eq. (S19.5) for each $j \neq j'$, which yields

$$\lim_{t\to\infty} b_{j'}(t) \equiv b_{j'}^* = \frac{\sum_{j \neq j'} A_j(t)}{A_{j'}(t)} \left(f\left(k^*\right) - (n+\delta+g)\, k^*\right) > 0,$$

that is, in contrast with all other countries, country j' receives net transfers in the long run. Using this in the flow international budget constraint (19.4) for country j', we have that $a_{j'}(t)$ also asymptotes to a constant given by

$$\lim_{t\to\infty} a_{j'}(t) \equiv a_{j'}^* = \frac{\sum_{j\neq j'} A_j(t)}{A_{j'}(t)} \frac{f(k^*) - (n+\delta+g)k^*}{r^* - n - g} > 0.$$

This completes the characterization of the asymptotic equilibrium. Asymptotically, per capita consumption in country j', $c_{j'}(t)$, grows at the constant rate g, while per capita consumption in any other country grows at a strictly smaller rate (since normalized consumption in any other country limits to 0). Country j' asymptotically maintains a positive normalized asset position (i.e. $a_{j'}^* > 0$) while every other country has a negative normalized asset position (i.e. $a_j^* < 0$), and resources asymptotically flow into country j' (i.e. $b_{j'}^* > 0$) out of every country $j \neq j'$ (i.e. $b_j^* < 0$).

We next note that the share of net world output (that is, net of investment) consumed in country j' tends to 1. To see this, note that $C_j(t) = A_j \exp(gt) L(t) \tilde{c}_j(t)$ and recall that $\tilde{c}_j(t)/\tilde{c}_{j'}(t) \to 0$ for any $j \neq j'$, which implies

$$\lim_{t\to\infty} \frac{C_{j'}(t)}{\sum_{j=1}^{J} C_j(t)} = \lim_{t\to\infty} \frac{1}{1 + \sum_{j\neq j'} \frac{A_j}{A_{j'}} \frac{\tilde{c}_j(t)}{\tilde{c}_{j'}(t)}} = 1,$$

proving that the share of world consumption in the patient country j' tends to 1. Relatedly, the asymptotic relative GNP of country j' is greater than its relative GDP. To see this, note that the GNP is the sum of domestic output and net international factor payments, that is

$$\begin{aligned} GNP_j(t) &= Y_j(t) + r(t) \mathcal{A}_j(t) \\ &= A_j(t) L(t) (f(k_j(t)) + r(t) a_j(t)). \end{aligned}$$

Then, for any $j \neq j'$, the asymptotic ratio of the GNPs is given by

$$\lim_{t\to\infty} \frac{GNP_j(t)}{GNP_{j'}(t)} = \lim_{t\to\infty} \frac{A_j}{A_{j'}} \frac{f(k^*) + r^* a_j^*}{f(k^*) + r^* a_{j'}^*} = \lim_{t\to\infty} \frac{A_j}{A_{j'}} \frac{f(k^*) + r^* a_j^*}{f(k^*) + r^* a_{j'}^*} < \frac{A_j}{A_{j'}},$$

where the inequality follows since $a_j^* < 0 < a_{j'}^*$, showing that the relative GNP of country j' is greater than its relative technology level due to the interest income on international assets. In contrast, the asymptotic ratio of the GDPs is exactly equal to the ratio of the technology levels, that is

$$\lim_{t\to\infty} \frac{GDP_j(t)}{GDP_{j'}(t)} = \lim_{t\to\infty} \frac{A_j(t) L(t) f(k(t))}{A_{j'}(t) L(t) f(k(t))} = \frac{A_j}{A_{j'}}.$$

Hence, in this model, the GDP and the GNP of countries will diverge since country j' will accumulate international assets and receive asset returns which will asymptotically increase its GNP beyond its GDP, while every other country's GNP will asymptotically be below the GDP.

Exercise 19.2, Part (d). The equilibrium in Part (c) is unrealistic since it requires all countries $j \neq j'$ to run a sustained current account deficit so large that they asymptotically export all of their surplus output to country j' as payments on accumulated debt. A country $j \neq j'$ may plausibly default on its debt and consume its surplus output, which would be better for the country even if it is subsequently cut off from world financial markets. Thus country j has a strong incentive to default and, anticipating this, country j' may choose not to lend to country j in the first place. Hence, due to the sovereign default risk we would expect there to be a bound on the normalized debt of a country.

We could reconcile the present model with these observations by making a reduced form assumption that $\mathsf{a}_j(t) \geq -\bar{\mathsf{a}}_j$ where $\bar{\mathsf{a}}_j$ is a bound on the debt to effective labor ratio the country can have without being tempted to default. We assume

$$\bar{\mathsf{a}}_j \in [0, \frac{(f(k^*) - (n + \delta + g) k^*)}{r^* - n - g}) \tag{S19.7}$$

so that the borrowing constraint binds in equilibrium. The equilibrium then features, for all $j \neq j'$,

$$\lim_{t \to \infty} \mathsf{a}_j(t) = -\bar{\mathsf{a}}_j \text{ and } \lim_{t \to \infty} b_j(t) = -(r^* - n - g)\bar{\mathsf{a}}_j > -(f(k^*) - (n + \delta + g) k^*)$$

$$\text{and } \lim_{t \to \infty} \tilde{c}_j(t) = (f(k^*) - (n + \delta + g) k^*) - (r^* - n - g)\bar{\mathsf{a}}_j > 0,$$

hence effective consumption per capita is no longer zero in the less patient countries $j \neq j'$. Moreover, effective consumption per capita in country j' is given by

$$\lim_{t \to \infty} \tilde{c}_{j'}(t) = f(k^*) - (n + \delta + g) k^* + \sum_{j \neq j'} \frac{A_j}{A_{j'}} (r^* - n - g)\bar{\mathsf{a}}_j,$$

and the share of world output that is asymptotically consumed in country j' is

$$\frac{\lim_{t \to \infty} A_{j'}\tilde{c}_{j'}(t)}{\lim_{t \to \infty} \sum_{j=1}^{J} A_j\tilde{c}_j(t)} = \frac{A_{j'}[f(k^*) - (n + \delta + g) k^*] + \sum_{j \neq j'} A_j (r^* - n - g)\bar{\mathsf{a}}_j}{\sum_{j=1}^{J} A_j [f(k^*) - (n + \delta + g) k^*]} < 1,$$

since $\bar{\mathsf{a}}_j$ satisfies (S19.7). Hence, when the countries face binding borrowing constraints, the share of world surplus consumed in country j' no longer tends to 1, which is arguably more realistic.

Exercise 19.3

Exercise 19.3, Part (a). The Euler equation in country j is given by $\dot{c}_j(t)/c_j(t) = (r(t) - \rho)/\theta$, which implies that the growth rate of normalized consumption $\tilde{c}_j(t) = c_j(t)/A_j(t)$ is given by

$$\frac{d\tilde{c}_j(t)/dt}{\tilde{c}_j(t)} = \frac{1}{\theta}(r(t) - \rho) - g. \tag{S19.8}$$

Integrating this equation, we have

$$\tilde{c}_j(t) = \tilde{c}_j(0) \exp\left(\int_0^t \frac{1}{\theta}(r(s) - \rho - \theta g) ds\right).$$

The same equation also holds for j', which implies $\frac{\tilde{c}_j(t)}{\tilde{c}_{j'}(t)} = \frac{\tilde{c}_j(0)}{\tilde{c}_{j'}(0)}$, that is, the ratio of the normalized consumption between any two country remains constant over time.

Exercise 19.3, Part (b). First note that the world normalized consumption and the world effective capital-labor ratio are respectively given by

$$\tilde{c}(t) = \frac{\sum_{j=1}^{J} A_j(t) L_j(t) \tilde{c}_j(t)}{\sum_{j=1}^{J} A_j(t) L_j(t)} = \frac{\sum_{j=1}^{J} A_j\tilde{c}_j(t)}{\sum_{j=1}^{J} A_j} \text{ and} \tag{S19.9}$$

$$k(t) = \frac{\sum_{j=1}^{J} A_j(t) L_j(t) k_j(t)}{\sum_{j=1}^{J} A_j(t) L_j(t)} = \frac{\sum_{j=1}^{J} A_j k_j(t)}{\sum_{j=1}^{J} A_j},$$

where we have used $L_j(t) = L(t)$ and $A_j(t) = A_j \exp(gt)$ for all j. Aggregating the resource constraint (19.2) over all countries, using the asset market clearing condition $\sum_{j=1}^{J} A_j b_j(t) =$

0, and substituting the expressions for $\tilde{c}(t)$ and $k(t)$ from Eq. (S19.9) we obtain the world resource constraint in effective labor units

$$\dot{k}(t) = f(k(t)) - \tilde{c}(t) - (n + g + \delta) k(t). \qquad (S19.10)$$

Next note that, by Proposition 19.1, $k_j(t) = k(t) = f'^{-1}(r(t) + \delta)$ for all t.[1] Then, aggregating Eq. (S19.8) over all countries and substituting $r(t) = f'(k(t)) - \delta$, we obtain the growth of the normalized world consumption as

$$\frac{d\tilde{c}(t)/dt}{\tilde{c}(t)} = \frac{1}{\theta}\left(f'(k(t)) - \delta - \rho\right) - g. \qquad (S19.11)$$

Hence, the world averaged variables, $\tilde{c}(t)$ and $k(t)$ satisfy the same equations (S19.10) and (S19.11) as the standard neoclassical model and the world equilibrium can essentially be represented by a single aggregate production function, as desired.

Exercise 19.3, Part (c). With free capital flows, the world economy is integrated in the sense that each household in each country faces the same prices for effective capital and labor. With CES preferences, each household has an indirect utility function that has a Gorman representation. Hence, there is a representative world consumer as predicted by Theorem 5.2. Also, even though each country has a different technology in production, by Theorem 5.4, these production possibility sets can also be aggregated. Hence, as we have seen in Part (b), the world equilibrium can be studied as a neoclassical closed economy with normalized consumption and capital levels $\tilde{c}(t)$ and $k(t)$. The aggregation results would not hold without free capital flows, since in that case, the consumers in each country would potentially face different prices for effective capital and labor. With different factor prices, the world economy is not integrated, and aggregation results, which are derived for a closed economy, cannot be applied to the world economy.

Exercise 19.3, Part (d). The easiest way to prove uniqueness and global stability is by noting that the integrated world equilibrium is isomorphic to a closed economy in which households have heterogenous initial asset levels and face the same prices $r(t), w(t)$ for effective capital and labor. The uniqueness and the global stability of the international equilibrium then follows from the analysis in Exercise 8.30.

Since the text takes a more direct approach to analyze the international economy, we also provide a direct proof for uniqueness of equilibrium using the notation and the approach in the text. Note that the world average variables, $\tilde{c}(t)$ and $k(t)$ satisfy the same equations (S19.10) and (S19.11) as the standard neoclassical model. Hence there is a unique saddle path $[\tilde{c}(t), k(t)]_t$ that satisfies Eqs. (S19.10) and (S19.11) such that $\lim_{t\to\infty}(\tilde{c}(t), k(t)) = (\tilde{c}^*, k^*)$. If $\tilde{c}(0)$ starts above the saddle path, the resource constraints are violated in finite time. If it starts below, the total asset holdings per effective labor, $\mathbf{a}_j(t) + k_j(t)$ (international assets and domestic capital), in at least one country would violate the transversality condition and this path cannot be optimal. Hence the saddle path is the unique equilibrium for the world average variables $[\tilde{c}(t), k(t)]_{t=1}^{\infty}$. Given the unique path for world variables, and in particular the world interest rate $r(t) = f'^{-1}(k(t) + \delta)$, the normalized consumption and asset positions, $\tilde{c}_j(t)$ and $\mathbf{a}_j(t)$, of each country can be obtained as follows. Recall that

---

[1]If countries start with different initial levels of capital per effective labor, $\{k_j(0)\}_{j=1}^{J}$, capital immediately flows between countries so that each country has $k(0) = \frac{\sum_{j=1}^{J} A_j k_j(0)}{\sum_{j=1}^{J} A_j}$ with the flows reflected in the asset positions $\{\mathbf{a}_j(0)\}_{j=1}^{J}$. Therefore, without loss of generality, we assume that $k_j(0) = k(0)$ for all countries, and international differences are captured by the initial asset positions $\{\mathbf{a}_j(0)\}_{j=1}^{J}$.

$\tilde{c}_j(t)$ satisfies Eq. (S19.8). Note also that after substituting for $b_j(t)$ and $k_j(t) = k(t)$, the resource constraint of country j can be written as

$$\dot{k}(t) + \mathsf{a}_j(t) = f(k(t)) - (g + n + \delta)\, k(t) - (g + n - r(t))\, \mathsf{a}_j(t) - \tilde{c}_j(t). \qquad (S19.12)$$

Since the paths of $k(t)$ and $r(t)$ are determined, Eqs. (S19.8) and (S19.12) constitute two differential equations in two paths of variables, $[\tilde{c}_j(t), \mathsf{a}_j(t)]_t$. Given the initial level of assets $\mathsf{a}_j(0)$, there exists a unique saddle path stable solution $[\tilde{c}_j(t), \mathsf{a}_j(t)]_t$ to these differential equations which also satisfy the transversality condition

$$\lim_{t\to\infty} (k(t) + \mathsf{a}_j(t)) \exp\left(-\int_0^t (r(s) - n - g)\, ds\right) = 0, \qquad (S19.13)$$

which corresponds to the unique equilibrium path for country j. This completes the proof that there exists a unique, globally stable world equilibrium path.

Exercise 19.4*

Exercise 19.4, Part (a). Recall that we have characterized the world equilibrium in Part (d) of Exercise 19.3. To solve for the asymptotic behavior of the equilibrium (which also corresponds to a steady state equilibrium), note that $\lim_{t\to\infty} d\tilde{c}(t) = 0$ thus Eq. (S19.11) implies $\lim_{t\to\infty} r(t) = \rho + \theta g$. Using this in (S19.8) shows $\lim_{t\to\infty} \tilde{c}_j(t) = \tilde{c}_j^*$, that is normalized consumption asymptotes to a constant in every country. Taking the limit of Eq. (S19.12) and using $\lim_{t\to\infty} k(t) = k^*$, we also have

$$\lim_{t\to\infty} \mathsf{a}_j(t) = f(k^*) - (g + n + \delta)\, k^* - \left(g + n + \delta - f'(k^*)\right) \lim_{t\to\infty} \mathsf{a}_j(t) - \tilde{c}_j^*,$$

which holds only if

$$\mathsf{a}_j(t) \to \mathsf{a}_j^* = \frac{f(k^*) - (g + n + \delta)\, k^* - \tilde{c}_j^*}{(g + n + \delta - f'(k^*))} \text{ and } \mathsf{a}_j(t) \to 0.$$

This proves that the borrowing constraint $\mathsf{a}_j(t) \geq -\phi k_j(t)$ does not bind on the asymptotic steady state equilibrium.[2]

The intuition for this result is as follows. Capital flows in this economy separate the investment and saving decisions in the sense that countries with similar production technologies invest similar levels of capital (i.e. $k_j(t) = k(t)$ for all j) while consuming and saving differently depending on their relative wealth (i.e. $\tilde{c}_j(t)$ is not necessarily the same). Asymptotically, there are still capital flows but countries settle on constant normalized debt levels, i.e. $\mathsf{a}_j(t)$ limits to a constant for all j. Since the borrowing constraint of this exercise puts a limit on the current account deficit in effective labor units, this constraint does not bind on the asymptotic steady state equilibrium.

Exercise 19.4, Part (b). To build the intuition, consider the extreme case as $\phi \to 0$, so there is no international borrowing. In this case, the world economy will be a collection of closed neoclassical economies. By our analysis in Chapter 8, the countries that start at different capital levels will converge at different rates to the steady state and they will have different prices, in particular different domestic interest rates $r_j(t)$ along the transition path. This intuition carries over to the case in which $\phi > 0$ and the countries do not necessarily have the same effective capital-labor ratios and the same domestic interest rates along the transition path.

---

[2]Note that there is a typo in the exercise statement. The borrowing constraint should take the form $\mathsf{a}_j(t) \geq -\phi k_j(t)$, since $\mathsf{a}_j(t)$ represents the asset position and thus $\mathsf{a}_j(t)$ is negative for a borrowing country.

In this case, the world equilibrium path consists of a sequence of local interest rates and allocations, and the world interest rate for international assets $\left[(r_j(t), k_j(t), \tilde{c}_j(t), \mathsf{a}_j(t))_{j=1}^J, r(t)\right]_t$ which are characterized as follows. The local interest rate $r_j(t)$ is equal to $f'(k_j(t)) - \delta$, hence is characterized given the sequence for effective capital-labor ratio. Given the international interest rate sequence $[r(t)]_t$, each country's allocations $\left[(k_j(t), \tilde{c}_j(t), \mathsf{a}_j(t))_{j=1}^J\right]_t$ are found by solving three differential equations. The first two differential equations are given by the Euler equation (S19.8) and the following analogue of Eq. (S19.12) in this case

$$\dot{k}_j(t) + \dot{\mathsf{a}}_j(t) = f(k_j(t)) - (g + n + \delta)k_j(t) - (g + n - r(t))\mathsf{a}_j(t) - \tilde{c}_j(t). \quad \text{(S19.14)}$$

The last differential equation takes a complementary slackness form. In particular, if $r_j(t) > r(t)$, or equivalently $k_j(t) < f'^{-1}(r(t) + \delta)$, then the country is borrowing constrained so it must be the case that $\mathsf{a}_j(t) = -\phi k_j(t)$. If $r_j(t) = r(t)$, then the country is not borrowing constrained and we have $k_j(t) = f'^{-1}(r(t) + \delta)$. We summarize this complementary slackness condition as follows

$$k_j(t) \le f'^{-1}(r(t) + \delta) \text{ with inequality only if } \mathsf{a}_j(t) = -\phi k_j(t). \quad \text{(S19.15)}$$

Hence, the equations (S19.8), (S19.14), and (S19.15) constitute three differential equations in three paths of variables $[k_j(t), \tilde{c}_j(t), \mathsf{a}_j(t)]_t$. These equations have a unique solution given the initial conditions $k_j(0), \mathsf{a}_j(0)$ and the transversality condition (S19.13), which characterizes the countries' allocations for a given international interest rate sequence, $[r(t)]_{t=0}$. Finally, the international interest rate sequence $[r(t)]_{t=0}^\infty$ is characterized such that the induced path for international assets $[\mathsf{a}_j(t)]_{t=0}^\infty$ clears the world capital market at all times, that is

$$\sum_{j=1}^J A_j b_j(t) = \sum_{j=1}^J A_j((r(t) - g - n)\mathsf{a}_j(t) - \dot{\mathsf{a}}_j(t)) = 0 \text{ for all } t.$$

This completes the characterization of the equilibrium.

As we have seen in part one, the steady state equilibrium for the economy with no borrowing constraints also satisfies all of the above requirements and continue to be the equilibrium of the economy with borrowing constraints. Moreover, any equilibrium $\left[(k_j(t), \tilde{c}_j(t), \mathsf{a}_j(t))_{j=1}^J, r(t)\right]_t$ in the economy with borrowing constraints will converge to this steady state. However, the equilibria in the economy with no borrowing constraints and borrowing constraints could differ along the transition path to steady state. To see this, consider some equilibrium path $\left[\left(k_j'(t), \tilde{c}_j'(t), \mathsf{a}_j'(t)\right)_{j=1}^J, r'(t)\right]_t$ for the economy with no borrowing constraints. It is possible that this path satisfies $\mathsf{a}_j'(t)/dt < -\phi k_j'(t)$ along the transition to the steady state, in which case the corresponding economy with borrowing constraints would have a different equilibrium path $\left[(k_j(t), \tilde{c}_j(t), \mathsf{a}_j(t))_{j=1}^J, r(t)\right]_t$ such that in some countries and for some periods the condition in Eq. (S19.15) holds as an inequality and the borrowing constraint binds.

For a concrete example, we consider the thought experiment in Corollary 19.1, that a fraction λ of the capital stock of country j is destroyed. We claim that the corollary does not hold in the economy with borrowing constraints, in particular, capital does not immediately flow to country j. Suppose the capital levels are immediately equalized, which implies $b_j(0) = \infty$ and consequently $\mathsf{a}_j(0) = -\infty$, that is, country j temporarily runs a very large current account deficit. This violates the borrowing constraint $a_j(t) \geq -\phi k_j(t)$ hence cannot be an equilibrium. Instead, Eq. (S19.15) shows that country j will have $k_j(t) < f'^{-1}(r(t) + \delta)$ and $a_j(t) = -\phi k_j(t)$ for a positive length of time, in particular, until the capital level $k_j(t)$ reaches the world level $k(t) = f'^{-1}(r(t) + \delta)$. Hence, in an economy with borrowing constraints, capital flows will be smoother and the equalization of capital stocks will take some time, which are relatively more realistic implications.

Exercise 19.11*

Equilibrium without Free Capital Flows. We first consider the world equilibrium with no capital flows. The equilibrium in this case can be represented by a path of world prices, country specific interest rates, country specific per capita allocations and capital intermediate intensity decisions $\left[p^K(t), p^L(t), \{r_j(t), c_j(t), k_j(t), x_j(t)\}_{j=1}^J \right]_t$ such that the intermediate and the final good production in each country is competitive, the trade balance equation (19.11) holds for all countries and in all periods, the representative consumer in each country behaves optimally, and the factor markets within countries and the international intermediate goods markets clear. We next characterize this equilibrium allocation.

First, normalizing the price of the final good to 1, the maximization by the intermediate good sector in country j implies that world prices satisfy

$$p_K(t) = f'(x_j(t)) \text{ and } p_L(t) = f(x_j(t)) - x_j(t) f'(x_j(t)) \text{ for each } j. \quad (S19.16)$$

This further implies that x_j is equated across countries, i.e.

$$\frac{f'(x_j(t))}{f(x_j(t)) - x_j(t) f'(x_j(t))} = \frac{p_K(t)}{p_L(t)}.$$

Since $x_j(t)$ is equal across countries, it is also equal to the ratio of capital-intensive intermediates to labor-intensive intermediates produced in the world, that is

$$x_j(t) \equiv x(t) = \frac{\sum_{j=1}^J Y_j^K(t)}{\sum_{j=1}^J Y_j^L(t)} = \frac{\sum_{j=1}^J B_j k_j(t)}{\sum_{j=1}^J A_j}, \text{ for all } t, \quad (S19.17)$$

where we have used the fact that $L_j(t) = L(t)$ for all j (cf. Eq. (19.15)). Hence, similar to the analysis in Section 19.3, due to free trade in intermediate goods, the ratio of capital-intensive to labor-intensive intermediates in each country is determined by a sum of the world capital-labor ratios. However, in this case due to productivity differences in the capital-intensive intermediate sector, country j's capital-labor ratio in the world average is weighted by the productivity parameter B_j.

Next, note that the differences in B_j cause a difference in countries' interest rates and the rates of accumulation of consumption and capital. In particular, the interest rate in country j is given by

$$r_j(t) = B_j p^K(t) - \delta = B_j f'(x(t)) - \delta$$

and, from the Euler equation, per capita consumption in country j grows according to

$$\frac{\dot{c}_j(t)}{c_j(t)} = \frac{1}{\theta}(r_j(t) - \rho) = \frac{1}{\theta}(B_j f'(x(t)) - \delta - \rho), \text{ for all } j \text{ and } t. \quad (S19.18)$$

Note also that the capital accumulation equation and trade balance for country j imply

$$
\begin{aligned}
\dot{k}_j(t) &= B_j k_j(t) p^K(t) + A_j p^L(t) - c_j(t) - (\delta + n) k_j(t) \\
&= (B_j f'(x(t)) - \delta - n) k_j(t) + A_j (f(x(t)) - x(t) f'(x(t))) - c_j(t) \quad (S19.19)
\end{aligned}
$$

where the second line substitutes the prices from Eq. (S19.16). Hence, the equilibrium is characterized by the $2J$ differential equations in (S19.18) and (S19.19) in $2J$ paths of variables $\left[(c_j(t), k_j(t))_{j=1}^J\right]_t$, J initial conditions for $k_j(0)$, and J transversality conditions

$$\lim_{t\to\infty} k_j(t)\exp\left(-\int_0^t \left(B_j f'(x(s)) - \delta - n\right) ds\right) = 0.$$

These equations completely characterize the equilibrium. The equilibrium path asymptotically tends to a steady state, which we characterize next.

Consider an equilibrium in which the capital-labor ratio in each country asymptotes to a constant, that is $k_j(t) \to k_j^*$ for each $j \in J$, which further implies $x(t) \to x^*$ by Eq. (S19.17). The resource constraint (S19.19) for country j can only be satisfied if $c_j(t)$ asymptotes to a constant c_j^* (which can also be zero). Let $m = \arg\max_j B_j$ denote the country with the highest productivity in capital intensive intermediates and suppose, for simplicity, that this country is unique. Eq. (S19.18) implies that $c_m(t)$ grows faster than any other $c_j(t)$ so that $c_m(t)/c_j(t)$ grows unbounded, which further implies

$$\lim_{t\to\infty} c_m(t) = c_m^* > 0 \text{ and } \lim_{t\to\infty} c_j(t) = 0 \text{ for } j \neq m.$$

Since $\dot{c}_m(t) \to 0$ and $c_m^* \neq 0$, Eq. (S19.18) implies

$$B_m f'(x^*) - \delta - \rho = 0, \tag{S19.20}$$

which uniquely pins down x^*. Since $c_j(t) \to 0$ for $j \neq m$, considering the limit of Eq. (S19.19), we have

$$k_j^* = \frac{A_j(f(x^*) - x^* f'(x^*))}{\delta + n - B_j f'(x^*)},$$

which pins down k_j^* for all $j \neq m$. Using Eq. (S19.17), k_m^* can also be uniquely solved for. Finally, considering the limit of Eq. (S19.19) for $j = m$ and Eq. (S19.20), we uniquely solve for c_m^* as

$$c_m^* = A_m\left(f(x^*) - x^* f'(x^*)\right).$$

We have thus solved for the asymptotic values $\left(k_j^*, c_j^*\right)_{j=1}^J$ and completed the characterization of the asymptotic steady state of the world equilibrium.

The equilibrium in this model has a number of predictions different than the model presented in Section 19.3. Unlike the model in Section 19.3, asymptotically consumption in the country with the greatest B_m grows relatively faster than other countries and the relative world consumption in this country tends to 1. Intuitively, the productivity differences in the intermediate good that uses the accumulating factor (capital) result in a greater divergence in income differences than productivity differences in the labor intensive intermediate sector. Also, unlike the model in Section 19.3, the present model features non-trivial transitional dynamics, since capital levels converge to their respective steady states at different speeds in countries with different productivity in the capital intensive intermediate sector (cf. Eq. (S19.19)).

Equilibrium with Free Capital Flows. Next, we consider the equilibrium with free capital flows, which can be represented by a sequence of world price of capital, world interest rates and country allocations $\left[p^K(t), p^L(t), r(t), \{c_j(t), k_j(t), x_j(t), \mathsf{a}_j(t)\}_{j=1}^J\right]_t$ such that the production of the intermediate and the final goods in each country is competitive, each country's international asset position satisfies the no-Ponzi scheme condition (19.5), international capital markets clear [cf. Eq. (19.6)], the representative consumer in each country optimizes, and the factor markets within countries and the international intermediate good markets clear. In this exercise, we follow the convention in Section 19.3 and let $k_j(t) = K_j(t)/L_j(t)$ and $\mathsf{a}_j(t) = \mathcal{A}_j(t)/L_j(t)$ represent capital and assets in per-capita units instead of effective labor units as in Exercises 19.3 and 19.4. Recall also that $L_j(t) = L(t)$ for all j.

As in the first part, let $m = \arg\max_j B_j$ denote the country with highest productivity in the capital intensive intermediate sector. Since the production technology in the capital intensive intermediate sector is linear, all physical capital would be located in country m so that[3]

$$k_j(t) = 0 \text{ for all } t \text{ and } j \neq m,$$

and all capital intensive intermediate production would take place in country m. This further implies

$$x_j(t) \equiv x(t) = \frac{\sum_{j=1}^{J} Y_j^K(t)}{\sum_{j=1}^{J} Y_j^L(t)} = \frac{B_m k_m(t)}{\sum_{j=1}^{J} A_j}, \text{ for all } t. \tag{S19.21}$$

Moreover, the world price of the capital-intensive intermediate good and the world interest rate is given by

$$p^K(t) = f'(x(t)) \text{ and } r(t) = B_m p^K(t) - \delta = B_m f'(x(t)) - \delta.$$

The resource constraint for country m has features of both resource constraints (S19.14) and (S19.19), and is given by

$$\begin{aligned}
\dot{k}_m(t) + \dot{\mathsf{a}}_m(t) &= p^K(t) B_m k_m(t) + p^L(t) A_m - c_m(t) - (\delta + n) k_m(t) + (r(t) - n)\mathsf{a}_m(t). \\
&= \left(B_m f'(x(t)) - \delta - n\right) k_m(t) \tag{S19.22} \\
&\quad + A_m \left(f(x(t)) - x(t) f'(x(t))\right) - c_m(t) + (r(t) - n)\mathsf{a}_m(t).
\end{aligned}$$

The resource constraint for country $j \neq m$ is simpler because $k_j(t) = 0$, and is given by

$$\dot{\mathsf{a}}_j(t) = A_j \left(f(x(t)) - x(t) f'(x(t))\right) - c_j(t) + (r(t) - n)\mathsf{a}_j(t). \tag{S19.23}$$

Using the international capital market clearing condition

$$\sum_{j=1}^{J} \frac{B_j(t)}{L(t)} = \sum_{j=1}^{J} \mathsf{a}_j(t) - (r(t) - n)\mathsf{a}_j(t) = 0,$$

Eqs. (S19.22) and (S19.23) can be aggregated to obtain the world resource constraint

$$\begin{aligned}
\dot{k}_m(t) &= \left(B_m f'(x(t)) - \delta - n\right) k_m(t) \\
&\quad + \left(\sum_{j=1}^{J} A_j\right) \left[f(x(t)) - x(t) f'(x(t))\right] - Jc(t), \tag{S19.24}
\end{aligned}$$

where the second line defines the world per-capita consumption $c(t) = \sum_{j=1}^{J} c_j(t)/J$. The intuition for Eq. (S19.24) is that all of the net surplus in the world flows into country m and contributes to the accumulation of k_m.

Next note that the representative household in each country faces the same interest rate $r(t) = B_m f'(x(t)) - \delta$ thus the Euler equations can be aggregated, which yields

$$\frac{\dot{c}(t)}{c(t)} = \frac{1}{\theta}\left(B_m f'(x(t)) - \delta - \rho\right). \tag{S19.25}$$

---

[3]Since all capital will flow to country m immediately, we can assume that $k_j(0) = 0$ for all $j \neq m$ and that all capital differences are captured by differences in initial assets, $\mathsf{a}_j(0)$.

Finally, aggregating the transversality conditions, we also have

$$\lim_{t \to \infty} k_m(t) \exp\left(-\int_0^t \left(B_m f'(x(s)) - \delta - n\right) ds\right) = 0. \qquad \text{(S19.26)}$$

Eqs. (S19.24) and (S19.25) constitute two differential equations in two paths of variables $[k_m(t), c(t)]_t$ (recall that $x(t)$ is a linear function of $k_m(t)$ in view of Eq. (S19.21)), and has a unique solution given $k_m(0)$ and the transversality condition Eq. (S19.26). For any given initial condition, $k_m(0)$, the unique solution starts on the saddle path and limits to a steady state (k_m^*, c^*). The steady state capital level is the solution to

$$B_m f'(x^*) - \delta - \rho = B_m f'\left(\frac{B_m k_m^*}{\sum_{j=1}^J A_j}\right) - \delta - \rho = 0,$$

and the steady state world consumption is solved from Eq. (S19.24). Moreover, given the path for $k(t), x(t)$ and $r(t)$, each country $j \neq m$'s per-capita consumption and asset holdings, $[c_j(t), \mathsf{a}_j(t)]_t$ are found by solving Eq. (S19.23) and the Euler equation along with the transversality condition and the initial asset holdings $\mathsf{a}_j(0)$. Country m's consumption can be solved as the residual of world consumption, $c_m(t) = Jc(t) - \sum_{j \neq m} c_j(t)$.

The equilibrium in this case is more similar to the analysis in Section 19.3 than the equilibrium in the first part. Unlike the first part and similar to Section 19.3, effective consumption per capita in all countries asymptote to a positive constant level. Intuitively, with free capital flows, the productivity differences in the capital intensive intermediate sector do not generate income differences since all world capital is used in production in country with the highest productivity. Hence, for a world economy in which free flow of intermediate goods may fail to generate convergence in income differences, free flow of factors create an additional force towards convergence, as demonstrated by this exercise.

Exercise 19.25*

We again consider the AK version of the model. The analysis applies without change and Proposition 19.10 holds also in this case, hence the equilibrium characterization is identical. Plugging Eq. (19.39) into Eq. (19.34), we have that the steady state output of country j relative to steady state world output satisfies

$$(Y_j(t) / Y(t))^* = \mu_j \left(\zeta_j \left(\rho_j + g^*\right)\right)^{(1-\varepsilon)/\tau}.$$

Hence, conditional on the other parameters, countries with lower discount rates, ρ_j, will be relatively poor since $1 - \varepsilon > 0$.

The intuition for this result is two-fold. First, countries with lower discount rates have higher capital levels, lower interest rates and relatively cheaper export goods in equilibrium as explained in Section 19.4.[4] Second, when $\varepsilon < 1$ countries with relatively cheaper export goods receive a smaller share of the world expenditure on exports and earn less export revenues (controlling for $\{\mu_j\}_j$). This effect can be seen most clearly in the trade balance equation (19.36): a lower $p_j(t)$ (and thus a lower $r_j(t)$) implies a lower $r_j(t)^{1-\varepsilon}$ and decreases the country's share of the world income. Intuitively, when $\varepsilon < 1$, the demand for each traded intermediate is sufficiently inelastic that raising the price does not decrease the demand much

---

[4]Recall that this is because of terms of trade effects. A country with lower discount rates tend to accumulate capital faster. This increases the supply of its exports relative to the supplies of other countries and reduces the relative price of its export goods. Since export goods use capital, this in turn lowers the interest rate. In equilibrium, the interest rate decreases just enough that capital in this country accumulates at the same rate as in the rest of the world.

and leads to higher profits. Hence, countries with low discount factors and low export prices end up with lower export revenues and lower income.

Note the immiserising growth pattern here: countries with low discount rates grow faster, and as a result, the price of their goods decreases so much that fast growth ends up making them relatively poorer. This counter-intuitive feature stems from two assumptions. First, we assume that production of all (capital and consumption) goods require an intermediate component that must be imported from other countries. Hence, capital accumulation in a country does not necessarily lead to comparable output growth since the country's production technology depends on imports, which the country must finance through exports. Second, with $\varepsilon < 1$, the demand for the country's goods is so inelastic that too much production causes strong price effects and reduces export revenues. With lower export revenues, the country can import less and thus produces less, hence the two assumptions together result in immiserising growth.

Viewed in this way, the second assumption, $\varepsilon < 1$, is particularly unpalatable and implausible. When $\varepsilon < 1$, producing more hurts export revenues, hence the government of every country has a strong incentive to decrease production of export goods. The same issues are also present when $\varepsilon > 1$, since the competitive pricing of export goods is not optimal for the country. In equilibrium, countries would want to tax export goods to some extent to increase the international price of their goods to monopoly pricing levels (see Exercise 19.26). The issue is amplified when $\varepsilon < 1$, since every country always has an incentive to reduce output (regardless of the world levels of output) and in fact every country would like to reduce output to levels close to 0. Hence, the price taking assumption in the model becomes much more difficult to maintain when we assume $\varepsilon < 1$. Therefore, it is sensible to assume $\varepsilon > 1$ in the present model, which also rules out immiserising growth.

Exercise 19.26 *

Exercise 19.26, Part (a). We claim that the path described by Eqs. (19.35) and (19.36) is no longer an equilibrium, since the social planner in country j can influence the supply and the price of the goods country j exports to the world. Let $\nu \in N(t)$ be an intermediate that can only be produced in country j. Using the CES aggregator for traded intermediates, the relative demand of good ν by the sector $k \in \{I, C\}$ in country $i \in \{1, .., N\}$ is given by

$$x_i^k(t, \nu) = p(t, \nu)^{-\varepsilon} \left(\int_0^N x_i^k(t, \nu)^{\frac{\varepsilon-1}{\varepsilon}} d\nu \right)^{\frac{\varepsilon}{\varepsilon-1}},$$

where we have also used the fact that the ideal price index of the basket of intermediates is chosen as the numeraire (cf. Eq. (19.32)). Summing the previous equation over all countries i and sectors k, we obtain the total demand for country j's goods as

$$\sum_{i=1}^J \sum_{k \in \{I,C\}} x_i^k(t, \nu) = p(t, \nu)^{-\varepsilon} \sum_{i=1}^J \sum_{k \in \{I,C\}} \left(\int_0^N x_i^k(t, \nu)^{\frac{\varepsilon-1}{\varepsilon}} d\nu \right)^{\frac{\varepsilon}{\varepsilon-1}}. \quad (S19.27)$$

Note also that the marginal cost of a unit capital in country j is the domestic rate of return to capital $r_j(t)$, thus the social planner in country j sets the price for the export good ν by solving

$$\max_{p(t,\nu)} (p(\nu, t) - r_j(t)) \sum_{i=1}^J \sum_{k \in \{I,C\}} x_i^k(t, \nu)$$

subject to the demand equation (S19.27). Assuming that each country is small the exports of country j do not affect the aggregated term on the right hand side of Eq. (S19.27), thus the social planner in country j faces an iso-elastic demand curve and the optimal price is given by

$$p_j(t) \equiv p(t, \nu) = \frac{\varepsilon}{\varepsilon - 1} r_j(t) \tag{S19.28}$$

for each export good ν of country j. In particular, note that $p_j(t)$ is greater than the competitive equilibrium price $r_j(t)$, thus a fully competitive equilibrium can no longer be an equilibrium if the social planner is making the domestic production decisions. Since each country has monopoly power for the goods it supplies to the world, a social planner can strategically undersupply its goods to raise the world price and increase the income of the export sector.

Exercise 19.26, Part (b). There is some room for interpretation in this problem regarding how strong the social planner's policy instruments are. As an extreme case, we could imagine a social planner who controls all of the allocations and production decisions within the country. As a simpler alternative, we could assume that the planner has a more restricted set of instruments, in particular, that she can influence the price of the export goods (so the competitive pricing $p_j(t) = r_j(t)$ is no longer required) but otherwise cannot interfere with the domestic competitive markets. It can be shown that these two policy alternatives result in the same allocations. Intuitively, once the social planner sets the international prices to maximize domestic income, the rest of the domestic economy is like a neoclassical economy and the welfare theorems apply at the domestic market, thus the planner cannot further improve over the equilibrium allocation. Therefore, without loss of generality we suppose that the planner can only influence production (and prices) in the export sector.

Under this assumption, the characterization of the equilibrium is similar to the fully competitive case with a few differences. We have noted in Part (a) that the optimal pricing decision for the planner is given by (S19.28). Using this, the analogue of the trade balance equation (19.34) in this case is

$$Y_j(t) = \mu_j p_j(t)^{1-\varepsilon} \sum_{i=1}^{J} Y_i(t) = \left(\frac{\varepsilon}{\varepsilon - 1} \right)^{1-\varepsilon} \mu_j r_j(t)^{1-\varepsilon} \sum_{i=1}^{J} Y_i(t). \tag{S19.29}$$

In this case, since the export sector is not competitive, the representative consumer will also receive profit income from the exports sector, which we denote by $\Pi_j(t) = \pi_j(t)\mu_j$ where $\pi_j(t)$ denotes the profits made by each traded intermediate monopolist. The output of a country is then given by

$$Y_j(t) = r_j(t) K_j(t) + \Pi_j(t). \tag{S19.30}$$

To make progress, we need to calculate the profit income. Note that both the consumption and the investment sectors have a Cobb-Douglas production function with the same share τ on traded intermediates. Thus every country (regardless of how it allocates resources between consumption and investment) spends the fraction τ of its income on intermediates, which implies

$$\sum_{i=1}^{J} \sum_{k \in \{I,C\}} \left(\int_0^N x_i^k(t, \nu)^{\frac{\varepsilon-1}{\varepsilon}} d\nu \right)^{\frac{\varepsilon}{\varepsilon-1}} = \tau \sum_{i=1}^{J} Y_i(t) = \tau \sum_{i=1}^{J} \left(r_i(t) K_i(t) + \Pi_i(t) \right).$$

Using this expression in Eq. (S19.27) and plugging in the optimal price from Eq. (S19.28), the profit income satisfies

$$
\begin{aligned}
\Pi_j(t) &= \mu_j \pi_j(t) = \mu_j \left(p_j(t) - r_j(t)\right) p_j(t)^{-\varepsilon} \tau \sum_{i=1}^{J} \left(r_i(t) K_i(t) + \Pi_i(t)\right) \\
&= \tau \mu_j \frac{1}{\varepsilon - 1} \left(\frac{\varepsilon}{\varepsilon - 1}\right)^{-\varepsilon} r_j(t)^{1-\varepsilon} \sum_{i=1}^{J} \left(r_i(t) K_i(t) + \Pi_i(t)\right).
\end{aligned}
\tag{S19.31}
$$

Using the trade balance equation (S19.29) and Eq. (S19.30), the sum on the right hand side of Eq. (S19.31) can be written in terms of $r_j(t) K_j(t) + \Pi_j(t)$ and the profit income in country j can be solved as

$$
\Pi_j(t) = \frac{\tau r_j(t) K_j(t)}{\varepsilon - \tau},
\tag{S19.32}
$$

which shows, in particular, that profits are linear in the capital income of the country. Plugging this in the expression for output (S19.30) and using the resulting expression in the trade balance equation (S19.29), we obtain

$$
r_j(t) K_j(t) = \left(\frac{\varepsilon}{\varepsilon - 1}\right)^{1-\varepsilon} \mu_j r_j(t)^{1-\varepsilon} \sum_{i=1}^{J} r_i(t) K_i(t).
\tag{S19.33}
$$

Eq. (S19.33) is the analogue of Eq. (19.36) in this environment and characterizes interest rates for a given distribution of capital levels. The Euler equation in this case is unchanged, and implies

$$
\frac{\dot{K}_j(t)}{K_j(t)} = \frac{r_j(t)^{\tau}}{\zeta_j} - \rho_j,
\tag{S19.34}
$$

which, given the interest rates, determines the evolution of capital levels. The world equilibrium is then determined by Eqs. (S19.33) and (S19.34), which is the analogue of Proposition 19.11 in this setup. The equilibrium is also saddle path stable and, starting from any distribution of capital, it tends to a steady state at which all capital levels grow at the same rate g^S. To calculate the steady state growth rate, we use $\dot{K}_j(t)/K_t(t) = g^S$ in Eq. (S19.34) which gives

$$
r_j^* = \left(\zeta_j \left(\rho_j + g^S\right)\right)^{1/\tau}.
$$

Plugging this in Eq. (S19.33), we have

$$
r_j^* K_j(t) = \mu_j \left(\frac{\varepsilon}{\varepsilon - 1}\right)^{1-\varepsilon} \left(r_j^*\right)^{1-\varepsilon} \sum_{i=1}^{J} r_i^* K_i(t).
$$

Aggregating the previous equation over j and substituting for r_j^* yields

$$
h\left(g^S\right) \equiv \sum_{j \in J} \mu_j \left(\frac{\varepsilon}{\varepsilon - 1}\right)^{1-\varepsilon} \left(\zeta_j \left(\rho_j + g^S\right)\right)^{(1-\varepsilon)/\tau} = 1.
\tag{S19.35}
$$

Note that $h\left(g^S\right)$ is strictly increasing with $\lim_{g^S \to \infty} h\left(g^S\right) = 0$. Thus if we assume

$$
h(0) = \sum_{j \in J} \mu_j \left(\frac{\varepsilon}{\varepsilon - 1}\right)^{1-\varepsilon} \left(\zeta_j \rho_j\right)^{(1-\varepsilon)/\tau} > 1,
\tag{S19.36}
$$

then there exists a unique g^S that solves Eq. (S19.35). We then obtain the analogue of Propositions 19.10 and 19.12 in this setup: under Assumption (S19.36), there exists a unique steady state equilibrium in which the capital stock and output in every country grows at the constant rate g^S that solves Eq. (S19.35).

Next, we compare Eq. (S19.35) with Eq. (19.38) that determines the growth rate g^* in the fully competitive economy. Since $\left(\frac{\varepsilon}{\varepsilon-1}\right)^{1-\varepsilon} < 1$ (recall that $\varepsilon > 1$) and $h\left(g^S\right)$ is strictly decreasing, we have $g^S < g^*$, that is, the world growth rate is lower when each social planners acts in the best interest of the country. We provide the intuition for this result in Part (c) below.

Exercise 19.26, Part (c). We consider the following thought experiment for the change in welfare. We consider a country j with a fixed capital level $K_j(t)$, and compare the welfare in this country when the world is on a fully competitive BGP equilibrium with the case in which the world is on a social planner BGP equilibrium. We have already noted that the growth rate is lower in the socially planned economy, however we also need to calculate initial consumption to make welfare comparisons between the two equilibria. In fact, our analysis below shows that the initial consumption level is greater in the socially planned economy, providing a counteracting effect for welfare.

First consider the welfare in the fully competitive BGP equilibrium. Substituting $p_j^I(t)/p_j^C(t) = \zeta_j$ in Eq. (19.31), we solve for initial consumption as

$$C_j(0) = \rho_j \zeta_j K_j(0). \tag{S19.37}$$

Consumption grows at the constant rate g^*, thus welfare can be calculated as

$$
\begin{aligned}
U_j(0) &= \int_0^\infty \exp\left(-\rho_j t\right) \log\left(C_j(0)\exp\left(g^* t\right)\right) dt \\
&= \frac{\log\left(C_j(0)\right)}{\rho_j} + g^* \int_0^\infty \exp\left(-\rho_j t\right) t\, dt \\
&= \frac{\log\left(\rho \zeta_j K_j(0)\right)}{\rho_j} + \frac{g^*}{\rho_j^2}. \tag{S19.38}
\end{aligned}
$$

Next we consider the socially planned BGP equilibrium. In this case, the representative consumer receives profit income on top of rental income, hence her flow budget constraint is

$$p_j^I(t)\dot{K}_j(t) + p_j^C(t)C_j(t) = r_j(t)K_j(t) + \Pi_j(t).$$

Integrating this constraint and using the transversality condition gives the lifetime budget constraint[5]

$$\int_0^\infty \exp\left(-\int_0^t r_j^e(s)\,ds\right) p_j^C(t)C_j(t)\,dt \le p_j^I(0)K_j(0) + \int_0^\infty \exp\left(-\int_0^t r_j^e(s)\,ds\right) \Pi_j(t)\,dt, \tag{S19.39}$$

---

[5]To derive this expression, first note that the flow budget constraint can be written in units of the time 0 numeraire as

$$
\exp\left(-\int_0^t r_j^e(s)\,ds\right)\left(\frac{d\left(p_j^I(t)K_j(t)\right)}{dt} - r_j^e(t)\left(p_j^I(t)K_j(t)\right)\right)
$$
$$
= \exp\left(-\int_0^t r_j^e(s)\,ds\right)\left(\Pi_j(t) - p_j^C(t)C_j(t)\right).
$$

Next note that the expression in the first line is equal to $d\left(\exp\left(-\int_0^t r_j^e(s)\,ds\right) p_j^I(t)K_j(t)\right)/dt$, thus integrating the flow budget constraint and using the transversality condition $\lim_{t\to\infty}\exp\left(-\int_0^t r_j^e(s)\,ds\right) p_j^I(t)K_j(t) = 0$ gives the lifetime budget constraint (S19.39).

where $r_j^e(t) = \left(r_j(t) + \dot{p}_j^I(t)\right)/p_j^I(t)$ denotes the interest rate in terms of the numeraire, or equivalently, the effective discount rate (see the discussion in Part (b) of Exercise 19.27). As usual, the Euler equation and log utility imply that consumption is a constant share of lifetime wealth, i.e.

$$p_j^C(0)\,C_j(0) = \rho_j\left(p_j^I(0)\,K_j(0) + \int_0^\infty \exp\left(-\int_0^t r_j^e(s)\,ds\right)\Pi_j(t)\,dt\right),$$

which is the analogue of Eq. (19.31) for the economy with social planners. Next note that $r_j(t) \equiv r_j$, $p_j^I(t) \equiv p_j^I$ and $p_j^C(t) \equiv p_j^C$ are constant on a BGP and $\Pi_j(t) = \tau r_j/(\varepsilon - \tau)\,K_j(t)$ from Eq. (S19.32) grows at rate g^S, which implies

$$C_j(0) = \rho_j\zeta_j\left(K_j(0) + \frac{\tau}{\varepsilon - \tau}\frac{K_j(0)}{1 - \frac{p_j^I}{r_j}g^S}\right).$$

Using $r_j^e = \frac{r_j}{p_j^I} = \rho_j + g^S$ (which follows from the Euler equation), we solve for the initial level of consumption as

$$C_j(0) = \rho_j\zeta_j K_j(0)\left(1 + \frac{\tau}{\varepsilon - \tau}\frac{\rho_j + g^S}{\rho_j}\right).$$

For a given capital stock, the initial level of consumption is greater than the initial consumption in the fully competitive equilibrium in Eq. (S19.37), since the household in the socially planned economy also receives profit income from the export sector which increases the consumption.

We next calculate the welfare in the socially planned economy as

$$
\begin{aligned}
U_j^S(0) &= \int_0^\infty \exp(-\rho_j t)\log\left(C_j(0)\exp(g^S t)\right)dt \\
&= \frac{\log\left(\rho\zeta_j K_j(0)\right)}{\rho_j} + \frac{g^S}{\rho_j^2} + \frac{1}{\rho_j}\log\left(1 + \frac{\tau}{\varepsilon - \tau}\frac{\rho_j + g^S}{\rho_j}\right).
\end{aligned}
$$

Comparing this expression with Eq. (S19.38), we obtain the difference in welfare as

$$U_j^S(0) - U_j(0) = \frac{1}{\rho_j^2}\left(g^S - g^*\right) + \frac{1}{\rho_j}\log\left(1 + \frac{\tau}{\varepsilon - \tau}\frac{\rho_j + g^S}{\rho_j}\right).$$

For typical calibrations of the model, the first (negative) term dominates and this expression is negative, that is, welfare is lower in the socially planned economy. Intuitively, welfare in the social planner's BGP equilibrium tends to be lower because of the beggar-thy-neighbor policies adopted by the social planners. Each planner is tempted to lower the supply of export goods and boost their price, which is good for the household taking import prices given. However, in equilibrium every social planner does the same, import prices increase and the relative price of each country's export goods remain (more or less) unchanged while the level of exports and imports are lowered. The end result is less-than-optimal trade, slower capital accumulation and slower growth which lowers welfare.

Exercise 19.26, Part (d). For analyzing trade in goods for which the supplier country has monopoly power (either because the country is the only producer as we assume following Armington (1969), or because there are trade costs and the country has a geographical advantage to supply the good cheaper than other producers), we expect the equilibrium in this exercise to be more plausible than the one analyzed in the text. Anti-trade sentiments are already high and export taxes are a source of revenue for governments. Therefore it is plausible to assume that governments would implement the beggar-thy-neighbor policies studied in this exercise. For an example, note that the oil cartel OPEC controls the supply of oil to increase the revenues for member countries. OPEC represents cooperation among multiple countries which is arguably even more difficult to sustain than cooperation within a single country, suggesting that the analysis in this exercise may be realistic. Note also that avoiding such beggar-thy-neighbor policies requires a world-wide cooperation of governments, which is very difficult as the ongoing Doha Round of trade negotiations suggests.

Exercise 19.27 *

Exercise 19.27, Part (a). Given the collection of varieties at time t $\{\mu_j(t)\}_j$, we define $N(t) \equiv \sum_{j=1}^{J} \mu_j(t)$. As in Eq. (19.32), we set the ideal price index of the basket of traded intermediates as the numeraire, that is we assume $\int_0^{N(t)} p_j(t,\nu)^{1-\varepsilon} d\nu = 1$. We let

$$X_j^k(t) = \left(\int_0^{N(t)} x_j^k(t,\nu)^{(\varepsilon-1)/\varepsilon} d\nu \right)^{\varepsilon/(\varepsilon-1)}$$

denote the aggregated basket of intermediates used by sector $k \in \{I, C\}$ in country $j \in \{1, .., J\}$. Recall that the consumption and investment goods are produced with technologies

$$
\begin{aligned}
C_j(t) &= \chi K_j^C(t)^{(1-\tau)(1-\gamma)} \left(L_j^E(t) \right)^{(1-\tau)\gamma} X_j^C(t)^\tau, \\
I_j(t) &= \zeta_j^{-1} \chi K_j^I(t)^{(1-\tau)} X_j^I(t)^\tau.
\end{aligned}
$$

Using this notation, a monopolist in country j for variety ν faces the isoelastic demand

$$x(t,\nu) = p(t,\nu)^{-\varepsilon} \sum_{i=1}^{J} \sum_{k\in\{C,I\}} X_i^k(t),$$

and has marginal cost equal to the rental cost of capital in country j, $r_j(t)$. Thus, the country j monopolists set prices given by

$$p_j(t) \equiv p_j(t,\nu) = \frac{\varepsilon}{\varepsilon-1} r_j(t), \tag{S19.40}$$

and their per-period profits are given by

$$
\begin{aligned}
\pi_j(t,\nu) &= \frac{r_j(t)}{\varepsilon-1} \left(\frac{\varepsilon}{\varepsilon-1} r_j(t) \right)^{1-\varepsilon} \sum_{i=1}^{J} \sum_{k\in\{C,I\}} X_i^k(t) \\
&= \frac{1}{\varepsilon} p_j(t)^{1-\varepsilon} \sum_{i=1}^{J} \sum_{k\in\{C,I\}} X_i^k(t). \tag{S19.41}
\end{aligned}
$$

Exercise 19.27, Part (b). Note that the labor market clearing condition is given by $L_j^R(t) + L_j^E(t) = 1$, hence we need to characterize the demand for labor in the R&D and the production sectors. First consider the R&D sector. The value function for a monopolist satisfies the Bellman equation

$$r_j^e(t) V_j(t,\nu) = \pi_j(t,\nu) + \dot{V}_j(t,\nu) - \delta V_j(t,\nu), \tag{S19.42}$$

where

$$r_j^e(t) \equiv \frac{r_j(t) + \dot{p}_j^I(t)}{p_j^I(t)} \tag{S19.43}$$

is the effective discount rate, that is, the interest rate for bonds denominated in the numeraire. To understand this expression, note that the ratio of the rental rate of capital to the price of capital $r_j(t)/p_j^I(t)$ is the interest rate for bonds denominated in capital. By no-arbitrage, the interest rate on numeraire bonds also takes into account the change in the price of capital goods $\dot{p}_j^I(t)/p_j^I(t)$, leading to the expression for the effective discount rate. Given the value function $V_j(t,\nu)$ that solves Eq. (S19.42), the free entry condition in country j implies

$$V_j(t,\nu)\,\eta \le w_j(t)\,, \text{ with equality if } L_j^R(t) > 0. \tag{S19.44}$$

In equilibrium, the free entry condition characterizes the demand for labor in the R&D sector: labor is allocated to R&D until the number of varieties increases and $V_j(t,\nu)$ decreases just enough that Eq. (S19.44) holds. Next consider the labor demand in the production sector. As labor is used only in the production of consumption goods, $L_j^E(t)$ can be found by considering the share of consumption in national income. In particular we have

$$(1-\gamma)(1-\tau)\,p_j^C(t)\,C_j(t) = L_j^E(t)\,w_j(t)\,, \tag{S19.45}$$

which characterizes the demand for labor in the production sector.

Exercise 19.27, Part (c). We consider a BGP equilibrium in which, for each country j, $r_j(t) \equiv r_j, \mu_j(t) \equiv \mu_j$ and $L_j^R(t) \equiv L_j^R > 0$ are constant while capital and consumption grow at the common constant rate g. We characterize the BGP equilibrium in two steps. First, we take the labor allocations $\left\{L_j^R\right\}_j$ as given and we characterize the resulting BGP equilibrium variables, in particular the growth rate g. Second, we solve for the allocations $\left\{L_j^R\right\}_j$ in terms of g so that the resulting BGP equilibrium variables satisfy the free entry conditions (S19.44). The growth rate g is then solved as a fixed point and the rest of the variables are characterized.

For the first step, consider a BGP allocation in which the R&D labor employment levels are constant and given by $\left\{L_j^R\right\}_j$. Note that the R&D technology equation is $\dot{\mu}_j(t) = \eta L_j^R - \delta\mu_j(t)$, thus the technology levels along the BGP are also constant and are given by

$$\mu_j = \frac{\eta}{\delta}L_j^R \text{ for each } j. \tag{S19.46}$$

Given a constant distribution of $\left\{L_j^R\right\}$ and $\left\{\mu_j\right\}_j$, the economy is very similar to the baseline case and the rest of the equilibrium variables are characterized similarly. We first show that the analogue of the trade balance equation Eq. (19.46) applies in this case. Note that the investment and the consumption technologies are both Cobb-Douglas with the same share τ of imports, hence no matter how the consumer splits her income between consumption and investment, she will spend τ of her wealth on imports. Thus the following trade balance similar to Eq. (19.46) holds in this case[6]

$$r_j(t) K_j(t) + w_j(t) = \mu_j \left(\frac{\varepsilon}{\varepsilon-1} r_j(t) \right)^{1-\varepsilon} \sum_{i=1}^{J} [r_i(t) K_i(t) + w_i(t)], \text{ for each } j \in \{1,..,J\},$$
(S19.47)

where we have substituted for $p_j(t)$ from Eq. (S19.40).

Second, we show that Eq. (19.35) also applies in this case and the analogue of Eq. (19.47) holds. To see these, note that log preferences imply that the consumer spends a constant fraction of her lifetime income on consumption today, i.e.[7]

$$p_j^C(t) C_j(t) = \rho_j \left[p_j^I(t) K_j(t) + \int_t^\infty \exp\left(-\int_t^z r_j^e(s)\, ds \right) w(z)\, dz \right],$$
(S19.48)

where recall that $r_j^e(t)$ is the effective discount rate given in (S19.43). Since $L_j^E(t) = 1 - L_j^R$ is constant in a BGP equilibrium, Eq. (S19.45) shows that wages are a constant multiple of the expenditure on consumption. Using this, the previous displayed equation can be simplified to[8]

$$\frac{\left(1 - L_j^R\right) w_j(t)}{(1-\gamma)(1-\tau)} = p_j^C(t) C_j(t) = \frac{\rho_j}{1 - \frac{(1-\gamma)(1-\tau)}{1-L_j^R}} p_j^I(t) K_j(t).$$
(S19.49)

This shows that consumers spend a constant fraction of the value of the capital stock as in the baseline economy analyzed in Sections (19.4). Eq. (19.35) then similarly follows from the Euler equation. Moreover, substituting for $p_j^I(t)$ from Eq. (19.33) into Eq. (S19.49), we obtain the analogue of Eq. (19.47) as

$$\frac{w_j(t)}{r_j(t) K_j(t) + w_j(t)} = \frac{(1-\gamma)(1-\tau)\rho_j}{\zeta_j^{-1} r_j(t)^\tau \left[1 - L_j^R - (1-\gamma)(1-\tau) \right] + (1-\gamma)(1-\tau)\rho_j}.$$
(S19.50)

Given a distribution $\left\{ L_j^R \right\}_j$ and a resulting distribution $\{\mu_j\}_j$, the equilibrium is then uniquely characterized by Eqs. (19.35), (S19.47) and (S19.50). As in the baseline case, given a distribution of capital stock $\{K_j\}_j$, Eqs. (S19.47) and (S19.50) uniquely determine the prices $\{w_j(t), r_j(t)\}_j$; and given the rental rates $\{r_j(t)\}_j$, Eq. (19.35) uniquely determines

---

[6]This expression is not entirely correct since the income of the representative household also includes profits from monopolistic firms, and some of this income is spent on R&D investment (i.e. as wage payments to R&D labor) which does not use traded intermediates. Incorporating these two effects into the trade balance equation changes nothing essential while considerably complicating the algebra, thus we ignore these effects in our analysis, which amounts to assuming that the gap between the period monopolistic profits and the period R&D investment is small relative to aggregate income. See Acemoglu and Ventura (2002) for an alternative version of the model that does not require this simplification.

[7]Consistent with our earlier simplifying assumption for the trade balance equation, we also ignore the shares of monopolistic firms in the lifetime income of the representative consumer.

[8]To show this step, note that log utility implies $p_j^C(t) C_j(t)$ grows at rate $r_j^e(t) - \rho_j$. By Eq. (S19.45), wages are a constant multiple of $p_j^C(t) C_j(t)$ so $w_j(t)$ also grows at rate $r_j^e(t) - \rho_j$, which implies $w(z) = w(t) \exp\left(\int_t^z (r_j^e(s) - \rho_j)\, ds \right)$. Plugging this into the lifetime budget of the household (in the RHS of Eq. (S19.48)) and using $w_j(t) = \frac{(1-\gamma)(1-\tau)}{1-L_j^R} p_j^C(t) C_j(t)$ from Eq. (S19.45) gives

$$p_j^C(t) C_j(t) = \rho_j \left[p_j^I(t) K_j(t) + p_j^C(t) C_j(t) \frac{(1-\gamma)(1-\tau)}{1-L_j^R} \int_t^\infty \exp\left(-\rho_j(z-t)\right) dz \right].$$

Rearranging this expression leads to Eq. (S19.49).

the evolution of the capital stock. Next we characterize the growth rate g on this BGP equilibrium (conditional on $\left\{L_j^R\right\}_j$). On a BGP, we have $\dot{p}_j^C(t) = 0$ and $\dot{p}_j^I(t) = 0$ thus the Euler equation (19.29) implies that the effective discount rate is constant and given by

$$g + \rho_j = r_j^e = r_j / p_j^I = \zeta_j^{-1} r_j^\tau, \tag{S19.51}$$

where the last equality uses Eq. (19.33). From the previous displayed equation, we solve for the rental rate in terms of the growth rate, that is $r_j = \left(\zeta_j / \left(g + \rho_j\right)\right)^{1/\tau}$. Substituting this in Eq. (S19.47), plugging in the expression for μ_j from Eq. (S19.46) and summing over all j, we obtain an equation that characterizes the growth rate g given the labor allocation $\left\{L_j^R\right\}_j$

$$\sum_{j=1}^{J} \left(\frac{\eta L_j^R}{\delta}\right) \left(\zeta_j \left(g + \rho_j\right)\right)^{(1-\varepsilon)/\tau} = \left(\frac{\varepsilon - 1}{\varepsilon}\right)^{1-\varepsilon}, \tag{S19.52}$$

which completes the first step.

For the second step, we solve for the unique $\left\{L_j^R\right\}_j$ which leads to equilibrium variables that satisfy the free entry conditions (S19.44). On a BGP equilibrium, profits are also growing at rate g, machines depreciate at rate δ and the effective discount rate is equal to $g + \rho_j$ (cf. Eq. (S19.51)). Combining these observations and the expressions for profits from Eq. (S19.41), the value function on a BGP is given by

$$\begin{aligned}
V_j(t) = \frac{\pi_j(t)}{g + \rho_j - g + \delta} &= \frac{1}{\varepsilon} p_j(t)^{1-\varepsilon} \frac{\sum_{i=1}^{J} \sum_{k \in \{I,C\}} X_i^k(t)}{\rho_j + \delta} \\
&= \frac{\frac{1}{\varepsilon} \left(\frac{\varepsilon}{\varepsilon-1} r_j\right)^{1-\varepsilon}}{\rho_j + \delta} \tau \sum_{i=1}^{J} \left[r_i K_i(t) + w_i(t)\right] \\
&= \frac{\tau}{\varepsilon} \frac{r_j K_j(t) + w_j(t)}{\mu_j \left(\rho_j + \delta\right)}, \tag{S19.53}
\end{aligned}$$

where the second line uses the fact that world exports have a share τ of total world income and Eq. (S19.40), and the third line uses Eq. (S19.47). On a BGP with positive research in every country, the free entry condition (S19.44) must be satisfied with equality, which after combining with the previous expression for the value function implies

$$\frac{\tau}{\varepsilon} \frac{r_j K_j(t) + w_j(t)}{\mu_j \left(\rho_j + \delta\right)} \eta = w_j(t).$$

Combining this expression with Eq. (S19.50) and substituting $\zeta_j^{-1} (r_j)^\tau = \rho_j + g$ from Eq. (S19.51) gives

$$\frac{\tau}{\varepsilon} \frac{\eta}{\mu_j \left(\rho_j + \delta\right)} = \frac{(1-\gamma)(1-\tau)\rho_j}{(\rho_j + g)\left[1 - L_j^R - (1-\gamma)(1-\tau)\right] + (1-\gamma)(1-\tau)\rho_j}.$$

Substituting for μ_j from Eq. (S19.46) and rearranging terms, we have

$$L_j^R(g) = \frac{1 + \frac{g}{\rho_j}\left(1 - (1-\gamma)(1-\tau)\right)}{\frac{\varepsilon}{\tau}\left(\frac{\rho_j}{\delta} + 1\right)(1-\gamma)(1-\tau) + 1 + \frac{g}{\rho_j}}, \tag{S19.54}$$

which solves the allocation of the labor force in country j in terms of the growth rate g. Plugging $L_j^R(g)$ into Eq. (S19.52) gives a single equation in terms of the parameters that determines the growth rate g. Assuming that the resulting solution for the world labor allocation satisfies $L_j^R(g) \in (0,1)$ for each j, this solution is the unique BGP equilibrium labor allocation and the corresponding g is the BGP growth rate, completing step two. Once we determine L_j^R in terms of the exogenous parameters, our analysis for step one determines the remaining equilibrium variables, completing the characterization of the BGP equilibrium.

The economic forces that lead to a BGP are diminishing returns due to international trade and specialization. From the baseline analysis in the text, we already know that a country cannot grow faster than other countries by accumulating capital, since it faces diminishing returns in the world market for its goods. Similarly, a country cannot innovate too many varieties, since it also faces diminishing returns in the number of varieties. To see this, suppose country j increases the number of its varieties from μ_j^1 to $\mu_j^2 > \mu_j^1$. Note that the share of world income that goes to expenditure on the basket of traded intermediates remains constant and equal to τ due to the Cobb-Douglas aggregator. Thus, assuming (for simplicity) that the price of all tradable goods are the same, country j increases its export revenues from the share of $\mu_j^1 \tau / \left(\sum_{i=1}^J \mu_i \right)$ of world income to the share $\mu_j^2 \tau / \left(\sum_{i=1}^J \mu_i \right)$ of world income, which implies that innovation features diminishing returns.[9] In particular, the share of world expenditure going to each variety decreases, which decreases the value of a new variety (cf. (S19.53)) and acts as a stabilizing force. Also when the country employs more labor in R&D, the supply of labor in production decreases and wages go up, which acts as another stabilizing force. Both of these forces imply that the countries' varieties are constant on a BGP.

Exercise 19.27, Part (d). Assume that there are many countries so changing the discount rate of a single country has a small effect on the world BGP growth rate g. Then, Eqs. (S19.54) and (S19.46) imply that an increase in the discount rate (typically) decreases the labor employed in the R&D sector and the number of varieties that the country produces, that is, less patient countries have fewer varieties and "worse technology" in equilibrium. Intuitively, the interest rate is higher in less patient countries, hence the value of being a monopolist is lower, which reduces innovation incentives and the equilibrium level of varieties.

Exercise 19.27, Part (e). We first claim that there cannot be balanced growth when the R&D sector uses both capital and labor. Note that this is a 2 sector AK economy (similar to Rebelo (1991)) hence the capital-labor ratio increases over time and the price of capital relative to labor decreases. Then, with a mixed R&D production technology, the cost of producing varieties relative to wages would also decrease. This in turn would increase the incentives to innovate and the number of varieties in the world, that is, there would be technological progress. But in an AK economy with technological progress, capital would grow at ever increasing rates (due to the growth in A) and there would not be balanced growth.

Next, consider the case in which the R&D sector uses only labor but the intermediate goods are produced using both capital and labor. We claim that nothing essential changes in this case and there is a BGP equilibrium with the same qualitative properties as in the baseline case. In this case, the unit cost of producing a variety would be different hence the monopolist profits per unit sold (given in Eq. (S19.41)) would be different. However, the expression for the value function in (S19.53) would remain the same. Intuitively, the share of traded goods

---

[9]Consider, for example, the extreme case in which innovation is so large that $\mu_j^1 \sim \sum_{i=1}^J \mu_j$. In this case additional innovation does not increase export revenues (for a given level of world income).

in world output is constant (due to the Cobb-Douglas production function) thus the demand changes just enough to offset any relative price changes, leading to the same expression for revenues, profits and the value function. Hence, the free entry condition (S19.44) could be solved following the same approach above. As the only essential difference, we would have to keep track of L_j^I (the amount of labor employed in the intermediate sector) along with L_j^R and L_j^E and the labor market clearing condition would take the form $L_j^R + L_j^E + L_j^I = 1$. If the varieties are also produced with a Cobb-Douglas production function using labor and capital, then the share of labor employed in the intermediate sector, L_j^I, would be a constant fraction of the share of labor employed in production, $L_j^E + L_j^I$. It follows that there exists a BGP equilibrium with similar qualitative properties as in the baseline case.

Exercise 19.28

From Eq. (19.54), it follows that an increase in ι weakly decreases $w^n(t)/w^s(t)$. Since all goods are traded at zero cost, $w^n(t)/w^s(t)$ is also a measure of the PPP adjusted income per capita and welfare in this model. Hence, increasing ι always weakly closes the relative income gap. With a higher ι, there is an increase in demand for Southern labor since more goods are imitated and produces in the South (cf. Eq. (19.53)). Since labor supply in the South is fixed, each Southern good is supplied at a lower relative scale and a higher relative world price (cf. Eqs. (19.51) and (19.50)), leading to an increase in the relative wage of Southern labor (cf. Eq. (19.49)).

The effects of ι on the PPP adjusted income in the North are ambiguous. On the one hand, more goods are imitated by the South, which reduces the price of these goods and increases the purchasing power of a Northern worker. On the other hand, the relative wage in the North decreases which works towards decreasing the welfare in the North. To see which of these effects dominates, we calculate the welfare of a Northern worker at the steady state for a given level of goods $N(t)$. First, consider the case in which the steady state is an equalization equilibrium. In this case, wages are already equalized and increasing ι has no effect on relative wages or relative prices, and hence no effect on the welfare of a Northern worker. So we focus on the second case, the specialization equilibrium. In this case, the number of new and old goods in equilibrium is given by

$$N^n(t) = \frac{\eta}{\eta + \iota} N(t), \text{ and } N^o(t) = \frac{\iota}{\eta + \iota} N(t).$$

Note that a Northern worker with wage $w^n(t)$ solves

$$\max_{[c(t,\nu)]_\nu} \left(\int_0^{N(t)} c(t,\nu)^{(\varepsilon-1)/\varepsilon} d\nu \right)^{\varepsilon/(\varepsilon-1)}$$

$$\text{s.t.} \quad \int_0^{N(t)} c(t,\nu) p(t,\nu) \leq w^n(t).$$

Using the Dixit-Stiglitz aggregator, the optimal value of this problem is equal to $w^n(t)/P$ where $P = \left(\int_0^{N(t)} p(t,\nu)^{1-\varepsilon} d\nu \right)^{1/(1-\varepsilon)}$ is the ideal price index. Recall that the price of old and new goods are given by $p^o(t) = w^s(t) < p^n(t) = w^n(t)$. Then, $w^n(t)/P$ can be written as

$$\left(\frac{w^n (t)^{1-\varepsilon}}{N(t) \left(\frac{\eta}{\eta+\iota} w^n (t)^{1-\varepsilon} + \frac{\iota}{\eta+\iota} w^s (t)^{1-\varepsilon} \right)} \right)^{1/(1-\varepsilon)}$$

$$= N(t)^{1/(\varepsilon-1)} \left(\frac{\eta}{\eta+\iota} + \frac{\iota}{\eta+\iota} \left(\frac{w^n(t)}{w^s(t)} \right)^{(\varepsilon-1)} \right)^{1/(\varepsilon-1)}$$

$$= N(t)^{1/(\varepsilon-1)} \left(\frac{\eta}{\eta+\iota} + \frac{\iota}{\eta+\iota} \left[\frac{\eta L^s}{\iota L^n} \right]^{(\varepsilon-1)/\varepsilon} \right)^{1/(\varepsilon-1)} .$$

The last two lines clarify the two effects we have identified. From the second line, for a given level of $w^n (t) / w^s (t)$ (which is greater than 1), increasing ι tends to increase Northern welfare since it lowers the aggregate price index P and increases the purchasing power in the North. The third in turn line shows that, increasing ι decreases $w^n (t) / w^s (t)$ (the term in brackets) and tends to decrease the welfare. Note that we have

$$\frac{d}{d\iota} \left(\frac{\eta}{\eta+\iota} + \frac{\iota^{1/\varepsilon}}{\eta+\iota} \left[\frac{\eta L^s}{L^n} \right]^{(\varepsilon-1)/\varepsilon} \right) = -\frac{\eta}{(\eta+\iota)^2} + \left[\frac{\eta/\iota + 1 - \varepsilon}{\varepsilon (\eta+\iota)^2} \right] \iota^{1/\varepsilon} \left(\frac{\eta L^s}{L^n} \right)^{(\varepsilon-1)/\varepsilon} . \quad \text{(S19.55)}$$

Hence, the steady state welfare in the North decreases in response to an increase in ι iff the expression in (S19.55) is negative. A sufficient condition for this to happen is $\varepsilon > \eta/\iota + 1$ (while still assuming that $(\eta L^s/\iota L^n)^{1/\varepsilon} > 1$ so we are in the specialization equilibrium).[10] The higher substitutability between goods, the lower the level of innovation in the North, and the higher the initial level of imitation, the more likely that this sufficient condition will hold and that the North will be worse off from an increase in imitation. We conclude that, in the Krugman (1979) model, increasing the rate of technology adoption closes the welfare gap between the North and the South, but may make the North better or worse off depending on the parameters of the model.

Exercise 19.29

Exercise 19.29, Part (a). The economy as described in the exercise does not admit a BGP equilibrium. Hence we analyze a slightly different economy in which the R&D technology in the North also uses labor and is given by

$$\dot{N}(t) = \eta N^n (t) L_N^R. \quad \text{(S19.56)}$$

We normalize the ideal price index to 1 at any t, i.e.

$$\left(\int_0^{N(t)} p(t,\nu)^{1-\varepsilon} d\nu \right)^{1/(1-\varepsilon)} = 1. \quad \text{(S19.57)}$$

We use subscripts $\{N, S\}$ to denote the allocations in the North and the South and we denote the aggregate consumption in country j with $C_j (t) = \left(\int_0^{N(t)} c_j (t)^{(\varepsilon-1)/\varepsilon} \right)^{\varepsilon/(\varepsilon-1)}$ for

---

[10]When ε is sufficiently large, the goods are more substitutable so both the relative prices and relative wages respond less to an increase in imitation, which shows that the two effects that we have identified are both weaker. It turns out that, for sufficiently large ε, the second effect dominates and the Northern labor is worse off from an increase in imitation.

$j \in \{N, S\}$. Optimization by the representative consumer in country $j \in \{N, S\}$ yields

$$c_j(t, \nu) = p(t, \nu)^{-\varepsilon} C_j(t) \text{ for each } \nu \in N(t) \text{ and } t \qquad (S19.58)$$

$$\frac{\dot{C}_j(t)}{C_j(t)} = \frac{1}{\theta}(r_j(t) - \rho) \text{ for each } t,$$

in particular, the demand for each good is iso-elastic. A monopolist in the North uses one unit of Northern labor to produce one unit and sells its product in both Southern and Northern markets, thus she solves

$$\max_{p(t,\nu)} p(t,\nu)^{-\varepsilon} (C_N(t) + C_S(t)) (p(t,\nu) - w_N(t)),$$

which leads to the optimal price

$$p(t,\nu) = \frac{\varepsilon}{\varepsilon - 1} w_N(t), \text{ for all } \nu \in N^n(t) \text{ and } t, \qquad (S19.59)$$

as desired. The monopolist's per period profits are given by

$$\pi(t,\nu) = \frac{1}{\varepsilon - 1} w_N(t) \sum_{j \in \{N,S\}} c_j(t,\nu), \text{ for each } \nu \in N^n(t). \qquad (S19.60)$$

Throughout, we assume $\varepsilon > 1$, since otherwise we have the counterintuitive result that growth of varieties reduces welfare (see Exercise 19.25).

Exercise 19.29, Part (b). Given $N^n(t), N^o(t)$ and the labor allocated to production in the North $L_N^E = 1 - L_N^R$, the static equilibrium is characterized by the allocation of $L_n^E(t)$ between old and new good sectors and wages $(L_N^n, L_N^o, w_N(t), w_S(t))$ such that markets clear and each worker in the North optimally chooses the sector to work. The price of each new and each old good is the same, which we respectively denote by $p^n(t)$ and $p^o(t)$. We also denote the demand in country j for each new and old good with $c_j^n(t)$ and $c_j^o(t)$. We denote the relative wages $w_N(t)/w_S(t)$ by $\omega(t)$.

First note that the price of the new goods $p^n(t)$ is characterized in Eq. (S19.59). The old goods $p^o(t)$ are produced competitively in the South (and perhaps also in the North) thus we have $p^o(t) = w_S(t)$. Next note that the supply of new and old goods are pinned down by total labor allocated to the production of each kind, which implies

$$\sum_{j \in \{N,S\}} c_j^n(t) = \frac{L_N^n}{N^n(t)} \text{ and } \sum_{j \in \{N,S\}} c_j^o(t) = \frac{L_S^o + L_N^o}{N^o(t)}. \qquad (S19.61)$$

Using these expressions for the price and the demand for goods in the first-order condition (S19.58), we have

$$\frac{L_S^o + L_N^o}{L_N^n} \frac{N^n(t)}{N^o(t)} = \frac{c_j^o(t)}{c_j^n(t)} = \left(\frac{p^o(t)}{p^n(t)}\right)^{-\varepsilon} = \left(\frac{w_S(t)}{\frac{\varepsilon}{\varepsilon-1} w_N(t)}\right)^{-\varepsilon}$$

which leads to an expression for relative wages

$$\omega(t) = \frac{\varepsilon - 1}{\varepsilon} \left(\frac{L_S + L_N^E - L_N^n}{L_N^n} \frac{N^n(t)}{N^o(t)}\right)^{1/\varepsilon}, \qquad (S19.62)$$

where we have used that all Southern labor is employed in the production of old goods and $L_N^n = L_N^E - L_N^n$ by labor market clearing in the North (recall that $L_N^E = L_N - L_R$ is the labor in the production sector).

As in the text, there are two cases to consider. If

$$\frac{\varepsilon - 1}{\varepsilon} \left(\frac{L_S}{L_N^E} \frac{N^n(t)}{N^o(t)} \right)^{1/\varepsilon} > 1, \tag{S19.63}$$

then we are in the specialization equilibrium with $L_N^n = L_N^E$, $L_N^o = 0$ and $\omega(t)$ is given by Eq. (S19.62) (or the left hand side of Eq. (S19.63)). Else if the condition in (S19.63) fails, then we are in the equalization equilibrium with $\omega(t) = 1$ and L_N^n found by solving Eq. (S19.62). Next note that substituting the prices for new and old goods in terms of wages, the ideal price index Eq. (S19.57) can be written as

$$N^n(t) \left(\frac{\varepsilon}{\varepsilon - 1} w_N(t) \right)^{1-\varepsilon} + N^o(t) w_S(t)^{1-\varepsilon} = 1. \tag{S19.64}$$

Having characterized $\omega(t) = w^N(t)/w^S(t)$, we can separately solve for $w_N(t)$ and $w_S(t)$ from the previous equation, which completes the characterization of the static equilibrium.

Exercise 19.29, Part (c). The value function of a monopolist who owns a new machine in the North satisfies the HJB equation

$$r_N(t) V(t, \nu) = \pi(t, \nu) + \dot{V}(t, \nu) - \iota V(t, \nu). \tag{S19.65}$$

Combining Eq. (S19.60) and Eq. (S19.61), per-period profits can be written as

$$\pi(t, \nu) = \frac{1}{\varepsilon - 1} L_N^n \frac{w_N(t)}{N^n(t)}.$$

Using this in the HJB Eq. (S19.65) and integrating, the net present discounted value of the monopolist owning the patent for product ν can be written as

$$V(\nu, t) = \int_t^\infty \exp \left(- \int_t^s (r(s') + \iota) ds' \right) \frac{1}{\varepsilon - 1} L_N^n \frac{w_N(s)}{N^n(s)} ds. \tag{S19.66}$$

This expression is different than the expression in Section 13.4 due to the presence of the ι term in the exponential discounting. This term captures the fact that, at flow rate ι, the monopolist's good is imitated and she loses the rents.

Exercise 19.29, Part (d). Given the R&D technology we have assumed in (S19.56), the free entry condition in an equilibrium with positive R&D is given by

$$\eta N^n(t) V(t, \nu) = w_N(t). \tag{S19.67}$$

We next consider a BGP equilibrium in which $N^o(t)$ and $N^n(t)$ grow at the same constant rate g, and the labor allocation in the North (L_N^n, L_N^o, L_N^R) is constant. In such an equilibrium, Eq. (S19.62) implies that $\omega(t)$ is constant and Eq. (S19.64) implies that $w_N(t)$ and $w_S(t)$ grow at rate $g/(\varepsilon - 1)$. Since we have normalized the ideal price index to 1, the consumption in each country grows at the same rate as wages, that is, $\dot{C}_j(t)/C_j(t) = g/(\varepsilon - 1)$. From the Euler equation for the North, this implies $r_N(t) = \rho + \theta g/(\varepsilon - 1)$. Using these in the value function (S19.66), we have

$$V(t, \nu) = \frac{1}{\varepsilon - 1} L_N^n \frac{w_N(t)}{N^n(t)} \frac{1}{\rho + \theta g/(\varepsilon - 1) + \iota - (g/(\varepsilon - 1) - g)},$$

where the $(g/(\varepsilon - 1) - g)$ term in the denominator captures the growth of $w_N(t)/N^n(t)$. Using the previous expression for the value function in the free entry condition (S19.67), we have

$$\eta \frac{1}{\varepsilon - 1} \frac{L_N^n}{(\theta - 1)\frac{g}{\varepsilon - 1} + g + \iota + \rho} = 1. \tag{S19.68}$$

Note also that, on a BGP, we have $\dot{N}^o(t) = \iota N^n(t)$, hence, $N^o(t)$ grows at the constant rate g only if

$$\frac{N^n(t)}{N^o(t)} = \frac{g}{\iota}.$$

Given this ratio between new and old goods, and using $L_N^E = 1 - L_N^R$, our static equilibrium characterization in Part (c) can be rewritten as

$$\omega = \max\left(1, \frac{\varepsilon - 1}{\varepsilon}\left(\frac{L_S}{1 - L_N^R}\frac{g}{\iota}\right)^{1/\varepsilon}\right)$$

$$L_N^n = \min\left(1 - L_N^R, \frac{1 - L_N^R + L_S}{1 + \left(\frac{\varepsilon}{\varepsilon - 1}\right)^\varepsilon \frac{\iota}{g}}\right). \tag{S19.69}$$

Note also that from the R&D technology in Eq. (S19.56), the growth rate is given by

$$g = \frac{\dot{N}(t)}{N(t)} = \eta\frac{N^n(t)}{N(t)}L_N^R = \eta\frac{g}{g + \iota}L_N^R,$$

hence $L_N^R = (g + \iota)/\eta$ on a BGP. Plugging this in Eq. (S19.69) and using the resulting expression in (S19.68), the world growth rate is uniquely solved from

$$\eta\frac{1}{\varepsilon - 1}\frac{\min\left(1 - \frac{g+\iota}{\eta}, \frac{1 - \frac{g+\iota}{\eta} + L_S}{1 + \left(\frac{\varepsilon}{\varepsilon - 1}\right)^\varepsilon \frac{\iota}{g}}\right)}{(\theta - 1)\frac{g}{\varepsilon - 1} + g + \iota + \rho} = 1. \tag{S19.70}$$

Exercise 19.29, Part (e). We claim that an increase in ι decreases the world growth rate g. To prove this, suppose, to reach a contradiction, that g increases in response to an increase in ι. Then, the numerator in Eq. (S19.70) would decrease and the denominator would increase, yielding a contradiction. This proves that the BGP growth rate is decreasing in ι. Intuitively, a higher rate of imitation reduces the growth rate in this economy since it discourages R&D activity in the North. Next we consider the welfare effects of an increase in ι. We have

$$U_j = \int_0^\infty \exp(-\rho t)\frac{C_j(t)^{1-\theta}}{1 - \theta}dt$$

$$= \frac{1}{1 - \theta}\frac{C_j(0)^{1-\theta}}{\rho - g_c(1 - \theta)}.$$

Hence, welfare is increasing in the initial level of consumption, $C_j(0)$ and in the growth rate $g_c = g/(\varepsilon - 1)$. The initial level of consumption is a complicated analytical expression that depends on all of the variables (including ι and g). Intuitively increasing ι tends to increase $C_j(0)$ due to reduced monopoly distortions, since after imitation takes place, competition eliminates the monopolistic mark-up. Therefore, on the one hand, increasing ι is bad for welfare since it decreases g_c, but on the other hand, it is good for welfare since it reduces static monopoly distortions. The net effect will depend on which force dominates.

The welfare forces we have described so far apply to Northern as well as Southern economies. There is a third welfare effect of reducing ι that effects North and South asymmetrically: a higher rate of imitation tends to decrease the relative wage of Northern workers. From the expression in Eq. (S19.62), as ι increases, the relative Northern wages (under plausible assumptions on parameters) tend to decrease. Intuitively, when imitation increases, the relative demand for new goods is lower (since there are relatively fewer new goods). Moreover, since innovation is discouraged, relatively more Northern labor is employed in production of new goods and the supply of new goods increases. These forces decrease the price of new goods and the wages in the North (see also Exercise 19.28).

Combining these effects on welfare, we note that Southern consumers may be worse off from an increase in the rate of imitation. They benefit from reduced monopoly distortions and enjoy higher relative wages, but on the other hand they get hurt through reduced innovation and reduced product variety in the future. The net effect on Southern welfare will be determined depending on the strength of these three economic forces. If innovation in North is sufficiently discouraged and the representative consumer in the South cares sufficiently about the future and/or has high intertemporal elasticity of substitution (i.e. low ρ and low θ), then an increase in imitation may make the Southern workers worse off.

Exercise 19.33

Exercise 19.33, Part (a). We characterize the BGP growth rate of each economy before and after trade opening. We denote by L^j the population in country j, and by L the world population.

Before Trade Opening. We conjecture a BGP equilibrium in which each country's knowledge stock $N^j(t)$ (and hence the world knowledge stock) grows at the same rate g. We first solve for the common world growth rate. The per-period profits for a monopolist in country j are constant and given by

$$\pi^j(t) = \beta \left(L^j - L_R^j \right).$$

The interest rate is also constant on a BGP (and the same in both countries) and V^j is given by

$$V^j(t, \nu) = \frac{\pi^j(t)}{r} = \frac{\beta \left(L^j - L_R^j \right)}{r}.$$

Using this expression in the free entry condition $\eta N(t) V^j(t, \nu) = w(t)$, and noting that the wages are given by $w(t) = \beta N^j(t) / (1 - \beta)$, we have

$$\frac{\eta \beta \left(L^j - L_R^j \right) N(t)}{r} = \frac{\beta}{1 - \beta} N^j(t). \tag{S19.71}$$

Adding up the previous equation for each country $j \in \{1, 2\}$, we get an equation that relates L_R and r,

$$\eta (L - L_R) = \frac{r}{1 - \beta}.$$

Next, note that summing the R&D technology equation $\dot{N}^j(t) = \eta N(t) L_R^j$ over $j \in \{1, 2\}$ yields $g = \frac{\dot{N}(t)}{N(t)} = \eta L_R$. Using this in the Euler equation for either country j, we have

$$g = \eta L_R = \frac{1}{\theta} (r - \rho),$$

as a second equation between L_R and r. Combining the two displayed equations, we uniquely solve for L_R as

$$L_R = \frac{(1 - \beta) \eta L - \rho}{\eta (\theta + 1 - \beta)}, \tag{S19.72}$$

and the world growth rate as

$$g = \frac{(1 - \beta) \eta L - \rho}{\theta + 1 - \beta}.$$

Next we turn to the allocation of labor within each country $j \in \{1, 2\}$. Since $N^1(t)/N^2(t)$ is constant, the R&D technology equation $\dot{N}^j(t) = \eta N(t) L_R^j$ implies $N^1(t)/N^2(t) = L_R^1/L_R^2$. Similarly, dividing Eq. (S19.71) for each country yields $N^1(t)/N^2(t) = (L - L_R^1)/(L - L_R^2)$. Combining these observations, we have

$$\frac{L_R^j}{L_R} = \frac{L^j - L_R^j}{L - L_R} = \frac{L^j}{L} = \frac{N^j(t)}{N(t)} \text{ for each } j.$$

In other words, countries' technology levels are proportional to their populations, and each country allocates the same share of its labor between the R&D and the production sectors, that is $L_R^j/L^j = L_R/L$ for each $j \in \{1, 2\}$. Then, the allocation of labor within countries is uniquely characterized using the expression for the world R&D labor L_R in Eq. (S19.72). The BGP allocation we have described will indeed be an equilibrium if the transversality condition also holds, that is, if $\rho > (1 - \theta) g$. This completes the characterization of the BGP equilibrium allocation. Note that there are transitional dynamics: on a BGP equilibrium, we have $N^1(t)/N^2(t) = L^1/L^2$, thus if the initial levels of technology are not proportional to population, the technology levels will adjust to this level along the transition path.

After Trade Opening. Suppose there is trade in intermediate goods. We assume that each country's intermediate goods are different. The integrated world economy is similar to a closed economy, hence the analysis is identical to the one in Section 13.2. We conjecture a BGP in which each country grows at the same constant rate g. The per-period profits of a monopolist are given by

$$\pi^j = \beta \left(L^1 - L_R^1 + L^2 - L_R^2 \right) = \beta (L - L_R).$$

The interest rate is constant on a BGP and the value function is given by

$$V^j = \frac{\eta \pi^j}{r} = \frac{\beta (L - L_R)}{r}.$$

Plugging this expression in the free entry condition $\eta N V^j = w = \beta N/(1 - \beta)$, we have

$$\frac{\eta \beta (L - L_R) N(t)}{r} = \frac{\beta}{1 - \beta} N(t), \tag{S19.73}$$

as the analogue of Eq. (S19.71). The interest can be solved as $r = \eta (1 - \beta)(L - L_R)$, which, by the Euler equation, implies

$$g = \frac{1}{\theta} \left(\eta (1 - \beta)(L - L_R) - \rho \right).$$

Combining this with the R&D technology equation that implies $g = \dot{N}(t)/N(t) = \eta L_R$, we solve for the growth rate as

$$g = \frac{(1 - \beta) \eta L - \rho}{\theta + 1 - \beta}. \tag{S19.74}$$

The BGP allocation with this growth rate will indeed be an equilibrium if the transversality condition is also satisfied, which is the case under the parametric restriction $\rho > (1 - \theta) g$. Note that there are no transitional dynamics in the integrated world equilibrium: starting from any $N_1(0), N_2(0)$, the economies immediately start growing at rate g as in the closed economy version of the model.

It follows that the growth rates in Parts 1 and 2 are identical. Comparing Eqs. (S19.71) and (S19.73) provides the intuition for this result. On the one hand, the left hand side is greater in (S19.73) since $L - L_R > L^j - L_R^j$, that is, each innovated machine is more profitable due to the larger market size. On the other hand, the right hand side is also greater in (S19.73), since $N\left(t\right) > N^{j}\left(t\right)$, that is wages and hence the cost of R&D are also greater due to better technology in the competing production sector. Since the world economy is already integrated in terms of knowledge flows, these effects exactly cancel each other in the BGP equilibrium and the growth rate remains identical. However, there are static gains from trade, i.e. each country's output is larger at every point after trade opening. To see this, note that output in country j before trade opening is given by

$$Y^{j}\left(t\right) = \frac{1}{1-\beta}N^{j}\left(t\right)L^{j},$$

whereas output in country j after trade opening is given by

$$\bar{Y}^{j}\left(t\right) = \frac{1}{1-\beta}N\left(t\right)L^{j}.$$

We have $\bar{Y}^{j}\left(t\right) > Y^{j}\left(t\right)$ since $N\left(t\right) > N^{j}\left(t\right)$, that is, due to the Dixit-Stiglitz love-for-variety in the final good sector, trade in intermediate goods increases output levels even though the output growth rates remain identical.

Exercise 19.33, Part (b). In this case, there are no knowledge flows and each economy is essentially a closed economy. The analysis is identical to Section 13.2. Before trade opening, we obtain as the analogue of Eq. (S19.71)

$$\frac{\eta\beta\left(L^{j}-L_{R}^{j}\right)N^{j}\left(t\right)}{r} = \frac{\beta}{1-\beta}N^{j}\left(t\right). \tag{S19.75}$$

and the growth rate of each economy is given by

$$g^{j} = \frac{\left(1-\beta\right)\eta L^{j}-\rho}{\theta+1-\beta}. \tag{S19.76}$$

After trade opening, the analysis in Part (a) continues to apply and the world growth rate is given by (S19.74).

Comparing Eq. (S19.76) with (S19.74), we have that the BGP growth rate increases in both countries after trade opening. To see the intuition, we compare Eq. (S19.75) with (S19.71). The market size and wage effects identified in Part (a) cancel each other also in this case. However, trade opening creates additional knowledge spillovers which increases the R&D incentives. In particular, note that the counterpart of the $N^{j}\left(t\right)$ term in Eq. (S19.75) is $N\left(t\right) > N^{j}\left(t\right)$ in Eq. (S19.73), which implies that the world growth rate is higher after trade opening. This analysis then suggests that, if the R&D sector uses scarce factors (such as labor), trade per se may not increase growth but it may increase growth indirectly by facilitating knowledge transfer.

Exercise 19.33, Part (c). The model suggests that trade can increase growth only if it also facilitates knowledge spillovers. There is some empirical evidence in favor of knowledge spillovers. For example Coe and Helpman (1995) show that R&D investment by own and by foreign countries increase a country's productivity growth. Moreover, R&D investment by trade partners has a greater effect relative to R&D investment by other countries, suggesting that trade facilitates knowledge spillovers. However, there are also micro level studies that analyze firms after they enter exports market, and those studies do not necessarily find an increase in firm productivity after they enter foreign markets. For example, Bernard and Jensen (1999) show that the more successful firms tend to enter the exports markets, however, once they enter, their productivity does not necessarily increase further. If one defines knowledge spillovers as knowledge flows from the industry to the production units (firms), the micro level studies cast doubt on the assumptions of the model in Part (a).

There is another interpretation of knowledge spillovers which is more consistent with both the macro and micro level evidence, and which makes the model in Part (a) more plausible. It could be that trade opening increases technology not because it increases knowledge spillovers per se, but it causes a selection of more productive firms within the industry as suggested by Melitz (2003) and increases industry level productivity. These effects would show in the aggregate or industry level productivity but not necessarily in the micro studies that consider the productivity of a particular firm. With this broad interpretation of spillovers, the specification in Part (b) (that trade increases "knowledge spillovers") makes more sense since the selection forces that increase productivity rely on increased competition (in product and labor markets) brought about by trade opening.

Chapter 20: Structural Change and Economic Growth

Exercise 20.3

Exercise 20.3, Part (a). The representative consumer chooses $\left[c^A(t), c^M(t), c^S(t), k(t)\right]_{t=0}^{\infty}$ to maximize (20.1) subject to (20.2) and the resource constraints (written in effective labor units)

$$\dot{k}(t) + \frac{1}{X(t)}\left[c^M(t) - p^A(t)c^A(t) - p^M(t)c^S(t)\right] = r(t)k(t) + \frac{w(t)}{X(t)} - (n+g)k(t). \quad \text{(S20.1)}$$

Here, $r(t)$ denotes the rental rate of capital which is also the interest rate since there is no depreciation.

Exercise 20.3, Part (b). From the first-order conditions for the consumption aggregator $c(t)$, the optimum consumption choice satisfies

$$p^A(t)\frac{c^A(t) - \gamma^A}{\eta^A} = \frac{c^M(t)}{\eta^M} = p^S(t)\frac{c^S(t) + \gamma^S}{\eta^S}. \quad \text{(S20.2)}$$

Substituting for prices $p^A(t)$ and $p^S(t)$ from Eq. (20.15) and using Eq. (20.2), the previous equation further implies that per-capita consumption is a constant multiple of the manufacturing consumption, that is $c(t) = \chi c^M(t)$ where $\chi \equiv \left(\frac{B^A\eta^A}{B^M\eta^M}\right)^{\eta_A}\left(\frac{B^S\eta^S}{B^M\eta^M}\right)^{\eta_S}$. Eq. (S20.2) also characterizes $c^A(t)$ and $c^S(t)$ in terms of $c^M(t)$, which after substituting into Eq. (S20.1) and using Eq. (20.15) to replace $p^A(t)$ and $p^S(t)$ shows that the consumer solves the following optimization problem

$$\max_{[c^M(t), k(t)]_{t=0}^{\infty}} \int_0^{\infty} \exp\left(-(\rho - n)t\right)\frac{\left[\chi c^M(t)\right]^{1-\theta} - 1}{1 - \theta}dt$$

$$\text{s.t. } \dot{k}(t) + \frac{1}{X(t)}\left[\frac{c^M(t)}{\eta^M} + B^M\left(\frac{\gamma^S}{B^S} - \frac{\gamma^A}{B^A}\right)\right] \quad \text{(S20.3)}$$

$$= r(t)k(t) + \frac{w(t)}{X(t)} - (n+g)k(t).$$

The current value Hamiltonian for this problem is

$$\hat{H}\left(t, k(t), c^M(t), \mu(t)\right) = \frac{\left[\chi c^M(t)\right]^{1-\theta} - 1}{1 - \theta}$$

$$+ \mu(t)\left[r(t)k(t) + \frac{w(t)}{X(t)} - (n+g)k(t) - \frac{1}{X(t)}\left(\frac{c^M(t)}{\eta^M} + B^M\left(\frac{\gamma^S}{B^S} - \frac{\gamma^A}{B^A}\right)\right)\right].$$

The first-order conditions are

$$
\begin{aligned}
\hat{H}_{c^M} &= 0 \Longrightarrow \chi^{1-\theta} c^M(t)^{-\theta} = \frac{\mu(t)}{\eta^M X(t)} \\
\hat{H}_K &= (\rho - n)\mu(t) - \dot{\mu}(t) \Longrightarrow -\frac{\dot{\mu}(t)}{\mu(t)} = r(t) - \rho - g.
\end{aligned}
$$

Combining these conditions and using the fact that $X(t)$ grows at rate g, we have the Euler equation

$$
\frac{\dot{c}^M(t)}{c^M(t)} = \frac{1}{\theta}\left(r(t) - \rho\right), \tag{S20.4}
$$

verifying the first part of Proposition 20.2.

Exercise 20.3, Part (c). Plugging the expression for prices in Eq. (20.15) in (S20.2), we derive Eq. (20.17) of the proposition.

Exercise 20.5

Exercise 20.5, Parts (a) and (b). We first characterize the differential equation system that determines the equilibrium in this economy. Note that from optimization in the manufacturing sector, the rental rate of capital is given by

$$
\begin{aligned}
r(t) &= B_M F_K\left(K_M(t), X(t) L_M(t)\right) \\
&= B_M f'\left(\frac{K_M(t)}{X(t) L_M(t)}\right) = B_M f'(k(t)),
\end{aligned}
$$

where the second line defines $f(x) \equiv F(x, 1)$ and uses the fact that F is constant returns to scale while the last equality uses Eq. (20.14). Using this expression for the interest rate, the Euler equation (S20.4) can be written as

$$
\frac{\dot{c}^M(t)}{c^M(t)} = \frac{1}{\theta}\left(B^M f'(k(t)) - \rho\right). \tag{S20.5}
$$

Next, note that constant returns to scale in the manufacturing sector implies $r(t)k(t) + w(t)/X(t) = B_M f(k(t))$, which, after plugging in the household's budget constraint (S20.3) gives the resource constraints

$$
\dot{k}(t) + \frac{1}{X(t)}\left[\frac{c^M(t)}{\eta^M} + B^M\left(\frac{\gamma^A}{B^A} - \frac{\gamma^S}{B^S}\right)\right] = B_M f(k(t)) - (n+g)k(t). \tag{S20.6}
$$

The equilibrium path $\left[c^M(t), k(t)\right]_t$ is characterized by the two differential equations (S20.5) and (S20.6), the initial condition $k(0)$, and the transversality condition given by

$$
\lim_{t \to \infty} k(t) \exp\left(-\int_0^t \left(B^M f'(k(s)) - n - g\right) ds\right) = 0. \tag{S20.7}
$$

Next we claim that if Condition (20.18) is not satisfied, then there is no CGP equilibrium. Consider a CGP equilibrium on which $c^M(t)$ grows at a constant rate g_c after some time T. From the Euler equation (S20.5), $k(t) = k^* = f'^{-1}\left((\theta g_c + \rho)/B^M\right)$ is constant for all $t \geq T$. Then, the resource constraint (S20.6) at any time $t \geq T$ can be written as

$$
B^M f(k^*) - (n+g)k^* = \frac{c^M(T)\exp((g_c - g)(t - T))}{\eta^M} + \frac{\exp(-g(t-T))}{X(T)} B^M\left(\frac{\gamma^A}{B^A} - \frac{\gamma^S}{B^S}\right).
$$

If $g_c > g$, then the right hand side exceeds the left hand side for sufficiently large t, leading to a contradiction. If $g_c < g$, then the right hand side goes to zero, but the left hand side is positive, leading to a contradiction. Hence, it must be the case that $g_c = g$. In this case, $\exp\left(-g\left(t - T\right)\right)\left(\gamma^A/B^A - \gamma^S/B^S\right)$ remains constant only if $\gamma^A/B^A - \gamma^S/B^S = 0$, that is, only if Condition (20.18) holds. It follows that Condition (20.18) is necessary for a CGP to exist.

Next, we claim that Condition (20.18) is sufficient for a unique CGP to exist. Suppose that Condition (20.18) holds and define normalized manufacturing consumption $\tilde{c}^M(t) = c^M(t)/X(t)$. The differential equation system (S20.5) and (S20.6) can be written in normalized variables as

$$\dot{k}(t) + \frac{\tilde{c}^M(t)}{\eta^M} = B^M f(k(t)) - (n + g)k(t). \qquad (\text{S20.8})$$

$$\frac{d\tilde{c}^M(t)/dt}{\tilde{c}^M(t)} = \frac{1}{\theta}\left(B^M f'(k(t)) - \rho\right) - g.$$

This system has a unique steady state at which $\tilde{c}^M(t) = \left(c^M\right)^*$ and $k(t) = k^*$ are constant and are implicitly defined by

$$f'(k^*) = (\rho + \theta g)/B^M \text{ and } \left(\tilde{c}^M\right)^* = \eta^M\left[B^M f(k^*) - (n + g)k^*\right]. \qquad (\text{S20.9})$$

Moreover, for any $k(0)$, there exists a saddle path $\left[\tilde{c}^M(t), k(t)\right]_t$ that converges to the steady state. The corresponding $\left[c^M(t), k(t)\right]_t$ also satisfies the transversality condition (S20.7) since we have $r^* - n - g = \rho - n + (1 - \theta)g > 0$ by Assumption 4. It follows that the equilibrium path is saddle path stable in normalized variables, and $c^M(t)$ and $K(t)/L(t)$ asymptotically grow at rate g. Moreover, if $k(0) = k^*$, then the equilibrium is at the steady state and $c^M(t)$ and $K(t)/L(t)$ grow exactly at rate g, that is, a CGP exists.

Next, to prove the rest of Proposition 20.4, we characterize the evolution of $c^A(t), c^S(t), c^M(t)$ and the allocation of labor to sectors in the CGP equilibrium. Since $\left(\tilde{c}^M\right)^*$ is constant on the CGP, we have $\dot{c}^M(t)/c^M(t) = g$. The expressions in Eq. (20.19) for the growth rates of $c^A(t)$ and $c^S(t)$ then follow from Eq. (20.17). Next, consider the resource constraints for each sector j at the steady state, which can be written in per-capita terms as

$$\frac{\dot{K}(t)}{K(t)}k^* X(t) + c^M(t) = B^M \frac{L^M(t)}{L(t)}X(t)f(k^*) \qquad (\text{S20.10})$$

$$c^A(t) = B^A \frac{L^A(t)}{L(t)}X(t)f(k^*)$$

$$c^S(t) = B^S \frac{L^S(t)}{L(t)}X(t)f(k^*).$$

Since $\dot{K}(t)/K(t)$ is constant and since $c^M(t)$ and $X(t)$ grow at rate g, the first equation implies that $L^M(t)/L(t)$ is constant, or equivalently, $\dot{L}^M(t)/L^M(t) = n$. Taking the time derivative of the second equation, we have $\frac{\dot{L}^A(t)}{L^A(t)} = \frac{\dot{c}^A(t)}{c^A(t)} + n - g$. Substituting for $\frac{\dot{c}^A(t)}{c^A(t)}$ from the first line of Eq. (20.19) and using the resource constraints (S20.10) leads to

$$\frac{\dot{L}^A(t)}{L^A(t)} = n - g\frac{\gamma^A L(t)/L^A(t)}{B^A X(t)f(k^*)},$$

which is the expression in (20.19). The expression for $\dot{L}^S(t)/L^S(t)$ is similarly obtained, completing the proof of Eq. (20.19). Finally, we note that the share of income accruing to capital on the CGP is given by

$$\frac{K(t)\,r(t)}{Y(t)} = \frac{K(t)\,B^M f'(k^*)}{B^M F(K(t),L(t)X(t))} = \frac{K(t)}{L(t)X(t)}\frac{f'(k^*)}{f(k^*)} = \frac{k^* f'(k^*)}{f(k^*)}$$

which is constant. This completes the proof of Proposition 20.4.

Exercise 20.6

Our analysis in Exercise 20.5 shows that when Condition (20.18) is satisfied, the equilibrium in normalized variables $(\tilde{c}^M(t), k(t))$ is saddle path stable and converges to the steady state $((\tilde{c}^M)^*, k^*)$. Moreover, the system in normalized variables is isomorphic to the standard neoclassical economy studied in Chapter 8, hence the saddle path is monotonic in k. In particular, if $k(0) < k^*$, then $k(t)$ increases towards k^*, and if $k(0) > k^*$, then $k(t)$ decreases towards k^* (cf. Proposition 8.7).

Exercise 20.8

Exercise 20.8, Part (a). A competitive equilibrium in this economy is a sequence of allocations $[L^A(t), L^M(t), Y^A(t), Y^M(t), c^A(t), c^M(t)]_t$ and prices $[p^A(t), p^M(t), w(t), p^Z(t)]_t$ such that the competitive production sectors maximize profits, consumers maximize utility, and all markets clear. We normalize the price of the manufacturing good, $p^M(t) = 1$ in each period.

Since the factor markets are competitive, from the agricultural final good production we have

$$w(t) = \zeta p^A(t) X(t) \left(\frac{L^A(t)}{Z}\right)^{\zeta-1} \text{ and } p^Z(t) = (1-\zeta)p^A(t)X(t)\left(\frac{L^A(t)}{Z}\right)^{\zeta}. \quad (S20.11)$$

and from the manufacturing good production we have

$$w(t) = X(t). \quad (S20.12)$$

Combining this with Eq. (S20.12), we have

$$p^A(t) = \frac{1}{\zeta}\left(\frac{L^A(t)}{Z}\right)^{1-\zeta}, \quad (S20.13)$$

which is a supply equation for labor in the agricultural sector.

From the demand side, the representative consumer solves

$$\max_{[c^A(t),c^M(t)]_t} \int_0^\infty \exp(-(\rho-n)t)\frac{1}{1-\theta}\left[\left((c^A(t)-\gamma^A)^{\eta^A}c^M(t)^{\eta^M}\right)^{1-\theta}-1\right]dt$$

$$\text{s.t.} \quad p^A(t)c^A(t) + c^M(t) = w(t).$$

Note that the representative consumer's problem is purely static since there are no savings in this economy. Assuming that there is an interior solution in which $c^A(t) > \eta^A$ and $c^M(t) > 0$ (we verify this assumption below), the static optimization of the consumer implies

$$\frac{p^A(t)\left(c^A(t)-\gamma^A\right)}{\eta^A} = \frac{c^M(t)}{\eta^M}.$$

We substitute the supply of $c^A(t), c^M(t)$ in this equation and use labor market clearing to get

$$\frac{p^A(t)}{\eta^A}\left(\frac{X(t)\left(L^A(t)\right)^\varsigma (Z)^{1-\varsigma}}{L(t)} - \gamma^A\right) = \frac{1}{\eta^M}\left(\frac{X(t)\left(L(t) - L^A(t)\right)}{L(t)}\right), \qquad \text{(S20.14)}$$

which is a demand equation for the agricultural sector that links price of the agricultural good to the amount of labor employed in agriculture.

The equilibrium level of $L^A(t)$ is determined by solving the supply and demand equations (S20.13) and (S20.14) jointly. Putting these equations together and defining $l^A(t) = L^A(t)/L(t)$, we have

$$f\left(l^A(t), t\right) \equiv l^A(t) - \frac{\gamma^A}{X(t)}\left(\frac{l^A(t)L(t)}{Z}\right)^{1-\varsigma} - \frac{\varsigma\eta^A}{\eta^M}\left(1 - l^A(t)\right) = 0, \qquad \text{(S20.15)}$$

which solves for the share of labor in agriculture, $l^A(t)$.

To complete the characterization of the equilibrium, we need to verify our assumption for an interior solution, that is, we need to check that fir each t there exists a solution $l^A(t)$ to Eq. (S20.15) which lies in $[0, L(t)]$. We also claim that the solution is unique when it exists. To show these claims, first suppose the parameters satisfy

$$g \geq n(1-\varsigma) \qquad \text{(S20.16)}$$

so that $L(t)^{1-\varsigma}/X(t)$ is non-increasing. If this term is increasing, then for sufficiently large t, $f\left(l^A, t\right)$ will be negative for all $l^A \in [0,1]$ and there will not be an interior solution. Under Condition (S20.16), note that $f(1, t)$ is increasing in t. Hence if we assume $f(1, 0) > 0$, then we have $f(1, t) > 0$ for all t. Since we also have $f(0, t) < 0$, it follows by the intermediate value theorem that for any t $f\left(l^A(t), t\right) = 0$ has an interior solution $l^A(t) \in (0, 1)$. The condition $f(1, 0) > 0$ can be rewritten as

$$X(0)Z^{1-\varsigma}(L(0))^\varsigma > \gamma^A L(0). \qquad \text{(S20.17)}$$

Next we claim that the solution to $f\left(l^A(t), t\right) = 0$ is unique when it exists. To see this, let $l^A \in [0, 1]$ be a solution and note that

$$\begin{aligned}
\frac{\partial f\left(l^A(t), t\right)}{\partial l^A(t)}\bigg|_{l^A(t)=l^A} &\equiv 1 - \gamma^A(1-\varsigma)\frac{\left(l^A(t)\right)^{-\varsigma}}{X(t)/L(t)^{1-\varsigma}Z^{1-\varsigma}} + \frac{\varsigma\eta^A}{\eta^M}\bigg|_{l^A(t)=l^A} \\
&= \frac{f\left(l^A(t), t\right)}{l^A(t)} + \varsigma\gamma^A\frac{\left(l^A(t)\right)^{-\varsigma}}{X(t)/L(t)^{1-\varsigma}Z^{1-\varsigma}} + \frac{\varsigma\eta^A}{\eta^M}\bigg|_{l^A(t)=l^A} \\
&= \frac{\varsigma\eta^A}{\eta^M} + \varsigma\gamma^A\frac{\left(l^A\right)^{-\varsigma}}{X(t)/L(t)^{1-\varsigma}Z^{1-\varsigma}} > 0,
\end{aligned}$$

where the third line uses $f\left(l^A, t\right) = 0$. This shows that the function $f(., t)$ is always increasing when it crosses the zero line, which further implies that it crosses the zero line only once and there is a unique solution $l^A(t) \in [0, 1]$, completing the proof of the claim.

Intuitively, Conditions (S20.16) and (S20.17) ensure that the agricultural productivity is always sufficiently high to produce the subsistence requirement γ^A for the population. We conclude that under Conditions (S20.16) and (S20.17), there exists a unique equilibrium path such that the share of labor in agriculture is the unique solution to Eq. (S20.15).

Exercise 20.8, Part (b). We claim that the unique solution $l^A(t)$ to Eq. (S20.15) is decreasing over time, that is, the labor share of manufacturing grows. To see this, recall that for each t the function $f(.,t)$ crosses the zero line from below. Moreover, by Condition (S20.16), the term $X(t)/L(t)^{1-\zeta}$ grows thus $f(l^A,t)$ is increasing in t for a given l^A, which implies that the $f(.,t)$ function shifts up over time. Since the function crosses zero from below, this further implies that the crossing point shifts to the left over time, that is $\frac{dl^A(t)}{dt} < 0$, proving our claim.

To see the intuition, we rearrange Eq. (S20.15) as

$$l^A(t) = h_t\left(l^A(t)\right) \equiv \frac{\eta^M}{\eta^M + \zeta\eta^A} \frac{\gamma^A}{X(t)/L(t)^{1-\zeta} Z^{1-\zeta}} l^A(t)^{1-\zeta} + \frac{\zeta\eta^A}{\eta^M + \zeta\eta^A}. \qquad (S20.18)$$

Note that if γ^A was equal to 0, the first term on the right hand side would be zero and there would be a balanced growth path in which a constant share of labor is employed in agriculture. The first term on the right hand side roughly corresponds to the amount of additional labor that needs to be employed in agriculture to satisfy the subsistence level of consumption. Due to sufficiently rapid technological progress (i.e. from Condition (S20.16) the productivity in agriculture, $X(t)L(t)^\zeta$ grows faster than the subsistence requirement, $\gamma^A L(t)$), this term decreases, and consequently, the share of labor employed in agriculture decreases. As technology progresses, less labor is required to cover the subsistence needs, and it is optimal to shift more of the labor to the manufacturing sector.

Exercise 20.8, Part (c). Since the production function is Cobb-Douglas, the shares of land and labor in agriculture are constant. More specifically, Eq. (S20.11) implies

$$\frac{p^Z(t)Z}{w(t)L^A(t)} = \frac{\zeta}{1-\zeta}$$

Substituting $w(t) = X(t)$ from Eq. (S20.12), we have

$$p^Z(t) = \frac{\zeta}{1-\zeta} L^A(t) X(t) = \frac{\zeta}{1-\zeta} l^A(t) L(t) X(t). \qquad (S20.19)$$

Hence, land rents increase in labor employed in the agricultural sector (which complements land in production) and technological progress in manufacturing (which increases the price of the agricultural good).

Plugging in the expression (S20.18) for $l^A(t)$, land rents can be rewritten as

$$p^Z(t) = \frac{\eta^M}{\eta^M + \zeta\eta^A} \frac{\gamma^A L(t)}{Z^{1-\zeta}} \left(l^A(t)\right)^{1-\zeta} + \frac{\zeta\eta^A}{\eta^M + \zeta\eta^A} X(t) L(t).$$

Note that it is possible for land rents to decrease along the equilibrium path. The second term is increasing, but the first term need not be increasing since $l^A(t)$ is decreasing and $L^A(t) = l^A(t) L(t)$ might also be decreasing (for example, it is decreasing when there is no population growth). Intuitively, land rents may be decreasing because of the demand side imbalance, which implies that the share of agriculture (and hence the share of land) in output is larger when productivity is lower. With technological progress, output increases but the share of land in output decreases, hence land rents may be decreasing if the second effect dominates.

Nevertheless, we claim that the first effect (increase in output) dominates in the long run and the land rents asymptotically grow at rate $g + n$. To see this, note that

$\lim_{t\to\infty} X(t)/L(t)^{1-\zeta} = \infty$ (from Condition (S20.16)) and thus Eq. (S20.18) implies that the demand side imbalance disappear and $l^A(t)$ tends to a constant level

$$l^A \to \left(l^A\right)^* = \frac{\zeta\eta^A}{\eta^M + \zeta\eta^A}.$$

It then follows from Eq. (S20.19) that land rents asymptotically grow at rate $n+g$. It follows that, in this economy, the returns to land can be non-monotonic, first decreasing as the economy goes through structural change towards manufacturing, but eventually increasing once the structural change is complete.

Exercise 20.9*

Our characterization in Exercise 20.5 also applies in this case and shows that the equilibrium path $\left[c^M(t), k(t)\right]_t$ is characterized by the differential equations (S20.5) and (S20.6) along with the initial condition $k(0)$ and the transversality condition (S20.7). Without Condition (20.18), the system can still be written in normalized variables $\left[\tilde{c}^M(t), k(t)\right]_t$ as

$$\dot{k}(t) + \frac{\tilde{c}^M(t)}{\eta^M} + \frac{B^M}{X(t)}\left(\frac{\gamma^A}{B^A} - \frac{\gamma^S}{B^S}\right) = B^M f(k(t)) - (n+g)k(t).$$

$$\frac{d\tilde{c}^M(t)/dt}{\tilde{c}^M(t)} = \frac{1}{\theta}\left(B^M f'(k(t)) - \rho\right) - g.$$

Note that this differential equation system is non-autonomous (time dependent) but converges to the autonomous system (S20.8) since $\lim_{t\to\infty} \frac{B^M}{X(t)}\left(\frac{\gamma^A}{B^A} - \frac{\gamma^S}{B^S}\right) = 0$. Consequently, there exists a path $\left[\tilde{c}^M(t), k(t)\right]_t$ that solves the non-autonomous system above and converges to the steady state $\left((\tilde{c}^M)^*, k^*\right)$ in Eq. (S20.9). The corresponding path $\left[c^M(t), k(t)\right]_t$ will also satisfy the transversality condition since we assume $\rho - n > (1-\theta)g$. Hence, $c^M(t)$ and $K(t)/L(t)$ asymptotically grow at rate g also when Condition (20.18 fails. Intuitively, with Stone-Geary preferences, the demand side imbalances disappear as $X(t)$ grows hence there is an asymptotic CGP equilibrium even when Condition (20.18) fails. However, as we have noted above, there is no CGP equilibrium in which $c^M(t)$ grows exactly at a constant rate after some period T.

Exercise 20.17

We assume that the production functions for the sectors are given by

$$Y_S(t) = A(t) K_S(t)^{\alpha_S} L_S(t)^{1-\alpha_S}$$
$$Y_M(t) = A(t) K_S(t)^{\alpha_M} L_S(t)^{1-\alpha_M},$$

where α_M, α_S (with $\alpha_M > \alpha_S$) denote the share of capital in each sector and $\dot{A}(t)/A(t) = g > 0$ denotes the common rate of Hicks-neutral technological progress. We could assume, as in Rebelo (1991), that only manufacturing goods are used in investment. However, this assumption will create an additional demand for investment (over services) that might grow as the economy accumulates capital. Instead, we want to isolate the standard demand side effect that tends to reallocate resources from manufacturing to services as the households' income increases. Therefore, we will solve an alternative exercise in which we assume that $C(t)$ is a final good (rather than a consumption aggregator) and investment goods are produced by a conversion technology using the final good. More specifically, instead of the consumption aggregator specified in the problem, suppose there is a competitive final good sector with the technology

$$Y(t) = \left(Y_S(t) + \gamma^S L(t)\right)^{\eta^S} Y_M(t)^{\eta^M}, \qquad (S20.20)$$

where $\eta^M = 1 - \eta^S$ and the final good is divided between consumption and investment $Y(t) = C(t) + I(t)$. Note that the final good production technology (S20.20) features a standard demand side effect similar to that in the exercise statement. We have normalized γ^S by the total population to ensure that population growth itself does not create a demand shift to services. Note also that this production technology has diminishing returns to scale in inputs $Y_S(t)$ and $Y_M(t)$, thus the competitive final good sector will make profits in equilibrium. We assume that the profits are distributed back to the representative consumer. We also normalize the price of the final good to 1, $p_Y(t) = 1$ and we denote the relative price of the service goods by $p(t) = p_S(t)/p_M(t)$.

We first characterize the static equilibrium for a given level of capital-labor ratio $k(t) \equiv K(t)/L(t)$ and the level of technology $A(t)$, which we later use to characterize the dynamic equilibrium. Our analysis for the static equilibrium (in particular, Lemma S20.1 below) shows that the relative price and the employment share of services will go up in response to capital deepening. The analysis for the dynamic equilibrium shows that, asymptotically, the demand side imbalance vanishes and consumption in manufacturing grows faster than services due to the supply side imbalance.

The Static Equilibrium. To characterize the static equilibrium, we consider the supply and the demand sides of the economy separately. Let $\kappa_S(t) = K_S(t)/K(t)$ and $\lambda_S(t) = L_S(t)/L(t)$ denote shares of factors allocated to services. On the supply side, we first derive a relationship between factor allocations $\kappa_S(t)$ and $\lambda_S(t)$. Profit maximization by the services and manufacturing producers gives

$$p_S(t)\alpha_S \frac{Y_S(t)}{K_S(t)} = r(t), \quad p_S(t)(1-\alpha_S)\frac{Y_S(t)}{L_S(t)} = w(t), \qquad (S20.21)$$

$$p_M(t)\alpha_M \frac{Y_M(t)}{K_M(t)} = r(t), \quad p_M(t)(1-\alpha_M)\frac{Y_M(t)}{L_M(t)} = w(t).$$

Combining these equations yields

$$k_S(t)\frac{1-\alpha_S}{\alpha_S} = k_M(t)\frac{1-\alpha_M}{\alpha_M} = \frac{w(t)}{r(t)}, \qquad (S20.22)$$

where we used $k_j(t) = K_j(t)/L_j(t)$ to denote the capital-labor ratio in a sector $j \in \{S, M\}$. Let $k(t) = K(t)/L(t)$ denote the aggregate capital-labor ratio at time t. Dividing Eq. (S20.22) by $k(t)$ gives

$$\frac{\alpha_S}{1-\alpha_S}\frac{\lambda_S(t)}{\kappa_S(t)} = \frac{\alpha_M}{1-\alpha_m}\frac{1-\lambda_S(t)}{1-\kappa_S(t)},$$

which further provides a relationship between $\lambda_S(t)$ and $\kappa_S(t)$

$$\kappa_S(t) = \left[1 + \frac{1-\alpha_S}{1-\alpha_M}\frac{\alpha_M}{\alpha_S}\frac{1-\lambda_S(t)}{\lambda_S(t)}\right]^{-1}. \qquad (S20.23)$$

Note that $\kappa_S(t)$ is increasing in $\lambda_S(t)$, that is, the resources are allocated together to the sectors.

Next we characterize $\lambda_S(t)$ given the relative price of services $p(t)$ and the capital-labor ratio $k(t)$. By Eq. (S20.21), we have

$$p_S(t)(1-\alpha_S)(k_S(t))^{\alpha_S} = w(t) = p_M(t)(1-\alpha_M)(k_M(t))^{\alpha_M}.$$

From Eq. (S20.22), we have that the capital-labor ratio in manufacturing is a constant multiple of the capital-labor ratio in services. Using this in the preceding equation, we have

$$p\left(t\right)\left(1-\alpha_S\right)\left(k_S\left(t\right)\right)^{\alpha_S} = \left(1-\alpha_M\right)\left(\frac{\alpha_M}{\alpha_S}\frac{1-\alpha_S}{1-\alpha_M}k_S\left(t\right)\right)^{\alpha_M},$$

which further yields

$$p\left(t\right)k_S\left(t\right)^{\alpha_S-\alpha_M} = \left(\frac{\alpha_M}{\alpha_S}\right)^{\alpha_M}\left(\frac{1-\alpha_M}{1-\alpha_S}\right)^{1-\alpha_M}. \qquad \text{(S20.24)}$$

Dividing by $k\left(t\right)^{\alpha_S-\alpha_M}$, the previous equation can further be written as

$$\frac{\lambda_S\left(t\right)}{\kappa_S\left(t\right)} = \left(\left(\frac{\alpha_M}{\alpha_S}\right)^{\alpha_M}\left(\frac{1-\alpha_M}{1-\alpha_S}\right)^{1-\alpha_M}\right)^{1/(\alpha_m-\alpha_S)} \left(p\left(t\right)\right)^{1/(\alpha_S-\alpha_M)}k\left(t\right).$$

Plugging Eq. (S20.23) in the preceding equation, we have:

$$\lambda_S\left(t\right) = \left[\frac{1-\alpha_S}{1-\alpha_M}\frac{\alpha_M}{\alpha_S}-1\right]^{-1} \qquad \text{(S20.25)}$$

$$\left[\frac{1-\alpha_S}{1-\alpha_M}\frac{\alpha_M}{\alpha_S} - \left(\left(\frac{\alpha_M}{\alpha_S}\right)^{\alpha_M}\left(\frac{1-\alpha_M}{1-\alpha_S}\right)^{1-\alpha_M}\frac{1}{p\left(t\right)}\right)^{1/(\alpha_M-\alpha_S)}k\left(t\right)\right],$$

which characterizes the resource allocation $\lambda_S\left(t\right)$ given the relative price $p\left(t\right)$ and the capital-labor ratio $k\left(t\right)$.

Eqs. (S20.25) and (S20.23) summarize the supply side of the economy. In particular, Eq. (S20.25) enables us to solve for $\lambda_s\left(t\right)$ given $k\left(t\right)$ and $p\left(t\right)$, and Eq. (S20.23) solves for $\kappa_S\left(t\right)$. Using also market clearing in capital and labor (that is, $\lambda_M\left(t\right) = 1-\lambda_S\left(t\right)$ and $\kappa_M\left(t\right) = 1-\kappa_S\left(t\right)$), these equations enable us to solve for $K_S\left(t\right), L_S\left(t\right), K_M\left(t\right), L_M\left(t\right)$ as functions of $p\left(t\right)$. Before we move on to the demand side, let us interpret Eq. (S20.25). We are particularly interested in how $\lambda_S\left(t\right)$ changes as $k\left(t\right)$ increases, i.e. in response to capital deepening. Since $\frac{1-\alpha_S}{1-\alpha_M}\frac{\alpha_M}{\alpha_S} > 1$ (from $\alpha_M > \alpha_S$), Eq. (S20.25) shows that, absent price effects $\lambda_S\left(t\right)$ tends to decrease in response to capital deepening. Intuitively, since manufacturing is the capital intensive sector, as the economy accumulates more capital it tends to reallocate resources towards manufacturing. However, there is a potentially counteracting price effect. In particular, Eq. (S20.25) also shows that $\lambda_S\left(t\right)$ is increasing in $p\left(t\right)$, that is, as services become more valuable the economy tends to reallocate resources towards services. From the analysis of the demand side below, we will see that increasing $k\left(t\right)$ tends to increase $p\left(t\right)$, hence the price effect counteracts the effect due to capital deepening. In fact, with the Cobb-Douglas production function, if there were no demand side imbalances these two effects would exactly cancel and $\lambda_S\left(t\right)$ would remain constant in equilibrium (see Proposition 20.6).

We next formally analyze the demand side. Given the production technology in (S20.20), the first-order conditions for the final good producers imply

$$\frac{p_S\left(t\right)\left(Y_S\left(t\right)+\gamma_S L\left(t\right)\right)}{\eta_S} = \frac{p_M\left(t\right)Y_M\left(t\right)}{\eta_M}.$$

Using market clearing in services and manufacturing sectors, this equation can be rewritten as

$$p\left(t\right)\frac{A\left(t\right)k_S\left(t\right)^{\alpha_S}L_S\left(t\right)+\gamma_S L\left(t\right)}{\eta_S} = \frac{A\left(t\right)k_M\left(t\right)^{\alpha_M}L_M\left(t\right)}{\eta_M}.$$

Using Eq. (S20.22) which relates $k_M(t)$ to $k_S(t)$, we have

$$p(t)\left(A(t)k_S(t)^{\alpha_S}L_S(t) + \gamma_S L(t)\right) = A(t)\frac{\eta_S}{\eta_M}\left(\frac{\alpha_M}{1-\alpha_M}\frac{1-\alpha_S}{\alpha_S}k_S(t)\right)^{\alpha_M}L_M(t).$$

Dividing by $A(t)L(t)k_S(t)^{\alpha_M}$ and simplifying, we have

$$p(t)k_S(t)^{\alpha_S-\alpha_M}\left(\lambda_S(t)+\gamma_S\frac{1}{A(t)k_S(t)^{\alpha_S}}\right) \tag{S20.26}$$

$$= \frac{\eta_S}{\eta_M}\left(\frac{\alpha_M}{1-\alpha_m}\frac{1-\alpha_S}{\alpha_S}\right)^{\alpha_M}(1-\lambda_S(t)).$$

This gives us a demand equation that links $p(t)$ to $K_S(t), K_M(t), L_S(t), L_M(t)$. In particular, absent any reallocation (had $\kappa(t)$ and $\lambda(t)$ been constant), and forgetting about the term with γ_S for now, increasing $k(t)$ increases $k_S(t)$ and increases $p(t)$ since $\alpha_S < \alpha_M$. Intuitively, increasing $k(t)$ makes manufacturing sector grow faster (since it is more capital intensive) and increases the price of services. As explained in Section 20.2.1, the reallocation effects cannot completely undo the faster growth in manufacturing thus the demand side forces tend to increase $p(t)$ in response to capital deepening.

The static equilibrium is determined by the supply Eqs. (S20.25) and (S20.23), the demand equation (S20.26), and market clearing in capital and labor. This constitutes a system with 5 equations in 5 unknowns, $K_S(t), K_M(t), L_S(t), L_M(t), p(t)$, which has a unique solution (given $k(t)$ and $A(t)$). Moreover, once we solve for these allocations, $p_S(t)$ and $p_M(t)$ can be determined from the profit maximization of the final good sector (i.e. as the marginal product of service and manufacturing goods given the technology (S20.20)). The following lemma characterizes the properties of the static equilibrium allocation, showing that the relative price and the employment of services increases in response to capital deepening.

LEMMA S20.1. *The static equilibrium allocations satisfy*

$$(i) \ \frac{\partial p(t)}{\partial k(t)} > 0, \ (ii) \ \frac{\partial \kappa_S(t)}{\partial k(t)} > 0, \ \frac{\partial \lambda_S(t)}{\partial k(t)} > 0.$$

Before we prove the claim, we provide an interpretation. Part (i) formalizes the price effect we have discussed above: as $k(t)$ increases, the manufacturing sector grows faster than services, hence the price of services go up. Reallocation effects can only partially offset this effect. Part (ii) shows that, labor and capital (which necessarily move together by Eq. (S20.23)) are reallocated to services. Intuitively, the supply side effects do not cause a reallocation in this economy due to the Cobb-Douglas aggregator, hence the effect of reallocation comes purely from the demand side. The demand side imbalances are such that the demand for services is increasing with income per capita (and thus increasing with capital deepening), which increases the price of services and causes a reallocation of resources towards the services sector.

PROOF. Using Eq. (S20.24), Equation (S20.26) can be rewritten as

$$\left(\frac{\alpha_M}{\alpha_S}\right)^{\alpha_M}\left(\frac{1-\alpha_M}{1-\alpha_S}\right)^{1-\alpha_M}\left(\lambda_S(t)+\frac{\gamma_S}{A(t)k_s(t)^{\alpha_S}}\right)=$$

$$\left(\frac{\alpha_M}{1-\alpha_M}\frac{1-\alpha_S}{\alpha_S}\right)^{\alpha_M}\frac{\eta_S}{\eta_M}(1-\lambda_S(t)).$$

Simplifying the expression and using Eq. (S20.24) once more, we have

$$
\lambda_S(t) + \frac{\gamma_S}{A(t)} \left[\left(\frac{\alpha_M}{\alpha_S} \right)^{\alpha_M} \left(\frac{1 - \alpha_M}{1 - \alpha_S} \right)^{1 - \alpha_M} \frac{1}{p(t)} \right]^{\frac{\alpha_S}{\alpha_M - \alpha_S}}
$$
$$
= \frac{1 - \alpha_S}{1 - \alpha_M} \frac{\eta_S}{\eta_M} (1 - \lambda_S(t)).
$$

Solving $\lambda_S(t)$ from this equation, we have

$$
\lambda_S(t) = \left[\frac{1 - \alpha_S}{1 - \alpha_M} \frac{\eta_S}{\eta_M} + 1 \right]^{-1} \left[\frac{1 - \alpha_S}{1 - \alpha_M} \frac{\eta_S}{\eta_M} - \frac{\gamma_S}{A(t)} \left[\left(\frac{\alpha_M}{\alpha_S} \right)^{\alpha_M} \left(\frac{1 - \alpha_M}{1 - \alpha_S} \right)^{1 - \alpha_M} \frac{1}{p(t)} \right]^{\frac{\alpha_S}{\alpha_M - \alpha_S}} \right].
$$
$$
\text{(S20.27)}
$$

Recall that Eq. (S20.25) is a supply side equation and provides an increasing relationship between $\lambda_S(t)$ and $p(t)$, which we denote by the function $\lambda_S^1(p(t))$. Eq. (S20.27) provides another increasing relationship between $\lambda_S(t)$ and $p(t)$, which we denote with the function $\lambda_S^2(p(t))$. The equilibrium is the intersection between these two curves. Note that, as $k(t)$ increases, $\lambda_S^1(p(t))$ curve shifts to the right and the $\lambda_S^2(p(t))$ curve remains unchanged. Hence, the effect of an increase in $k(t)$ depends on how the two increasing curves $\lambda_S^1(p(t))$ and $\lambda_S^2(p(t))$ intersect: either $\lambda_S(t)$ and $p(t)$ both go down or they both go up. We next prove that $\lambda_S^1(p(t))$ and $\lambda_S^2(p(t))$ curves always intersect in a way such that both $\lambda_S(t)$ and $p(t)$ go up. To see this, note that both curves have the form

$$
\lambda_S^i(p(t)) = D_i - E_i p(t)^{-B_i},
$$

for some constants D_i, E_i, B_i. Moreover, we have

$$
D_1 = \left[\frac{1 - \alpha_S}{1 - \alpha_M} \frac{\alpha_M}{\alpha_S} - 1 \right]^{-1} \frac{1 - \alpha_S}{1 - \alpha_M} \frac{\alpha_M}{\alpha_S}
$$
$$
> \left[\frac{1 - \alpha_S}{1 - \alpha_M} \frac{\eta_S}{\eta_M} + 1 \right]^{-1} \frac{1 - \alpha_S}{1 - \alpha_M} \frac{\eta_S}{\eta_M} = D_2
$$

and $B_1 = 1/(\alpha_M - \alpha_S) > \alpha_S/(\alpha_M - \alpha_S) = B_2$. At the intersection point $(\bar{\lambda}_S(t), \bar{p}(t))$, we also have

$$
D_1 - E_1 \bar{p}(t)^{-B_1} = D_2 - E_2 \bar{p}(t)^{-B_2},
$$

which implies $E_1 \bar{p}(t)^{-B_1} > E_2 \bar{p}(t)^{-B_2}$ since $D_1 > D_2$. Combining this with $B_1 > B_2$, we have

$$
\left. \frac{d\lambda^1(p(t))}{dp(t)} \right|_{(\bar{\lambda}_S(t), \bar{p}(t))} = \frac{B_1 E_1 \bar{p}(t)^{-B_1}}{\bar{p}(t)} > \frac{B_2 E_2 \bar{p}(t)^{-B_2}}{\bar{p}(t)} = \left. \frac{d\lambda^2(p(t))}{dp(t)} \right|_{(\bar{\lambda}_S(t), \bar{p}(t))}.
$$

That is, in the $(\lambda_S(t), p(t))$ plane (where $p(t)$ corresponds to the y axis), the supply curve $\lambda_S^1(p(t))$ is increasing faster than $\lambda_S^2(p(t))$ (at the crossing point) so that $\lambda_S^1(p(t))$ crosses $\lambda_S^2(p(t))$ from below. Hence, when $k(t)$ increases, $\lambda_S^1(p(t))$ curve shifts to the right and both $p(t)$ and $\lambda_S(t)$ increase. Eq. (S20.23) then further implies that $\kappa_S(t)$ increases, completing the proof of the claim. □

The Dynamic Equilibrium. The analysis so far has characterized the static variables given $k(t)$ and $A(t)$. We now consider the dynamic equilibrium. The representative consumer maximizes

$$\max_{[c(t),k(t)]_t} \int_0^\infty \exp\left(-\left(\rho - n\right)t\right) \frac{c(t)^{1-\theta}}{1-\theta} dt$$

s.t. $Y_S(t)$ and $Y_M(t)$ are solved from the static eq. given $k(t)$ and $A(t)$.

$$\dot{k}(t) = \frac{(Y_S(t) + \gamma_S L(t))^{\eta_S} Y_M(t)^{\eta_M}}{L(t)} - c(t) - (n+\delta)k(t), \text{ and} \qquad \text{(S20.28)}$$

$$\frac{\dot{A}(t)}{A(t)} = g, \frac{\dot{L}(t)}{L(t)} = n. \qquad \text{(S20.29)}$$

The consumer's dynamic optimization is equivalent to

$$\frac{\dot{c}(t)}{c(t)} = \frac{1}{\theta}\left(r(t) - \rho\right), \qquad \text{(S20.30)}$$

and the transversality condition

$$\lim_{t\to\infty} k(t) \exp\left(-\int_0^t \left(r(s) - n\right) ds\right) = 0. \qquad \text{(S20.31)}$$

The dynamic equilibrium path $[k(t), c(t)]_t$ is then characterized by two differential equations (S20.28) and (S20.30) given the initial condition $k(0) \equiv K(0)/L(0)$ and the transversality condition (S20.31) [and given the exogenous processes for technology and population in (S20.29)].

We assume that the technological progress g is large enough so that there is growth and capital accumulation in this economy at all points in time. Hence, $k(t)$ grows on the dynamic equilibrium path. Lemma S20.1 then suggests that $p(t)$ increases over time.[1] Since $A(t)$ also grows, the term in Eq. (S20.27) that contains γ^s gets smaller and limits to 0, hence we have

$$\lim_{t\to\infty} \lambda_S(t) = \lambda_S = \left[\frac{1-\alpha_S}{1-\alpha_M}\frac{\eta_S}{\eta_M} + 1\right]^{-1} \frac{1-\alpha_S}{1-\alpha_M}\frac{\eta_S}{\eta_M}. \qquad \text{(S20.32)}$$

In other words, in this economy, demand side imbalances fade out as the economy grows and all that remains are the supply side imbalances. Since the final good production is Cobb-Douglas, as Section 20.2 demonstrates, the supply side imbalances are completely offset by price effects and the allocation of labor (and capital) between sectors tends to an intermediate constant, that is

$$\lambda_S(t) \to \lambda_S^* \in (0,1) \text{ and } \kappa_S(t) \to \kappa_S^* \in (0,1).$$

To characterize the asymptotic behavior of consumption and the capital stock, we consider a CGP equilibrium in which $c(t)$ grows at an asymptotically constant rate g_c. Then, from the Euler equation, $r(t)$ is also asymptotically constant at $r = \theta g_c + \rho$. From the resource constraint (S20.28), the capital-labor ratio $k(t)$ also asymptotically grows at rate g_c. It follows that $k_S(t) = (\kappa_S(t)/\lambda_S(t))k(t)$ and $k_M(t)$ asymptotically grow at rate g_c. Recall that,

$$\begin{aligned} Y_M(t) &= A(t)K_M(t)^{\alpha_M} L_M(t)^{1-\alpha_M} = A(t)k_M(t)^{\alpha_M} \lambda_M(t) L(t) \\ \text{and } Y_S(t) &= A(t)K_S(t)^{\alpha_S} L_S(t)^{1-\alpha_S} = A(t)k_S(t)^{\alpha_S} \lambda_S(t) L(t). \end{aligned}$$

---

[1]Strictly speaking, Lemma S20.1 does not prove this claim since the static equilibrium values also depend on $A(t)$, which is changing over time. Below, we verify this conjecture by showing that $p(t)$ asymptotically grows at a positive constant rate.

Hence, asymptotically, $Y_M(t)$ grows at rate $\alpha_M g_c + n$ and $Y_S(t)$ grows at rate $\alpha_S g_c + n$. Using Eqs. (S20.32) and (S20.25), we have that $k(t) / \left(p(t)^{1/(\alpha_M - \alpha_S)} \right)$ limits to a constant, thus $p(t)$ asymptotically grows at the positive rate $g_p = (\alpha_M - \alpha_S) g_c$. Intuitively, the manufacturing sector asymptotically grows faster (since $\alpha_M g_c + n > \alpha_S g_c + n$) and the price of services grows just enough to offset the difference so that the share of both sectors, $p_M(t) Y_M(t)$ and $p_S(t) Y_M(t)$ remain constant.

We next calculate the growth rate g_c in terms of the exogenous variables. From Eq. (S20.21), we have $r(t) = p_S(t) A(t) \alpha_S (k_s(t))^{\alpha_S - 1}$. Since the interest rate is constant on a BGP and $g_c = g_k$, we have

$$g_{p_S} + g + (\alpha_S - 1) g_c = 0,$$

which determines the growth rate in terms of the growth rate of the price of services g_{p_S}. To find g_{p_S}, note that the production function (S20.20) asymptotes to a constant returns to scale function thus $\lim_{t \to \infty} \left(\frac{p_S(t)}{\eta_S} \right)^{\eta_S} \left(\frac{p_M(t)}{\eta_M} \right)^{\eta_M} = p_Y(t) = 1$. This implies that $p(t) = p_S(t) / p_M(t)$ asymptotically grows at the constant rate $g_c (\alpha_M - \alpha_S)$ and thus

$$g_{p_S} = g_c (\alpha_M - \alpha_S) \frac{\eta_M}{\eta_M + \eta_S}.$$

Combining the two displayed equations, we solve

$$g_c = \frac{g}{1 - \alpha_M \frac{\eta_M}{\eta_M + \eta_S} - \alpha_S \frac{\eta_S}{\eta_M + \eta_S}} \tag{S20.33}$$

as the growth rate in this economy. The allocations we have described will indeed correspond to an asymptotic CGP if the transversality condition, $\rho > (1 - \theta) g_c$, is satisfied where g_c is given by the formula in (S20.33).

Asymptotically, production (and hence consumption) of manufacturing goods grows faster. Note that, when there is only the demand side reallocation effect towards the services (as in the model analyzed in Section 20.1), consumption of services grows faster than manufacturing. However, this is not necessarily the case in the present model since there is also the supply side effect that manufacturing sector is more capital intensive. In fact, in the limit, the demand side imbalance becomes insignificant and the remaining supply side effect makes consumption of manufacturing goods grow faster.

Exercise 20.19*

The equilibrium of this economy is a path of allocations $\left[\begin{array}{l} [x(\nu, t)]_{\nu \in N(t)}, L^M(t), L^A(t), \\ C^A(t), C^M(t), Z^M(t), N(t) \end{array} \right]_t$ and prices $\left[p^A(t), p^M(t), r(t), w(t) \right]_t$ such that firms in the agricultural and manufacturing sectors maximize profits, consumers maximize utility, the R&D sector maximizes profits, the evolution of $N(t)$ is determined by the free-entry condition and all markets clear. We normalize the price of the manufacturing sector to one, i.e. $p^M(t) = 1$ for each t. Let $L^A(t)$ be the share of labor employed in agriculture. We conjecture an equilibrium in which $L^A(t) \equiv L^A$ is constant. Since the letter η is used as the share of agriculture in output, we use ζ to denote the number of varieties produced by a unit investment in R&D, that is, the R&D technology is given by $\dot{N}(t) = \zeta Z(t)$.

We first characterize the demand side. The representative consumer solves

$$\max_{[c^A(t), c^M(t), a(t)]_t} \int_0^\infty \exp(-\rho t) \left(c^A(t) - \gamma^A\right)^\eta c^M(t)^{1-\eta} \, dt$$

s.t. $\dot{a}(t) = r(t) a(t) + w(t) - c^M(t) - p^A(t) c^A(t),$

where $a(t)$ denotes the per capita assets in this economy. The static first-order conditions give

$$\frac{p^A(t) \left(c^A(t) - \gamma^A\right)}{\eta} = \frac{c^M(t)}{1 - \eta}. \tag{S20.34}$$

In the equilibrium that we conjecture, we have $c^A(t) = B^A G(L^A)$ which is constant. Then the dynamic first-order condition for the choice of $c^M(t)$ along the equilibrium path gives

$$g \equiv \frac{\dot{c}^M(t)}{c^M(t)} = \frac{1}{\eta}(r(t) - \rho). \tag{S20.35}$$

From the profit maximization of the manufacturing final good producers, the demand for each variety is given by

$$x(\nu, t) = p(\nu, t)^{-1/\beta} \left(L - L^A\right)$$

which shows that the optimal price is $p(\nu, t) = \frac{1}{1-\beta}(1 - \beta) = 1$ and the optimal quantity is $x(\nu, t) = L - L^A$. The monopolists' per-period profits are then given by $\pi(\nu, t) = \beta(L - L^A)$. In a positive growth equilibrium, the no-arbitrage condition is given by $\zeta V(\nu, t) = 1$, which implies that the value function is constant over time. Since the profits are constant, the value function is constant only if the interest rate is constant $r(t) = r$. This further implies $V(\nu, t) = \zeta \beta(L - L^A)/r$, which after plugging into the free entry condition characterizes the interest rate as

$$r = \zeta B(L - L_A). \tag{S20.36}$$

From the maximization of the final good sector, wages are given by

$$w(t) = \frac{\beta}{1 - \beta} N(t).$$

Using this in the profit maximization for the agricultural sector, we have

$$B^A G'(L^A) = w(t)/p^A(t) = \frac{\beta}{1 - \beta} \frac{N(t)}{p^A(t)}, \tag{S20.37}$$

which completes the characterization of the supply side.

We next combine the demand and the supply side equations to solve for the equilibrium. Using Eq. (S20.36) in (S20.35), the growth rate in the manufacturing sector is given by

$$g = \frac{\dot{c}^M(t)}{c^M(t)} = \frac{1}{\eta}\left(\zeta \beta(L - L^A) - \rho\right). \tag{S20.38}$$

Moreover, the resource constraint for the manufacturing good implies

$$L c^M(t) = \frac{1}{1 - \beta} N(t)(L - L^A) - (1 - \beta) N(t)(L - L^A) - \frac{\dot{N}(t)}{\zeta}. \tag{S20.39}$$

Since $c^M(t)$ grows at the constant rate g, there is a unique level of $c^M(0)$ so that, the previous differential equation for $N(t)$ has a stable solution. For this choice of $c^M(0)$, $N(t)$ also grows at rate g and Eq. (S20.39) can be rewritten as

$$c^M(t) = \left(\frac{1}{1 - \beta}(L - L^A) - (1 - \beta)(L - L^A) - \frac{g}{\zeta}\right) \frac{N(t)}{L}.$$

Next, substituting this expression for $c^M(t)$, using $c^A(t)L = B^A G(L^A)$ and substituting for $p^A(t)$ from Eq. (S20.37), the demand equation (S20.34) implies

$$\frac{\beta}{1-\beta}\frac{N(t)}{B^A G'(L^A)}\left(B^A G(L^A) - \gamma^A L\right) = \frac{\eta}{1-\eta}\left(\frac{\beta(2-\beta)}{1-\beta}(L-L^A) - \frac{g}{\zeta}\right)N(t),$$

which is satisfied if and only if L^A is a solution to

$$\frac{1}{1-\beta}\frac{1}{G'(L^A)}\left(G(L^A) - \frac{\gamma^A}{B^A}L\right) = \frac{L-L^A}{1-\eta}\left(\frac{\eta(2-\beta)}{(1-\beta)} - 1\right) + \frac{\rho}{\zeta(1-\eta)}, \qquad \text{(S20.40)}$$

where we also used the expression for the growth rate in (S20.38). This shows that employment in agriculture is indeed constant on this equilibrium and characterizes L^A. The path that we have described will be an equilibrium if the solution L^A to this equation lies in $(0, L)$ and the growth rate g in Eq. (S20.38) satisfies $\rho > (1-\eta)g$ so that the transversality condition holds. Note that there is no transitional dynamics in the equilibrium we describe: starting at $t = 0$, varieties and production in manufacturing grow at the constant rate g.

Note a few properties of the BGP equilibrium. The output in the manufacturing sector grows at rate g while the agricultural output is constant, thus there is structural change in the sense that relative production (and consumption) of manufacturing increases. However, the share of labor employed in the manufacturing sector remains constant. Intuitively, the demand side ensures that the price of the agricultural goods (relative to the manufacturing goods) also grows at rate g, which exactly offsets the technological progress in manufacturing and allows for a constant labor share to be employed in agriculture.

Next consider an increase in B^A. From (S20.40), when $\eta(2-\beta) > (1-\beta)$ (which is to say that the share of agriculture is sufficiently large), an increase in B^A always decreases L^A. A reduction in L^A in turn increases the growth rate of the economy in (S20.38). The intuition for this result is as follows. If there were no demand side imbalance (towards agriculture), this economy would only have supply side imbalances with a Cobb-Douglas aggregator. Then growth in manufacturing would be completely offset by price effects and the share of labor in manufacturing would remain constant. In addition to the supply side effects, the economy also has a demand side imbalance towards agriculture which shifts some labor towards agriculture. With a higher B^A, the subsistence requirement of the economy can be satisfied with less labor thus some labor gets allocated to manufacturing. With more labor employed in manufacturing, the standard market size effect increases innovation and hence the endogenous growth rate of the economy.

Chapter 21: Structural Transformations and Market Failures in Development

Exercise 21.1

Once we allow individuals to make a non-trivial portfolio decision, each individual still has two options. She can join the financial coalition and earn $Q > q$ with certainty as the idiosyncratic risk is shared or she can invest some part of her endowment in the risky asset, not join the financial coalition and earn the random return $Q + \varepsilon$. Note that by relaxing the assumption that each individual has to invest either all or none of her wealth in the risky saving technology we do not have to consider the option of investing in the riskless asset separately as choosing a riskless portfolio is contained in the option of investing a part of the endowment in the risky asset while not joining the financial coalition. The benefit of choosing the second option over the first one is, that she does not have to pay the fixed costs ξ to join the coalition. Let us denote the values from these options as $V_i^{FC}(W_i(t), R(t+1))$ for joining the financial coalition and $V^R(W_i(t), R(t+1))$ for choosing the risky asset. It is clear that the first option is exactly the same as given in the book (Section 21.1), i.e.

$$
\begin{aligned}
V_i^{FC}\left(W_i\left(t\right), R\left(t+1\right)\right) &= \log\left(\frac{1}{1+\beta}\left(W_i\left(t\right)-\xi\right)\right) + \beta\log\left(\frac{\beta R\left(t+1\right)Q}{1+\beta}\left(W_i\left(t\right)-\xi\right)\right) \\
&= \log\left(\frac{1}{1+\beta}\left(\frac{\beta R\left(t+1\right)Q}{1+\beta}\right)^{\beta}\left(W_i\left(t\right)-\xi\right)^{1+\beta}\right).
\end{aligned}
$$

The value of investing in the risky asset without joining the financial coalition is given by

$$
\begin{aligned}
V_i^R\left(W_i\left(t\right), R\left(t+1\right)\right) &= \max_{\{c(t),s(t),x(t)\}} \log c(t) + \beta\mathbb{E}_t\log c(t+1) \\
\text{s.t. } W_i\left(t\right) &= c(t) + x(t)s(t) + (1-x(t))s(t) \\
c(t+1) &= [x(t)s(t)q + (1-x(t))s(t)(Q+\varepsilon)]R(t+1) \\
x(t) &\in [0,1],
\end{aligned}
$$

where $x(t)$ denotes the share of savings invested in the riskless asset. Note that as $x(t) = 1$ is always available, we will have

$$
V_i^R\left(W_i\left(t\right), R\left(t+1\right)\right) \geq V_i^N\left(W_i\left(t\right), R\left(t+1\right)\right)
$$

where recall $V_i^N\left(W_i\left(t\right), R\left(t+1\right)\right)$ was defined as the value of investing everything in the risky asset. Let us write the maximization problem a little bit more compact by replacing $c(t+1)$ and $c(t)$. This yields

$$
V_i^R\left(W_i\left(t\right), R\left(t+1\right)\right) \tag{S21.1}
$$
$$
= \max_{\{s(t),x(t)\in[0,1]\}} \log(W_i(t)-s(t)) + \beta\mathbb{E}_t\log[x(t)s(t)q + (1-x(t))s(t)(Q+\varepsilon)]R(t+1).
$$

309

The necessary conditions for an interior solution for this problem are given by

$$\beta\mathbb{E}_t\left[\frac{x(t)q+(1-x(t))(Q+\varepsilon)}{x(t)s(t)q+(1-x(t))s(t)(Q+\varepsilon)}\right] = \frac{1}{(W_i(t)-s(t))} \tag{S21.2}$$

$$\beta\mathbb{E}_t\left[\frac{q-Q-\varepsilon}{x(t)q+(1-x(t))(Q+\varepsilon)}\right] = 0. \tag{S21.3}$$

First of all, realize that (S21.2) still determines the individual's optimal savings conveniently as

$$s(t) = \frac{\beta}{1+\beta}W_i(t), \tag{S21.4}$$

i.e. total savings are exactly the same as in the model where we did not allow for a portfolio choice. This is a very convenient property of the log utility functions. (S21.3) then shows that the maximizing portfolio share $x^*(t)$ is determined as a function of Q and q *only* (and the distribution of ε). In particular, the optimal portfolio share does *not* depend on the capital stock as it is neither dependent on $W_i(t)$ or $s(t)$ (which would introduce a dependence on the current capital stock) nor on $R(t+1)$ which would introduce a dependency on the future capital stock $K(t+1)$ (and hence on the current capital stock via the accumulation equation). Therefore we can write the maximizing portfolio share as

$$x^*(t) = x(Q,q). \tag{S21.5}$$

To see that (S21.3) determines $x(Q,q)$ uniquely, note that

$$\frac{\partial}{\partial x}\mathbb{E}_t\left[\frac{q-Q-\varepsilon}{xq+(1-x)(Q+\varepsilon)}\right] = -\mathbb{E}_t\left(\frac{q-Q-\varepsilon}{xq+(1-x)(Q+\varepsilon)}\right)^2,$$

so that the LHS of (S21.3) is strictly decreasing in x. Furthermore note that $0 \le x(Q,q) < 1$ as for $x=1$ we get that

$$\mathbb{E}_t\left[\frac{q-Q-\varepsilon}{q}\right] = \frac{q-Q}{q} < 0,$$

as ε is a mean-zero shock. Hence, the individual will never hold a riskless portfolio. the intuition is that when holding the riskless portfolio, the consumer is locally risk neutral so that the risk induced by the marginal unit of the riskless asset (which has a higher expected return) is only of second order. Additionally, we have for $x=0$ that

$$\mathbb{E}_t\left[\frac{q-Q-\varepsilon}{Q+\varepsilon}\right] = \mathbb{E}_t\left[\frac{q}{Q+\varepsilon}\right] - 1 = q\left(\mathbb{E}_t\left[\frac{1}{Q+\varepsilon}\right] - \frac{1}{q}\right).$$

Hence, x will be interior as long as $\mathbb{E}_t\left[\frac{1}{Q+\varepsilon}\right] > \frac{1}{q}$ (which does not follow from our assumption that $\mathbb{E}_t[Q+\varepsilon] = Q > q$ but will be satisfied if Q is big enough or the support of ε is small). For notational simplicity and without loss of generality as no results are dependent on this assumption, let us suppose this is the case. The most important implication of (S21.5) is, that all individuals who invest a positive amount of funds in the risky sector will invest exactly the same fraction of their savings. It is precisely this property which implies that all qualitative results go through even though we allow here for a meaningful portfolio choice. Too see this formally, substitute (S21.4) and (S21.5) into (S21.1) to get the value of investing a positive amount in the risky sector as

$$V_i^R\left(W_i\left(t\right),R\left(t+1\right)\right)$$

$$= \log\left(\frac{W_i(t)}{1+\beta}\right) + \beta\mathbb{E}_t\log\left(\frac{\beta R(t+1)}{1+\beta}W_i(t)[x(Q,q)q+(1-x(Q,q))(Q+\varepsilon)]\right)$$

$$= \log\left(\frac{W_i(t)}{1+\beta}\right) + \beta\log\left(\frac{\beta R(t+1)}{1+\beta}W_i(t)\right) + \beta\mathbb{E}_t\log\left([x(Q,q)q+(1-x(Q,q))(Q+\varepsilon)]\right)$$

$$= \log\left(\frac{1}{1+\beta}\left(\frac{\beta R(t+1)}{1+\beta}\right)^\beta W_i(t)^{1+\beta}\right) + \Xi(Q,q)$$

where we defined $\Xi(Q,q) = \beta\mathbb{E}_t\log\left([x(Q,q)q+(1-x(Q,q))(Q+\varepsilon)]\right)$ as this term is only a function of the exogenous parameters Q and q. In order to characterize the optimal behavior we just have to compare the two values V_i^{FC}, and V_i^R. Joining the financial coalition is preferred as long as

$$V_i^{FC}\left(W_i\left(t\right),R\left(t+1\right)\right) \geq V_i^R\left(W_i\left(t\right),R\left(t+1\right)\right)$$

$$\log\left(\frac{(W_i(t)-\xi)^{1+\beta}}{1+\beta}\left(\frac{\beta R(t+1)Q}{1+\beta}\right)^\beta\right) \geq \log\left(\frac{W_i(t)^{1+\beta}}{1+\beta}\left(\frac{\beta R(t+1)}{1+\beta}\right)^\beta\right) + \Xi(Q,q)$$

$$\frac{W_i(t)-\xi}{W_i(t)} \geq \left(\exp\left(\Xi(Q,q)\right)Q^{-\beta}\right)^{1/(1+\beta)}$$

$$W_i(t) \geq \frac{\xi}{1+(\exp\left(\Xi(Q,q)\right))Q^{-\beta})^{1/(1+\beta)}} \equiv \hat{W}.$$

This is a very convenient result, because it again shows that there will be a cutoff level of wealth $\hat{W}$ characterizing the optimal behavior. In particular, $\hat{W}$ does not depend on the capital stock and therefore is not dependent on time. This being said, the equilibrium takes the following form: those individuals with $W_i(t) < \hat{W}$ will hold a risky portfolio where the share of risky assets is given by $1 - x(Q,q) > 0$. Those individuals with $W_i(t) \geq \hat{W}$ will pay the fixed costs, join the financial coalition and enjoy the riskless return Q. Hence, the investment decision is still characterized by a cut-off rule so that the qualitative results *on the aggregate level* derived in Section 21.1 are not changed. In particular note that the capital accumulation will still be deterministic as the shocks ε are purely idiosyncratic. However, now there are fluctuations in consumption as some individuals choose a risky portfolio and might get a bad draw from the underlying stochastic shock.

Exercise 21.6

Exercise 21.6, Part (a). The easiest way to see why the problem above in fact characterizes the equilibrium allocation of workers to tasks is a simple application of the Welfare Theorems laid out in Section 5.6. The production sets of this economy satisfy the requirements for an application of the Second Welfare Theorem (Theorem 5.7), i.e. they are cones and are convex. Let us furthermore assume that the consumption side of this economy is characterized by individuals endowed with utility functions that are quasi-concave and satisfy local non-satiation. Then the Second Welfare Theorem implies that we can find prices and transfers such that a Pareto optimal allocation can be decentralized as a competitive equilibrium. But the allocation of labor across sectors that solves the maximization problem in (21.31) will be the allocation chosen in *any* Pareto optimal allocation. Hence, any equilibrium in this economy will have a labor allocation across sectors characterized by (21.31). To sustain such an allocation as an equilibrium, consider a price system of the following form: let w_L and w_H be the current wage rate for skilled and unskilled workers respectively. Taking these prices as given, a firm with access to technology h will employ L low skilled and hL high skilled workers Such a firm will have a profit of

$$\pi(h) = A_h L - w_L L - w_H h L = (A_h - w_L - w_H h)L.$$

Now note that we need to have

$$A_h - w_L - w_H h \leq 0 \qquad \forall h \qquad\qquad \text{(S21.6)}$$

for (w_L, w_H) to be equilibrium prices. Otherwise the firm with access to the technology for which (S21.6) was violated would demand an infinite amount of labor. But (S21.6) is exactly identical to (21.32) where the respective wages are replaced by the respective Lagrange multipliers.

Exercise 21.6, Part (b). To derive the first-order conditions given in (21.32) let us set up the Lagrangian for the maximization problem. In particular let us explicitly incorporate the non-negativity constraints on labor inputs $L(h)$. The Lagrangian is given by

$$\mathcal{L} = \int_0^{\bar{h}} A_h L(h)\,dh + \lambda_L \left(L - \int_0^{\bar{h}} L(h)\,dh \right) + \lambda_H \left(H - \int_0^{\bar{h}} h L(h)\,dh \right) + \int_0^{\bar{h}} \mu(h) L(h)\,dh$$

where $\lambda_L, \lambda_H, [\mu(h)]_{h \in [0,\bar{h}]}$ are the multipliers associated with the two resource constraints and the non-negativity constraints. Note especially there is a continuum of constraints associated with the constraint that labor inputs cannot be negative. The necessary conditions for this problem are given by

$$\frac{\partial \mathcal{L}}{\partial L(h)} = A_h - \lambda_L - \lambda_H h + \mu(h) = 0 \qquad \forall h \in [0,\bar{h}] \qquad\qquad \text{(S21.7)}$$

$$\lambda_L \geq 0, \quad \lambda_L \left(L - \int_0^{\bar{h}} L(h)\,dh \right) = 0 \qquad\qquad \text{(S21.8)}$$

$$\lambda_H \geq 0, \quad \lambda_H \left(H - \int_0^{\bar{h}} h L(h)\,dh \right) = 0$$

$$\mu(h) \geq 0, \quad \mu(h) L(h) = 0 \qquad \forall h \in [0,\bar{h}], \qquad\qquad \text{(S21.9)}$$

where (S21.8) to (S21.9) are the respective complementary slackness conditions. (S21.7) then implies that for all h, it will be true that

$$A_h = \lambda_L + \lambda_H h - \mu(h) \leq \lambda_L + \lambda_H h,$$

as $\mu(h) \geq 0$ (see (S21.9)). Furthermore note that we will necessarily have $\lambda_L > 0$, i.e. the resource constraint for low skilled labor will be binding. This follows immediately from the fact that the technology A_0 does not require any high skilled labor so that the maximand could be increased by using that technology if there was additional low skilled labor. Additionally, the resource constraint for high skilled labor will also be binding as A_h is increasing in h. Intuitively, if there were some idle skilled workers, you would use the low skilled workers now employed with technology A_0 together with those skilled workers in the sector with high technology A_h. This would increase the total amount of goods produced. Hence we will also always have $\lambda_H > 0$.

Exercise 21.6, Part (c). To derive sufficient conditions such that the solution involves all skilled workers to be employed with the "highest" technology $\bar{h}$ let us again consider the necessary conditions in (S21.7) to (S21.9) So suppose there is such a solution. In such a solution the resource constraint for skilled labor will be binding so that $\lambda_H > 0$. Additionally it is clear that the non-negativity constraint for the $\bar{h}$-technology is *not* binding, i.e. $\mu(\bar{h}) = 0$. Hence (S21.7) implies that

$$A_{\bar{h}} = \lambda_L + \lambda_H \bar{h}.$$

Additionally we know that there will be no sector active requiring *some* skilled labor. This follows from the fact that all skilled labor is used in the $\bar{h}$-sector. The low skilled labor which has not been used yet (recall that we assumed that $H/L < \bar{h}$) will therefore be employed with the A_0 technology so that $\mu(0) = 0$. Hence we also get that

$$A_0 = \lambda_L.$$

These equations are sufficient to pin down the multipliers on the resource constraint. We get that $\lambda_L = A_0$ and $\lambda_H = (A_{\bar{h}} - A_0)/\bar{h}$. For this to be solution to the problem, the non-negativity constraints will have to be binding for all $h \in (0, \bar{h})$, i.e.

$$\mu(h) = \lambda_L + \lambda_H h - A_h = A_0 + \frac{(A_{\bar{h}} - A_0)}{\bar{h}} h - A_h > 0 \qquad \forall h \in (0, \bar{h}).$$

Hence a sufficient condition in terms of exogenous parameters is

$$A_h < A_0 + \frac{(A_{\bar{h}} - A_0)}{\bar{h}} h = \frac{\bar{h} - h}{\bar{h}} A_0 + \frac{h}{\bar{h}} A_{\bar{h}} \qquad \forall h \in (0, \bar{h}). \tag{S21.10}$$

This is a very intuitive condition: the technology of all "intermediate" sectors $h \in (0, \bar{h})$ has to be below the convex combination of the two sector 0 and $\bar{h}$. If that is the case, i.e. if A_h is convex as a function of h, then it is the case that the solution to this problem involves full specialization in that only the extreme sectors 0 and $\bar{h}$ are employed.

Exercise 21.6, Part (d). To come up with an example where the highest sector is not used, let us consider a case where (S21.10) is not satisfied. So suppose that technology A_h is given by

$$A_h = \begin{cases} A_0 + \gamma h & \text{if } h \le h^C \\ A_0 + \gamma h^C + (h - h^C)\kappa & \text{if } h > h^C \end{cases} \tag{S21.11}$$

where $\gamma > \kappa$. Hence the technology is continuous and piecewise linear, where the slope is higher for lower technologies. With this technology is easy to verify that (S21.10) is violated. This is simply due to the fact that for technology h^C we get that

$$\begin{aligned} \frac{\bar{h} - h^C}{\bar{h}} A_0 + \frac{h^C}{\bar{h}} A_{\bar{h}} &= \frac{\bar{h} - h^C}{\bar{h}} A_0 + \frac{h^C}{\bar{h}} \left(A_0 + \gamma h^C + (\bar{h} - h^C)\kappa \right) \\ &= A_0 + \frac{h^C}{\bar{h}} \left(\gamma h^C + (\bar{h} - h^C)\kappa \right) \\ &= A_0 + h^c \gamma + \frac{h^C}{\bar{h}} (\bar{h} - h^C)(\kappa - \gamma) \\ &< A_0 + h^c \gamma = A_{h^c}. \end{aligned}$$

Hence, whereas the condition in (S21.10) required A_h to be a convex function of h, the technology in our example given in (S21.11) is concave in h.

Note however that this was only derived as a sufficient condition for a solution where *only* the $\bar{h}$-technology is used with high skill labor. Hence we need to be a little more careful to show that in this example *no* worker will be employed in the $\bar{h}$ sector. Let us prove this by contradiction. Suppose technology $\bar{h}$ is used. Then we get that

$$\lambda_L = A_0 \text{ and } \lambda_H = \frac{A_{\bar{h}} - A_0}{\bar{h}}$$

as shown above. But now note that

$$\lambda_H = \frac{A_{\bar{h}} - A_0}{\bar{h}} = \frac{\gamma h^C + (\bar{h} - h^C)\kappa}{\bar{h}} = \kappa + \frac{h^C}{\bar{h}}(\gamma - \kappa) < \gamma$$

so that for $h < h^C$ we have

$$A_h - \lambda_L - \lambda_H h + \mu(h) = A_0 + \gamma h - \lambda_L - \lambda_H h + \mu(h) = (\gamma - \lambda_H)h + \mu(h) > 0$$

which violates the first-order condition in (S21.7). Hence, $\bar{h}$ cannot be the only sector employing skilled labor.

So suppose that *some* workers are employed in that technology. Hence, $\mu(\bar{h}) = 0$. Above we showed that there will be some other sector h using skilled workers Hence, such a solution features

$$A_{\bar{h}} = \lambda_L + \lambda_H \bar{h} \tag{S21.12}$$

$$A_h = \lambda_L + \lambda_H h. \tag{S21.13}$$

Suppose first that $h > h^C$. Then we get that $A_{\bar{h}} - A_h = (\bar{h} - h)\kappa$. Additionally we get from (S21.12) and (S21.13) that $A_{\bar{h}} - A_h = (\bar{h} - h)\lambda_H$. Hence,

$$\lambda_H = \kappa. \tag{S21.14}$$

But then consider some sector $h' \leq h^C$. Assume this sector is not active. This is the case if

$$A_{h'} = A_0 + \gamma h' < \lambda_L + \lambda_H \bar{h} = A_0 + \kappa h',$$

which contradicts our assumption $\gamma > \kappa$. As h' is arbitrary, all technologies $h' \leq h^C$ will be active so that $\mu(h') = 0$ for all $h' \leq h$. But then it is clear that we get from the two first-order conditions for sectors h' and h'' with $h' < h'' \leq h^C$ that

$$A_{h''} - A_{h'} = \gamma(h'' - h') = (h'' - h')\lambda_H,$$

so that

$$\lambda_H = \gamma,$$

which contradicts (S21.14). Hence, $h > h^C$ cannot be active.

Suppose now that some sector $h \leq h^C$ is active. From the first-order conditions we get $A_{\bar{h}} - A_h = \lambda_H(\bar{h} - h)$. But from the definition of the technology we have

$$A_{\bar{h}} - A_h = A_0 + (\gamma - \kappa)h^C + \bar{h}\kappa - A_0 - \gamma h$$
$$= (\gamma - \kappa)(h^C - h) + (\bar{h} - h)\kappa,$$

so that

$$\lambda_H = \kappa + (\gamma - \kappa)\frac{h^C - h}{\bar{h} - h} < \gamma$$

where the last inequality follows from $h^C < \bar{h}$. This however violates the first-order condition (S21.12) for technology $h + \Delta$. To see this, note that

$$A_{h+\Delta} = A_h + \Delta\gamma = \lambda_L + \lambda_H h + \Delta\gamma > \lambda_L + \lambda_H(h + \Delta),$$

which violates (S21.12). So if technology $\bar{h}$ is active, no other sector employing skilled labor can be active. However we showed above that this is impossible too. Hence, with the technology given in (S21.11) there will be no workers employed with the $\bar{h}$-technology.

Exercise 21.6, Part (e). With the results derived above it should be clear that an equilibrium exists where more then two technologies are being used in equilibrium. Let us again consider the necessary conditions for the maximization problem above and suppose that the technologies $h'' > h'$ are being used. Those technologies have to satisfy

$$A_{h''} - A_{h'} = (h'' - h')\lambda_H.$$

This shows that for all sectors which are being used in equilibrium we need that the production increase from using a more skill-intensive technology is proportional to the additional amount of skilled labor used. Additionally we need that it exceeds the increase from all technologies h which are *not* used in equilibrium, because for h to not being used we need that

$$A_{h''} - A_h = \lambda_L + h''\lambda_H - \lambda_L - h\lambda_H + \mu(h) = (h'' - h)\lambda_H + \mu(h) > (h'' - h)\lambda_H,$$

where we used that $\mu(h) > 0$ as h is not being used. To see how this can be an equilibrium, suppose that equilibrium wages for skilled and unskilled labor are given by w_S and w_L respectively. The profit from employing one unit unskilled and h'' units skilled labor using technology h'' is then given by

$$\pi'' = A_{h''} - w_S h'' - w_L.$$

Similarly, using the unit of unskilled labor and the h' complementary units of skilled labor with technology h' gives a profit of

$$\pi' = A_{h'} - w_S h' - w_L,$$

so that

$$\pi'' - \pi' = A_{h''} - w_S h'' - A_{h'} + w_S h' = (h'' - h')(\lambda_H - w_S).$$

This shows that for $\lambda_S = w_S$ the profit from using the two technologies is the same. Hence, firms are indifferent from using either of those technologies so that an equilibrium exists, where two technologies are used.

Note however, then whenever such an equilibrium exists, there also exists another equilibrium where only one technology is used and the A_0 technology employs the residual unskilled labor. Hence, there is no loss of generality to consider only two firms A_h and A_0, where the A_h firm uses $\frac{H}{h}$ units of unskilled labor and the A_0 firm uses the residual $L - \frac{H}{h}$ units of unskilled labor.

Exercise 21.12

Exercise 21.12, Part (a). We have to show two things. First of all we have to show that all banks will necessarily engage in monitoring. Then we have to show that equilibrium borrowing rates will be given by $i = r + m$. To show the first claim, suppose that there was an equilibrium where no monitoring takes place and some individuals receive a positive amount of credit. For this to be an equilibrium, all individuals have to maximize utility. But this implies that all individuals will default on their loan as running away does not have any negative consequences (recall that they will never be caught and that the model is a two period model so that no long-term contracts are possible) but strictly increases the income available at the end of the life. This however cannot be an equilibrium, because banks are losing money on their loans. Hence there are two potential equilibria. In the first one, no loans are given at all. In the second one, banks incur monitoring expenses. Let us first show that there is no equilibrium where no loans are made. As shown in subsection 21.6.2, the critical wealth level for an individual to invest in education if she would have to take out a loan at rate i was given by

$$x \geq f \equiv \frac{(2+r)\,w_u + (1+i)\,h - w_s}{i-r}.$$

Assuming that the initial wealth distribution has positive mass over its whole support, there will be positive demand for loans at rate i as long as $f < h$. To see that this is always the case, note that

$$f = \frac{(2+r)\,w_u + (1+i)\,h - w_s}{i-r} < h \iff (2+r)\,w_u + (1+r)h < w_s,$$

which is the case from our assumption (21.55). Additionally note that

$$\lim_{i \to \infty} \frac{(2+r)\,w_u + (1+i)\,h - w_s}{i-r} = h.$$

Using this we can characterize the demand function for loans. Let wealth x be distributed by G_t. The demand for loans at time t as a function of the interest rate i is then given by $D_t(i) = \int_{f(i)}^{h}(h-x)dG_t(x)$ which satisfies $D_t(i) > 0$ and $\lim_{i \to \infty} D_t(i) = 0$ by our analysis above. This proves that we will never have an equilibrium where no loans are provided. Because if so, then there would be a profitable deviation from banks offering loans at an interest rate $i > r + m$ and exerting monitoring effort. From the argument above, there would be positive demand for those loans and the offering bank would make positive profits. Hence, all equilibria are characterized by a positive number of credit contracts traded and banks exerting monitoring efforts.

This being said we now have to show that there is no equilibrium involving a borrowing rate of $i > r + m$. This follows from a typical Bertrand competition argument. Suppose there was an equilibrium with a borrowing rate $i > r + m$ and N banks. Then there exists one bank (say bank 1) with profits π_1 satisfying

$$\pi_1 < \int_{f(i)}^{h} (i - r - m)(h - x)dG_t(x). \tag{S21.15}$$

To understand (S21.15) note that individual x takes out a loan of size $h - x$ and the bank serving that client makes a profit $(i - r - m)(h - x)$ on that loan. With N banks being active, there has to exist one bank which does not serve the whole market. Hence, the inequality in (S21.15) is strict. So let us write $\int_{f(i)}^{h}(i - r - m)(h - x)dG_t(x) - \pi_1 = \Delta$. By lowering interest rates to $i - \varepsilon$ and attracting the whole market bank 1 could increase its profits as

$$\int_{f(i-\varepsilon)}^{h} (i - \varepsilon - r - m)(h - x)dG_t(x) - \pi_1$$

$$= \Delta - \left(\int_{f(i)}^{h} (i - r - m)(h - x)dG_t(x) - \int_{f(i-\varepsilon)}^{h} (i - \varepsilon - r - m)(h - x)dG_t(x) \right) > 0$$

for ε small enough. Hence the above cannot be an equilibrium. This proves that the unique equilibrium will be characterized by banks offering credit contracts at the rate $i = r + m$ and exerting monitoring efforts. With $m > 0$ this of course implies that $i > r$. But this is exactly the case analyzed in subsection 21.6.2 as the choice of i was arbitrary. Hence, a model like this provides a simple microfoundation for the version of the Galor-Zeira model analyzed in subsection 21.6.2.

Exercise 21.12, Part (b). Consider now the case where monitoring involves a fixed costs M. By the same arguments as above, there will be no equilibrium where banks do not monitor. If banks do provide a loan and monitor the repayment, they must exactly break-even. This follows again from Bertrand competition in the banking sector. Hence consider a bank offering a loan of size $h - x$. Let us denote the amount of money the consumer borrowing $h - x$ pays back by $i(x)(h - x)$, i.e. $i(x)$ is the effective interest rate the consumer x is charged. For the bank to break even, this amount has to cover the costs of providing the loan, i.e.

$$i(x)(h - x) = r(h - x) + M,$$

where we used that the costs of each unit of capital are given by r and the fixed costs M are incurred whenever any monitoring takes place. Hence, the equilibrium borrowing rate is given by

$$i(x) = r + \frac{M}{h - x}, \tag{S21.16}$$

which immediately shows that the average borrowing rate is decreasing in the size of loan as the fixed monitoring costs are split across more "borrowing units". Let us now analyze the model in subsection 21.6.2 where the borrowing rate is given by (S21.16).

Again it is clear that no individual with $x \geq h$ will take out a loan. Instead those individuals will invest in education (as the educational investment is efficient) and will leave bequests of

$$b_n\left(x\left(t\right)\right) = \delta\left(w_s + \left(1 + r\right)\left(x\left(t\right) - h\right)\right).$$

Now consider an individual with $x < h$. Clearly there are no incentives to take out a higher, nor a smaller loan as (S21.16) shows that $i(x) > r$. As in subsection 21.6.2 we have to compare the income at the end of the life to decide if it is worth to take out a loan. By taking out a loan, the individual generates an income at the end of her life of

$$y_s(x) = w_s + (1 + i(x))(x - h).$$

This equation simply states that the only source of income the individual generates are the skilled wages at the end of the life (recall that you cannot work while you are young because you spend the time getting educated) and that the loan $h - x$ including the interest on this loan has to be paid back. Using (S21.16) we get that

$$y_s(x) = w_s + (1 + r)(x - h) - M. \tag{S21.17}$$

If the individual does not invest in education, her income is given by

$$y_u(x) = (1 + r)(x + w_u) + w_u. \tag{S21.18}$$

This follows from the fact that without investing in education you earn w_u in every period and you earn an interest rate of r for any unit of savings (which are given by the initial wealth endowment x plus the first period wages w_u). Hence, in order to characterize the optimal investment decision, individuals invest in education if and only if $y_s(x) \geq y_u(x)$. Using (S21.17) and (S21.18) this implies that

$$w_s \geq (2 + r)w_u + (1 + r)h + M. \tag{S21.19}$$

The crucial implication of (S21.19) is that this condition does *not* depend on the individual's wealth! Hence, if (S21.19) is satisfied, then *all* individuals will invest in education, whereas if (S21.19) is violated, *no* individual with $x < h$ will invest in education. The intuition for this result is that we can interpret this debt contract as a fixed decrease in the skill premium. This is especially apparent in (S21.17) where the *effective* high skill wage after having taken out a loan to finance education is given by $w_s - M$. Hence this model is mathematically equivalent to one with perfect capital markets (i.e. everyone can borrow at rate r) but where poorer people have a lower return to education - they earn $w_s - M$ instead of w_s. Hence the educational decision should not depend on the individuals income x but only if it is efficient given that skilled wages are effectively lower. And investment is efficient if and only if (S21.19) is satisfied. Using this result we can characterize the correspondence describing equilibrium dynamics as

$$\text{If } w_s \geq (2+r)w_u + (1+r)h + M, \text{ then}$$

$$x(t+1) = \begin{cases} b_s(x(t)) = \delta(w_s + (1+r)(x(t) - h) - M) & \text{if } x(t) < h \\ b_n(x(t)) = \delta(w_s + (1+r)(x(t) - h)) & \text{if } x(t) \geq h \end{cases}.$$

$$\text{If } w_s < (2+r)w_u + (1+r)h + M, \text{ then}$$

$$x(t+1) = \begin{cases} b_u(x(t)) = \delta((1+r)(w_u + x(t)) + w_u) & \text{if } x(t) < h \\ b_n(x(t)) = \delta(w_s + (1+r)(x(t) - h)) & \text{if } x(t) \geq h \end{cases};$$

The equilibrium dynamics are relatively simple. Observe first that all those loci representing $x(t+1)$ as a function of $x(t)$, are parallel to each other as each unit of initial wealth $x(t)$ earns a return of r. Then consider the second case, i.e. the case where $w_s < (2+r)w_u + (1+r)h + M$ so that poor individuals do not invest in education. With the same parametric configuration as in subsection 21.6.2 it is therefore clear that we have the same two stable states $\bar{x}_U$ and $\bar{x}_S$ displayed in Figure 21.9. However, we do not have the steeper locus for individuals taking out loans at the higher rate i so that this model does not feature the unstable steady state x^*. Instead the function representing equilibrium dynamics is not continuous and the jump occurs of course at $x = h$. If we have $w_s \geq (2+r)w_u + (1+r)h + M$ where everyone invests in education, the two parts of the function representing the dynamics differ just by the constant amount M by which the part for $0 < x(t) < h$ is shifted down. Hence there are two cases. If M is sufficiently small so that the lower part of the locus is always above the 45 degree line (i.e. $\delta(w_s - M) > h$), there is a unique steady state given by $\bar{x}_S$ to which all dynasties will monotonically converge. If on the other hand M is high enough so that the the function representing the dynamics crosses the 45 degree line in the interval $0 < x(t) < h$, there are two steady states which are stable. Again there is no unstable steady state as x^* in Figure 21.9.

Summing up we can distinguish two cases. If M is sufficiently high, there will be two stable steady states and the long-run evolution will be similar to the economy characterized in subsection 21.6.2 (although we might have all people investing in education). If M is small enough, the behavior of the economy will be very different: all individuals will invest in education and even though poor individuals have to pay the extra amount M to cover the monitoring costs, it is small enough such that there is only one steady state and all dynasties converge to it.

Exercise 21.12, Part (c). If individuals cannot be prevented from running away by incurring monitoring costs, the analysis gets a little more involved. We assume that contracts take the following form: if an individual with wealth x takes out a loan of size z the interest charged is equal to $i(z, x)$. After receiving the loan, the individual decides if he wants to run away or not. In case he runs away, the bank gets λy with probability p, where y is the income (including wage payments) of the individual. In case the individual does not run away, the bank gets $(1 + i(z, x))z$. Let us now characterize the contracts that can occur in equilibrium. First of all note that we will have $i(z, x) \geq r$, as r are the banks' opportunity costs. This implies that individuals will never want to take out more money than necessary, i.e. conditional on taking out a loan, an individual with wealth x will take out a loan of size $h - x$. Then note that Bertrand competition in the banking sector will make sure that banks cannot make positive profits. In particular, this implies that $i(h - x, x) = r$, whenever the individual does not run away in equilibrium. So consider the decision to run away. By not running away and paying the interest $i(h - x, x)$, utility is given by

$$\log(w_s - (1 + i(h - x, x))(h - x)) + \log((1 - \delta)^{1-\delta}\delta^\delta).$$

If the individual runs away, utility is given by

$$(1-p)\log(w_s) + p\log((1-\lambda)w_s) + \log((1-\delta)^{1-\delta}\delta^\delta) = \log(w_s) + p\log(1-\lambda) + \log((1-\delta)^{1-\delta}\delta^\delta),$$

as the end of period income when the loan is not repaid is given by w_s and the individual is caught with probability p (and then has to pay λw_s). Hence, the individual does not run away if

$$\log(w_s - (1 + i(h - x, x))(h - x)) \geq \log(w_s) + p\log(1 - \lambda). \qquad (S21.20)$$

By the zero profit condition of banks, equilibrium interest rates $i(h - x, x)$ will be given by r whenever (S21.20) holds true. Using this, we get that the condition for banks being able to lend at rate r is given by

$$\log(w_s - (1 + r)(h - x)) \geq \log(w_s) + p\log(1 - \lambda).$$

As $1 - \lambda < 1$ we have that $\log(1 - \lambda) < 0$. Hence the condition is clearly satisfied for x close enough to h. Furthermore, the LHS is strictly decreasing in x. Hence, by continuity there will exists $\hat{x}$, such that

$$\log(w_s - (1 + r)(h - \hat{x})) = \log(w_s) + p\log(1 - \lambda), \qquad (S21.21)$$

i.e. someone with wealth $\hat{x}$ will be exactly indifferent between repaying his loan with interest r and running away[1]. All individuals with $x \in (\hat{x}, h]$ will be strictly better repaying the loan. Hence, whenever $h > x \geq \hat{x}$, the banking sector will be willing to lend $h - x$ at interest rate r. What about the individuals with $x < \hat{x}$? First of all note that there is no way to provide loans, where default is prevented. To induce repayment, interest rates would have to be lowered. But at interest rates below r, banks would make losses. Hence, whenever $x < \hat{x}$, the banking sector will not provide finance where orderly repayment takes place in equilibrium. So *if* a bank lends to someone with $x < \hat{x}$, there will be default in equilibrium. The net payoff of the bank when lending to someone with wealth $x < \hat{x}$ is given by

$$\pi^B(x) = p\lambda w_s - (1 + r)(h - x), \qquad (S21.22)$$

where the first term is expected amount the bank can recover and the last term contains the opportunity costs of capital. From (S21.21) we know that

$$\log(w_s - (1 + r)(h - \hat{x})) = \log\left((1 - \lambda)^p w_s\right)$$

which implies

$$(1 + r)(h - \hat{x}) = [1 - (1 - \lambda)^p]\, w_s. \qquad (S21.23)$$

As $\pi^B(x) \leq \pi^B(\hat{x})$ for all $x < \hat{x}$ (see (S21.22)), we therefore find that

$$\begin{aligned}
\pi^B(x) &\leq \pi^B(\hat{x}) \\
&= (p\lambda - [1 - (1 - \lambda)^p])\, w_s \\
&= (p\lambda + (1 - \lambda)^p - 1)\, w_s.
\end{aligned}$$

---

[1]Note that if $\hat{x} < 0$, everyone in this economy can get a loan at interest rate r.

But as both p and λ are smaller than one, we get that[2]

$$p\lambda + (1-\lambda)^p < 1.$$

Hence we find that

$$\pi^B(x) < 0 \text{ for all } x < \hat{x},$$

so that no loans are made to individuals with wealth below $\hat{x}$. The intuition for this result is the following: as consumers in this economy are risk-averse and banks are risk-neutral, banks would have to make expected losses for the consumers to prefer the lottery over the safe project. To see this, note from (S21.21) that the certainty equivalent of getting w_s with probability $1-p$ and $(1-\lambda)w_s$ with probability p for the consumer with income $\hat{x}$ is given by

$$w_s - (1+r)(h-\hat{x}).$$

By risk aversion, this certainty equivalent is smaller than the expected payoff, i.e.

$$w_s - (1+r)(h-\hat{x}) < p(1-\lambda)w_s + (1-p)w_s.$$

Rearranging terms yields

$$p\lambda w_s - (1+r)(h-\hat{x}) < 0.$$

But the term on the LHS is exactly the expected payoff of the bank (see (S21.22)). Hence, whenever the consumer choose to run away, i.e. chooses to take the risky over the safe payoff, the bank strictly prefers not to make the loan as she would need to be subsidizing the consumer for him to be willing take the risk.

This captures the typical commitment problem with incomplete capital markets. If individuals are too poor, they cannot commit to not run away so that no loans are made in equilibrium. This analysis established that the loan market in the model takes the following form. All individuals with $x > h$ do not take out a loan because they can pay for their educational expenses out of their own wealth. Individuals with $x \in [\hat{x}, h]$ take out a loan of size $h - x$ and pay an interest rate of r. Finally, the poor agents with $x < \hat{x}$ cannot find credit on the market and therefore are not able to invest in education. Note also that in this case, the educational decision is straightforward. As education is efficient at an interest r (recall that we assumed that $w_s > (1+r)h + (2+r)w_u$), all agents that can get credit at this interest rate, will want to do so and incur the education expenditures. Hence, the end of period income as a function of initial wealth is given by

$$y(x) = \begin{cases} (2+r)w_u + (1+r)x & \text{if } x < \hat{x} \\ w_s + (1+r)(x-h) & \text{if } x \geq \hat{x} \end{cases},$$

where recall $\hat{x} < h$ as shown above. As bequests are just a fraction δ of this income, the equilibrium correspondence describing the dynamic behavior of wealth is given by

$$x(t+1) = \begin{cases} \delta\left[(2+r)w_u + (1+r)x(t)\right] & \text{if } x(t) < \hat{x} \\ \delta\left[w_s + (1+r)(x(t)-h)\right] & \text{if } x(t) \geq \hat{x} \end{cases}. \tag{S21.24}$$

---

[2]To see this, define $f(\lambda) = p\lambda + (1-\lambda)^p$. As $f(0) = 1$ and $f(1) = p$ and

$$\begin{aligned} f'(\lambda) &= p - p(1-\lambda)^{p-1} \\ &= p\left[\frac{(1-\lambda)^{1-p} - 1}{(1-\lambda)^{1-p}}\right] < 0, \end{aligned}$$

we get that

$$f(\lambda) = p\lambda + (1-\lambda)^p < 1 \text{ for all } \lambda \in (0,1].$$

How will this equilibrium correspondence look like? First of all note that it is discontinuous at $x = \hat{x}$, as

$$(2+r)w_u + (1+r)\hat{x} - (w_s + (1+r)(\hat{x} - h)) = (2+r)w_u - w_s + (1+r)h < 0$$

from our assumption that education is (strictly) efficient. Secondly note that both parts (i.e. for both $x(t) < \hat{x}$ and $x(t) \geq \hat{x}$) of the equilibrium correspondence in (S21.24) will have a slope equal to $\delta(1+r)$ so that they are parallel as everyone in this economy is borrowing and lending and interest rate r. This shows that if $\delta(1 + r) < 1$ and w_s is high enough (in particular we need that $w_s + (1+r)(\hat{x} - h) > \hat{x}$) and w_u is low enough (so that $\delta[(2 + r)w_u + (1 + r)\hat{x}] < \hat{x}$), there will be two steady states, both of which are locally stable. The low steady state x_L^* is given by

$$x_L^* = \delta\left[(2+r)w_u + (1+r)x_L^*\right] = \frac{\delta(2+r)}{1 - \delta(1+r)}w_u$$

and the high steady state x_H^* is given by

$$x_H^* = \delta\left[w_s + (1+r)(x_H^* - h)\right] = \frac{\delta}{1 - \delta(1+r)}\left(w_s - (1+r)h\right).$$

Furthermore, the dynamics are very simple. All dynasties starting with $x(0) < \hat{x}$ will converge to x_L^* and all dynasties with $x(0) \geq \hat{x}$ will converge to x_H^*. Within those two regions $[0, \hat{x})$ and $[\hat{x}, \infty)$ convergence is monotone in the sense that

$$\begin{array}{ll}
x(t) \text{ increases towards } x_L^* & \text{if } \quad x(0) < x_L^* \\
x(t) \text{ decreases towards } x_L^* & \text{if } \quad x_L^* < x(0) < \hat{x} \\
x(t) \text{ increases towards } x_H^* & \text{if } \quad \hat{x} \leq x(0) < x_H^* \\
x(t) \text{ decreases towards } x_H^* & \text{if } \quad x_H^* < x(0).
\end{array}$$

This characterizes the equilibrium dynamics in this economy.

Exercise 21.12, Part (d). Let us now analyze the responsiveness of educational investments in each of these models. We have shown that the model characterized in the first part is exactly the model analyzed in subsection 21.6.2. The analysis in this section showed that the set of individuals investing in education S_1^{ED} (where we identify individuals with their wealth levels) was given by

$$S_1^{ED} = \left\{ x \,\bigg|\, x \geq \frac{(2+r)w_u + (1+r+m)h - w_s}{m} = f \right\}.$$

As the threshold f is decreasing in w_s, more individuals will invest in education. In particular, if w_s increases to $w_s + \Delta$, all individuals with wealth x satisfying

$$f - \frac{\Delta}{m} \leq x < f$$

will now invest in education but did not do so before.

For the model analyzed in the second part, the education response is very different. There we showed that depending on parameters, either the entire population will invest in education or no individual with $x < h$ will be willing to invest in education (as the interest rate required to so would be too high). The crucial condition for educational investment was

$$w_s \geq (2+r)w_u + (1+r)h + M, \tag{S21.25}$$

i.e. if this condition is satisfied, everyone will invest in education. Hence the response to an increase in the skill premium is discontinuous. There will be no response whenever (S21.25) was satisfied before *or* if (S21.25) was violated and still is violated after the change. If however the increase in the skill premium Δ is such that

$$w_s < (2+r)w_u + (1+r)h + M < w_s + \Delta,$$

suddenly everyone with $x < h$ will start investing in education. Hence there might either be no response at all or the response is substantial. Additionally, the high steady state is shifted to the right as w_s increases.

In the third model, the set of individuals investing in education was characterized by a wealth cut-off $\hat{x}$, such that all individuals with $x \geq \hat{x}$ incurred educational expenses. Hence to characterize the educational response to an increase in the skill premium we have to analyze how $\hat{x}$ changes in w_s. In (S21.23) $\hat{x}$ was defined by

$$(1+r)(h - \hat{x}) = [1 - (1-\lambda)^p] w_s, \qquad (S21.26)$$

so that

$$\frac{\partial \hat{x}}{\partial w_s} = -\frac{1 - (1-\lambda)^p}{1+r} < 0.$$

Hence, the number of people investing in education, which are characterized by $x > \hat{x}$, increases when the skill premium increases. The reason is that an increase in the skill premium increases the amount of money banks can confiscate in case the individual runs away and is caught. This reduces the incentive to default on the loan and the marginal agent $\hat{x}$ will now be strictly better off to repay the loan. This can also be seen from (S21.26) which shows that for given $\hat{x}$, the RHS will increase, i.e. the net costs of running away are increasing in w_s, so that paying back the loan becomes relatively cheaper (note that $(1+r)(h - \hat{x})$ is the amount agent $\hat{x}$ pays back). Hence, the incentive constraint will be relaxed so that some people can now get a loan who could not have gotten one before. Via this channel an increase in the skill-premium will cause a higher level of aggregate educational expenses. This analysis (especially the difference between the first and the third and the second model) shows that the exact mechanism how credit market imperfections are modelled is absolutely crucial for the comparative statics the model delivers.

Chapter 22: Institutions, Political Economy and Growth

Exercise 22.2

Note first that we have to drop the assumption of risk-neutrality on the middle class producers' behalf. The reason is that in equilibrium the production side will have a similar structure like the AK-economy characterized in Chapter 11 (see especially subsection 11.4). Hence, the equilibrium interest rate will be constant so that with risk neutrality, there will not be an interior solution for the problem of the middle class agents. Let us for simplicity assume that middle class producers have a utility function given by $u(c) = \log(c)$.

We will see that the assumption of risk aversion complicates the analysis significantly. As this exercise is less about the exact structure of the equilibrium tax sequence and more about the growth effects of taxation, our presentation will concentrate on the main issues. For a full analysis of a similar economy with risk averse agents we refer to Exercise 22.17.

So consider the problem of middle class producers. The most important effect of introducing risk aversion will be seen to lie in the fact that choices made at time t will depend on the entire path of future taxes $\{\tau(s)\}_{s=t}^{\infty}$. Hence, we have to introduce this path of future taxes as a state variable for the entrepreneurs' problem. To do so let us introduce some notation. Middle class producers face a tax sequence $\{\tau(t)\}_{t=0}^{\infty}$, which they take as given. The problem is still stationary in the sense that once the current level of capital and future taxes $\{\tau(s)\}_{s=t}^{\infty}$ are controlled for, the problem will not depend on calender time. Hence we can write the recursive formulation of the problem of the middle class as

$$V(K, \{\tau(s)\}_{s=m}^{\infty})$$
$$= \max_{\{K',L\}} \left\{ \log \left[(1 - \tau(m))F(K, AL) + (1 - \delta)K - K' - wL \right] + \beta V(K', \{\tau(s)\}_{s=m+1}^{\infty}) \right\},$$

where

$$0 \leq K' \leq (1 - \tau(m))F(K, AL) + (1 - \delta)K - K' - wL$$

and where we already substituted the budget constraint

$$C(t) = (1 - \tau(t))F(K(t), A(t)L) + (1 - \delta)K(t) - K(t+1) - w(t)L(t). \qquad (S22.1)$$

Like in the exposition given in section 22.2, let us without loss of generality assume that $L_i(t) = 1$ (note that this exercise assumes that there is a measure one of entrepreneurs, i.e. $\theta^m = 1$). Using this, the first-order condition and the Envelope Condition are given by

$$\beta V_K(K', \{\tau(s)\}_{s=m+1}^{\infty}) = \frac{1}{\pi^C(K, \{\tau(s)\}_{s=m}^{\infty})}$$

$$V_K(K, \{\tau(s)\}_{s=m}^{\infty}) = \frac{1}{\pi^C(K, \{\tau(s)\}_{s=m}^{\infty})} \left[(1 - \tau(m))F_K(K, A) + (1 - \delta) \right],$$

where we denoted consumption by the policy function π^C, i.e. $C(m) = \pi^C(K(m), \{\tau(s)\}_{s=m}^{\infty})$. Combining these optimality conditions, the middle class' optimal consumption and capital choice is determined by the Euler equation

$$\frac{\pi^C(K', \{\tau(s)\}_{s=m+1}^{\infty})}{\pi^C(K, \{\tau(s)\}_{s=m}^{\infty})} = \beta \left[(1 - \tau(m+1)) F_K(K', A) + (1 - \delta) \right]. \tag{S22.2}$$

As (S22.2) describes the capital choice of all agents, all middle class' agents will chose the same capital level $K_i(t) = K(t)$. Hence, the endogenous total factor productivity term is given by

$$A(t) = B \int_0^1 K_i(t)\, di = B \int_0^1 K(t)\, di = BK(t).$$

Substituting this in (S22.2) and reintroducing the time indices, we get that

$$
\begin{aligned}
\frac{C(t+1)}{C(t)} &= \beta \left[(1 - \tau(t+1)) F_K(K(t+1), BK(t+1)) + (1 - \delta) \right] \\
&= \beta[(1 - \tau(t+1)) F_K(1, B) + (1 - \delta)],
\end{aligned}
\tag{S22.3}
$$

where we used the fact that F has constant returns to scale in K (and increasing returns in K and L). Note especially that $F_K(1, B)$ is a constant like in the AK-economy. Hence the middle class producers' problem is characterized by the Euler equations, the resource constraint and the transversality conditions. For a given tax sequence $\{\tau(t)\}_{t=0}^{\infty}$, these equations determine the entire path of allocations $[[K_i(t), C_i(t)]_{t=0}^{\infty}]_{i=0}^1$.

To complete the description of the equilibrium (and in particular to learn about the growth consequences of taxing entrepreneurs) we have to determine the optimal tax sequence $\{\tau(t)\}_{t=0}^{\infty}$. The budget constraint of the government is still given by

$$T^w(t) + \theta^m T^m(t) + \theta^e T^e(t) \leq \tau(t) \int_{S^m} F(K_i(t), A(t) L_i(t))\, di,$$

where the only difference to (22.8) is the changed production structure (which now depends on the (endogenous) TFP term). As the elite's only income is generated by tax revenues, the optimal solution will involve

$$T^w(t) = T^m(t) = 0$$

so that

$$C^e(t) = T^e(t) = \frac{\tau(t)}{\theta^e} \int_0^1 F(K_i(t), A(t) L_i(t))\, di. \tag{S22.4}$$

Using that

$$F(K_i(t), A(t) L_i(t)) = F(K(t), BK(t)) = K(t) F(1, B),$$

the elite's consumption level in (S22.4) is given by

$$C^e(t) = T^e(t) = \frac{1}{\theta^e} \tau(t)\, K(t) F(1, B). \tag{S22.5}$$

Assuming that the agents of the elite are still risk-neutral, the problem of the elite is given by

$$\max_{\{\tau'(t)\}_{t=0}^{\infty}} V^E \left(\{\tau'(t)\}_{t=0}^{\infty} \right) = \max_{\{\tau'(t)\}_{t=0}^{\infty}} \sum_{t=0}^{\infty} \beta^t \left(\frac{1}{\theta^e} \tau'(t)\, K(t, \{\tau'(t)\}_{t=0}^{\infty}) F(1, B) \right),$$

where $K(t, \{\tau'(t)\}_{t=0}^{\infty})$ denotes the entrepreneur's optimal capital choice for a given tax sequence $\{\tau'(t)\}_{t=0}^{\infty}$. Note that the elite realizes that those capital choices depend on the whole sequence of taxes and that each entrepreneur i will choose the same capital level if she faces the same tax sequence. For the purpose of this exercise we actually do not have to solve this problem. So let us just note that under regularity conditions, this problem will have an interior solution, say $\{\tau^*(t)\}_{t=0}^{\infty}$. In particular one can also show that there is an equilibrium where taxes are constant, i.e. $\tau^*(t) = \tau^* > 0$. As a formal proof in a similar environment (although an environment which does not feature growth) is contained in exercise 22.17, we will not provide the details of the argument here.

To finally show that those distortionary taxes $\tau^* > 0$ reduce the growth rate of the economy, we will show that there exists a BGP where the growth rate of the economy will be given by the growth rate of capital which in turn will be reduced if the middle class faces distortionary taxes. To see this, note first that total output in this economy is given by

$$Y(t) = \int_0^1 Y_i(t)di = \int_0^1 F\left(K_i(t), A(t)L_i(t)\right)di = F(1,B)K(t),$$

i.e. output grows at the same rate as the economy's capital stock. Using (S22.5) it is also clear that the consumption level of the elite is also proportional to the capital stock if taxes are constant because $C^e(t) = \frac{1}{\theta^e}\tau^* K(t) F(1,B)$. Workers are only endowed with labor, i.e. their consumption level if given by the current wage rate. Wages however are given by

$$
\begin{aligned}
w(t) &= A(t)F_L\left(K_i(t), A(t)L_i(t)\right) = A(t)F_L\left(K(t), A(t)\right) = BK(t)F_L\left(K(t), BK(t)\right)\\
&= BK(t)F_L\left(1,B\right),
\end{aligned}
$$

i.e. are also proportional to the capital stock. This shows that the consumption level of the middle class given in (S22.1) satisfies

$$
\begin{aligned}
C(t) &= (1-\tau^*)F(K(t), A(t)) - K(t+1) - BK(t)F_L\left(1,B\right)\\
&= (1-\tau^*)F(1,B)K(t) - K(t+1) - BK(t)F_L\left(1,B\right)
\end{aligned}
$$

so that

$$\frac{C(t)}{K(t)} = (1-\tau^*)F(1,B) - BF_L\left(1,B\right) - \frac{K(t+1)}{K(t)}. \qquad (S22.6)$$

Along the BGP, final output $Y(t)$ grows at a constant rate so that $\frac{K(t+1)}{K(t)}$ is constant. Hence the RHS of (S22.6) is constant which shows that entrepreneurial consumption is proportional to capital too. Hence, along the BGP we have that

$$g^* = \frac{Y(t+1)}{Y(t)} = \frac{C(t+1)}{C(t)} = \frac{K(t+1)}{K(t)}.$$

From (S22.3) however it is then clear that

$$g^* = \beta[(1-\tau^*)F_K(1,B) + (1-\delta)]$$

and therefore

$$\frac{\partial g^*}{\partial \tau^*} = -\beta F_K(1,B) < 0.$$

This shows that distortionary taxation will reduce the growth rate of the economy. The intuition is the following: the source of growth in this economy is the endogenous labor-augmenting technology term $A(t)$ which is determined by the investment decisions of middle class producers. In equilibrium, the economy will have the same structure as an AK-economy so that capital accumulation is the only source of growth. Distortionary taxes however reduce the return to capital so that capital accumulation will be lower as entrepreneurs will reduce their savings. This in turn reduces the growth rate of the economy.

The most important aspect of this exercise is, that it shows that most results about the distortionary taxation can be generalized to environments which feature (endogenous) growth. The analysis however becomes harder (as illustrated by this exercises, where we did not present a closed form solution) and often intractable. This is the reason why the discussion in the book mostly focuses on economies without growth.

Exercise 22.3

To analyze the case of the middle class deciding about the tax policies, let us first note that *given* the policy vector $p^t = \{\tau(s), T^w(s), T^m(s), T^e(s)\}_{s=t}^{\infty}$ the unique competitive equilibrium is still characterized by Proposition 22.1. In particular, the equilibrium capital ratio $\hat{k}(\tau(t))$ is given by

$$\hat{k}(\tau(t)) \equiv (f')^{-1}\left(\frac{\beta^{-1} + \delta - 1}{1 - \tau(t)}\right) \tag{S22.7}$$

and equilibrium wages are given by

$$\hat{w}(\tau(t)) = (1 - \tau(t))\left[f(\hat{k}(\tau)) - \hat{k}(\tau(t))f'(\hat{k}(\tau))\right]. \tag{S22.8}$$

Using this, the per period consumption level of the representative middle class agent is

$$C^m(t) = (1 - \tau(t))F(K_i(t), L_i(t)) - (K_i(t+1) - (1-\delta)K_i(t)) - w(t)L_i(t) + T^m(t).$$

Using that $L_i(t) = L^* = 1/\theta^m$ this can be written as

$$
\begin{aligned}
C^m(t) &= L^*(1-\tau(t))f\left(\hat{k}(\tau(t))\right) - L^*\hat{k}(\tau(t+1)) + (1-\delta)L^*\hat{k}(\tau(t)) \\
&\quad - (1-\tau(t))\left[f(\hat{k}(\tau(t))) - \hat{k}(\tau(t))f'(\hat{k}(\tau))\right]L^* + T^m(t) \\
&= \left[-\hat{k}(\tau(t+1)) + (1-\delta)\hat{k}(\tau(t)) + (1-\tau(t))\hat{k}(\tau(t))f'(\hat{k}(\tau))\right]\frac{1}{\theta^m} + T^m(t) \\
&= \left[-\hat{k}(\tau(t+1)) + \beta^{-1}\hat{k}(\tau(t))\right]\frac{1}{\theta^m} + T^m(t),
\end{aligned}
$$

where the last line uses that (S22.7) implies that

$$(1 - \tau(t))f'(\hat{k}(\tau)) = \beta^{-1} - (1-\delta).$$

To solve for $T^m(t)$ we can use the government's budget constraint, which is given by

$$\theta^m T^m(t) + \theta^e T^e(t) + T^w(t) = \tau(t)\int_{S^m} F(K_i(t), L_i(t))di = \tau(t)f(\hat{k}(\tau(t))).$$

Clearly the middle would want to set $T^e(t) = T^w(t) = 0$. Hence we get that

$$T^m(t) = \frac{1}{\theta^m}\tau(t)f(\hat{k}(\tau(t))),$$

so that the consumption level of the representative middle class agent is given by

$$C^m(t) = \frac{1}{\theta^m}\left[-\hat{k}(\tau(t+1)) + \beta^{-1}\hat{k}(\tau(t)) + \tau(t)f(\hat{k}(\tau(t)))\right].$$

Using this, we can write the *policy* problem of the middle class agent recursively as

$$
\begin{aligned}
&V^m(\tau, [\hat{k}_i(\tau)]_{i \in S^m}) \\
&= \max_{\tau' \in [0,1]} \left\{\left[\beta^{-1}\hat{k}(\tau) + \tau f(\hat{k}(\tau)) - \hat{k}(\tau')\right]\frac{1}{\theta^m} + \beta V^m(\tau', [\hat{k}_i(\tau')]_{i \in S^m})\right\},
\end{aligned}
$$

where the capital stocks $[\hat{k}_i(\tau)]_{i \in S^m}$ are given in (S22.7). The Envelope Condition is given by

$$V_\tau^m(\tau, [\hat{k}_i(\tau)]_{i \in S^m}) = \left[\beta^{-1}\frac{\partial \hat{k}(\tau)}{\partial \tau} + f(\hat{k}(\tau)) + \tau f'(\hat{k}(\tau))\frac{\partial \hat{k}(\tau)}{\partial \tau}\right]\frac{1}{\theta^m}. \tag{S22.9}$$

As the first-order condition is given by

$$\frac{\partial \hat{k}(\tau')}{\partial \tau'}\frac{1}{\theta^m} = \beta V_\tau^m(\tau',[k_i(\tau')]_{i\in S^m}),\qquad (\text{S22.10})$$

(S22.9) and (S22.10) together imply that

$$V_\tau^m(\tau,[\hat{k}_i(\tau)]_{i\in S^m}) - \beta^{-1}\frac{\partial \hat{k}(\tau)}{\partial \tau}\frac{1}{\theta^m} = \left[f(\hat{k}(\tau)) + \tau f'(\hat{k}(\tau))\frac{\partial \hat{k}(\tau)}{\partial \tau}\right]\frac{1}{\theta^m} = 0,$$

so that the optimal tax rate is implicitly defined by

$$f(\hat{k}(\tau)) + \tau f'(\hat{k}(\tau))\frac{\partial \hat{k}(\tau)}{\partial \tau} = 0.\qquad (\text{S22.11})$$

From (S22.7) we get that

$$\frac{\partial \hat{k}(\tau)}{\partial \tau} = \frac{\beta^{-1}-(1-\delta)}{(1-\tau)^2}\frac{1}{f''(\hat{k}(\tau))},$$

so that (S22.11) yields

$$\begin{aligned}
0 &= f(\hat{k}(\tau)) + \tau f'(\hat{k}(\tau))\frac{\beta^{-1}-(1-\delta)}{(1-\tau)^2}\frac{1}{f''(\hat{k}(\tau))}\\
&= f(\hat{k}(\tau)) + \frac{\tau}{1-\tau}\left(\frac{\beta^{-1}-(1-\delta)}{(1-\tau)^2}\right)^2\frac{1}{f''(\hat{k}(\tau))},\qquad (\text{S22.12})
\end{aligned}$$

where the second equality uses (S22.7). Hence, (S22.7) and (S22.12) provide us with two equations in two unknowns (k,τ) which we can (in principle) solve. We are only interested if $\tau > 0$. To see that this is the case, note that

$$\hat{k}(0) = (f')^{-1}(\beta^{-1}+\delta-1) > 0,$$

so that (S22.12) is not satisfied for $\tau = 0$ as $f(\hat{k}(0)) > 0$. In particular note that the LHS of (S22.12), i.e. the term

$$f(\hat{k}(\tau)) + \frac{\tau}{1-\tau}\left(\frac{\beta^{-1}-(1-\delta)}{(1-\tau)^2}\right)^2\frac{1}{f''(\hat{k}(\tau))}$$

describes the marginal returns of setting a higher tax rate. As $f(\hat{k}(0)) > 0$, this shows that the marginal return of a tax increase at $\tau = 0$ are positive. Hence, the middle class will indeed want to tax themselves. Although this might seem to be a strange result at first sight, the result is sensible. The intuition why the middle class would exert taxes on themselves is the following. Given that all markets are competitive, middle class producers make zero profits beyond the competitive return on their capital which they themselves are endowed with. By imposing a tax which middle class producers will take as given after the tax is set, perfect competition will ensure that middle class producers earn zero profits *after the tax is paid for*. Hence, equilibrium wages will be lower - both via the direct tax effect (see (S22.8)) and the slowed down capital accumulation. Those tax dollars will however be distributed among the middle class producers so that the possibility to tax themselves represents an inefficient mechanism how the middle class can transfer resources from workers to themselves. The same intuition would also apply when the whole population are the beneficiaries of the tax receipts. This would tend to reduce the incentives to impose distortionary taxes, the basic intuition however would still go through - taxes will still be a measure to reduce wages and transfer resources to the middle class.

Exercise 22.8

Note first that the assumption that power shifts *permanently* from the elite to the middle class simplifies the task of comparing $V^e(E)$ and $V^e(M)$ considerably. So let us derive $V^e(M)$, i.e. the value of the elite when the middle class is in political power. As this value function will be dependent on the tax policy the middle class chooses, we have to solve the policy problem of middle class producers. As we assumed that Condition 22.1 did not hold, wages are equal to zero. For a given policy sequences $\{\tau^e(t), \tau^m(t)\}_{t=0}^{\infty}$ the maximizing capital-labor ratio as a function of the tax rate was given by (see (22.20))

$$k(\tau^m) = (\beta(1 - \tau^m))^{1/(1-\alpha)} A_i. \tag{S22.13}$$

Together with the governments budget constraint

$$T^w(t) + \theta^m T^m(t) + \theta^e T^e(t) \leq \phi \int_{S^m \cup S^e} \tau^i(t) F(K_i(t), L_i(t)) \, di + R^N \tag{S22.14}$$

we can solve for the consumption level of the representative middle class agent as

$$C^m(t) = \bar{L}[f(k(\tau^m(t))) + (1-\delta)k(\tau^m(t)) - k(\tau^m(t+1))] + T^m(t). \tag{S22.15}$$

As the optimal policy sequence as decided upon by the middle class will involve

$$T^w(t) = T^e(t) = 0,$$

we can combine (S22.14) and (S22.15) to get

$$
\begin{aligned}
C^m(t) &= \bar{L}[f(k(\tau^m(t))) + (1-\delta)k(\tau^m(t)) - k(\tau^m(t+1))] + \frac{R^N}{\theta^m} + \\
&\quad \frac{\phi}{\theta^m}\bar{L}\tau^m(t)f(k(\tau^m(t))) + \frac{\phi}{\theta^m}\bar{L}\tau^e(t)f(k(\tau^e(t))) \\
&= \bar{L}\left[f(k(\tau^m(t)))\left(1 + \frac{\phi}{\theta^m}\tau^m(t)\right) + (1-\delta)k(\tau^m(t)) - k(\tau^m(t+1))\right] \\
&\quad + \frac{\phi}{\theta^m}\bar{L}\tau^e(t)f(k(\tau^e(t))) + \frac{R^N}{\theta^m}.
\end{aligned}
$$

The middle class will set $\{\tau^e(t)\}_{t=0}^{\infty}$ to maximize their lifetime utility. But as $\tau^e(t)$ only appears in the equation of $C^m(t)$ (and not in $C^m(t+1)$) this is just a static problem, i.e. the middle class will tax the elite according to

$$\tau^e(t) = \arg\max_{\tau} \tau f(k(\tau)).$$

This is intuitive as it requires that $\tau^e(t)$ is set to maximize the tax revenues the middle class gets from the elite. The necessary first-order condition is given by

$$f(k(\tau^e(t))) + \tau f'(k(\tau^e(t)))\frac{\partial k(\tau^e(t))}{\partial \tau} = 0. \tag{S22.16}$$

As we are still in the case of the canonical Cobb-Douglas model, (S22.16) simplifies to

$$\frac{1}{\alpha}(A^m)^{1-\alpha}k^{\alpha} - \tau(A^m)^{1-\alpha}k^{\alpha-1}k\frac{1}{(1-\alpha)(1-\tau)} = 0,$$

which yields the optimality condition $\frac{\alpha\tau}{(1-\alpha)(1-\tau)} = 1$, or rather

$$\tau^e(t) = \tau^e = 1 - \alpha.$$

Additionally note that $\tau^m(t) = 0$. The reason is that there is excess labor supply, i.e. wages will be zero. Recall that exercise 22.3 showed that middle class producers would want to tax themselves if this would decrease wages (as it would represent a possibility to extract resources from workers). With excess labor supply wages are not dependent on the tax rate (they are equal to zero) so that taxing themselves does not have benefits and taxes will be zero. Given this policy choice by the middle class, the consumption level of the elite when the middle class is in power is given by

$$
\begin{aligned}
C^e(t) &= (1 - \tau^e)\bar{L}f(k(\tau^e)) + (1 - \delta)\bar{L}k(\tau^e) - \bar{L}k(\tau^e) \\
&= (1 - \tau^e)\bar{L}f(k(\tau^e)) - \bar{L}k(\tau^e) \\
&= \bar{L}\left[\alpha\frac{1}{\alpha}(A^e)^{1-\alpha}(\beta\alpha)^{\alpha/(1-\alpha)}(A^e)^\alpha - (\beta\alpha)^{1/(1-\alpha)}A^e\right] \\
&= \bar{L}A^e(\beta\alpha)^{\alpha/(1-\alpha)}(1 - \alpha\beta) \tag{S22.17}
\end{aligned}
$$

where the second line explicitly used our assumption that $\delta = 1$ and third line used (S22.13) to arrive at

$$
k(\tau^e) = (\beta(1 - \tau^e))^{1/(1-\alpha)}A^e = (\beta\alpha)^{1/(1-\alpha)}A^e.
$$

Using this expression for consumption, we can solve for the value of the elite when the middle class is in power as

$$
V^e(M) = \bar{L}A^e(\beta\alpha)^{\alpha/(1-\alpha)}(1 - \alpha\beta) + \beta V^e(M) = \frac{1}{1 - \beta}\bar{L}A^e(\beta\alpha)^{\alpha/(1-\alpha)}(1 - \alpha\beta).
$$

Note that it is precisely here where the assumption of a permanent power shift simplifies the analysis - otherwise we could not have solved $V^e(M)$ without knowledge of $V^e(E)$. From here we can now show that in this model

$$
V^e(E) > V^e(M).
$$

To do so we show that per period consumption of the elite under elite control is strictly higher than under the control of the middle class. Let us denote the elite's consumption level under the control of the elite and the middle class by $C^e(E)$ and $C^e(M)$ respectively. The analysis in section 22.4.2 established that

$$
\begin{aligned}
C^e(E) &= \beta^{\alpha/(1-\alpha)}A^e\bar{L}/\alpha + [\phi\beta^{\alpha/(1-\alpha)}\tau^m(1 - \tau^m)^{\alpha/(1-\alpha)}A^m\theta^m\bar{L}/\alpha + R^N]/\theta^e \\
&\geq \beta^{\alpha/(1-\alpha)}A^e\bar{L}/\alpha.
\end{aligned}
$$

Using (S22.17) we therefore get that a sufficient condition for $C^e(E) > C^e(M)$ is

$$
\beta^{\alpha/(1-\alpha)}A^e\bar{L}/\alpha > \bar{L}A^e(\beta\alpha)^{\alpha/(1-\alpha)}(1 - \alpha\beta).
$$

This however will be satisfied as

$$
1 > \alpha^{1/(1-\alpha)}(1 - \alpha\beta).
$$

As the elite gets a higher consumption level in every period when they themselves are in power, they strictly prefer being in power, i.e.

$$
V^e(E) > V^e(M)
$$

as required.

Exercise 22.16

Exercise 22.16, Part (a). If Condition 22.1 fails to hold, labor demand will fall short of labor supply so that wages will always be equal to zero. Hence, the factor price manipulation motive is absent. If $\phi = 0$, then it is furthermore the case that the tax revenue the elite might extract from the middle class cannot be used as consumption of the elite. Hence the only channel why the consumption level of the middle class matters for the utility of the elite is via the possibility of political replacement. Recall that we assumed that probability of political replacement was given by $\eta(t) = \eta(\theta^m C^m(t))$. It will still be true that the elite will be better off being in power than being governed by the middle class (see the solution to Exercise 22.8). Hence, the only objective regarding the choice of τ and g is to reduce the consumption of the middle class to increase the probability of political survival $1 - \eta(t)$ (recall that we assumed that $\eta'(.) > 0$). As middle class consumption is increasing in g and decreasing in τ, the utility of the elite is strictly increasing in the tax rate and decreasing in the productivity of the middle class. Therefore it is clear that $g = 0$ and setting the maximal tax rate is the optimal action for the elite. This shows that any MPE will feature $g = 0$. To see that this will also be true for all SPE, note that the decision to block the technology can be taken only once at $t = 0$. So suppose there was a SPE where $g = 1$. From then on, the unique SPE will be characterized by $\tau(t) = \bar{\tau}$ as this yields the maximal utility the elite can attain (in the sense that it would minimize middle class consumption). But this will also be the unique SPE in case the elite would have set $g = 0$. As the utility of the elite will be higher when the productivity of the middle class is lower, the unique SPE will involve $g = 0$.

Exercise 22.16, Part (b). As we restrict ourselves to MPE and the maximization problem of the elite is stationary, the optimal tax rate will be a function of g, but constant over time. Let us denote those optimal tax rates by $\hat{\tau}(1)$ and $\hat{\tau}(0)$ respectively. Following the analysis in Section 22.4.2 we can therefore write the utility of the elite as a function of g as[1]

$$
\begin{aligned}
V^e(E, g) &= \beta^{\alpha/(1-\alpha)} A^e \bar{L}(1 - \beta a)/a + [\phi \beta^{\alpha/(1-\alpha)} \hat{\tau}(g)(1 - \hat{\tau}(g))^{\alpha/(1-\alpha)} A(g)^m \theta^m \bar{L}/\alpha]/\theta^e \\
&\quad + R^N/\theta^e + \beta \left[(1 - \eta[\hat{\tau}(1), g]) V^e(E, g) + \eta[\hat{\tau}(1), g] V^e(M) \right],
\end{aligned} \tag{S22.18}
$$

where we used that the elite's value under the control of the middle class does not depend on g. This is a direct consequence of our assumption that wages are equal to zero and hence will be independent of $A^m(g)$ once the middle class gains power. The elite will therefore prefer to block the technology of the middle class if $V^e(E, 0) - V^e(E, 1) > 0$. To make some progress here, let us first determine the consumption level of middle class entrepreneurs. Taking taxes as given and employing $\bar{L}$ units of labor each, the after tax consumption of each entrepreneurs as a function of g is given by

$$
\begin{aligned}
C^m(g) &= (1 - \hat{\tau}(g)) \bar{L} \frac{1}{\alpha} [\beta(1 - \hat{\tau}(g))]^{\frac{\alpha}{1-\alpha}} A^m(g) - [\beta(1 - \hat{\tau}(g))]^{\frac{1}{1-\alpha}} A^m(g) \\
&= \bar{L} A^m(g) (1 - \hat{\tau}(g))^{\frac{1}{1-\alpha}} \beta^{\frac{\alpha}{1-\alpha}} \frac{1 - \alpha\beta}{\alpha},
\end{aligned} \tag{S22.19}
$$

---

[1]Note that the expression is slightly different than the one given in the book (the equation after (22.30)). This is due to the fact that there is a small typo in the book, i.e. the term $(1 - \beta a)$ is missing. To derive our expression, note that the elite would not want to tax itself given that there is excess labor supply and equilibrium wages are zero. Recall that this will not be true if wages were not zero (see exercise 22.3). The per-period consumption level of the elite will therefore be given by

$$
C^e(t) = \bar{L} \left(f(k(t)) - k(t+1) + (1 - \delta)k(t) \right).
$$

As $\delta = 1$ and $k(t) = [\beta(1 - \tau(t)]^{1/(1-\alpha)} A^e$ (see (22.20)), we get that

$$
\begin{aligned}
C^e(t) &= \bar{L} \left(\frac{1}{\alpha} (A^e)^{1-\alpha} \beta^{\alpha/(1-\alpha)} (A^e)^\alpha - \beta^{1/(1-\alpha)} A^e \right) \\
&= \bar{L} A^e \beta^{\alpha/(1-\alpha)} \left(\frac{1}{\alpha} - \beta \right) \\
&= \bar{L} A^e \beta^{\alpha/(1-\alpha)} (1 - \beta\alpha) \frac{1}{\alpha}
\end{aligned}
$$

as given in (S22.18).

where we used the optimal capital-labor ratio given in (22.20). To construct an example where the elite would want to prevent the middle class from adopting the efficient technology even if they can extract taxes from them, suppose for simplicity that $A^m(0) = 0$, i.e. the elite can effectively block the middle class from producing at all. The best way to think about this assumption is not from a purely technological perspective but rather as a regulation where middle class producers are prevented from entering the market in the first place. Let us furthermore assume that $\eta(0) = 0$, which captures the idea that power is firmly in the hands of the elite as long the middle class does not have any resources. Hence, $\eta\left[\hat{\tau}(0), 0\right] = 0$ so that (S22.18) implies

$$V^e(E, 0) = \left(\beta^{\alpha/(1-\alpha)} A^e \bar{L}(1 - \beta a)/a + R^N/\theta^e\right) \frac{1}{1 - \beta}. \qquad (S22.20)$$

Let us for expositional purposes also assume that $\eta(\theta^m C^m(1)) = 1$ whenever $C^m(1) > 1$, i.e. if the middle class will consume a positive amount, then it will take over the political power with certainty. This assumption is not crucial, it merely simplifies some calculations. Hence, the function $\eta(.)$ takes the simple form

$$\eta(x) = \begin{cases} 0 & \text{if } x = 0 \\ 1 & \text{if } x > 0 \end{cases}.$$

Note in particular this this implies that $\eta'(x) = 0$ whenever $x > 0$.

Using this, we have to consider two cases to solve for the value function of the elite given in (S22.18). Suppose the elite chooses $\hat{\tau}(1) < 1$. Then it follows from (S22.19) that $C^m(1) > 0$, so that the elite's value if given by

$$V^e(E, 1) = \beta^{\frac{\alpha}{1-\alpha}} A^e \bar{L}(1 - \beta a)/a + [\phi \beta^{\frac{\alpha}{1-\alpha}} \hat{\tau}(1)(1 - \hat{\tau}(1))^{\frac{\alpha}{1-\alpha}} A(1)^m \theta^m \bar{L}/\alpha + R^N]/\theta^e + \beta V^e(M), \qquad (S22.21)$$

as $\eta(\theta^m C^m(1)) = 1$. If however the elite decides to allow the technology adoption but then decides to set $\hat{\tau}(1) = 1$, its value is given by

$$\begin{aligned} V^e_{\tau=1}(E, 1) &= \beta^{\alpha/(1-\alpha)} A^e \bar{L}(1 - \beta a)/a + R^N/\theta^e + \beta V^e_{\tau=1}(E, 1) \\ &= \frac{\beta^{\alpha/(1-\alpha)} A^e \bar{L}(1 - \beta a)/a + R^N/\theta^e}{1 - \beta}. \end{aligned} \qquad (S22.22)$$

Note that we indexed the value function by $\tau = 1$ to indicate that this refers to the case where the elite confiscates the entire output of middle class producers. But (S22.22) and (S22.20) now show that

$$V^e_{\tau=0}(E, 1) = V^e(E, 0).$$

This is intuitive as both these policies do not generate any tax revenues (either the middle class has a productivity level of zero or they do not accumulate any capital) but allow the elite to cling to their power. Hence let us without loss of generality assume that the elite does not consider the option of allowing technology adoption ($g = 1$) and then taxing the entire returns. Hence, the two values of the elite are $V^e(E, 1)$ (given in (S22.21)) and $V^e(E, 0)$ (given in (S22.20)).

Now note that $V^e(E, 1)$ depends on the value of the elite once the middle class has taken over power, i.e. $V^e(M)$. In this context the only incentive of the middle class to tax the elite once they are in power is to extract tax revenues as there is no scope for factor price manipulation (as wages are zero) and we assume that the middle class will never get replaced once they are in power. This implies that the middle class will set taxes to maximize tax revenue, i.e. will set $\tau^e_M = 1 - \alpha$ (see the solution to Exercise 22.8 for the derivation), where

τ_M^e denotes the tax rate imposed on the elite by the middle class. The consumption level of the elite under middle class control $C^e(M)$ will therefore be given by

$$
\begin{aligned}
C^e(M) &= (1-\tau_M^e)\frac{1}{\alpha}\bar{L}(A^e)^{1-\alpha}k(\tau_M^e)^\alpha - \bar{L}k(\tau_M^e) + (1-\delta)\bar{L}k(\tau_M^e) \\
&= (1-\tau_M^e)\frac{1}{\alpha}\bar{L}A^e(\beta(1-\tau_M^e))^{\alpha/(1-\alpha)} - \bar{L}A^e(\beta(1-\tau_M^e))^{1/(1-\alpha)} \\
&= \bar{L}A^e(\beta\alpha)^{\alpha/(1-\alpha)}(1-\beta\alpha),
\end{aligned}
$$

where the second line used $\delta = 1$ and the fact the optimal capital-labor ratio is given in (22.20) as

$$
k(\tau_M^e) = A(\beta(1-\tau_M^e))^{1/(1-\alpha)}.
$$

Note that this is of course the same expression as (S22.19) when taxes are given by $\tau = 1-\alpha$. Hence we get that

$$
V^e(M) = C^e(M) + \beta V^e(M) = \frac{1}{1-\beta}\bar{L}A^e(\beta\alpha)^{\alpha/(1-\alpha)}(1-\beta\alpha).
$$

Substituting this in (S22.21) we find that

$$
\begin{aligned}
V^e(E,1) &= \beta^{\alpha/(1-\alpha)}A^e\bar{L}(1-\beta a)/a + [\phi\beta^{\frac{\alpha}{1-\alpha}}\hat{\tau}(1)(1-\hat{\tau}(1))^{\frac{\alpha}{1-\alpha}}A(1)^m\theta^m\bar{L}/\alpha + R^N]/\theta^e \\
&\quad + \frac{\beta}{1-\beta}\bar{L}A^e(\beta\alpha)^{\alpha/(1-\alpha)}(1-\beta\alpha) \\
&= \beta^{\alpha/(1-\alpha)}A^e\bar{L}\frac{1-\beta a}{\alpha}\left(1+\frac{\beta}{1-\beta}\alpha^{1/(1-\alpha)}\right) \\
&\quad + [\phi\beta^{\alpha/(1-\alpha)}\hat{\tau}(1)(1-\hat{\tau}(1))^{\alpha/(1-\alpha)}A(1)^m\theta^m\bar{L}/\alpha + R^N]/\theta^e.
\end{aligned}
$$

Hence, the elite will block the technology whenever $V^e(E,0) > V^e(E,1)$, i.e.

$$
\frac{\beta^{\frac{\alpha}{1-\alpha}}A^e\bar{L}\frac{1-\beta a}{\alpha}+R^N/\theta^e}{1-\beta} > \beta^{\frac{\alpha}{1-\alpha}}A^e\bar{L}\frac{1-\beta a}{\alpha}\left(1+\frac{\beta}{1-\beta}\alpha^{\frac{1}{1-\alpha}}\right) + [\phi\beta^{\frac{\alpha}{1-\alpha}}\hat{\tau}(1)(1-\hat{\tau}(1))^{\frac{\alpha}{1-\alpha}}A(1)^m\theta^m\bar{L}/\alpha + R^N]/\theta^e.
$$

To ease the interpretation, let us rearrange this condition as

$$
\frac{\left[\beta^{\frac{\alpha}{1-\alpha}}A^e\bar{L}\frac{1-\beta a}{\alpha}\left(1-\alpha^{\frac{1}{1-\alpha}}\right)+R^N/\theta^e\right]\beta}{1-\beta} > \frac{[\phi\beta^{\frac{\alpha}{1-\alpha}}\hat{\tau}(1)(1-\hat{\tau}(1))^{\frac{\alpha}{1-\alpha}}A(1)^m\bar{L}]\theta^m}{\alpha\theta^e}. \quad \text{(S22.23)}
$$

(S22.23) illustrates the basic trade-off the elite is facing. Consider the first the LHS. By blocking economic entry of the middle class it can capture the rents from natural rents because it can ensure to stay in power. Furthermore they do not face the taxes which the middle class is going to impose once entry occurs (this is captured by the term $(1-\alpha^{1/(1-\alpha)})$). As the elite will never be replaced, this payoff is multiplied by $\beta/(1-\beta)$. On the other hand, the RHS incorporates that they lose the tax returns the middle class could pay if entry was allowed. The comparative statics results are intuitive. Distortionary blocking of economic development gets more likely the higher the rents of natural resources and the more productive the elite (i.e. the higher A^e). On the other hand, the elite will accommodate entry of the middle class if they are very productive (i.e. $A(1)^m$ is high), the state capacity (i.e. the ability of the state to efficiently extract resources governed by ϕ) is higher and the more numerous the middle class is vis-a-vis the elite.

Up to now we left the general expression $\hat{\tau}(1)$ to clearly identify the source of the benefits of not blocking entry, i.e. the tax returns. However we can also solve for $\hat{\tau}(1)$ explicitly. The optimal tax rate is given by

$$\tau^* = \arg\max_\tau \tau(1-\tau)^{\alpha/(1-\alpha)} = 1 - \alpha.$$

This is intuitive: without taxes affecting the political replacement (recall that $\eta'(x) = 0$), the elite will tax the middle class to maximize tax revenues. Using this, (S22.23) reduces to

$$\frac{\left[\beta^{\frac{\alpha}{1-\alpha}} A^e \bar{L} \frac{1-\beta a}{\alpha}\left(1 - \alpha^{\frac{1}{1-\alpha}}\right) + R^N/\theta^e\right]\beta}{1-\beta} > \frac{[\phi\beta^{\frac{\alpha}{1-\alpha}}(1-\alpha)(\alpha)^{\frac{\alpha}{1-\alpha}} A(1)^m \bar{L}/\alpha]\theta^m}{\theta^e},$$

which is just a parametric condition as required.

Exercise 22.16, Part (c). Up to now we have stressed the fact that many distortions arise simply because we restricted attention to a limited set of instruments. Hence, many distortions would not exist if the elite would have access to more efficient means to transfer resources from middle class producers to themselves. For example in the baseline model analyzed in Section 22.2 the equilibrium would feature no distortionary taxation but only lump-sum taxes. This simply reflects the fact that in this framework the elite is only concerned to redistribute resources from the middle class to itself and in equilibrium they will chose the most efficient way to do this. This intuition however is changed when other concerns like the factor manipulation motive or the possibility of political replacement become more prominent. To see this, let us consider the example from above but now assume that Condition 22.1 holds, i.e. there will be full employment in this economy and wages will be positive. We will show that it is this feature which will induce the elite to choose distortionary policies although it has access to lump-sum taxes. Suppose for simplicity that the elite has only two fiscal instruments, namely the lump sum tax T^m and the technology choice g. This of course is restrictive in that we do not allow the elite to distort the economy by imposing distortionary taxes τ^m on the middle class. For the point we want to make here however, this is not decisive. We just want to see if the elite would block the technology choice of the middle class (which is of course an inefficient policy choice) in spite of having lump-sum taxes available.

Again we assume that the probability of replacement $\eta(.)$ is an increasing function of the consumption level of the middle class. This immediately implies that the elite would want to impose the highest lump-sum taxes possible, i.e. would set a lump-sum tax of $T^m = C^m(t) = Y^m(g) - w(t)\bar{L}$. In contrast to our analysis above however wages are not zero but will be equal to the lowest marginal product of producers in this economy. The marginal product of labor is given by

$$\frac{\partial Y(t)}{\partial L} = \frac{1-\alpha}{\alpha}A_i(t)^{1-\alpha}\left(\frac{K_i(t)}{L(t)}\right)^\alpha = \frac{1-\alpha}{\alpha}A_i(t)^{1-\alpha}\left[\beta^{1/(1-\alpha)}A_i(t)\right]^\alpha = \frac{1-\alpha}{\alpha}\beta^{\alpha/(1-\alpha)}A_i(t),$$

where we used the optimal capital-labor ratio $K_i(t)/L_i(t)$ given in (22.20). Hence, equilibrium wages in this economy are given by

$$w(t) = \frac{1-\alpha}{\alpha}\beta^{\alpha/(1-\alpha)}\min\{A^e, A^m(g)\} \equiv w(g), \qquad \text{(S22.24)}$$

where we explicitly denoted the dependence of the equilibrium on the decision of the elite. This already suggests why the inefficient blocking of technological adoption might occur in equilibrium - it is a mechanism to reduce equilibrium wages. For a given choice of g, the receipts from the lump sum taxation are given by

$$T^m = Y^m(g) - w(t)\bar{L} = \bar{L}\frac{1}{\alpha}\beta A^m(g) - \bar{L}w(t) = \bar{L}\frac{1}{\alpha}[A^m(g)\beta - (1-\alpha)\beta^{\alpha/(1-\alpha)}\min\{A^e, A^m(g)\}].$$

Let us assume that

$$A^m(1) > A^e > A^m(0),\qquad\qquad\text{(S22.25)}$$

i.e. the elite is more productive than the middle class if and only if technology adoption is prevented. As the entire surplus of the middle class is extracted via lump-sum taxation, i.e. post-tax consumption of the middle class is equal to zero, the probability of replacement does *not* depend on g, i.e.

$$\eta(t) = \eta(\theta^m C(1)) = \eta(\theta^m C(0)) = \eta(0) \equiv \eta.$$

To analyze the decision to block or not block the technological adoption of the middle class we again have to compare the values of the elite. Using (S22.18) we find that

$$
\begin{aligned}
V^e(E,g) &= \frac{\beta^{\frac{\alpha}{1-\alpha}}A^e\bar{L}(1-\beta a) - \bar{L}w(g)\alpha}{\alpha} + \frac{\theta^m(Y^m(g) - w(g)\bar{L}) + R^N}{\theta^e}\\
&\quad + \beta\left[(1-\eta)V^e(E,g) + \eta V^e(M)\right]\\
&= \frac{\frac{\beta^{\frac{\alpha}{1-\alpha}}A^e\bar{L}(1-\beta a) - \bar{L}w(g)\alpha}{\alpha} + \frac{\theta^m(Y^m(g)-w(g)\bar{L})+R^N}{\theta^e} + \beta\eta V^e(M)}{1-\beta(1-\eta)}\qquad\text{(S22.26)}
\end{aligned}
$$

so that

$$
\begin{aligned}
V^e(E,1) - V^e(E,0) &= \frac{\bar{L}(w(0)-w(1)) + \frac{\theta^m}{\theta^e}\left[Y^m(1) - Y^m(0) + (w(0)-w(1))\bar{L}\right]}{1-\beta(1-\eta)}\\
&= \frac{\frac{\theta^m+\theta^e}{\theta^e}\bar{L}(w(0)-w(1)) + \frac{\theta^m}{\theta^e}\left[Y^m(1)-Y^m(0)\right]}{1-\beta(1-\eta)}.
\end{aligned}
$$

Note that the difference in values $V^e(E,1) - V^e(E,0)$ does *not* depend on $V^e(M)$ as the replacement probability does not depend on g. Hence, the terms including $V^e(M)$ cancel out. From here we can conclude that the elite would want to block the middle class from adopting the efficient technology whenever $V^e(E,1) - V^e(E,0) < 0$, i.e. when

$$
\begin{aligned}
0 &> (\theta^m + \theta^e)\bar{L}(w(0) - w(1)) + \theta^m[Y^m(1) - Y^m(0)]\\
&= (\theta^m + \theta^e)\bar{L}\frac{1-\alpha}{\alpha}\beta^{\alpha/(1-\alpha)}(A^m(0) - A^e) + \theta^m\bar{L}\frac{1}{\alpha}\beta[A^m(1) - A^m(0)],
\end{aligned}
$$

where the second line used (S22.24) and (S22.25). To facilitate the intuition, let us write this condition as

$$(\theta^m + \theta^e)\bar{L}\frac{1-\alpha}{\alpha}\beta^{\alpha/(1-\alpha)}(A^e - A^m(0)) > \theta^m\bar{L}\frac{1}{\alpha}\beta[A^m(1) - A^m(0)].$$

From there it is apparent that technology is blocked, when the gains from lower equilibrium wages (on the LHS) exceed the benefits from higher lump-sum taxes (on the RHS). The comparative static results are also intuitive. The higher $A^m(1)$, the higher the incentives of the elite to not block adoption from the middle class. The reason is that given our assumption in (S22.25), $A^m(1)$ will never determine equilibrium wages but will only increase the resources the elite can extract. If on the other hand the elite is very productive, i.e. A^e is high, there are bigger incentives to block technology adoption from the middle class. This is also intuitive: if the elite does not block the technology of the middle class, it will be A^e that determines equilibrium wages. Hence, if A^e is high it is more profitable to block the technology adoption by the middle class as this will reduce equilibrium wages by relatively more compared to the case where A^e is low. This shows that if the elite has access to efficient means of resource extraction, they might still use inefficient policies (like blocking technology adoption) due to the factor price manipulation motive.

Exercise 22.17

To see that entrepreneurs' capital accumulation is characterized by (22.61) let us write the entrepreneurs' problem recursively. The current capital stock is the state variable and the sequence of taxes $\{\tau(t)\}_{t=0}^{\infty}$ is taken as given. Hence, the recursive formulation is given by

$$V(k, \{\tau(s)\}_{s=m}^{\infty}) = \max_{\{k'>0,c>0\}} \left\{ \log(c) + \beta V(k', \{\tau(s)\}_{s=m+1}^{\infty}) \right\}$$

$$\text{s.t. } c + k' = f(k) = (1 - \tau(m))Ak^{\alpha}.$$

As this will be a crucial part of the solution it is worthwhile to pause for second and observe that we parametrize the value function by the entire sequence of future taxes. Hence if today's taxes are $\tau(m)$, tomorrow's value function is dependent on $\{\tau(s)\}_{s=m+1}^{\infty}$. Substituting the constraint we therefore get

$$V(k, \{\tau(s)\}_{s=m}^{\infty}) = \max_{k' \in [0,(1-\tau(m))Ak^{\alpha}]} \left\{ \log((1-\tau(m))Ak^{\alpha} - k') + \beta V(k', \{\tau(s)\}_{s=m+1}^{\infty}) \right\},$$

which yields the first-order condition

$$\frac{1}{(1-\tau(m))Ak^{\alpha} - k'} = \beta V'(k', \{\tau(s)\}_{s=m+1}^{\infty}) \qquad (S22.27)$$

and the Envelope Condition

$$V'(k, \{\tau(s)\}_{s=m}^{\infty}) = \frac{\alpha(1-\tau(m))Ak^{\alpha-1}}{(1-\tau(m))Ak^{\alpha} - k'}. \qquad (S22.28)$$

Iterating (S22.28) forward, combining it with (S22.27) and denoting the policy function by $k' = \pi(k, \{\tau(s)\}_m)$ yields

$$\frac{1}{(1-\tau)Ak^{\alpha} - \pi(k, \{\tau(s)\}_m)} = \frac{(1-\tau')\beta\alpha A\pi(k, \{\tau(s)\}_m)^{\alpha-1}}{(1-\tau')A\pi(k, \{\tau(s)\}_m)^{\alpha} - \pi(\pi(k, \{\tau(s)\}_m), \{\tau(s)\}_{m+1})}, \qquad (S22.29)$$

where $\tau = \tau(m)$ and $\tau' = \tau(m+1)$. To solve this problem, let us conjecture a specific solution. In particular, let us conjecture that

$$\pi(k, \{\tau(s)\}_{s=m}^{\infty}) = \kappa(1 - \tau(m))Ak^a,$$

where κ is to be determined. The most important part of this guess of the policy function is that it is only dependent on the current tax rate $\tau(m)$. With this conjecture we get that

$$\pi(\pi(k, \{\tau(s)\}_{s=m}^{\infty}), \{\tau(s)\}_{s=m+1}^{\infty}) = \kappa(1 - \tau(m+1))A(\kappa(1-\tau(m))Ak^a)^{\alpha}.$$

To simplify the notation let $\tau(m) = \tau$ and $\tau(m+1) = \tau'$. Using this, (S22.29) yields

$$\frac{1}{(1-\tau)Ak^{\alpha}(1-\kappa)} = \frac{(1-\tau')\beta\alpha A [\kappa(1-\tau)Ak^a]^{\alpha-1}}{(1-\tau')A [\kappa(1-\tau)Ak^a]^{\alpha} - \kappa(1-\tau')A (\kappa(1-\tau)Ak^a)^{\alpha}},$$

from which it can be verified that

$$\kappa = \alpha\beta.$$

Hence, the capital accumulation policy function is indeed given by

$$\pi(k(t), \tau(t)) = k(t+1) = \alpha\beta(1 - \tau(t))Ak(t)^a \qquad (S22.30)$$

as required in (22.61). Note especially that we in principle allowed for capital accumulation to depend on the entire sequence of future taxes. However it turns out that the solution conveniently takes the easy form that future tax rates do not matter for current decisions once current taxes are controlled for. The reason for this is deeply rooted in the combination of log preferences and full depreciation. We know that with those preferences the income and the substitution effect exactly cancels out, i.e. controlling for lifetime wealth, an increase in the price of future consumption versus current consumption would leave current consumption (and savings) unchanged. With full depreciation however, lifetime wealth is just given by current output $(1 - \tau(t))Ak(t)^\alpha$, i.e. does not depend on future taxes either. Hence, future taxes do neither affect the saving rate nor lifetime wealth, so that current savings are not dependent on future taxes. Current savings however are equal to tomorrow's capital stock as there is full depreciation. Hence, it is only the current tax rate that affects capital accumulation.

Let us now turn to the problem of the elite. Their per period consumption level is equal to the tax proceeds, i.e. it is given by

$$c^e(t) = \tau(t)y(t) = \tau(t)Ak(t)^\alpha.$$

Writing the problem of the elite recursively, yields the formulation

$$V^e(k) = \max_{\tau \in [0,1]} \left\{ \log(\tau Ak^\alpha) + \beta V^e(k'(\tau)) \right\}. \tag{S22.31}$$

Note that τ is of course *not* a state variable for the elite. Along the equilibrium path however, we know exactly how the future capital stock k' depends on current taxes - it is exactly given by (S22.30). Substituting this into (S22.31) yields the required formulation

$$V^e(k) = \max_{\tau \in [0,1]} \left\{ \log(\tau Ak^\alpha) + \beta V^e(\alpha\beta(1 - \tau)Ak^a) \right\}. \tag{S22.32}$$

That the endogenous value function V^e is differentiable for $k > 0$ and strictly concave follows from Theorem 6.4 in Chapter 6. To see this, let us check that the assumptions in Theorem 6.4 are satisfied. That the instantaneous utility function is strictly concave and continuous is obvious. Furthermore, the correspondence G is simply given by $G(k) = [0, Ak^\alpha]$, which is compact-valued, continuous and nonempty. That the limit condition required in Assumption 6.1 also holds follows from the following observation. Consider the capital accumulation of entrepreneurs if taxes were zero. This would be given by

$$k(t + 1) = \alpha\beta Ak(t)^a.$$

By the usual argument, this process has a finite steady state k^* starting from any $k(0)$. But then it is clear that in this taxless economy we would have

$$k(t) \leq \max\{k(0), k^*\}.$$

With taxes there will of course be less capital for all $t > 0$ so that per period consumption by the elite is bounded from above by

$$\tau(t)Ak(t)^\alpha \leq Ak(t)^\alpha \leq A\left(\max\{k(0), k^*\}\right)^\alpha,$$

which is the consumption level they would get if capital accumulation was given as in the taxless economy but the elite could extract all the resources. Hence we get that

$$\lim_{T \to \infty} \sum_{t=0}^{T} \beta^t \log(c^e(t)) < \lim_{T \to \infty} \sum_{t=0}^{T} \beta^t \log(A\max\{k(0), k^*\}^\alpha) = \frac{\log(A\max\{k(0), k^*\}^\alpha)}{1 - \beta} < \infty,$$

which verifies that the limit exists and is finite as required in Assumption 6.1. This proves the strict concavity of V^e. To prove differentiability of the value function, simply apply Theorem 6.6 and note that the instantaneous utility function is differentiable.

Using this result, we can use (S22.32) to get the Euler equation of the elite. The first-order condition is given by

$$\frac{1}{\tau} - \beta (V^e)'(k') \alpha \beta A k^a = 0.$$

Using that from (S22.30) we know that $k' = \alpha \beta (1 - \tau(t)) A k^\alpha$, the above simplifies to

$$\frac{1}{\tau} = \beta^2 (V^e)'(k') \alpha A k^a = \beta (V^e)'(k') \frac{k'}{1-\tau} \tag{S22.33}$$

as required. The Envelope Condition reads

$$
\begin{aligned}
(V^e)'(k) &= \frac{\alpha}{k} + \beta (V^e)'(k') \alpha^2 \beta (1 - \tau) A k^a \frac{1}{k} = \frac{\alpha}{k} \left(1 + \beta (V^e)'(k') \alpha \beta (1 - \tau) A k^a \right) \\
&= \frac{\alpha}{k} \left(1 + \beta (V^e)'(k') k' \right). \tag{S22.34}
\end{aligned}
$$

Using the conjecture $V^e(k) = \eta + \gamma \log k$, it is clear that $(V^e)'(k) = \gamma \frac{1}{k}$ so that (S22.34) reduces to

$$\gamma \frac{1}{k} = \frac{\alpha}{k} \left(1 + \beta \gamma \frac{1}{k'} k' \right),$$

which can be solved for

$$\gamma = \frac{\alpha}{1 - \alpha \beta}$$

as required. The policy function for the elite can then be solved from (S22.33). Using the expression for $(V^e)'(k')$ and γ, (S22.33) simplifies to

$$\frac{1}{\tau} = \frac{\beta \alpha}{1 - \alpha \beta} \frac{1}{k'} \frac{k'}{1 - \tau} = \frac{\beta \alpha}{1 - \alpha \beta} \frac{1}{1 - \tau},$$

so that indeed

$$\tau = 1 - \alpha \beta.$$

Hence, the optimal tax rate is independent of the state variable, i.e. the capital stock in the economy. Again this constancy of the optimal tax rate is heavily dependent on the logarithmic preferences. To see this more clearly, note that we can write the elite's problem as.

$$V^e(k) = \max_{(1-\tau)' \in [0,1]} \left\{ \log(A k^\alpha - (1 - \tau) A k^\alpha) + \beta V^e(\alpha \beta (1 - \tau) A k^a) \right\}.$$

This problem however is isomorphic to the problem of a consumer with a current level of resources $A k^\alpha$ having to decide on consumption and saving. In this context, $(1 - \tau)$ would be the saving rate. Savings earn a gross return of $\alpha \beta$. But with log preferences we know that the saving rate will be constant and so are taxes in this example.

To finally study the dynamics of capital in this economy, (S22.30) and $\tau = 1 - \alpha \beta$ imply that

$$k(t + 1) = \alpha \beta (1 - \tau(t)) A k(t)^a = (\alpha \beta)^2 A k(t)^a.$$

Clearly this economy will have a unique steady state given by

$$k^* = \left((\alpha \beta)^2 A \right)^{1/(1-\alpha)}.$$

Furthermore, it can be shown by the usual arguments that convergence to this steady state will be monotone and that the system will be globally stable, i.e. $k(t)$ will converge to k^*

for any initial condition $k(0)$. Hence the dynamics of the capital stock will qualitatively be similar to the dynamics of the standard neoclassical growth model.

Exercise 22.22*

Exercise 22.22, Part (a). Consider the game with two parties. Let us assume that individuals' preferences are symmetric, i.e. for individual i with bliss point α_i, we assume that $p \succ p'$, whenever $|\alpha_i - p| < |\alpha_i - p'|$. Note that this assumption is not innocuous but for the purpose of this exercise no intuition is lost by just considering this case. Let $p_A(q_A, q_B)$ be the probability that party A wins, when it offers platform q_A and party B offers q_B. For simplicity we assume that voters randomize whenever they are indifferent between q_A and q_B. Then, $p_A(q_A, q_B)$ is given by

$$p_A(q_A, q_B) = \begin{cases} 1 & \text{if } |\tfrac{1}{2} - q_A| < |\tfrac{1}{2} - q_B| \\ 0 & \text{if } |\tfrac{1}{2} - q_A| > |\tfrac{1}{2} - q_B| \\ \tfrac{1}{2} & \text{if } |\tfrac{1}{2} - q_A| = |\tfrac{1}{2} - q_B| \end{cases},$$

i.e. party A wins the election, when it is closer to the midpoint $\frac{1}{2}$. Obviously we have $p_B(q_A, q_B) = 1 - p_A(q_A, q_B)$. To characterize the equilibrium of this game, let us derive the best response function of both parties. Let $BR_i(q_j)$ the best response function of party i when party j offers platform q_j. As parties are assumed to maximize the probability of winning, $BR_i(q_j)$, is given by

$$BR_i(q_j) = \begin{cases} \{q \in [0,1] \mid |\tfrac{1}{2} - q| < |\tfrac{1}{2} - q_j|\} & \text{if } q_j \neq \tfrac{1}{2} \\ \tfrac{1}{2} & \text{if } q_j = \tfrac{1}{2} \end{cases}, \tag{S22.35}$$

i.e. for any q_j party i just wants to get closer to the midpoint (but she is indifferent among all platforms conditional on being closer). From there we can conclude that the unique equilibrium in this game is given by $(q_A, q_B) = \left(\frac{1}{2}, \frac{1}{2}\right)$. To see this, note that an equilibrium corresponds to a fixed point of the best responses. Hence, the median voter outcome $(q_A, q_B) = \left(\frac{1}{2}, \frac{1}{2}\right)$ is an equilibrium because it is a fixed point of the best response functions, i.e.

$$BR_A\left(\frac{1}{2}\right) = \frac{1}{2} = BR_B\left(\frac{1}{2}\right).$$

To prove that the equilibrium is also unique, suppose there was another equilibrium for example involving $q_B > \frac{1}{2}$. From (S22.35) we get that

$$q_A \in (1 - q_B, q_B). \tag{S22.36}$$

But given q_A in (S22.36), (S22.35) implies

$$BR_B(q_A) \neq q_B.$$

Hence, there is no equilibrium involving policies which are not equal to $\frac{1}{2}$.

Now suppose the parties try to maximize their vote share. In that case, the analysis is a little different, as the best response functions are discontinuous. The best response functions is given by

$$BR_A(q_B) = \begin{cases} \emptyset & \text{if } q_B < \frac{1}{2} \\ \emptyset & \text{if } q_B > \frac{1}{2} \\ \frac{1}{2} & \text{if } q_B = \frac{1}{2} \end{cases} \tag{S22.37}$$

To see why $BR_A(q_B) = \emptyset$ whenever $q_B \neq 1/2$, consider $q_B < 1/2$. First of all note that

$$q < q_B \implies q \notin BR_A(q_B)$$

as proposing q would give a vote share smaller than $1/2$ whereas proposing $q_B + \varepsilon$ would deliver a vote share which is strictly higher than $1/2$ as long as ε is sufficiently small (i.e. satisfies $q_B + \varepsilon < 1/2$). Similarly we get that

$$q = q_B \Longrightarrow q \notin BR_A(q_B),$$

as $q_B + \varepsilon$ would yield a higher vote share by the same argument as above. Finally suppose $q > q_B$. Then consider $\tilde{q} = q - 1/2(q - q_B) < q$. Clearly, $\tilde{q}$ is closer to q_B so that $\tilde{q}$ will yield a higher vote share than q. As $q > q_B$ was arbitrary, this shows that

$$q > q_B \Longrightarrow q \notin BR_A(q_B),$$

so that indeed

$$BR_A(q_B) = \emptyset.$$

the case for $q_B > 1/2$ is analogous. Although the best response function looks different than the one in the "maximize the probability of winning"-case, the equilibrium outcome is the same, i.e. both parties will offer the bliss point of the median voter, i.e. $q_A = q_B = \frac{1}{2}$. To see this, note that (q_A, q_B) is an equilibrium whenever

$$BR_A(q_B) = q_A \text{ and } BR_B(q_A) = q_B,$$

where $BR_i(.)$ is given in (S22.37). But the only fixed point of these mappings is given by $q_A = q_B = \frac{1}{2}$. Hence, with two parties, both the outcome and the intuition of the game is the same regardless if parties maximize their vote share or the probability of winning - each party wants to be closer to the median voter as the competing party.

Exercise 22.22, Part (b). Consider the case of three parties trying to maximize the probability of winning. As this game has a continuum of equilibria in pure strategies, let us characterize their structure. To do so, let us show which policy choices *cannot* be equilibria. Without loss of generality let us suppose that $p^A \leq p^B \leq p^C$.

- *There is no equilibrium with $p^A = p^B = p^C = p$.* Suppose there was such an equilibrium. If $p < 1/2$ ($p > 1/2$), each party could win with probability one by proposing $p + \varepsilon$ ($p - \varepsilon$). If $p = 1/2$, each party could also win with probability one by proposing $p + \varepsilon$, as the other parties share (roughly) $1/2$ of the votes, whereas the deviating party gets $1/2$ of the votes alone.
- *There is no equilibrium with $p^A = p^B = p < p^C$ and party A or B wins.* Again, party C could win with probability one by offering $p + \varepsilon$ ($p - \varepsilon$) if $p < 1/2$ ($p > 1/2$). By the same argument there does not exist an equilibrium with $p^A < p^B = p^C = p$ and party B or C winning with probability one.
- *There is no equilibrium with $p^A < p^B < p^C$ and some parties are tying.* Party A (C) could move to $p^B - \varepsilon$ ($p^B + \varepsilon$) and win with probability one.
- *There is no equilibrium with $p^A < p^B < p^C$ and party B winning with probability one.* If $q^B \geq 1/2$ ($q^B \leq 1/2$), party A (C) could move to $1/2 - \varepsilon$ ($1/2 + \varepsilon$) and win with probability one.

This leaves us with two potential equilibrium configurations. Either we can have $p^A = p^B = p < p^C$ and party C winning with probability one (or similarly we could have $p^A < p^B = p^C = p$ and party A winning with probability one). Or we can have $p^A < p^B < p^C$ and either party A or party C winning with probability one. The intuition why there are equilibria with these configurations is, that there are no profitable unilateral deviations. Consider the first case. Clearly there is no incentive for party C to change its behavior. But party A and B cannot improve their winning probability either, because once, one of the parties moves to get closer to C, the party "left behind" attracts more voters. Hence, if party A moves towards C, it will be party B who will win (and vice versa). Hence, there are equilibria which such configurations. The intuition for the other case is the same. Suppose party A wins. Whenever B moves sufficiently to the left for A not to win, it will be party C who wins and vice versa. It can be verified that there is a continuum of those equilibria, i.e. there are various choices for q^A, q^B and q^C which are consistent with equilibrium.

Exercise 22.22, Part (c). Consider now the case where the parties maximize their vote share. To show that there is no equilibrium in pure strategies, suppose first there was an equilibrium where all the parties chose the same platform q. By randomization, each party would get a third of the votes. This cannot be an equilibrium as there is an incentive to deviate to $q + \varepsilon$ if $q \leq \frac{1}{2}$ and $q - \varepsilon$ if $q \geq \frac{1}{2}$. Such a deviation would give the deviating party a vote share of at least $\frac{1}{2} - \varepsilon$. Hence, there is no equilibrium where all parties propose the same platform. So suppose there is an equilibrium where the policies are different (not necessarily all of them). Without loss of generality assume that $p^A < p^B \leq p^C$. Then there is a profitable deviation for party A, to propose the platform $\tilde{q} = p^B - \varepsilon > p^A$. By doing so, the party would increase its vote share, so that $p^A < p^B \leq p^C$ could not have been an equilibrium. Hence, there are also no equilibria, where parties offer different platforms. This proves the claim, that the game does not have any equilibrium in pure strategies.

Exercise 22.22, Part (d). Let us now consider a mixed strategy equilibrium. A mixed strategy f is a probability distribution on $[0, 1]$ (not necessarily with full support). Hence let f_C and f_B be given and consider party A. We conjecture that all parties play a symmetric mixed strategy on the support $[\alpha, 1 - \alpha]$, with $\alpha < 1/2$. To characterize the equilibrium we need to find f and α. The vote share of party A when proposing a policy q^A is given by

$$S^A(q^A) = 2 \int_\alpha^{q^A} f(x)F(x) \left(1 - \frac{q^A + x}{2}\right) dx + 2 \int_{q^A}^{1-\alpha} f(x)(1 - F(x)) \left(\frac{q^A + x}{2}\right) dx$$

$$+ 2 \int_\alpha^{q^A} \int_{q^A}^{1-\alpha} f(x)f(y)\frac{y - x}{2} dy dx. \tag{S22.38}$$

where F denotes the cdf corresponding to the density f. To understand this equation, note that there are 3 scenarios that can happen. First of all we can have that $q^A \geq x = \max\{q^B, q^C\}$. If so, party A gets $1 - q^A + \frac{q^A - x}{2} = 1 - \frac{q^A + x}{2}$ of the votes. What is the probability that this happens? Suppose first that $q^B \geq q^C$, i.e. $x = q^B$. The probability that $x \geq q^C$ is given by $F(x)$ as party C mixes according to f. Hence, $\int_a^{q^A} f(x)F(x) \left(1 - \frac{q^A + x}{2}\right) dx$ gives exactly party $A's$ expected vote share *conditional* on $q^A \geq q^B \geq q^C$. As the case of $q^C \geq q^B$ is entirely symmetric, $\int_a^{q^A} f(x)F(x) \left(1 - \frac{q^A + x}{2}\right) dx$ appears twice in the expression of the expected votes share of party A. The second term in (S22.38) has exactly the same interpretation for the case of $q^A \leq \min\{q^B, q^C\}$. Finally, we could have $q^B \leq q^A \leq q^C$ or $q^C \leq q^A \leq q^B$. This is captured in the second line. The vote share for party A if $q^B = x < q^A < q^C = y$ is given by

$$\frac{q^A - x}{2} + \frac{y - q^A}{2} = \frac{y - x}{2}.$$

The probability for $q^B = x$ and $q^C = y$ is given by $f(x)f(y)$. Again there are two configurations how this case can occur.

For party A to be willing to mix over the support, she has to be indifferent between all policies in the support. In particular she has to be indifferent between $q^A = \alpha$ and $q^A = 1 - \alpha$.

Using (S22.38) we get that

$$
\begin{aligned}
S^A(\alpha) &= 2\int_\alpha^{1-\alpha} f(x)(1-F(x))\left(\frac{\alpha+x}{2}\right)dx \\
&= \alpha\int_\alpha^{1-\alpha} f(x)(1-F(x))dx + \int_\alpha^{1-\alpha} f(x)(1-F(x))xdx \\
&= \alpha - \alpha\int_\alpha^{1-\alpha} f(x)F(x)dx + \frac{1}{2} - \int_\alpha^{1-\alpha} f(x)F(x)xdx,
\end{aligned}
$$

where we used that $\int_\alpha^{1-\alpha} f(x)dx = 1$ and $\int_\alpha^{1-\alpha} f(x)xdx = \frac{1}{2}$. Similarly we have that

$$
\begin{aligned}
S^A(1-\alpha) &= 2\int_\alpha^{1-\alpha} f(x)F(x)\left(1-\frac{1-\alpha+x}{2}\right)dx \\
&= \int_\alpha^{1-\alpha} f(x)F(x)(1+\alpha-x)dx \\
&= (1+\alpha)\int_\alpha^{1-\alpha} f(x)F(x)dx - \int_\alpha^{1-\alpha} f(x)F(x)xdx.
\end{aligned}
$$

Combining these two equations we get that

$$
S^A(1-\alpha) - S^A(\alpha) = (1+2\alpha)\int_a^{1-\alpha} f(x)F(x)dx - \alpha - \frac{1}{2}.
$$

As party A has to be indifferent, we need that f and α has to be such that $S^A(1-\alpha) = S^A(\alpha)$, i.e.

$$
(1+2\alpha)\int_\alpha^{1-\alpha} f(x)F(x)dx - \alpha - \frac{1}{2} = 0. \tag{S22.39}
$$

Let us conjecture that parties play uniform strategies on $[\alpha, 1-\alpha]$. We will come back to this conjecture below. If f is a uniform density on $[\alpha, 1-\alpha]$ it is clear that

$$
f(x) = \begin{cases} \frac{1}{1-2\alpha} & \text{if } x\in[\alpha, 1-\alpha] \\ 0 & \text{otherwise} \end{cases}.
$$

Then we get that

$$
\begin{aligned}
\int_a^{1-\alpha} f(x)F(x)dx &= \frac{1}{1-2\alpha}\int_a^{1-\alpha} \frac{x-\alpha}{1-2\alpha}dx \\
&= \left(\frac{1}{1-2\alpha}\right)^2\int_0^{1-2\alpha} xdx = \frac{1}{2},
\end{aligned}
$$

so that (S22.39) is clearly satisfied. Hence, if the other two parties play according to a uniform strategy on $[\alpha, 1-\alpha]$, party A is indeed indifferent between playing the upper and lower policy of the common support. This shows that our conjecture of parties playing uniform strategies is at least a potential solution. For it to be an equilibrium we further have to show two things. First of all we need to show that party A is indeed indifferent between all policies in the support. Formally this means that

$$
\frac{\partial S^A(q^A)}{\partial q^A} = 0, \quad \text{for all } q^A \in [\alpha, 1-\alpha]. \tag{S22.40}
$$

Secondly we have to show that it could not do better to propose a policy outside the support, i.e.

$$
S^A(q) \le S(\alpha), \quad \text{for all } q \notin [\alpha, 1-\alpha].
$$

Let us first consider the first requirement, which will determine the parameter a (which, recall is still an endogenous variable). Differentiating (S22.38) yields

$$\frac{\partial S^A(q^A)}{\partial q^A} = 2f(q^A)F(q^A)\left(1 - q^A\right) - \int_\alpha^{q^A} f(x)F(x)dx \qquad (S22.41)$$

$$+ \int_{q^A}^{1-\alpha} f(x)(1 - F(x))dx - 2f(q^A)(1 - F(q^A))q^A$$

$$+ f(q^A)\int_{q^A}^{1-\alpha} f(x)\left(q^A - x\right)dx - f(q^A)\int_\alpha^{q^A} f(x)\left(x - q^A\right)dx.$$

Defining $f(x) = \frac{1}{1-2\alpha} \equiv \bar{f}$, (S22.40) and (S22.41) imply that

$$0 = 2F(q^A)\left(1 - q^A\right) - \int_\alpha^{q^A} F(x)dx + \int_{q^A}^{1-\alpha} (1 - F(x))dx$$

$$-2(1 - F(q^A))q^A + \bar{f}\left[\int_{q^A}^{1-\alpha} \left(x - q^A\right)dx - \int_\alpha^{q^A} \left(q^A - x\right)dx\right]$$

$$= 2\left[F(q^A) - q^A\right] + \left(1 - \alpha - q^A\right) - \int_\alpha^{1-\alpha} F(x)dx \qquad (S22.42)$$

$$+ \left[\int_\alpha^{1-\alpha} \bar{f}x dx - q^A \int_\alpha^{1-\alpha} \bar{f}dx\right].$$

Now note that

$$\int_\alpha^{1-\alpha} \bar{f}dx = \int_\alpha^{1-\alpha} f(x)dx = 1 \text{ and } \int_\alpha^{1-\alpha} \bar{f}x dx = \int_\alpha^{1-\alpha} f(x)x dx = \mathbb{E}[x] = 1/2$$

and

$$\int_\alpha^{1-\alpha} F(x)dx = \int_\alpha^{1-\alpha} (x - \alpha)f(x)dx = 1/2 - \alpha$$

so that (S22.42) reduces to

$$0 = 2\left[\frac{q^A - \alpha}{1 - 2\alpha} - q^A\right] + 1 - \alpha - q^A - 1/2 + \alpha + 1/2 - q^A$$

$$= 2\alpha\frac{2q^A - 1}{1 - 2\alpha} + 1 - 2q^A.$$

Hence,

$$\frac{2\alpha}{1 - 2\alpha} = 1$$

which requires that $\alpha = 1/4$.

This shows that if parties B and C play uniform strategies with support $[1/4, 3/4]$, party A is indifferent between all policies on $[1/4, 3/4]$, i.e. party A's best response is also a uniform distribution on $[1/4, 3/4]$. Note in particular that the support $[1/4, 3/4]$ is the unique solution under the conjecture that the distribution played is indeed uniform.

Finally we also have to show that party A would not want to propose a policy outside the support. So consider some $q^A < \alpha$. From (S22.38) we get that for $q^A < \alpha$

$$
\begin{aligned}
S^A(q^A) &= \int_\alpha^{1-\alpha} f(x)(1 - F(x))\left(q^A + x\right) dx \\
&= \bar{f}^2 \int_\alpha^{1-\alpha} (1 - \alpha - x)\left(q^A + x\right) dx \\
&= \bar{f}\left[(1-\alpha)q^A \int_\alpha^{1-\alpha} f(x)dx + (1 - \alpha - q^A)\int_\alpha^{1-\alpha} xf(x)dx - \int_\alpha^{1-\alpha} x^2 f(x)dx\right] \\
&= 2\left[\frac{q^A}{4} + \frac{3}{8} - \int_\alpha^{1-\alpha} x^2 f(x)dx\right],
\end{aligned}
$$

where the last lines uses that $\alpha = 1/4$ and $\bar{f} = 2$. This however shows that $S^A(q^A)$ is strictly increasing for all $q^A \le \alpha$, so that

$$
S^A(q^A) \le S^A(\alpha) = S^A(z), \quad q^A \le \alpha \text{ and } z \in [\alpha, 1 - \alpha]
$$

as required. Similarly we can also show that $S^A(q^A) \le S^A(1 - \alpha)$ whenever $q^A \ge 1 - \alpha$.

This establishes that there is a unique symmetric equilibrium where all parties play uniform strategies. It is given by a uniform mix over the support $[1/4, 3/4]$. Note that we did not establish that there do not exist other symmetric, i.e. not necessarily uniform equilibria. This however is the case as shown in Shaked (1982).

Exercise 22.27

Exercise 22.27, Part (a). To find the preferred tax rate for each agent, we have to derive the indirect utility function as a function of the policy variable (here the tax rate τ). Hence we have to solve for individuals' (equilibrium) income as a function of the tax rate. Equilibrium wages and interest rates are given by

$$
r = (1-\alpha)K^{-\alpha}H^\alpha = (1-\alpha)(\lambda k)^{-\alpha}\left[(1-\lambda)\int h d\mu(h)\right]^\alpha = Y\frac{1-\alpha}{\lambda k} \quad \text{(S22.43)}
$$

$$
w = \alpha(\lambda k)^\alpha\left[(1-\lambda)\int h d\mu(h)\right]^{\alpha-1} = \alpha(\lambda k)^\alpha((1-\lambda)\mu_h)^{\alpha-1} = \frac{Y\alpha}{(1-\lambda)\mu_h} \quad \text{(S22.44)}
$$

where the mean level of human capital is denoted by $\mu_h = \int h d\mu(h)$. Using this, we can derive individual income. Let $I^K(\tau, k)$ and $I^H(\tau, h)$ denote the income of capitalists with capital k and workers with human capital h as a function of the tax rate and the respective endowment. Substituting (S22.43) and (S22.44), we get that

$$
\begin{aligned}
I^K(\tau, k) &= (1-\tau)rk + (\tau - v(\tau))(\lambda rk + (1-\lambda)w\mu_h) \\
&= Y[\frac{1-\alpha}{\lambda}(1-\tau) + \tau - v(\tau)] \\
I^H(\tau, k) &= (1-\tau)wh + (\tau - v(\tau))(\lambda rk + (1-\lambda)w\mu_h) \\
&= Y[\frac{\alpha}{1-\lambda}(1-\tau)\frac{h}{\mu_h} + \tau - v(\tau)].
\end{aligned}
$$

The optimal tax rate is the one that maximizes individual income. Let $\tau^K(k)$ and $\tau^H(h)$ denote the preferred tax rate of capitalists and workers, when the respective individual has a factor endowment of k and h respectively. Consider first the capitalists. Let us first look for an interior solution. The FOC for capitalists is given by

$$\frac{\partial I^K(\tau^K(k), k)}{\partial \tau} = Y[-\frac{1-\alpha}{\lambda} + 1 - v'(\tau^K(k))] = 0,$$

which implies

$$v'(\tau^K(k)) = v'(\tau^K) = 1 - \frac{1-\alpha}{\lambda}.$$

Note that the capitalists' preferred tax rate does not depend on k (and hence we write $\tau^K(k) = \tau^K$). By the Inada condition $v'(1) = \infty$ and the fact that v is increasing, this implies that $\tau^K < 1$. By the convexity of v it is also clear that if there is an interior solution it is unique. The necessary and sufficient condition for the existence of an interior solution is then just, that $v'(0) < 1 - \frac{1-\alpha}{\lambda}$ which (by the fact that $v'(0) = 0$) implies that

$$\tau^K > 0 \Leftrightarrow 1 > \frac{1-\alpha}{\lambda} \Leftrightarrow \lambda > 1 - \alpha. \tag{S22.45}$$

(S22.45) contains a very intuitive condition. As taxes are given back lump sum, capitalists get a fraction λ of the tax bill. As taxes are proportional to the factor payments and (given the Cobb-Douglas structure) capital earnings amount to a fraction $(1-\alpha)$ of output, capitalists are net receivers of taxes if $\lambda > 1 - \alpha$. Hence, the preferred tax rate by capitalists is given by

$$\tau^K = \begin{cases} 0 & \text{if } \lambda < 1 - \alpha \\ (v'^{-1}(1 - \frac{1-\alpha}{\lambda}) & \text{if } \lambda \geq 1 - \alpha \end{cases}. \tag{S22.46}$$

Consider now the workers. By the same reasoning as above, if the preferred tax rate of a worker indexed by h is interior, it is given by

$$\tau^H(h) = v'^{-1}(1 - \frac{\alpha}{1-\lambda}\frac{h}{\mu_h}).$$

Note that in contrast to τ^K, the preferred tax rate of worker h does depend on his level of human capital h. Again the Inada conditions ensure that $\tau^H(h) < 1$. The solution is interior if $1 > \frac{\alpha}{1-\lambda}\frac{h}{\mu_h}$. This is also intuitive: for the worker with $h = \mu_h$, there is no gain from redistribution *within* the group of workers so he prefers positive taxes if and only if workers get more of the tax receipts than their share of factor payments (i.e. if $(1 - \lambda) > \alpha$). If $h < \mu_h$, the respective worker even gains from redistribution within the group of workers so that poorer workers favor higher taxes. This is also true for interior solutions as

$$\frac{\partial \tau^H(h)}{\partial h} = -\frac{\alpha}{\mu_h(1-\lambda)}\frac{1}{v''(\tau^H(h))} < 0 \tag{S22.47}$$

i.e. the preferred tax rate is decreasing in h. Hence, the preferred tax rate is given by

$$\tau^H(h) = \begin{cases} 0 & \text{if } \frac{1-\lambda}{\alpha} < \frac{h}{\mu_h} \\ (v'^{-1}(1 - \frac{\alpha}{1-\lambda}\frac{h}{\mu_h}) & \text{if } \frac{1-\lambda}{\alpha} \geq \frac{h}{\mu_h} \end{cases}. \tag{S22.48}$$

For the preferences over tax rates to be single peaked, a sufficient condition is that the indirect utility function is concave. From above we get that

$$\frac{\partial^2 I^H(\tau, h)}{\partial \tau^2} = \frac{\partial^2 I^K(\tau, k)}{\partial \tau^2} = -Y v''(\tau),$$

so that single peakedness is satisfied as v is convex, i.e. $v'' > 0$.

Let us now characterize the equilibrium tax rate. Given the single-peakedness of preferences over policies we can apply the MVT to determine the equilibrium tax rate τ^*. Note that we do allow voters to vote strategically but sincere voting is still weakly dominant so that the unique equilibrium outcome in weakly dominant strategies features the median ranked bliss point. To characterize the equilibrium tax rate we therefore just have to determine who will be median voter. Doing so shows that there exists a unique equilibrium tax rate τ^*, which is given by

$$
\tau^* = \begin{cases} \tau^K & \text{if } \lambda \geq \frac{1}{2} \\ \tau^H(h^P) & \text{if } \lambda < \frac{1}{2} \text{ and } \tau^H(h^P) > \tau^K \\ \tau^H(h^R) & \text{if } \lambda < \frac{1}{2} \text{ and } \tau^H(h^R) < \tau^K \\ \tau^K & \text{if } \lambda < \frac{1}{2} \text{ and } \tau^H(h^P) \leq \tau^K \leq \tau^H(h^R) \end{cases}, \qquad \text{(S22.49)}
$$

where

$$
h^P = \left\{ h \mid (1-\lambda) \int_{-\infty}^{h^P} d\mu(h) = \frac{1}{2} \right\} = F^{-1}\left(\frac{1}{2(1-\lambda)} \right) \qquad \text{(S22.50)}
$$

$$
h^R = \left\{ h \mid (1-\lambda) \int_{h^R}^{\infty} d\mu(h) = \frac{1}{2} \right\} = F^{-1}\left(1 - \frac{1}{2(1-\lambda)} \right), \qquad \text{(S22.51)}
$$

and we defined

$$
F(x) = \int_{-\infty}^{x} d\mu(h).
$$

To see why equilibrium taxes are given in (S22.49), let us go through the different cases.

Case 1, $\lambda \geq \frac{1}{2}$. In this case, the median voter will be a capitalist so that equilibrium taxes will be the preferred tax rate of capitalists $\tau^K(k)$ as given in (S22.46).

Case 2, $\lambda < \frac{1}{2}$. In this case, capitalists alone are not in the majority. So consider a coalition of poor (i.e. low human capital) workers. h^P as defined in (S22.50) is exactly the worker such that all the workers to the left of h^P would have a measure of $1/2$ in the population. Note that all workers to the left of h^P have a preferred tax rate which is higher than $\tau^H(h^P)$. So if $\tau^H(h^P) > \tau^K$, h^P will indeed be the median voter as one half of the population will prefer higher taxes than $\tau^H(h^P)$ and one half of the population (λ capitalists and the $(1-\lambda)\int_{h^P}^{\infty} d\mu(h)$ rich workers) will prefer lower taxes. Hence, $\tau^H(h^P)$ is the equilibrium tax rate if $\tau^H(h^P) > \tau^K$ and $\lambda \leq 1/2$.

Case 3. Similar to Case 2, let us now consider a coalition of rich (i.e. high human capital workers). In this case h^R is defined to be the workers such that workers to the right represent exactly one half of the population. Recall that all workers with $h > h^R$, would prefer a lower tax rate. Hence, $\tau^H(h^R)$ is the equilibrium outcome if the rest of the population prefers higher taxes than $\tau^H(h^R)$. We clearly have that $\tau^H(h) > \tau^H(h^R)$ whenever $h < h^R$. Additionally we also need that the capitalists would want to see higher taxes, i.e. $\tau^K > \tau^H(h^R)$. This shows that $\tau^H(h^R)$ is the equilibrium outcome if $\tau^K > \tau^H(h^R)$ and $\lambda \leq 1/2$.

Case 4. This case comprises the situations where Cases 2 and 3 fail because the preferred tax rate of the capitalists is on the "wrong" side of the threshold. To see this, consider Case 2 but let $\tau^K > \tau^H(h^P)$. In this case the size of the population that prefers (weakly) higher tax rates than $\tau^H(h^P)$ is given by

$$
(1-\lambda) \int_{-\infty}^{h^P} d\mu(h) + \lambda = \frac{1}{2} + \lambda > \frac{1}{2}
$$

so that h^P is not the median voter. Intuitively, h^P is already so rich that the capitalists could form a coalition with some of the poorer agents (specifically, with a measure $\frac{1}{2} - \lambda$ of them) to get a majority of the population voting for higher taxes. So what will the equilibrium in this case look like? Clearly equilibrium taxes cannot be lower than $\tau^H(h^P)$ as a majority of the population prefers higher taxes. Hence there are two possibilities. Either a measure $\frac{1}{2} - \lambda$ and the capitalists prefer taxes which are weakly higher than τ^K in which case $\frac{1}{2} - \lambda + \lambda = \frac{1}{2}$ of the population would prefer tax rates which are weakly higher than τ^K so that τ^K will be the equilibrium outcome. On the other hand it could also be the case that there are no $\frac{1}{2} - \lambda$ workers who would prefer (weakly) higher taxes than τ^K. Formally, define $\tilde{h}$ as

$$(1 - \lambda) \int_{-\infty}^{\tilde{h}} d\mu(h) = \frac{1}{2} - \lambda$$

and let $\tau^H(\tilde{h}) < \tau^K$. By construction there is then more than one half of the population which prefers taxes lower than τ^K and all of these are workers. Hence, the rich workers with $h \in [h^R, \infty]$ would be in the majority if $\tau^H(h^R) < \tau^K$ in case the equilibrium would be as in Case 3. This shows that the equilibrium is given by τ^K if $\lambda < 1/2$ and $\tau^H(h^P) \leq \tau^K \leq \tau^H(h^R)$.

Having derived the equilibrium taxes we can now consider the comparative statics exercises. First of all note, that none of the equilibrium tax rates depend on the level of capital k. This is both due to the Cobb-Douglas structure in that individual capital earnings rk are proportional to output Y and due to the homogeneity among capitalists (i.e. the distribution of capital is degenerate - note that τ^H is dependent on μ_h). To determine the consequences of an increase in the number of capitalists λ we have to recognize that there are two effects. First of all the preferred tax rate of any voter changes as τ^K and $\tau^H(h)$ are functions of λ. But secondly, an increase in λ will also change the decisive voter itself. From (S22.46) we see that τ^K is weakly increasing in λ as (in the case of $\lambda \geq 1 - \alpha$) we have that

$$\frac{\partial \tau^K}{\partial \lambda} = \frac{1}{v''(\tau^K)} \frac{1 - \alpha}{\lambda^2} > 0. \qquad (S22.52)$$

This is intuitive: the capitalists as a class get $1 - \alpha$ from the wage bill but a fraction λ from the tax payments. Hence, the bigger λ the higher the rents they can extract from the workers so they will prefer higher taxes.

Given this reasoning it is also intuitive that workers will tend to prefer lower taxes if they are in the minority. This is seen from the preferred tax rate of worker h in (S22.48). If $\frac{1-\lambda}{\alpha} > \frac{h}{\mu_h}$ (so that the solution is interior), the change in her preferred tax rate is given by

$$\frac{\partial \tau^H(h)}{\partial \lambda} = -\frac{1}{v''^H(h))} \frac{\alpha}{(1 - \lambda)^2} \frac{h}{\mu_h} < 0. \qquad (S22.53)$$

If $\frac{1-\lambda}{\alpha} \leq \frac{h}{\mu_h}$, $\frac{\partial \tau^H(h)}{\partial \lambda} = 0$ as $\tau^H(h) = 0$ for those workers.

However, a change in λ does not leave the median voter unchanged. If $\lambda \geq \frac{1}{2}$, the distinction does not matter, as all capitalists are homogenous in their preferred tax policies. If $\lambda < \frac{1}{2}$ however, the human capital (and therefore the preferred tax rate) of the median voter changes. Upon totally differentiating (S22.50) and (S22.51) we get that

$$\frac{dh^P}{d\lambda} = \frac{\int_{-\infty}^{h^P} dF(h)}{(1 - \lambda)\mu(h^P)} > 0, \qquad (S22.54)$$

and

$$\frac{dh^R}{d\lambda} = -\frac{\int_{h^R}^{\infty} dF(h)}{(1 - \lambda)f(h^R)} < 0. \qquad (S22.55)$$

These results are intuitive. If the share of capitalists λ increases, a bigger share of workers is needed account for one half of the population. Hence the decisive agent of the poor coalition

h^P needs to be richer and the decisive agent of the rich coalition h^R needs to be poorer. As workers' preferred taxes are (for given λ) decreasing in h (see (S22.47)), the effect of an increase in λ on the equilibrium tax rate is ambiguous. If $\tau^* = \tau^K$, equilibrium taxes will increase as seen from (S22.52). If on the other hand $\tau^* = \tau^H(h^P)$ or $\tau^* = \tau^H(h^R)$ we get that

$$\frac{d\tau^*}{d\lambda} = \frac{\partial \tau^H(h^P)}{\partial \lambda} + \frac{\partial \tau^H(h)}{\partial h}\bigg|_{h=h^P} \times \frac{dh^P}{d\lambda} < 0 \qquad (S22.56)$$

$$\text{and } \frac{d\tau^*}{d\lambda} = \frac{\partial \tau^H(h^R)}{\partial \lambda} + \frac{\partial \tau^H(h)}{\partial h}\bigg|_{h=h^R} \times \frac{dh^R}{d\lambda} \gtrless 0 \qquad (S22.57)$$

as $\frac{\partial \tau^H(h)}{\partial \lambda} < 0$ (see (S22.53)), $\frac{\partial \tau^H(h)}{\partial h} < 0$ (see (S22.47)) and $\frac{dh^R}{d\lambda} < 0$ and $\frac{dh^P}{d\lambda} > 0$ as shown in (S22.54) and (S22.55). Hence the effect of an increase in λ on the equilibrium tax rate depends crucially on the identity of the median voter. Intuitively, if the median voter is a poor worker (see (S22.56)) equilibrium taxes will decrease because the median voter will have to be richer (and hence prefers lower taxes) and will furthermore prefer lower taxes because he is a worker whose share of the population decreased. If on the other hand the median voter is a rich worker (see (S22.57)) the effect is ambiguous. By being a worker, he prefers lower taxes (this is the $\frac{\partial \tau^H(h)}{\partial \lambda}$ term). But as the decisive voter will get poorer (as $\frac{dh^R}{d\lambda} < 0$), he will prefer higher taxes. Hence, an increase in the share of capitalists might increase or decrease taxes depending on who is the median voter.

Exercise 22.27, Part (b). Now consider the case of two-dimensional taxes. As interest rates and wages are still given by the expressions in (S22.43) and (S22.44), individual incomes are given by

$$
\begin{aligned}
I^K(\tau_k, \tau_h, k) &= (1-\tau_k)rk + (\tau_k - v(\tau_k)\lambda rk + (\tau_h - v(\tau_h)(1-\lambda)w\mu_h \\
&= (1-\tau_k)Y\frac{1-\alpha}{\lambda} + (\tau_k - v(\tau_k))(1-\alpha)Y + (\tau_h - v(\tau_h))\alpha Y \\
I^H(\tau_k, \tau_h, h) &= (1-\tau_h)wh + (\tau_k - v(\tau_k)\lambda rk + (\tau_h - v(\tau_h)(1-\lambda)w\mu_h \\
&= (1-\tau_h)Y\frac{\alpha}{1-\lambda}\frac{h}{\mu_h} + (\tau_k - v(\tau_k))(1-\alpha)Y + (\tau_h - v(\tau_h))\alpha Y,
\end{aligned}
$$

where τ_k and τ_h denotes the tax on capital and labor income respectively. To determine the optimal tax rates, let us again first look for interior solutions. Again it is clear that the convexity of v will ensure that those solutions are unique (if they exist). The FOC for the capitalists are given by

$$\frac{\partial I^K(\tau_k^K(k), \tau_h^K(k), k)}{\partial \tau_k} = Y(1-\alpha)[-\frac{1}{\lambda} + 1 - v'(\tau_k^K)] = 0 \qquad (S22.58)$$

$$\frac{\partial I^K(\tau_k^K(k), \tau_h^K(k), k)}{\partial \tau_h} = Y\alpha(1 - v'(\tau_h^K))) = 0. \qquad (S22.59)$$

Note that again neither the capitalists' preferred tax rate on capital τ_k^K or labor income τ_h^K depends on k or μ_h. The solutions for these optimality conditions are intuitive. (S22.59) directly implies that $\tau_h^K = v'^{-1}(1) \equiv \tau^*$, i.e. the capitalists' optimal tax rate for workers equates the marginal transfer to the marginal distortion. (S22.58) then shows that τ_k^K will be equal to zero. To see this, note that the marginal utility of a higher tax rate is negative at $\tau_k^K(k) = 0$, as

$$-\frac{1}{\lambda} + 1 - v'(0) = -\frac{1-\lambda}{\lambda} < 0.$$

This is also intuitive: as there is no inequality among the capitalists, they value taxes only if they induce transfers from the workers to themselves. But capital taxes are not paid by the workers.

The situation for the workers is slightly different. First of all it is obvious that the preferred tax rate on capital will also be given by $\tau_k^H(h) = v'^{-1}(1) = \tau^*$, i.e. they will also equate the marginal value of taxes with the marginal distortion. To determine the optimal tax rate on wage income however, inequality among the workers will play a role. The FOC is given by

$$\frac{\partial I^H(\tau_k^H(h), \tau_h^H(h), h)}{\partial \tau_h} = Y\alpha\left(-\frac{1}{1-\lambda}\frac{h}{\mu_h} + 1 - v'(\tau_h^H(h))\right) = 0,$$

so that worker h's optimal tax rate on human capital income is given by $\tau_h^H(h) = \max\{0, \tilde{\tau}_h^H(h)\}$, where $\tilde{\tau}_h^H(h)$ solves the equation

$$v'(\tilde{\tau}_h^H(h)) = 1 - \frac{h}{(1-\lambda)\mu_h}.$$

Again we see that for h small enough (i.e. for $h < (1-\lambda)\mu_h$), worker will prefer to tax themselves as they will gain from tax payments made by the richer workers. Hence the optimal tax rates are given by

$$(\tau_k^K(k), \tau_h^K(k), \tau_k^H(h), \tau_h^H(h)) = (0, \tau^*, \tau^*, \tau_h^H(h)), \tag{S22.60}$$

$$\text{where } \tau_h^H(h) = \begin{cases} 0 & \text{if } h \geq (1-\lambda)\mu_h \\ v'^{-1}\left(1 - \frac{h}{(1-\lambda)\mu_h}\right) & \text{if } h < (1-\lambda)\mu_h \end{cases}.$$

Let us now turn to the voting equilibrium.

PROPOSITION S22.1. *Suppose that $\lambda < \frac{1}{2}$. Then there exists a voting equilibrium $(\tau_k^{EQ}, \tau_h^{EQ})$ if and only if $\tau_h^H(h^R) = 0$, where h^R is defined in (S22.51) and $\tau_h^H(h)$ is given in (S22.60). If the equilibrium exists, it is given by*

$$(\tau_k^{EQ}, \tau_h^{EQ}) = (\tau^*, 0)$$

where $\tau^* = v'^{-1}(1)$.

PROOF. We will first show that $\tau_k^{EQ} = \tau^*$. Suppose this is not the case, i.e. there is equilibrium $(\tilde{\tau}_k, \tilde{\tau}_h)$ with $\tilde{\tau}_k \neq \tau^*$. Then consider the platform $(\tau^*, \tilde{\tau}_h)$. This platform will be preferred by all workers so that it will win the pairwise competition against $(\tilde{\tau}_k, \tilde{\tau}_h)$ as workers are in the majority. Hence $(\tilde{\tau}_k, \tilde{\tau}_h)$ could not have been an equilibrium. As $\tilde{\tau}_h$ was arbitrary, this proves that $\tau_k^{EQ} = \tau^*$ if an equilibrium exists. Let us now prove that there is no equilibrium whenever $\tau_h^H(h^R) > 0$. We first show that there is no equilibrium with $\tau_h^{EQ} \neq \tau_h^H(h^R)$. Suppose there is an equilibrium $(\tau^*, \tilde{\tau}_h)$ and $\tilde{\tau}_h \neq \tau_h^H(h^R)$. Then consider the platform $(\tau^*, \tau_h^H(h^R))$. If $\tilde{\tau}_h < \tau_h^H(h^R)$, all capitalists and all workers with $\tau_h^H(h) > \tilde{\tau}_h$ will vote for $(\tau^*, \tau_h^H(h^R))$. Hence $(\tau^*, \tau_h^H(h^R))$ will get a measure of votes larger than $\lambda + (1-\lambda)\int_{-\infty}^{h^R} d\mu(h) = 1/2$. Hence $\tilde{\tau}_h > \tau_h^H(h^R)$. But if $\tilde{\tau}_h > \tau_h^H(h^R)$, the platform $(\tau^*, \tau_h^H(h^R))$ will get a measure of votes larger than $(1-\lambda)\int_{h^R}^{\infty} d\mu(h) = 1/2$. Hence $\tilde{\tau}_h > 0$ and $\tilde{\tau}_h \neq \tau_h^H(h^R)$ cannot be an equilibrium. But now suppose there is an equilibrium $(\tau^*, \tau_h^H(h^R))$ with $\tau_h^H(h^R) > 0$. Then consider the platform $(\tau^* - \varepsilon, \tau_h^H(h^R) - \eta)$. For $\eta = 0$ this will make capitalists strictly better off but does not have any first-order effect on workers, as $\frac{\partial I^H(\tau_k, \tau_h, h)}{\partial \tau_k}\Big|_{\tau_k = \tau^*} = 0$. Hence there exists η and ε small enough such that

$(\tau^* - \varepsilon, \tau_h^H(h^R) - \eta)$ will get the votes of the capitalists and all the workers with $h > h^R$. This population has a mass of $\lambda + (1 - \lambda) \int_{h^R}^{\infty} d\mu(h) > 1/2$ so that $(\tau^* - \varepsilon, \tau_h^H(h^R) - \eta)$ will win the pairwise competition and $(\tau^*, \tau_h^H(h^R) > 0)$ could not have been an equilibrium. This shows that there is no equilibrium if $\tau_h^H(h^R) > 0$. Finally consider the platform $(\tau^*, 0)$ if $\tau_h^H(h^R) = 0$. As $(1 - \lambda) \int_{h^R}^{\infty} d\mu(h) = 1/2$ prefers $(\tau^*, 0)$ over all available policies, $(\tau^*, 0)$ is an equilibrium. This proves the proposition. $\qquad \square$

The intuition for this result is the following. With workers representing the majority of the population, capital taxes will always be high in equilibrium. A potential contender platform can therefore always win the capitalists'' approval by proposing lower capital taxes. For a small decrease, this will leave the workers indifferent up to second order effects. To win a majority, this contender platform will have to change the taxes on labor income. By decreasing labor taxes, the platform will get all the rich agents with $h > h^R$. This group has a measure of $1/2$ so that new platform will surely win a pairwise competition. By increasing taxes however, the new platform will not win a majority as all agents with $h > h^R$ will prefer the old platform for both reasons that capital taxes are higher and that labor taxes are lower. Hence, if the platform $(\tau^*, \tau_h^H(h^R))$ can be beaten, then only via a decrease in the tax rate on labor income. The case of $\tau_h^H(h^R) = 0$ then exactly ensures that such a variation is not possible so that an equilibrium exists.

This potential non-existence of equilibrium follows from the fact that once we introduce a second dimension, the preferences do not satisfy single-crossing over the two-dimensional policy space anymore. They are single peaked in both dimensions individually but not once we consider the (τ_k, τ_h) space. Hence there are situations in which a Condorcet winner (and hence a voting equilibrium) does not exist in this economy.

To sensibly talk about comparative statics in λ, we have to assume that parameters (and the distribution of human capital F) is such that a Condorcet winner exists. As above we have to consider the intensive margin (worker h's preferred policy changes) and the extensive margin (where the identity of the decisive voter changes). Let us first consider the equilibrium tax on capital income $\tau_k^{EQ} = \tau^*$. As τ^* does not depend on λ, the capital tax remains unchanged if the share of capitalists increases. To analyze the effect on the equilibrium tax on labor, note that we have seen above that a Condorcet winner will involve $\tau_h^{EQ} = \tau_h^H(h^R) = 0$. Although (S22.55) above showed that $\frac{dh^R}{d\lambda} < 0$, i.e. the median voter changes, this shows that the voting equilibrium in this economy requires that the new median voter h^R will still satisfy $h^R \geq (1 - \lambda)\mu_h$ so that his preferred tax rate is still equal to zero. Hence, if a Condorcet winner exists, neither equilibrium tax rate will change if the share of capitalists λ increases.

Exercise 22.27, Part (c). Let us now consider the case of sequential voting. We will see that in this case existence of equilibrium is guaranteed as those simultaneous changes of tax rates that were responsible for breaking the equilibrium in Part (b) are infeasible. Let solve the game using backwards induction. We still assume that $\lambda < 1/2$.[2] Taking τ_k as given, the vote about the labor income tax rate will be a standard problem where the median voter theorem applies: the policy variable is one-dimensional and voters have single peaked preferences by the convexity of v. Furthermore we saw above (see (S22.60)), that $\tau_h^K = \tau^* > \tau_h^H(h)$, $\forall h$, i.e. the capitalists favor the highest labor income taxes in the population. Hence, the equilibrium tax rate on labor income τ_h^{EQ} is given by $\tau_h^H(h^R)$ as

---

[2]The case of $\lambda > 1/2$ would of course be trivial. With capitalists being in the majority, the equilibrium tax rate will be given $(\tau_k^{EQ}, \tau_h^{EQ}) = (0, \tau^*)$ as there is no conflict if interest among the capitalists. An increase in λ would not change the equilibrium at all, as τ^* is not dependent on λ (see (S22.59)).

defined above. Given that the unique equilibrium outcome in the second stage is $\tau_h^H(h^R)$ and is independent of τ_k, the first stage will also feature an equilibrium determined by the median voter theorem. As workers are in the absolute majority and all agree on the τ_k dimension, the equilibrium capital tax rate will be given by $\tau_k^{EQ} = \tau^*$. Hence, in the case of sequential voting there is a unique equilibrium given by $(\tau^*, \tau_h^H(h^R))$. Note that this equilibrium exists irrespective of $\tau_h^H(h^R) = 0$ or $\tau_h^H(h^R) > 0$.

The equilibrium in independent of k (as both τ^* and $\tau_h^H(h)$ and the determination of h^R is). The comparative statics with respect to λ are again similar to above. As

$$\frac{d\tau^*}{d\lambda} = 0$$

the equilibrium tax on capital does not change. The change in the equilibrium labor tax is again (see (S22.57)) given by

$$\frac{d\tau^*}{d\lambda} = \frac{\partial \tau_h^H(h^R)}{\partial \lambda} + \left.\frac{\partial \tau_h^H(h)}{\partial h}\right|_{h=h^R} \times \frac{dh^R}{d\lambda} \gtrless 0,$$

i.e. the change in the labor tax is ambiguous as $\frac{dh^R}{d\lambda} < 0$, $\frac{\partial \tau_h^H(h^R)}{\partial \lambda} > 0$ and $\frac{\partial \tau^H(h)}{\partial h} < 0$. The intuition is the same as above: as the human capital of the median voter declines, i.e. the decisive voter gets poorer, the extensive margin calls for a higher equilibrium tax rate. The intensive margin however, still implies that the preferred tax rate will decrease as only workers pay the labor tax but capitalists get a share of the receipts. If the share of capitalists increases, workers will therefore prefer lower taxes. Hence, the effect of an increase in the capitalist population on equilibrium labor taxes is ambiguous.

Chapter 23: Institutions, Political Economy and Growth

Exercise 23.12

Exercise 23.12, Part (a). In order the characterize the Markov Perfect Equilibrium of this game, let us be precise about the timing. In every period the rich first decide if they want to extend the franchise. If the franchise is extended, the poor will set the tax rate forever and there will be no revolution as the poor cannot revolt against a democracy. If the franchise is not extended, the rich set the tax rate and it is implemented. It is only after taxes are set, that the poor decide if they want to start a revolution. If no revolution is started, the game will commence with the next period. If on the other hand the poor do start a revolution, no future actions will be taken and the poor get their payment of $\mu(t)$ in all future periods. Given this timing, we are now in the position to define the MPE of this game.

Before doing so, let us make the following observation which will simplify the notation. Given that individuals have the option to hide their money from taxation at a cost of ϕ, we would in principle have to consider this decision as a part of the agents' strategy. Such a strategy will however be trivial. In particular, the optimal strategy will involve individuals hiding their money whenever the taxes they face exceed ϕ. Given that it will never be optimal for any party deciding about the taxes to set higher taxes, we can without loss of generality analyze this game by just imposing ϕ as an upper bound on the tax rate.

Following the definition given in Appendix C, a Markovian strategy is a mapping from the space of payoff-relevant states K_i to the action space A_i, i.e. a pure Markovian strategy is given by $\hat{\sigma}_i : K_i \to A_i$, where $i = 1, 2, ..., N$ denotes the respective player. A MPE in this economy is therefore a profile of Markovian strategies $\hat{\sigma}^* = (\hat{\sigma}_1^*, ..., \hat{\sigma}_N^*)$ such that there does not exist i who has any (not necessarily Markovian) profitable deviation taking $\hat{\sigma}_{-i}^* = (\hat{\sigma}_1^*, ..., \hat{\sigma}_{i-1}^*, \hat{\sigma}_{i+1}^*, .., \hat{\sigma}_N^*)$ as given. Hence in order to define a MPE in this economy we first have to define the set of payoff relevant states and the actions available.

Given the timing above, the payoff-relevant states are different for the poor and the rich. For the rich, we could take the payoff relevant state as given by $\chi(t) \in \{R, P\}$ which denotes which party is in power. However, given our timing above, the rich do not have any actions once the poor are in power, i.e. once $\chi(t) = P$. Hence we will define the actions for the rich only in case $\chi(t) = R$, so that the state variable for the rich is trivially be given by $\chi(t) = R$.

For the poor the situation is slightly more complicated. For them, the typical element of their payoff relevant state space is given by $(\chi(t), p(t), \mu(t))$, where $p(t)$ is the policy vector in t if the rich are in power, i.e. it consists of the tax rate and of the franchise offer. Hence in contrast to the rich, current policies *are* part of the payoff-relevant state as the poor will make their decision to seek a revolution dependent on those policies.

The action spaces for the two groups R and P (i.e. for all individuals in those groups) are then given by

$$A_R = \{(E,(NE,\tau)) \text{ where } \tau \in [0,\phi]\}$$

$$A_P = \begin{cases} \tau \in [0,\phi] & \text{if } \chi(t) = P \text{ or } p(t) = E \\ \{NR, R\} & \text{otherwise} \end{cases},$$

where E and NE denote the decision to either extend or not extend the franchise respectively and R and NR refers to the decision to start a revolution or keep the rich in power. Note that we define the action space of the rich in a way such that there is no further tax setting decision when the franchise is extended. Similarly, A_P incorporates already that if the franchise is extended or the poor are in power, the only choice the poor have is the tax rate τ. This being said, a Markov Perfect Equilibrium in this economy is a strategy profile $\hat{\sigma}^* = (\hat{\sigma}_R^*, \hat{\sigma}_P^*)$ with a typical element $\hat{\sigma}_R^* \in A_R$ and $\hat{\sigma}_P^*(\chi(t), p(t), \mu(t)) \in A_P$ such that there does not exist a profitable deviation.

Exercise 23.12, Part (b). To show the required results we have to derive the optimal strategies for the rich and the poor. The fact that $\mu(t) = \mu^l$ simplifies the problem considerably as the strategies will be stationary. Characterizing the optimal strategy of group i means of course finding the function σ^i which maximizes groups i's utility for any realization in their state space. Let us analyze the poor first and consider the decision whether or not to start a revolution. Clearly this decision will be dependent on current and future taxes. It is here where the restriction to Markovian strategies simplifies the discussion a lot. As the state variable for the rich does not change as long as there is no revolution, the tax rate chosen by the rich τ^R will also be constant. Hence the decision of the poor can be characterized by simply comparing the per-period utilities starting next period (note that current taxes have to be paid regardless of the revolution decision). By starting a revolution each individual gets $\mu^l/(1-\lambda)$ in all future periods. By keeping the rich in power, each poor individual gets

$$U_P(\tau^R) = (1 - \tau^R)\frac{1-\theta}{1-\lambda} + \tau^R = \frac{1 - \theta + \tau^R(\theta - \lambda)}{1-\lambda}, \tag{S23.1}$$

where τ^R is the tax rate, the rich set and we used the fact that the lump sum transfer from taxation is just given by

$$T = (1 - \lambda)\tau^R \frac{1-\theta}{1-\lambda} + \lambda\tau^R \frac{\theta}{\lambda} = \tau^R.$$

(S23.1) shows that the per period utility of the poor is increasing in τ^R so that the worst outcome the poor can get by keeping the rich in power will involve $\tau^R = 0$. This however would imply $U_P(0) = \frac{1-\theta}{1-\lambda}$ which would still exceed the payoff from starting a revolution as we assumed $\mu^l < 1 - \theta$. In case the poor are in power, (S23.1) shows that they prefer the maximum amount of taxation, i.e. $\tau = \phi$. Hence the optimal strategy of the poor is given by

$$\sigma^P(\chi(t), p(t), \mu^l) = \begin{cases} \phi & \text{if } \chi(t) = P \text{ or } p(t) = E \\ NR & \text{if } \chi(t) = R \text{ and } NE \in p(t) \end{cases}.$$

The decision problem of the rich is simpler. For the rich we have

$$U_R(\tau) = (1 - \tau)\frac{\theta}{\lambda} + \tau = \frac{\theta - \tau(\theta - \lambda)}{\lambda},$$

so that the rich favor low taxes (as $U_R(\tau)$ is decreasing in τ). Given that the poor will never start a revolution, there are also no benefits of offering a higher tax rate. What about extending the franchise? We showed above that the poor will press for higher taxes once they have the chance. Hence, the rich would very much prefer to stay in power. The optimal strategy of the rich is therefore given by

$$\sigma^R = (NE, 0)$$

As the rich hold power initially, it is clear that *along the equilibrium path* the franchise will never be extended and taxes will always be equal to zero.

Exercise 23.12, Part (c). Let us again characterize the optimal strategies. From the analysis above it is clear that the behavior of the poor once they are in power is exactly the same as above - they will impose the maximum amount of taxation given by ϕ. What about their decision to start a revolution? As now $\frac{\mu^l}{1-\lambda} > \frac{1-\theta}{1-\lambda}$, they would prefer a revolution *if* the rich still set taxes to zero (recall that (S23.1) showed that $U_p(0) = \frac{1-\theta}{1-\lambda}$). So let σ^R be the optimal strategy of the rich. As the strategy is Markovian it will be characterized by a constant tax rate τ^R as the payoff relevant state variable $\chi(t)$ does not change as long as the rich are in power. The poor will be (weakly) better off keeping the rich in power and not seeking a revolution as long as the per-period payoffs (as of tomorrow) of not revolting will be (weakly) higher, i.e. as long as

$$(1 - \tau^R)\frac{1 - \theta}{1 - \lambda} + \tau^R \geq \frac{\mu^l}{1 - \lambda}. \tag{S23.2}$$

As the LHS of (S23.2) is increasing in τ^R and

$$\frac{1 - \theta}{1 - \lambda} \leq \frac{\mu^l}{1 - \lambda} \leq \frac{(1 - \phi)(1 - \theta) + \phi(1 - \lambda)}{1 - \lambda} \tag{S23.3}$$

by assumption, there is a unique level of taxes $\hat{\tau}^R$ such that (S23.2) holds with equality. In particular, (S23.3) implies that $\hat{\tau}^R$ will satisfy

$$0 < \hat{\tau}^R < \phi. \tag{S23.4}$$

The optimal strategy of the poor is therefore given by

$$\sigma^P(\chi(t), p(t), \mu^l) = \begin{cases} \phi & \text{if } \chi(t) = P \text{ or } p(t) = E \\ NR & \text{if } \chi(t) = R \text{ and } p(t) = (NE, \tau^R \geq \hat{\tau}^R) \\ R & \text{if } \chi(t) = R \text{ and } p(t) = (NE, \tau^R < \hat{\tau}^R) \end{cases}.$$

Now consider the rich when they are in power. Taking σ^P as given (in particular that taxes will be given by ϕ in case $\chi(t) = P$), their future per-period payoff when extending the franchise is given by

$$U_R(E|\sigma^P) = (1 - \phi)\frac{\theta}{\lambda} + \phi.$$

What about staying in power and setting a tax rate τ? Using σ^P and the fact that the rich will lose everything if a revolution takes place, their future payoff is given by

$$U_R((NE, \tau)|\sigma^P) = \begin{cases} (1 - \tau)\frac{\theta}{\lambda} + \tau & \text{if } \tau \geq \hat{\tau}^R \\ 0 & \text{if } \tau < \hat{\tau}^R \end{cases}.$$

As $(1 - \phi)\frac{\theta}{\lambda} + \phi$ is decreasing in τ, the rich will set exactly $\tau = \hat{\tau}^R$. This will prevent a revolution and the franchise does not have to be extended. As $\hat{\tau}^R < \phi$ (see (S23.4)) it is also clear that

$$U_R((NE, \hat{\tau}^R)|\sigma^P) = (1 - \hat{\tau}^R)\frac{\theta}{\lambda} + \hat{\tau}^R > (1 - \phi)\frac{\theta}{\lambda} + \phi = U_R(E|\sigma^P),$$

so that the optimal strategy of the rich is given by

$$\sigma^R = (NE, \hat{\tau}^R).$$

Along the equilibrium path the franchise is never extended and taxes are given by $\hat{\tau}^R$. The condition on μ^l was crucial to ensure that $\hat{\tau}^R \leq \phi$. If that condition does not hold, there do not exist high enough taxes such that a revolution is prevented without extending the franchise.

Exercise 23.12, Part (d). There is the possibility of the franchise being extended once we do not restrict ourselves to Markovian strategies. To see this we have to introduce some additional notation. Once we allow for non-Markovian strategies, a strategy σ_i is a map from the set of histories to the sets of actions. The actions in each period are still the same as above. So what is a history? As all past actions are observable, a history for the rich in time t is given by

$$h_t^R = [\{\tau_s\}_{s=0}^{t-1}, \{\gamma_s\}_{s=0}^{t-1}],$$

where $\gamma_s \in \{NE, E\}$. Hence, in every period t the rich "observe" (recall) all past tax rates and their extension offers. The histories for the poor are slightly different. They are given by

$$h_t^R = [\{\tau_s\}_{s=0}^{t-1}, \{\gamma_s\}_{s=0}^{t-1}, p(t)],$$

i.e. in addition to the information the rich base their decision on the poor also observe the tax rate and the extension decision (i.e. the policy vector $p(t)$), which the rich are proposing at t. To construct an equilibrium which features franchise extension if $\mu^l > 1 - \theta$ (i.e. especially if $1 - \theta < \mu^l < (1 - \phi)(1 - \theta) + \phi(1 - \lambda)$ where we saw that there was no franchise extension in the MPE), suppose that the poor were expecting the rich to set zero taxes in the future and to not offer a franchise extension. Today, the poor face a tax rate of τ^R and no franchise extension was offered. The value (as of tomorrow) of starting a revolution is given by

$$V^P(R) = \sum_{s=0}^{\infty} \beta^s \frac{\mu^l}{1-\lambda} = \frac{1}{1-\beta} \frac{\mu^l}{1-\lambda}, \tag{S23.5}$$

as each poor agent gets $\frac{\mu^l}{1-\lambda}$ in all periods in the future. The value (as of tomorrow) of not starting a revolution today but only in the next period is given by

$$V^P(NR) = \frac{1-\theta}{1-\lambda} + \beta \sum_{s=0}^{\infty} \beta^s \frac{\mu^l}{1-\lambda} = \frac{1-\theta}{1-\lambda} + \frac{\beta}{1-\beta} \frac{\mu^l}{1-\lambda}, \tag{S23.6}$$

where the first term $\frac{1-\theta}{1-\lambda}$ is the expected payoff conditional on believing that the rich will set a tax rate of zero in the future. As long as $\mu^l > 1 - \theta$, (S23.5) and (S23.6) therefore show that $V^P(R) > V^P(NR)$, i.e. the poor prefer to start a revolution today *if* they expect that the rich will set zero taxes in the future. Hence, whenever they have these expectations and are faced with a situation where no franchise extension is offered, the poor will start a revolution.

Taking this strategy as given, the rich have to decide on their tax rate and franchise decision. By offering the franchise extension, they will get a payoff

$$V^R(E) = \sum_{s=0}^{\infty} \beta^s \frac{\theta - \phi(\theta - \lambda)}{\lambda} = \frac{1}{1-\beta} \frac{\theta - \phi(\theta - \lambda)}{\lambda}, \tag{S23.7}$$

where $\frac{\theta - \phi(\theta - \lambda)}{\lambda}$ denotes the per-period payoff of being governed by the poor, who will set a tax rate of ϕ in all periods. By not offering the franchise extension and setting a tax rate τ^R, the value of the elite will be given by

$$V^R(NE, \tau^R) = \frac{\theta - \tau^R(\theta - \lambda)}{\lambda}, \tag{S23.8}$$

where we used that the poor will start a revolution when the franchise is not extended so the the rich will only get the current payoff and zero in all future periods. Comparing (S23.7) and (S23.8) we see that

$$V^R(E) > V^R(NE, \tau^R) \text{ for } \beta \text{ sufficiently close to } 1.$$

This intuitive. By not extending the franchise the rich generate benefits in the present (i.e. they do not face the high taxes ϕ) but it is costly in the future as they get zero instead of $\frac{\theta - \phi(\theta - \lambda)}{\lambda}$ in all future periods. Hence, when the rich are patient enough, the costs will outweigh the benefits so that extending the franchise will indeed be optimal for the rich. Hence, there is an equilibrium where the franchise is extended as long as the poor expect the rich not to extend the franchise and to set zero taxes in all future periods. So now we have to argue why this can occur in equilibrium. To see this, consider the situation of the rich. We have to show that in this equilibrium, the rich would actually want to set zero taxes. We have seen above that the decision to start a revolution will only depend on the franchise offer. If the franchise extension is offered, the poor will be in power in the future, if it is not offered, a revolution will occur. Hence, the rich will set taxes to maximize their current payoff. But as the rich are net payers, they strictly prefer zero taxes. Intuitively, in the proposed equilibrium, whenever the rich are in power it will be the last period. As there are no long-term benefits of setting higher taxes, setting zero taxes is optimal. The poor should therefore expect that in equilibrium the rich will set zero taxes in the future. This shows that there is an extension of the franchise now, although the MPE did not feature franchise extension (for the same parameters).

To see that there will never be an extension of the franchise if the revolutionary threat is low enough (in particular if $\mu^l < 1 - \theta$), note that in every equilibrium the future utility of the poor by not starting a revolution today is bounded from below by

$$V^P(NR) \geq V^P(\{\tau_t^R\}_{t=0}^\infty),$$

where $V^P(\{\tau^R\}_{t=0}^\infty)$ is the value of the poor if they will never start a revolution in the future and just face the taxes the rich set. As this is always an option, the equilibrium value of the poor has to be higher. And as the value of the poor is increasing in the tax rate, it is also clear that

$$V^P(\{\tau_t^R\}_{t=0}^\infty) \geq V^P(\{\tau_t^R = 0\}_{t=0}^\infty) = \frac{1}{1-\beta}\frac{1-\theta}{1-\lambda}.$$

The value of starting a revolution is given by

$$V(R) = \frac{1}{1-\beta}\frac{\mu^l}{1-\lambda}.$$

Hence as long as $\mu^l < 1 - \theta$, the threat of a revolution is never credible as in every equilibrium that poor will get at least $1 - \theta$ per period. But given that the poor will never start a revolution and that the rich prefer to stay in power, the franchise will never be extended if $\mu^l < 1 - \theta$.

Exercise 23.12, Part (e). The reason why the predictions between the MPE and SPE differ is the following: if we restrict ourselves to Markovian strategies, the policies set by the rich will have to be constant over time because they are functions of the payoff-relevant state variables which do not change as long as the rich are in power (in fact this is the only payoff-relevant state variable for the rich as argued above). Hence, we simply can not construct an equilibrium like the one here, where even though the rich offer a franchise extension today and set taxes τ^R, in the future the poor expect the rich to never extend the franchise again and set zero taxes. This would clearly be a non-stationary strategy which is ruled once we restrict ourselves to MPE. From a more economic perspective, the more permissible concept of SPE (recall that every MPE is subgame-perfect, but not every SPE is also an equilibrium in Markovian strategies) can be interpreted as allowing for equilibria where there is less commitment on the side of the rich. The MPE can be seen as an equilibrium where the rich set taxes today and commit to set the same taxes tomorrow. In the SPE this commitment device is not necessarily available. We can construct equilibria where the poor expect the rich to set zero taxes in the future and in those equilibria these expectations are correct. Note in particular that this possibility of commitment is valuable for the rich. In the MPE analyzed in Part (c), the payoff of the rich was given by

$$V^R(MPE) = \frac{1}{1-\beta}\frac{\theta - \hat{\tau}^R(\theta - \lambda)}{\lambda},$$

where $\hat{\tau}^R$ was defined in (S23.2) and satisfied $0 < \hat{\tau}^R < \phi$. In the SPE the payoff of the rich is given by

$$V^R(SPE) = \frac{1}{1-\beta}\frac{\theta - \phi(\theta - \lambda)}{\lambda},$$

as the franchise is extended immediately. As $\hat{\tau}^R < \phi$, it is clear that

$$V^R(MPE) > V^R(SPE).$$

Hence, the possibility of commitment is valuable for the rich. Note however, that this does not mean that the MPE is better than *every* SPE. In particular this cannot be true as the MPE is of course a SPE. Hence, we simply showed that some equilibria (which can be interpreted as not featuring commitment) are sustainable in the SPE and cannot occur as MPE.

Which of these concepts is more satisfactory depends a lot on the specific context, to which this model is applied, in particular on the information structure and the coordination possibilities within the groups. To make this statement clear, observe first that the poor are doing better in the SPE characterized in Part (d) than in the MPE of Part (b) as

$$V^P(SPE) = \frac{1}{1-\beta}\frac{1-\theta+\phi(\theta-\lambda)}{\lambda} > \frac{1}{1-\beta}\frac{1-\theta+\hat{\tau}^R(\theta-\lambda)}{\lambda} = V^P(MPE).$$

So suppose we want to model the interaction between the poor and the rich and allow that within the poor there is an organization trying to influence the decision-making of the poor. This organization can do the math and realize that this particular SPE yields a higher value for the poor. In particular, this organization knows that all it has to do for this equilibrium to emerge, is to convince people that tomorrow (whatever the rich were doing in the past) the rich will set zero taxes and never offer an franchise extension again. Once the poor hold those expectations, the franchise will be extended in the SPE. So if we think that organizations determining opinions or expectations in their constituency are important, the SPE might be a better framework as it gives those expectations a bigger role. If on the other hand we think of the political arena as a more anonymous place, the MPE might be a better model as it captures the idea that people might presume that if conditions (i.e. the state variables) do not change, the policies should not change either.

Exercise 23.12, Part (f). Before we characterize the equilibrium, let us be precise about the timing of events. We presume here that the value of $\mu(t)$ is realized at the beginning of the period, i.e. in particular before the rich decide about extending the franchise. Hence the current state $\mu(t)$ now has to be part of the state space of each party. Let us first consider the strategy of the poor. Again it is clear from the discussion above that in case they are in power, they will set a tax rate of $\tau^P = \phi$. What about the decision to start a revolution? Let us construct a MPE where the poor start a revolution if and only if $\mu(t) = \mu^h$ *and the franchise is not extended*. Hence let us conjecture the following strategies and confirm that those strategies (under appropriate parametric restrictions) are a MPE. Let

$$\sigma^P(\chi(t), p(t), \mu(t)) = \begin{cases} \phi & \text{if } \chi(t) = P \text{ or } E \in p(t) \\ R & \text{if } \chi(t) = R, NE \in p(t) \text{ and } \mu(t) = \mu^h \\ NR & \text{if } \chi(t) = R, NE \in p(t) \text{ and } \mu(t) = \mu^l \end{cases} \quad (S23.9)$$

and

$$\sigma^R(\mu(t)) = \begin{cases} E & \text{if } \mu(t) = \mu^h \\ (NE, 0) & \text{if } \mu(t) = \mu^l \end{cases}. \quad (S23.10)$$

To show that these strategies constitute a MPE, we have to show that there are no profitable deviations. In order to study the incentives of the poor to stick tho their proposed strategy, let us first introduce some notation. Let $V^P(NR; \mu)$ and $V^P(R; \mu)$ be the value of the poor agents if the current state is μ, the franchise was not extended and they do or do not start a revolution respectively. Additionally let $V^P(E)$ be the value of the poor when the franchise extension is offered. What are those objects? Clearly we have that

$$V^P(E) = \frac{1}{1-\beta} \frac{1 - \theta + \phi(\theta - \lambda)}{1 - \lambda}, \quad (S23.11)$$

as once the franchise is extended, the poor set a tax rate of $\tau = \phi$ in all future periods. The value to start a revolution is given by

$$V^P(R; \mu) = \frac{1 - \theta}{1 - \lambda} + \frac{\beta}{1 - \beta} \frac{\mu}{1 - \lambda}, \quad (S23.12)$$

where the first term $\frac{1-\theta}{1-\lambda}$ is the payoff of the poor given that the rich set taxes of zero and the second term is the (discounted) value of receiving $\mu \in \{\mu^l, \mu^h\}$ in all periods of the future. Finally consider the value of the poor to not start a revolution. It is given by

$$V(NR; \mu) = \frac{1 - \theta}{1 - \lambda} + \beta\left((1 - q)V(NR; \mu^l) + qV(E)\right). \quad (S23.13)$$

To understand (S23.13), note that by not starting a revolution, the poor agent gets $\frac{1-\theta}{1-\lambda}$ today (as equilibrium taxes are zero). In the next period we will either have $\mu(t+1) = \mu^l$, which happens with probability $1 - q$ and in which case in equilibrium neither the franchise will be extended nor a revolution will take place so that the future value is equal $V(NR; \mu^l)$. If the state $\mu(t+1) = \mu^h$ occurs (which happens with probability q), the equilibrium strategies prescribe that the franchise will be extended so that poor get a value of $V(E)$. Having defined these objects we are in the position to prove that the strategies in (S23.9) and (S23.10) constitute a MPE.

Let us first consider the poor. We have to check that not starting a revolution if $\mu = \mu^l$ is (weakly) preferred to starting a revolution, i.e. that

$$V(NR; \mu^l) \geq V^P(R; \mu^l). \quad (S23.14)$$

Using (S23.13) and (S23.11) we get that

$$
\begin{aligned}
V(NR; \mu^l) &= \frac{1-\theta}{1-\lambda} + \beta \left((1-q)V(NR; \mu^l) + qV(E) \right) \\
&= \frac{1}{1 - \beta(1-q)} \left[\frac{1-\theta}{1-\lambda} + \frac{\beta q}{1-\beta} \frac{1 - \theta + \phi(\theta - \lambda)}{1-\lambda} \right] \\
&= \frac{1}{1-\beta} \frac{1-\theta}{1-\lambda} + \frac{1}{1 - \beta(1-q)} \frac{\beta q}{1-\beta} \frac{\phi(\theta - \lambda)}{1-\lambda}.
\end{aligned}
\tag{S23.15}
$$

From (S23.12) we get that

$$
V^P(R; \mu^l) = \frac{1-\theta}{1-\lambda} + \frac{\beta}{1-\beta} \frac{\mu^l}{1-\lambda}.
$$

Hence for (S23.14) to be satisfied, we need that

$$
1 - \theta + \frac{q}{1 - \beta(1-q)} \phi(\theta - \lambda) \geq \mu^l.
\tag{S23.16}
$$

Note that for $q = 1$ this is just the condition

$$
\mu^l \leq 1 - \theta + \phi(\theta - \lambda) = (1 - \phi)(1 - \theta) + \phi(1 - \lambda)
$$

which we encountered already in Part (c). Hence if (S23.16) holds true, the poor would not want to start a revolution if $\mu = \mu^l$.

Now consider $\mu = \mu^h$. We have to show that the poor would actually want to start a revolution, i.e. we have to show that the threat is credible. From (S23.12) we get that

$$
V^P(R; \mu^h) = \frac{1-\theta}{1-\lambda} + \frac{\beta}{1-\beta} \frac{\mu^h}{1-\lambda}.
$$

The value of not starting a revolution is again given by (S23.15) where we used that in accordance with the single deviation principle both parties play their equilibrium strategies in the future. Hence, in the MPE we need that

$$
V^P(R; \mu^h) \geq V^P(NR; \mu^h)
$$

which is the case if

$$
1 - \theta + \frac{q}{1 - \beta(1-q)} \phi(\theta - \lambda) \leq \mu^h.
\tag{S23.17}
$$

Again note that for $q = 0$ we get that (S23.17) reduces to $\mu^h > 1 - \theta$, which was necessary for there to exist an equilibrium where franchise extension takes place. So given the strategy of the rich, (S23.16) and (S23.17) are the two conditions we need to verify that the strategy of the poor is indeed a best response.

Let us now turn to the analysis of the strategy of the rich. To check that the rich are behaving optimally is considerably easier. Setting a tax rate of $\tau = 0$ is optimal as the rich prefer low taxes and the revolution decision of the poor is not dependent on the tax rate. What about the franchise decision? Clearly the rich would prefer the franchise extension to the revolution but would rather stay in power themselves. Hence, $\mu(t) = \mu^h$ triggers the extension of the franchise as otherwise the poor would start a revolution and the the franchise is not extended when $\mu(t) = \mu^l$ as there is no revolutionary threat by the poor.

This shows that the strategies above constitute an MPE as long as (S23.16) and (S23.17) are satisfied. In particular note that there is the extension of the franchise on the equilibrium path because as long as $q < 1$ the state $\mu(t) = \mu^h$ will be reached with probability one so that the franchise will be extended at some point. Note that the option of franchise extension is useful for the rich. The reason is that at some point the revolutionary potential of the poor will be high enough (i.e. whenever $\mu(t) = \mu^h$) so that only the possibility of franchise extension can save the rich from a revolution.

Exercise 23.12, Part (g). By construction such an equilibrium will have to have the feature that the strategy of the rich will be such that the extension of the franchise is never offered (on the equilibrium path) and the poor will never start a revolution (in equilibrium) as in this case there would be a profitable deviation - the rich could simply offer the extension of franchise. Also, as we assume that the unique MPE does not feature franchise extension, the SPE we need to construct has to feature non-Markovian strategies. The additional degree of freedom non-Markovian provide us with is the possibility to condition current actions on past variables. As these are not payoff relevant, Markovian strategies were restricted to not use this information. We now show that we can construct a SPE without extension in cases where the unique MPE features franchise extension on the equilibrium path. Consider the following construction. Recall that in Part (d) we showed that there is a SPE with franchise extension if the poor expect zero taxes in the future. So consider the following equilibrium. Let the rich set some tax rate $\bar{\tau} < \phi$ and the franchise extension is not offered. The poor also expect that taxes will be $\bar{\tau}$ in the future as long as $\bar{\tau}$ was set in the past. By not starting a revolution the poor will have a future value of

$$V^P(NR) = \frac{\beta}{1-\beta} U^P(\bar{\tau}).$$

By starting a revolution when $\mu(t) = \mu$, the poor will have a future value of

$$V^P(R,\mu) = \frac{\beta}{1-\beta}\mu.$$

Hence the poor will abstain from a revolution if

$$U^P(\bar{\tau}) \geq U^P(\mu). \tag{S23.18}$$

As we assumed that $U^P(\phi) > \mu^h$, i.e. the utility when taxes are at their maximum value is higher than the expected value of starting a revolution, we can find $\bar{\tau}$ close enough to ϕ such that (S23.18) will be satisfied for μ^h. Then it is also satisfied for $\mu^l < \mu^h$. Hence, as long as the poor expect that taxes will be equal to $\bar{\tau}$, no revolution will be triggered. Once $\tau \neq \bar{\tau}$ is observed however, the poor expect that taxes will be equal to zero in the future. We showed above that this can occur in an SPE, i.e. that those expectations yield a SPE where the poor start a revolution whenever no franchise extension is made and that those expectation are consistent with SPE in that setting zero taxes is actually a best response for the rich. By sticking to the equilibrium strategy, the rich get a future payoff of

$$V^R(\bar{\tau}, NE) = \frac{1}{1-\beta}\frac{\theta - \bar{\tau}(\theta - \lambda)}{\lambda}.$$

By deviating, the rich get

$$V^R(\tau, NE) = \frac{\theta - \tau(\theta - \lambda)}{\lambda} \quad \text{for } \tau \neq \bar{\tau}$$

$$V^R(E) = \frac{1}{1-\beta}\frac{\theta - \phi(\theta - \lambda)}{\lambda}.$$

Note that $V^R(\tau, NE)$ only consists of the current payoff $\frac{\theta - \tau(\theta - \lambda)}{\lambda}$ as in equilibrium the poor will start a revolution whenever $(\tau, NE) \neq (\bar{\tau}, NE)$ is observed. As $\bar{\tau} < \phi$, it is clear that

$$V^R(\bar{\tau}, NE) > V^R(E).$$

Furthermore we also see that

$$V^R(\bar{\tau}, NE) \geq V^R(\tau, NE) \quad \text{for } \beta \text{ sufficiently high.}$$

Hence the equilibrium strategies characterized above constitute a SPE in this game. This shows that in this equilibrium there will be no franchise extension along the equilibrium path but taxes will be equal to $\bar{\tau}$ and the rich will stay in power. The non-Markovian nature of this equilibrium comes from the fact that the poor are allowed to have history-dependent punishment strategies, i.e. once $\tau \neq \bar{\tau}$ is observed, the rich are punished by a revolution in equilibrium. The crucial point of course is that this threat is credible if the poor believe that future taxes will be equal to zero. Hence, a one-shot deviation from the rich alters the expectations of the poor entirely. This is not possible in a MPE. Such a response by the poor will impose discipline on the rich to set high taxes throughout which in turn will make an extension of the franchise unnecessary. Therefore, similar to our discussion in Part (e), once we consider SPE, there are many ways to sustain diligent behavior via choosing history-dependent punishments to off-the-equilibrium-path observations. In the example here, this possibility actually helps the elite (recall that in the example in Part (d), the rich were worse off) because it effectively represents a commitment device to high taxes in the future which in turn make revolutions not profitable. This however eliminates the threat for the rich to extend the franchise so that they can cling to the political power on the equilibrium path forever.

References

Acemoglu, Daron (2002) "Directed Technical Change." *Review of Economic Studies*, 69, pp. 781-810.

Acemoglu, Daron (2003) "Patterns of Skill Premia." *Review of Economic Studies*, 70, pp. 199-230.

Acemoglu, Daron (2009) *Introduction to Modern Economic Growth.* Princeton University Press, Princeton, NJ.

Acemoglu, Daron, Simon Johnson and James Robinson (2002) "Reversal of Fortune: Geography and Institutions in the Making of the Modern World Income Distribution." *Quarterly Journal of Economics*, 117, pp. 1231-1294.

Acemoglu, Daron and Jaume Ventura (2002) "The World Income Distribution." *Quarterly Journal of Economics*, 117, pp. 659-694.

Aghion, Philippe and Peter Howitt (1992) "A Model of Growth through Creative Destruction." *Econometrica*, 60, pp. 323-351.

Aiyagari, S. Rao (1993) "Uninsured Idiosyncratic Risk and Aggregate Saving." Federal Reserve Bank of Minneapolis, Working Paper No. 502.

Arrow, Kenneth J., Hollis B. Chenery, Bagicha S. Minhas, and Robert Solow (1961) "Capital-Labor Substitution and Economic Efficiency." *Review of Economics and Statistics*, 43, pp. 225-250.

Armington, Paul S. (1969) "A Theory of Demand for Products Distinguished by Place and Production." *International Monetary Fund Staff Papers*, 16, pp. 159-178.

Ben-Porath, Yoram (1967) "The Production of Human Capital and the Life Cycle of Earnings." *Journal of Political Economy*, 75, pp. 352-365.

Blackwell, David (1965) "Discounted Dynamic Programming." *Annals of Mathematical Statistics*, 36, pp. 226-235.

Blanchard, Olivier J. (1985) "Debt, Deficits, and Finite Horizons." *Journal of Political Economy,* 93, pp. 223-247.

Blanchard, Olivier J. and Stanley Fischer (1989) *Lectures on Macroeconomics.* MIT Press, Cambridge, MA.

Bernard, Andrew B. and J. Bradford Jensen (1999) "Exceptional Exporter Performance: Cause, Effect, or Both?" *Journal of International Economics*, 47, pp. 1-25.

Caballero, Ricardo J. (1990) "Consumption Puzzles and Precautionary Savings." *Journal of Monetary Economics*, 25, pp. 113-136.

Chamberlain, Gary and Charles A. Wilson (2000) "Optimal Intertemporal Consumption under Uncertainty." *Review of Economic Dynamics*, 3, pp. 365-395.

Coe, David T. and Elhanan Helpman (1995) "International R&D Spillovers." *European Economic Review*, 39, pp. 859-887.

Clark, Gregory (2005) "The Condition of the Working Class in England, 1209-2004." *Journal of Political Economy*, 113, pp. 1307-1340.

Diamond, Peter (1965) "National Debt in a Neoclassical Growth Model." *American Economic Review*, 55, pp. 1126-1150.

Dixit, Avinash K. and Joseph E. Stiglitz (1977) "Monopolistic Competition and Optimum Product Diversity." *American Economic Review*, 67, pp. 297-308.

Habakkuk, John (1962) *American and British Technology in the Nineteenth Century: Search for Labor-Saving Inventions.* Cambridge University Press, Cambridge.

Krugman, Paul (1979) "A Model of Innovation, Technology Transfer, and the World Distribution of Income." *Journal of Political Economy*, 87, pp. 253-266.

Lucas, Robert E. (1978) "Asset Prices in an Exchange Economy." *Econometrica*, 46, pp. 1426-1445.

Lucas, Robert E. (1993) "Making a Miracle." *Econometrica*, 61, pp. 251-272.

Malthus, Thomas R. (1798) *An Essay on the Principle of Population.* W. Pickering, London.

Mas-Colell, Andreu, Michael D. Whinston and Jerry R. Green (1995) *Microeconomic Theory.* Oxford University Press, New York.

Melitz, Mark (2003) "The Impact of Trade on Intra-Industry Reallocations and Aggregate Industry Productivity." *Econometrica*, 71, pp. 1695-1725.

Michel, Philippe (1982) "On the Transversality Condition in Infinite Horizon Optimal Problems." *Econometrica*, 50, pp. 975-985.

Michel, Philippe (1990) "Some Clarifications on the Transversality Condition." *Econometrica*, 58, pp. 705-723.

Rebelo, Sergio (1991) "Long-Run Policy Analysis and Long-Run Growth." *Journal of Political Economy*, 99, pp. 500-521.

Rivera-Batiz, Luis A. and Paul M. Romer (1991) "Economic Integration and Endogenous Growth" *Quarterly Journal of Economics*, 106, pp. 531-555.

Romer, Paul M. (1987) "Growth Based on Increasing Returns Due to Specialization." *American Economic Review*, 77, pp. 56-62.

Romer, Paul M. (1990) "Endogenous Technological Change." *Journal of Political Economy*, 98, 71-102.

Shaked, Avner (1982) "Existence and Computation of Mixed Strategy Nash Equilibrium for 3-Firms Location Problem." *Journal of Industrial Economics*, 31, pp. 93-96.

Shell, Karl (1971) "Notes on the Economics of Infinity." *Journal of Political Economy*, 79, pp. 1002-1011.

Samuelson, Paul A. (1975) "Optimum Social Security in a Life-Cycle Growth Model." *International Economic Review*, 16, pp. 539-544.

Solow, Robert M. (1956) "A Contribution to the Theory of Economic Growth." *Quarterly Journal of Economics*, 70, pp. 65-94.

Solow, Robert M. (1957) "Technical Change and the Aggregate Production Function." *Review of Economics and Statistics*, 39, pp. 312-320.

Stokey, Nancy, Robert E. Lucas and Edward C. Prescott (1989) *Recursive Methods in Economic Dynamics.* Harvard University Press, Cambridge, MA.

Zeldes, Stephen P. (1989) "Optimal Consumption with Stochastic Income: Deviations from Certainty Equivalence." *Quarterly Journal of Economics*, 104, pp. 275-298.